Introduction
to
SOCIAL WELFARE

Introduction

to

SOCIAL

WELFARE

Second Edition

WALTER A. FRIEDLANDER

Professor of Social Welfare   University of California at Berkeley

PRENTICE - HALL, INC.

Englewood Cliffs, New Jersey

PRENTICE-HALL SOCIOLOGY SERIES

Herbert Blumer, Editor

First printing ...... January, 1961
Second printing ...... June, 1961
Third printing .... May, 1962

HV
91
J .F7
1961

PRINTED IN THE UNITED STATES OF AMERICA

49700 — C

Foreword

ORGANIZED SOCIAL WELFARE has been elevated to a position of great importance in our nation. It is being called upon to extend its services greatly and to execute them skillfully. This requires more social workers and a continuous effort to increase their professional competence. Nothing is more important in the recruitment of prospective workers and in their training than giving them an introduction to the field. This introduction should include a thorough discussion of social welfare—its scope, its tasks, its perspective, its principles, and its problems. It also should awaken genuine interest, stimulate eagerness to respond to the challenges of the field, and cultivate professional dedication.

The field of social welfare is undergoing continuous development and diversification into specialized areas. Research has become a recognized part of the social-welfare endeavor. Efforts are being made to achieve greater effectiveness through periodic reappraisal and reformulation of guiding principles. Similarly, constant attention is being given to devising new methods of practice, and other disciplines are being studied for possible contributions to the field.

To depict this broad and diversified field of endeavor, to present what is basic and sound in the accumulated knowledge, and to portray what is important in the new lines of development are major undertakings. That Dr. Friedlander has achieved distinction in this field is attested to by the wide adoption of the first edition of his book. It has been used in 96 of the 114 colleges in the United States offering an undergraduate social-work sequence, and in most of the graduate schools of social work.

v

The second edition brings the topic up to date and improves on the presentation of the dynamics of social welfare and its role in our society. Dr. Friedlander's scholarship, skill, and dedication are evidenced by the quality of his revision.

HERBERT BLUMER
University of California
Berkeley

Preface to Second Edition

IN OUR MODERN INDUSTRIAL SOCIETY, social welfare has become such an important part of our life and our culture that an understanding of its fundamental philosophy, structure, and functions becomes necessary for every educated citizen. It is generally accepted that government agencies and private citizen groups, organized in religious charities or humanitarian philanthropy, are indispensable in order to relieve suffering, poverty, sickness, and delinquency and counteract waste of human capacities. This book explains how social welfare concepts and services have developed through tradition, experience, and sociological changes. We need an historical and a philosophical perspective in order to comprehend the present complicated system of social welfare, its principles, its legal framework, and its effect on our fellow citizens.

The aim of this book is to serve particularly three groups of readers: (1) those who are looking forward to, or are already employed in, positions in the fields of public assistance, social insurance, recreation, group work, public employment services, in correctional institutions, probation, and parole services, or related activities for which graduate professional training is not always required; (2) those who plan to take up, or are engaged in, studies of graduate social work, or who are working in responsible positions and want to inform themselves through this survey of the development, the basic ideas, and the present system of social welfare, and (3) citizens interested in volunteer work in the social services.

The fundamental concepts, the historic perspective, and the main phases of social welfare organization are presented in nontechnical

vii

language; professional jargon is avoided as much as possible. References are given predominately to books and journals available in most college and university libraries and in many public libraries.

The author is indebted to Dr. Herbert Blumer, General Editor of the Prentice-Hall Sociology Series, Professor of Sociology and Social Institutions and Director of the Institute of Social Sciences, University of California in Berkeley, Mr. Alfred W. Goodyear and Mr. Robert L. Bull of Prentice-Hall, Inc., for their advice, guidance, and improvements on the manuscript, and to his wife, Li Bergmann Friedlander for her invaluable assistance. He also wishes to express his appreciation to his faculty colleagues in colleges and schools of social work, particularly at the School of Social Welfare, University of California in Berkeley, and to Professor Ernest B. Harper, School of Social Work, Michigan State University, and Professor Thomas F. Lewin, New York School of Social Work, Columbia University, who helped in the preparation of this revised edition. The author is grateful to the publishers and authors of books and professional publications for information and materials which were used in this work (although he alone is responsible for the philosophy and content of this book).

Berkeley, California

WALTER A. FRIEDLANDER

Table of Contents

3. (Cont.)

Part II. Social Work Processes

Part III. Social Welfare Programs and Practice

Introduction
to
SOCIAL WELFARE

I.

The Historical Development of Social Welfare

1.

Introduction: The Concept of Social Welfare

THE CONCEPT and the term "social welfare" in the sense of a scientific program have only recently developed in connection with the social problems of our industrial society. Poverty, sickness, suffering, and social disorganization have existed throughout the history of mankind, but the industrial society of the nineteenth and twentieth centuries had to face so many social problems that the older human institutions—family, neighborhood, church, and local community—could no longer adequately meet them. The need for a broader system of social services resulted. In the following chapters we shall briefly analyze how human society dealt with destitution, maladjustment, and physical and mental ills and how the family and the tribe, the church, private philanthropy, and the community, under the influence of humanitarianism, in turn assumed the responsibility for satisfying people's needs. But, it was only about one hundred years ago that the magnitude of social problems made it necessary to organize, under private and public initiative, social services for the needy. Since that time, government has taken an increasingly greater responsibility for the well-being of the citizens. In addition to the development of humanitarian ideas with emphasis on our responsibility for others, the progress of the biological and social sciences provided new tools for investigating the causes of poverty, of human deficiencies, and of dissatisfaction, the aim being to cure or to alleviate social problems.

3

A number of studies have tried to establish a concise terminology for the concepts of "social welfare," the "social services," "social work," and "social security." No universally accepted agreement has been reached.[1]

For this study, we suggest the following definitions. "Social welfare" is the organized system of social services and institutions, designed to aid individuals and groups to attain satisfying standards of life and health, and personal and social relationships which permit them to develop their full capacities and to promote their well-being in harmony with the needs of their families and the community.[2] "Social work" is a professional service, based upon scientific knowledge and skill in human relations, which assists individuals, alone or in groups, to obtain social and personal satisfaction and independence. It is usually performed by a social agency or a related organization. The term "social welfare" has a broader implication than professional social work. Finally, the term "the social services" is often used in a very general sense; Harry M. Cassidy[3] defined it as "those organized activities that are primarily and directly concerned with the conservation, the protection, and the improvement of human resources" and includes as social services: social assistance, social insurance, child welfare, corrections, mental hygiene, public health, education, recreation, labor protection, and housing.[4]

---

[1] Karl de Schweinitz, *The Art of Helping People out of Trouble* (Boston: Houghton, 1924); Helen L. Witmer, *Social Work: An Analysis of a Social Institution* (New York: Farrar & Rinehart, 1942), pp. 3-10; Alice Cheyney, *Nature and Scope of Social Work* (New York: American Association of Social Workers, 1926); Harry M. Cassidy, *Social Security and Reconstruction in Canada* (Boston: Humphries, 1943), pp. 13-17; and, Joseph P. Anderson, "Social Work as a Profession," *Social Work Year Book* (1945), p. 446.

[2] Harold L. Wilensky and Charles N. Lebeaux, *Industrial Society and Social Welfare* (New York: Russell Sage Foundation, 1958), p. 17 defines *social welfare* as those formally organized and socially sponsored institutions, agencies, and programs which function to maintain or improve the economic conditions, health, or interpersonal competence of some parts or all of a population; and *social work* as an occupation or profession, a group of people with more or less specific training and skills, who occupy key positions, along with other groups, in the provision of welfare services.

[3] *Op. cit.*, p. 13.

[4] *Social Work* has been recently defined by Prof. Werner W. Boehm: "Social work seeks to enhance the social functioning of individuals, singly and in groups, by activities focused upon their social relationships which constitute the interaction between man and his environment. These activities can be grouped into three functions: restoration of impaired capacity, provision of

Education and labor legislation contribute to people's well-being and physical and mental growth, but they have not been included in our definition of social welfare. Social welfare services are administered by public or private organizations, and the structure and functions of these services will be discussed. The objective of social welfare is to secure for each human being the economic necessities, a decent standard of health and living conditions, equal opportunities with his fellow citizens, and the highest possible degree of self-respect and freedom of thought and action without interfering with the same rights of others.

By "social security" we understand a program of protection provided by society against those contingencies of modern life—sickness, unemployment, old-age dependency, industrial accidents, and invalidism—against which the individual cannot be expected to protect himself and his family by his own ability or foresight.[5] This general goal of social protection, as a rule, is secured through the various forms of public assistance, social insurance, and frequently preventive health and welfare services. In general use, the term social security does not embrace private social welfare activities, which are, however, an important part of the system of social welfare in most countries. The social philosophy which has led to the origin of the concept of social welfare, as one essential cultural characteristic of modern society, has fundamentally changed during the centuries of human history. We shall trace its essential elements in the following chapters in order to understand the present-day meanings and the reactions of the public toward the question of social welfare.

This book does not attempt to teach the methods and professional skills of social work. They are based upon knowledge of human behavior and motivation, the dynamics of human relationships, the sociological, economic, and political structure of our society, knowl-

---

individual and social resources, and prevention of social dysfunction." *Objectives of the Social Work Curriculum of the Future* (New York: Council on Social Work Education, 1959), p. 54. A brief definition of social work suggested by the United Nations Secretariat is "social work is an activity designed to help towards a better mutual adjustment of individuals and their social environment." *The Development of National Social Service Programmes* (New York: United Nations, 1960).

5 Maurice Stack, "The Meaning of Social Security," William Haber and Wilbur J. Cohen (editors), *Readings in Social Security* (Englewood Cliffs, N.J.: Prentice-Hall, Inc., 1948), pp. 41-45.

edge of the community and of the social services, and upon the practical application of social work techniques in supervised field work. This study will present an analysis of the structure and functions of social welfare in their evolution up to the present, and of the underlying social philosophy.[6]

Social work is both a science and an art and is carried on in six different forms based upon a common core of knowledge and skill which we call "generic social work." [7] The six processes of social work are: (1) *social casework,* which helps the individual client to effect better social relationships and a social adjustment that makes it possible for him to lead a satisfying and useful life; (2) *social group work,* which helps people to participate in the activities of a group for their intellectual, emotional, and physical growth, and for the achievement of goals considered desirable by society; (3) *community organization,* the process of planning and developing social services in order to meet the health and welfare needs of a community or larger unit; (4) *social welfare administration,* the process of organizing and directing a social agency; (5) *social welfare research,* inquiry into the validity of the structure and methods of social work; and (6) *social action,* the organized group process for solving general social problems, and furthering social welfare objectives by legislative, social, health, or economic progress.

Social work has drawn its knowledge and insight from political science, psychology, sociology, economics, medicine, psychiatry, anthropology, biology, history, education, and philosophy, but, by synthesis, it has developed into a science of its own. As a profession, social work depends upon the body of knowledge based upon these other social sciences, the specific structure and function of social welfare activities, and the skill and responsibility which is required for each professional performance. As a helping process, social work

---

[6] The reader will find valuable information on current theory and practice of social welfare in the *Social Work Yearbook,* published by the National Association of Social Workers.

[7] The official interpretation of social work by the Armed Forces is narrower: "Social work is that process which deals directly and differentially with persons who have problems relating primarily to their social situation and which endeavors, individual to individual, to understand what help is needed, and to assist the individual to find and utilize the help indicated." *Social Work Journal,* Vol. XXXII, No. 1 (January 1951), p. 43.

assists people with problems of social and emotional adjustment and helps them to achieve greater social and personal satisfaction and independence.

Selected Bibliography *

*Abbott, Edith, *Social Welfare and Professional Education,* 2nd ed. Chicago: University of Chicago Press, 1942.

Barnes, Harry E., and Oreen Ruedi, *The American Way of Life,* 2nd ed. Englewood Cliffs, N.J.: Prentice-Hall, Inc., 1950.

*Bisno, Herbert, *The Philosophy of Social Work.* Washington, D.C.: Public Affairs Press, 1952.

Cassidy, Harry M., *Social Security and Reconstruction in Canada.* Boston: Humphries, 1943.

Cheney, Alice, *Nature and Scope of Social Work.* New York: American Association of Social Workers, 1926.

*de Schweinitz, Karl, *The Art of Helping People Out of Trouble.* Boston: Houghton, 1924.

Ellwood, Charles A., *A History of Social Philosophy.* Englewood Cliffs, N.J.: Prentice-Hall, Inc., 1938.

*Fink, Arthur E., Everett E. Wilson, and Merrill B. Conover, *The Field of Social Work,* 3rd ed. New York: Holt, 1955.

*Kahn, Alfred J. (editor), *Issues in American Social Work.* New York: Columbia University Press, 1959.

Kelso, Robert W., *The Science of Public Welfare.* New York: Holt, 1928.

*Konopka, Gisela, *Eduard C. Lindeman and Social Work Philosophy.* Minneapolis: University of Minnesota Press, 1958.

MacIver, Robert, *The Contribution of Sociology to Social Work.* New York: Columbia University Press, 1931.

Merrill, Francis E., and H. Wentworth Eldridge, *Culture and Society.* Englewood Cliffs, N.J.: Prentice-Hall, Inc., 1952.

Miles, Arthur P., *An Introduction to Public Welfare.* Boston: Heath, 1949.

Stroup, Herbert Hewitt, *Social Work: An Introduction to the Field.* New York: American Book (Revised ed.), 1960.

*Witmer, Helen L., *Social Work: An Analysis of a Social Institution.* New York: Farrar & Rinehart, 1942.

---

* Publications of particular value for the reader in this and the following bibliographies are marked with an asterisk (*).

2.

Old World Background

I. SOCIAL PROBLEMS

Modern anthropology and sociology have shown that with the beginning of human society the feeling of belonging, and the readiness to provide mutual protection, were just as influential as the selfish desire to dominate weaker human beings. Dating from this early phase of human development, mutual assistance can be called one of the fundamental drives which compensates for destroying or enslaving fellow men. Mutual aid served as the means of protection for family or tribe against the hostile world. The role of the head or chief was mainly that of protector against human enemies as well as against wild animals.

With the growth of tribes and the beginnings of religion, the priests assumed leadership in providing protection for the helpless, widows and orphans, and the sick. Religious devotion became the most powerful incentive for benevolence and charity. We find this motive in ancient religions, the Vendidad and Hindu philosophy, in Assyrian, Babylonian, and Egyptian codes, in Greek and Roman customs—particularly, however, in Jewish and Christian religious teachings.[1] Charity was motivated primarily by the desire to receive

---

[1] Amos G. Warner, *American Charities,* 3rd ed. (New York: Crowell, 1919), pp. 4-6; Stuart A. Queen, *Social Work in the Light of History* (Philadelphia: Lippincott, 1922), pp. 267-307; and Gisela Konopka, *Eduard C. Lindeman and Social Work Philosophy* (Minneapolis: University of Minnesota Press, 1958), pp. 84-88.

the grace of God or to secure the merits of good deeds for eternal life, but a genuine feeling of pity for the widows and orphans may well have been a reason that the demands of the churches for the relief of the poor were willingly followed. To relieve the distress of the unfortunate became, in Jewish and Christian concepts, an important religious duty. It was essential to the church as moral force, to the giver as a means of satisfaction and hope, to the destitute and to the community as a welcome aid. The teaching of the prophets in Israel and of St. Paul, St. Augustine, St. Francis, and St. Thomas Aquinas in the Christian church gave the recipient of alms dignity whereas almsgiving enobled the generous donor. The early Christians helped one another when facing poverty and persecution but the medieval church entrusted the administration of charity to the bishops, the local priest, and the deacons. With the growing influence of the church and the acceptance of Christianity as state religion, institutions for the poor were established in the monasteries, serving as orphanages, as homes for the old, the sick, and the handicapped, and as refuge for the homeless, continuing the tradition of the Greek *xenodochia* (guest houses). Particularly active in distributing alms to the poor were the Franciscans, founded by Saint Francis d'Assisi, and the Hospitallers, established by Guy de Montpelliers. They devoted their main activity to missionary preaching, collecting alms, and distributing relief to the destitute. Under these circumstances mendicancy grew throughout Europe since asking for alms was not only an easy way of making a living but was also socially respected because it was shared with the missionaries and monks, with students of the universities, and with the Crusaders on their way to the Holy Land. Although the church praised charity and almsgiving, the state did not take the same attitude. Beginning with the statute of Charlemagne in 800, secular authorities threatened to prohibit mendicancy and fined citizens who would give alms to able-bodied beggars. These decrees aimed to force serfs and rural laborers to stay on the manors, and to protect peasants and travelers against robbery by vagrant beggars. This conflict between church and state existed until the end of the Middle Ages.

The older church institutions in which charity was rendered—monasteries, abbeys, and convents—were partly replaced by the "hospitals" (*hôtels de Dieu*) which administered to old and sick persons, orphans, abandoned children, and pregnant women. They became the main agency of medieval charity. Hospitals were founded with the help of donations from kings, dukes, and members of the aristocracy. However, only some of the destitute found shelter and refuge in these institutions; many wandering beggars remained on the roads and were a curse with which local and state governments were unable to cope. The difference in ideology regarding beggars was not the only conflict in the field of charity between the church and the secular authorities. Another conflict arose over mismanagement of church institutions and hospitals and the abuse of funds, which led to criticism, measures of control, and the setting up of boards of supervision by the states. In order to stop vagrancy and mendicancy, many European states enacted repressive statutes imposing brutal penalties, but none really succeeded in wiping out vagabondage.

Still more violent became the conflict between church and state in the sixteenth century, during the period of the Reformation. In Germany, Martin Luther appealed in an open address, "Appeal to the Christian Nobility of the German Nation" (1520), to the princes to forbid begging and to organize in all parishes a "common chest" for the receipt of money, food, and clothes to assist the needy. Luther requested that regular contributions in addition to voluntary gifts be made to these chests. A similar plan for relief was carried out in Zurich, Switzerland, by the Protestant Reformator Ulrich Zwingli, in 1525. France, Austria, and the Scandinavian countries developed programs which resembled the Lutheran concept; the responsibility for the collection of funds and the distribution of relief to destitute, sick, and orphans was assumed by local authorities, but the church wardens played the leading role in relief administration.[2]

Although these methods recognized the legal responsibility of the community for the maintenance of the poor, they did little to change the social conditions of destitute families. The idea that the fate of the individual poor deserved attention was first conceived by the Spanish philosopher Juan Luis Vives in the sixteenth century. Vives was educated in Paris and lived most of his life in Belgium. A friend of Erasmus of Rotterdam and of Sir Thomas More, he was one of the noted scientists of his time. He developed a concise program of poor relief for the Consuls and the Senate of the city of Bruges in

---

[2] Karl de Schweinitz, *England's Road to Social Security* (Philadelphia: University of Pennsylvania Press, 1949), pp. 36-38.

Flanders under the title *"De Subventione Pauperum."* [3] He proposed dividing the city into parish quarters, assigning two senators with a secretary to each quarter in order to investigate the social conditions of every pauper family, and providing for aid through vocational training, employment, and rehabilitation, instead of the customary distribution of alms. For the aged and unemployable Vives asked commitment to a hospital (almshouse). These foresighted ideas were not practiced, however, in Continental Europe for a long time.

It was two and one-half centuries later that the methods of Vives' plan were applied in practice. This was done in Hamburg in 1788, where a reform of poor relief introduced a district system of investigation and distribution of relief to individual paupers through volunteer committees appointed by the Senate. The city was divided into sixty quarters following a plan suggested by Professor Busch, city senator and commissioner of public relief. Each quarter had about the same number of poor families. Each commission consisted of three respectable citizens who served without compensation. The investigations were directed by regulations of a central board composed of five senators and ten other citizens. The sixty commissions acted at the same time as agents of the "central poor house," interviewed the poor, inquired about their health, earnings, and morals, and determined the individual needs of each family. Children and adolescents were trained in elementary courses and in an industrial school attached to the central orphan asylum. [4]

A similar system of relief was inaugurated by an American tory, Benjamin Thompson, later Count of Rumford, in Munich in 1790. In order to prevent the begging of sturdy paupers, he founded a "military workhouse" which manufactured the clothing for the army. With the help of volunteer district commissions, able-bodied beggars were recruited for this workhouse. It also provided raw materials for home industry to persons in poverty who wanted to earn their living. Both the Hamburg and the Munich relief systems were financed by taxation and by collections of voluntary gifts. Although the system

---

[3] Juan Luis Vives, *Concerning the Relief of the Poor or Concerning Human Need,* A Letter Addressed to the Senate of Bruges. Translated by Margaret M. Sherwood, New York School of Philanthropy, 1927.

[4] K. de Schweinitz, *op. cit.* pp. 91-99; and, Walter Friedlander and Earl Dewey Myers, *Child Welfare in Germany Before and After Naziism* (Chicago: University of Chicago Press, 1940), pp. 39-44.

was actually used first in Hamburg, it was called the *Elberfeld system*. The city of Elberfeld introduced the same plan in 1853 and financed it exclusively from public taxation. The volunteers of the Elberfeld commissions lived in the same quarter as the poor whom they supervised, and thus were closely acquainted with their conditions. Later a large number of other European cities adopted this program.

The most important reformer of the charities of the Catholic Church was Father Vincent de Paul in France who was active during the seventeenth century. This young priest had been captured by Tunisian pirates and sold as a galley slave. Sharing for a number of years the fate of the most unfortunate, he devoted his life after his escape to the improvement of charities, especially for prisoners and their families, orphans, illegitimate children, and the sick and hungry. He succeeded in arousing interest among the aristocracy and at the royal court, and obtained large foundations for the establishment of hospitals, orphanages, and foundling asylums. Not satisfied with such spectacular success, he persuaded the ladies of the court to devote themselves to personal services for the destitute and sick. He organized a lay order, the "Ladies of Charity," whose members visited the poor in their homes, distributing food and clothes. In order to improve the methods of nursing the sick and handicapped, in 1633 Father Vincent founded another order, the "Daughters of Charity," composed of young women of the peasant class who wanted to devote themselves to charitable work. They were trained in nursing the poor and became the forerunners of the social worker. The ideas of Father Vincent caused important reforms to be made in the entire charity program under Catholic auspices, not only in France, but also in other countries.

II. EARLY CHARITIES IN ENGLAND

In medieval England, care of the poor was an activity of the church. To give alms to the destitute, blind, and lame was a religious duty, and a means of salvation from the threat of divine punishment after death. Since the main motive for almsgiving was the salvation of the soul of the donor, he usually had little concern for the human being who received his charity. Beginning in the fourteenth century, however, some distinction was made between two classes of the poor: the able-bodied poor who could earn their living, and the impotent poor who were unable to work—the blind, the lame, the aged, the sick, young children, and pregnant women. For the care of the poor the church devoted from one-fourth to one-third of the tithes and offerings collected from its parishioners.

Relief to the destitute was first distributed by the priest of the parish, with the help of the churchwardens and deacons. In the thirteenth and fourteenth centuries, religious orders and church institutions relieved the parish churches from most of the duties of caring for the poor. In the fifteenth century more than a thousand monasteries, convents, hospitals, and abbeys provided shelter, alms, food, and clothes for the poor or for wandering beggars. Many institutions were maintained by endowments donated for charitable purposes by members of the royal house and the aristocracy. Although daily distributions of food were made at the convent gate and shelter was granted to the homeless, little was done to change the social conditions of the poor so that they might become self-supporting again.

Whereas the church was by far the most important charitable institution of this period, its work was supplemented from the twelfth to the fifteenth century by the relief activities of the guilds. Craft and merchant guilds, rural fraternities, and social or church guilds were organized primarily for the purpose of mutual self-help, brotherhood, and fellowship. Therefore, they supported first their own sick or needy members, and their widows and orphans, but they also organized charities for the poor of the town. Particularly in times of droughts and famines, they distributed barley and corn to the destitute, fed them on certain feast days, and offered free lodgings to poor travelers.

Until the fourteenth century, the King and Parliament did not concern themselves with the charities of the church and the guilds. With the slow disappearance of feudalism and the social changes resulting from a new economic order which freed the serfs and employed agricultural labor for wages, the King and his nobles faced the problem of how to maintain order among the laborers and prevent vagrancy. The emancipation of the rural laborer from serfdom on the manor created new problems. Formerly the serf and his family were fed and clad by the lord, and the lady cared for the old and the sick. Emancipation gave the laborer and his family the freedom to

14 OLD WORLD BACKGROUND

wander, but it deprived him of his former security. In times of unemployment, sickness, old age, and invalidity, he was forced to go begging. At the beginning of the Industrial Revolution the manufacture of wool opened some work to the laborer, but resident workers were hired first. During the summer, workers migrated from one part of the country to another in order to find work in harvesting the crops. Soldiers returning from the wars in France often preferred to live in the towns rather than to go back to their hard, low-paid work and dependency on the manor. These social conditions increased the danger of poverty.

The first poor law in England was based upon a national catastrophe.[5] In 1348, the plague or "Black Death," brought in from the Levant on ships carrying infected rats killed two-thirds of the entire English population within two years. It caused a severe shortage of labor on the manors and resulted in a steep rise in wages. Urged by the landed gentry, King Edward III issued the *Statute of Laborers* of 1349. It ordered that able-bodied laborers without means must accept employment from any master willing to hire them and forbade them to leave their own parish. Citizens were not allowed to give alms to able-bodied beggars. The *Statute of Laborers* became the first of many laws in the development of the "Erastian State" in which secular power replaced clerical authority. It was designed to prevent vagrancy and begging, and to force the rural worker to stay on the land. Cruel punishment such as being put into the stocks, being whipped, branded, or mutilated by cutting off the ears and the nose, being condemned to the galleys, and finally hanged was ordered for beggars and vagrants. When the expanding woolen industry made sheep raising more profitable for the gentry than growing grain crops, tilled land was converted into pasture. Only a small number of shepherds were needed to replace the large numbers of rural laborers, and the unemployed families joined the ranks of former soldiers and sailors unable to find work.

The first constructive measure taken by government for relief of the poor was the statute of Henry VIII in 1531. It provided that

---

[5] The description of the development of social welfare in England presented in Karl de Schweinitz, *England's Road to Social Security, 1349 to 1947* (Philadelphia: University of Pennsylvania Press, 1949) is recommended for further study. See also Brian Tiernay, *Medieval Poor Law* (Berkeley: University of California Press, 1959).

mayors and justices of the peace should investigate applications of the aged and paupers unable to work who were maintained by the parish. They were to be registered and licensed to beg in an assigned area. This law was the beginning of a recognition of public responsibility for the poor, but it still threatened brutal punishment for other beggars and vagrants.

The Reformation brought a fundamental change in the entire system of charities and relief for the poor in England. One of its features was the secularization of the monasteries and hospitals which had been the primary source for the relief of the destitute. The influence of the guilds had vanished during the fifteenth century. Other benevolent foundations which formerly provided aid to needy groups no longer did so, and with the confiscation of church property by Henry VIII it became necessary to provide otherwise for the care of the poor. Therefore, the *Statute of 1536* established the first plan of public relief under the auspices of the government in England. It ruled that paupers could be registered in their parishes only after they had resided for three years in the county. The parish had to maintain the "impotent poor" from voluntary contributions of the parishioners through church collections. Able-bodied beggars were forced to work, and idle children from five to fourteen years of age were taken away from their parents and indentured. In 1562, the *Statute of Artificers* was issued which regulated wages and hours of labor and sought to increase the skill of artisans by an apprentice system. It required that vagrants and vagabonds be forced to hard labor and that unemployed beggars between twelve and sixty years of age be hired out as servants. However, voluntary collections proved to be insufficient for the support of the poor. Their ranks had been swelled by disbanded monks, nuns, and by thousands of families formerly sheltered or employed in monasteries and convents. As work became scarce and the price of food rose, vagrancy and begging increased. In 1563, Parliament had to adopt compulsory measures to finance parish poor relief. Each householder was compelled by law to make a weekly contribution based upon property and income.

In 1572, Queen Elizabeth signed a statute of Parliament that introduced a *general* tax to provide funds for *poor relief* and established overseers of the poor to administer the new law. The *Statute of 1572* marked the final recognition that the government was responsible for providing aid to people who could not maintain themselves. In 1576 "houses of correction," supplied with wool, hemp, flax, and iron, were established in which the able-bodied poor, particularly young persons, were forced to work.

The *Statute of 1597* confirmed that the churchwardens and four substantial householders were to be appointed as overseers of the poor by the justices of the peace. Almshouses should be erected for the impotent poor, the old, the blind, the lame, and those unable to work, and parents and children were made liable for each other's maintenance.

III. THE ELIZABETHAN POOR LAW OF 1601

The *Poor Law of 1601*, often referred to as "43 Elizabeth," was a codification of the preceding poor relief legislation. Its only new feature was the establishment of liability for support to grandparents as well as to parents in need. The statute represented the final form of poor law legislation in England after three generations in which public opinion had been greatly excited about the necessary provisions for the poor in a period of political, religious, and economic changes that required government action. The law confirmed the responsibility of the parish—the local community—for the maintenance of the poor who were not supported by their relatives. The parish's responsibility to aid the destitute was limited to persons who had been born there or who had at least lived in the parish for three years. This question of "residence" or "settlement right" as one of the important requirements for the receipt of public relief has remained a vital issue in public assistance up to the present time.

The *Poor Law of 1601* did not permit the registration of a person as being in need of charity whenever his relatives, husband or wife, parents or children were able to support him. The "principle of relatives' responsibility" or "family responsibility" means that relatives have to assume the primary obligation for supporting the poor, and that public relief authorities aid the destitute only if the family cannot maintain him. This question of family responsibility also has persisted in being a serious problem in public assistance. The law distinguished three classes of the poor:

(1) *The Able-bodied Poor.* They were called "sturdy beggars"

and were forced to work in the "house of correction" or "work-house." Citizens were forbidden to give them alms, and paupers who arrived from other parishes were returned to the place where they had last dwelt for a year. A beggar or "valiant vagabond" who refused to work in the house of correction was put in the stocks or in jail.

(2) *The Impotent Poor.* These were people unable to work—the sick, the old, the blind, deaf-mute, the lame, the demented, and mothers with young children. They were to be placed in the alms-house where they were to help within the limits of their capacities. If the impotent poor had a place to live and it seemed less expensive to maintain them there, the overseers of the poor could grant them "outdoor relief," usually "in kind," sending food, clothes, and fuel to their homes.

(3) *Dependent Children.* These were orphans, foundlings, and children who had been deserted by their parents or whose parents were so poor that they could not support them. These children were to be placed out to any citizen who was willing to take them without a charge. If no such "free home" was available, the child was to be given to the lowest bidder. Children of eight years and older who were able to do some domestic and other work were indentured with a townsman. Boys were taught the trade of their master and had to serve until their twenty-fourth birthday. Girls were brought up as domestic servants and remained in indenture until they were twenty-one years of age or married.

The "overseers of the poor" administered the poor law in the parish. They were appointed by the justices of the peace or magistrates. Their function was to receive the application of the poor person for relief, to investigate his condition, and to decide whether he was "eligible" for relief. The overseers decided whether the applicant and his family should be placed in the workhouse or almshouse, were to be "sold out," or should receive aid in their own home. As a rule, an old disused building served as almshouse and workhouse. In the work-house the inmates were forced to do hard labor, under the supervision of a superintendent who was appointed by the overseers of the poor. The overseers had to collect the poor tax assessed upon land, houses, and tithes of all inhabitants, and to register assessment and payments. The poor tax was the main source for the financing of poor relief. It was supplemented by private donations and bequests, and by the use of fines for the violation of certain statutes.

The *Poor Law of 1601* set the pattern of public relief under governmental responsibility for Great Britain for three hundred years. It established the principle that the local community—the parish— had to organize and finance poor relief for its residents, provide sustenance to the unemployable and children, and work to the ablebodied. It still maintained many of the earlier features of repression and disdain for the destitute, but it also accepted an obligation for the aid of people who could not provide for themselves. The fundamental provisions of the Elizabethan *Poor Law* were incorporated into the laws of the American colonies and have remained an important element even in the present concepts of public assistance and in the considerations of the public in regard to social legislation.

A. The Settlement Act of 1662

Since each parish was responsible for the maintenance of its own poor, it wanted to protect itself against an additional burden created by the moving in of poor persons from other communities who might ask for relief. The gentry, however, were anxious to retain on the land rural laborers who were needed for the cultivation of the estates. Following the pressure of both the parishes and the gentry, Charles II enacted in 1662 the *Law of Settlement*. It empowered the justices of the peace to return to his former residence any newcomer who, in the opinion of the overseers of the poor, might at some future date become a public charge. Within forty days after arrival, the overseers had to investigate and might request from the justice of peace that the newcomers be expelled. However, if the new family was able to rent property for ten pounds sterling a year or to deposit this sum, it was exempted from the threat of removal.

This statute was the expression of an extreme parochialism. It discriminated against the common laborer who could not afford a deposit or a rent of ten pounds sterling a year. It represented a post-feudal attempt to force the rural workers to stay in their villages, although the industrial development of the towns offered greater promise for them. Difficulties arose in some towns when the overseers, eager to get rid of paupers, offered them bribes to go clandestinely to another parish. Therefore, in 1686, King James II ruled that the prescribed forty days for investigation should be counted only from the date on which the newcomer sent a written report on his abode and his family to the overseers or the churchwardens. A few years later, in 1691, King William III required that an announcement of the arrival of newcomers be posted in the church. Despite these legal amendments, frequent disputes between townships arose over the question of whether or not laborers had gained settlement in a parish. Litigation before the courts and useless transportation of families and witnesses cost the country a great deal of money. Furthermore, the statute prevented workers from going during harvest time to other counties where they were badly needed. These economic conditions made necessary further changes in the administration of the settlement law. Mobility of labor was finally achieved by the introduction of the "certificate," a document issued by the parish authorities which guaranteed that the township would pay the cost of maintenance of the bearer if he should be in need. Thereafter, each community requested such a certificate from newcomers. It was not until 1795 that the *Act of 1662* was amended so that a newcomer could not be sent back to his former residence until he actually had applied for relief. Even so vagabonds, "disorderly persons," and unmarried pregnant women could still be forcibly expelled immediately.

B. Workhouses and Outdoor Relief

During the second half of the seventeenth century, the English were in fierce commercial competition with the Dutch, who had succeeded in developing an efficient industry and trade. English economists admired the absence of beggars in the streets and the productive operation of the Dutch almshouses, in which inmates manufactured goods for export. The desire to keep raw materials, wool and mining iron in England and to produce finished goods for export led to the training of the poor for industry. Following the *Workhouse Act of 1696,* workhouses in Bristol and other cities instructed the inmates, adults and children, in spinning, knitting, linen weaving, lace work, and in the manufacture of nets and sails. However, these experiments had no economic success since the unemployed poor had no particular training and could not compete with workshops employing skilled foremen and laborers. In 1722, the overseers were authorized to make contracts with private manufacturers who employed the paupers, and relief was refused to any person not willing to enter the workhouse. This "workhouse test" forced families to give up their homes and to live in the workhouse as in a prison, the men separated from their wives and children. Many paupers preferred to live in utmost poverty with their families rather than to move to the workhouse or "house of correction." Workhouses conducted by private contractors attempted to make profits by spending as little as possible for equipment and repair and for the food and clothing of the inmates, but the work of the tired and hungry inhabitants was so inadequate that the contractors still operated at a loss. The mistreatment of the inmates, the lack of fresh air and proper sanitation, and the immorality in the overcrowded wards aroused serious criticism from ministers and social reformers such as Jonas Hanway, Joseph Townsend, Richard Burn, John Scott, and Thomas Gilbert. The first of the crusaders for a reform of the workhouse, Jonas Hanway, spent several years in the study of these institutions. He exposed the appalling rate of infant mortality in the workhouses where sometimes 82 per cent of all babies under one year of age died. In 1761, on the incentive of Hanway, Parliament attempted to improve these conditions by the registration of all infants in workhouses, and in 1767 the removal from the workhouse of all children under six years and their placement with foster families was ruled.

One of the most persistent reformers of the workhouse was Thomas Gilbert. As a magistrate he knew of the failures of the poor laws, but as member of the House of Commons he could appraise them with more effect. The *Poor Law Amendment of 1782,* known as the "Gilbert Act," abolished the "contractor system" of the workhouse, replaced the honorary overseers of the poor by salaried "guardians of the poor," and reversed the principle of "indoor relief" by the provision that persons able and willing to work should be maintained in their own homes until employment was procured.

Economic changes in England, however, were a continuous source of increasing poverty. For centuries the poor man had used the "commons" of the village. He had grown vegetables, potatoes, barley, and wheat for his family, had grazed his sheep, geese, pigs, or cows, and had thus supplemented the meager earnings from his small field or from working as a tenant farmer. The "enclosure movement" which began in the fourteenth century, enlarged the holdings of the landed aristocracy, but took away from the poor peasant the livestock and products that had made it possible for him to maintain his family. Moreover, many peasants lived on the common land and thought they owned it. With the "enclosure," they became "squatters," landless poor, and were forced to move. In industry, the invention of power machinery, driven by wind or water, transferred production from villages and small towns to larger cities where water transportation was available. The place of manufacture shifted from the home of the craftsman to the larger workshop and mill. The growth of industry tended to increase the number of workers, but the new machinery in the mills replaced many of the hand weavers, thus creating unemployed paupers and vagrants.

C. Partial Relief

The war with France from 1793 to 1815, following the French Revolution, increased the cost of living. Disabled war veterans refused to go to the poorhouse with their families and insisted upon receiving poor relief in their own homes. Magistrates and guardians became concerned with the suffering of the poor and considered means to increase wages or to secure a minimum wage. In May 1795, a conference of poor-law officials of Berkshire County at Speenhamland decided to establish "a table of universal practice," which determined the amount of relief on the basis of the local cost of bread needed for the sustenance of the family. This so-called "bread scale" was to be used also to supplement wages of laborers whose earnings were less than this minimum subsistence. The new practice spread to other places and was approved by Parliament by the *Speenhamland Act of 1795*. The statute authorized relief allowances in the homes of the poor, according to the size of the family, either for their support or to supplement low wages. It led to widespread use of outdoor relief for old, infirm, and handicapped persons.

As a result of these measures, wages and the general standard of living were lowered. More and more persons received full or partial relief and, therefore, contributed to the need for higher poor tax rates. Employers became accustomed to paying substandard wages and to referring workers to the guardians of the poor. Relief destroyed the worker's incentive to do a good job and tended to keep wages down to the bread scale.

It is not difficult to understand why such a system was severely criticized. The opposition centered on the granting of relief to persons in their own homes, that is, "outdoor relief." This practice was held responsible for the economic and moral failure of the program. In reality, it was not just the method of "direct" or "outdoor" relief which caused undesirable effects, but rather the failure to secure minimum wages that would maintain the worker, and the lack of administrative ability for constructive use of poor relief. With the increasing cost of the poor rate, dissatisfaction among taxpayers was aggravated by the uneven distribution of this burden. Communities with a large number of paupers frequently had few wealthy merchants so that the poor tax had to be collected from householders of modest income. Another criticism of poor law practice was based upon the economic theory of laissez-faire, as presented in Adam Smith's *Wealth of Nations*.[6] It postulated that the state should not interfere with private economy so that the manufacturer could reap the profits of production. Supporters of Smith's doctrine, such as Jeremy Bentham and Reverend Joseph Townsend, suggested a gradual decrease and, finally, the elimination of public poor relief. The most influential representative of this theory was another clergyman, Thomas R. Malthus. In his famous *Essay on Population,* which appeared in 1798, he explained that the food supply increased only in arithmetic progression, the population in geometric progression, and that agriculture, therefore, was unable to feed a steadily increasing population—a situation, he claimed, that made war, famine, and pestilence necessary to stem this dangerous growth. Malthus disapproved of poor relief because it tended to encourage paupers to have more children in order to get relief for them, and tended to raise the price of food, which again impoverished the entire working class.

Although the opposition of the classical economists to public relief had a theoretical, financial, and commercial basis, objection of others, such as John Stuart Mill, to the poor law practices was founded upon humanitarian and moral considerations. Reverend Thomas Chalmers (1780-1847), a parish minister in the small community of Kilmany, Scotland, organized a program of private charity on the principle of neighborly aid. An eloquent preacher, he

---

[6] *An Inquiry Into the Nature and Causes of the Wealth of Nations,* published in 1776.

was called to Glasgow in 1814, and found there an expensive system of poor relief, financed from public taxes and from church collections. Chalmers opposed the impersonal character and inefficiency of this charity. At Kilmany he had visited each home of the parish, and he resumed this custom at the large Tron parish in Glasgow with its 11,000 members. His visits revealed numerous personal and health problems which had been unknown before. After four successful years, Chalmers was called to organize the St. John parish in a very poor section of Glasgow. He accepted on condition that he would be given full control over the administration of relief. He divided this parish into twenty-five districts, with about 400 parishioners each, under the guidance of a deacon who investigated relief applications. The surprising result was that during four years only twenty new applicants, from a parish population of 8,000, were found in need.

Based upon this experience, Chalmers proclaimed that the prevalent practice of public and church relief was wasteful, demoralized the pauper, destroyed his will to support himself; that it eliminated the will of his relatives, friends, and neighbors to help; and that it failed to use the readiness of philanthropists to aid the poor. Chalmers suggested the following procedure: (1) each case of distress be carefully investigated, the cause of destitution determined, and the possibilities of self-maintenance of the pauper developed; (2) if self-support was not possible, relatives, friends, and neighbors be encouraged to care for orphans, the aged, the sick and handicapped; (3) if the need of the family could not thus be met, some wealthy citizens be found to maintain the family; (4) only if none of these measures succeeded, the deacon of the district should ask for the help of the congregation.

Chalmers' important contribution to the field of charity was his philosophy of personal, parochial relief. He developed the principle of investigating each case of destitution on an individual basis and of attempting a solution of the cause of distress. Chalmers, like his contemporaries, considered personal failures as the main cause of poverty and overlooked the economic and social factors outside the power of the individual. Nevertheless, his concept that a personal interest in the fate of the destitute is essential, was important to the progress of relief work. Fifty years after Chalmers' pioneer work, the London Charity Organization Society organized a program of relief that was, in the main, based upon Thomas Chalmers' ideas. They laid the first foundation for the individual approach in social work which today we call "case work."

IV. POOR LAW REFORM OF 1834

Severe opposition to the poor law practice, the rising flood of pauperism, and the heavy increase in the poor tax burden, led in 1832 to the appointment of a "Royal Commission for Inquiring into the Administration and Practical Operation of the Poor Laws." Its chairman became Professor Nassau W. Senior, a noted economist, and its secretary, Edwin Chadwick, a brilliant young lawyer, who had studied under Jeremy Bentham. The Commission undertook for two years in every county of England an extensive survey of poor law administration and rendered its report in 1834. The report emphasized that the prevailing practice of poor relief had failed to bring children and able-bodied adults to work and had made them "permanent paupers" instead of self-supporting citizens, particularly through the introduction of "partial relief." Poor tax rates were used as subsidies to farmers, landlords, storekeepers, and manufacturers. The six main recommendations of the report were: (a) to abolish "partial relief" as provided under the Speenhamland system; (b) to place all able-bodied applicants for relief in the workhouse; (c) to grant "outdoor relief" only to the sick, the old, the invalid, and to widows with young children; (d) to coordinate the administration of relief of several parishes into a "poor law union"; (e) to make the conditions of poor relief recipients less desirable than those of the lowest paid worker in the community *(Principle of "Less Eligibility");* and (f) to establish a central board of control to be appointed by the King.

These recommendations were enacted August 14, 1834, a statute known in England for one hundred years as The New Poor Law.

"Poor Law Unions" were formed by neighboring parishes. They were administered by a Board of Guardians, composed of representatives of each parish with a paid staff, and managed a common workhouse and almshouse. In order to develop a uniform poor law policy, a Permanent Royal Poor Law Commission was appointed with three commissioners; Edwin Chadwick was its first secretary and George Coode, assistant secretary. Fifteen assistant commissioners visited poor law unions, attended meetings of the boards of guardians, and inspected workhouses and almshouses.

The application of the legal principle of less eligibility meant that poor relief was granted to the destitute in such a meager amount and in such a derogatory way that its receipt put the poor in a condition less desirable than that of the lowest paid laborer in the community. By maintaining this principle the boards of guardians thought to force relief applicants to accept any type of labor rather than ask for public support. This concept has persisted in public assistance in many parts of the world. The public is afraid that destitute persons prefer to receive poor relief to exerting themselves in unpleasant manual work; the amount of assistance, therefore, should be less than the wage earned by a low-paid worker and should not provide a higher standard of living than can be earned by honest work. But, in cases of large families, the maintenance of the children might require a higher amount than some underpaid workers earn, and for this reason the old idea of "less eligibility" is still a controversial issue.

From the point of view of financial economy, the reform of 1834 was a success. It reduced the cost of poor relief between 1834 and 1837 by more than one-third; two hundred workhouses were constructed and old institutions improved. Able-bodied poor were forced to go to the workhouse with their families as a test of their economic need. No separate buildings for almshouses and workhouses were established, however, as had been recommended by the Commission in 1834. Old and young people, sturdy and ill, feeble-minded, insane, and cripples were placed in the same institution. Families were broken up, because women, young boys and girls, the aged, crippled, and infirm were assigned to separate wards of the workhouse. Mothers were permitted to care for their young children in the so-called "nursery" only at prescribed hours. Under a rigid discipline, inmates were forced to hard labor as much as their physical strength permitted and were treated not much differently than convicts. No wonder that the workhouse was very unpopular, and hated by the working class. Disraeli said in a famous address that the reform bill of 1834 pronounced that to be poor in England was a crime.

The reform of 1834 meant a resumption of the rigid, repressive measures of the *Poor Law of 1601*. It reduced the expenditures for poor relief, but made life in the workhouse so unbearable that the poor asked for relief only when there was no other way to survive. These methods did not consider the danger of mass poverty in periods of unemployment and economic depression. Therefore, some poor law unions introduced "a work test outside the workhouse," and permitted the poor to receive outdoor relief in their homes. In order to maintain uniform practices, the *Outdoor Relief Regulation Order of 1852* upheld the principle of "less eligibility." These measures were violently resented by the working class who called the workhouse the "bastille." The interest in the poor was awakened by such humanitarians as Charles Dickens who published his "Oliver Twist" with its description of workhouse life in 1837 and 1838, and by members of Parliament who disliked the power entrusted to the poor law commissioners. The Poor Law Commission also had internal difficulties. Edwin Chadwick was an energetic, aggressive reformer, not content with the cautious actions of the commissioners. In 1847, the Commission was replaced by a Poor Law Board whose president had a seat in the House of Commons. The four other members of the Board were appointed by the Crown. Edwin Chadwick became General Commissioner of the Poor and supervised investigations into the causes of poverty and the means of an effective social reform.

Earlier surveys made by the poor law commissioners with the assistance of medical inspectors, especially Dr. Southwood Smith, had revealed that widespread prevalence of disease among the lower classes was a major cause of destitution. Disease deprived the laborer and his family of the means of livelihood and made them dependent upon public relief. Disease among the poor was caused mainly by unhealthy housing and living conditions and by malnutrition. In urban slums people lived in overcrowded quarters, and often adolescents and children of both sexes slept in one bed. This led to promiscuity, quarrels, delinquency, immorality, and rapid spread of contagious diseases. Many workingmen as boarders lived with families in the same room. Often seven to ten used one sleeping room, or lived in damp, dark cellars without any ventilation. All over England the poorer quarters were without water supply and drainage; drinking water was often polluted in rivers or deficient pipelines. There were usually no outside toilets and no sewers in the streets. The refuse was thrown into the public gutter, and there existed no scavenger service or regular street cleaning, although occasionally this was done by inmates of the workhouse. Another cause of epidemics was the failure to bury the dead, among the poor, until the poor law guardians assumed the cost of the funeral.

On the initiative of Edwin Chadwick, the Poor Law Board brought these conditions to the attention of Parliament. Chadwick thus became the first pioneer of public hygiene. He developed a program of protection against contagious diseases by sanitary provisions for water systems, sewage, and drainage. He also advocated the establishment of parks and flower gardens for the recreation of the population. Due to his insistence, free public vaccination against cholera, typhus, and smallpox was introduced in 1840. The *Public Health Act* of August 31, 1848, established a General Board of Health, and Edwin Chadwick served as one of its members. The Board supported local authorities in the fight against epidemics, in the improvement of housing conditions in the slums, and in the establishment of sanitation. In spite of his devoted service, Edwin Chadwick again found severe opposition. After six years he was dismissed because the House of Commons felt that he entrusted too much power to a central health authority, and because the physicians complained that he infringed upon vested interests of the medical profession. Undertakers and water-supply companies also complained that their profits were curtailed by the regulations of the Board of Health.

Chadwick was a prophet far ahead of his contemporaries. It took many decades before his vision of a system of government providing under central direction decent aid to the poor, a sound public health protection, adequate housing, recreation, and public schools for the entire population became an accepted concept of society.

V. CHILD LABOR AND FACTORY LEGISLATION

Until the beginning of the nineteenth century, social policy in England had been used to suppress the laboring classes in the interest of the land owners, the manufacturers, and the merchants. Pauper children were set to work by "selling" them to farmers, by indenture to craftsmen, or by hard labor in almshouses. The development of the textile mills in the nineteenth century, however, offered an unprecedented opportunity to use the poorhouse children. They were offered to textile manufacturers as cheap labor. The fate of these children became deplorable. Some were as young as four, five, or six years of age, and there was no legal limitation of their working hours. So-called "slappers" held them awake by whipping them when they fell asleep. A typical day of such a poor child leased out to a textile mill was as follows: The children got up at four to five in the morning. The younger ones had to pick up cotton waste from the factory floor all day. Children of six or seven years were put to the spinning wheel or to the loom where their small, deft, flexible fingers could throw the thread quicker than adults. The children usually had half an hour for a frugal breakfast and an hour for a lunch of similar quality. During working hours they had to stand and were not allowed to leave their work place, outside of the meals, to go to the toilet or to get a drink of water. The latter was strictly prohibited, and if it did occur, the hapless child was brutally punished by whipping. As a rule, the child's labor was completed after five or six in the evening, often hours later, so that the working day was sometimes sixteen to eighteen hours long. The lack of sleep, of fresh air and sunshine, of rest and of any vacation made many of these children undernourished, weak, and sick. Many died in their teens, when they had worked themselves to death.[7]

The first step in the direction of their protection was taken by the *Health and Morals Act of 1802,* passed on the initiative of Sir Robert Peel, who objected to the use of young children in labor camps at the textile mills. The statute of 1802 restricted the working hours of "pauper apprentices" to twelve hours a day, and forbade night work for children. The law applied, however, only to pauper children leased out from the poor houses. Cotton-mill owners, however, hired children directly from their parents and continued to exploit them without any limit of working hours.

Concerned about these conditions, Sir Robert Peel, Robert Owen, John Wood, and John Fielden pursued the demand for a protection of working children against mistreatment and overwork which was so destructive to their health. In Parliament Michael Sadler, Anthony Ashley Cooper (later the Earl of Shaftesbury), R. Cobden, and James Graham became the advocates of child labor legislation. This movement led to the enactment of the *Factory Act of 1833,* which

---

[7] Grace Abbott, *The Child and the State,* Vol. I (Chicago: University of Chicago Press, 1938), pp. 138-152.

prohibited the employment of children under nine in the textile industry and limited daily working hours for children. At the suggestion of Edwin Chadwick, the law introduced the appointment of factory inspectors under a central, national office. An amendment of the *Factory Act of 1847* ordered a daily maximum of ten working hours for women and children under eighteen years.

The industrial development of England and the economic crises which accompanied the introduction of modern machinery led to several periods of unemployment. Local boards of guardians were forced to borrow money in order to maintain the workhouses or to provide public works in times of widespread unemployment. Even so, the conditions in numerous workhouses were unbearable. Most workhouses had inadequate sanitary facilities, poor ventilation, and lack of medical and nursing care for the sick and the aged. The beds were so short that inmates were unable to sleep well. Above all, superintendents and attendants were, as a rule, ignorant and callous people. Legislative reforms led to an expansion of the supervisory powers of the Poor Law Board. In 1871, the Local Government Board was founded, and took over the functions of the Board of Health and of the Poor Law Board. The new board maintained the policy of advocating the workhouse test and of warning the boards of guardians against a liberal granting of outdoor relief. The Local Government Board failed to recognize that such stern treatment usually fell upon broken-down, depressed, and feeble persons who could not obtain employment and needed encouragement and help for their rehabilitation.

VI. PRISON REFORM

Since the Middle Ages, prisons had been the place of severe human suffering. The medieval dungeons, often situated without light and air in the deep, humid cellars of old castles, were not much different from the prisons used during the seventeenth to the nineteenth century. The convicts suffered from hunger and cold, neglect and brutal beatings. The prison population consisted not only of offenders convicted for crime but also included persons who could not pay their civil debts. Nevertheless, all inmates were forced to pay the jailer for their upkeep since he and his assistants lived off the money they extorted from the prisoners and their families and friends. Some charitable donations provided prisoners with bread, beef, and broth on Sundays and holidays, but did not change the miserable conditions in the prisons and on the floating jail-hulks on the Thames.

In 1681, Thomas Firmin began to free hundreds of unfortunate debtors from prison by paying their small debts and the jailers' fees, and other philanthropists followed his example. In 1700, a meeting of the Society for Promoting Christian Knowledge advocated that jailers found guilty of extortion and mistreatment should be dismissed.

The demand for a reform of the prisons was rising throughout the eighteenth century. Among the early reformers who became deeply concerned about the inhuman treatment of the victims of penal institutions was General Oglethorpe. One of his friends, a young architect Castell, had been imprisoned for debt in the London Fleet prison, in 1728; after he was forced to spend all his money for his upkeep, he was sent to the "sponging house" in spite of his plea that he would die there because it was infected with smallpox. His fear proved justified, he contracted the disease and died. The House of Commons appointed a committee of inquiry with Oglethorpe as chairman. The investigations led to some improvements, especially the prohibition of sale of liquors in prisons.

The work of prison reform found its strongest advocate in another philanthropist, John Howard. He was born 1726 as son of a well-to-do London tradesman. He was of delicate health, a quiet, self-enclosed, deeply religious young man without ambitions for honors and conformity. The death of his father left him at the age of sixteen heir to a considerable fortune. He traveled through France and Italy and became interested in the relief of the people of Lisbon, which had been destroyed in the earthquake of 1755. He decided to sail to Lisbon in order to organize a relief action. The ship on which he was sailing was captured by a privateer, and together with other passengers and the crew he was brought to Brest and confined to a filthy, dark dungeon as a prisoner of war. During the following months, Howard and his companions were dragged through several other prisons along the French coast, and he discovered that everywhere the conditions were the same—unhealthy, cold quarters (without light and air), insufficient food, no bedding, no blankets, and brutal treatment. Howard finally suceeded in being released under his pledge to find an exchange in England. There he began telling of his horrible adversities. This experience became the root of Howard's life work for prison reform. During the following decade, he improved housing conditions of his tenants, on his estate, whom he encouraged by low rent and active support to reconstruct their homes, to education of their children, and to participate in church and recreational activities. After making studies of prisons in France, Italy, Switzerland, and Holland, Howard was nominated Sheriff of Bedford, in 1773, at the age of forty-six. In general, the office was a post of honor, but Howard took his assignment seriously and devoted his time to its duties. He sat in the courts during the trials and visited all prisoners in the jails of the county. His conscience was aroused when defendants accused of crimes, but not found guilty, were often dragged back to jail, after already having suffered months of unjust imprisonment before trial because they could not pay the fees to the jailer. In surrounding counties, John Howard found the same conditions of prisons that had shocked him when he was incarcerated in France. Debtors who could not pay their debts were treated like felons who had committed serious crimes, and men were hanged as certainly for stealing a pair of shoes as for arson or murder. The job of feeding the prisoners was farmed out to the highest bidder. Tap-selling of beer and liquor induced the jail-keeper to encourage drunkenness and orgies under his eyes. Because no separation between the sexes was properly secured, temptation and vice were prevalent. The prisoners were kept in idleness, whereas Howard had observed that in continental countries the prison inmates were put to work. The jailers and their helpers were coarse and ignorant men, selected for their brutality and insensibility to human suffering. The decayed, insecure buildings led to the use of irons, clubs, and whipping to prevent escape.

Many prisons had no water supply, and the excrements of a large mass of prisoners accumulated in heaps of poisonous feculence within the precincts. The prisoners were forced to sleep upon muddy floors and a rotten mass of litter in their cells while the stench of the manure oozed into them. No wonder that prisoners died from cold and from the "gaol-fever." No ventilation or light was available in the overcrowded cells. The prisoners did not receive religious or moral comfort, since most of the prison chaplains were rough, idle men who preferred to drink and gamble with the debtors. John Howard's sense of justice was aroused, and he recorded his distressing observations with the conclusion that a more searching investigation was necessary. In the House of Commons, John Howard was invited to speak as an expert on prison questions. He continued his studies on travels to the European continent and published, in 1777, his work, *On the State of the Prisons in England and Wales, with Preliminary Observations and an Account of Some Foreign Prisons and Hospitals,* written with the aid of his friends Reverend Densham and Dr. Price. The book was received with unusual interest by the public and was highly praised. Although it led to improvements in English prisons, to better food and ventilation, to the cleaning of cells, to the supply of bedding and blankets, and to medical care in cases of "gaol-fever," John Howard was not satisfied. He continued his travels to the European countries and the Near East in order to help other countries in prison reform. On such a journey he died in Russia, in 1789.

Another pioneer in prison reform was Elizabeth Fry (1780-1845). As a Quaker she followed her religious inspiration to visit the infamous Newgate prison, known as "hell upon earth." Using the influence of her wealthy banker husband, she succeeded in starting a school for the children in the prison and in employing one of the women convicts as teacher. She then introduced, for the adult women, knitting and lace embroidery work, which improved their morale and created new hope in their lives. Her interest in the personal fate of the inmates brought a new spirit of order, industry, and religion into their habits. Her methods inspired other philanthropists to make similar attempts in other penal institutions in England.

Despite some improvements brought about by the reformers, jails and prisons remained backward in England as long as they were under local administration. It was not until 1877, when the *Prison Act* transferred the administration of penal institutions to a central organization—the National Prison Commission—that reform of the entire correctional system started. Until this time most jails and prisons did not separate young offenders from hardened criminals. As a result, they became "schools of vice" where the youngsters as novices were introduced into the skills of crime. The lack of segregation and of protection by the jailers had often calloused the young delinquent against the feeling of responsibility for his fellow men, while his greed for money and his drives for violence and lust were developed. In 1894, a parliamentary committee investigated the penal institutions and requested the separation of young offenders from older convicts, and their special treatment with vocational training. One of the committee members, Sir Evelyn Ruggles-Brise, visited the United States, in 1897, and studied the youth reformatory at Elmira, New York. Stimulated by his observations, the first separate institution for the treatment of young delinquents in England was established at the Rochester Prison near Borstal. From this school, the entire new program of special correction of young offenders received the name "Borstal System."

For a long time, the Courts of Chancery in England had jurisdiction over neglected and dependent children. In criminal cases, however, children over seven years of age were treated as adults. The first legal protection for delinquent children was created by the *Juvenile Offenders Act of 1847,* which limited the criminal persecution of children under fourteen years of age and of adolescents under sixteen years to specific cases of crime. Special children's courts which replaced the criminal courts were introduced in England only in 1912, after the previous experience of juvenile courts in the United States had been studied.

VII. SOCIAL REFORM AND CHARITY ORGANIZATION

Three main factors influenced the social philosophy and practice of poor relief in England during the nineteenth century: the social reform movements, the Charity Organization Societies, and social research. These three developments were possible through the initiative of individuals deeply devoted to philanthropy and human progress.

A. Social Reform

Important elements in the development of social reform caused by the rapid industrialization of England were the Chartist, Christian Socialist, and the trade-union movements.

At the turn of the century, the *Combination Laws of 1799 and 1800* prohibited workers, under the threat of severe penalties, from forming trade unions in order to obtain higher wages or better working conditions. It was not until 1824 that, on the initiative of Francis Place, this legislation was repealed. Even with this advance, however, political discrimination against the working class remained effective. Laborers were excluded from suffrage when this civic privilege, in 1832, was extended to the middle class and the professions. The Chartist movement, beginning in the 1830's as the political voice of labor, attempted to obtain suffrage and secret vote by ballot for all citizens, but it failed in spite of riots and petitions to Parliament with millions of signatures. Thereafter, the disappointed workers turned their interest from political aims to more practical methods of improving their economic conditions. In 1844, the Chartists opened the first cooperative store owned by the workers themselves at Rochdale. The example for consumers' cooperatives had been presented by the philanthropist Robert Owen in his textile mills at New Lanark. Owen started his career as a poor boy, but gained a large fortune as a manufacturer in the textile industry. He recognized that decent wages and sanitary working conditions attracted the best workers and made the industry profitable. He established a model industrial community, providing low-cost housing with gardens, sanitation, and playgrounds; cooperative stores selling at cost; and a library and recreation facilities for workers and their families. Several other manufacturers in various parts of England followed the example of Robert Owen.

Another approach for the improvement of social conditions of the workers was taken when trade unions began to organize mutual benefit plans for their members, providing aid in case of sickness, accidents, unemployment, invalidism, and old age. The success of cooperative and mutual aid enterprises led to the establishment of the Trades Union Congress as a national federation. Under the leadership of Richard Cobden and John Bright the congress campaigned for the extension of suffrage to laborers, which was granted to urban workers by Parliament through the *Reform Bill of 1867*. After the first trade union representatives had been elected to the House of Commons in 1874, agricultural workers, rural householders, and miners were enfranchised in 1884. An amendment to the *Poor Law of 1894* made elective officers the members of the boards of guardians, which administered poor relief. Women as well as labor representatives became eligible for membership. The influence of the social reform movement freed workers from the continuous threat of destitution, and the trade-union movement made labor a new participating force in government, rather than a mere object of pity and poor relief.

After the collapse of the Chartists, in 1848, a group of religious and intellectual reformers under the guidance of Frederick Denison Maurice, Charles Kingsley, and J. M. Ludlow pursued the idea of improving social conditions of the working class through education. They appealed to the church to assist the masses in their desire for cultural and social emancipation. The Christian Socialists sponsored cooperative associations among the workers of various industries, and they developed night classes for adult education for which they found idealistic teachers among clergymen and university faculties. The Christian Socialist movement laid the groundwork for a sympathetic understanding between labor and the church, which is still characteristic of England. The "Working Men's College" in East London, founded by F. D. Maurice in 1854, was the most famous of these adult schools.

British socialism had its roots in the ideas of the social reformers, particularly those of Robert Owen. In addition to his work in connection with his own factories, Owen had conceived a general plan to establish cooperative rural communities in which agricultural and industrial products would be exchanged to make their population self-supporting. He proposed that educational and cultural facilities be included in such an organization. Robert Owen appealed to his friends and other wealthy citizens to assist the working class in its attempt to gain self-respect, education, and independence. The socialist philosophy was further developed by Karl Marx and Friedrich Engels, who lived in exile in England. Marx's influence as a theoretical philosopher was profound, but his political and economic ideas were not widely accepted among British labor. Of the groups interested in social reform, the most influential became the Fabian Society, which was founded in 1883. Among its leading members were Bernard Shaw, Sidney and Beatrice Webb, Sidney Olivier, and Graham Wallas. The Fabians did not, in contrast to Marx's philosophy, advocate a revolutionary socialist action in order to achieve a classless society; rather, they embarked upon such practical reforms as women's suffrage, wage and hours legislation, housing projects, and education. Their influence upon the practice and legal background of poor relief was, however, delayed until the social legislation at the beginning of the twentieth century accepted their basic concepts.

B. Housing Reform

Since the beginning of the nineteenth century, the expanding industries attracted hundreds of thousands of workers and their families to the towns. It was obvious that this rapidly growing urban population could not be housed easily in the cities unless construction was stepped up to increase the housing facilities available to the industrial workers. Several philanthropists exposed the serious danger to the health and morale of the working class from unsatisfactory housing conditions. Old mansions left by wealthy owners of mills and factories were split up into tenements with small apartments or single rooms for the workers' families. Near the mills, gardens and open spaces were quickly filled with shoddy constructions, erected without regard to sanitation, ventilation, or security against fire hazards. In order to make the maximum of profits, the builders in new industrial areas were bent on squeezing the largest possible number of dwellings on to every acre of land. In contrast, a few model cottages were established by some philanthropic employers. At their initiative, the Metropolitan Association for Improving the Dwellings of the Industrious Classes was founded in 1842, in London. Following suggestions of Edwin Chadwick, several cities enforced the clearance of the worst slums in order to avoid the grave danger of cholera and typhus. The interest of the public in housing reform was aroused by the writings of John Stuart Mill, Thomas Carlyle, John Ruskin, and Charles Dickens who were concerned about the poverty and degradation of the working masses. Thus, Parliament also became aware of the need of social reform.

Outstanding in the fight against unhealthy housing and the exploitation of the workers in the slum tenements was Octavia Hill, an admirer of John Frederick Denison Maurice and a member of the Christian Socialists. With the help of her friend, the philosopher John Ruskin, Octavia Hill started, in 1864, a philanthropic scheme of rebuilding slum tenements in London. She rented sanitary, decent living quarters at low prices to working families who could not afford to pay higher rents. In this project she enlisted a number of ladies as volunteers, who collected the monthly rent from the residents, and, at the same time, advised the families in economic home management and sound leisure time activities. Octavia Hill was convinced that the personal influence of these volunteer rent collectors encouraged the workers and their families to better training, to self-respect, and to an education of their children which would secure them the skills of higher paid trades and regular jobs. In 1865, Octavia Hill was also one of the founders of the Commons Society in London, which began to build recreational facilities, parks, and gardens in various districts of London.

C. The Charity Organization Society

The Poor Law Reform of 1834 did not bridge the widening gulf between the growing wealth of the manufacturers and mill owners and the severe pauperization of the steadily increasing masses of industrial workers. Philanthropists became concerned in saving either individuals whom they personally knew or certain groups of the poor, such as the children, and the blind, lame, or crippled people, from the degradation and cruel treatment of the mixed almshouse.

In periods of economic crises and unemployment, public concern became particularly strong, and many charitable societies with various purposes were endowed and organized. In newspapers, donations for the poor were solicited, and a large number of philanthropic agencies were established. In the 1860's several business crises occurred, and in London almost all churches and about one hundred charitable agencies distributed alms in money, food, clothes, and fuel tickets. Private charity societies began to face the usual criticism that they were wasting money and that by their alms and gifts they induced people to become beggars. Private charities still considered poverty as a personal fault of the poor, just as did the boards of guardians in public relief.

In order to overcome the chaos created by charitable church groups and philanthropic societies, the Reverend Henry Solly recommended, in 1868, establishing a board coordinating the activities of private and public charities. In 1869 the Society for Organizing Charitable Relief and Repressing Mendicity was founded in London, to be renamed soon after the Charity Organization Society, (frequently abbreviated, C.O.S.). The leading spirit of the Society was

Sir Charles Stewart Loch, who served from 1875 to 1915 as its secretary. Among other well-known members of the Society were the Reverend Richard Green, Edward Denison, Octavia Hill, and the Reverend Samuel Barnett. In its principles, the Charity Organization Society was guided by the theories of Thomas Chalmers, that the individual was responsible for his poverty and that acceptance of public relief destroyed the self-respect of the pauper and led him to subsist on alms. The Society also followed Chalmers' thought that the pauper be asked to exert all his abilities for maintaining himself. To carry out these principles, the Charity Organization Society set up an inquiry department where the poor law guardians, charity societies, and individual philanthropists were given information about an applicant for relief. This innovation caused the unmasking of many "professional beggars" and people who received aid from several relief agencies. The Charity Organization Society used the German method of the "Elberfeld System." It divided the city into small districts, each of which was administered for relief distribution by a group of citizens serving as volunteer commission. Great confidence was bestowed upon the activities of well-to-do volunteers, who would take a strong personal interest in the poor families assigned to them. They were to assist the families with money, clothes, and food, but the main emphasis was placed on their moral influence that would change the way of life of the poor. In larger districts, the direction of the work of these volunteers was entrusted to a paid "agent" of the Charity Organization Society.

The Society was opposed to an extension of public poor relief and supported the tendency among its members to reduce government expenditures for the poor. It encouraged, however, the growth of private charities, the giving of donations and bequests in their behalf, and the initiative among the volunteers for bringing individual aid to families in distress.

The example of the London Charity Organization Society of 1869 was followed in other large cities in England and Scotland, and nine years after the foundation of the Society in London, this movement reached the United States. It developed cooperation between poor relief and private charities, succeeded in eliminating some fraudulent setups, prevented duplication of support, and strengthened the concept of rehabilitation of the poor. It formed the groundwork for casework as individual aid, on the one hand, and for community organization, on the other.

D. The Settlement House

Among the Christian Socialists, Edward Denison took a new approach in the endeavor to help the underprivileged gain education. As a volunteer of the Society for the Relief of Distress in London, in 1867, he became convinced that the mere distribution of alms was futile. He abandoned his comfortable life and moved to Stepney, a poor quarter in East London, in order to live with the people in this slum district. There Denison taught Bible classes, history, and economics. The inhabitants of Stepney found him reluctant to give them the customary meat and coal tickets unless he was certain they were in dire need, but he was generous with time spent in listening to their personal problems and offered his counsel when he felt they were oppressed.

The idea of living among the people who needed help was most effectively demonstrated by Canon Samuel Augustus Barnett. Born in Bristol, 1844, he had studied theology at Oxford and accepted in 1873, the post of Vicar of St. Jude's Church in Whitechapel in East London, one of the poorest parishes in the diocese. Barnett was encouraged by his fiancee, Henrietta Rowland, who had worked under Octavia Hill. After their marriage Henrietta became her husband's co-worker. In Whitechapel the Barnetts found a great proportion of the 8,000 parishioners unemployed or sick, and living in filthy, overcrowded tenements. The Barnetts went to Oxford and Cambridge and discussed with university students the conditions they had encountered in St. Jude's. They invited them to come to live with them in Whitechapel in order to study the life of the underprivileged, to help in their education, and to render personal aid. Among those who followed Vicar Barnett's invitation was Arnold Toynbee, an enthusiastic and gifted young Oxford graduate. He was outstanding among his colleagues because of his devotion and the warm, personal contact he had established with the families of the parish. Unfortunately he was of poor health, contracted tuberculosis, and died in 1883, before reaching his thirtieth birthday. In his memory, a number of his friends built, in 1884, a university settlement in the Whitechapel district and called it "Toynbee Hall." It was the first settlement house in the world.

Canon Barnett was elected the first warden of the settlement house. Toynbee Hall had three main objectives: (1) education and cultural development of the poor, (2) information for the students and other residents of the settlement regarding the conditions of the poor and the urgent need for social reforms, and (3) a general awakening of popular interest in social and health problems, and in social legislation. The basic purpose of the settlement was to contact educated men and women with the poor for their mutual benefit, so that by common work and studies they could exercise a cultural influence beyond the teaching of special subjects. The settlement offered not just classes for children and adults. Toynbee Hall brought to the people in this quarter heretofore inaccessible educational opportunities. The attitude of a superior "lady bountiful" which still prevailed in charity societies was replaced by cooperation and learning on the part of both instructors and workers attending lectures and discussion groups.

E. Social Research

Social research was a third important factor that influenced the social philosophy and the practice of poor relief in England. The first of a long series of social studies was undertaken by Edwin Chadwick when he was secretary of the Poor Law Commissioners; it dealt with health and sanitary conditions of the working classes. The report was published in 1842, and became the start of the public health movement. Another stimulus to public concern and philanthropic endeavor was found in the articles of Henry Mayhew on "London Labour and the London Poor," published in 1849 in the London *Morning Chronicle*. These articles made a deep impression on such people as Octavia Hill and awakened their social conscience. They contributed as well to the rise of the movement of the Christian Socialists. The most important social survey, however, was made by a wealthy businessman, Charles Booth. He hired, in 1886, a staff of interviewers and conducted the research as his private enterprise. The study investigated people by trades, their living and labor conditions, working hours and wages, and unemployment. Booth was determined to get the true facts, and his staff worked

systematically and with precision. The study was not limited to
destitute people. It covered thousands of employed workers' families. The results of Booth's study, which was published yearly,
showed that one-third of the London population was living on, or
below, the "poverty line." The findings of Booth's studies disproved
the previous theory of poverty always being the fault of the individual. They also showed that the deterrent features of the poor laws
were no solution, and that human suffering from destitution was
often created by insufficient wages, environment, inadequate housing,
and unhealthy sanitary equipment. The results of this research were
supported by another study, *Poverty, A Study of Town Life,* conducted by R. Seebohm Rowntree in the city of York and published
in 1901. It revealed that in the small city of York 27.84 per cent of the
entire population were living in poverty. Through these findings
of social research, the necessity of introducing more effective measures of social reform became evident.

VIII. THE POOR LAW COMMISSION OF 1905

At the beginning of the twentieth century, the people of England faced the grave threat of unemployment. It was most serious
in the coal mining regions. Due to technical superiority of the United
States mines, and more favorable production and transportation
conditions in the European continental coal industries, a number
of British mines were unable to compete and were forced to dis-
continue operations. Others needed fewer workers, and some closed
because their coal supply was exhausted. As a result, masses of
unemployed coal miners and their families asked for relief. However,
it was not possible to put entire communities into the workhouse,
as required by the *Poor Law of 1834.* Some mining towns applied
to Parliament for aid. Private charities found themselves unable to
support tens of thousands of jobless families for unlimited periods,
and national emergency funds had to be appropriated. The Liberal
Party, in 1905, promised a reform of the poor laws and aid to the
unemployed. After its victory, the new government embarked upon
a policy of social reform. A "Royal Commission on the Poor Laws
and Relief of Distress," with Lord George Hamilton as chairman,
was appointed. Among its eighteen members, were Sir Charles Loch,

Octavia Hill, and Helen Bosanquet, but only four composed an aggressive minority: Mrs. Beatrice Webb (representing the Fabian Society), George Lansbury (Trade Unions and Labour Party), Francis Chandler (Trade Unions), and the Reverend Prebendary, later Bishop H. Russell Wakefield. In press discussions, the meetings of the Commission were cited as "The Webbs Against the Poor Law." Beatrice Webb was morally supported by her husband, although he was not a member of the Commission.

Sidney Webb's father had served on one of the London boards of guardians, and his son inherited from him a concern for the fate of the workers and the poor. From the time he was sixteen years of age, Sidney Webb worked for a living. He became an official with the London City Council and accepted the role of economic analyst with the Fabian Society. His wife, Beatrice Potter Webb, came from a wealthy London business family. During her studies she became interested in economic and political theory. After serving for some time as a visitor for a district committee of the London Charity Organization Society and as a rent collector in a philanthropic housing project, she assisted Charles Booth as an investigator in his study on the conditions of workers at the docks and in the "sweat" industries of London. In 1890, she undertook, on her own, a study of the cooperative movement and, during its preparation, met Sidney Webb, who advised her in this research. After the completion of the work, they decided to study together the trade union movement. They were married in 1892, and completed many studies in the field of labor conditions, economics, political science, and social legislation.

Beatrice Webb insisted, in the Royal Commission, upon a critical investigation of the poor law philosophy and its results. The extent of economic distress which the investigation revealed was appalling. The official statistics showed that 928,621 persons were receiving public relief, among them 300,000 children living under most unfavorable conditions.

The Poor Law Commission agreed upon the following recommendations: (1) poor law unions and boards of guardians should be replaced by county councils, reducing the number of local relief administrations by three-quarters; (2) the punitive character of poor relief should be abolished in favor of a humane public assistance program; (3) mixed almshouses should be abolished, mentally deficient and mentally ill patients should be treated in hospitals, and children placed in foster homes or residential schools; and (4) national pensions for the aged, free hospital treatment for the poor, gratuitous public employment services, and a program of social insurance with unemployment and invalidity benefits should be introduced.

However, there were fundamental differences of opinion between the majority and minority of the Commission. The majority wanted a mild reform of the old poor law and advocated close cooperation with private charities. The minority demanded the abolition of the poor law. As a result of the work of the Commission the way for fundamental progress in social legislation was opened. Sidney and Beatrice Webb founded a "Committee for the Prevention of Destitution," which worked with the trade unions for social reform.

Already during the sessions of the Royal Commission social legislation had started. The *Provision of Meals Act of 1906* organized free school lunches in the elementary schools; the *Education Act of 1907* provided medical examinations of school children; the *Old Age Pensions Act of 1908* secured a weekly pension of five shillings for deserving poor persons over seventy years of age.

A. Employment Services and Social Insurance

Large-scale unemployment forced Parliament to pass the *Unemployed Workmen Act of 1905*. For unemployed workers it provided relief administered by local distress committees which tried to find jobs for them. Following the proposal of the Royal Commission, the *Labor Exchange Act of 1909* empowered the Board of Trade (comparable to the Department of Commerce in the United States) to set up labor exchanges (employment services) to help employers find competent workers, help workers find jobs, and to increase the mobility of labor.

In the field of *social insurance legislation,* the urgent need for protection of injured workers led, in 1897, to the enactment of the *Workmen's Compensation Act.*[8] Earlier legislation, the *Fatal Ac-*

---

[8] The first compulsory social insurance legislation had been enacted in Germany. On the initiative of Chancellor Bismarck who pursued political as well as economic goals, the German Parliament had passed a sickness insurance law in 1883, an industrial accident insurance law (corresponding to workmen's compensation) in 1884, and old age and invalidity insurance in 1889. The German program did not include an unemployment insurance law because the problem

cidents Act of 1846 and the *Employers' Liability Act of 1880,* had proved insufficient to help the injured worker and his family. The statute of 1897 established the legal right of compensation for the injured worker independent of any fault of the employer or his crew. No machinery for public administration, however, was provided. The injured workers and the widows and orphans of those killed in industrial accidents were forced to sue the employer before the courts. This led to long delays and high expenses, which the workers could not afford, or settlements which deprived the injured worker or his survivors of most of his compensation.

The need for protection of the workers in periods of unemployment proved to be an urgent problem. The report of 1909, therefore, proposed the establishment of a system of compulsory unemployment insurance. On a visit to the European continent, in 1908, David Lloyd George was impressed with the operation of the German sickness insurance plan, and recommended insurance with unemployment and health benefits. This twofold program was enacted by the *National Insurance Act of 1911* which was prepared by Sir Hubert Llewellyn-Smith and William H. Beveridge.

Beveridge was the son of a Scotch judge, had been born in India, and studied law and economics at Oxford where he was a brilliant student. Greatly influenced by the work and the ideas of Sidney and Beatrice Webb, he left a successful law practice after one year of activity at the London Bar in order to accept the position as subwarden at Toynbee Hall. There he lived among the East London workers and studied particularly the conditions of the unemployed families. In 1909, he published his first book *Unemployment—A Problem of Industry.*

After the enactment of the *Labor Exchange Act of 1909,* Churchill appointed William Beveridge to organize the labor exchanges. When the *National Insurance Act* was passed, it was natural that Beveridge was called upon to take responsibility for the setup of the unemployment insurance plan.

---

of unemployment was not of major importance during the 1880's in Germany. Many other countries in Central and Northern Europe followed the German example. Some of them chose instead of the German system of compulsory insurance the way of voluntary insurance legislation. Denmark enacted in 1891 an old-age pensions act which did not require contributions from the insured workers nor from the employers.

The *National Insurance Act of 1911* established compulsory health insurance for workers of modest income. The program was financed by contributions of the insured workers and their employers, and grants from Parliament. It was administered by "approved societies," nonprofit organizations established either by trade unions, mutual aid societies, employers, or commercial insurance companies. The latter were interested in carrying health insurance because their agents could sell other policies, particularly accident and death insurance, to families when they collected health insurance contributions. The insured worker received only medical treatment from a practitioner who prescribed medicine. The worker received no hospital care or treatment by a medical specialist and no insurance for his family. Cash allowances during the time of sickness were limited to twenty-six weeks, after this period a reduced disablement benefit was paid. Maternity benefit was given at confinement to insured women workers and to the wives of insured men.

In 1925, the *Widow's, Orphans' and Old Age Contributory Pensions Act* extended the principle of social insurance to men over sixty-five, women over sixty years of age, and to widows, orphans, and dependent children under fourteen (or under sixteen years of age when in school). Contributions from the insured workers and their employers were collected by the "approved societies," together with health insurance contributions. Local post offices paid the benefits, and the claims were adjudicated by local branch offices of the Ministry of Health. For both contributions and benefits a "flat rate system" was used so that uniform amounts were paid throughout the country.

The program of social insurance was fundamentally different from poor relief. Its contributions and benefits were determined by law. Payments were made upon the arrival of contingencies—old age, sickness, widow- and orphanhood, unemployment—without regard to the financial situation of the individual, insured person. There was no disgrace in receiving benefits from funds to which the insured himself or the husband or father had contributed. Psychologically, people were stimulated to save money, because they were anxious to have funds in addition to the social insurance benefits which merely covered basic necessities. Thus, the initiative toward economic independence of the insured persons was not suppressed.

B. Changing Social Policy

World War I absorbed the unemployed and even created a labor shortage. Toward the end of the war, the *Representation of People Act of 1918* abolished the disfranchisement for recipients of poor relief. In 1919, the central poor law agency, the Local Government Board, was replaced by the Ministry of Health, which administered poor relief, public health, sanitation, health insurance benefits, as well as public housing and town planning.

The *Local Government Act of 1929* led to a fundamental reform of the public relief structure. It abolished the poor law unions and boards of guardians and assigned public relief to the *county councils* and in metropolitan areas to borough councils, concentrating the administration in 145 counties. Public assistance committees were appointed that were composed of members of the county councils and other citizens. In each county, a "guardians committee" acted as voluntary investigators of relief applications. The *National Economy Act of 1931* introduced "Unemployment Assistance" payments from the Exchequer (the national treasury) to unemployed persons who had exhausted, or were not eligible for, unemployment insurance benefits. The administration of assistance was placed by the *Unemployment Act of 1934,* in the Unemployment Assistance Board.

IX. SOCIAL WELFARE DURING WORLD WAR II

At the outbreak of the war in 1939, the Unemployment Assistance Board was charged with payment of war victim allowances and its name was changed to National Assistance Board. The *Old-Age Pensions Act of 1940* provided for additional pensions based upon individual need, particularly for medical care.

In the field of health services, the war demand increased efforts for the treatment of tuberculosis, cancer, and venereal diseases. Important changes were made in the coordination of hospital facilities. When the outbreak of the war seemed imminent, in 1939, an "Emergency Hospital Scheme" coordinated the voluntary and public hospitals and clinics. Modern health treatment centers, consultation services, and rehabilitation clinics were set up. An extension of medical research and an expanded program for training of young physicians were undertaken.

Serious problems were created in England during World War II, by the necessity of evacuating hundreds of thousands of women, children, and the old, infirm, and sick from the large cities.

The population in England found it hard to understand the many regulations regarding air raid protection, rationing, shelters, war damage compensation, family allowances for wives and children of men in the Armed Forces, rent control, taxes, and evacuation schedules, so that reliable information became necessary. Following London's example, over 1,000 Citizens' Advice Bureaus were established to meet this need, especially for information for servicemen on furlough regarding the whereabouts of their evacuated families. The bureaus rendered free advice on questions arising out of the war, gave legal opinion, and issued forms for applications. The Citizens' Advice Bureaus did not dispense assistance but referred applicants for material help to social agencies. Their staff consisted of trained social workers, lawyers, administrative officials, and volunteers borrowed from both public and voluntary social agencies. The services of the Citizens' Advice Bureaus proved to be so valuable, that a large number has been maintained to give community information services.

X. THE BEVERIDGE REPORT

In a dramatic hour of the war, when in June 1941 bombs were continuously falling near Westminster Hall, England began a revolutionary reform of her entire social welfare program. Arthur Greenwood, Labour Minister of Reconstruction, appointed, with the unanimous consent of Parliament, an Interdepartmental Committee on Social Insurance and Allied Services under the chairmanship of Sir (now Lord) William Beveridge, in order to survey the structure and the efficiency of the British social services and to make recommendations for necessary reforms. After World War I, Beveridge was Director of the London School of Economics, and in 1937 he became Master of the noted University College at Oxford. This explains why the challenging task of a re-examination of the entire social insurance and welfare program was entrusted to him. The Beveridge Committee included representatives of all organizations of public assistance, social insurance, pensions, health, and economic affairs. The committee's investigations included hundreds of hearings of citizens' groups, ranging from chambers of commerce, manufacturers' associations, and commercial insurance companies to labor unions, consumers' cooperatives, and the Fabian Society. Sir William's report attempted to find a way to gain "Freedom from Want" taking into consideration the fact that personal and economic suffering in modern industrial society was, as a rule, caused by disruption or loss of earning power. It emphasized that, in addition to "want," four other "giants" also prevent human well-being: "disease," "ignorance," "squalor," and "idleness."

The Beveridge Report devised a system of social security in which the program of social insurance is only one, although the most important, of several measures. Without losing a bold look into the future, recommendations were based on past experience in England. The goal of social security was to guarantee a basic level of income for every citizen with his own efforts, so that his initiative to secure for himself and his family more than a mere subsistence minimum should not be stifled.

It inaugurated a comprehensive system of social security based upon five programs: (1) a unified, comprehensive, and adequate program of *social insurance;* (2) *public assistance* as a national program for aiding people who were not sufficiently protected through social insurance benefits; (3) *children's allowances* (now called "family allowances") providing a weekly benefit for each child after the first; (4) comprehensive free *health and rehabilitation services* for the entire population; and (5) the *maintenance of full employment* through public works in order to prevent mass unemployment in economic crises.

The proposal aimed to protect the entire population, not just the working class. It was conceived as a unified plan, to be administered by one national agency (now called Ministry of Pensions and National Insurance) integrating the vast number of uncoordinated, overlapping efforts that had been made in the past. Six basic principles were suggested for the procedure: (1) unified administration, (2) comprehensive coverage, (3) flat rate of contributions,

(4) flat rate of benefits, (5) adequacy of all benefits to meet basic needs of the recipients, and (6) classification of the population.[9]

Lord William emphasized that the underlying social philosophy of his plan was to secure the British people against want and other social evils, and that social security could be rendered while preserving the personal freedom, enterprise, and responsibility of the individual for his family. The Beveridge Report became the foundation of the modern social welfare legislation of Great Britain and a model for other countries.

XI. ENGLAND'S SOCIAL SECURITY PROGRAM

The structure of the present British social security program follows the recommendations of the Beveridge Report, although certain changes have been made. The Ministry of National Insurance coordinates the program. Its administration comprises two main sections: (1) a comprehensive social insurance scheme for old-age, invalidity, and health insurance (*National Insurance Act of 1946*); and (2) workmen's compensation (*Industrial Injuries Act of 1946*). A system of *family allowances* was established by the *Family Allowance Act of 1945*. *Public assistance* is provided according to the *National Assistance Act of 1948* through the National Assistance Board, a division of the Home Office. The Ministry of Public Health administers a broad program of public health services based upon the *National Health Service Act of 1946*. The family allowances have been in effect since August 1, 1946, and the other parts of the program since July 5, 1948.

The backbone of the entire social security plan is the *social insurance system*. It includes health insurance, unemployment insurance, old-age (superannuation) and invalidity insurance, workmen's compensation, and special grants for marriage, child birth, and funeral

---

[9] The Report suggested six groups: (1) employees; (2) employers and self-employed persons; (3) housewives; (4) adult persons who are not gainfully employed, for example, cripples, invalids, insane; (5) retired persons above working age; and (6) children below working age. The *National Insurance Act of 1946* (see below) reduced the classification scheme to three groups: (1) employed persons, gainfully occupied in Great Britain under a contract of service; (2) self-employed people, gainfully occupied, but under no control of an employer; and (3) nonemployed persons. See D. Marsh, *op. cit.*, p. 83; and, M. Hall, *op. cit.*, pp. 31-38.

expenses. It protects over thirty-five million people against the dangers of sickness, unemployment, old age, invalidism, death of the breadwinner, and industrial injuries. The insured population is divided into three categories: (a) employed persons; (b) the self-employed—employers, members of the professions, independent artists, and artisans; and (c) nonemployed people—mostly married women in their own household.

In the original legislation of 1946, contributions and benefits of the social insurance program were flat rate payments, the same amount for the members of each of the three categories: adult men, adult women, and working boys and girls under eighteen years of age. Benefits were paid in case of retirement, invalidity, unemployment, before and after child birth, and higher benefits under the industrial accident insurance program to totally or partially disabled workers and their dependents. Supplementary benefits are paid to the wife of the retired worker, to his widow after his death, and to his first child under 16 years of age, while family allowances are paid to subsequent children in the family.

The *National Insurance Act of 1959* amended this principle of a unified flat rate system of contributions and benefits and introduced an additional graduated program of contributions and benefits for the retirement pensions of workers and employees. These graduated contributions are related to the insured person's remuneration and are paid by the insured worker and by his employer. The graduated contributions, however, do not affect the maternity, sickness, unemployment, and survivor benefits, nor do they apply to self-employed and nonemployed persons who continue to be insured under the original system of flat rate contributions and flat rate benefits. For the last two categories the national treasury pays one-third of the contributions.

Graduated contributions and the corresponding graduated retirement benefits related to the earnings of insured persons who earn more than £9 up to £15 a week are covered under the supplementary plan of 1959. They may be "contracted out" to approved private insurance companies or to retirement pension systems for public employees. In 1958, about 9 million employees, one-third of the total working population in England, were covered by such private or civil service retirement plans. Private pension plans must meet legal requirements securing the solvency of the companies and must provide retirement payments and the reservation of pension rights equivalent to the official graduated pension benefits under the national insurance program.[10]

Three types of *maternity benefits* are provided: (1) a *maternity grant* which permits the mother to make the necessary purchases for the baby; and either (2) a weekly *attendance allowance* for four weeks, or (3) a *maternity allowance* for eighteen weeks. To qualify for the first two benefits, twenty-six contributions in the year preceding the confinement are required; the maternity allowance requires forty-five contributions during the same period and that the mother does not work and submits to medical examinations. An additional *home confinement grant* is paid if no maternity ward was used for the delivery.

After the death of her husband, a widow has a claim to a widow's allowance for an adjustment period of thirteen weeks. After this time, she receives a weekly guardian's benefit for each of her dependent children, as long as they are under sixteen years of age. Orphans who have lost both parents receive the same orphan's benefit. Death benefits are given in case of the loss of either husband or wife to the survivor, so that funeral expenses can be met.[11]

The administration of the social insurance benefits is carried out through the Ministry of Pensions and National Insurance and its regional and local offices, with the help of local advisory committees. Medical boards and medical appeal tribunals decide questions of health damage and capacity to work. Independent local appeal tribunals hear grievances of the insured persons. Employees of the National Assistance Board, usually, are not professionally trained social workers. Private social agencies offer personal counseling to beneficiaries of public assistance and social insurance benefits.

The second part of the British social security system is *family allowances*. They are paid upon application to every family with

---

[10] The rates of contributions may be reduced or increased by order of the treasury in order to assist in the maintenance of employment or to combat inflation in accordance with the economic needs of the country. The law provides also for a review every five years to adjust the rates of benefits. See also, "New Graduated Retirement Benefits in Great Britain," *Social Security Bulletin,* Vol. 23, No. 9 (September 1959), pp. 4-9.

[11] The various grants also are adjusted to changing living standards. A "special child's allowance" is paid to a divorced mother after the death of her former husband.

two or more children under sixteen years of age, without regard to the financial condition of the family. The allowance is paid to the mother, until the year after the child's sixteenth birthday, if he is in school or in apprenticeship. The family allowance is based upon the consideration that, in our industrial society, wages are paid for the work rendered. For this reason, families with numerous children barely earn enough for a decent living, whereas a single worker might be able to live well on the same earning. The family allowance represents, therefore, a mutual sharing between society and parents in the expenses for the upbringing, the education, and the preservation of health of children. The family allowance of eight shillings a week does not cover the entire cost of the rearing of the children. All children receive free school lunches or dinners, recreation, and health services, in such as a free day camp or summer vacation home. Family allowances are financed from national taxation; in 1959, 8,750,000 children in 3,500,000 families received family allowances in Great Britain.

The third part of the social security system is *public assistance.* Under the *National Assistance Act of 1948,* public assistance replaced the poor law through two new schemes: (1) financial assistance to persons in economic need, administered by the National Assistance Board and its twelve regional and 350 local offices; and (2) institutional and individual services, administered by the county councils. In urgent cases the local office immediately may grant emergency relief. Old, blind, deaf, crippled, and disabled persons are encouraged in their efforts to earn a part of their living. National assistance is granted according to general regulations, but the applicant's individual conditions are considered. The applicant has a right of appeal against the decision of the local office to the National Assistance Board. The Board assumes financial responsibility for vagrants and "casual poor persons" who formerly were supported by the local authorities.

County councils, as local authorities, provide *welfare services* distinct from financial aid. These services include old people's homes and hostels for infirm, blind, deaf, mentally deficient, crippled, and handicapped persons. The residents pay their board from their own income or insurance benefits. If their income is insufficient, the National Assistance Board pays the difference, including a small amount for pocket money. The county provides instruction, workshops, vocational training, and cultural and recreational activities, and it employs the staff of the hostels as well as social workers who give casework service to the residents. Private social agencies may be asked by the county to accept old and handicapped people into their institutions and to provide individual care by their social work staffs and volunteers.

The care of orphans, and neglected and deserted children remains the responsibility of the county councils. The children are placed either in foster families or in children's institutions. Under the provisions of the *Children Act of 1948,* each county council appoints a Children's Committee as the authority for child care with a Children's Officer as head of its staff. The children remain under the protection of the committee until they are eighteen years of age. The court may appoint the county council to serve as legal guardian of the child. The central supervisory authority for the care of dependent children is the Home Secretary who is assisted by an Advisory Council on Child Care. Private agencies and children's institutions that receive children or place them in foster homes are registered with the Home Office, and have to meet established standards of care.

A Central Training Council in Child Care has organized two types of special training. The first, developed in cooperation with the universities, trains "boarding-out officers"—social workers who explore suitable foster homes and supervise the children placed in these families. The second type, established with the help of local education authorities, prepares house mothers, house fathers, and other resident workers for children's homes.

The county councils use facilities of voluntary social agencies for the accommodation of children and adults who need institutional placement, special treatment, vocational training, recreation, and skilled social work service. The counties grant subsidies to private organizations which provide welfare services. Each county council has an advisory committee with whom the area officer meets, usually every second month, in order to ask advice for individual cases. Adoption was introduced as a legal measure in 1926; the *Adoption Act of 1950* regulates the process of adoption and the protection of the child, of his mother, and of the adopting parents.

The *Disabled Persons (Employment) Act of 1944* requires industrial or commercial enterprises with a regular working force of twenty or more workers to employ disabled persons. The quota is assigned annually by the Minister of Labor; it is usually 3 per cent of the working force of the plant. No disabled person is forced to register, but the law entitles the registered disabled worker to attend vocational training courses, without charge, to complete his interrupted apprenticeship, and to receive vocational guidance. He also has the right for reinstatement to be employed in private industry and priority on employment in occupations designated as appropriate for disabled workers by the Minister of Labor, such as car park attendant or electric elevator operator. "Re-employ factories" provide jobs for severely disabled persons under particular legal protection, with safety measures and special production methods. Other factories voluntarily offer employment to registered, severely handicapped workers.

Special care is given by the National Assistance Board to "persons without a settled way of life." They are divided into two groups: (1) those able to work and (2) the unemployables, particularly the invalid, aged, and sick. *Reception centers* permit individual observation and diagnosis and separate the unsettled from their habitual life on the road or in the city slums. After the diagnosis has been made, a treatment plan is developed. The treatment is provided in *re-establishment centers,* which provide the unsettled with the opportunity to adjust to work, to accept vocational training, and to use workshop facilities. The centers combine strict discipline with a sympathetic approach to the individual's problems and attempt to bring the unsettled person back to normal life and work. The second category of the unsettled, old, sick, and invalid vagabonds are cared for in *casual wards* where they receive medical and custodial treatment; many of these wards are affiliated with hospitals.

The Public Health Service

Among modern British social legislation, none has provoked so much attention and heated controversy as the *National Health Service Act of 1946,* which came into force on July 5, 1948, and marks a fundamental change in the attitude toward health. It provides medical care free of charge to all British citizens who apply for it. Already, during the war, in 1942, the Medical Planning Commission of the British Medical Association had recommended a program of medical care for the entire people. The Churchill government first introduced the plan, which was enacted in 1946 under Prime Minister Atlee.

The National Health Service system is not "socialized medicine." The patient is not compelled to use the service; if he takes advantage of the service, he may choose his family doctor, dentist, hospitals, and specialists. Physicians, dentists, pharmacists, and nurses are not forced to work for the Health Service, either; they may continue private practice.

The Health Insurance program secures financial benefits during illness while the patient loses his income. It protects the insured and his family against destitution. Distinguished from the Insurance program, the National Health Service provides medical examination, diagnosis, treatment free of charge in the doctor's office or at the patient's home, and hospitalization. The health service supplies the necessary medicines, artificial limbs, and appliances. Services are obtained through the family doctor with whom the patient has registered, if he wants to use the health service. A change of the family physician is possible any time, and the physician also may remove a patient from his list when he no longer wishes to serve him. The family doctor prescribes medicines, hearing aids, and appliances, which the patient receives at the pharmacy.[12] Since the Amendment of 1951, one-half of the cost of dentures and eyeglasses is charged to patients who are able to afford this contribution. Prescriptions for old-age pensioners and ex-servicemen are free of charge. The family physician refers the patient whenever necessary to specialists, hospitals, and clinics. If a patient is taken sick while away from home, he may consult any doctor in the Health Service for free treatment as a "temporary resident."

Dental treatment does not require previous registration and includes fillings, removing infected teeth, and repairing dentures. For more complicated and expensive dental work, the patient needs an approval by the local Dental Estimate Board. Under the auspices of the local public health authorities, priority in preventive and curative dental clinics is given to expectant mothers and young children.

The Public Health Service Plan is widely used in England. Ninety-

---

[12] The statute of 1946 did not provide a fee for medicines and appliances. The introduction of a fee, however, was felt necessary in 1949 to avoid the abuse of drugs and medicines and to prevent too heavy expenditures under the health service. It was increased to one shilling for each item on the prescription in 1956. The Minister of Health is authorized to regulate the fees. Patients have to pay for replacement of appliances which have been lost or damaged through carelessness.

seven per cent of the population have registered with a family physician in the Service. About 97 per cent of all general physicians, over 94 per cent of the dentists, and the great majority of medical specialists, opticians, and pharmacists offer their services under the health plan. The list of local physicians, general practitioners and specialists, dentists, optometrists, and pharmacists is available to the public at the post offices and at public libraries. Among the citizens registered for the Service are, of course, people of means who expect from the family physician the same medical attention which they formerly received as private patients. This will not be possible always, due to the larger number of patients involved, but this fact assists in the maintenance of high standards of medical care.

Physicians in the National Health Plan receive a "capitation payment" for each registered patient which is determined by the Ministry of Public Health after consultation with the medical association. Each doctor may accept 3,500 patients, and 2,000 more, if he employs an assistant. Doctors with a small clientele receive a "loading payment," young physicians an "initial practice allowance." Elderly doctors are entitled to a "hardship payment," and special fees are granted for doctors with less than 500 patients, for the treatment of emergencies and temporary residents, and for home calls in maternity cases and rural districts. Supplements are granted to doctors working in difficult and unpopular areas. Dentists, ophthalmologists, opticians, and pharmacists are paid, according to their individual services, on the basis of an approved fee schedule. Medical specialists receive their remuneration on a part-time or full-time salary basis, with special awards for qualified professional services. Government grants are available for physicians who attend medical postgraduate refresher courses, who accept young assistant doctors for training, and who are engaged in medical research.

The administration of the National Health Service is organized, according to the three branches of the Service, into: (a) general medical and dental services, (b) hospital and specialist services, and (c) local government services. The general medical and dental services are administered by 138 Executive Councils established by the counties as local health authorities. They review the patients' lists of the physicians, allocate patients whom no doctor wants to accept, and refuse in "over-doctored areas" the admission of new general practitioners until there is need for them.

Hospital and consultant physicians' services are administered by fourteen Regional Boards, whose areas are designated by a Central Medical Practices Committee. After consultation with the medical executive councils, the local medical associations, and senior staffs of the hospitals in the area, the Regional Board appoints "management committees" for hospitals in the region, takes measures for coordination of hospitals, and develops regional health policies and public health planning.

Each of the fourteen regions is connected with a university medical school which uses one or several "voluntary teaching hospitals" for the training of medical and dental students. The university teaching hospitals retain their legacies, gifts, and endowments for research and fellowship. Endowments of other hospitals are pooled in a Hospital Endowments Fund. Hospital management committees and regional medical boards use the fund for the development and improvement of hospital facilities, equipment, and research. The broad representation of noted members of the medical, dental, and pharmaceutical professions on these boards enables them to give leadership in the planned expansion of hospitals and clinics throughout the entire country and to work toward higher standards and effective health policies. Under the health plan, about 2,700 hospitals with 500,000 beds are available. Professional and technical improvements and an amalgamation of small and inefficient hospitals were achieved.[13] Two hundred and fifty denominational hospitals have been "disclaimed," and continue to operate under private management. The regional hospital boards negotiate the contracts with specialists (medical consultants).

The 146 local health authorities provide for maternity and child welfare services, midwifery, home nursing, health visiting, and after-care of the sick. They arrange for domestic help in time of confinement and sickness, for vaccination and immunization, and for ambulance services for emergency transportation to hospitals or clinics. Domestic help under the Home Help Service is free to families who cannot afford to pay for a homemaker, whereas other families pay a moderate weekly charge. The local health authority employs a

---

[13] An increasing number of British hospitals have "almoner's departments," staffed by medical social workers. Mental hospitals and psychiatric clinics employ psychiatric social workers. Two public medical services have not been incorporated: the Schools Medical Service, controlled by the Minister of Education, and the Industrial Medical Service, under the Minister of Labor.

medical officer and his staff under the direction of a "health committee." In cases of home confinement, free midwife service and a
maternity outfit is granted, and in the cases of home nursing, such
articles as crutches and wheel chairs for the sick room and for
convalescence. Tubercular patients receive medical care and public
assistance benefits. After the patient returns from the hospital or
tuberculosis sanitarium, a social worker or a visiting nurse assumes
after-care. By the establishment of child guidance and mental hygiene
clinics, local health authorities help in the prevention of mental diseases.

Special attention is given to expectant and nursing mothers, infants and young children under five years of age. The maternity
and child welfare services of the counties provide free prenatal and
postnatal care with obstetric and pediatric examination and treatment. Expectant mothers and young children are entitled to milk,
cod-liver oil, and orange juice at a reduced price, but free of charge to
mothers who cannot afford to pay for it.

In schools, free medical inspections, dental treatment, and special
attention to blind, visually handicapped, epileptic, and crippled children are provided. Some counties employ medical social workers
under the title "welfare officer" for services for children, the aged,
and the handicapped.

The cost of the National Health Service is high. Funds contributed
by the social insurance program to the health service cover about 13
per cent of the entire health service budget. The remainder is financed
by national and some local taxes. Administrative cost of the National
Health Service amounts to only 2.5 to 3 per cent of the expenditure.

The final success of the health service depends upon the cooperation of the public and of the professions. The statute provides for the
future establishment of additional health centers by the counties,
when financial and technical conditions permit. At these centers,
family doctors, medical specialists, and dentists have their offices for
both the health service and their private practice, with laboratory and
pharmaceutical facilities.

The public in England often regards the health service as part of
the social insurance plan and as a return for the weekly social insurance contribution. In fact, the health service is available to everyone independent of his coverage under the social insurance program.

XII. PRIVATE SOCIAL SERVICES

For centuries England has been noted for the important role that private charities have played in its society as pioneers of the various social services, and for the numerous volunteers active in the field of social work. The recent expansion of public welfare and the social insurances has still left wide opportunities for the activities of private social agencies. The public authorities encourage voluntary agencies to continue their work in personal aid to old, sick, handicapped, and young persons. Characteristic examples of present social services provided under the auspices of voluntary agencies are maternity and old-age homes, health visiting, home nursing, midwives' services, ambulances and transportation aid; care of mothers and babies; clinics and sanitariums for tubercular patients; hostels for mentally defective children and adults; and after-care service for the sick. Other activities of private social agencies include probation and parole for juveniles and adults; social clubs for adolescents, the aged, and the unemployed; marriage guidance councils; child guidance clinics; disaster relief; visiting old people in their homes or in institutions; and managing "village halls" (rural cultural and education centers).

The essential functions of private social agencies in these fields in England today are: (1) carrying on new experiments and developing new forms of social work which may later be taken over by public agencies when they have proved successful; (2) supplementing public social services when certain persons or particular needs are not covered by public services, limited in funds and by legal provisions, and because individual care and counseling is required; (3) interpreting social work to the public, particularly through citizens' advice bureaus, and by informing legislators and public agencies of the special problems which have escaped their attention; and (4) performing social surveys in order to determine the social and health needs of a community and the quest for social legislation—plus providing the stimulation of public authorities to take the necessary action.

Volunteers participate in private social agencies in Great Britain, particularly in youth groups, advisory bureaus, and child care work affiliated with the schools, and probation, but they often work under instruction and supervision of trained professional workers. Volunteers are particularly active in work with aged and handicapped persons. Subsidies to private agencies are frequently granted by the counties and the various ministries of the national government. Committees of the counties' public assistance and health programs are composed mainly of volunteers. Nearly all voluntary social agencies are represented in the National Council of Social Service, which was founded in 1919. More than one hundred national organizations are members of the Council, among them the Family Welfare Association (successor to the Charity Organization Society). The National Council encourages the setup of local "councils of social services" and "rural community councils" to coordinate the work of local agen· cies. It has been difficult, however, to finance some of the local private agencies because endowments and contributions are scarce, due to the economic conditions of postwar England.

The recent extension of public social services has, however, led to a certain duplication of work and overlapping between public and private social work activities. Some private social agencies still maintain a critical attitude toward public social services, with the argument that private organizations have a superior social philosophy and practice based upon the old principle of "voluntary action" for which there is at present scarcely any proof. In the interest of economy and efficiency, it seems desirable to achieve an elimination of overlapping services and a coordination of public and private activities to meet the social needs of the population.

Recipients of public assistance payments are entitled to be members of advisory councils, grievance committees, and appeal tribunals. The participation of laymen and of recipients of social aid, as well as of the professions, secures their understanding of the social problems these institutions must face in carrying out their objectives. The broad representation of the public on both public and private boards, in England, secures deeper understanding of the social problems and a democratic interpretation. In the United States, we have been more hesitant to admit recipients of assistance to boards of public and private social agencies.

Voluntary agencies are now able to concentrate on their real task, on the difficult, intangible problems of bringing aid to human beings in need of understanding and encouragement, and, especially, on the prevention of juvenile delinquency.

XIII. JUVENILE DELINQUENCY

In 1908, the *Prevention of Crime Act* had authorized the courts to order special treatment of young delinquents and introduced the *Borstal System* as part of the national penal program. When the *Children's Act of 1912* established juvenile courts and probation services, Borstal institutions grew in number and became more specialized in the nature of their methods of education, vocational guidance, and occupational training. The age of young offenders who might be admitted to Borstal institutions was raised to twenty-three years, and the maximum time of institutional treatment in Borstal schools to four years. The Commissioner of the Borstal institutions is a member of the National Prison Commission. He decides, upon the recommendations of his staff, how long the individual young offender shall remain in the institution. Education is entrusted to teachers, housemasters, and matrons who, under a cottage system, live together with the youngsters. Disciplinary officers are separated from the other educational staff. A preliminary observation of each offender in a clinical setting enables the governor of the Borstal institution to select the specific school, the type of vocational training, and the personnel which promise the most effective adjustment of the juvenile delinquent. The Borstal schools use the volunteer assistance of the surrounding communities. A "visiting committee" of interested citizens gets acquainted with the boys and maintains contact with them. Youth groups in the town visit the schools and invite the boys to take part in sports, games, and recreation. Other volunteers teach technical skills and handicraft, and arrange for such recreational activities as musical performances and dramatic plays. The vocational training in Borstal schools is directed toward practical skill with no makeshift work. Competition with free labor on the general market has been avoided by manufacturing goods approved by labor unions. After the young offender is released, he remains under parole supervision, which is carried out by trained parole officers or by volunteers instructed by the Borstal Association.

The Juvenile Courts, first created by the *Children's Act of 1912,* have helped in discouraging juvenile delinquency. In 1920, the *Juvenile Court Metropolis Act* provided that the Home Secretary could select, for the juvenile courts, magistrates with previous experience and special qualifications for dealing with young offenders, so that, in the courts, higher standards of procedure and more effective adjustment of youth could be obtained. In England, the juvenile court consists of the magistrate, as presiding judge, and of two lay justices (often teachers, physicians, social workers, or members of charitable agencies), one of whom must be a woman. The *Children and Young People Act of 1933* emphasized the need of action toward the welfare of the young offender. The court has the power to remove the young delinquent from his home or from undesirable surroundings and secure his effective education and training. The court's sessions are not open to the public or to the press; only witnesses, the parents or guardian of the child and the probation officer or investigating social worker are admitted.

In their work of protection and adjustment of children and young persons the juvenile courts depend upon the aid of public and private child welfare agencies, child guidance clinics, and probation services. Probation for minors is widely used in Great Britain. If it is necessary to remove the child from his own family, foster homes are selected and supervised by child protective agencies or by chapters of the Borstal Association. There are also "hostels" and "probation homes" for young offenders who cannot be placed in a foster family. For the adjustment of difficult and seriously delinquent children and adolescents the Borstal institutions and "approved schools" [14] are used. The value of preventive services, such as recreation and youth group activities, is well recognized, and these clubs and recreation groups receive financial support from private organizations, the counties, and the national government. The "approved schools," in contrast, are classified according to their special training equipment and their staff skills. There are separate schools for girls and boys, and the various age groups and particular difficulties of the children are taken into consideration.

---

[14] The "approved schools" correspond to licensed training schools or industrial schools in the United States. For an analysis of the Borstal institutions, see William Healy and Benedict Alper, *Criminal Youth and the Borstal System* (New York: The Commonwealth Fund, 1941); and Lionel W. Fox, *The English Prison and Borstal Systems* (London: Routledge and Kegan Paul, 1952).

Selected Bibliography

*Abbott, Grace, *The Child and the State*. Chicago: The University of Chicago Press, 1938.

Barnett, Henrietta O., *Canon Barnett, His Life, Work, and Friends*. London: J. Murray, 1918 and 1921.

Bell, E. Moberly, *The Life of Octavia Hill*. London: Constable, 1938.

Bellows, Reverend H. W., *John Howard, His Life, Character and Service*. Chicago: John Howard Association, 1948.

*Beveridge, Sir William, *Social Insurance and Allied Services*. New York: Macmillan, 1942.

*————, *Voluntary Action: A Report on Methods of Social Advance*. London: G. Allen, 1949.

Booth, Charles, *Life and Labour of the People of London* (10 vols.). Longmans, 1900-1911.

Bosanquet, Helen, *The Poor Law Report of 1909*. London: Macmillan, 1909.

Bourdillon, A. F. C., *Voluntary Social Services. Their Place in the Modern State*. London: Methuen, 1945.

Chalmers, Thomas (abridged and edited by Charles R. Henderson), *The Christian and Civic Economy of Large Towns*. New York: Scribner, 1900.

*Cohen, Emmeline W., *English Social Services, Method and Growth*. London: G. Allen, 1949.

Cole, Margaret, *Beatrice Webb*. New York: Harcourt, 1946.

*de Schweinitz, Karl, *England's Road to Social Security, 1349-1947*, 3rd rev. ed. Philadelphia: University of Pennsylvania Press, 1947.

Finer, S. E., *The Life and Times of Sir Edwin Chadwick*. London: Methuen, 1952.

Grunhut, Max, *Penal Reform—A Comparative Study*. Oxford: Clarendon Press, 1948.

*Hall, M. Penelope, *The Social Services of Modern England*. London: Routledge and Kegan Paul, 1952.

Hammond, J. L., and Barbara Hammond, *The Village Labourer, 1760-1832*. London: Longmans, 1912.

*Healey, William, and Benedict S. Alper, *Criminal Youth and the Borstal System*. New York: The Commonwealth Fund, 1941.

Hene, Derek H., *The British Health Service*. London: Shaw, 1953.

Hill, Octavia. *Homes of the London Poor*. London: Macmillan, 1883.

*Hobman, Daisy L., *The Welfare State*. London: Murray, 1953.

Hovell, Mark. *The Chartist Movement*. Manchester, England: The University Press, 1925.

Jones, Dorsey D., *Edwin Chadwick and the Early Public Health Movement in England,* University of Iowa Studies in the Social Sciences, Vol. IX, No. 3. Iowa City: University of Iowa, 1931.

Loch, Sir Charles S., *Charity and Social Life: A Short Study of Religious and Social Thought in Relation to Charitable Methods and Institutions.* London: Macmillan, 1910.

Macadam, Elisabeth, *The Social Servant in the Making.* London: G. Allen, 1945.

Manson, Julius, *The British Health Service.* New York: League of Industrial Democracy, 1952.

*Marsh, David C., *National Insurance and Assistance in Great Britain.* London: Pitman, 1951.

Means, James H., *Doctors, People, and Government.* Boston: Little, 1953.

Mendelsohn, Ronald, *Social Security in the British Commonwealth.* Oxford: Blackwell, 1953.

Mess, Henry A., *Voluntary Social Services Since 1918.* London: Routledge and Kegan Paul, 1948.

*Morris, Charles (editor), *Social Case Work in Britain.* London: Faber, 1950.

Moss, John, *The Duties of Local Authorities Under the National Assistance Act, 1948.* London: Hadden, Best, 1948.

Osborn, Phyllis, "The National Assistance Program of Great Britain," *Social Service Review,* Vol. XXXII, No. 3 (March 1958), pp. 24-32.

Pimlott, John A. R., *Toynbee Hall, Fifty Years of Social Progress, 1884-1934.* London: Dent, 1935.

*Rathbone, Eleanor, *Family Allowances.* London: G. Allen, 1949.

*Robson, William A., *Social Security,* 3rd ed. London: G. Allen, 1949.

Rowntree, B. Seebohm, *Poverty, A Study of Town Life.* London: Macmillan, 1903.

———, and G. R. Lavers, *English Life and Leisure: A Social Study.* London: Longmans, 1951.

Shenfield, B. E., *Social Policies for Old Age.* London: Routledge and Kegan Paul, 1957.

Steinbicker, Carl R., *Poor Relief in the Sixteenth Century.* Washington: Catholic University Press, 1937.

Stevenson, Allan C., *Recent Advances in Social Medicine.* London: Churchill, 1950.

Tierney, Brian, *Medieval Poor Law.* Berkeley: University of California Press, 1959.

Traill, H. D., *Social England.* London: Cassell, 1897.

Watt, Hugh, *Thomas Chalmers and the Disruption,* 2nd rev. ed. Edinburgh: Nelson, 1943.

Webb, Beatrice, *My Apprenticeship.* London: Longmans, 1926.

———, *British Poor Law Will Endure.* London: Oxford University Press, 1928.

Webb, Sidney, *The Break-up of the Poor Law* (Being Part One of the Minority Report of the Poor Law Commission). London: Longmans, 1909.

———, and Beatrice Webb, *English Poor Law Policy.* London: Longmans, 1910.

———, *The Prevention of Destitution.* London: Longmans, 1912.

Whitney, Janet, *Elizabeth Fry, Quaker Heroine.* London: Harrap, 1937.

*Wooton, Barbara, *An Appraisal of Social Science and Social Pathology.* London: G. Allen & Unwin, 1959.

*Younghusband, Eileen L., *Social Work in Britain.* Edinburgh: Constable, 1951.

———, *Report of the Working Party on Social Workers in the Local Authority Health and Welfare Services.* London: Ministry of Health, 1959.

3.

History of Voluntary and Public Social Services in the United States: 1600 to the Present

I. EARLY DEVELOPMENT: LOCAL CHARITIES

As early as the beginning of the seventeenth century, the colonists (most of them coming from England) brought with them the customs, laws, and institutions of the mother country. In general, they were vigorous persons who came to the New World in order to gain freedom to worship, better economic opportunities, to rule themselves or to seek adventure. They found a vast land of forests, fertile valleys, an abundance of wild game, and fish in the lakes and rivers. Few of the new settlers had substantial means—most had only meager belongings—but they were willing to work hard for their living as farmers, hunters, or traders. The isolated settlements of the new frontier were subject to the dangers of Indian assaults, of wild animals, and of natural disasters.

Various cultural backgrounds influenced their attitude to welfare problems, particularly British Puritan, Scotch, English Catholic, Anglican, Dutch, and French, as well as the Quaker traditions. Most followed a strict code of behavior, and disapproved of drinking, gambling, and other vices. They demanded thrift and industrious work which was necessary for the survival of their community and tested religiosity by demonstration of material success. The Puritans had a horror of laziness and poverty because they considered idleness a sin and the source of unhappiness and crime, and poverty a proof of low moral quality. They were also anxious to avoid the heavy taxes common in England where some parishes spent as much as one-third of their total revenues for poor relief. From the English tradition, the colonists inherited the concept that paupers, beggars, and vagrants were criminals, and this accentuated their contempt for those who asked for support from the parish.

Most paupers were widows and orphans and the sick, old, and invalid persons. But there was another category of involuntary immigrants that the mother countries, especially England, wanted to get rid of. At the order of English courts, demented and maimed persons and convicted offenders were deported as "involuntary servants" to work for a number of years. Others were kidnapped by traders and sea captains and sold as servants to colonists. Under the apprenticeship laws, dependent children were also deported from the poorhouses to the Colonies. The majority of the involuntary servants became self-supporting, law-abiding citizens, but some of them were weak, sick, or unwilling to work.

In contrast to the thickly populated European countries from which they emigrated, the settlers lived in scattered places, as farmers and hunters, on the ragged edge of existence, and struggled hard to wrench a bare living from the soil and the woods. They were so involved in their own problems of survival that they gave little thought to the needs of others unable to face the hardships of frontier life. Since land was cheap and labor scarce, beggars able to work were not given alms. Still, the aged, the sick, and women with young children needed help. The traditional resources of the mother country, such as church institutions, endowed charities, hospitals, and almshouses did not exist in the settlements. The local parish had to take care of its destitute. As in England, the colonists were eager to prevent those who might become a public charge from entering the settlement or who seemed objectionable for religious, political, or moral reasons. Such persons were deported, and the Colonies sometimes even paid the passage back to Europe when the individual settlement could not afford the expense.

When the number of paupers increased to the point that some

action had to be taken, overseers or supervisors of the poor were appointed in the parish or township. They had to assess and to collect a poor tax, to investigate the resources of relief applicants, and to dispense relief to the paupers. Frequently, the overseer held other functions, too, such as councilman or town treasurer; later, in many places, his position became a full township office.

The Colonies adopted the *Elizabethan Poor Law,* at least in principle. Every town made provisions for the maintenance of the poor, supplying food, clothing, firewood, and household essentials. They had to be residents for a statutory period, varying between three months and five years. Following English tradition, newcomers often were "warned out," that is, ordered to leave the community unless they could provide security by bond of a resident in good standing. If members of such a family were found begging, they were whipped in the market place and forcibly returned to their former residence. Since many immigrants arrived without means, ship masters who brought them over had to deliver passenger lists and to deposit bond that no passenger would become a public charge for five years. Residents responsible for the arrival of paupers had to indemnify the town.

Poor relief was given mainly in two forms: (1) either as "outdoor relief" in kind (food, clothes, fuel), or (2) by "farming out" or "selling out" the pauper to the lowest bidder. A special type of farming out, was the placement of widows and infirm and aged paupers, for short periods, from house to house. Older children were "indentured"; the town did not pay for them as they worked for their maintenance.

The cost of poor relief was met by the poor tax and certain fines that were imposed for refusal to work at harvest time, for selling bread or butter at short weight, for not attending public worship, or for illegally bringing a pauper into the Colony. If a town failed to make appropriations for poor relief, the county courts assessed the town and disposed of the funds.

Whatever the cause of his distress the pauper was treated as a morally deficient person. He had to swear to the "pauper's oath" and his name was entered on the "poor roll" exhibited in the city hall or in the market place. Local newspapers published the names of all paupers, with the amount of their relief allowances. In Pennsylvania, paupers had to wear the Roman letter "P" on the shoulder of the right sleeve. Old and invalid indigents who had resided for a long time in the parish were considered "worthy poor," if they complied with the moral standards of the neighborhood; all others, particularly strangers and newcomers, were considered "unworthy poor." Disfranchisement of paupers prevailed everywhere. The repressive, punitive character of poor relief, as it had developed in England, was maintained in the New World.

Especially harsh was the treatment of "wanderers" or vagabonds; they were adjudged "rogues" to be "stripped naked from the middle upward, be openly whipt on his or her naked body, not exceeding the number of fifteen stripes" [1] and ordered to leave the parish. Idlers and beggars were often confined to the jail, the "bridewell," or the house of correction. The main purpose of this practice was to spare the citizens of the Colony taxes for poor relief.

In Virginia and North Carolina, using the English parish system, churchwardens and vestrymen acted as overseers of the poor, levied pauper taxes, distributed relief, and farmed out the indigent. In 1785, county overseers of the poor were appointed as a consequence of the separation of church and state. In Louisiana, a French Colony, religious charities, according to French tradition, took care of the poor. Children were cared for in orphanages, the sick and the aged in hospitals.

Orphans, abandoned and illegitimate children remained a major problem of the southern states; many were born to Negro, Indian, and mulatto women and others to white servants who were not permitted to care for the child. In the eighteenth century, impoverished Negro slaves and freed mulatto servants became another group requiring poor relief. Illegitimate children and orphans were "bound out" in order to save poor relief expenses.

There were two fundamental differences between the English and the American poor law practice in the seventeenth and eighteenth centuries. In England, the general method of poor relief was to place the paupers into poorhouses and workhouses; in the Colonies, only in some larger cities were a few almshouses and houses of correction established. In England, legacies, endowments, and bequests pro-

---

[1] Marcus W. Jernigan, *Laboring and Dependent Classes in Colonial America, 1607-1783* (Chicago: University of Chicago Press, 1931), p. 201.

vided substantial funds for the support of the poor in hospitals, asylums, and orphanages; in the Colonies, private charities played an insignificant role until the end of the eighteenth century.

The first almshouse was established as early as 1657 at Rensselaerswyck, New York. Plymouth Colony ordered the construction of a workhouse in 1658, and Boston set up an almshouse in 1660. The legislature of Massachusetts ruled in 1699 that vagabonds, beggars, and disorderly persons should be put to work in houses of correction. During the eighteenth century some Colonies began to use almshouses and workhouses in large cities, instead of boarding out the paupers with families. Most smaller towns continued, however, to farm out the poor by "auctioning them off" to the lowest bidder. Other towns "contracted" with a resident to take care of all paupers in town for a stipulated sum. This method secured the taxpayers against unexpected expenses for poor relief but did not protect the poor against brutal treatment, inadequate care, hunger, and exploitation.

Besides public poor relief, church charities during the Colonial period provided some relief but limited their aid to members of the congregation. The minister, his wife, and deacons visited the sick, widows, and orphans. Assistance was denied to people who neglected admonitions of the minister or whose moral behavior, laziness, drinking, or gambling were criticized in the parish. Churches financed their charity by collections among their members, offerings at the religious services, and appeals for funds in cases of emergency.

A second characteristic type of private charities in America were the National Benevolent Societies, fraternal orders of various nationality groups. The first was founded in Boston among Scottish immigrants in 1657. Other benevolent societies for the English (St. Andrew's Societies), the Irish, the French, the Dutch, and the Germans were organized in the eighteenth and nineteenth centuries.

A third type of private charity was the *philanthropic association* founded for humanitarian motives in order to aid groups in special need. Examples are the Philadelphia Society for Alleviating the Miseries of Public Prisoners, founded in 1787; the Massachusetts Charitable Fire Society of 1794, for the victims of fire; and the New York Society for the Relief of Poor Widows with Small Children, founded in 1798. Endowments to charities became important during the nineteenth and twentieth centuries. Founders of private charities assigned in their wills the administration of endowed funds to a board of trustees who incorporated the foundation according to state laws.

II. THE WAR BETWEEN THE STATES AND THE ALMSHOUSE

The American Revolution was influenced by the desire of the people for liberty, by their resentment of British governmental oppression, and by the French equalitarian philosophy of Jean Jacques Rousseau. During the final years of the eighteenth and the early years of the nineteenth century, the ideals of individual freedom and self-help grew in importance and inspired humanitarian movements for the abolition of slavery, for general public education, women's rights, a better treatment of the poor, the mentally ill, of reform of prisons, and for religious tolerance.

During the first decades of the nineteenth century, the parishes and counties complained about rising expenses for poor relief. In Massachusetts and Connecticut, the state governments had at least assumed the cost for those paupers who were "unsettled" or were "warned out." In New York, Laws on the State Poor provided state funds for refugees fleeing from the Indians, or from the British armies. In general, the maintenance of the poor remained the responsibility either of the town or township, or of the county. Some midwestern and the western states made the counties responsible for the administration of the poor laws, whereas in New England and the eastern states the township continued to provide poor relief.

The growing burden of the expenses for poor relief on local government resulted from two causes: (1) the number of poor increased with the total increase in population; and (2) in times of failure of crops and lack of suitable employment, other "able-bodied persons" also applied for poor relief, often granted them by the overseer of the poor as a political or personal favor. This "spoil system of poor relief" led to the support of families who might have been able to maintain themselves.

Large cities in Rhode Island, New Hampshire, New York, Virginia, Connecticut, Delaware, Virginia, and Pennsylvania had established poorhouses and considered them the most economic and effective means to care for the poor. In 1821, the General Court of Massachusetts appointed a committee to investigate the pauper laws of the Commonwealth. Under the chairmanship of Josiah Quincy, the committee suggested to the legislature the adoption of five principles: (1) that outdoor relief was wasteful, expensive, and destructive to the morals of the poor; (2) that "almshouses" were the most economic mode of relief, because in a "house of industry" each pauper was set to work according to his ability, the result being that the able-bodied earned their maintenance and contributed to the support of the impotent group; (3) that the poor be employed in agricultural work; (4) that a board of citizens should supervise the almshouse; and (5) that intemperance was considered the most powerful and universal cause of pauperism.

Two years later, in 1823, the New York legislature instructed Secretary of State J. V. N. Yates to collect information on the expense and operation of the poor laws. The Yates Report, rendered in 1824, divided the poor into two classes—those under permanent support and the "temporary poor." Among the first class, 35 per cent were unable to work because of age, infirmity, blindness, and physical and mental handicaps; 38 per cent were children under fourteen years of age. The remaining 27 per cent, however, were considered able to earn their living if proper arrangements were made. The report criticized that sturdy beggars and "profligate vagrants" were encouraged to become "pensioners of public relief" because overseers granted them aid without careful examination. The complicated system of legal settlement led to expensive litigation between towns and counties; that paupers suffered by their cruel removal from one town to another; and that the "farmed out" paupers were mistreated and "tortured" by their keepers. Education and morals of the children were neglected, and they grew up in filth, idleness, ignorance, and disease "to become early candidates for the prison or the grave." No adequate provisions were made for setting the paupers to work. On the basis of these findings, the Yates Report recommended the following measures: (1) to establish in each county a "house of employment," providing a farm for agricultural work and education of the children; (2) to procure a workhouse (or "penitentiary") for sturdy beggars and vagrants, with enforced hard labor; (3) to levy an excise tax on whisky distilleries in order to raise the funds for poor relief; (4) to rule that one year's residence in a county of New York con-

stitutes a legal settlement; (5) to abolish "the orders of removal" and
the appeals in poor law litigation; (6) to order that no healthy male
between eighteen and fifty years of age be placed on the pauper list;
and (7) to punish street begging and the bringing of paupers into
the state.[2]

Following the Quincy and Yates Reports, Massachusetts, New
York, and most states of the Union established almshouses and
workhouses and placed relief applicants into these institutions. Immediately after the release of the Yates Report, the state of New
York passed, in 1824, the *County Poor House Act,* which transferred the management of the almshouse from the township to the
county.

The War Between the States ended with the abolition of slavery
through the Thirteenth Amendment; the Constitutional authority of
the Federal government, which became responsible for the welfare
of the people, under the Fifteenth Amendment, was interpreted by
the courts and the administration as restricting the Federal role.

Unfortunately, the introduction of almshouse care did not have
the effect of improving the conditions of the poor which the legislators
had hoped for. The first almshouses had sheltered the old and the
sick. Now the poor families who had been supported in their own
homes, and persons who were boarded out to families, were forced
into the almshouses. There the old and sick were thrown together with
tramps and vagabonds, with blind, deaf-mutes, cripples, idiots, epileptics, and insane people. Children, orphans, foundlings, unmarried
mothers with their children, prostitutes, and criminals were put in
these houses, often without separation of the sexes and age groups.
There were no sanitary facilities, and old cots and straw were used
instead of beds. The almshouse usually was a dilapidated building,
bequested to the town or cheaply bought at auction. Its management
frequently was assigned to a jobless political supporter of the overseer or to an old farm couple unable to continue regular work and
unqualified for the care of children and adults. For the education of
the children in the almshouse there were no funds nor personnel able
to teach. Sometimes, 20 to 25 per cent of the inmates were idiots or

---

[2] The text of the Quincy and Yates Reports may be found in Sophonisba P.
Breckinridge, *Public Welfare Administration in the United States* (Chicago:
University of Chicago Press, 1935), pp. 30-54.

insane. The almshouses became a "human scrap heap" and did not fulfill the hope that had been raised in a reform of the care of the poor.

A. Medical Care for the Poor

From the beginning of American Colonial history, the hardships of frontier life, unwholesome situations on immigrant ships, climatic conditions, natural disasters, and battles with Indians caused injuries and illness among the settlers. Because doctors were few and lived long distances from their patients, their services were expensive. Under these circumstances, it became necessary for the towns to provide for the medical treatment and maintenance of the indigent sick. Such statutory provisions were enacted in Rhode Island in 1662, in Connecticut in 1673, and in New York in 1687. If a destitute patient needed medical care the overseer of the poor or the justice of peace arranged for the service of a physician. Sometimes an annual contract was made between the overseer and a physician to care for all assigned paupers. In New York, pauper patients were boarded out to families, and the city paid for their maintenance and nursing.[3] During the seventeenth century, there were no hospitals in the Colonies, and it was not before the second half of the eighteenth century that the first private hospitals were built. Because the poor law authorities were reluctant to spend money for paupers, they assumed the responsibility for payment of surgical treatment for poor patients, only after they had approved the expense or had been ordered to do so by the court. In emergencies, especially when the patient's life was endangered, physicians cared for him and later sued the poor law authorities for their fees.

In some Colonies physicians were engaged by the Colony, not by the individual towns, to "attend upon the poor generally in the county."[4] Pauper patients had no free choice of a physician. These doctors frequently were not the most competent or the best trained and the contracts granted them rather low compensation.

Mentally disturbed and feeble-minded patients—children as well as adults—were usually left with their families and without special care.

---

[3] David M. Schneider, *History of Public Welfare in New York, 1609-1866* (Chicago: University of Chicago Press, 1938), p. 84.

[4] Edith Abbott, *Public Assistance; American Principles and Policies* (Chicago: University of Chicago Press, 1940), p. 358.

The violently insane and the deformed were considered to be possessed by the devil. The colonists attempted to drive out the "evil spirit" by whipping the unfortunate victim, by shackling him to stakes at the market place, or throwing him into coarse pens, leaving him to hunger and cold. Other mental patients were locked up in attics, basements, and outhouses; were put into strait jackets; chained to a wall of their homes; or confined to the local jail. When the family could not pay for the maintenance of an insane patient, the overseers farmed the "lunatic" out to people willing to take him, just as was done with lame, blind, and crippled indigents.

The first hospitals for indigent patients in the Colonies were the infirmaries or sick wards of the almshouses.[5] When the city of New York established, in 1736, its Public Workhouse and House of Correction, a physician was engaged as medical officer for the infirmary. Bellevue Hospital in New York was started, in 1794, as a "pesthouse"; and a "fever hospital ward" for patients suffering from contagious diseases was added in 1825. When most counties established almshouses during the period following the Quincy and Yates Reports, they also took care of the indigent sick. Only in larger almshouses were the sick paupers separated from other inmates and placed into a "sick bay" or infirmary, and even there medical care was limited to emergency operations and rare visits of the doctor. In general, sick inmates of the almshouse were left to the attention of the matron, or, more often, of other inmates. It was not until the end of the nineteenth century that Massachusetts and Rhode Island set up "almshouse hospitals," and that special wards in almshouses were set aside for the medical care of sick paupers.

The first hospitals were established as private charity institutions, for example, the Almshouse and Infirmary of the Society of Friends in Philadelphia, but after some time it became necessary for cities, counties, or the states to grant subsidies to the hospitals. During the nineteenth century, the separation of the hospital from the almshouse became necessary. In Washington, Oregon, Nevada, and California, the lack of almshouses caused counties to set up hospitals. The rapid development of medical and sanitary science in the nineteenth century contributed greatly to the improvement of medical facilities in

---

[5] Bernhard J. Stern, *Medical Services by Government* (New York: Commonwealth Fund, 1946), p. 15.

the county hospitals. An important stimulus to the raising of standards was the beginning awareness of the dangers for the entire community of epidemics and contagious diseases.

B. Characteristics of Public Poor Relief

The deplorable conditions in the poorhouses led to three major changes in poor relief during the nineteenth century: (1) Private charity societies took the initiative in establishing orphanages and asylums because they objected to the placement of children and helpless invalid and old people in mixed almshouses where they were forced to live with vagrants, rogues, prostitutes, mentally disturbed patients, and criminals. Private relief societies were often affiliated with churches, fraternal orders, or national benevolent associations, and they became the leading, progressive element in American social welfare during the past century. (2) The states themselves assumed responsibility for certain classes of the poor, such as the insane, the feeble-minded, and convicted offenders for whom there were no adequate local facilities. (3) Some local public relief authorities, under the influence of state boards of charity, began to question the old concepts of poor relief with their humiliating, deterrent treatment of the poor. As a whole, however, public poor relief was still following the pattern of the Elizabethan Poor Law.

Changes of the underlying principles and improvements in the practice of poor relief were rather slow and sporadic as a result of sociological and economic factors.

C. The Practice of Poor Relief

The spirit of the English poor laws dominated most of the Colonial laws, whether or not they used degrading terminology in speaking of "paupers." The public, with few exceptions, maintained its resentment against the poor tax burden and its contempt for people unable to take care of themselves in a society which identified economic prosperity and success with efficiency and virtue under the influence of Herbert Spencer's "Social Darwinism," advocated in this country by William Graham Sumner, the militant defender of a laisser-faire policy and of individualism. Some of the most cruel forms of treatment of the poor, such as the whipping after the "warning out" and the posting of the poor roll at the market place, were gradually abandoned, but there remained the spirit of unwillingness to recognize the aid for the poor as socially necessary and justified.[6] The abuses of corrupt local politicians to maintain their positions with the help of poor relief did not make it popular with the people. However, indigent families were still subject to such humiliation that they would rather starve than go on relief. An example of this attitude [7] is the case of a Kansas farmer's family. A severe drought that caused a failure of the crop, in 1878, forced them to ask for county relief when both husband and wife fell ill. When the family with their two children was put into the poor farm, the husband left, after he recovered from his illness, in order to take a job as a farm hand and his wife with the two children remained at the poor farm until he could earn money. The superintendent of the poor farm bound out the eight-year-old son of the couple for ten years, against the child's will and without the consent of his parents. When the parents asked for the boy, the courts refused to release the child. This treatment of parents and child characterizes the disregard of their human rights and their feelings in the practice of the old poor laws.[8]

D. Inadequate Relief Funds

Due to the principle of local responsibility for general poor relief, the towns, parishes, or counties had to raise from local taxes the funds for the care of the poor. The various states differed in their legislation regarding the tax power of municipalities and counties, but generally the "general property tax" on real estate was the sole source of revenue for the local government. Small towns and thinly populated rural counties, therefore, were unable to raise sufficient funds for poor relief.

E. Settlement and Removal

In order to protect the taxpayers against the financial burden of additional indigents, settlement laws made elaborate provisions limit-

---

[6] Nathan E. Cohen, *Social Work in the American Tradition* (New York: Dryden Press, 1958), pp. 22-32.

[7] E. Abbott, *op. cit.*, pp. 125-179.

[8] Grace Browning and Sophonisba P. Breckinridge, *The Development of Poor Relief Legislation in Kansas* (Chicago: University of Chicago Press, 1935), pp. 130-133.

ing the eligibility for public relief to lawful residents who had been in the community, county, or state for a prescribed period. Nobody could acquire legal settlement when he had been "warned out" or had applied for public or private aid during this period. The required time of settlement varied widely, but, as a rule, it was between one and five years. Persons without legal settlement applying for poor relief were sent back to the last place of residence.

F. Family Responsibility

Parents and adult children were legally obliged to support one another if in need, and in some states even grandparents, grandchildren, brothers, and sisters had to support their relatives. The enforcement of this obligation often led to the prosecution of unwilling relatives with little income, which sometimes brought about open hostility between them.

III. SOCIAL SERVICES UNDER STATE AUSPICES

The legal principle that the town or county was responsible for poor relief and the development of private charities within the community indicates that institutions for relief and charity were local in character. For certain groups of the poor—the insane, the feebleminded, the blind, the deaf-mute, the criminal, and the delinquent—the resources of the community were insufficient. A more powerful authority had to assume responsibility. The states, therefore, had to establish the necessary provisions for the care and treatment of these people in special institutions. This change developed gradually during the eighteenth and nineteenth centuries.

The various state institutions were administered by separate boards of directors or trustees, and at first there was no cooperation whatever between these boards nor a unified plan in using the available facilities. Finally, for financial and practical reasons, the states coordinated the use of their institutions and developed uniform standards of care in hospitals, asylums, and correctional institutions.

A. The Care of the Insane

Mentally ill or "distraught" persons were, since colonial times, as a rule kept by their families locked or chained in a barred room or jailed with beggars and criminals. The nature of mental illness was not understood.[9] However, since 1732, they received hospital care in the almshouse of Philadelphia and later, in 1753, in the Pennsylvania Hospital. The first institution to be established especially for the mentally ill was the Eastern State Hospital at Williamsburg, Virginia, founded in 1773. With the progress of medicine and natural science, physicians became optimistic about the possibility of curing mental diseases.

Ten years after the opening of the hospital at Williamsburg, the outstanding psychiatrist of this period, Dr. Benjamin Rush, joined the medical staff of the Pennsylvania Hospital in Philadelphia and became a member of the medical faculty of the University of Pennsylvania. Dr. Rush had visited England and France and was greatly impressed by the work of Philippe Pinel at the Bicêtre Hospital in Paris. Instead of the cruel method of chaining the insane to the walls in the dungeon-like basements and the whipping of unruly patients, he advocated their humane treatment, blood-letting, and occupation of the patients in the hospital. Inspired by these ideas, Dr. Benjamin Rush, in 1783, introduced the new methods to the Pennsylvania Hospital and taught them to medical students at the university. In thirty years of devoted service to the mentally ill he won the title of "The Father of American Psychiatry." Recognizing the importance of the diseases of the mind, Dr. Rush insisted that mental patients should no longer be considered incapable of human reactions and left in cold, dark, and windowless wards. He introduced cold and hot baths, placed the patients in heated and ventilated rooms, assigned them simple work as "occupational therapy," and trained male and female attendants to nurse the patients with kindness. He separated the sexes and the violent from the quiet patients, as well as the chronic from acute cases of mental illness. He removed the iron rings which had been used for chaining the patients to the wall, and changed the attitude of giving mere custodial care to giving active cure.

The Eastern State Hospital remained for nearly half a century the only hospital reserved for mental patients. In 1817, the Friends Asylum at Frankford, Pennsylvania was opened as a private institu-

9 Albert Deutsch, *The Mentally Ill in America* (New York: Columbia University Press, 1949), pp. 32, 47-48; and, Milton Greenblatt, *et al.* (editors), *The Patient and the Mental Hospital* (Glencoe: Free Press, 1957).

tion, and in 1824 the state of Kentucky opened the Eastern Lunatic Asylum at Lexington. Maryland, Massachusetts, Pennsylvania, Connecticut, Ohio, and New York followed in building institutions for the mentally ill and deficient. These mental hospitals, however, could accommodate only a small fraction of the mentally ill. Many dependent insane and feeble-minded remained neglected, and, often, poor law commissioners failed to commit insane paupers to the state hospitals that charged the county higher rates. They preferred to keep the insane, who could not remain with their families, in local jails, houses of correction, and almshouses.

The great pioneer for the care of the mentally ill was a woman without medical training, Dorothea Dix.[10] Born in 1802, she left her parents after an unhappy childhood to live with her wealthy grandmother in Boston. At the age of fourteen she opened a school at Worcester and, after completing her education, the Dame School (in Boston, in 1821), which became a famous institution for girls. Miss Dix became acquainted with the leading citizens of New England who sent their children to her school. In 1836 health reasons forced her to take a rest in England. After her return to Boston, in 1841, a young divinity student asked her help in speaking at a Sunday service to women convicts at the East Cambridge jail. Miss Dix was deeply shocked to find the women in their cells, many of them mentally deranged, in bare, filthy, and unheated quarters. This caused her to enlist the help of influential friends—the statesman Charles Sumner and the physician Dr. Samuel G. Howe—to investigate the jail with her and to mobilize the Boston press. Her findings aroused Dorothea Dix's suspicion that conditions in other institutions might be similar. Without any public authority, Miss Dix visited every almshouse, workhouse, jail, and prison in Massachusetts. After talking with the inmates and with the keepers, she explored possibilities of improvements. On the advice of her friends, Miss Dix submitted in 1843 a memorial to the state legis-

---

[10] Dorothea Dix's life and work is described in Edith Abbott, *Some American Pioneers in Social Welfare* (Chicago: University of Chicago Press, 1937); Helen E. Marshall, *Dorothea Dix, Forgotten Samaritan* (Chapel Hill: University of North Carolina Press, 1937); and, Francis Tiffany, *Life of Dorothea Lynde Dix* (Boston: Houghton, 1890). Dorothea Dix published several books for children, among them, *Hymns for Children* (Boston: Munroe & Francis, 1825) and, *American Moral Tales for Young Persons* (Boston: L. Bowles & Greene, 1832).

lature in which she described the shocking conditions which she had found. Insane patients and idiots were chained to the walls in cold cellars, beaten with rods, lashed, and confined in cages and pens. One man was in a close stall for seventeen years, and a young girl, naked in a barn, was the prey for the boys of the village. Another patient had been chained in an outhouse in winter so that his feet had been frozen. Although some politicians and overseers tried to obstruct Miss Dix's survey, public indignation and the influence of Charles Sumner, Horace Mann, Dr. Samuel Howe, and Dr. Luther Bell led the legislature to pass a bill providing for immediate relief of the insane and the enlargement of the state lunatic hospital at Worcester. After this success, Dorothea Dix decided to continue her investigations of the conditions of the insane and feeble-minded in other states. In Rhode Island, she received large donations from two philanthropists, Cyrus Butler and Nicholas Brown, for an asylum. In New Jersey, Miss Dix convinced the legislature of the necessity of building a mental hospital at Trenton. She traveled many thousands of miles and inspected hundreds of almshouses and jails. By her accurate, reliable reports of the suffering of mental patients, she convinced eleven state legislatures of the necessity of constructing or increasing the capacity of mental hospitals. She became the crusader for the mentally ill.

Her observations convinced Dorothea Dix that, with the growth of industrialization, mental diseases would increase, and that it would be necessary to obtain federal grants from Congress for the future care of the insane. In 1848, she submitted a memorial to Congress and pleaded that 5,000,000 acres of land be given to the states for the care of indigent insane. When her proposal was rejected, she repeated her request in 1849, suggesting the land grant should be used also for blind and deaf-mute persons. After much delay, Congress passed the bill in 1854. The bill provided for 10,000,000 acres of land for care of insane persons and 2,250,000 acres for maintenance and training of blind and deaf-mutes (*12¼ Million Acre Bill*). However, President Pierce vetoed the bill on constitutional grounds because "the power for relief of the needy or otherwise unfortunate members of society" was vested in the states and not conferred upon the Federal government. There was bitter debate in Congress, but the veto was not overruled, and it established for eighty years a principle of abstention by the Federal government from the field of social welfare. But Dorothea Dix's life work had made the public aware of the sufferings of the mentally disturbed patients and had caused the building of thirty-two hospitals in our country.

B. Care for the Mentally Deficient

For a long time the feeble-minded (idiots, imbeciles, and morons) shared the fate of the psychotic (insane). They were kept at home without proper care or were committed to jails or poorhouses whenever their families were unable or unwilling to keep them. The first attempt to educate a feeble-minded child was made in France, in 1799, when Dr. Jean Marc Gaspard Itard in Paris trained an idiot boy found by hunters exposed in the woods. In 1837, Dr. Edouard Seguin opened a private school for feeble-minded children in Paris. His work found recognition throughout Europe, and in 1848, he followed an invitation to the United States to address legislatures and medical societies in several states. In the meantime, studies of the conditions of the mentally deficient had been made in Massachusetts and New York, and the first state School for Idiots and Feeble-minded Youth was opened in South Boston, Massachusetts, in 1848. Dr. Samuel Gridley Howe, who was appointed its director, had studied the treatment of mentally deficient children in Paris.[11] The Massachusetts school developed new methods of training of feeble-minded children under Dr. Walter E. Fernald. New York built a state school for feeble-minded children at Albany in 1851. Pennsylvania granted state subsidies to a private school for idiots in Germantown in 1854, and Ohio and Connecticut followed in 1857 and 1858. Other states established mental institutions during the following decades. Many private institutions were first supported by state grants, and later were taken over by the state when private funds were insufficient.

Other provisions for mentally deficient children were the establishment of separate classes in elementary schools and of special schools in larger cities. These schools taught subnormal children

---

[11] For information on Samuel Howe's life and work, see Julia W. Howe, *Reminiscence* (Boston: Houghton, 1900); and, Laura E. Richards, *Samuel Gridley Howe* (New York: Appleton-Century-Crofts, Inc., 1935). The problem of mental deficiency is discussed in Richard L. Masland, *et al., Mental Subnormality—Biological, Psychological, and Cultural Factors* (New York: Basic Books, 1958).

who were mentally so retarded that they could not profit by the regular school program. In order to enable the mentally deficient to become self-supporting, the states also have organized programs of vocational education, guidance, and placement services.

C. Care of the Blind

Indigent blind persons had been objects of private and public charity for a long time, and the almshouses sheltered many blind children and adults. The first attempt to educate blind children was made in Paris, in 1784, by Valentin Haüy. His school set patterns for other European institutions. A Boston physician, Dr. John D. Fisher, visited the school for the blind in Paris and aroused interest in Boston for an institution for blind children. In 1832, the Massachusetts Asylum for the Blind, under the direction of Dr. Samuel Gridley Howe, was opened.

Samuel G. Howe (1801-1876) graduated from Harvard Medical School in 1824 and joined the Greeks in their fight for independence. Before returning to the United States, Dr. Howe observed in France new methods of teaching the blind and mentally deficient. Before opening the school in Boston, Dr. Howe returned to Europe to study the methods of education of the blind in England, France, and Germany and to recruit experienced teachers for the new asylum. The school soon became too small for the growing number of blind students and moved to a mansion donated by Colonel Thomas H. Perkins. The institution later was named Perkins Institute and Massachusetts School for the Blind.

Dr. Howe's outstanding success was Laura Bridgman, a seven-year-old blind and deaf girl. She was brought to Dr. Howe as a hopeless idiot. Dr. Howe taught her, with years of patient work, to read, speak, and become an intelligent, thoughtful woman. She became, after Dr. Howe's death, one of his biographers. Together with his friend Horace Mann, Dr. Howe achieved a reform of the Boston school system, the training of teachers, and the education of deaf-mute children.[12]

---

[12] Gabriel Farrell, *The Story of Blindness* (Cambridge, Mass.: Harvard University Press, 1956); Berthold Loewenfeld, *Our Blind Children: Growing and Learning with Them* (Springfield, Ill.: Thomas, 1956); and, Jacobus Ten Broek and Floyd W. Matson, *Hope Deferred: Public Welfare and the Blind* (Berkeley: University of California Press, 1959).

The Perkins Institution offered training of the blind in academic studies, in music, and gymnastics and developed mechanical and domestic skills for vocational preparation. Michael Anagnos established the Howe Memorial Press, a Reference Library on Blindness and the Blind, and a kindergarten for blind children.

In 1832, a second school, the New York Institution for the Blind, was set up under the direction of Dr. John D. Russ, and was later known as The New York Institute for the Education of the Blind. There, in 1863, a modification of the French Braille system of raised print was introduced.

The third pioneer institution for the blind was established in Philadelphia, in 1833, by Dr. Julius Friedlander, with emphasis on industrial training and vocational guidance. These three schools served as examples for most other states. In 1837, Ohio opened the first public institution for the blind that was financed entirely by taxation.

In day schools blind children are taught together with sighted children, but the blind receive special instruction in reading, writing, and arithmetic. Now all states educate blind children, either in special classes or at home.

The prevention of blindness was first stressed by Dr. Park Lewis in New York. There, the State Commission for the Prevention of Blindness, organized under Miss Louise Schuyler in 1908, was devoted, primarily, to spreading the knowledge of prophylaxis of ophthalmia neonatorum, an eye infection occurring at childbirth. The Commission, now named the National Society for the Prevention of Blindness, extends its program to the entire country, includes other diseases which may lead to blindness, and promotes safety programs in industry for the protection of eye sight.

The first state to enact special legislation for the financial maintenance of the blind was Indiana, which passed a statute concerning the indigent blind as early as 1840. Other states followed—Ohio in 1898, Illinois in 1903, and Wisconsin in 1907. Before the enactment of the *Social Security Act,* in 1935, twenty-nine states had passed special statutes on blind relief. There were, however, among social workers and among the blind themselves, differences of opinion over whether or not special relief was undermining the initiative of the blind in their attempt to learn a trade or a profession and thus to become self-reliant citizens. This desire of the blind to be respected as normal human beings deserves recognition, appreciation, and encouragement. The number of blind persons in the United States is estimated at about 320,000.

D. The Care of the Deaf and Deaf-Mute

Different from the blind, the deaf and deaf-mute have found in human society less sympathy and help. Their inability to understand the world around them has been a source of irritation or ridicule to others. If the deaf were poor, they were treated as idiots, left to their families, or placed in poorhouses. The first scientific training of deaf-mute children, in the eighteenth century, was undertaken by Jacob Rodriges Pereire of Bordeaux, France. Based upon Pereire's method, the first school for deaf-mute children was founded in Paris, in 1760 by the Abbé Charles Michel de l'Epée. Students of his school founded other institutions for the deaf and deaf-mute in Europe. At the same time, John Braidwood opened a school for the deaf in Edinburgh, Scotland.

An attempt to teach the deaf in the United States was made in New York when, in 1810, Dr. John Stanford, a minister, found a number of deaf children on his visits to the almshouse and offered them religious education. In 1812, John Braidwood, Jr., a grandson of the founder of the Edinburgh institution, came to America and tried to open schools for the deaf in Virginia, New York, and Baltimore. He had no success since the public was apathetic to the fate of the deaf, and Mr. Braidwood was not familiar with American customs.

When at Hartford, Connecticut in 1815 Alice Cogswell, the deaf daughter of a physician, was in need of education, friends of the family took up a collection and sent Dr. Thomas H. Gallaudet to Europe in order to study the methods of teaching the deaf. In England the disillusioned Braidwood family prevented him from observing their work, but in Paris Abbé Sicard, director of the Paris school for the deaf, instructed him in the art of training the deaf. He also sent one of his best teachers, Lautent Clerc, with Dr. Gallaudet to America where both opened the first American Asylum for the Deaf at Hartford, in 1817.

The first *public* residential school for the deaf was the Central College at Danville, Kentucky, organized in 1823. Other states followed the Kentucky pattern—Ohio in 1829, Virginia in 1838, Indiana in 1844, Tennessee in 1845, Georgia in 1846, and California in 1861. Private as well as public institutions for the deaf, in their early development, had the character of charities and were primarily devoted to the education of poor deaf children. The first day school for deaf children was opened in New York, in 1869. In the beginning, sign language was taught; more recently, the oral method and lipreading have been emphasized. Frequently, both methods are combined. In 1864, Congress granted funds for the organization of the Columbia Institute for the Deaf and Dumb in Washington, D.C. Thus, of all the handicapped groups, the federal government first assumed responsibility for the education of the deaf. Today, most states have residential schools for the deaf.

The deaf are no longer treated as charity cases, but as people of normal intelligence, permitted to participate in such occupations as they can perform. There are about 175,000 deaf and 10,000,000 hard-of-hearing persons in the United States. Emphasis is laid upon their education, not on public assistance.

Private societies, such as the American Society for the Hard-of-Hearing, support the work for the prevention of deafness by informing the public about the danger of scarlet fever. They procure hearing aids for people who cannot afford to buy them, and urge the medical examination of preschool children, so that medical treatment and education may start early.

E. The "State Poor"

Since local poor relief was granted only to residents who had acquired legal settlement, towns refused to take care of other paupers who had recently arrived, or who had been "warned out." The urgent needs for food and medical care of such unfortunates, however, could not fully be denied. For this reason, the Colonial legislature of Massachusetts assumed the payment of the necessary expenses for these "state paupers" in 1675. Other Colonies took similar measures, particularly during such emergencies as attacks by Indian tribes, inundations, and other natural disasters. In New York State, relief at the expense of the state treasury, was granted those refugees from the wars against the Indians and, in 1778, to the survivors of veterans in the War of the Revolution.

The assumption of state responsibility for persons without legal settlement and without an earlier residence to which they could be returned became a necessity, because townships or counties refused to care for such persons in need.[13] The beginning of industrial production in the New England States attracted agricultural workers from the farms to look for jobs in the towns. If they lost their jobs, the period of legal settlement often had not been attained, so that the number of "state poor" greatly increased during the nineteenth century and sometimes was almost as high as that of the resident poor under township relief.

Another group of needy persons who were considered a responsibility of the Colonies and later the states, rather than of local government, were the disabled veterans. For the veterans, various provisions were enacted during the Colonial period. Immediately after the Revolution the Federal government became the main source of their support, while the states continued to grant veterans and survivors of veterans additional pensions and special privileges.

F. Crime and Delinquency

During the Middle Ages and up to the sixteenth century, many crimes were punished by death or exile. Prisoners were detained, usually tortured before sentence, and incarcerated, often for life, in dungeons of castles or towers. No consideration was given to their health, and they lived or died under the worst conditions. In the Colonial period a large number of crimes against persons or property was punished by hanging or by banishment from the Colony. Persons arrested were held by the sheriff or his deputies in the local jail. This frequently was not a safe place because outbreaks of desperate criminals and attacks by gangs of friends of the convicted person were not rare, but no other facilities existed until the latter part of the eighteenth century.[14] The growing population, the

---

[13] The states paid a lump sum for the relief of these "state poor" to the towns, which delegated it to a contractor. Frequently, both the towns and the contractors wanted to profit from this appropriation so that very meager care resulted for the poor.

[14] The typical jail was a "catch-all" for dangerous criminals, minor offenders, debtors, and destitute people. There was no separation of prisoners by crime, age, or sex. Debauchery and promiscuous intercourse were frequent. The

deportation of convicts from Australia and England to America, and the changing economic structure of our country led to an increase in serious crimes. However, the influence of French humanitarianism made it difficult to continue the death sentence as punishment for minor crimes. As the number of convicted offenders became larger, the communities began looking to the states for protection. Pennsylvania was the first to establish a state penal institution. In 1790, the legislature decided to convert the local jail at Walnut Street in Philadelphia into a state prison. Since its founding by William Penn, Pennsylvania lived under the influence of the philosophy of the Religious Society of Friends (Quakers). They were convinced that the divine power in every human being could achieve his reformation and that the sinner left to meditation would repent and give up his sin. In accordance with this philosophy, prisoners in the state prison in Philadelphia were segregated into two groups. Those convicted for such serious crimes as murder, arson, adultery, burglary, and manslaughter were confined to solitary cells without communication with other prisoners. Others who had committed minor offenses were lodged in dormitories, and lived in groups. The new method meant a classification of the prisoners according to the nature of their offense; it was a step toward differentiation of treatment and rehabilitation. Under this Pennsylvania system of prisons, which was accepted by other states (New York, Virginia, Massachusetts, Vermont), more humane treatment and less corporal punishment were exercised. The system was optimistic in hoping for an inner reformation of the convict. The lack of qualified and devoted personnel (due to low wages of the warden and guards), overcrowding of the institutions, idleness of the convicts, lack of sufficient funds for proper management, and political scandals, led to a failure of this type of prison management.

A second type of state prison was introduced at Auburn, New York, in 1816. It differed from the Pennsylvania plan inasmuch as the prisoners were confined only at night to solitary cells, but had to work during the day in congregate prison workshops. The plan of reformation by isolation was abandoned; confinement to a single

---

jailers demanded fees from all prisoners, regardless of whether or not they had been acquitted by the court. See Orlando Lewis, *The Development of American Prisons and Prison Customs* (New York: American Prison Association, 1922), p. 13.

cell was used only as a disciplinary measure. Following the example of the prison at Ghent (Belgium), the Auburn prison was built in a star shape with cell blocks opening onto a gallery which could be easily watched by one guard in the center of the building at each floor. The Auburn system was widely accepted, and well-known prisons, such as Sing Sing in New York (1825) and San Quentin in California (1852), followed its pattern.

Prison reform in the United States, the introduction of humane treatment of the convicts, and the use of work as a means of rehabilitation was influenced by experiences of the English reformers (particularly John Howard) [15] and by the penal philosophy of Beccaria and Lombroso. In this reform it proved important to segregate young offenders from hard-boiled criminals; this resulted in the establishment, in 1876, of a special institution in Elmira, New York. The reformatory was used for young convicts between sixteen and thirty years of age, and later, also, for older first offenders. Its main purpose was to prevent the "habitual criminals" from infecting younger offenders. The first prison for women was established at Sherborn, Massachusetts, in 1879, and most states followed by building separate penal institutions for women.

In prisons and penitentiaries, as well as reformatories, employment in workshops equipped with modern industrial machinery, and agricultural and road-building work are provided for the prisoners. The present method, therefore, is called the industrial prison system. The production of goods in prisons or by prison gangs hired by farmers, mill owners, and manufacturers presented serious competition with free labor. Employers, workers, and labor unions objected to this competition so that Federal and state legislation finally limited the use of prison labor. Modern industrial machinery, and the production of goods, is necessary in order to train the prisoners for useful work.

IV. STATE BOARDS OF CHARITIES

The increasing number of state institutions for the handicapped and delinquent in the nineteenth century created a chaotic state of administration. These institutions were based upon special state legis-

---

[15] See Chapter 2.

lation and each placed under the administration of a separate board of directors. Each board requested, annually, higher appropriations from the legislature. There was no uniform policy in principles of management, treatment of inmates, budgets, or personnel standards in institutions, even within the same state. The lack of coordination between the various institutions and of intelligent use of their facilities was strongly felt.

The first state to create a central agency for the supervision of all state charitable institutions was Massachusetts, which organized a State Board of Charities in 1863. The Board had an able secretary in Mr. Frank S. Sanborn. Dr. Samuel Gridley Howe served from 1864 for ten years as its president. He initiated a survey of the existing statutes and regulations of the lunatic asylums, state hospitals, almshouses, industrial schools, and charitable institutions for which Massachusetts granted annual subsidies.[16] Dr. Howe recommended methods for humane treatment of the poor in all these institutions and for efficient management; these were published, in 1866, under the title *Principles of Public Charities*. They emphasized the family system in placing children and adults in the community whenever it was not absolutely necessary to keep them in almshouses, hospitals, or asylums. Members of the Massachusetts Board of Charities inspected not only the state almshouses, lunatic asylums, reform schools, and prisons, but also, local almshouses and jails. Information and data collected from the inspections were summarized and submitted to the legislature. In five years, the State Board of Charities succeeded in reducing substantially the number of "state paupers," by introducing a plan of classification for all inmates of state institutions, and in establishing order in the administration of all state charity institutions. In 1869, a "state visiting agent" was appointed to attend the trials of juvenile delinquents before the courts in order to assume care for the children who were not committed to reform schools. The state agent became a forerunner of the juvenile probation officer.

The advantages of a central state charity agency were soon recognized in other states. They followed the example of Massachusetts, in that each established its own State Board of Charities and Cor-

---

16 Frank J. Bruno, *Trends in Social Work* (New York: Columbia University Press, 1957), pp. 31-43.

rection. In the meantime, Massachusetts had added, in 1869, an agency of coordination in the field of public health—the State Board of Health. Its example stimulated other states to organize such boards, first California in 1870 and the District of Columbia in 1871.

The main results of the activities of the State Boards of Charities were: (1) better care and protection of dependent children whom they removed from the poorhouses, and placed in licensed children's asylums or in foster homes with standards set by the state boards; (2) more uniform and efficient administration of local public relief; (3) the decrease of pauperism and economic suffering in industrial districts by the protection of immigrants; (4) improvement in the care of the mentally ill. The State Boards also were instrumental in the foundation of a nationwide organization representing the field of social welfare. In 1865, the American Social Science Association was established, which preceded the Conference of Boards of Public Charities, now the National Conference on Social Welfare.[17]

In the western states, the counties, rather than cities and townships, assumed the responsibility for poor relief. In California, even counties were unable to meet the problems of the Gold Rush of 1850, when tens of thousands of immigrants arrived after long, strenuous travels. Mining towns had no facilities for medical care nor public relief of any kind. Thus, for the first years of California's statehood, the state government was forced to assume the sole responsibility for the maintenance of the sick and of orphans. Orphanages founded by religious societies were first maintained partly by municipal subsidies, later by the state. In 1853, the counties, under the Boards of Supervisors, assumed the responsibility for the care of the aged and the sick, which was regulated by a state *Poor Law of 1855*.

Upon the requests of various citizens' groups and social agencies, the legislature established a State Board of Charities and Corrections, in 1903, for the supervision of the charitable, correctional, and penal institutions of the state, the counties, and cities. In 1913, Children's Agents in the State Board of Control were appointed to supervise children's institutions and children in foster care for whom state aid was paid; their activities were, in 1921, assigned to the Bureau of

---

17 Frank J. Bruno, *op. cit.*, pp. 3-7; and, Harry L. Lurie, "The Development of Social Welfare Programs," *Social Work Year Book* (1960), pp. 28-29.

Children's Aid in the Department of Finance. Finally, in 1925, the functions of supervision and control of state agencies were consolidated in the Department of Public Welfare which was renamed, in 1927, the State Department of Social Welfare. This illustration of the California development is characteristic of the haphazard legislation and the slow development of systematic organization of welfare functions in the western states.

V. PRIVATE SOCIAL AGENCIES AND CHARITY ORGANIZATIONS

The inadequacies of the mixed poorhouses that were harmful to the poor, and especially to children and young people who were forced to live with vagrants, criminal elements, prostitutes, and sick and mentally disturbed persons, were the main incentive for the foundation of private social agencies during the nineteenth century. As we have seen, religious charities and philanthropic relief societies were already in existence, but their activities were limited to aid for some special local groups. One of the first organizations which attempted to find a constructive remedy for people in economic distress was the New York Society for the Prevention of Pauperism, created in 1817. Its aim was to determine scientifically what were the causes of poverty and to develop means of rehabilitation instead of the mere palliative of financial relief. In a survey made under the auspices of the Society, the following causes of poverty were found: ignorance, idleness, intemperance, lack of thrift, imprudent hasty marriages, lotteries, pawnbrokers, houses of prostitution, gambling, and the large number of charitable institutions. The Society divided New York City into districts and assigned to each district two or three volunteer "visitors of the indigent" as its agents. It introduced bills in the city council in order to prohibit street begging and to restrict saloons, which were considered a primary cause of destitution. The Society established an employment bureau and a savings bank and encouraged the foundation of mutual aid and mutual life insurance groups to protect their members against economic hazards. It provided supplies for home industrial employment of women. The studies of the Society revealed the lack of cooperation between the various charitable organizations and the need for constructive rehabilitation of the poor families.

In Boston, the Reverend Joseph Tuckerman, a Unitarian minister and city missionary, was appointed by the Massachusetts legislature, in 1832, to conduct a survey of the conditions of the poor. His investigations pointed out the influence of low wages and unemployment, which did not permit the unskilled worker and his family to buy the bare necessities of life. He recommended securing better housing facilities for the poor, compulsory school attendance for all children, and providing an individual consideration of the conditions and needs of each family in distress.[18]

After a severe winter in 1843, which caused large-scale unemployment in New York, the Association for Improving the Condition of the Poor was founded in order to coordinate the disorganized relief measures of the large number of church and other charitable societies which had been set up to give relief. The Association, under the able leadership of Robert Hartley, criticized indiscriminate almsgiving without knowledge of the individual needs of the applicants and the lack of constructive measures to make the poor families self-supporting. The Association requested that each applicant for relief be visited in his home by either a volunteer or an employee of the charity society so that the family could be counseled.

The city was divided into twenty-one districts with 225 sub-districts, each of them assigned to one "friendly visitor." The Association did not grant money, but the visitor might enlist financial aid from relatives or friends of the poor, or from relief societies. The Association attempted to restrict lotteries, gambling, and drinking, and it organized the foundation of the New York Juvenile Asylum in 1851, the Society for the Relief of the Ruptured and Crippled in 1853, and the New York Children's Aid Society in 1854. Similar associations were established in other cities. These associations had certain success in the line of social reform, but they did not accomplish the desired cooperation between the numerous relief and charity societies. These agencies jealously guarded the favor of wealthy citizens for contributions to their own institutions and refused to cooperate in a systematic plan for relief and rehabilitation.

---

18 Daniel T. McColgan, *Joseph Tuckerman, Pioneer in American Social Work* (Washington: Catholic University of America, 1940); and, Robert H. Bremner, *From the Depths—the Discovery of Poverty in the United States* (New York: New York University Press, 1956).

A. The Charity Organization Societies

During the economic depression of 1873, the public again became aware of the inadequacy and disorganization of public and private relief, and its interest in the work of the London Charity Organization Society was aroused. The Reverend S. Humphreys Gurteen who had been previously in London and was acquainted with the Charity Organization Society, organized, in 1877, in Buffalo, New York the first society of this type in the United States. Its aim was to help the poor more effectively and to avoid waste of funds, competition, and duplication of work among the relief societies. Within ten years, twenty-five charity organization societies were founded. Among their leaders were Josephine Shaw Lowell in New York, Robert T. Paine and Zilpha D. Smith in Boston, Amos G. Warner in Baltimore, and the Reverend Oscar McCulloch in Indianapolis. The main principles of the Charity Organization Societies (C.O.S.) were: (1) cooperation of all local charity agencies under a board of their representatives; (2) a central "confidential register"; and (3) an investigation of the social condition of every applicant by a "friendly visitor" in order to determine the need and the individual measures necessary in each individual case.

The founders of the societies represented the "bourgeois benevolence," wealthy citizens who felt morally obligated to alleviate the suffering of the poor and hoped thus to minimize political unrest and industrial strife. The members of the board, manufacturers, bankers, and merchants, wanted to be respected in their communities as religious and philanthropic benefactors and civic leaders. Their economic and political philosophy influenced the attitude of the visitors. They believed that poverty was caused by personal fault, idleness, negligence, mismanagement, drinking, gambling, and vice. They hoped that by giving friendly advice, by helping in procuring employment or, sometimes, by giving a loan, they could strengthen the moral fiber of the indigent and encourage them to become self-supporting.

Although this doctrine was originally the accepted social philosophy of the C.O.S., the visitors found that there were other factors that caused destitution, when they became more intimately acquainted with the conditions of "their families." They recognized that unhealthy neighborhood and housing conditions prevented the maintenance of health and morals, that low wages did not allow the purchase of adequate food and clothes even with careful housekeeping and thrift. Jobs were scarce in periods of economic depressions, and it was not the fault of the unemployed worker that he could not find a new position. In times of sickness or unemployment, families became the victims of "loan sharks" who caused them to go into debt for years by charging high interest and heartlessly demanding money. Others lost their meager savings by fraud. The practical experiences of the visitors thus revealed that the concept of individual fault did not stand the test of honest analysis. They began to ask for measures which would fundamentally change those social conditions, and became advocates of social reform. In order to implement the findings of their members, Charity Organization Societies became active in promoting social legislation for improvement of housing, clearance of slums, and better enforcement of tenement legislation, as well as in measures for prevention and treatment of tuberculosis, widespread among the poverty-stricken classes. Some societies established employment bureaus, loan societies, workshops, laundries, lumberyards, wayfarers' lodges and shelters, and legal-aid bureaus. Training centers were set up for the rehabilitation of handicapped people, the blind, the deaf and crippled, and for domestic training of girls. Hospitals, dispensaries, and visiting nurses' services, recreation and summer camps, nurseries for young children, fresh-air playgrounds, and related facilities were organized under the auspices of Charity Organization Societies. They supported the movement for child labor legislation and the organization of special courts for children and adolescents. Many active workers and volunteers of the Charity Organization Societies felt the need for a deeper understanding of the behavior of individuals and of social and economic problems and asked for special training for social work. Such study was first suggested by Anna L. Dawes of Pittsfield, Massachusetts, in 1893. Mary Richmond, in 1897, formulated the plan for the establishment of the Training School for Applied Philanthropy, which organized the first social work courses in New York in 1898.[19] Out of

---

[19] Edith Abbott, *Social Welfare and Professional Education,* rev. ed. (Chicago: University of Chicago Press, 1942), pp. 20-21; Frank J. Bruno, *op. cit.,* pp. 138-144; and, Arthur S. Link, *American Epoch: A History of the United States since the 1890's* (New York: Knopf, 1955).

requests within the Charity Organization Societies grew the recognition of the need of professional education for social work. Another characteristic of the Charity Organization Societies was that their members desired for themselves, and for the public, reliable information on social and health conditions and on the activities of the societies. The result was the publication of a magazine, *Charities Review,* in New York in 1891, which merged in 1910 with several related journals and became one of the leading professional publications under the title, *The Survey.* This was published until 1952, and has greatly contributed to the theoretical and practical development of social work.

The Charity Organization Societies did not attempt to reform public poor relief. They followed Thomas Chalmers' belief that receipt of public poor relief weakened the initiative and moral strength of the indigent. In several cities—Brooklyn, New York, Baltimore, Philadelphia, Washington, St. Louis, Kansas City, Missouri, and San Francisco—the Charity Organization Societies convinced the city councils that public outdoor relief could be abolished and might be dispensed by private relief agencies. Some societies received public subsidies, for several years, for saving the municipal treasury the expense for public outdoor relief.

In their programs the Charity Organization Societies faced two conflicting tasks. They had been organized to achieve better coordination and integration of the existing relief societies and to improve the health and social resources of the community. However, vested interests among member agencies often resented recommendations for changes of methods of work, so that some societies were forced to establish divisions for service to families in need. These divisions conflicted with the activities of other relief societies, which objected because the C.O.S. had not been founded to set up rival organizations. Therefore, at the suggestion of Francis H. McLean, Director of the Russell Sage Foundation, functions of the Charity Organization Societies were separated. In 1908, in Pittsburgh, Pennsylvania, a Council of Social Agencies was founded as the social welfare coordination and planning body. It was composed of representatives of all member social agencies, and The Associated Charities of Pittsburgh was organized as a family welfare society. This pattern was applied in most of the C.O.S. They assumed the title Council of Social Agencies for their planning and coordinating activities,[20] while United Charities, Federated Charities, and so forth were established as nondenominational family and children's services. The Council of Social Agencies had difficulties in raising its operating funds from the public because administrative functions do not appeal to the donors. Thus, in 1913, in Cleveland, the need for joint financing of all private charity work, including the activities of the Council of Social Agencies, was recognized, and led to the establishment of a Community Chest as the organization for collecting private contributions and donations and for distributing them fairly to the social agencies.

One of the main arguments that C.O.S. had used in their criticism of public relief was that they were able to operate cheaper than poor law authorities and would save taxpayers money. Local governments, states, and even Congress had for a long time supported the work of private charities by subsidies for institutions, schools, hospitals, and for relief services to children and adults. In Pennsylvania, in 1889, almost one-third of the public expenses for charities and corrections was spent in subsidies to private charities, and in New York City, in 1890, the percentage of expenditure for support of private charities from public taxes was still higher. This practice was widely used throughout the country.[21]

The main point in favor of public subsidies to private relief societies was that they were more economic. They relied upon endowments, donations, and voluntary contributions, and often had only minor expenses for salaries and wages; particularly was this true of sectarian agencies which used the service of volunteers and religious orders. Another argument was that private charities had a wholesome moral influence upon the clients, and were directed by devoted people, not by "bureaucrats" or political appointees. The "spoils system" in public service had indeed caused mismanagement and inadequacies in public relief. Some philanthropists also thought that relief from private charities would not burden the poor with the stigma of pauper relief and was less degrading.

However, there were valid arguments against tax-supported subsidies to private charities: the objection that public funds should

---

[20] Councils of similar nature had been set up before in New York City, Rochester, and Elmira, New York (Frank Bruno, *op. cit.,* p. 194).

[21] Amos G. Warner, Stuart A. Queen, and Ernest B. Harper, *American Charities and Social Work* (New York: Crowell, 1930), pp. 185-189.

not be spent for denominational or private purposes; that private charity encouraged pauperism and frequently duplicated public efforts; and, that public subsidies would weaken the willingness of sponsors to contribute to private charities. From the point of social philosophy, the subsidy system had definite weaknesses. Our country's characteristics are self-reliance, pride of independence, and neighborly aid to people in distress. It seemed inconsistent for private charity to ask for the help of the same government that was criticized in its relief administration as corrupt and inefficient.

The concept of public subsidy to private agencies made necessary the introduction of certain safeguards whenever public tax funds were used to subsidize private social work. The formula "public control must go where public money goes" expresses this trend. This principle requires the following measures: (1) the methods and standards of the private agency have to be approved by the public organization granting the subsidy; (2) the private agency and institution has to permit inspections by government representatives; (3) the organization has to keep accounts, has to allow their auditing, and has to render reports; (4) the admission policy of the private institution needs approval by the public subsidizing agency; and (5) the private agency agrees to ask for a uniform rate of subsidy for each needy client or patient per month or day.[22] The general trend seems to be toward limiting the use of public funds for public social welfare activities, leaving the maintenance of private social agencies to their own membership, to donations and foundations, and to financial campaigns through Community Chests, United Funds, and national agencies.

B. Youth Services and Settlement Houses

Youth Services. Social group work, in the professional term, dates from about twenty-five years ago. Organizations with a planned purpose of meeting the needs of young persons, especially in big cities, began their work a century ago. The first society of this type was founded, in 1844, in England by a draper, George Williams,

---

[22] An analysis of the principles involved in public subsidies in social work is to be found in Arlien Johnson, *Public Policy and Private Charities* (Chicago: University of Chicago Press, 1931); see also, Wayne McMillen, "Financing Social Welfare Services," *Social Work Year Book* (1957), pp. 260-267.

who attempted to bring the young drapers of London back to a Christian way of life. With this purpose in mind, he founded the first Young Men's Christian Association (YMCA).

A retired American sea captain, J. V. Sullivan, who had founded the Marine Mission for seamen, was impressed by the success of the London YMCA, gathered together young men, and established in Boston, in 1851, the first American YMCA, which spread in a few years to many other cities of the United States. The purpose of this organization was the improvement of the spiritual and mental conditions of young men, the establishment of living quarters at low price with decent, sanitary facilities, particularly for young men who came to the large cities to find work and who could not afford to pay room and board in more expensive homes.

In 1860, the first Boys' Club was founded in Hartford, Connecticut, by a church women's group, in order to give young boys an opportunity to pursue games and sports, music, dancing, and dramatic activities. Other Boys' Clubs spread quickly over the country, frequently under the auspices of church groups or civic organizations which desired to attract the children by games, play, and crafts, rather than leaving them to the doubtful influences of city streets. The Jewish Center movement traced its origin to the "literary societies of young people," in the 1840's, who wanted to get together for lectures and discussions.

The first Young Women's Christian Association (YWCA) in the United States was founded in Boston, in 1866, under the leadership of Lucretia Boyd, and in New York, in 1867, by Grace Dodge. They provided clean, low-rent housing and a cultural center for girls and young women who came to the cities from other parts of the country in order to work. Girls found it difficult to rent rooms in a decent neighborhood for prices they could afford to pay.

Following the example of the English foundation of the Boy Scouts by Sir Baden-Powell, the American Boy Scouts were organized in 1910; a few years later a similar movement for girls was created by Juliette Low in 1912 under the title of "Girl Guides." The Campfire Girls were established in 1911 following the planning of a group of educators, under the leadership of Dr. Luther Gulick; their activities were not limited to outings and hiking, but included, as did most of the other youth organizations, games, singing, workshops, and educational and cultural activities in meetings and club discussions. The American Junior Red Cross is composed of nearly twenty million school children, engaged in health, safety, and recreational programs. The 4-H Clubs, sponsored by the U.S. Department of Agriculture, state colleges and counties, develop in rural youth ten to twenty years of age, ideals and high standards for farming, home skills, and cultural life in the rural community.

The motives for the foundation of these organizations were, of course, different. Frequently, there were religious reasons with the idea of strengthening in children and adults in poor neighborhoods the interest and the devotion to a religious life and to counteract the demoralizing influences of slums, filth, and crime. Many organizations started with such motivation, but all agencies in this field had also the sincere desire to advance the moral, intellectual, spiritual, as well as the physical and social, well-being of children, young people, and adults whom they invited to join their activities, to develop a sound body and a healthy character. They wanted to help underprivileged children and young people to have social pleasure and recreational advantages which they were lacking in their families, and tried to overcome limitations, prejudice, and injustices based upon low economic status and difference in race, color, and religion.

The Settlement House Movement. The development of modern industry brought masses of workers and their families into the cities. They lived in overcrowded quarters, without comfort, sufficient space for their children, and without relatives and friends. Even more forlorn were the large numbers of immigrants arriving in the United States who were needed as industrial labor. They were living in slums and in unsanitary surroundings of overcrowded flats or shabby shacks around the factories, railroad yards, docks, or stock yards. Little of promise from an educational or cultural standpoint could be expected in neighborhoods where poverty went hand in hand with sickness and ignorance. There was little mutual understanding among the poor who came from different racial and religious backgrounds and spoke different languages. The need for the creation of a new sense of neighborhood spirit in order to make good citizens out of underprivileged families in slum conditions had first been felt by Canon Samuel Barnett and his friends at Toynbee Hall in London. Toynbee Hall gave the inspiration to American visitors that educated persons living in such a neighborhood together with the poor and sharing life with the underprivileged would be a valiant factor in overcoming dangers of social and spiritual disorganization. Stanton Coit and Charles B. Stover were the first Americans to transplant the idea of the settlement house to this country. After a study of Toynbee Hall and European experiments, they founded, in 1887, the Neighborhood Guild of New York City, later changed to the University Settlement House. One of the most important social settlements in the United States became Hull House in Chicago, founded by Jane Addams and Ellen Gates Starr, in 1889.[23]

Jane Addams, one of the great pioneers in American social work, was born in Cedarville, Illinois, in 1861. Since her childhood she had wanted to live among the poor. Her travels with Ellen Starr in Europe, the observation of living conditions in Italy and London, and the remarkable success of the Barnetts at Toynbee Hall strengthened Miss Addams' desire to create a similar cultural center in Chicago. They did not plan a new charity, but they built the settlement house as a place for the working people (particularly new immigrant groups of various nations and religions), where they might enjoy life in the new country with its opportunities, in order to develop those higher moral and intellectual qualities upon which depend values of living in a democracy. Hull House, the settlement on the west side of Chicago, on Halsted Street, was open to large groups of foreign immigrants in the neighborhood: Bohemians, Italians, Germans, Greeks, Polish and Russian Jews, and Irish newcomers. Among the residents who joined Jane Addams in devoted work at Hull House were Florence Kelley, Julia Lathrop, Edith and Grace Abbott, Mrs. J. T. Bowens, Graham Taylor, and Alice Hamilton.[24] Although, at first, the neighborhood was distrustful of the aims of the newcomers, some people accepted the invitation to visit the settlement house, began to

---

[23] Jane Addams, *Twenty Years at Hull House* (New York: Macmillan, 1910), pp. 121-127; Lorene M. Pacey, *Readings in the Development of Settlement Work* (New York: Association Press, 1950); and, Allen F. Davis, "Raymond Robbins: The Settlement Worker As Municipal Reformer," *Social Service Review,* Vol. 33, No. 2 (June 1959), pp. 131-141.

[24] In this connection, the leading role of Jane Addams as a pacifist, in the international women's movement, in the fight for women's suffrage and for civil liberty, in foreign relief for the children after the end of World War I, for school reform, and tolerance in religious and racial questions can only be indicated. Among her books are the following: *Democracy and Social Ethics* (1902), *Newer Ideals of Peace* (1907), *The Spirit of Youth and the City Streets* (1909), *Twenty Years at Hull House* (1910) and, *The Second Twenty Years at Hull House* (1930). Jane Addams died May 21, 1935.

ask for advice and came to work with the residents. Deserted women, injured workmen, widows, families unable to pay their installments on furniture asked for counsel. To meet the needs of the neighborhood, a day nursery and kindergarten were established, followed by various clubs for boys and girls, and an art gallery. Discussion and study groups, a school of music, dramatics and arts, classes in rhythm and dancing, and workshops for children and adults developed. The residents became active in promoting factory legislation, better housing, adequate wages and working hours, arbitration of labor disputes, free employment services, and other social reforms. Jane Addams and her co-workers lectured to civic groups to convince them of the need of social legislation, child labor protection, prohibition of night work for women and children, juvenile courts, and probation services.

The experiences of Hull House helped in the development of other settlement houses. We might mention here College Settlement for Women in New York, Andover House in Boston (later called South End House), founded by Robert A. Woods, and Chicago Commons organized by Professor Graham Taylor. Lillian Wald and Mary Brewster founded Henry Street Settlement in New York; Mary Kingsbury Simkhovitch, the Cooperative Social Settlement (later, Greenwich House) in New York; Mary McDowell, the University of Chicago Settlement near the stockyards. Other early settlement houses were Gaylord White Union Settlement attached to Union Theological Seminary, New York; Goodrich House in Cleveland; the Irene Kaufman Settlement, Pittsburgh, Pennsylvania; Telegraph Hill Neighborhood House, San Francisco; and Flanner House, Indianapolis.

Residents of settlement houses became champions of social reform. Living among the poorest classes of industrial workers and immigrants, they recognized the damage done by unsanitary housing conditions, overcrowded flats, low wages, night work for women and children. From the settlement houses came the call for slum clearance, for special juvenile courts to deal with young offenders, and for the organization of the Consumers' League to help the housewife and to protect the health of the family. They requested housing legislation, supported the prevention of tuberculosis, and organized child labor committees. Settlement houses attempted to develop among the poor and the low-paid working class a feeling of self-respect; their resident staff let the neighborhood share the advantage of higher education, culture, and knowledge by living and working together in the settlement house.

Hospitality, friendliness, education, information, and getting acquainted with one another in the neighborhood was the main pattern of their activities. They worked in slums and congested areas in an endeavor to demonstrate by life experience their firm belief in democracy, human equality, and dignity. They fought for equal opportunities for the poor and handicapped and for the abolition of prejudice and discrimination against people because of their skin, religion, race, and foreign birth. Important tools in this fight for human values, education, and cultural development of the underprivileged, were various activities of the settlement houses: boys' and girls' clubs, playgrounds, kindergartens, adult education classes in languages, economic and legal problems, hygiene, labor relations, handicraft, the study of American history and its institutions, and discussion groups. These activities with children, adolescents, and adults emphasized the need of adjustment of the immigrant groups arriving from many countries. They were organized to acquaint newcomers with their new environment and to help them understand the morals, customs, and laws of the United States. Other informal study groups were devoted to cultural and civic affairs, to economic and health problems, and to the development of creative abilities in art classes and workshops, dramatic and literary groups.

The settlement houses are working toward a rebuilding of understanding and cooperation of neighbors in city quarters, where there is frequently a lack of good will, hostility, disunity, and bitter competition, aggravated by low wages, poor working conditions, and neglect of sanitary housing facilities. Immigrant groups in these neighborhoods arrive with unrealistic, exaggerated ideas about American opportunities and wealth. They have to go through difficult periods of economic deprivation, discrimination because of their language and foreign background, dangers to their health, and humiliation until they become settled in the new country. The settlement houses assist the immigrants to go through such trying periods by strengthening their feelings of being welcome and accepted in the new country, by maintaining some of their native skills in arts and crafts, and by encouraging their pride in cultural values which they brought from their homes.

VI. FEDERAL PARTICIPATION IN THE SOCIAL SERVICES

Until the end of the nineteenth century, social services under private and public auspices maintained their local character. Only to a limited extent, statewide systems for a few special groups of people were established, which we discussed above. One of the new trends in social welfare in the twentieth century is the recognition of the need to consider problems of social welfare on the national scale, using the experience of local and state organizations to introduce effective measures throughout the country.

This development was not a rapid one. It faced the traditional resistance of local and state interests, which insisted on their autonomy. Until the depression of 1930, the participation of the Federal government was only a half-hearted and partial one. The leadership in nationwide organization was taken by private organizations, particularly the National Child Labor Committee (1904) and the National Consumers' League (1899).

The Constitution of the United States did not contain a specific principle regarding the responsibility of the Federal government with respect to social welfare. The power of Congress to provide for the "general welfare of the people" (Article 1, Section 8) was a rather general clause and did not refer especially to the setup of public social services. This fact explains the veto of President Pierce against Dorothea Dix's suggestion of federal land grants to the states for mental hospitals. For certain categories of persons, however, the Federal government could not refuse to accept responsibility, and these five groups are sometimes called the "Federal Wards." They are the Indians, the immigrants, passengers and crews of seagoing vessels, the veterans, and offenders of federal laws.

A. Social Services for the Indians

The Continental Congress founded, in 1775, departments of Indian affairs in order to improve the relations with the Indian tribes and to protect their land against seizure without treaty. In 1789, a Bureau of Indian Affairs was organized in the War Department, which regulated treaties for land purchase, schools for Indian children, and some medical care.[25] In 1849, when the Gold Rush in California lured large masses of migrants to the West, the Bureau was reorganized as the Office of Indian Affairs, under the Department of Interior in order to placate the Indian tribes. After the War Between the States, a Board of Commissioners arranged for reservations on which the Indians might live without interference from the whites. These reservations would include schools and health facilities. In 1887, the *Allotment Act* provided for a distribution of land to Indian families to be held in trust by the United States so that it could not be sold. Unfortunately, the aims of the law were not fulfilled. The land was largely "rented" to white men, and the Indians lost nearly 60 per cent of their original property. The Indian Service of the Department of the Interior, meanwhile, employed experts on land use to help the Indians in the reservations to learn more effective methods of agricultural production and husbandry, and a medical supervisor to improve the health services.

In 1924, all Indians received United States citizenship, but the poverty of the tribes continued with a few exceptions. On the basis of Lewis Meriam's survey in 1928, the appropriations for education of Indian children were increased, and in 1934, the Indian Reorganization Act provided protection for the Indian tribes by incorporation of the land and support of agricultural training and production, schools, and medical care. The Act attempted to secure the Indians civic and cultural freedom, to restore their own management of their affairs, to prevent further depletion of natural resources in the reservations, and to develop a sound economy which would make the Indians independent of outside support. With the help of this program under the Bureau of Indian Affairs, the number of Indians is now increasing and has grown from 1933, when it was only 200,000, to more than 400,000. However, the average income of an Indian farm family in most reservations is still only about one-third of that of a white farm family. Some tribes, such as the Navahos and Hopis, whose grazing lands were insufficient for their growing population, have suffered severe hardship.

---

[25] Through the *Indian Removal Act of 1830,* the Indians were forced, however, to leave all their lands east of the Mississippi, although they met in the West hostile native tribes unwilling to let them in.

The schools for Indians on the reservations are still not adequate to secure education for all Indian children. The death rate among the Indians is far above the national average. Although the Indians are entitled to receive free medical service, available hospitals, tuberculosis dispensaries, and sanitation and health centers need further expansion. The funds allocated for relief administered to Indians are too low to meet the need of the many indigent Indians. Social services are rendered in the states through the Indian Agency set up by the Bureau of Indian Affairs for each tribe. The payment of public assistance to the Indians in the states is frequently difficult because their economic need and their legal eligibility are not proved. The lack of adequate appropriations for the Bureau of Indian Affairs makes it difficult to attract well-qualified physicians, teachers, nurses, and social workers needed for medical care, preventive health work, education, and counseling on the reservations. In order to create self-maintaining Indian tribes, the irrigation of unproductive and arid land, the introduction of productive home industries and other industrial manufacturing, and native crafts will be necessary.[26] Experiences on the reservations prove that with patient education, and with industrial and technical training, the Indians will be able to become self-supporting, and to maintain their native culture and dignity; but as long as the tribes remain on the reservations, special educational, health, and social services will be absolutely needed. For Indians who leave the reservations to live in urban communities, the Bureau of Indian Affairs offers relocation and placement services.

B. The Immigrants

With regard to new immigrants, the Colonies and later the states assumed measures of control primarily to protect their citizens against health and moral dangers and financial burdens which the newcomers might engender. Supplementing many state statutes, the Federal *Passenger Act of 1819* required medical inspection of all arriving immigrants, in order to control their health status. In 1882,

---

[26] Voluntary organizations, working in the interest of the Indians, include the Indian Rights Association, the Association on American Indian Affairs, the Institute on Ethnic Affairs, various Indian native organizations, and the American Friends Service Committee.

the Federal government assumed most of the control over immigration (thus replacing the states), introduced a head tax for immigrants, and prohibited the naturalization of foreign-born Orientals. In 1891, the Bureau of Immigration in the Treasury Department became the administrative Federal agency. It was transferred to the Department of Commerce and Labor in 1903 and was called Bureau of Immigration and Naturalization, in 1906. Under changing laws and regulations, admission of immigrants became more difficult. Persons considered of immoral character, likely to become public charges, and contract laborers hired abroad were excluded. In 1917 the *Burnett Bill* introduced a literacy test. After the end of World War I, in a period of intense isolationism, the so-called *Quota System Law of 1921* and the *Immigration Act of 1924* were passed. They limited the annual number of immigrants to a total of 153,774; for each nationality group, however, the limit was set at a maximum of 3 per cent of the estimated number of this national background residing in the United States in 1910, with a minimum of 100 for each country. The new policy towards immigration was discriminatory and restrictive. Immigrants from England, Ireland, and northern and western Europe were favored over those from southern and eastern Europe, where pressure to emigrate was high. The *Oriental Exclusion Law of 1924* virtually stopped immigration from the Far East. As a consequence, immigration which had averaged, in the decade before 1914, over 1,000,000 per year fell during the decade preceding World War II to a yearly average of 53,000. In 1940, the Bureau of Immigration and Naturalization was transferred to the Department of Justice under a Commissioner for Immigration and Naturalization.

The Federal immigration services have been mainly agencies for legal control and administration of naturalization procedure. When the *Alien Registration Act of 1940* required the registration of all immigrants and alien residents, the Bureau of Immigration and Naturalization developed an Educational Services Division, which helped immigrants prepare for naturalization by providing them with textbooks, pamphlets, and home-study courses. Most language and citizens' classes are conducted by local boards of education and voluntary social agencies. Recently, the naturalization of Chinese nationals was permitted (1943), as well as that of East Indians (1946) and Philippinos (1946), but the annual immigration quota of these countries is small: China, 105; India, 100; Ceylon, 100; the Philippines, 100; Japan, 185; and Korea, 100.[27]

Social work for immigrants in the form of counseling, case work, and group work is rendered by private social agencies, particularly the International Institutes; Protestant, Catholic, and Jewish welfare agencies; the International Social Service (formerly International Migration Service); Travelers' Aid Societies; settlement houses; and other voluntary groups. The Department of State and the American Consulates administer immigration procedure abroad.

After World War II, the *Displaced Persons Act of 1948* permitted the admission of 415,744 refugees and victims of Nazi forced-labor camps. The Act also allowed 15,000 refugees who were already in the United States for temporary asylum, as well as war orphans, to remain here. The Act was severely criticized for its religious and ethnic discrimination, but an amendment of 1950 corrected some of its faults. A three-man Displaced Persons Commission administered the Act, working closely with accredited voluntary social agencies. Private agencies, through their state and local committees, were providing assurances of housing and employment, affidavits of support, and placement with relatives and friends. Several states organized commissions for resettlement of displaced persons, conducted surveys on employment opportunities, and coordinated the resettlement work carried on by public and private agencies.[28]

Since the enactment of the *Immigration Act of 1917,* immigrants could not apply for public assistance within five years after their arrival without being faced with deportation. More recently, however, immigration authorities have interpreted the provisions of the laws that displaced persons and other immigrants are not subject to deportation if they become ill, develop a mental disability, lose a job and are forced to apply for public assistance. Physical or mental illness must not have existed prior to the immigrant's entry to the United States. After the displaced person applies for public assist-

---

[27] F. Campbell Bruce, *The Golden Door: The Irony of Our Immigration Policy* (New York: Random House, Inc., 1954); and, Frank L. Auerbach, *The Immigration and Naturalization Act: A Summary of Its Principal Provisions* (New York: Common Council for American Unity, 1952), pp. 18-23.

[28] See Arthur Greenleigh, "Aliens and Foreign Born," *Social Work Year Book* (1957), pp. 105-110; the article explains the controversial nature of our immigration policies.

ance, he has to show that the cause of his need for public aid did not prevail before his immigration to this country.

On January 1, 1953, President Truman's Commission on Immigration and Naturalization submitted recommendations, evaluating the immigration and naturalization policies. All major religious creeds had asked the President to appoint the Commission. The Commission expressed its conviction that immigration has given strength to this country not only in manpower, new industries, and prosperity, but also in new ideas, inventions, and new culture that have enriched our nation. It is contrary to the traditional American spirit to view every alien with suspicion or with hostility. Although immigrants certainly need the United States, we also need immigrants.[29] On the basis of these considerations the Commission believed that our present immigration laws flout fundamental American traditions and ideals, display lack of faith in America's future, damage American prestige and position among other nations, and ignore the lessons of the American way of life. It recommended that our present immigration law should be completely rewritten.

The *Internal Security Act of 1950* ordered that aliens report their present residence each year between January 1 and 10 to the Federal Immigration and Naturalization Service. They receive an Alien Registration Receipt Card which is added to their visa. Displaced persons receive on arrival a provisory registration card for their legitimation. The *McCarran-Walter Act of 1952,* which was passed over a veto of President Truman, excluded alien members or affiliates of the communist or other totalitarian parties and those who advocate the doctrines of world communism or totalitarianism. It maintains the outdated quota system for immigration. Its discriminatory nature was severely criticized by Protestant, Catholic, and Jewish religious groups as unfair to ethnic and religious minority groups, an attitude that is foreign to fundamental American principles. The law went into effect in 1952. It may be hoped that the Act will be amended

---

[29] President's Commission on Immigration and Naturalization, *Whom Shall We Welcome?* (Washington, D. C.: Government Printing Office, 1953), pp. XIV-XV; Frances J. Brown and Joseph S. Roucek (editors), *One America: the History, Contributions, and Present Problems of Our Racial and National Minorities,* rev. ed. (Englewood Cliffs, N. J.: Prentice-Hall, Inc., 1952); and, William S. Bernard and Arthur Greenleigh, "Aliens and Foreign Born," *Social Work Year Book* (1960), pp. 106-112.

so that its discriminatory character and its legal ambiguities be removed.

C. Federal Public Health Service

The first Federal program in the field of public health was the Marine Hospital Service which, in 1798, provided medical care and hospitalization for American seamen. In 1878, foreign quarantine was made a responsibility of the Marine Hospital Service. Emergency funds for the prevention of epidemics were appropriated in 1883, and a hygienic laboratory added in 1887. Foreign and interstate quarantine became the full responsibility of the Federal service in 1893. Its name was changed to Public Health and Marine Hospital Service in 1902, when cooperation with the states and responsibilities of the service were expanded and the Pan American Sanitary Bureau was established. The research activities of the agency were broadened and the name changed again to United States Public Health Service in 1912. Venereal disease control was added in 1918, two hospitals for narcotic drug addicts and the Mental Hygiene Division in 1930. At the same time the National Institute of Health was developed as an expanded research and laboratory division of the Public Health Service.

Under the *Social Security Act of 1935,* the Public Health Service became, first, a part of the agencies under the Social Security Board, and its activities in grants-in-aid to the states, in cancer research, and in control of venereal diseases were expanded. With the establishment of the Federal Security Agency, in 1939, the Public Health Service became an independent agency under the Federal Security Administrator and is now a major part of the Department of Health, Education and Welfare. In 1944, the *Public Health Service Act* codified the provisions on Federal public health activities, and expanded research and tuberculosis control. Under the *Hospital Survey and Construction* ("Hill-Burton") *Act of 1946* the U.S. Public Health Service allocates grants-in-aid to the states, counties and cities for determination of medical needs and for construction or expansion of hospitals, health centers and clinics. Special attention has recently been given to research and development of facilities for prevention and treatment of mental diseases, cancer, heart diseases, and for dental care.

Research activities of the U.S. Public Health Services are conducted through the National Institutes of Health, which now comprise cancer, mental health, heart, dental, experimental biology, and microbiology research.

Other Federal health activities are administered by the U.S. Children Bureau, the Social Security Administration, and the Food and Drug Administration (under the Department of Health, Education and Welfare), the Department of Agriculture, and the Veterans Administration.

D. War Veterans

Already in the New England Colonies pensions for war veterans disabled in their military service and for their survivors were an accepted practice. The Continental Congress, in 1776, continued to provide pensions for invalid veterans and the widows of soldiers who had died in the Revolutionary War, and the Federal government accepted this concept after the adoption of the Constitution. After the War Between the States, the benefits granted to the veterans as "Federal wards" were limited to pensions, land grants, and the care of severely mutilated veterans in The National Asylum for Disabled Volunteer Soldiers and Sailors. Since 1833, the Federal Bureau of Pensions took over the veterans pensions. Under the impact of World War I, the benefits of war veterans were supplemented by hospitalization, vocational rehabilitation, and government life insurance after the *War Risk Insurance Act of 1917* established an insurance compensation in case of death and disability caused by war injuries. The administration of Federal veterans benefits still was spread among many agencies which led to "red tape" and delay in the operations. In order to create a more efficient organization, the Veterans Bureau was established in 1921, and in 1930 the Veterans Administration, as a further step in the consolidation of Federal activities for veterans. The Veterans Administration coordinated the work formerly done by the Bureau of Pensions, the War Risk Insurance Bureau, the Board of Vocational Education, and the National Home for Disabled Volunteer Soldiers.

During World War II, a new social philosophy, regarding the duties of the nation for its veterans, developed. Until this time, it was assumed that pensions for the disabled and the survivors of those who lost their lives in the war was the main task. The new concept expanded this program by assisting all veterans to regain a position in the community after their return equal to that which they would have obtained if they had not been absent in military service. Vocational rehabilitation, medical care, and educational benefits were strengthened or newly added for the returning veterans. The veterans of the Korean War are entitled to similar privileges as those of the two World Wars.

In addition to these Federal services for veterans, the states also established benefits for veterans who had been residents of the state for a certain period, and, during World War II, these supplementary state plans were enlarged.[30]

E. Offenders Against Federal Laws

Federal wards of a different nature were those persons who had violated Federal laws and were sentenced to prison by Federal courts. Because the Federal government first had no facilities for convicted offenders, it committed them to state prisons and penitentiaries for which the Federal courts paid. In 1890, the establishment of Federal prisons was enacted by Congress. They were expanded and improved after prison riots at Leavenworth in 1919. The U.S. Department of Justice introduced parole services for discharged prisoners and, under the *Federal Probation Act of 1925*, a system of probation. In 1930, the Federal Bureau of Prisons was organized, which developed pioneer methods in effective care and rehabilitation of the inmates of the Federal prisons, under the leadership of Sanford Bates and his successor, James V. Bennett. Vocational training (with the aim of preparing the prisoner for a job after his release), recreational and educational facilities, medical and dental care, and religious and cultural activities in the Federal prisons and penitentiaries became examples for other institutions. The Federal penal institutions were classified into penitentiaries for serious crimes with separation of intractable, older offenders from habitual, but tractable offenders, reformatories, correctional institutions for short-term offenders, one medical center for mentally and physically maladjusted convicts, the National Training School for Boys, two detention headquarters, and Federal prison camps. The United States Probation Systems is attached to the Administrative office of the United States Courts. It investi-

---

[30] For more details, see Chapter 15.

gates the social condition and background of an offender appearing before a Federal court and supervises offenders selected for probation and persons released from Federal correctional institutions on parole or on "conditional release." It also refers juvenile delinquents to local juvenile courts for probation services.[31]

VII. THE WHITE HOUSE CONFERENCES

More important evidence of the trend in the social welfare scene in the twentieth century, in order to recognize the need for a national policy instead of local efforts and piecemeal state legislation, occurred in the field of child welfare. It began in 1909, when President Theodore Roosevelt, at the suggestion of a New York lawyer, invited leading workers of child welfare agencies from all over the country to the White House for a "Conference on the Care of Dependent Children." The Conference adopted a platform that children should not be taken away from their families for reasons of poverty, and that normal children who had to be removed from their own families should be placed in foster homes rather than in children's institutions. If children, for special reasons, had to be placed in orphanages or other children's institutions, these should be operated on the cottage plan with small units for the children instead of the large dormitories often used until this time. Children's agencies should be licensed for their work and should be inspected by state authorities. Two recommendations of the Conference were of special importance: first, that the states should enact mothers' pension laws in order to enable widows and deserted women to keep their children; and second, that the Federal government should establish a Federal children's agency. The first recommendation led, in 1911, to legislation of mothers' pensions or allowances laws in several states; Illinois was the first to do this.

The second proposal of the Conference of 1909 resulted in the creation of the Children's Bureau by Congress in 1912. This idea had been conceived by Lillian Wald and Florence Kelley and was vigorously endorsed by social agencies and citizens' groups. President

[31] Negley K. Teeters and John Otto Reinemann, *The Challenge of Delinquency* (Englewood Cliffs, N. J.: Prentice-Hall, Inc., 1950), pp. 627-628; and, Norman V. Lourie, "Juvenile Delinqency," *Social Work Year Book* (1960), pp. 344-355.

Taft nominated Julia Lathrop, prominent social worker and close friend of Jane Addams at Hull House in Chicago, as the first chief of the Bureau. The Children's Bureau was the first active agency of the Federal government in social welfare (as distinguished from education and public health). The purpose of the agency was to act as a clearing house for the entire country, "to investigate and report upon all matters pertaining to the welfare of children and child life among all classes of our people," especially the questions of infant mortality, birth rate, orphanages, juvenile courts, child labor, and social legislation on children. The Children's Bureau's investigations greatly influenced the practice of child care and legislation for the protection of children. A third administrative function was assigned to the Bureau by Congress through the Federal child labor laws, the *Maternity and Infancy Act of 1921* (*Sheppard-Towner Act*), the *Social Security Act of 1935* and the *Fair Labor Standard Act of 1939*. The Children's Bureau was first placed in the Department of Commerce and Labor, in 1913, in the newly separated Department of Labor; in 1946 it was transferred to the Federal Security Agency, and it is now one of the bureaus of the Social Security Administration in the U.S. Department of Health, Education and Welfare.

Another suggestion of the White House Conference of 1909 was the establishment of a voluntary nationwide organization for the development of standards for child care and protection. This organization was founded, in 1920, under the title Child Welfare League of America. Its membership consists of voluntary and public child welfare agencies and institutions which meet the standards set by the League, and of individual members; it publishes a monthly journal, *Child Welfare*.

The second White House Conference, held in 1919 upon invitation of President Woodrow Wilson, was prepared by the U.S. Children's Bureau and called "The Children's Bureau Conference on Child Welfare Standards." It discussed problems of child labor, juvenile delinquency, and dependent children that had been aggravated by World War I, plus the topics of the health of mothers and young children, needs of the preschool and school child, and child welfare legislation. This Conference led to the enactment of the *Maternity and Infancy Act of 1921* and to the setup of child welfare divisions in many states.

The third "White House Conference on Child Health and Protection," called by President Herbert Hoover, convened in 1930. It concentrated on the health needs of children, with special emphasis upon the physically and mentally handicapped child, education, medical care, and health protection of children. The principles of the Conference were announced as "The Children's Charter," [32] asking for spiritual and moral training for every child, understanding of his personality, a home with love and security, protection from birth through adolescence, proper schooling, recreation, and preparation for citizenship and parenthood. For rural children, the Conference demanded equal services as for urban children; for blind, deaf, crippled, and mentally handicapped children, special care, treatment and training; and the establishment of necessary health and welfare services.

President Franklin D. Roosevelt called the fourth "White House Conference on Children in a Democracy" under the theme "Our Concern—Every Child." When the Conference met in January 1940, the war in Europe was raging and the Conference studied the effects of the democratic and fascist philosophies on child care and education. It affirmed the interdependence of social and economic security, tolerance, health education, and opportunity for personal growth for the welfare of children. To follow up its recommendations, the Conference formed a voluntary National Citizens Committee, which remained active during World War II for the protection of children. The rejection of many young men for physical and mental defects demonstrated that more attention needed to be given to the health of all children.

The "Midcentury White House Conference on Children and Youth" held in December, 1950 was the fifth in the series of the conferences. It was invited by President Harry Truman. The conference had the motto "For every child a fair chance for a healthy personality," but it was held under the shadow of the Korean War. The Conference emphasized the emotional factor in the development of children and the specific aspects of adolescence, rather than those of younger children. It was aware that the child and adolescent should be regarded as a whole personality and not be treated as separate entities. Characteristic of this fifth White House Conference was that

[32] Reproduced in N. Teeters and J. Reinemann, *op. cit.*, p. 626; see also, Maurice O. Hunt, "Child Welfare," *Social Work Year Book* (1960), pp. 154-155.

young delegates as representatives of youth organizations participated with full rights.

The Conference made recommendations for the use of research and professional skills, for education for parenthood, for the strengthening of the parents' confidence in their own educational abilities, for broader opportunities for children to gain knowledge of nature and social experiences, for better training in the professions regarding human behavior and cultural influences, and an intensification of studies and preparation for child services. Other recommendations were the establishment of local health services, hospitals and schools without racial discrimination, free college and university education, school lunches, nursery schools, and guidance and counseling in schools and social agencies.

The Conference expressed its firm belief in the principle of separation of church and state and its opposition to the use of public schools for religious education, which remains an important task of the family. Also suggested were expansion of recreation with participation of youth in its planning, extension of social insurance and public assistance, the use of social and psychological knowledge in the treatment of children before courts, and coordination of preventive services for children among private agencies and public authorities. Improvement of methods in child labor protection, adoption and foster care, and special care of handicapped children and children in migratory families were demanded.

The sixth White House Conference on Children and Youth was held in Washington March 27 to April 2, 1960 with the focus on the study of children and youth in a changing world.[33] The Conference had as its two main topics "The World Around the Young" and "The Young in the World." Emphasis was placed on "opportunities for children and youth to realize their full potential for creative life in freedom and dignity." The Conference meetings discussed the ideals and values of our civilization, their changes, and the effects of scientific and technical developments, population pressures, and world events on youth. The Conference evaluated the influence of the environment in which the young generation grows up and the necessity of improving urban, suburban, and rural communities. It studied

---

[33] Katherine B. Oettinger, "The Growth and Meaning of White House Conferences on Children and Youth," *Children,* Vol. 7, No. 1 (January-February 1960), pp. 3-8.

the problem of mobility in our country, the shifts in population, and their impact on education, health, social, and cultural relations of youth. The effects of economic conditions in our "affluent society" (Professor John Galbraith) were a topic of the Conference, unemployment, inadequate family income, work of the mother, and changing employment conditions. The Conference also studied the stages of development from infancy to maturity with special emphasis on the problems of adolescents, of education in response to particular needs for different groups of gifted, retarded, and handicapped children, work facilities, and the responsibilities of young persons as citizens to the community and the nation. Questions of physical, mental, and social handicaps of the young were discussed, as well as the serious problems of broken families and of maladjustment of children under consideration of the causes, diagnosis, and treatment of these conditions and possibilities of rehabilitation of emotionally disturbed and delinquent children.

Representatives of youth organizations participated together with adult members of the Conference actively in its deliberations. The recommendations adopted by the Conference will have considerable impact upon the development of child welfare and youth services, education, and youth employment by follow-up plans and activities in the states for the years to come.

VIII. THE REVOLUTION OF THE SOCIAL SERVICES IN THE DEPRESSION

The economic depression which started with the crash of the New York Stock Exchange in October 1929 marked a complete change in the principles and practice of American social welfare, particularly in poor relief. Until this time, public relief had been managed mainly by political appointees in cities or counties, overseers, or supervisors of the poor. They identified poverty with vice or idleness, and distributed relief on a starvation level, ranging from ten cents to seventy cents per day. Only in forty large cities, were trained social workers on the staff of public relief agencies. Private family welfare agencies existed in about four hundred larger cities, and self-respecting families in financial need went to voluntary agencies, which "protected them" from the disgrace of applying for "pauper aid." Public expenditures for poor relief had slowly been increased during the two preceding decades, but private agencies emphasized that their methods for preventing destitution and for achieving rehabilitation were more economic and, therefore, justified subsidies from taxation.

When, due to the Depression, the number of unemployed increased from 2,860,000 in the spring of 1929 to over 4,000,000 in January 1930, the public in the larger cities looked to the voluntary welfare agencies as the main source of financial support for the steadily growing mass of unemployed. The local private welfare agencies attempted to aid the new applicants who never before had asked for relief. Many unemployed used up their savings whenever they could get payments from the banks that had not closed; others tried to borrow money from relatives, friends, the grocer, and baker, but credit was quickly exhausted and did not keep the family fed and rent or mortgage paid. In a few months, the private social agencies had spent their entire annual budget, exhausted their reserves, or incurred debts in order to continue their activities. By the spring of 1930, all private agencies (as well as public relief offices) were deeply alarmed. The public expected that the private agencies would meet their obligation, but this trust did not fill the exhausted coffers. The Association of Community Chests and Councils issued frantic appeals to industry and to local Chests to secure the necessary funds by a special emergency campaign. However, the results of this effort were spent in a few months, due to the fact that unemployment increased, in the spring of 1930, to over 4,600,000. Several severe droughts which afflicted Arkansas, Kentucky, Louisiana, Mississippi, Oklahoma, and Texas aggravated economic conditions.

President Hoover refused to consider Federal aid to states which applied for help. He thought the American way of handling the emergency, which might be of only short duration, was through private charities, supported by voluntary donations—not by tax money. In August 1930, he called a conference of governors and appointed an Emergency Committee for Employment, under the chairmanship of his personal friend, Colonel Arthur Woods. This Committee followed Hoover's philosophy and appealed to Community Chests, private industry, and the public to supply money for the support of the unemployed. It also requested free services from hospitals and dispensaries, and that child care and recreation agencies accept more children. These well-meant pleas, however, had as little success as the Committee's slogans, "Spread the work" (suggesting that persons should be employed on part-time work) and "Give a job." In April 1931, Colonel Woods resigned and his successor was Fred C. Croxton, an experienced social worker.[34]

During this time the number of unemployed increased; by September 1930 it exceeded 5,000,000, and all over the country municipal and county relief offices had to support a larger and larger amount of unemployed families. Public relief was slowly taken out of its "Cinderella" role and became one of the principal functions of government. Many states were at first reluctant to assume financial responsibility, since their own taxes had decreased due to losses in business, tax delinquencies, and lower production. But in 1931, Massachusetts, New York, Oklahoma, California, New Hampshire, and Maryland were forced to provide state unemployment relief in order to avoid starvation of the unemployed families. The unemployed numbered, in the spring of 1931, over 8,000,000, and their number steadily increased. Not only employees and industrial workers lost their jobs; with the decreasing purchasing power of a large proportion of the entire population, over 750,000 farmers went bankrupt between 1930 and 1933, and 54.1 of every 1,000 farms were forcibly sold in 1932, because the farmers were unable to pay their mortgages or tax returns.

President Hoover maintained his belief that private charity should continue in meeting distress, and, encouraged by his pronouncements, private social agencies still hoped that with a decrease in unemployment they would be able again to take care of the unemployed and their families. They stated the emergency required a combination of the resources of private philanthropy, government, and business. Because their hesitancy delayed the urgently needed appropriations for relief from state legislatures eager to avoid higher taxation for relief funds, counties and cities saw no way of accepting more of the responsibility for mass relief in behalf of local government. The Depression, however, grew more severe. The repeated appeals of Community Chests and private charities no longer could raise the funds necessary to maintain the unemployed. In New York the first Temporary Emergency Relief Administration was organized,

---

[34] Josephine C. Brown, *Public Relief, 1929-1939* (New York: Holt, 1940), pp. 63-71; and, John K. Galbraith, *The Great Crash 1929* (Boston: Houghton, 1955).

with Harry L. Hopkins as executive director. He was a trained social worker with experience in settlement house work, family welfare, Red Cross, and health services. He immediately established uniform policies and standards of relief for the entire state. Other states soon followed the example of New York, so that at the end of 1932 twenty-four states had granted appropriations for disaster relief or emergency relief for the unemployed.[35]

The means of private charities became exhausted. Local and state funds proved to be inadequate to protect the growing millions of unemployed against hunger, cold, suffering, and despair, and the requests for Federal action were heard more frequently every month. Families were broken up in the vain, hectic attempt of the husband and father to find work. Disease increased, and sick people did not receive medical care. Children were passed around among neighbors because the parents had no food or were looking for jobs. The number of suicides mounted. Tuberculosis and malnutrition in children grew dangerously, and most savings of the middle class had been lost. In Congress, Senators Edward Costigan and La Follette introduced bills for Federal aid to provide emergency relief, and the governors of several states claimed the unemployment problem could not be solved without Federal support. But the opposition of the Hoover cabinet, the chambers of commerce, and some citizen's organizations remained firm. Several bills providing Federal funds for relief were passed, but vetoed by President Hoover. Finally, he consented to sign the *Emergency Relief and Construction Act of 1932*. It authorized the Reconstruction Finance Corporation (RFC) to loan the states, counties, and cities $300,000,000 for relief and public work relief projects.[36] Numerous applications from states, counties, and cities immediately made it necessary that an expert should determine the real need of the various states. Fred Croxton was, therefore, appointed head of the Emergency Relief Division of the Corporation. Loans were given on an emergency basis, not exceeding the expenses for one month, so that neither adequate machinery could be set up nor projects developed to secure employment of large numbers of people out of work or to be of permanent

---

[35] National Resources Planning Board, *Security, Work and Relief Policies* (1942), p. 29.

[36] The loans of the RFC were to be refunded by 1935, but legislation in 1934 and 1938 repealed this provision.

value to the community. The local administrators never knew what funds for work relief would be available for the next month, so that no planning was possible in an operation from hand to mouth, which only supplied bare subsistence to the unemployed.

When Franklin D. Roosevelt was elected President in November 1932, the economic depression had reached its depth. The people hoped the new President would cope with an unemployment of 15,000,000 workers, which was depriving thousands of families of their homes and farms and forcing them to live on meager relief without a real hope for recovery. In his inaugural address, on March 4, 1933, President Roosevelt analyzed this economic breakdown:

> Values have shrunken to fantastic levels; taxes have risen; our ability to pay has fallen; . . . the withered leaves of industrial enterprise lie on every side; farmers find no market for their produce; the savings of many years in thousands of families are gone.
> More important, a host of unemployed citizens face the grim problems of existence, and an equally great number toil with little return. . . . The only thing we have to fear is fear itself—nameless, unreasoning, unjustified terror which paralyzes needed efforts to convert retreat into advance.

In some states 40 per cent of the total population were receiving relief, in some counties even as much as 90 per cent.

In this period of despair, the New Deal succeeded in re-establishing new confidence and a balance in the economic system of the nation. It replaced profiteering and speculation by stabilization, and enforced essential humanitarian measures for the suffering, deprived masses of the population.[37]

The first major legislation under President Roosevelt in the fight against depression, unemployment, and economic apathy was the *Federal Emergency Relief Act of 1933*. It represented a radical change in Federal relief policy. It abolished the principle of short loans to the states and substituted for it a new concept of Federal responsibility for human welfare, because, under our economic system, the individual has little control over and influence upon the national production in periods of crisis. Federal grants to the states

---

[37] Thomas H. Greer, *American Social Reform Movements* (Englewood Cliffs, N. J.: Prentice-Hall, Inc., 1949), pp. 266-268; Arthur M. Schlesinger, Jr., *The Coming of the New Deal* (Boston, Houghton, 1959); and, Harry L. Lurie, *op. cit.,* pp. 37-39.

were provided to assist the states in meeting the urgent needs of their citizens.

The administration of the new law was assigned to the Federal Emergency Relief Administration (FERA), and President Roosevelt appointed Harry L. Hopkins its administrator. FERA was an independent agency directly under the President. The initial appropriation of Congress was $500,000,000, one half of which was to be given as grants to states on a matching basis (25 per cent Federal, 75 per cent state and local funds). The other half was given, without matching provision, to states whose resources were depleted or whose unemployment was so grave that no matching could be expected. Congress appropriated additional funds later, so that, until the end of FERA in 1936, the amount of $3,088,670,625 was allocated for this program. After October 1933, FERA was authorized to grant the funds to the states without a matching requirement at the discretion of the administrator. The two main functions of FERA were: (1) to administer the grants to the states for unemployment relief which was exclusively distributed by public welfare agencies and (2) to control proper use of the Federal grants and to establish satisfactory relief standards in the interest of the unemployed.

The organization of FERA was divided into five divisions:

(1) The *Federal Work Division* provided grants to the states for work relief projects conducted by states or communities. They were approved, supervised, and, in special instances, administered by FERA, which advised in engineering problems, labor relations, working conditions, and safety measures. An Emergency Education Program for unemployed teachers and the Surplus Commodities Distribution were administered by the Work Division.

(2) The *Division of Relations with States* supervised the state relief programs through field representatives and regional offices in cooperation with the State Emergency Relief Administrations. In many states, they were the beginning of state welfare departments. A Social Service Section in the Division supervised the standards of relief. Each local relief administrator had to employ at least one experienced social worker on his staff and a qualified supervisor for every twenty workers, in order to make social investigations of need and to assure a reliable and nonpolitical administration of Federal funds.

(3) *Division of Special Programs*—the particular needs of the tens of thousands of migratory workers who were looking for work in

other states made it necessary to establish the Federal Transient Bureau. This supervised the policies and standards of relief to migratory workers who had no legal residence and, in some states with numerous migrants, the setup of migratory labor camps with sanitary facilities.

(4) *The Division of Research, Statistics, and Finance* conducted surveys and investigations, collected accurate data on the relief population, and issued regular relief statistics to provide the necessary information for a fair administration of the vast grant-in-aid program to the states.

(5) *The Rural Rehabilitation Division* provided aid to farmers, agricultural workers, and tenants; rehabilitation on the farm by grants for livestock, seeds, farm equipment, repair, and debt adjustment; resettlement of farmers removed from submarginal land; homesteads for tenants and farm workers.

A special service of the Work Division stimulated the voluntary organization of "self-help cooperatives" among farmers to improve methods of buying and selling, common use of expensive tractors and agricultural machinery, and the organization of prepaid medical and dental treatment programs. Free advice by agricultural specialists and home economists was made available to the farmers.

Among the first rules issued by FERA was that all Federal grants were to be administered only by public agencies. It was prohibited, therefore, to delegate distribution of Federal relief to private charities, a widespread custom before this period. All state plans were carefully reviewed, and the insistence of FERA on employment of trained social workers and qualified personnel helped in an efficient control of the entire program.

The FERA program had as its objective to provide work for the unemployed and to use appropriations exclusively for persons who were able to work but had lost their jobs because of the Depression. Local authorities attempted to place their unemployables—sick, old, and infirm persons and mothers with young children—on the federal relief rolls, but the surveys of the Research Division revealed this practice and led to the elimination of unemployable people from FERA grants. The standards for relief developed by FERA required that consideration be made of the amount of money that would be needed to pay for adequate living conditions and medical care, and that relief should be given by cash instead of the commissary system, which had been frequently used by local relief offices. Useful public work was considered superior to direct relief, which endangered the self-respect and technical skill of the recipient.

In order to provide jobs for the unemployed, FERA immediately began to cooperate with the U.S. Employment Service and the Federal Emergency Public Works Administration. A special National Re-employment Service was organized, supported by FERA funds, to find jobs for as many unemployed as possible. The work relief projects in most states were not too satisfactory and employed only about 1,000,000 (mostly unskilled) workers. In order to introduce more adequate opportunities for the unemployed, the President created the Civil Works Administration by Executive Order of November 9, 1933 as a means of promoting recovery through the employment at regular wages of 4,000,000 unemployed workers. It was thought of as "a shot in the arm" for the economic system that would bring about a rapid increase of purchasing power which would set normal pro-duction and consumption again in motion. The main difference be-tween the FERA and the Civil Works Administration (CWA) was that CWA was exclusively operated by the Federal government; it used many skilled workers in teaching and supervision, and it paid union wages. The administrator of CWA was also Harry Hopkins, an appointment which guaranteed close cooperation with FERA. One-half of the workers in CWA were taken from the emergency work relief rolls; the other half were people in general need of jobs. The program went into effect with remarkable speed and employed at its peak, in January, 1934, 4,260,000 persons. It was so costly, ex-penditures for the six-month period amounted to $863,965,000, that Congress decided to liquidate it only shortly after it had been under-taken. The liquidation was completed in July 1934 after the Civil Works Administration had functioned only four and one-half months. The workers were transferred again to the FERA program, which took over many unfinished projects of the CWA. The period of CWA operation was too short to draw reliable conclusions regarding its economic, social, and psychological effect.

With the close of the work projects of the Civil Works Admin-istration, the FERA organized a threefold program of employment. The first was an Emergency Work Relief Program, set up to help urban communities with over 5,000 population; the second, the Rural Rehabilitation Program was set up to assist farmers to become self-supporting again; and the third was a resettlement plan to relocate landless rural workers, and was the beginning of a land utilization program to be continued later under the Department of Agriculture. In addition to these work relief programs, direct relief was granted to people who could not be employed on work projects.

The administration of this huge unemployment relief program under FERA was extremely difficult. It was carried on as a new venture in a confused and disturbed economic situation in which state and local authorities, as well as private social agencies, had to orient themselves to new principles and methods. It is not surprising, therefore, that severe criticism of the FERA operations was mixed with recognition for its unusually effective policies in the field of public welfare. Its strict separation from the regular activities of state and local public welfare agencies unfortunately prevented the immediate influence of the new concepts of public responsibility on the policies of cities and counties that social workers had expected.[38] But the acceptance of government responsibility for the relief of economic distress was definitely established as social philosophy during this period, and it was also recognized that people had a right to assistance without losing thereby respect for their dignity and their worth as human beings.

A. The Works Projects Administration

As the FERA had been set up only as a temporary measure and the Federal government felt that it should not assume responsibility for direct relief to people unfit for employment, President Roosevelt decided in May 1935 to substitute a work relief program under centralized Federal control with the title Works Progress Administration (WPA), later (in 1939) to be named Works Projects Administration. The *Emergency Relief Appropriations Act of 1935* provided the necessary funds. Originally it was hoped that private industry and the Public Works Administration would be able to absorb most of the unemployed people, but it soon became evident that the Works Progress Administration (WPA) would have to supply the jobs itself.

---

[38] Edith Abbott, *Public Assistance*, Vol. I (Chicago: University of Chicago Press, 1940), pp. 669-690; Donald S. Howard, *The WPA and Federal Relief Policy* (New York: Russell Sage Foundation, 1943); and, Arthur M. Schlesinger, *op. cit.*, Chapter 16.

Its objective was to employ 3,500,000 people on relief. The WPA established the policies, administered the program, approved the projects presented by local and state governments, and reviewed the certifications of workers on the projects to ascertain whether they were in economic need and employable. The state and local governments selected useful work projects which were of value to the communities and provided funds for materials and supervision. The WPA paid the wages of the workers, which amounted to an average of $54.25 a month. Congress excluded certain types of projects, such as military production, slum clearance and demolition work, and theater production projects, in order to avoid competition with private industries.

The wages in WPA were different from the earlier FERA method of family budget; they were a "security wage" without relation to family size and dependents. The wage provided a "minimum security income" which varied according to local standards and the skill of the worker. At least 120, later 130 hours of labor were required per month. An unfortunate limitation for WPA was that every worker had to be taken from public relief rolls, and small communities did not have sufficient skilled workers to be hired as foremen and supervisors for the projects. The fact that in each family only one member might be employed under WPA was a hardship on large families.

The administration of WPA was assigned to Harry L. Hopkins immediately under the President. Six regional field representatives supervised local projects. In 1939, the agency was called Works Projects Administration and was merged with the Federal Works Agency. With exception of some Federal projects, WPA projects were prepared and sponsored by cities, counties, and states. During its entire function, WPA furnished jobs for 7,800,000 individuals who had been unemployed.

The WPA projects have contributed greatly to the improvement of economic, health, welfare, and cultural facilities of our country. The construction work provided 470,000 miles of highways, bridges, roads and streets; and 90,000 public buildings, among them 132 new, and 1,500 enlarged hospitals, medical and dental clinics, visiting nursing stations, libraries, schools, and museums. Three and one-half million acres of swamp land were drained to eliminate the danger of malaria, 12,000 water mains constructed and repaired, and 18,000 miles of storm and sanitary sewers built. A large number of play-grounds and parks, sport fields and swimming pools for recreation, airports for national defense, soil and water conservation works, and flood control and reforestation projects were part of the WPA activities. Unemployed professional persons, artists, sculptors, painters, musicians, teachers, day-nursery teachers, nurses, librarians, and recreation leaders were given jobs in their own fields for the benefit of communities. They taught classes and courses which could not have been offered otherwise. The arts projects brought new cultural stimulation, and the theatre and concert projects gave enjoyment to the people. Valuable research projects for unemployed writers and scientists created such books as the *American Guide Series*.

In spite of these achievements, the WPA was not able to overcome severe criticism. The great costs of a public works program, the lack of conscientious labor on some projects, and the fact that WPA took away some private business were the main sources of complaint. As WPA never had sufficient funds to give work to all unemployed, those unable to get WPA jobs were among its opponents. Contractors were dissatisfied because they wanted to do construction work themselves; organized labor was uneasy because it feared that the low WPA wages would keep down union wages. The WPA was accused of engaging in political activities, particularly in the plays of the theatre projects and in paintings and murals of some artists. Much of this criticism may have been rather factional and biased, but the legal limitations and the lack of certainty about the continuation and financing of the projects made it impossible to develop the program in an ideal form. Since 1940, most projects were devoted to the defense effort, and when industries and production absorbed all available labor, the WPA was closed in 1943.

Social workers in the Works Project Administration program applied their skill in interviews with applicants asking for emergency employment. They had objected earlier to the punitive policies of the poor law authorities, which tended to degrade the poor and to create a demoralized pauper class. In the principles of the work program, they found an opportunity to treat the applicant with respect, to maintain his human dignity and his feeling of usefulness, and to use the work relief assignment as a means for his economic rehabilitation.

B. Work Programs for Unemployed Youth

Even in normal times it is not always easy for youth in a highly industrialized society to obtain work without special education, training, and experience, but the Depression aggravated this problem. Under the New Deal two programs were developed to aid youth prepare for satisfactory employment and to prevent enforced idleness and unhappiness. The first of these programs was the Civilian Conservation Corps, the other the National Youth Administration.

The law on the Civilian Conservation Corps (CCC) was the first social legislation enacted under President Franklin D. Roosevelt, who signed the bill on March 31, 1933. It authorized the President to establish a nationwide chain of forest camps for unemployed youth. The aim was to supply healthy surroundings, adequate food, training and vocational education, and at the same time to assist in the conservation of our country's national resources. Unemployed youth between the ages of seventeen and twenty-five (later twenty-three) who were unmarried, in need of work, out of school, and physically and mentally fit for vigorous work could enroll for a CCC camp. In addition, war veterans and Indians were entitled to enroll; they usually were employed in the administration of the camps or in supervision of the work. Campers received thirty dollars a month, of which twenty-five dollars was sent home for the support of their families; in 1939 this compensation was reduced to twenty-two dollars. The camps of wooden barracks and tents (mostly army material) were set up in national and state forests and parks. The boys and young men built fire towers and fire breaks, forest nurseries, truck and hiking trails, and emergency airfields. They worked in forest insect and tree disease control and planted over three billion new trees. They constructed roads in parks and rural areas, built dams to forestall soil erosion, cleared forests from blister rust and tree beetles, cleaned the streams for fish and fowl, and drained mosquito infested marsh land. They assisted in flood control by constructing irrigation and drainage ditches and dams and helped to create recreational facilities by developing trails, picnic grounds, and vacation camps. The young men applied for CCC at the local welfare office. About 37 per cent came from broken homes. Most of them came from relief families, but this was no condition for their eligibility.[39]

The President appointed Robert Fechner, general vice-president of the International Association of Machinists and lecturer on labor problems at Harvard University, as director of the emergency conservation work. The boys received, in 1,500 camps, medical care and preliminary training, conditioning them for forest work, education in subjects from elementary to high school levels, and vocational and technical training. In 1939, the admission requirement of having to be in financial need was abolished, and the Civilian Conservation Corps was placed under the Federal Security Agency.

Among the criticism voiced against the CCC program were lack of integration with other Federal agencies, the secondary role of the educational activities, and that it competed with local training programs better fitted for urban youth. In fact, the Corps improved greatly the physical and mental health and the fitness of its members, their education and vocational skill, maturity, morale, and self-confidence. It employed during its operation 2,662,000 men, of whom 2,209,000 were young persons. Fourteen thousand Indians were employed on Indian reservations, doing work on drainage and improvement of land. About 260,000 enrollees were war veterans for whom no age limit was imposed. The normal time of enrollment was for six months, with the possibility of re-enrollment for up to two years. During the last years of its operation, from 1940 to 1942, the CCC shifted to defense, industrial training and installation of public utilities. In 1942, contrary to the advice of the President, Congress decided to terminate the CCC program because it was too expensive and rural districts needed young agricultural workers.

The second work program for youth was the National Youth Administration (NYA). Already, in 1934, a student-aid plan had been financed by the Federal Emergency Relief Administration, which also had set up a few resident camps and schools for unemployed women.[40] When, in 1935, almost 3,000,000 young people received emergency relief from public funds, President Roosevelt felt it imperative to establish a special program which would preserve the

---

[39] John D. Guthrie, *Saga of the CCC* (Washington, D. C.: American Forestry Association, 1942), pp. 5-7.

[40] Palmer O. Johnson and Oswald L. Harvey, *The National Youth Administration* (Washington, D. C.: Advisory Committee on Education, 1938), pp. 6-7.

energy and skill of unemployed young women and men. He created the National Youth Administration by executive order of June 26, 1935 as an independent unit within the Works Progress Administration. Two main programs were established: (1) a *student-aid* plan of part-time work with financial assistance to needy high school, college, and graduate students sixteen to twenty-four years of age, to enable them to continue their education, and (2) an *out-of-school* work program consisting of part-time employment on work projects designed to give experience and training to unemployed youths of eighteen to twenty-five years of age. In addition to these two main activities, the NYA established junior guidance and placement services in cooperation with the public employment services, training courses for recreational leaders, some resident projects for experience in cooperative living between rural and urban youth, and health examinations for its members.

The administration of NYA was headed by Aubrey Williams as executive director, and by a National Advisory Committee representing labor, business, agriculture, education, church, and welfare groups. The organization was decentralized through five regional offices, a state youth administrator in every state with a volunteer advisory committee, and district and local directors and advisory committees to meet local needs. In 1939, the NYA was transferred to the Federal Security Agency, and in September 1942 to the War Manpower Commission. In July 1943 Congress withdrew the appropriations and ordered the liquidation of the NYA. In its eight years, NYA had served 4,800,000 young men and women, helping them continue their education or training them for employment. It discontinued January 1, 1944.

The student-aid program provided 1,514,000 students in secondary schools with monthly allowances, between three and six dollars, which covered carfare, shoes, and incidental expenses. College students received up to twenty dollars (graduate students up to thirty dollars) a month. They were selected by the schools on the basis of economic need and scholarship. Their activities in school ranged from maintenance and clerical help to tutoring, library, and research work. The out-of-school program aimed primarily at giving youths between eighteen and twenty-five years of age experience and confidence in their ability to work. It helped 2,700,000 youths by employing them on such projects as the construction of community centers, playgrounds, tennis and basketball courts, parks, and swimming pools, making furniture for children's institutions and schools, and repairing of fire equipment. All projects were devised by public authorities, who provided materials, equipment, and supervision. The allocation of federal funds of the NYA was made on the basis of the total youth population of every state. All youths were registered with the public employment services which, in some instances, were assisted by vocational guidance and placement through a special junior employment section.

In the central office of the NYA, a Division of Negro Affairs protected the particular interests of the Negro minority and secured their full share in educational and training facilities.

The main objections to the NYA came from the school authorities, who protested that a Federal agency controlled the education program, that the activities of the regular schools were duplicated, and that NYA was too costly. In fact, the funds allocated to NYA were never adequate to meet the need for continued schooling, so that it was forced to limit the allowances to modest supplements. One of the valuable fruits of NYA and CCC work was the introduction of work experience into the educational program of American schools.

C. Rural Rehabilitation

In rural regions with poor soil, or under the one-crop system, the Depression brought disaster. Farmers lost their part-time jobs in industries, their unemployed children returned from industrial centers, and they could not meet their installment rates or buy feed and seed. Many lost their land to the mortgage holder. The Federal Emergency Relief Administration, following examples in Texas and Alabama, first offered loans to farmers as well as some subsistence homesteads.

In 1935, President Roosevelt established the Resettlement Administration in order to continue the agricultural program of the FERA,[41] which was succeeded, in September 1937, by the Farm Security Administration. It provided two programs, "rehabilitation" and "social services." The first included: (1) loans to farmers, tenants, and sharecroppers on easy terms for the purchase of land, farm equip-

---

[41] U.S. Department of Agriculture, *History of the Farm Security Administration* (1940), pp. 2-4.

ment, seed, feed, and livestock, with counseling on efficient farm management; (2) purchase of farms or homesteads with payment in installments running as long as forty years; (3) setup of farm cooperatives for the joint purchase of tractors, elevators, or purebred sires and for common use of the equipment; and (4) a "debt adjustment service," including legal advice and economic aid. The social services program organized voluntary prepaid medical and dental care at an annual cost, varying from fifteen to forty-five dollars per family. It provided cash grants in emergencies, such as sickness and accidents, and set up migrant camps (partly permanent and partly mobile) with sanitation, medical, and dental service. In the national defense program the Farm Security Administration resettled farm families whose land was used for army needs, established emergency housing for war workers in dormitories and trailers, and erected public housing projects in defense areas.

In 1946, the Farmers Home Administration in the U.S. Department of Agriculture became the successor of the Farm Security Administration. The new agency grants three types of credit to farmers: (1) *farm ownership loans,* amortized over a forty-year period, to enable the farmer to purchase a family-size farm or to improve, enlarge, or repair the farm; (2) *insured mortgages* to guarantee, for a period of forty years, the loans of private lenders so that farmers may purchase or improve farms; and (3) *production and subsistence* loans (up to $3,500) to allow farmers to purchase on reasonable rates and terms, seed, livestock, feed, fertilizer, and farm equipment and to refinance debts and bolster family subsistence in emergencies. Loans carry no more than 5 per cent interest, and veterans and disabled veterans receive preference. The field staff of the Farmers Home Administration still gives individual advice in farm management to farmers who ask for loans or help.

IX. A PERMANENT SOCIAL SECURITY PROGRAM

Although temporary emergency measures for relief and work projects under the FERA were carried on, it became evident that a permanent organization of the welfare system of the country, with the Federal government sharing in its expenditures, was necessary. In his message to Congress on June 8, 1934, President Roosevelt announced that a bill would be presented to provide security against the great disturbing factors in life, especially unemployment and old age. On June 29, 1934 he appointed a Committee on Economic Security consisting of Miss Frances Perkins, Secretary of Labor, as chairman and the secretaries of the Treasury, of Agriculture, the Attorney General, and the Federal Emergency Relief Administrator as members. In the preparation of legislation, the Committee enlisted the help of a Technical Board of Economic Security, consisting of government experts in Federal, state, and local public agencies, with Arthur J. Altmeyer as chairman. The Committee also was aided by an Advisory Council on Economic Security, composed of experts who were not connected with public agencies and under the chairmanship of President Frank Graham of the University of North Carolina. He had a professional staff, with Professor Edwin E. Witte as executive director.[42]

On January 15, 1935 the Committee on Economic Security submitted its report to President Roosevelt, who transmitted it, under the title *Economic Security Bill,* to Congress. After certain amendments and changes the *Social Security Act* became law on August 14, 1935. Thus, the fundamental Federal law in the field of social welfare in the United States was created. The Social Security Act introduced three main programs: (1) a program of *social insurance,* consisting of a Federal old-age insurance system and of a Federal-state system of unemployment compensation, (2) a program of *public categorical assistance* supported by Federal grants-in-aid for three groups, including Old-Age Assistance, Aid to the Needy Blind, and Aid to Dependent Children, to which a fourth category, Aid to the Permanently and Totally Disabled, was added in 1950, and (3) a program of *health and welfare services,* providing for Maternal and Child Health Services, Services for Crippled Children, Child Welfare Services, Vocational Rehabilitation, and Public Health Services. The last two programs later were based on different legal foundations, the *Vocational Rehabilitation Act of 1943 and the Public Health Service Act of 1944.*

The *Social Security Act* placed the Federal administration of the three programs under a new agency, the Social Security Board. The

---

[42] Social Security Board, *Social Security in America* (1937), pp. III-V, 515-517; and, Wilbur J. Cohen, "The First Twenty Years of the Social Security Act, 1935-1960," *Social Work Year Book* (1960), pp. 49-62.

three members of the Board were appointed by the President of the United States for terms of six years, but not more than two could belong to the same political party. The Board's first chairman was John G. Winant; his successor was Arthur J. Altmeyer. The Board was established as an independent agency under the President, but an amendment of 1939 placed the Social Security Board, together with other agencies, under the newly created Federal Security Agency. At this time, the U.S. Public Health Service was grouped together with other Federal units concerned with health problems, but child welfare services remained under the administration of the U.S. Children's Bureau. In 1946, a reorganization of the Federal Security Agency abolished the Social Security Board and replaced it by the Social Security Administration under a single Commissioner for Social Security. Under Presidents Franklin D. Roosevelt and Harry Truman, the change of the Federal Security Agency into a cabinet department was proposed in several bills. But it wasn't until 1953 that President Eisenhower's first Reorganization Plan succeeded in establishing the Department of Health, Education and Welfare with that department's secretary as a member of the Cabinet. The Social Security Administration, the Public Health Services, the Office of Education, and the Office of Vocational Rehabilitation are important branches of the Department.

The amendments to the Social Security Act, particularly those of 1950, 1952, 1954, 1956, and 1958, increased the numbers of people eligible for old-age and survivors' insurance and unemployment compensation. These amendments strengthened the operations of the public assistance programs and the various health and welfare services, and indicated modern society's increasing recognition of responsibility for the preservation of the welfare of all people.

The role of private social agencies fundamentally changed during the Depression. At the start of the Depression, private agencies soon exhausted all their funds and were forced to abandon the dispensation of economic aid that was considered, until this date, as one of their main functions. Public welfare departments in cities and counties took over the main responsibility for the relief of the financially distressed. Private social agencies still are granting some economic aid to persons who are not eligible for public assistance, and if it is necessary in order to make casework and counseling services effective; they are rendering such financial help as cannot be given by public agencies. The basic distinction between the present functions of public and private agencies is that private social agencies emphasize casework services for personal and behavior questions, adjustment in family and environmental problems, and the providing of group work and recreational facilities not supplied by public authorities. Private agencies no longer assume the main responsibility for economic support of people in financial need, but supplement the assistance given by public welfare agencies. Private agencies still engage in health services for tuberculosis, cancer, venereal diseases, heart ailments, infantile paralysis, and rheumatic fever and in children's services, particularly for adoption and child placement, institutional care for children and adults, vocational guidance, and training. Often, these services are coordinated with those offered under public auspices.

X. WAR AND POSTWAR PROBLEMS

The main problems which social services faced during World War II were family separation caused by the absence of husbands, fathers, and fiancés in the armed services or in war industries, and children left without proper care and supervision by working mothers. There also were general health and moral difficulties caused in communities by mass living in military training locations and inadequate conditions in war industries areas. Often, public and private agencies had to meet these increased problems with inadequate personnel, depleted by the call of social workers to service with the armed forces. Finally, war services endangered the maintenance of regular peace-time programs for the aged, the handicapped, the sick, and children.

In order to solve these problems, a nationwide effort of coordination of all available resources was attempted under the guidance of the Office of Community War Services, which was organized under the Federal Security Agency. The Office was guided by an Interdepartmental Advisory Council, with representatives of all Federal agencies engaged in health and welfare work. Five central committees dealt with: (1) health and medical care, (2) family security, (3) nutrition, (4) social protection, and (5) community organization for health and welfare. The twelve regional offices of the Federal Security Agency established a similar coordination, their regional directors serving at the same time as directors of community war services. State and local defense councils in cooperation with public and private social agencies carried programs and suggestions to the people. In the defense industrial areas, medical and dental facilities, sanitation, water supply, hospitals, clinics, schools, and housing often were lacking, so that a tremendous effort to provide them was imperative. The funds for the construction and operation were made available through the so-called *Lanham Act* (*Community Facilities Act*) *of 1940*. They enabled communities to build housing for war workers and families of service men, hospitals, schools, water and sewage systems, and child care centers freeing mothers for work in war industries.

A serious problem was the lack of recreational facilities for service men on furlough and for war workers in cities in which the population had suddenly increased to many times its former size. The recreation sections of the regional offices of the Community War Services joined their efforts with state and local defense committees and with the United Service Organization (USO). This agency was created in 1941 by six private social agencies—the YWCA, YMCA, the National Catholic Community Service, the Jewish Welfare Board, the Salvation Army, and the National Travelers Aid Association.[43] Their cooperation resulted in the establishment of centers for servicemen with facilities for social activities, music, dramatic performances, dances, hobby clubs, discussion groups, libraries, and reading and writing rooms. They arranged for invitations to servicemen for family dinners, concerts, and theatres. USO agencies, and particularly Travelers Aid, offered counseling and casework service to servicemen, war workers, and transients who had personal problems. More than 1,000 USO centers were operating during the war. The American Red Cross provided medical and casework services in military camps and assisted the families of the servicemen through its Home Service Division. Private social agencies, together with public welfare departments cooperated with the defense councils in giving civil protection, improving nutrition during rationing and war shortages,

---

[43] Federal Security Agency, *Health, Welfare, and Related Aspects of Community War Services* (October 1942); Helen R. Wright, *Social Service in Wartime* (Chicago: University of Chicago Press, 1944); and, Reginald Robinson, *Serving the Small Community* (New York: Association Press, 1959).

and (with the support of public health authorities) in rendering "social protection" against venereal diseases.

A. The Japanese Evacuation

One event during World War II deserves discussion from the point of view of social welfare: the evacuation of the population of Japanese descent from the states on the West Coast. The Japanese are one of the small minorities (about 127,000 persons) in our country. Almost 120,000 of them lived in California, Oregon, and Washington. Immediately after Pearl Harbor a wave of suspicion, hatred, and fear against persons of Japanese ancestry engulfed the Pacific Coast. Military leaders were afraid of sabotage and the danger of support of an enemy attack. Racial prejudice was combined with dislike of economic competition. Truck farmers, merchants, laundrymen, restaurant, fruit- and vegetable-market owners, and fishermen urged the removal of Japanese from the West Coast. Others argued that an evacuation would be necessary in order to protect the Japanese-Americans against harm from mob violence. After the President authorized the evacuation of military zones, Japanese-Americans were asked to move voluntarily from the Pacific Coast inland. Of 100,000 in California 10,000 followed this suggestion, hastily sold their business, land, and property, and tried to settle in the neighboring states. But they encountered difficulties. Utah, Nevada, Wyoming, and Arizona prevented them from entering their territory because they considered them "dangerous." On March 2, 1942 General De Witt ordered their removal from the Western Coast areas. President Roosevelt created the War Relocation Authority on March 18, 1942 as a civilian agency to carry out the evacuation. Social workers with other citizens were concerned about the constitutionality of this measure, since 75,000 of the group were American citizens. However, they assisted in the relocation process at the registration centers. They did their best to advise the Japanese about the disposal of their property, the storage of furniture and equipment, and the safekeeping of valuables, but many Japanese were so upset that they sold everything at great loss and patiently accepted being placed behind barbed wire in ten relocation centers, which were established by the evacuees themselves, in desert regions under the command of the army engineers. The War Relocation Authority sought to make life in these centers as bearable as possible. Crowded army barracks (without sufficient privacy for families with many children), lack of constructive work, limited and inadequate wages, and shortage of health and sanitary facilities and teachers for the schools in the camps were serious handicaps. The anxiety about the future and the hostility of the press—and sometimes of the guards and surrounding population—created problems and led, in a few instances, to riots. Japanese who were considered "disloyal" were segregated in Tule Lake, California, while, in the other relocation camps, an intensive outplacement program was carried out.

With the help of local committees, on which members of the American Friends Service Committee, of the YWCA, the YMCA, and the Federal Council of Churches of Christ were particularly active, 41,000 persons left the centers and worked in communities all over the country. Life in the relocation centers was trying, especially for adolescents who lost the traditional oriental respect for their helpless and often embittered parents. Juvenile delinquency, family discord, and political strife were rampant. The removal of families to outside communities served to solve many difficulties which social workers in the centers tried to alleviate. When Japanese-Americans were permitted to volunteer for army service, the spectacular record of their combat units, particularly in Italy, helped to restore their own self-respect and caused a change in public opinion. The War Relocation Authority encouraged the return of the evacuees to their old communities or to places of their own choice as soon as it was permitted by Presidential order in 1945. Many older evacuees had suffered under the internment and had lost their initiative so that they first preferred to stay in the camps, a typical damage of "institutionalization." But with the aid of placement officers of the War Relocation Authority and local committees the difficulties of finding housing, jobs, and acceptance in the communities were finally solved.[44]

---

[44] U.S. Department of the Interior, War Relocation Authority, *WRA: A Story of Human Conservation* (Washington, D. C.: Government Printing Office, 1947); Dorothy S. Thomas and Richard S. Nishomoto, *The Spoilage* (Berkeley: University of California Press, 1946); Alexander H. Leighton, *The Governing of Men* (Princeton: Princeton University Press, 1945); and, Dorothy Swaine Thomas, *The Salvage: Japanese American Evacuation and Resettlement* (Berkeley: University of California Press, 1952).

B. Health and Welfare in Civil Defense

The *Federal Civil Defense Act of 1951* provided for preparing the country for emergency action in case of an enemy attack and organized a Federal Civil Defense Administration. Among the civil defense measures to be taken in case of an air attack or atomic bombardment are warning, protection of citizens, restoration of communications, medical, health, and sanitation services, and emergency welfare activities.[45] The possibility of an atomic bombing has greatly increased the danger of mass destruction of human life and of entire communities. However, the abhorrence of people for a suicidal war makes it difficult for the public to develop realistic awareness of this danger and creates an atmosphere of apathy which does not secure an effective protection against disaster situations.

It is anticipated that in case of such a disaster, many families will be left homeless, without food, clothing, without a place to eat, sleep, and rest, and without money. In order to preserve civilian morale in such a situation, efficient welfare services are necessary. Social workers may have to evacuate families or children, to relocate refugees, and they may have to provide mass feeding, clothing, shelter, and financial aid to destitute people.

It is desirable to give such emergency help as rapidly as possible. The victims of an enemy attack immediately should receive aid until they can again take care of themselves and can resume their normal work and life. Necessary emergency welfare services have to include information centers, field hospitals, shelter, canteens, and a registration service. The existing hospitals, clinics, and dispensaries would be used for emergency health measures, but supplementary facilities might have to be established if necessary. In each state, the chief health officer takes charge of all civil defense health and medical services. Social workers advise evacuees and refugees about locating relatives and friends and refer them to public assistance, medical care, and child care services. They would also counsel them regarding their legal rights for insurance benefits and other allowances, employment

---

[45] Wilbur J. Cohen and Evelyn F. Boyer, "Federal Civil Defense Act of 1950: Summary and Legislative History," *Social Security Bulletin*, Vol. 14, No. 4 (April 1951), pp. 11-16; Ralph E. Pumphrey, "Social Work and National Defense, *Social Work Year Book* (1954), pp. 500-505; and, Robert C. Edson, "Disaster Relief," *ibid.*, (1960), pp. 218-223.

services, retraining and vocational rehabilitation facilities, and temporary settlement.

The social and health problems created by the establishment of new plants and installations in many defense communities, some of them in isolated areas, also require serious attention. Workers and their families in congested areas near defense factories are seriously threatened by hardships, inadequate housing and health provisions, and lack of hospitals and schools. In 1953, in one trailer camp, 2,000 children were left without any playground or supervision, forced to crawl under the wheels of automobiles and trailers. In a southern community, a trailer camp was set in rigid rows under the blazing sun, endangering the health of women and children. An open ditch served as the sewage system near a large concentration of huts used as dwelling places for defense workers' families. Defense housing projects sometimes are full of dust and flies. Their inhabitants are without decent recreational facilities, lonely, and frustrated, and frequently in need of schools, health centers, nursing facilities, water supply, sewage disposal, and recreational and cultural life.

In many communities, classified as "critical defense housing areas," there are no Community Chests or Councils of Social Agencies. Often, the social agencies are understaffed and not able to assume the additional responsibilities of meeting the problems created due to the large defense industries, military encampments or training centers, and of preparing for the people's protection in case of an atomic attack.

Under the auspices of the National Welfare Assembly, the nationwide coordinating body of private social welfare agencies, most of the funds for the civil defense needs of the country are raised in a unified campaign by the United Defense Fund which, at the local level, is coordinated with the activities of the Community Chests. The United Defense Fund (UDF) is composed of six organizations: (1) The United Community Defense Services, (2) The United Service Organizations, (3) The American Social Hygiene Association, (4) The National Recreation Association, (5) The United Seamen's Service, and (6) the American Relief for Korea.

Recreation and welfare activities, including personal and family counseling for members of the armed forces, are the responsibility of the United Service Organizations. The USO, which had been very active during World War II, merged in 1951 with the Associated Services for the Armed Forces. USO is now composed of the YMCA,

YWCA, Salvation Army, National Catholic Community Service, National Jewish Welfare Board, National Travelers Aid Association, and "Camp Shows, Inc." These coordinated agencies provide wholesome leisure-time activities for military personnel to meet the religious, spiritual, social, cultural, and welfare needs of men and women in the Armed Forces. USO shares these services with the American Red Cross, whose field directors and staffs offer assistance to military personnel in camps and hospitals and supplement recreation programs overseas. The American Red Cross maintains preparation for disaster relief in cooperation with the Armed Forces, Federal, state, and local governments, and private organizations. It assists in the planning and preparation of emergency relief measures.

The Air Force organized, in 1951, an Office of Community Services in order to make available recreational and social welfare resources of the communities to members of the Air Force and their families.

The United Community Defense Services, in cooperation with the American Red Cross, provide defense programs for civilian welfare and health, which supplement the preparations of state and local governments for disaster relief in case of an emergency. United Community Defense Services (UCDS) is a federation of fourteen nonprofit national organizations [46] founded in 1951 at the suggestion of the National Welfare Assembly and the Community Chests and Councils of America. UCDS offers advice to defense communities by making fact-finding surveys which determine the health and welfare needs of the population and enable the community to organize and finance an effective civilian defense social welfare program. It assists the community in the establishment and temporary financing of emergency programs, including health services, child care, and recreation, where community resources cannot meet these needs. UCDS is engaged in the recruitment of nurses, social workers, and volunteers for defense service and emergency preparations. UCDS pays partic-

---

[46] These are: (1) American Social Hygiene Association, (2) Child Welfare League, (3) Committee on Careers in Nursing, (4) Family Service Association, (5) YWCA, (6) Catholic Community Service, (7) Committee on Social Work in Defense Mobilization, (8) Federation of Settlements and Neighborhood Centers, (9) Organization for Public Health Nursing, (10) Probation and Parole Association, (11) Recreation Association, (12) Travelers Aid Association, (13) Urban League, and (14) AFL-CIO Community Services Committee.

ular attention to the development of the resources of underprivileged minority groups and to the establishment of interracial cultural cooperation. Finally, UCDS conducts research to discover the scope of the defense impact and to interpret to the public the importance of preparedness for emergency action.

Separate defense programs are carried on by: (1) the American Social Hygiene Association for the prevention and cure of venereal diseases, (2) the National Recreation Association in the field of physical education and recreational activities, (3) the United Seamen's Service at ports for members of the merchant marine, and (4) the American Relief for Korea for the rehabilitation of the country which had so severely suffered during the war.

In the field of civil defense, neither Congress nor the majority of States have yet taken the full-hearted action to secure the best available protection for the population. In the area of welfare service, the public welfare departments, with the support of the social agencies coordinated under the United Defense Fund and with the aid of the American Red Cross, are expected to provide most of the social services in an emergency. Civil defense and disaster protection is financed mainly through private contributions, state and local funds, and is left to local initiative. It seems doubtful whether this arrangement provides the necessary preparedness and sufficient security under present conditions.

Selected Bibliography

Abbott, Edith, *Historical Aspects of the Immigration Problem; Select Documents.* Chicago: University of Chicago Press, 1926.

———, *Public Assistance. American Principles and Policies,* Vol. I. Chicago: University of Chicago Press, 1940.

*———, *Some American Pioneers in Social Welfare: Select Documents with Editorial Notes.* Chicago: University of Chicago Press, 1937.

*Abbott, Grace, *The Child and the State: Select Documents with Introductory Notes,* 2 vols. Chicago: University of Chicago Press, 1938.

Adams, Grace, *Workers on Relief.* New Haven: Yale University Press, 1939.

*Addams, Jane, *Forty Years at Hull House.* New York: Macmillan, 1935.

*———, *Twenty Years at Hull House: with Autobiographical Notes.* New York: Macmillan, 1910.

———, *et al., Philanthropy and Social Progress.* New York: Crowell, 1893.

Bakke, E. Wight, *Citizens Without Work: A Study of the Effects of Unemployment Upon the Worker's Social Relations and Practices.* New Haven: Yale University Press, 1940.

Bernard, William S., and Arthur Greenleigh, "Aliens and Foreign Born," *Social Work Year Book* (1960), pp. 106-112.

*Best, Harry, *Blindness and the Blind in the United States.* New York: Macmillan, 1934.

————, *Deafness and the Deaf in the United States.* New York: Macmillan, 1943.

Breckinridge, Sophonisba P., *Public Welfare Administration in the United States,* 3rd impression. Chicago: University of Chicago Press, 1935.

*Bremner, Robert H., *From the Depths: The Discovery of Poverty in the United States.* New York: New York University Press, 1956.

Brown, Francis J., and Joseph S. Roucek, *One America: The History, Contributions, and Present Problems of Our Racial and National Minorities,* rev. ed. Englewood Cliffs, N.J.: Prentice-Hall, Inc., 1945.

*Brown, Josephine C., *Public Relief, 1929-1939.* New York: Holt, 1940.

Browning, Grace, and Sophonisba P. Breckinridge, *The Development of Poor Relief Legislation in Kansas.* Chicago: University of Chicago Press, 1935.

Bruce, J. Campbell, *The Golden Door: The Irony of Our Immigration Policy.* New York: Random House, Inc., 1954.

*Bruno, Frank J., *Trends in Social Work: As Reflected in the Proceedings of the National Conference on Social Work, 1874-1956.* New York: Columbia University Press, 1957.

Cahn, Frances and Valeska Bary, *Welfare Activities of Federal, State, and Local Governments in California, 1850-1935.* Berkeley: University of California Press, 1936.

Clarke, Helen I., *Principles and Practice of Social Work.* New York: Appleton-Century-Crofts, Inc., 1947.

*————, *Social Legislation,* 2nd ed. New York: Appleton-Century-Crofts, Inc., 1957.

*Cohen, Nathan Edward, *Social Work in the American Tradition.* New York: Dryden Press, 1958.

Coit, Stanton, *Neighborhood Guilds: An Instrument of Social Reform.* London: Sonnenschein, 1891.

Corner, George W., *The Autobiography of Benjamin Rush.* Princeton: Princeton University Press, 1950.

Creech, Margaret D., *Three Centuries of Poor Law Administration.* Chicago: University of Chicago Press, 1936.

*Deutsch, Albert, *The Mentally Ill in America: A History of Their Care and Treatment from Colonial Times.* New York: Columbia University Press, 1946.

Devine, Edward J., *When Social Work Was Young.* New York: Macmillan, 1939.

Dix, Dorothea L., *Memorial to the Legislature of Massachusetts, 1843,* Vol. VI. Boston: Old South Leaflets (1889).

Duffus, R. L., *Lillian Wald: Neighbor and Crusader.* New York: Macmillan, 1938.

Fechner, Robert, "The Civilian Conservation Corps Program," *Annals of the American Academy of Political and Social Science,* Vol. 194 (November 1937), pp. 129-140.**

Feder, Leah, *Unemployment Relief in Periods of Depression.* New York: Russell Sage Foundation, 1936.

Fosdick, Harry Emerson, *On Being a Real Person.* New York: Harper, 1943.

French, Richard Slayton, *From Homer to Helen Keller: A Social and Educational Study of the Blind.* New York: American Foundation for the Blind, 1932.

Greer, Thomas H., *American Social Reform Movements: Their Pattern Since 1865.* Englewood Cliffs, N.J.: Prentice-Hall, Inc., 1949.

Guthrie, John D., *Saga of the CCC.* Washington, D.C.: American Forestry Association, 1942.

Henderson, Charles R., *Modern Methods of Charity.* New York: Macmillan, 1904.

Hopkins, Harry L., *Spending to Save.* New York: Norton, 1936.

Howard, Donald S., *The WPA and Federal Relief Policy.* New York: Russell Sage Foundation, 1943.

Howe, Julia W., *Reminiscences (1819-1899).* Boston: Houghton, 1900.

*Jenergan, Marcus W., *Laboring and Dependent Classes in Colonial America, 1607-1783.* Chicago: University of Chicago Press, 1931.

Johnson, Arlien, *Public Policy and Private Charities.* Chicago: University of Chicago Press, 1931.

Johnson, Palmer O., and Oswald L. Harvey, *The National Youth Administration.* Washington, D.C.: Advisory Committee on Education, 1938.

Kelso, Robert W., *The History of Public Relief in Massachusetts, 1620-1920.* Boston: Houghton, 1922.

*————, *The Science of Public Welfare.* New York: Holt, 1928.

Kieley, James F., *Account of Origin, Growth and Work of the CCC.* Washington, D.C.: Department of the Interior, National Park Service, 1938.

** This journal will be referred to as *Annals.*

Kluckhohn, Clyde, and Dorothea Leighton, *The Navaho*. Cambridge: Harvard University Press, 1946.

Lane, Marie D., and Francis Steegmuller, *America on Relief*. New York: Harcourt, 1938.

*Lee, Porter, *Social Work as Cause and Function*. New York: Columbia University Press, 1937.

*Leighton, Alexander H., *The Governing of Men*. Princeton: Princeton University Press, 1945.

Lewis, Orlando, *The Development of American Prisons and Prison Customs, 1776-1845*. New York: Prison Association, 1922.

Linn, James W., *Jane Addams: A Biography*. New York: Appleton-Century-Crofts, Inc., 1935.

Lorwin, Lewis L., *Youth Work Programs, Problems and Policies*. Washton, D.C.: American Youth Commission, American Council of Education, 1941.

McColgan, Daniel T., *A Century of Charity*. (2 vols.). Milwaukee: Bruce, 1951.

McWilliams, Carey, *Prejudice: Japanese Americans*. New York: Little, 1944.

Mangold, George, *Problems of Child Welfare*, 3rd ed. New York: Macmillan, 1936.

Marshall, Helen E., *Dorothea Dix: Forgotten Samaritan*. Chapel Hill: University of North Carolina Press, 1937.

Meriam, Lewis, *et al.*, *The Problem of Indian Administration*. Baltimore: Johns Hopkins Press, 1928.

Miles, Arthur P., *An Introduction to Public Welfare*, Chapter 4. Boston: Heath, 1949.

Pintner, R., J. Eisenson, and M. Stanton, *The Psychology of the Physically Handicapped*. New York: Appleton-Century-Crofts, Inc., 1931.

*Queen, Stuart Alfred, *Social Work in the Light of History*. Philadelphia: Lippincott, 1922.

*Rich, Margaret E., *A Belief in People: A History of Family Social Work*. New York: Family Service Association of America, 1956.

Richards, Laura E., *Letters and Journals of Samuel Gridley Howe*, 2 vols. Boston: Dana Estes & Co., 1909.

————, *Samuel Gridley Howe*. New York: Appleton-Century-Crofts, Inc., 1935.

Robinson, Reginald, *Serving the Small Community*. New York: Association Press, 1959.

Sanborn, Franklin B., *Doctor Samuel Gridley Howe, The Philanthropist*. New York: Funk, 1891.

Schneider, David M., *History of Public Welfare in New York, 1609-1866.* Chicago: University of Chicago Press, 1938.

————, and Albert Deutsch, *The History of Public Welfare in New York State, 1867-1940.* Chicago: University of Chicago Press, 1941.

Schwartz, Harold, *Samuel Gridley Howe, Social Reformer (1801-1876).* Cambridge: Harvard University Press, 1956.

Simkhovitch, Mary K., *Neighborhood: My Story of Greenwich House.* New York: Norton, 1938.

*Stroup, Herbert Hewitt, *Social Work: An Introduction to the Field,* rev. ed. New York: American Book, 1960.

Sunley, Emil W., *The Kentucky Poor Law, 1792-1936.* Chicago: University of Chicago Press, 1942.

Thomas, Dorothy S., *The Salvage: Japanese American Evacuation and Resettlement.* Berkeley: University of California Press, 1952.

Thurston, Henry W., *The Dependent Child: A Story of Changing Aims and Methods in the Care of Dependent Children.* New York: Columbia University Press, 1930.

U.S. Displaced Persons Commission, *The DP Story.* Washington, D.C.: Government Printing Office, 1952.

*U.S. National Resources Planning Board, *Security, Work and Relief Policies.* Washington, D.C.: Government Printing Office, 1942.

Wald, Lillian D., *The House on Henry Street.* New York: Holt, 1915.

————, *Windows on Henry Street.* Boston: Little, 1934.

Warner, Amos G., Stuart A. Queen, and Ernest B. Harper, *American Charities and Social Work.* New York: Crowell, 1930.

Watson, Frank Dekker, *The Charity Organization Movement in the United States.* New York: Macmillan, 1922.

Weber, Gustavus, and Lawrence F. Schmeckebier, *The Veterans Administration, Its History, Activities and Organization.* Washington, D.C.: Brookings Institution, 1934.

Wilson, Howard E., *Mary McDowell: Neighbor.* Chicago: University of Chicago Press, 1928.

Wise, Winifred E., *Jane Addams of Hull House: A Biography.* New York: Harcourt, 1935.

Woods, Robert A., and Albert J. Kennedy, *The Settlement Horizon—A National Estimate.* New York: Russell Sage Foundation, 1922.

*Worcester, Daisy Lee W., *Grim the Battles.* New York: Exposition Press, 1954.

*Wright, Helen R., *et al., Social Service in Wartime.* Chicago: University of Chicago Press, 1944.

Zimand, Savel, *Public Health and Welfare: The Citizen's Responsibility —Selected Papers of Homer Folks.* New York: Macmillan, 1958.

II.

Social Work
Processes

Introduction to Part II

SOCIAL WORK ACTIVITIES may be classified into six types: social casework, social group work, and community organization—the three basic methods of social work—and social welfare administration, social welfare research, and social action—three ancillary activities which are necessary to establish, maintain, and operate social services. Social work process is the interaction between the client and the social worker; between the members of a group with one another and with the group worker; and between individuals and groups in the community. Social casework and social group work are carried out in direct, personal contact with the people who use the social services; here, Helen L. Witmer's definition of social work applies: ". . . to give assistance to individuals in regard to the difficulties they encounter in their use of an organized group's services or in their own performance as a member of an organized group." Although there is no uniform theoretical agreement over whether or not all six activities should be classified as social work,[1] they are important tools in our modern social welfare program. They all require certain common skills which may be called generic social work qualifications, but the methods applied in the six processes differ.[2]

---

[1] Helen L. Witmer, *Social Work: An Analysis of a Social Institution* (New York: Farrar & Rinehart, 1942), pp. 121, 123; and, Herbert H. Stroup, *Community Welfare Organization* (New York: Harper, 1952), p. 126.

[2] A detailed analysis of the methods of social casework, social group work, and community organization, with illustrations and interpretations, is given in Walter A. Friedlander (editor), *Concepts and Methods of Social Work* (Englewood Cliffs, N. J.: Prentice-Hall, Inc., 1958).

4.

Social Casework

I. DEVELOPMENT OF THE CASEWORK PROCESS

During the last quarter of the nineteenth century, the workers of the Charity Organization Societies were influenced in their ideas and practice by the recognition of the widespread economic and spiritual distress among the masses of low-paid manual laborers, the sick, and unemployed in the industrial large cities. They realized the lack of helpful, constructive relief given by the poor law authorities and their apathy toward the suffering of the destitute. They also became aware of the waste of energy and funds resulting from the lack of cooperation and information, and the confusion and duplication of effort which existed among private charitable agencies. The Charity Organization Societies accepted Thomas Chalmers' theory that public poor relief was not effective, and that the individual client needed "rehabilitation" so that he could support himself and his family. They sought to achieve this goal by making personal visits to the poor, by giving advice, admonitions, and financial aid. In each case, the rehabilitation of the poor person was to be carried on after a careful investigation of his conditions and discussions with the applicant and the people in his surroundings. This was the beginning of casework.

In their method of finding a social solution for the personal and economic problems of a client, the Charity Organization Societies spent money for vocational training, tools and equipment, rent for setting up a workshop or a small business, for food, clothes, and rent of a room or an apartment for the maintenance of the family. These measures were, however, merely incidental to the real purpose of rehabilitating the client. The volunteers and agents of the relief societies considered themselves representatives of the community; they visited the applicant and collected facts on his conditions, family relations, experiences, and abilities. The findings were submitted to a committee representing the local charities that decided which action should be taken, with the aim of restoring the client to self-support. In this task the "friendly visitor" continued the personal contact with the client, gave him advice and directions to become independent. It was expected that the client follow the suggested plan. The necessary funds for rehabilitation, however, were solicited from well-to-do citizens by employed agents of the Charity Organization Society. The personal contact of the volunteer was thus separated from the measures of financial assistance because the societies thought that the mixing of both would impair the moral and educational influence and the personal relationship between the friendly visitor and the client.

II. CHANGING CASEWORK PHILOSOPHY

The approach of the "friendly visitors" was based upon the assumption that the client was in his precarious condition due to some fault in his behavior. This moral foundation of the early casework approach became questionable when the "friendly visitors" began to realize that frequently the cause of distress was not a character defect, but the social conditions under which the client lived. Such conditions were illness of the client or of his family, numerous children, unsanitary, overcrowded housing, low wages, debts, undernourishment, inadequate education, and training. This recognition of the influence of environment on the individual was supported, at the turn of the century, by the scientific findings of the "school of environmental determinism" in anthropology, biology, sociology, and economics. Novelists, sociologists, and political scientists exposed the social evils of industrial society and emphasized the need for fundamental social reforms in working conditions and wages, in the establishment of schools, housing, hospitals and clinics, in the prevention of communicable diseases, and the abolition of night work for women and children.

The effect of these experiences was that the Charity Organization Societies became concerned with finding ways of advocating social legislation that would prevent destitution, disease, and social disorganization. But, though measures of social reform were improving the living conditions of the poverty stricken and the low income group, there were still many families in dire want and distress. They needed understanding, helpers to listen to them and to advise them so that they might make the right use of such community services as clinics, hospitals, employment bureaus, legal aid, training facilities, and adult education. Under these circumstances, social agencies continued to carry on casework in recognition of the fact that social reform did not solve all individual problems. Social workers also became aware of the fact that their interest should not be limited to the individual applicant, especially the breadwinner of the family, but that each member of the family deserved their attention and should be considered in relation to his environment.

The experiences of social workers revealed a serious conflict of values in our civilization. Modern industrial society was inclined to embrace a theory of "Social Darwinism" that its unfit members should be eliminated as a natural process, and that interference with such elimination was harmful to a healthy society. However, religious thought and humanitarian philosophy respect the divine nature of man and demand that every human being be assisted whatever his failures might be. These two value systems contradict each other. Social workers accepted the "Humanitarian Ethos" as their concept of responsibility of society for the welfare of individuals in the community. Our general public, however, often is still ambivalent about following one or the other of the two conflicting concepts and is uncertain whether to accept rugged individualism or humanitarian philosophy.[3]

In 1911, Porter R. Lee, director of the New York School of Social Work, stated that social casework is "the method of effecting the understanding of the needs, resources, and reactions of individuals." [4] But there still remained at this time a paternalistic, domineering at-

---

[3] H. Witmer, *op. cit.*, pp. 55, 167-169, 172; Barrows Dunham, *Man Against Myth* (Boston: Little, 1947), pp. 59-60, 64-65; and, Herbert Bisno, *The Philosophy of Social Work* (Washington, D. C.: Public Affairs Press, 1952), pp. 30-41.

[4] Porter R. Lee, "Social Function of Case Work," *National Proceedings of Conference of Charities and Corrections* (1911), pp. 260-266.

titude in the relation of the social worker toward the client who came to ask for advice and help. Although, in theory, it was proclaimed "casework must work with and not for the individual," in practice, the caseworker considered himself the best and the only objective judge in what was the right solution for the client, because of his experience in social questions. Another factor in social casework practice at this period before World War I strengthened the dominant role of the social worker. Social agencies took advantage of the growing number of persons who received training either in special courses or in the newly established schools of social work and employed them instead of untrained volunteers. This meant that the paid social worker assumed most functions in the agency: the initial interview with the applicant, social investigation of his home and his environment, the social diagnosis of the facts found in this investigation, and the development of a plan for treatment or rehabilitation of the applicant and his family. In 1917, Mary E. Richmond, director of the Charity Organization Division of the Russell Sage Foundation, first described this method.[5] Social agencies no longer submitted the findings of social investigations to a local committee, so that the social caseworker became the decisive element in the process of aiding the client.

However, social agencies found that their aim of rehabilitation of children and adults could not be achieved by counseling alone. Frequently substantial financial assistance was needed in order to maintain families during the period of readjustment, retraining, and rehabilitation, and, in some instances, for long periods. Family welfare and child protective agencies still aimed at supporting people who were not in need of institutionalized care using funds collected from private donors and contributors. They prevented, by this practice, the public from being aware of the necessity of improving the facilities of public relief authorities, of providing adequate budgets, and competent administration of public relief.

---

[5] Mary E. Richmond, *Social Diagnosis* (New York: Russell Sage Foundation, 1917). See also Gordon Hamilton, *Theory and Practice of Social Casework* (New York: Columbia University Press, 1947), pp. 11-12, 19; Helen H. Perlman, *Social Casework: A Problem-solving Process* (Chicago: University of Chicago Press, 1957), pp. 84-96; and, Henry S. Maas, "Social Casework," in *Concepts and Methods of Social Work* (Englewood Cliffs, N. J.: Prentice-Hall, Inc., 1958), pp. 18-23.

III. SOCIAL DIAGNOSIS AND THERAPY

Mary Richmond and the early practitioners of social casework required a thorough investigation of the facts and data of the life of the individual who was in need of help. Through social diagnosis, they attempted to analyze these findings and to determine the underlying causes for social and personal difficulties of the client. After this critical examination, followed the interpretation of the specific conditions for the behavior and the reactions of the client, based upon his individual personality. The therapy was planned upon the preceding investigation and the social diagnosis; it was frequently directed toward external improvements in the environment, living conditions, and type and location of work, which were considered of primary importance in the initial period of casework practice.

Methods and practice of social casework were also deeply influenced by the recognition of the scientific development of psychology and psychiatry in this country. There were important contributions from the social sciences, such as the studies of child growth by G. Stanley Hall, the investigations of sex problems by Havelock Ellis, and the invention of intelligence tests by Binet and Simon in France and their introduction in the United States by H. H. Goddard. Another decisive influence was the foundation of the mental hygiene movement by Clifford Beers after the publication of his experiences as a mental patient in his book, *A Mind that Found Itself,* in 1908. These ideas shifted the fundamental interest of social work from economic and sociological emphasis toward psychological and emotional problems of the client. Important factors in this development were the discoveries of Sigmund Freud, psychoanalysis and dynamic psychology, and the work of Freud's followers, Otto Rank, C. G. Jung, Alfred Adler, and others who founded their own schools.

Before this period, only a few social workers had been employed in mental hospitals, especially in children's wards; they helped the psychiatrists in securing information about the case history and the family conditions of the patient, and took care of the patient after his discharge. Some general hospitals felt the need to employ social caseworkers to assist the physician in his diagnosis and treatment by collecting the data on the patient's earlier illnesses and reporting on his social and economic conditions. These social workers were aware of the necessity to make use of the resources of the patient's family as well as of the facilities of the community, of social agencies, employers, and friends in order to preserve and strengthen the results of medical treatment.

During World War I, the interest of social workers took a further turn from environmental factors to the psychological aspects of human behavior for which psychiatry, psychology, and biology had laid the groundwork. The immediate reason for this intensified psychological concern of social workers was the establishment of "home service divisions" through the American Red Cross where social workers assisted families whose husbands were serving with the armed forces. These families were different from former clients of the Charity Organization Societies and of the poor relief agencies; most of them had never before been in contact with social agencies. These families, whose husbands served overseas, were typical American people, a cross section of the entire country. Because the Red Cross is maintained by voluntary contributions of the population, its job was to be of service to these families, and the old "lady bountiful" attitude was out of place for servicemen's families.[6] The same was true for Red Cross workers serving in hospitals and field stations with the fighting armies in Europe. The large number of neuropsychiatric patients suffering from "shell-shock" created a heavy demand for psychiatric social workers who were trained, for the first time, at Smith College in 1918. Because of the war shortage of psychiatrists, psychiatric social workers were given for the first time substantial responsibility in the treatment of psychoneurotic patients and worked in close contact with the psychiatrists in the armed forces. In this work, emphasis was placed on the fact that human behavior is not arbitrarily chosen or accidental, but is the result of a lifelong development as well as of family and surroundings upon the organism and the emotions of the individual.

In our society, some people have serious difficulties to decide in the conflicts between their own desires and the demands of society. Frequently, the patient is not conscious of the motivations for his

---

6 Virginia Robinson, *A Changing Psychology in Social Work* (Chapel Hill: University of North Carolina Press, 1930), p. 53.

behavior and attempts to conceal by apparent rationalizations the true motives for his actions. The findings of Sigmund Freud about "the unconscious" have shown that emotions govern our behavior more than reason. Freud emphasized that the experiences in early childhood frequently determine the personality development of the adult. This gave new insights to social workers who tried to incorporate psychiatric theories into their concepts.

The first implication of psychiatric theories for casework was the demand that the caseworker had to secure more detailed facts in order to understand the personality, the motivations, and the emotional needs of the client. This task, however, required more knowledge and skill than the caseworker mastered and also more time for the work on each individual case. For this reason, after World War I, family and children's agencies began to employ trained psychiatric social workers to help clients with difficult emotional maladjustments. Under these circumstances, caseworkers had to sacrifice the concept of working with the entire family as a unit, because the problems of the family group were not identical with the specific emotional and personality problems of the individual client, whether child or adult.

With a better psychological understanding of human behavior and a more realistic evaluation of economic problems, social casework changed its approach to the client. The full respect of the caseworker for the personal dignity and worth of the client as a human being represents the process of "democratization" of casework. The caseworker accepts the client as he is; he does not attempt to mold him as he would like him to be. The change in approach led, in the beginning, from an active influence of the caseworker upon the client to an attitude of pronounced "passivity." For some time, caseworkers barely spoke to the client, merely listened to his explanations and tried to accept his statements as well as the motivations which he revealed. The silence of the caseworker forced the client to speak but often did not give him sufficient help in making his own decisions. Progress in casework technique was made when the caseworker began to see that effective help for the client was achieved only by the full understanding of his ideas and feelings, making this the core of diagnosis and therapy. This enabled the client to work out his emotional problems in a way he chose himself. He has the "right of self-determination" in how much he likes to accept the advice of the caseworker and to use the aid of the social agency or of other community resources.[7]

Since the late 1930's, casework has attempted to avoid the extremes of domination or of passivity in relation to the client, and to achieve an equilibrium between these opposite approaches. Caseworkers have learned that social, economic, psychological, and cultural factors influence each individual, and that the concern of casework is not only the client as an individual, but in his relation to his family and community. As the capacity for self-help varies among human beings, the caseworker has to assume the responsibility for helping the client to find satisfactory solutions for his individual problems. The caseworker refrains from moral judgments of the client's behavior, but this does not imply that he approves of attitudes which are harmful to the client himself or to others and which lead to asocial or criminal action. Certain limitations are set by social and cultural standards, sometimes unwritten laws, which may not be violated in our society. The reactions of the community toward ethnic and religious minority groups, toward Negroes, Mexicans, Orientals, Indians, or toward recent immigrants require understanding and special consideration by the caseworker.

There are individuals and families who are not willing to come to a social agency to ask for help on their own initiative. Such "resistive families" are found particularly in cases of family discord, child neglect, in cases of criminal and asocial behavior, and juvenile delinquency. They deny their need for guidance, assistance, and treatment. Here, the social worker or probation officer has to take the initiative, has to call in the home of the family, and has to try to understand psychologically the reactions of the clients in order to modify patiently their hostile, defiant attitude. In dealing with a delinquent juvenile gang, a "street corner worker" first may have to join them in order to be accepted and to gain their confidence before he is able to influence their behavior. We call this approach

---

[7] Bertha C. Reynolds, "Between Client and Community," *Smith College Studies in Social Work,* Vol. V (1934), pp. 98-99; Grace Marcus, *Some Aspects of Relief in Family Case Work* (New York: Columbia University Press, 1947), p. 70; H. Witmer, *op. cit.,* pp. 170-179; and, Anita J. Faatz, *The Nature of Choice in Casework Process* (Chapel Hill: University of North Carolina Press, 1953).

"supportive" or "aggressive casework," or "out-reaching" social work.[8]

IV. INFLUENCE OF PSYCHOLOGICAL THEORIES

In social casework we deal with human feelings and human behavior. For this reason, professional training of social workers includes the study of motivations, the dynamics of human behavior, and the application of psychology in working with people. There are two basic orientations in social casework today which use such a dynamic psychological approach: the "diagnostic" or "dynamic school" and the "functional school." Both schools apply psychological knowledge in order to understand the client, relate their work to the individual needs of the client, and use the dynamics of relationship in order to help the client in his development. They differ from each other fundamentally, however, in the psychological scheme which they use. In the following paragraphs the psychological scheme of each is sketched briefly. The student who wishes to understand more fully and more clearly the differences between them should consult the references in the footnote.[9]

The *diagnostic casework theory* derives its philosophy and methods from the theory of personality which was created by Sigmund Freud and his followers and applies the principles of "dynamic psychiatry" in the social casework approach. Diagnostic casework accepts personality organization as a composite of differentiated and interacting elements which react on each other but which also are

---

[8] Sylvan S. Furman (editor), *Reaching the Unreached* (New York: New York City Youth Board, 1952); New York City Youth Board, *How They Were Reached* (New York, Monograph No. 2, 1954); Fritz Redl, *Controls from Within* (Glencoe, Ill.: The Free Press, 1952); Kermit T. Wiltse, "The 'Hopeless' Family," *Social Welfare Forum* (1958), pp. 135-153; and, Sidney Love and Herta Mayer, "Going Along with Defenses in Resistive Families," *Social Casework,* Vol. 40, No. 2 (February 1959), pp. 69-74.

[9] Cora Kasius (editor), *A Comparison of Diagnostic and Functional Casework Concepts* (New York: Family Service Association of America, 1950), pp. 7-13; G. Hamilton, *op. cit.,* pp. 258-262; Grace Marcus, "Family Casework in 1948," *Journal of Social Casework* (now called *Social Casework*) Vol. 29, No. 7 (July 1948), pp. 261-270; and, Isabel L. Stamm, "Ego Psychology in the Emerging Theoretical Base of Casework," in Alfred J. Kahn (editor), *Issues in American Social Work* (New York: Columbia University Press, 1959), pp. 80-109.

influenced by the people in one's environment and by the social and economic conditions in which one lives. Conscious as well as unconscious influences are regarded as determining our human values, behavior, and self-control. Social workers need to comprehend the effects of emotional experiences on human behavior, especially the emotions in early childhood, the feelings of anxiety, frustration, guilt, and tensions caused by the conflict between the "id" (the primitive drives for gratification of all needs) and the "ego" (the socialized force of the individual that becomes aware of its part in human society and of the values of religion, ethics, and civilization).

The relationship to parents, siblings, and persons in the environment play an important role in the life experiences of the individual. In Freudian psychology the ego holds the key position in the psychic structure. It performs the most important functions of maintaining a balance between the inner drives and the superego. The superego is the ideal that a person forms of a human being that is usually absorbed from childhood experience with parents, particularly the father. It consists of a synthesis of the rules of desirable conduct, of prohibitions and inhibitions impressed upon the child by his parents and his environment. The development of the superego creates the human conscience. The ego reconciles the psychic, emotional needs of the individual with the demands of reality and society. The ego is influenced by inner emotions and external factors, and it functions in self-preservation, perception, reality testing, organization, planning, and judgment. An understanding of the human personality structure, of intrapsychic conflicts and their influence upon behavior, is required in order to achieve change and improvement in attitude. Deviations from normal psychic functions may be recognized, classified, and changed by therapy. The type and intensity of therapeutic action necessary depends upon the nature and the extent of the psychosocial disturbance of the individual client. Therapy attempts to remove the disturbance between the individual's emotional needs and the facts of his physical and social environment, and helps the client to change and to increase his ego capacity. Diagnostic casework encourages the client to discuss his difficulties and develops a planned treatment directed to the goal of helping the client to resolve his inner conflicts, to mobilize his ego strength, and to lessen environmental pressures by social planning. The diagnostic caseworker assumes the responsibility for evaluating the client's problems and for establishing supportive measures which help him to adjust according to his individual needs.

Functional casework is taught primarily at the School of Social Work of the University of Pennsylvania and is based upon the theory of "will therapy," developed by Otto Rank. This theory centers around the assumption of an organizing force, the "will," in the human personality. It concludes that the interaction of inner instinctual drives of the individual and environmental influences is directed by the individual's autonomous yearning for his "self." This self is the result of transcendental forces composed of inner and environmental experiences by means of the will. Personality growth is achieved by relationships with others, primarily between mother and child, through "projection" of one's needs upon the other person. Because such projection cannot lead to complete union in reality, limitations are either accepted or frustration results because of refusal to recognize reality. The client is encouraged to overcome his disturbances and anxieties by his will to solve his psychic problem. The functional caseworker attempts to help the client to release his innate capacity. Because psychic disturbances are caused by a destructive use of the relationships of the client, functional casework seeks to replace it by new relationships conducive to constructive use of his "self" and those of other people. In this process, the client directs himself toward his change of attitude, whereas, the functional caseworker helps him to release his energies toward self-responsibility and self-acceptance. Functional casework calls its function the "helping process" and does not use the diagnostic term "treatment." It is convinced that the client's use of his "self" toward his own goals, and with his free choice, are his right, but also his own responsibility. The functional approach does not refer to general norms as does the diagnostic school. The "helping process," according to the functional approach, is limited by the agency setting. The needs of the client can be met only within the framework of agency function, which is considered the keynote. The "client must find his own satisfying solution and ultimate adjustment" among the services which the social agency offers.

Diagnostic casework attempts to help the client adjust to normal behavior. It measures success in terms of how far the client approaches normal behavior. This approach aims at more effective treatment through the use of increasing scientific knowledge of the forces affecting human behavior and social adjustment; it seeks objective criteria for measuring and predicting casework results.

The functional theory operates on the assumption that the client himself must determine his goals and choices within the framework of agency services. Its measure of progress is how far the client achieves this self-direction.

The two schools of social casework are different in their theoretical philosophy, but, representatives of both schools accept their mutual differences in philosophy and their implications in practice. It is recognized that each school is contributing to the body of knowledge and skill of social casework.

Social workers have been concerned about whether or not social casework might use Carl R. Rogers' *client-centered therapy* as the psychological basis for a particular functional approach. Professor Rogers characterizes his method as "self-directed therapy," which permits the client to gain full confidence in the therapist or counselor and complete awareness of his own personality, so that the client himself can overcome his anxieties and feel able to cope with his problems.[10]

In fact, some social workers use an "eclectic theory" in applying elements of various schools of psychology as the basis of their approach to the client. The discussion about the specific values of the various schools of psychology in their application for social work has not been closed. An analysis of their essential elements for the practice of social work permits hope that in the future some synthesis between the two psychological methods may be worked out. Such a synthesis might develop new effective skills of social work in helping the client.

V. CASEWORK PROCEDURE

The modern casework agency offers well-defined services to the client. The caseworker explains these services clearly and discusses

---

[10] The reader may find more information on this specific type of psychotherapy in Carl R. Rogers, *Counseling and Psychotherapy, Newer Concepts in Practice* (1942), and *Client-Centered Therapy, Its Current Practice, Implications, and Theory* (Boston: Houghton, 1951); and on psychological theories in Ruth L. Monroe, *Schools of Psychoanalytic Thought* (New York: Dryden Press, 1955); Gerald S. Blum, *Psychoanalytic Theories of Personality* (New York: McGraw, 1953); and, Herbert H. Aptekar, *The Dynamics of Casework and Counseling* (Boston: Houghton, 1955).

with the client in what way he wants to use the agency's facilities and how they may help him in a solution of his problems. No aid is imposed upon the client. He has to decide whether or not he wants to accept the agency's help. The caseworker explains to the client what his own abilities of solving his problems are, and what the agency may contribute. Thus, the client gains an understanding of the economic and emotional elements which cause his problems. Casework attempts to awaken the strength for self-help in the client and to restore his ability for self-support, thereby maintaining his self-respect and human dignity.

Present-day social casework is facing a number of serious problems. Casework skills are required in all social agencies which work with families and children, with delinquents and adult offenders, and with aged persons. However, many workers, particularly in public welfare agencies and probation and parole services, have no adequate professional training or competence for it. Some social agencies that want to employ caseworkers with full graduate training and supervised field work experience find it difficult to hire them, because working conditions, salaries, supervision, or the local situation are not desirable. The education of sufficient graduate social work students is impeded by the lack of good field work agencies with qualified supervisors and technical facilities.[11]

Another problem confronting social casework is the lack of highly skilled and experienced caseworkers in some social agencies. In these agencies, there is a heavy turnover and loss of trained workers who wish to take up family life, or who transfer to agencies which are more attractive. There is, furthermore, need for research studies which attempt to evaluate the successes and failures of casework, to determine the situations in which casework is helpful, and where it does not operate with effect. Many caseworkers are inclined to look at each client as a new, unique phenomenon, but fail to recognize the types of human needs and reactions from which a general professional experience can be drawn. Examples of research studies in evaluation of casework efficiency are presented in J. McV. Hunt, *et al., Testing Results in Social Casework; A Field-Test of the Movement Scale* (New York: Family Service Association of America, 1950), and,

---

[11] Helen Harris Perlman, "Social Casework," *Social Work Year Book* (1960), pp. 535-540; and, Florence Hollis, "Social Casework," *Social Work Year Book* (1957), pp. 525-531.

Lilian Ripple, "Factors Associated with Continuance in Casework Service," *Social Work,* Vol. 3, No. 1 (January 1957).[12]

Technical methods of recording casework need simplification, clerical operations need streamlining, and the procedure of conferences and consultations needs concentration and more concise action.

Casework services still need to be interpreted to the public, in fact more than health or recreation services, in order to gain in the community fuller understanding of their value and increased moral and material support.

The following are trends in present casework practice: (1) caseworkers gain a sharpened concept of the function of social diagnosis and treatment in relation to the facilities of the social agency; (2) caseworkers develop increasing skill in relating their understanding of the client's tensions, fears, and frustration to his social environment and economic conditions; (3) the caseworker, it is recognized, should take the initiative in "supportive," "out-reaching," or "aggressive" casework which is necessary with certain types of clients; (4) social agencies, both private and public, are showing a growing awareness of the need for trained, skilled caseworkers in an adequate proportion to the number of clients who need their services, and demonstrating an understanding for the importance of giving early individual and family counseling concerning problems of adjustment; (5) in this period of many social changes, casework is willing to apply its skills to new problems and to work in a team relationship with other professional groups whenever this is essential to help the clients.

Selected Bibliography

Aptekar, Herbert, *Basic Concepts in Social Casework*. Chapel Hill: University of North Carolina Press, 1941.

———, *The Dynamics of Casework and Counseling*. Boston: Houghton, 1955.

Benedek, Therese, *Insight and Personality Adjustment*. New York: Ronald, 1946.

*Garret, Annette, *Interviewing: Its Principles and Methods*. New York: Family Welfare Association of America, 1942.

---

12 Jane Hanford, "Maximum Use of Casework Service," *Selected Papers in Casework* (1951), pp. 8-10. Case illustrations of social casework practice are discussed in Henry S. Maas, "Social Casework," *op. cit.,* pp. 16-115.

*Gordon, Henrietta, *Casework Services for Children: Principles and Practice*. Boston: Houghton, 1956.

*Hamilton, Gordon, *Theory and Practice of Social Casework,* 2nd ed. New York: Columbia University Press, 1951.

*Hollis, Florence, *Social Casework in Practice: Six Case Studies*. New York: Family Welfare Association of America, 1939.

Kardiner, Abraham, *The Individual and His Society*. New York: Columbia University Press, 1939.

*Kasius, Cora, *Principles and Techniques in Social Casework*. New York: Family Service Association of America, 1950.

*Lowry, Fern, *Readings in Social Casework*. New York: Columbia University Press, 1939.

*Maas, Henry S., "Social Casework," in Walter A. Friedlander (editor), *Concepts and Methods of Social Work*. Englewood Cliffs, N.J.: Prentice-Hall, Inc., 1958, pp. 15-115.

Paradise, Viola, *Toward Public Understanding of Casework: A Study of Casework Interpretation in Cleveland*. New York: Russell Sage Foundation, 1948.

Perlman, Helen H., "The Basic Structure of the Casework Process," *Social Service Review,* Vol. 34, No. 3 (September 1953), pp. 308-315.

————, "Freud's Contribution to Social Welfare," *Social Service Review,* Vol. 31, No. 2 (June 1957), pp. 192-202.

————, *Social Casework, A Problem-solving Process*. Chicago: University of Chicago Press, 1957.

Regensburg, Jeanette and Selma Fraiberg, *Direct Casework with Children*. New York: Family Service Association of America, 1957.

Reynolds, Bertha Capen, *Learning and Teaching in the Practice of Social Work*. New York: Farrar & Rinehart, 1942.

*Richmond, Mary E., *Social Diagnosis*. New York: Russell Sage Foundation, 1917.

————, *What Is Social Casework? An Introductory Description*. New York: Russell Sage Foundation, 1922.

*Robinson, Virginia, *A Changing Psychology in Social Work*. Chapel Hill: University of North Carolina Press, 1930.

Rogers, Carl R., *Counseling and Psychotherapy*. Boston: Houghton, 1942.

Taft, Julia, *Counseling and Protective Service as Family Casework: Functional Approach*. Philadelphia: University of Pennsylvania Press, 1946.

Taylor, Robert K., "Identification and Ego-directed Casework," *Social Work,* Vol. 5, No. 1 (January 1960).

*Witmer, Helen Leland, *Social Work: An Analysis of a Social Institution*. New York: Farrar & Rinehart, 1942.

5.

Social Group Work

SOCIAL GROUP WORK is centered around a "group." It does not concentrate on the individual alone. It emphasizes the education, development, and cultural growth of the members of the group. It is frequently carried on in voluntary activities during leisure time, under the guidance of a group worker. Although work with groups has concerned agencies identified with the social welfare movement for many years, the first recognition of such work as a social work process occurred in the second decade of this century.[1] The social group work process emphasizes the possibilities for the development and social adjustment of the individual through voluntary group action and the use of an association with others in a group as a means of furthering socially desirable objectives. This process is determined by the objectives of the agency, the dynamic forces and adjustive efforts within the group itself, the group worker's skill of observation and interpretation of adjustive and formative efforts within the group, and in the selection and application of an effective group work technique toward constructive results.[2]

---

[1] See Gertrude Wilson and Gladys Ryland, *Social Group Work Practice. The Creative Use of the Social Process* (Boston: Houghton, 1949), pp. 7-16.

[2] William I. Newstetter, "What Is Social Group Work?" *National Conference of Social Work, 1935,* pp. 291-300; Juanita Luck Cogan, "Social Group Work," *Social Work Year Book* (1960), pp. 540-549; and, Gisela Konopka, *Group Work in the Institution* (New York: Whiteside, 1954).

I. BASIC CONCEPTS OF SOCIAL GROUP WORK

Social casework is a helping relationship between an individual (the caseworker) with another individual (the client). Social group work, however, is characterized by the fact that it is carried out in a group setting, and the helping process deals with individuals in their relationship as members of a group.

Gisela Konopka defines the activities of the social group worker as follows: "The group worker enables various types of groups to function in such a way that both group interaction and program activity contribute to the growth of the individual and the achievement of desirable social goals." [3]

We are aware that human beings do not grow up isolated from others. Children are born into a family; later they join with other children in informal groups. Adolescents and adults usually join a church, lodge, or other social group, following the natural desire for companionship, belonging, and recognition. In most instances, social casework also is concerned not exclusively with the individual client, but with his family and environment because they play an important role in causing or alleviating personal problems of the individual. The caseworker functions as a member of a group, just as everyone else in our society.

The social group worker, however, is primarily concerned with the relationship among the members of the group and between the members and himself. The group worker functions mainly through his participation in the interaction between the individuals in the group, but he is not a regular member, identifying himself with the others, absorbed by the activities of the group as such. The worker's functions are guided by his professional understanding of group life and by the individual member's need for his help or for withholding his assistance. This knowledge permits the group worker to give professional service to the group as a whole and to each individual member of the group. In order to be able to assume this responsibility, the group worker needs to be aware of his professional self. He has to control his personal impulses, values, and preferences,

---

[3] The ideas and functions of group work are described in more detail in Gisela Konopka, "The Method of Social Group Work," in Walter A. Friedlander (editor), *Concepts and Methods of Social Work* (Englewood Cliffs, N. J.: Prentice-Hall, Inc., 1958), p. 118 (definition), and pp. 116-200.

and to concentrate upon making it possible for the members of the group to obtain the achievements and personal as well as cultural satisfactions which the group and its activities offer.

Methods of working with groups may be classified into five categories:

(1) The *dictatorial or authoritarian method:* The leader orders, the members obey.

(2) The *personification method:* The members imitate the group worker and attempt to be like him, but they do not explore and find their own abilities.

(3) *The preceptive method:* The worker gives instructions, the group members carry them out, learn skills; but they are not detecting their own resources and capacities.

(4) The *manipulative method:* The group worker goes with the group through a phase of planning and decision-making. In fact, the group is only accepting a prearranged program of the leader, and is deceived into believing that the group itself came to the decision.

(5) The *enabling method:* The group worker helps the members to participate with full responsibility in the life of the group, in its planning and program, in developing their own ideas, skills, and personal attitudes, and to make their own decisions regarding the purposes and actions of the group.[4]

In a democratic society, only the last of these methods is considered as the desirable way of achieving the aims of positive, constructive group life. It helps the individual members enjoy the satisfaction derived from being accepted as a part of the whole, to express themselves, and to participate in the collective action of the group.[5]

II. DEVELOPMENT AND CHARACTERISTICS OF SOCIAL GROUP WORK

The orientation in the early settlement houses and in other group work agencies was first of a religious and missionary nature, with the

---

[4] G. Wilson and G. Ryland, *op. cit.,* pp. 60-61; and, Harleigh Trecker, *Group Work Foundations and Frontiers* (New York: Association Press, 1955).

[5] Alan F. Klein, *Society—Democracy—and the Group* (New York: Womans Press, 1953); and, Helen U. Phillips, *Essentials of Group Work Skill* (New York: Association Press, 1957).

purpose of encouraging church participation and Sunday schools, and of protecting their members from the moral dangers of city life. But the young people who joined the groups were often more attracted by activities from which they hoped to gain material advantage, education, or pleasure. Similar motives frequently induced children and adolescents in poor quarters to join group work agencies. When, in the beginning of the twentieth century, Boy Scouts and other groups for boys and girls were founded, which no longer centered in under-privileged neighborhoods but appealed to middle- and upper-class children as well, the nature of group work organizations and their methods changed. A different use of the group work process was made when mental hospitals and child guidance clinics began to introduce recreational programs as a method of therapy for mentally ill, mentally defective, and nervous patients. In other group activities, the emphasis changed from the mere participation in physical education, sports, crafts, and discussions—to the effect the group activities had on the individual member's personal growth and in the collective life of the group. To learn to share experiences with others, to give and take, to clarify differences of opinion and judgment without hostility and frustration, to yield in good spirit to decisions of the majority is even more important for the development of personality than the learning of special skills. The process changed from routine direction of activities to conscientious consideration of the desires and needs of the individuals in the group and of those factors which would make the group as a whole the educational and cultural experience the members hoped for, from which they could gain a feeling of belonging together and of mutual solidarity.

The group work process relies upon scientific, critical elements to measure the interaction among group members, the results of guidance and mutual stimulation from within the group, and the forces which determine the action of gangs and related groups which oppose direction toward socially accepted goals and outside leadership.

The group work process attempts to achieve the following objectives: to provide experiences which integrate the essential needs of the individuals who form the group; to encourage wholesome mental and social attitudes on the part of each participant toward his place in the group and in society; to achieve skill in some leisure-time pursuit; and to provide experience in acceptable social behavior, and in collective, positive activities rather than useless or destructive ones.

III. PRACTICE OF SOCIAL GROUP WORK

The practice of social group work is determined by the nature and the objectives of the social agency which provides the service, and by the needs which the group and its individual members want to satisfy in their group experience. There are four different levels of activities in which the group worker is engaged:

(1) "Basic" social group work, the practice with "primary groups," such as children, adolescents' and adults' clubs, sport and recreation groups, and study and discussion societies.

(2) Supervision of other group workers, professionals and volunteers.

(3) Administration of social group work agencies or other organizations through which group work is offered.

(4) Community organization, planning, and coordination of group work activities.[6]

We shall discuss, in this chapter, mainly the first type of group work, with primary social groups. Group workers most commonly work with this group, whereas supervision, administration, and community organization in the realm of group work are assigned to a smaller number of experienced and professionally trained people.[7]

Group work organizations in the field of recreation may be classified into four categories according to their activities:

(1) Agencies with programs primarily providing recreation and informal education, such as public recreation and adult education in schools, extension divisions of colleges and universities, YWCA, YMCA, boys' and girls' clubs, senior citizens' clubs, and similar private organizations.

(2) Agencies conducting recreational and educational programs

---

[6] G. Wilson and G. Ryland, *op. cit.,* pp. 27, 69-78; and, Nathan E. Cohen, "Implications of the Present Scene for Social Group Work Practice," *Social Welfare Forum* (1955), pp. 48-60.

[7] Harleigh B. Trecker, "Community Planning for Group Work," in Charles Hendry (editor), *A Decade of Group Work* (New York: Association Press, 1948), pp. 124-132.

combined with religious, ideological, and social purposes, such as churches, young people's and women's groups, clubs interested in civic information, adult and workers' education societies.

(3) Agencies primarily concerned with other objectives which conduct recreational and educational programs as a support of their main functions, such as settlement houses and community centers (whose main purpose is the establishment of constructive, cooperative neighborhood relations, and the improvement of living and health standards), public housing projects, clubs of labor unions, of factories, and of such youth groups, as the 4-H Clubs, which fundamentally want to function as "character-building," vocational, or occupational organizations.

(4) Agencies which provide therapy to patients in need of physical, mental, and emotional adjustment (hospitals, rehabilitation centers, mental and child guidance clinics); they use group work as one of the means for achieving their therapeutic objective.[8]

Social group work usually is thought of in connection with leisure time and recreational activities. It is of particular importance, however, in the setting of an institution, such as a children's home, an orphanage, an industrial school, or an old-age home. In institutions the daily life requires an understanding of human behavior, and the capacity to establish personal ties with members of "living groups" as well as of "interest groups" or clubs which may form themselves in the institution.[9] Houseparents, teachers, instructors, and administrators assist children or adults to adjust to the demands of group living, and at the same time to develop or to preserve their own personality and cultural satisfaction. The trained social group worker is able to assist, in an institutional setting, in developing the constructive aspects of group living, and encouraging the group members to present their ideas, ingenuity, skills, and abilities. He is aware of the dangers of "boss-rule," or dictatorship, and of uncooperative leaders, who subdue other members and make them

---

[8] Grace L. Coyle, *Group Work with American Youth* (New York: Harper, 1948), pp. 6-18; and, Gisela Konopka, "Group Work and Therapy," in Charles Hendry (editor), *op. cit.,* p. 41.

[9] A stimulating discussion of such functions in children's homes is to be found in the chapter by Netta Berman, "The Group Worker in a Children's Institution," in Susanne Schulze (editor), *Creative Group Living in a Children's Institution* (New York: Association Press, 1951), pp. 117-125.

lose their individuality or exclude those whom they do not like. Disturbed and overaggressive members of an institution, frequently found in correctional settings, have special problems of their own. These are complicated by the fact that in the institutional setting there are increased difficulties in planning and carrying out of leisure-time activities, recreational and educational programs, and of bringing to the staff an understanding of group dynamics and group therapy. The group worker takes the initiative in developing recreation for patients and for the staff whenever the institution is not close enough to other sources for providing for leisure time and cultural activities.

The main objective in the social group work process is to stimulate the initiative, the group consciousness, and self-direction in the group. The group worker does not assume the initiative himself, but makes the group members the active, creative forces. The group's program is the framework within which the group experience occurs. The interaction between the group members, learning to be a member of a society, understanding of different opinions and values, accepting majority decisions as a good sport, are important factors with creative values for personality growth, especially in the development of young persons. The social group worker needs a knowledge of individual and group behavior and of social conditions as well as the ability to work efficiently with groups of people. His leadership requires skill to awake in the members of the group their creative abilities and to develop constructive, socially acceptable activities. His function is to help each individual in the group gain satisfaction and enjoyment through the group relations and activities, and to assist the group as a social unit to find its own objective.[10] The group members have the satisfaction of being with others of their own age, of developing social attitudes and skills, of finding creative outlets for their cultural, artistic, or social abilities, which might never have been discovered without such group stimulation.

The following sample of group work in practice illustrates this social work process.

---

[10] Grace L. Coyle, "Social Group Work," *Social Work Year Book* (1954), pp. 480-486; Audrey Trecker and Harleigh B. Trecker, *How to Work With Groups* (New York: Womans Press, 1952); and, Clara Kaiser, "The Advance of Social Group Work," *Social Welfare Forum* (1955), pp. 35-47.

Kids in trouble [11]

Roberto

Roberto, a boy of slight build and dark complexion, looks older than his 15 years. He has gone in gangs with older boys for several years, and consequently, when he was 12, he appeared before the Juvenile Court, charged with stealing. Since, he has had a probation officer and has been taken in by the police twice, but not on charges serious enough to bring him before the court again. The probation officer reports that Roberto's home is small and physically inadequate, but that the family relations are pleasant enough.

When Roberto was in the seventh grade, his gang started going to a community center in the neighborhood. They had a weekly recreation program of sports, swimming, and dancing, but even here most of the boys were older than Roberto. Much destruction of the building took place, and the solution for the Center, a year later, was to divide the group and form a smaller club for boys and girls who were Roberto's age, many of whom also had juvenile court records.

From the beginning, Roberto was loyal in attendance, but very moody, showing enormous distrust of the club leader, who was a woman. For several months he would not talk with the leader, but took great delight in mocking the way she spoke. He seemed to hope that she would be angry about this, but when she only laughed with him, he dropped this mockery. During this sullen, quiet period with Roberto, the leader always invited him to join in activities, but never insisted that he do so.

His favorite activity was to listen to bop records, and occasionally he danced, usually alone. While the other club members planned parties, played ping-pong and basketball, had crafts and dramatic groups, he sat, saying nothing, by the record player. Only once, however, did he outwardly cause trouble, this being on a day when his phonograph records were not available. He got a gang of boys together and they wandered around restlessly, eventually throwing a table down the stairs. When the club leader pointed out that club

---

[11] The author is indebted to Miss Gertrude Wilson, Professor of Social Welfare, University of California, Berkeley, for this case illustration.

groups must pay for damage to the building, Roberto admitted that he was responsible and would pay himself, rather than have the whole group pay.

In planning their club program, the group asked to have dancing lessons. With this activity, the club leader saw a change in Roberto's attitude. He received a great deal of recognition from the club leader, the members, and the dancing teacher, because he was the best dancer and learned new steps very quickly. When complimented about this, he dropped his tough outward appearance and was more like a shy, modest kid.

Recently, Roberto was elected an officer of the club, and he took his responsibility very seriously. He personally tried to see that all the members' behavior was good at the last dance, and everyone reported that it was the best party the club had had.

IV. GROUP WORK IN OTHER SETTINGS

A. Cooperation Between Casework and Group Work Agencies

It is an accepted idea by now that a close cooperation between caseworkers and group workers helps the people whom social work serves. But it took a long time until this concept took hold among social workers. Caseworkers often turn to group work agencies, such as the "Y's," girls' or boys' clubs, and the 4-H Clubs, for help in behalf of individual children in need of recreation, of companionship, or of developing art and music skills. Experience in group living assists the child or youngster who has difficulties in his family or school, who is lonely or frustrated, or who suffers from excessive sibling rivalry to find new friends, to feel accepted, to develop his ability to get along with others, and to gain initiative and self-reliance.[12]

The caseworker who must refer a child or adolescent to a group

---

[12] Gertrude Wilson, *Group Work and Case Work—Their Relationship and Practice* (New York: Family Welfare Association of America, 1941); Gordon Hamilton, *Theory and Practice of Social Case Work* (New York: Columbia University Press, 1951), pp. 235-236, 242-244; and, Harleigh B. Trecker, *Group Work—Principles and Practice* (New York: Womans Press, 1948), pp. 101-102.

work agency considers the child's personality, environment, and age in deciding which type of group will be most helpful for him. In an "interest group" the child is attracted by the specific activities carried out in the group. In the "club group" the referred child may find other children of his age who, with the help of the worker, are willing to accept him into their society. A successful referral requires that the group worker has a keen understanding of the personality and emotional needs of the child, knowledge of symptomatic behavior, the skill to deal sympathetically with the individual child as well as with the group as a whole. Such referrals are made by children's and family welfare agencies, public welfare departments, hospitals, child guidance clinics, and churches. In making a referral, the caseworker finds out which available group, in its composition and leadership, will best serve the needs of the child, and where he promises to be an asset to the other members. Under such circumstances, group experience may help the child make a successful adjustment.

However, the group worker might find a member of the group who needs a personal, intensified relationship and individual assistance which the group worker cannot give, perhaps because there is not enough time to devote to him without neglecting the rest of the group. In such instances, the group worker will, with the consent of the child or adolescent, and of the parents, refer him to a casework agency for individual treatment. The child remains in the group as long as he is able to enjoy his participation. A cooperative relationship between the group worker and the caseworker may be of help to the child who desires help from both workers and proves capable of using it.

In other cases of referral, the social worker of the agency to which the child is referred assumes the immediate relationship with the child in such a way that the child can attach himself fully to the new worker without conflict from the referral worker. The referral worker, in these cases, restricts himself to following the development of the child through occasional conferences with the new worker.

B. Group Work With Adults and With Aged Persons

Work with groups of young adults, middle-aged and elderly persons has gained importance. There is increasing recognition that skilled group work process would make this work more valuable and effective for the members of the groups.[13]

During recent decades, the proportion of the older generation, over sixty-five years of age, to the total population has steadily increased due to the progress in medical science, geriatrics, and improved living standards. Our country has developed its cultural and recreational institutions with strong emphasis on the needs and habits of children and youth and, until recently, has given little attention to the leisure-time needs of older persons. The growing importance of the older citizen's group requires more consideration, not only in measures of social and economic security, but also in cultural activities and recreation.

With the introduction of old-age insurance and of old-age retirement provisons in civil service and in industrial health and welfare plans, an increasing number of the over 15,000,000 persons aged sixty-five years and older will be unable to obtain jobs in industry. Their life threatens to become dull and lonely without work so that satisfactory recreational facilities become more and more important for them. The first awareness of this change of emphasis was shown, when the William Hodson Center in New York City and settlements in Chicago, primarily the Olivet Institute, in 1940, organized the first "Golden Age Clubs" for elderly people. Other cities, Cleveland, Cincinnati, Philadelphia, followed, and at present recreational facilities for older citizens are offered in many cities.

The organization of leisure time for the aged may be planned by a group of citizens in cooperation with a settlement house, a family welfare agency, a church, or a community center which is ready to provide the meeting place and the facilities for group activities.

Lists of the names of older people living in the selected neighborhood are collected. Visits to the aged, a personal letter of invitation, or announcements in the local press might start the work. As in other recreational activities, programs would be arranged according to the interests and preference of the members of the group after it

---

13 Leland P. Bradford, "Adult Education as Group Work," L. K. Hall, "Group Work in Religious Education," Eleanor G. Coit and Orlie Pell, "Group Work in the Workers' Education Setting," in Charles Hendry (editor), *op. cit.,* pp. 52-76; Ira De Reid, *et al., Minority Groups: Segregation and Integration* (New York: Columbia University Press, 1955); and, Malcolm S. Knowles (editor), *Handbook of Adult Education in the U.S.* (Chicago: Adult Education Association, 1960).

was organized. They could include games, arts and crafts; music, movies, or television; a discussion of topics of actual cultural or political importance; or just an opportunity of getting together socially and talking with people of like situation. Simple refreshments are important because some old folks rarely have an opportunity of enjoying meals in the company of others. Members of the clubs are limited to those sixty years of age or older, many of them widows or widowers, or couples without children or relatives in the community. There should be no discrimination according to sex, faith, or race, nor as to financial status.

Group activities in homes for the aged have also become an important factor in modern institutional care. They are necessary for the well-being of older people. Their own active participation in the program is essential. But, in a home for the aged, the question of health sets limitations to recreational activities, discussions, and dramatic performances.[14]

V. GROUP THERAPY

The term "group therapy" is frequently used, but often not clearly defined. A great variety of activities, including group discussions with psychiatrists or psychiatric social workers, group meetings in mental hygiene clinics or psychopathic hospitals, or acting in psychodrama, are called group therapy. Careful selection of a suitable group of companions by the group worker is an essential condition for success and for predicting the probable influence of the members of the group upon one another.

The primary objective of such groups is to function as a medium for carrying out therapy for their members. Such groups have been composed of individuals who were unable to participate in normal group activities with others of the same age, who could not relate

---

[14] Herbert Shore, "Group Work Program Development in Homes for the Aged," *Social Service Review,* Vol. XXVI, No. 2 (June 1952), pp. 181-194; Jerome Kaplan, *A Social Program for Older People* (Minneapolis: University of Minnesota Press, 1953); James H. Wood, *Helping Older People Enjoy Life* (New York: Harper, 1953); Gordon J. Aldridge, "Old Age as a Social Problem," *Journal of Public Law,* Vol. 2, No. 2 (Fall 1954), pp. 333-339; and, Leo W. Simmons, *Toward Better Understanding of the Aging* (New York: Council on Social Work Education, 1959).

to people, and were either too shy and withdrawn, or so hostile and aggressive, that they could not function in a normal group.

Group therapy has its own value as therapy. It is not just a simpler, quicker process than individual treatment. It is based upon the curative or socializing effect of a group, and upon the development of friendly contacts in a secure atmosphere of help provided by the group leader in a controlled environment. In this interaction of the patients with each other, each one feels more secure as he discovers that other members of the group have similar, or even worse, problems, and that his own difficulties are not caused by a unique failure or inadequacy. This recognition permits the patient to identify himself with other members of the group, lessens his anxiety, and develops his readiness to try to help the others, while, at the same time, adjusting himself to the group. This experience encourages the patient, it gives him a feeling of solidarity and of getting along with other people. The entire process is made possible through the relationship between the group therapist and the members of the group.[15] In general, group therapy develops a feeling of unity between the group members. Therapists, as a rule, are careful to avoid that patients express their feelings of suppressed hostility, aggression, and related drives too forcefully, because it would distort the therapeutic climate of the group; it has to be left to individual treatment.

Changes in environment are disturbing to adults and to children with whom group therapy has been practiced. Samuel R. Slavson, one of the outstanding pioneers in the field of child guidance and group therapy, characterizes his method as "activity group therapy," in which the therapeutic effect is produced by the active participation of disturbed or neurotic children or adults in such a group which permits them to act out or talk about their anxieties, fears, or aggressive feelings. The patient, who represses his spontaneity because he is afraid of being rebuked or of losing prestige, may be encouraged to talk about his problems when he sees others in the group freely expressing themselves. In order to achieve such results, the group should be composed of a small number of patients of the same

---

[15] Robert Plank, "An Analysis of a Group Therapy Experiment," *Human Organization*, Vol. 10, Nos. 3 and 4 (Fall and Winter, 1951), pp. 5-21, 26-36; and Dorwin Cartwright, and Alvin Zander, *Group Dynamics: Research and Theory* (Evanston, Ill.: Row, 1953).

sex and of the same age.[16] The group therapy setting must be informal; it must permit a confidential relation between the therapist and the members of the group.

In such therapeutic groups, even children of preschool age play out their anxieties, tensions, and fantasies. They use for their expression various toys and materials, such as animals, dolls, figures of families, wood blocks, plastics, water colors, and finger paints. The social worker or psychiatrist gives them interpretations of their actions and plays. More intensive psychotherapy is used for disturbed children of elementary school age for whom different materials are offered in order to permit them in their play group to express their feelings.

The success of group therapy with children and adults depends upon a competent group therapist who needs, at least, to meet the qualifications for individual therapy. Since World War II, psychiatric patients have been treated by group therapy in military and veterans hospitals, and clinics. In 1943, the American Group Therapy Association was founded. It provides for its members—psychiatrists, psychiatric social workers, group therapists, and clinical psychologists—information on research and new experiences, conferences, and exchange of ideas.

VI. TRENDS IN SOCIAL GROUP WORK PRACTICE

Among new elements in the development of social group work, we may emphasize the following trends:

(1) The democratic principle of self-determination is recognized as the genuine American method of social group work. The older form of authoritarian leadership is in the process of being discarded. Democracy implies respect for the personal dignity of each group member. It precludes enforcing the leader's own ideas as long as these ideas are not accepted by the majority of the group.

The professional staff of the group work agency needs to have faith in the democratic ideal and in human dignity, as well as in

[16] Samuel R. Slavson, *An Introduction to Group Therapy* (New York: Commonwealth Fund, 1943), pp. 1-2; and, Grace L. Coyle, "Group Work in Psychiatric Settings," *Social Work*, Vol. 4, No. 1 (January 1959).

people's ability to learn and to decide for themselves what they want to do. This idea requires that the group workers work *with* the group, not *for* the group.

(2) Certain group work methods are being applied to the expanding program of mass recreation, frequently under the guidance of public recreation departments, schools, and colleges. However, the need for the setup of smaller groups is recognized as being necessary in order to offer individualized services for people who desire personal attention and help.

(3) Recreational agencies now accept the need for employment of trained, professional social workers who are able to give competent supervision to volunteer leaders and to work with such groups which need skill, understanding, and experience. The development of the administration and community relations of group work agencies also requires professional skills.

(4) It is now recognized that under professional leadership, individual members in groups receive more attention, based upon the group worker's understanding of psychiatric concepts of human needs. A new teamwork is developed in which group workers join together with caseworkers, psychiatrists, psychologists, and sociologists to help solve personality problems of group members.

(5) Professional leadership has already stimulated a broad literature in the field of social group work and the development of scientific research in which social psychology, sociology, and sociometry contribute to a critical evaluation of the validity of group work methods.

(6) The tasks and objectives of leisure-time and recreational agencies are being clarified. An adjustment of the program of recreational agencies is under way to meet the actual, essential needs of the community.

(7) In many communities, a sincere concern about desirable interracial and intergroup relations is now established. It is leading to mutual understanding and respect among different ethnic and religious groups. Organizations are being encouraged in which membership is open to everyone regardless of creed, race, color, sex, and economic status.

(8) The forces of intergroup relations are finding recognition in new provinces: in groups of the aged; in churches, factories, labor unions, cooperatives; and in reformatories, prisons, and institutions for mentally defective patients. Group dynamics is beginning to play

an important role in improving relations between management and workers in industry.[17]

(9) Social agencies, professional associations, and schools of social work encourage professional education and attempt to develop the most suitable curriculum for training in group work, as well as criteria for the selection of students.

(10) Professional social workers are assuming the responsibility for improving their own competence and skill, for assisting the schools of social work in their teaching methods, and for raising the quality of group work practice. They are attempting to achieve a commonly accepted classification of jobs and the establishment of salaries commensurate with their responsibilities.

(11) Public authorities, such as municipal welfare departments, boards of education, and recreation commissions are assuming financial responsibilities and are sponsoring group work services, particularly for teen-agers, and the aged.

Selected Bibliography

Birren, James E. (editor), *Aging and the Individual*. Chicago: University of Chicago Press, 1960.

Blumenthal, Louis H., *Administration of Group Work*. New York: Administration Press, 1948.

Burgess, Ernest W. (editor), *Aging in Western Culture*. Chicago: University of Chicago Press, 1960.

Cartwright, Dorwin, and Alvin Zander, *Group Dynamics: Research and Theory*. Evanston, Ill.: Peterson, 1953.

Coyle, Grace L., *Group Experience and Democratic Values*. New York: Woman's Press, 1947.

————, *Group Work with American Youth*. New York: Harper, 1948.

Donahue, Wilma (editor), *Education for Later Maturity*. New York: Morrow, 1955.

*Hendry, Charles E. (editor), *A Decade of Group Work*. New York: Association Press, 1948.

*Kaiser, Clara, "Characteristics of Social Group Work," *Social Welfare Forum* (1957), pp. 158-169.

---

[17] Paul M. Limbert, "Major Trends and Developments in Professional Aspects of Group Work," in Charles Hendry (editor), *op. cit.*, pp. 141 ff., 148-149; Herman D. Stein and Richard A. Cloward, *Social Perspectives in Behavior* (Glencoe: Free Press, 1959); and, Marjorie Murphy, *The Social Group Work Method in Social Work Education*, Curriculum Study, Vol. XI (New York Council on Social Work Education, 1959).

————, (editor), *The Objectives of Group Work*. New York: Association Press, 1936.

Klein, Alan F., *Society, Democracy, and the Group*. New York: Womans Press, 1953.

*Konopka, Gisela, *Group Work in the Institution*. New York: Whiteside, 1954.

*————, "The Method of Social Group Work" (Walter A. Friedlander, editor), *Concepts and Methods of Social Work*, Chapter III. Englewood Cliffs, N.J.: Prentice-Hall, Inc., 1958.

————, *Therapeutic Group Work with Children*. Minneapolis: University of Minnesota Press, 1949.

McCaskill, Joseph C., *Theory and Practice of Group Work*. New York: Association Press, 1930.

Mathiasen, Geneva, and Edward H. Noaks, *Planning a Home for the Aged*. New York: Dodge, 1960.

Phillips, Helen U. (editor), *Achievement of Responsible Behavior Through Group Work Process*. Philadelphia: University of Pennsylvania Press, 1950.

————, *Essentials of Group Work Skill*. New York: Association Press, 1957.

Murphy, Marjorie, *The Social Group Work Method in Social Work Education*, Curriculum Study, Vol. XI. New York: Council on Social Work Education, 1959.

Murray, Clyde E., Marse G. Bowens, and Russell Hogrefe (editors), *Group Work in Community Life*. New York: Association Press, 1959.

*Schulze, Susanne, *Creative Group Living in a Children's Institution*. New York: Association Press, 1951.

Slavson, S. R. (editor), *Practice of Group Therapy*. New York: International Universities Press, 1947.

*Sullivan, Dorothea F. (editor), *Readings in Group Work*. New York: Association Press, 1952.

*Trecker, Harleigh B., *Group Work Foundations and Frontiers*. New York: Whiteside, 1955.

*————, *Social Group Work: Principles and Practice*. 2nd ed. New York: Whiteside, 1955.

Wilson, Gertrude, *Group Work and Case Work*. New York: Family Service Association of America, 1941.

————. "Social Group Work Theory and Practice," *Social Welfare Forum* (1956), pp. 143-159.

*———— and Gladys Ryland, *Social Group Work Practice*. Boston: Houghton, 1949.

6.

Community Organization

I. PRINCIPLES

"Community Organization" is the social work process of establishing a progressively more effective adjustment between the social welfare needs and the community resources within a geographic area.[1] In our discussion here we consider those phases of community life that are devoted to social welfare. We are aware, however, that the life of the local community includes the planning and coordination of education, housing, transportation, water and sewage supply, and other necessities of human living as well as social and health services, and that an integration of these essential elements in community planning is indispensable. Instead of the term "Community Organization" some social workers prefer "Social Welfare Planning," "Social Inter-Group Work Process," "Social Welfare Organization," or "Social Engineering." The three main objectives of community welfare organization are: (1) to determine the social needs, (2) to arrange for careful and conscientious planning to meet the needs of the population, and (3) to mobilize the forces of the community in the best way to achieve this goal.

---

[1] Various definitions are discussed in Wayne McMillen, *Community Organization for Social Welfare* (Chicago: University of Chicago Press, 1949), pp. 20-22. See also Herbert H. Stroup, *Community Welfare Organization* (New York: Harper, 1952), pp. 138-148.

Clarence King [2] has emphasized that all social work programs in our country can accomplish their purpose only if they are accepted by the majority of the people. This is one of the tasks of community organization; citizen participation in welfare organization is the essential factor in this process of social work. We need in our democratic society the working together of all groups of the population in the development, maintenance, and the reorganization of institutions for health, welfare, and recreation. This principle applies to all types of social work, but particularly to community welfare organization. Because citizens have insight into the social needs of their communities and because their permanent support of a new or an expanded program of services is indispensable, their responsible initiative in the planning and in the setting up of welfare and health services is necessary.

To mobilize the citizens for social welfare programs requires the knowledge and skills of the "community organizer," the professional worker. Volunteers are engaged not only in the community organization process but also in other phases of social work such as family and child care. The social and psychological elements that influence citizens in their decisions about participation in community projects are of vital importance in a democracy. The increased interest in volunteer services is an indication of the growing willingness of citizens to offer their time and energy in order to assist in meeting social needs. Such interest must be recognized and encouraged.

It is necessary to distinguish the underlying social philosophy, which is the same in community organization as in casework or group work, from the special skills or techniques applied to achieve an efficient coordination and integration of community resources for health and welfare. The objectives of community organization are: (1) to help citizens find the ways best suited for the provision of health and welfare services, for the improvement of the social environment, and for prevention of suffering; (2) to encourage cooperative

[2] *Organizing for Community Action* (New York: Harper, 1948), p. 22; Arthur Hillman, *Community Organization and Planning* (New York: Macmillan, 1950), pp. 13-14; and, Genevieve W. Carter, "Social Community Organization. Methods and Processes," in Walter Friedlander (editor), *Concepts and Methods of Social Work* (Englewood Cliffs, N. J.: Prentice-Hall, Inc., 1958), pp. 210-213, 227-228.

efforts for the purpose of common human welfare; (3) to construct, for individuals and groups, the channels of mutual understanding on problems of health and welfare and the means of communication essential to common action.

Community organization does not relieve citizens, as individuals or as civic groups, of their social responsibilities. Rather it attempts, by exchange of ideas and experiences, to clarify the social responsibility of the community, citizens, and government authorities to take the necessary measures to meet social and health needs.

Within the framework of community organization, the social worker has the task of contributing his professional knowledge, skill, and experience. From his awareness of social conditions, the social worker is able to share with other citizens the recognition of health and welfare needs. He is qualified to stimulate in the community the necessary surveys and research in order to establish facts and prepare a plan for improving conditions. He is able to assist in giving the interpretation of social needs to his clients, to the neighborhood, and to social groups in the community.

II. HISTORY OF COMMUNITY ORGANIZATION

Community organization has its main roots in the charity organization movement in the United States. The need for coordination of the work of charities and philanthropic societies had been recognized earlier, but its realization became one of the objectives of the Association for Improvement of Conditions of the Poor which was founded in New York City in 1843.[3] Charity Organization Societies, whose development in this country began in Buffalo in 1877, recognized that their principal goal was to coordinate the existing charities and relief societies, to avoid overlapping and duplication of services, and to encourage cooperation between social agencies instead of rivalry and competition. To find solutions for these problems, special councils or boards were established in Charity Organization Societies of Rochester, N.Y., Elmira, N.Y., and in New York City in 1882. These councils were composed of representatives of the major charities in the city. Francis H. McLean favored the idea that a

---

[3] See Chap. 3, p. [93] supra; and Campbell G. Murphy, "Community Organization for Social Welfare," *Social Work Year Book* (1960), pp. 186-188.

separate body assume the responsibility for coordination of welfare agencies and planning of programs. His idea was carried out when, in 1908, the Associated Charities of Pittsburgh, Pa., organized a Community Welfare Council.[4] Similar councils, usually called "Council of Social Agencies," were set up in Milwaukee in 1909, in St. Louis in 1911, in Cincinnati and Cleveland in 1913, in Minneapolis in 1916, and in Chicago in 1917. In 1960, 700 Community Welfare Councils were members of the national federation, "United Community Funds and Councils." Their objectives are coordination of social welfare activities and inter-agency cooperation between public and private social agencies, the raising and maintaining of standards of service, development of community leadership in the promotion of health and welfare, and social planning. Because the quality of service often varies among agencies, community welfare councils are able to raise these standards by requiring a certain level of performance as a condition of council membership. Since some social agencies and institutions developed according to the initiative of individual philanthropists or of independent religious and humanitarian groups, social welfare councils now provide the means of investigating social needs of the community and of coordinating agency efforts, with agreement on division of work and on basic policies.

The financing of charities was from the very beginning a major interest of the Charity Organization Societies. The vast and increasing number of relief societies, charitable institutions, and other social agencies in large cities led to continuous solicitation of donations and contributions from well-to-do citizens. Almost every day bankers, businessmen, lawyers, and physicians were approached by one or another group of citizens, hospitals, dispensaries, or orphanages, which competed for the favor of the donors. The donors could not understand why such a variety of agencies was necessary since many of them seemed to do the same work. Some became hostile and refused contributions, others asked for a change in agency collection policies. This demand of the public was made for still another reason. A number of fraudulent, unscrupulous "entrepreneurs" asked for donations for charities with impressive titles and betrayed the

---

[4] Frank Bruno, *Trends in Social Work* (New York: Columbia University Press, 1948), p. 194. W. McMillen, *op. cit.*, pp. 416-417, considers the Milwaukee council the first independent council because the Pittsburgh organization remained part of the Associated Charities for a year.

trust of the benevolent people they approached. Some social agencies that hired skillful fund raisers were able to collect substantial contributions, often much more than their services warranted, whereas others of vital importance to the community had to operate on a starvation level because they lacked efficient fund-raising facilities.

Previous attempts at combined fund-raising for charities had been made in Liverpool by Reverend A. Hume in 1873, by the Associated Charities of Denver, Colorado in 1887, by Federations of Jewish Charities in Boston in 1895, and by the Charity Organization Society of Elmira, N.Y. in 1910. Earlier, the YMCA's had introduced a community-wide campaign for raising money for their activities. Another element in the development of joint financing of social agencies was the "charity work endorsement committees," which, at the turn of the century, were sponsored by chambers of commerce and commercial associations. At last in Cleveland, in 1913, the first "Community Chest," as a special organization for the financing of social work, was founded under the title "Federation for Charity and Philanthropy" on the initiative of Major Newton D. Baker. It substituted one organization and one campaign for fifty-three drives and collections, and succeeded in tripling the number of donors to charity. In a few years, fifteen metropolitan cities introduced Community Chests, and during both world wars many war chests followed the same pattern. In 1960, about 2,000 Community Chests and United Funds conducted fund-raising campaigns for health and welfare services.[5] The main objective of the Community Chest is to procure the necessary funds for the operations of its member agencies. But it also aims at a fair and constructive distribution of the collected funds so that the participating agencies may best serve the interests of the population and improve and expand their services as needed. In order to carry on its campaign successfully and to obtain the necessary contributions for private agencies, the chest has to interpret for the public the programs and policies of the different social agencies.

----

[5] Lyman S. Ford, "Community Chests," *Social Work Year Book* (1951), p. 117; Allen T. Burns, *Community Mobilization for Human Needs* (New York: Community Chests and Councils, 1938); Guy Thompson, "Community Chests and United Funds," *Social Work Year Book* (1957), pp. 175-179; and, Ida C. Merriam, "Financing Social Welfare Services," *ibid., 1960,* pp. 267-277.

III. STRUCTURE OF COMMUNITY ORGANIZATION

The agencies that carry on the process of community organization may be divided into two groups: those operating on the local level, and those active on a state, national, or international level. For the purpose of our discussion only the first group will be considered.

In a city, or large county of metropolitan character, community organization, as a rule, is performed by the following organizations: (1) Community Welfare Council, (2) Community Chest, (3) Coordinating Council, (4) Neighborhood Council, (5) the Social Service Exchange, and (6) individual social agencies.

(1) *A Community Welfare Council* or *Council of Social Agencies* exists in almost every city with a population of 100,000 or more, for the purpose of community-wide planning and coordination of the local health, welfare, and recreational services. The organization of the Councils is not uniform, but the following features are characteristic of most of them. They are composed of representatives of all social agencies of welfare, health, and recreation which maintain standards acceptable to the Council. Often, some individuals, such as the mayor of the city and outstanding persons in the field of philanthropy, health, welfare, and culture are members. The social agencies represented usually include public agencies, such as the department of public welfare, the public health department, the recreation and park commission, the board of education, and the juvenile court. Because public agencies are maintained by taxes, they participate in the work of the Community Welfare Council without an interest in receiving financial support from money-raising campaigns. However, some private agencies also may be members of the Council without sharing in general collections for health and welfare purposes. Each social agency participating in the Council is usually represented by two members, one the president or another member of the board of directors, and the other a professional social worker, in most instances the executive of the agency. In large cities or counties the council establishes a number of divisions, such as family welfare, child care and adoption, recreation, health and medical care services, and care for the aged, with committees to direct each division. Sometimes the Council conducts a separate "Social Planning Bureau," a statistical and research bureau, and a public in-

formation division. An example of the organization of a Council is presented in Chart 1. The functions of a Community Welfare Council are frequently classified into the following six activities: [6]

(a) *Coordination.* The meetings of the Council with its lay board and staff members present to the public and private social agencies and to the citizens a full picture of the health and welfare work performed in the community. Usually, the Council distributes a bulletin and other pertinent information among its members. In these ways, members have an opportunity to share experiences, to develop mutual understanding, and to work together. Meetings and conferences permit them to identify common problems, to explore unmet needs of the population, and to eliminate duplication of effort. Thus, the Council operates as a clearing house, permitting better service for the community.

(b) *Fact-Finding.* Often, social and health conditions in the community must be investigated to determine the causes and the complexity of problems, the available resources for health and welfare services, and the cost and distribution of such services. Therefore, social research and surveys are necessary to acquire reliable knowledge of conditions that need change. Sometimes, it is advisable to request "outside" experts or consultants to conduct such a survey because they are not biased in regard to the conservation of the existing social services and are able to compare conditions with those in other cities or regions. Committees in charge of evaluation of social surveys should be composed both of laymen and professional workers. They should convey the findings and recommendations of the survey, not only to the members of the council, but also to the general public.

(c) *Joint Action.* The advantage of a Community Welfare Council is that it combines a large number of organizations, and mobilizes, through its board and lay members, important forces in the community. As a result, it is able to conduct joint careful planning on the basis of research and examination of the prevailing conditions, and to enlist the support of many groups in carrying out the measures recommended by its fact-finding committee.

---

[6] Campbell G. Murphy, "Community Organization for Social Welfare," *Social Work Year Book* (1960), pp. 186-191; Howard F. Gustafson, "Community Welfare Councils," *ibid.*, pp. 191-198; and, Arthur Hillman, *Sociology and Social Work* (Washington: Public Affairs Press, 1956), pp. 43-45.

Chart 1. *Organizational Structure of a Community Welfare Council.*

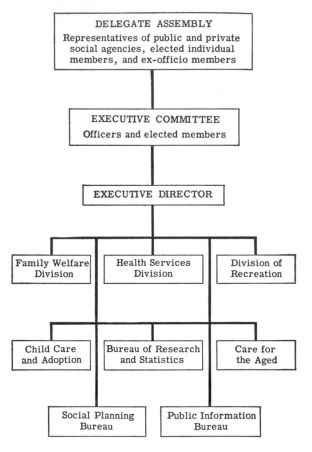

(d) *Improving the Quality of Service.* The observation and evaluation of the quality of services rendered by the social agencies of the
community is an important function of the council. The council attempts to improve inadequate services by consulting with board
members and by providing intensive staff training courses.

(e) *Common Services.* There are certain welfare activities that
are of value to the entire community. Such activities as the compilation of a central index, usually called a "social service exchange," or
the maintenance of a central volunteer bureau, are the proper responsibility of a Community Welfare Council. Other services include

a central information bureau, or a research and statistical bureau or institute. Further possibilities might include a joint intake bureau for casework, child care, and guidance services.

(f) *Developing Public Understanding.* One of the essential objectives of the Community Welfare Council is to bring the value of the work of social agencies to the attention of the people and to enlist their understanding, concern, and active participation in these services.[7] Social surveys have shown that a large percentage of the citizens have a very vague notion of what social agencies do and why they are necessary. To bring the facts to the people and to impart to them clear, objective, basic information about health and social conditions, and the role of social and health agencies is a real challenge for the community welfare council. Such councils may be effective in developing community leaders—lay persons who have a clear understanding of the need for health and welfare services and who are able to convey their knowledge to the people.

(2) *The Community Chest* was formed because private social agencies depend upon voluntary contributions for the financing of their services and their personnel. A cooperative method of raising the necessary funds for these activities is required to avoid dissatisfaction and hostility among the people who are called upon for contributions to private social agencies and to secure a fair support for all essential welfare organizations. As a rule, the Community Chest or the United Fund is governed by a board of directors which represents, not only social agencies that are members of the Chest, but also citizens constituting a broad cross-section of the population of the area. In large cities, these representatives form a delegate association of the Community Chest and elect a board of directors, which supervises the operations of the Chest and sets up its policies. The management of the Chest is directed through an executive committee and its officers (president, secretary, and treasurer), as well as through the executive director who usually is appointed by the board of directors. There are laymen and representatives of other social agencies on both the board of directors and on the executive committee of the Chest.

---

[7] See Genevieve Carter, *op. cit.,* pp. 201-209; Lucy P. Carner, "The Youth and Government Project," *National Conference of Social Work, Selected Papers in Group Work and Community Organization* (1952), pp. 12-16; and, Leonard W. Mayo, "Relationships Between Public and Voluntary Health and Welfare Agencies," *Child Welfare,* Vol. XXXIX, No. 1 (January 1960), pp. 1-5.

Frequently, they represent the public welfare department, the board of education, the health department, and the recreation commission. They advise the Chest concerning the population's need for voluntary health, recreation, and welfare services, and support the endeavor to raise funds for private agencies. The most important work of the Chest is entrusted to the budget committee and to the campaign committee. The budget committee is composed of some members of the executive committee, other lay persons and representatives of the community welfare council. Prior to the annual campaign, usually in September, all participating social agencies submit a detailed budget for the subsequent year and request a certain share in the funds to be raised by the drive. The budget committee carefully studies the requests, compares them with former budgets, and discusses each agency's request with its representatives. The budget committee then estimates the total amount of money that may be raised by the campaign and revises, in view of this estimate, the plan for the allocation of funds to the individual agencies. The adjusted budget is submitted to the executive committee or to the board of directors for approval.

The campaign committee is in charge of the preparation of the annual drive. It invites church, civic, and youth organizations to enlist volunteers for a house-to-house canvass. It appoints special subcommittees and captains for individual contributions and special drives among industries, department houses, service clubs, banks, professional associations, and organized labor groups. The committee supervises the campaign which usually lasts no longer than one month or six weeks. An illustration of the pattern of Chest organization is shown in Chart 2.

In order to carry on a successful campaign, the Community Chest has to interpret to the population, the year round, the necessity, as well as the extent and quality, of recreational, health, and welfare services offered in the community. That a close working relationship with the community welfare council is necessary in this respect is obvious considering that both agencies have similar objectives. The Chest's interpretation of the need for health and welfare services is a cooperative effort with the public information task of the Council and is usually carried out after joint planning. From the financial point of view, the Community Chest promotes the most efficient, coordinated, and well-integrated services. The Chest avoids duplications of work, conducts research regarding the social and health

Chart 2. *Organizational Structure of a Community Chest.*

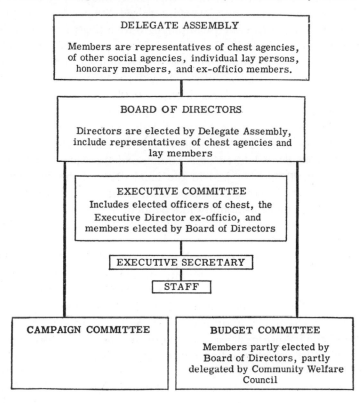

<table>
<tr><td>

DELEGATE ASSEMBLY

Members are representatives of chest agencies, of other social agencies, individual lay persons, honorary members, and ex-officio members.

</td></tr>
</table>

BOARD OF DIRECTORS

Directors are elected by Delegate Assembly, include representatives of chest agencies and lay members

EXECUTIVE COMMITTEE
Includes elected officers of chest, the Executive Director ex-officio, and members elected by Board of Directors

EXECUTIVE SECRETARY

STAFF

CAMPAIGN COMMITTEE

BUDGET COMMITTEE
Members partly elected by Board of Directors, partly delegated by Community Welfare Council

needs, and encourages careful planning and evaluation of projects and welfare operations.

Because the Community Chest assumes the responsibility for the financial support of private social agencies, for the fund-raising campaign, and for a fair distribution of the collected contributions, the Community Welfare Council is free to concentrate its attention upon social surveys and research, coordination of health, welfare, and recreation services, and program planning.

The principle of joint fund-raising for welfare purposes, as represented by the Community Chest, is basically sound, but Chests and United Funds have not been able to raise the necessary money because the larger health agencies refuse to participate. During recent years, the amount of contributions for health and welfare services collected from federated campaigns was about one-fifth of the total, but the large national health agencies raised 80 per cent of their funds outside of the federated campaign. Public taxes and social insurance benefits are used substantially for payment of social and health services, and it is expected that the rising level of middle-class family income and social insurance benefits enable more people to pay fees for social and health services.

A number of important health and welfare agencies, especially the American Red Cross, the National Tuberculosis Association, the National Foundation, the American Heart Association, the National Society for Crippled Children and Adults, and the American Cancer Society, frequently do not join in the local drive of the community chests and insist in carrying on their own campaigns. Citizens have been dissatisfied by near-monthly independent appeals of these health or welfare organizations made in addition to the annual campaigns of the Community Chest.[8]

In general, Community Chests welcome special donations and bequests which are made independently of the regular, annual campaign. In some metropolitan cities, a separate Community Fund has been organized in order to receive and administer such donations and bequests for charitable purposes and health and welfare services. The Fund has its own by-laws, a board of directors which determines the policy of the agency, and an executive who is responsible for the administration and the allocations of the money, stocks, bonds, and other properties. There is planned cooperation between the Fund and the local Chest.

In some cities, the Community Welfare Council and the Community Chest are combined in a single organization. In other instances, where a separate Council and Chest operate, the necessary teamwork is secured by the employment of one executive and staff for both the Council and the Community Chest. Both organizations share offices and other facilities and have common research and public relations

---

[8] F. Emerson Andrews, "Fund Raising" in Ernest B. Harper and Arthur Dunham (editors), *Community Organization in Action* (New York: Association Press, 1959), pp. 266-274; Harold J. Seymour, "The Successful Fund-Raising Campaign," *ibid.*, pp. 275-279; Margaret M. Fellows and Stella A. Koenig, *Tested Methods of Raising Money* (New York: Harper, 1959); John R. Seeley, *et al., Community Chest: A Case Study on Philanthropy* (Toronto: University of Toronto Press, 1957); and, Ida C. Merriam, "Financing Social Welfare Services," *Social Work Year Book* (1960), pp. 267-277.

committees. The Community Welfare Council usually participates in the selection of the members of the budget committee of the Community Chest.

(3) *The Coordinating Council* is a citizen's group created for coordinating the social forces of a municipal district in order to deal with specific social problems (primarily juvenile delinquency). The first Coordinating Council was founded in 1919, in Berkeley, California, by Professor August Vollmer. A preceding social survey at an elementary school had revealed that 90 per cent of truant and delinquent children were in families under economic stress, and that a coordination of the social services of the community was needed in order to prevent juvenile delinquency by proper care, treatment, and guidance.

This Coordinating Council achieved successful cooperation of public authorities and private social agencies in the area and developed a child guidance clinic, vocational counseling, a social service exchange, and broad educational programs. Following this example, similar Coordinating Councils were established in San Francisco, Los Angeles, and other cities in California. Later, Coordinating Councils were organized in New York, Illinois, and St. Paul, Minnesota. Coordinating Councils maintain a cooperative relationship with the local Community Welfare Council, and are represented at its delegate body or board of directors. Their main objective is the prevention of juvenile delinquency; but some Coordinating Councils have given attention to other social problems. They differ in their functions from Community Welfare Councils because they place emphasis on specific social questions, and enlist the participation of local civic groups and individuals who are not members of the Community Welfare Council.[9]

(4) *The Neighborhood Council* is a citizens' committee which is organized to improve social conditions that are of particular importance to a certain neighborhood. Some of the neighborhood councils have grown from planning committees in settlement houses; others have been encouraged by a Council of Social Agencies, a Parent-Teacher Association, or other civic or religious societies. Social

---

[9] W. McMillen, *op. cit.,* p. 324; A Hillman, *Community Organization and Planning* (New York: Macmillan, 1950), pp. 218-227; and, August Vollmer, "Crime Can Be Checked," *Community Organization,* Vol. VII (March-April 1939), pp. 3-4.

workers usually participate in the work of Neighborhood Councils as individuals or as representatives of their social agencies, but they are a minority; laymen form the majority of the council. The Neighborhood Council is not concerned with the wide range of social welfare and health questions as is the Community Welfare Council, or very urgent special problems as the Coordinating Council.

The Neighborhood Council frequently attempts to improve the local facilities for recreation, parks and playgrounds, or summer camp facilities for school children. It may be concerned with the establishment of a community center, the improvement of sanitary or housing conditions within the area, the founding of a consumers' cooperative to restrict high living costs, or the setting up of garbage collection policies. During World War II, many Neighborhood Councils took part in the work of the Civilian Defense Program and shared with other groups the responsibility for planning. The local character of the Neighborhood Council permits an intensified interest of its members. In some cities, as in Pittsburgh, Pennsylvania, all Neighborhood Councils have founded a Federation, and use the professional staff of the Federation for their programs and activities.

(5) *The Social Service Exchange* is a federation of welfare and health agencies which maintains a central, confidential register, and a cooperative clearing service which lists all persons known to health and welfare agencies. Sometimes the title "Social Service Index" or "Confidential Exchange" is used. The concept of the Exchange was brought to our country with the Charity Organization Society from England. The purpose of the Social Service Exchange is clearance so that each social agency knows whether or not persons applying for aid or service receive similar or other care by another organization, and that fraud, duplication of efforts, and waste are avoided. The Social Service Exchange has four functions: (1) to register social agency records as referred to the Exchange; (2) to supply, on request of a member agency, information about previous registrations of the person or family in the index; (3) to notify the member agencies, previously aiding the person, of the new inquiry; and (4) to provide data for studies and research. Thus, the Social Service Exchange promotes cooperation and exchange of information among social agencies serving the same person or family. Criticism of the Exchange has recently advocated that it should be abolished; but rather a revision of its functions may be needed.

The Social Service Exchange is organized either by the Community Welfare Council, the Community Chest, or an individual public or private agency (for instance, a public welfare department or a private family service agency), or it is established as an independent organization.

The financing of the social service exchange is either assumed by the sponsoring agency, such as the Community Chest, the Community Welfare Council, a public welfare department or a private agency, or by member agency fees. The latter may be arranged according to the size of work load of agencies so that the budget of the Exchange is assessed in advance, or according to the prorate use of the Exchange by each agency.

The equipment of the Exchange consists of a card index to the case records of the member agencies. A separate card for each family contains surname, first names, woman's maiden name, birth dates of parents and children, the address, and a note on cross references. There is usually a street and house card for all registered persons as well. Inquiries and information are exchanged on simple, printed forms. Most Social Service Exchanges serve a city or a county.

Since 1951, a number of Social Service Exchanges were discontinued, and the value of the Exchange has been questioned.[10] The main reasons for the closing of the Exchange were the cessation of registration and use by public welfare and health departments, the increasing expenses of the exchange, the fact that selective registration was made instead of registration of all clients, specialization of agencies, and changes in social work philosophy which refuse to use information from other sources than the client. The United Community Funds and Councils of America has established research on the value of the Social Service Exchange and its role in inter-agency communication. Whether the exchange will continue to operate, will depend upon the conviction of social agencies as to its value, upon competent professional personnel, and a sufficient use by the cooperating agencies.

(6) *Community Organization by Individual Social Agencies* is ex-

---

[10] Morton I. Teicher, "Let's Abolish the Social Service Exchange," *Social Work Journal,* Vol. 33, No. 1 (January 1952), pp. 28-31; Stephen L. Angell and Frank T. Greving, "A New Look at the Social Service Exchange," *Social Work Journal,* Vol. 36, No. 1 (January 1955); and, Kenneth I. Williams, "Social Service Exchanges," *Social Work Year Book* (1960), pp. 559-563.

ecuted by high-standard agencies, such as family welfare agencies, child protective or child care agencies, adoption societies, and health services. This secondary function of these agencies may be concerned with the development of recreational facilities in cooperation with lay groups and public authorities, establishment of a mental hygiene clinic or other joint treatment facilities, or the raising of funds for such special goals as the construction of a clinic or hospital. Individual agencies are active in community organization where no community welfare council has been established.

We have discussed so far the structure of local community organization. On the state level only a few State Councils of Social Work coordinate the services of public and private welfare and health agencies. But there are a variety of advisory committees and commissions and State Conferences of Social Work in which representatives of public and private social agencies work together with lay persons for the purpose of better use of resources. Certain organizations have been set up on a regional basis, comprising several states, such as the Regional Conferences of the Child Welfare League of America and the Southern Regional Council, which attempts to improve civic, economic, and racial conditions of the Negro population in the southern states.

National organizations in the field of social welfare under public and private auspices are also interested in the process of developing adequate standards, and enlisting public support. Their large number makes integration and coordination on the national level difficult. The National Social Welfare Assembly represents voluntary health and welfare agencies as their central national organization. The Assembly encourages cooperation of public and private social welfare programs and attempts planning of field services with states and local communities on the national level. Community organization is carried on by the National Association of Social Workers,[11] by various national organizations of religious and humanitarian character, and by such agencies as the American Public Welfare Association, the Child Welfare League of America, the Family Service Association of America, and the United Community Funds and Councils of America.

---

[11] Ray Johns, *The Co-operative Process Among National Social Agencies* (New York: Association Press, 1946), pp. 112, 253-254; and, Leonard W. Mayo and Robert M. Webb, "National Organizations in Social Welfare," *Social Work Year Book* (1960), pp. 408-416.

The U.S. Department of Health, Education and Welfare assists in the improvement of standards of service by studies, research, publications, and conferences.

On the *international level* the functions of most organizations are concerned with welfare and health services in foreign countries and devoted to achieving international cooperation and integration of methods, skills, and resources. The activities of UNRRA during and after World War II, the United Nations, Department of Social Affairs, the Economic and Social Council (ECOSOC), the World Health Organization, and UNESCO are examples of agencies, active in international community organization.[12]

Selected Bibliography

Andrews, F. Emerson, *Philanthropic Giving.* New York: Russell Sage Foundation, 1950.

————, *Corporation Giving.* New York: Russell Sage Foundation, 1952.

Baker, Helen Cody, and Mary Swain Routzahn, *How To Interpret Social Welfare.* New York: Russell Sage Foundation, 1947.

Beam, Kenneth S., *Coordinating Councils in California.* Sacramento: California Department of Education, Bulletin No. 11, 1938.

*Buell, Bradley, and Associates, *Community Planning for Human Services.* New York: Columbia University Press, 1952.

Carner, Lucy P., "The Youth and Government Project," *National Conference of Social Work, Selected Papers in Group Work and Community Organization,* 1952, pp. 12-16.

*Carter, Genevieve W., "Social Work Community Organization Methods and Processes" (Walter A. Friedlander, editor), *Concepts and Methods of Social Work.* Englewood Cliffs, N.J.: Prentice-Hall, Inc., 1958, pp. 201-282.

Cohen, Nathan E., "Reversing the Process of Social Disorganization" (Alfred J. Kahn, editor), *Issues in American Social Work* (New York: Columbia University Press, 1959), pp. 138-158.

Colcord, Joanna C. (revised by Donald S. Howard), *Your Community; Its Provision for Health, Education, Safety, and Welfare.* New York: Russell Sage Foundation, 1947.

Community Chests and Councils, *Community Organization for Health and Welfare on a State-Wide Basis.* New York: 1946.

---

[12] International organizations and their activities are discussed in Chapter 16 infra.

————, *Health and Welfare Planning in the Smaller Community.* New York: 1945.

————, *Labor Participation in Organized Health and Welfare Activities Other Than Fund Raising.* New York: 1943.

Dahir, James, *Communities for Better Living: Citizen Achievement in Organization, Design and Development.* New York: Harper, 1950.

Danstedt, Rudolph T., "Current Conflicts in the Approach to Community Organization," *Social Service Review,* Vol. XXIV, No. 1 (March 1950), pp. 67-73.

Dimock, Marshall, *The Executive in Action.* New York: Harper, 1945.

*Dunham, Arthur, *Community Welfare Organization.* New York: Crowell, 1958.

*Green, Helen D., *Social Work Practice in Community Organization.* New York: Whiteside, 1954.

Gunn, Selskar M., and Philip S. Platt, *Voluntary Health Agencies: An Interpretive Study.* New York: Ronald, 1945.

*Harper, Ernest B., and Arthur Dunham, *Community Organization in Action.* New York: Association Press, 1959.

Harrison, Shelby M., and F. Emerson Andrews, *American Foundations for Social Welfare.* New York: Russell Sage Foundation, 1946.

Hiller, Robert I., *The Education and Work Experience of Community Organization Practitioners.* New York: Community Chests and Councils of America, 1949.

*Hillman, Arthur, *Community Organization and Planning.* New York: Macmillan, 1950.

Howard, Donald S., *Community Organization: Its Nature and Setting.* New York: American Association of Social Workers, 1947.

Jenkins, Edward C., *Philanthropy in America.* New York: Association Press, 1950.

Johns, Ray E., *The Cooperative Process Among National Social Agencies.* New York: Association Press, 1946.

*King, Clarence, *Organizing for Community Action.* New York: Harper, 1948.

Klein, Philip, *et al., A Social Study of Pittsburgh.* New York: Columbia University Press, 1938.

Kraus, Hertha, "Community Organization in Social Work: A Note on Choices and Steps," *Social Forces* (October 1948).

Lippitt, Ronald, *et al., The Dynamics of Planned Change.* New York: Harcourt, 1958.

*McMillen, Wayne, *Community Organization for Social Welfare,* 6th impression. Chicago: University of Chicago Press, 1954.

*Murphy, Campbell G., *Community Organization Practice*. Boston: Houghton, 1954.

Nisbeth, Robert A., *The Quest for Community*. New York: Oxford University Press, 1953.

North, Cecil C., *The Community and Social Welfare: A Study in Community Organization*. New York: McGraw, 1931.

Pettit, Walter W., *Case Studies in Community Organization*. New York: Appleton-Century-Crofts, Inc., 1928.

*Ross, Murray G., *Case Histories in Community Organization*. New York: Harper, 1958.

*————, *Community Organization Theory and Principles*. New York: Harper, 1955.

Routzahn, Mary B., and Evart G. Routzahn, *Publicity for Social Work*. New York: Russell Sage Foundation, 1928.

Ruml, Beardsley, and Theodore Geiger, *The Manual of Corporate Giving*. Washington: National Planning Association, 1952.

Sanderson, Dwight, and Robert A. Polson, *Rural Community Organization*. New York: Wiley, 1939.

*Schottland, Charles I., *Community Organization 1958*. New York: Columbia University Press, 1958.

Seeley, John R., *et al., Community Chest: A Case Study in Philanthropy*. Toronto: University of Toronto Press, 1957.

Sorensen, Roy, *The Art of Board Membership*. New York: Association Press, 1950.

*Stroup, Herbert Hewitt, *Community Welfare Organization*. New York: Harper, 1952.

Taylor, Eleanor K., *Public Accountability of Foundations and Charitable Trusts*. New York: Russell Sage Foundation, 1953.

Warren, Roland L., *Studying Your Community*. New York: Russell Sage Foundation, 1955.

7.

Ancillary Social Welfare Processes

I. SOCIAL WELFARE ADMINISTRATION

The administration of public and private social agencies is designed to achieve the full effect of the services for which they have been established. The principles that rule the administration of social welfare organizations will be discussed in this chapter. Administration of social agencies translates the provisions of social legislation and the aims of private philanthropy and religious charities into the dynamics of services and benefits for humanity. Management of social agencies is oriented to aid people in the most efficient way possible; it has been briefly described as the art of human relations.[1]

The skills of administration are not limited to social welfare settings. They are derived from public administration and from the techniques of business management. But the special objective of social services—to help human beings—is an element which distinguishes the management of social agencies from that of commercial and industrial enterprises and from other activities that do not directly deal with human beings.

---

[1] Karl de Schweinitz, *People and Process in Social Security* (Washington, D.C.: American Council on Education, 1948), p. 20. Other definitions are "facilitating activities necessary and incidental to the giving of direct service by a social agency" (Arthur Dunham) or "the process of transforming social policy into social service" (John C. Kidneigh); Arthur H. Kruse, "Administration of Social Agencies," *Social Work Year Book* (1960), 79-85.

Social work administration involves making judgments and using professional knowledge and skill which differ from those required in business administration, or even in the management of schools, hospitals, and churches.[2]

Administration of public social agencies is complicated by the specific roles legally assigned to the three levels of government: Federal, state, and local. The administration is determined by laws and statutes, its budget by decisions of the legislative body that allocates the annual appropriations and indirectly influences the appointment of personnel. Our constitutional principle of the separation of powers has not always been observed in the administration of public welfare, because courts have assumed administrative functions, such as the disbursement of mothers' pensions, orphans' allowances, and workmen's compensation. The trend, however, is toward an assignment of executive functions to administrative bodies.

Policies in public welfare administration are primarily established at the state level by state departments of public welfare. The policies of Federal agencies (such as veterans' services, old-age and survivors' insurance), are determined by the Federal government. Public Welfare Administration, like other government operations, requires clear objectives, and policies, an efficient organizational structure, with precise staff organization, sound methods of selection, recruitment, and promotion of personnel, decent working conditions, and fiscal accounting and control as guarantees for responsible management.

There are, nevertheless, important differences from other types of government functions. Social service administration requires thorough experience with the philosophy and methods of social welfare, knowledge of social legislation and social work practice. Above all, public welfare administration demands a sincere appreciation of and devotion to the specific objectives of social welfare and its inherent social philosophy. This identification with the aims and function of social welfare is required not only of the executive of a social agency and his assistants, but of the entire staff.

A. Functions of Welfare Administration

The main administrative functions of a private or public social

---

[2] Sue Spencer, *The Administration Method in Social Work Education* (New York: Council on Social Work Education, 1959), p. 17.

agency may be divided into nine activities: (1) fact-finding; (2) analysis of social conditions and of services to meet human needs; (3) decision on the best way of reaching this objective; (4) planning and allocating resources; (5) setting up organizational structure and work assignments; (6) staffing the agency; (7) supervising and controlling personnel and finances; (8) recording and accounting; and (9) supplying financial resources.[3] The first four functions may be characterized as "enterprise determination," the other five as "enterprise execution." [4]

(1) Fact-finding depends upon the social agency's program and objectives which, in turn, are determined by whether the agency is a public institution or a private organization. Fact-finding requires research of the social or health conditions which make the planned services of the agency necessary. In case of a public agency, the results of the research findings are submitted to the legislative body which decides about the action to be taken (for instance, the establishment of a child guidance clinic by the county board of supervisors). A private social agency might be set up when the results of the preceding research are presented to a community welfare council or to a group of interested citizens (for instance, proving the need for the foundation of an adoption agency for children of minority groups).

(2) An analysis of the social problems which the agency serves permits it to make an estimate of the type and number of services that will be needed, and to evaluate the trends for the future, based upon statistical data of previous experiences.

(3) After the agency makes a diagnosis of present social needs, it must make a decision on which alternative course of action to follow, considering its resources, both personal and financial, as well as deciding how it can make the most constructive use of personnel and equipment.

---

[3] John C. Kidneigh, "Administration of Social Agencies," *Social Work Year Book* (1957), pp. 76-78; Spencer, *op. cit.,* pp. 26-32; and, Walter Friedlander, *Concepts and Methods of Social Work* (Englewood Cliffs, N. J.: Prentice-Hall, Inc., 1958), pp. 288-292.

[4] William Brownrigg, *The Human Enterprise Process and Its Administration* (University, Ala.: University of Alabama Press, 1954); Spencer, *op. cit.,* p. 26; Peter Drucker, *The Practice of Management* (New York: Harper, 1954); and, Herbert Simon, *Administrative Behavior* (New York: Macmillan, 1957).

(4) Planning and allocating resources is carried out, on the basis of the preceding choice of alternatives, while considering how the objectives of the social agency may best be realized. The immediate and long-range goals of the agency are clarified, and policies developed which direct the work of the agency in order to meet the changing needs of its clients.

(5) Setting up the organizational structure of the agency leads to a distribution of duties to the members of the staff with a clear definition of responsibilities concerning their work, delegation of authority, and supervision; a description of staff and line services, and the establishment of standardized operations. It includes the delegation of everyone's authority, so that each member of the staff knows exactly what his assignment and responsibilities are.

(6) Personnel administration determines policies on recruitment and employment in the agency, on tenure, promotions, salaries, vacations, and working conditions. A fair evaluation of the performance of the staff is necessary to ensure efficient service and good morale. Rules for retirement and dismissal, in-service-training, and grievance procedures are part of personnel administration.

(7) Control of the agency's operation secures the proper function of the organization and the attainment of its objectives. It requires coordination of the staff's activities, supervision, and regular communication, consultation services, staff conferences, and financial control measures.

(8) Recording and accounting for all essential activities and material expenses of the agency are necessary in order to provide a reliable analysis of its budgetary operations which have to be reported to its governing body and to the membership or legislative authority under which the social agency works. It allows for an evaluation of the efficiency of the operations and suggests possible improvements. It may be used for recommendations for modifications of the social policy of the agency.

(9) The mobilization of the financial resources of the agency depends upon its nature and structure. In public agencies, the administration of the budget requires negotiations for the allocation of funds with the Federal, state, or local government; in private welfare organizations, money from special campaigns or

the Community Chest is relied upon for funds. Budget controls guarantee that the money received is spent economically and in accordance with the policies and rules of the agency. Budgeting also describes the allocation of the funds available to the branches and divisions of the agency so that each of them can operate most effectively.

B. Organizational Structure

The structure of public social agencies is part of the Federal, state, or local government setup. The organization, as a rule, is determined by law or statute as well as by the size of the population and the territory served by the social agency. The legislative body influences the organization, personnel, and content of services by appropriating or withholding funds for the operation of the agency. In private social agencies, either the members or a board of directors exercise the power of ultimate control.

Usually, the governing board of a public or private welfare agency is a commission, such as the board of a state public welfare department, a county welfare commission, or the board of directors of a voluntary family welfare agency. Sometimes a single administrator replaces the governing board. He may be supported by an advisory board. In private agencies, the board of directors usually is composed of lay persons. The board and its committees decide upon policies, support the mobilization of the necessary resources, and assist in public relations.

The *executive* is the chief administrative officer of the agency. Usually, he is appointed by the board or by another authority, such as the governor of the state, the county board of supervisors, or the city council. He is responsible for the management of the agency and for carrying into effect the program and the policies of the agency that are adopted by the board or by statute. The executive represents the authority of the governing board, but, as the chief of the staff, he also maintains the interrelation between the board and the personnel of the agency. The executive is responsible for presenting to the board all essential information so that it can decide upon realistic policies.

As the head of the staff, the executive carries the following responsibilities. In personnel management, he must recruit, promote, and dismiss staff members, following the general personnel policy established by the governing body of the agency. Authority of the executive concerning personnel matters should be exercised in cooperation with the staff. The executive remains the final authority in cases where differences arise, and in the judgment of discipline and competence. He is responsible for carrying out clearly the outlined personnel policies and for the procedure to be followed in handling grievances. The executive decides on staff coordination, assignments, and staff development. He is responsible for delegating authority to the members of the staff in connection with assigning duties, leaving sufficient freedom for all of them to exercise their initiative and ingenuity. The executive interprets board policies, community realities, and professional knowledge to the staff and enables its members to participate in advance studies, institutes, and community activities. Communication between the executive and the staff is essential. The members of the staff should have the opportunity to present their experiences, observations, and recommendations in personal contact and at staff meetings to supervisors and to the executive, or, on special occasions, to the board of directors.[5]

The executive is responsible for the establishment of subdivisions of the social agency, such as departments and district or branch offices, and for coordination and cooperation among divisions. It is also his duty to distribute the agency's functions into line, staff (executive and policy functions), and auxiliary services.

The *staff* (personnel) varies according to the nature and size of the agency. In larger agencies, the staff consists of one or more assistant directors, supervisors, social workers, clerical and maintenance workers, and sometimes other professional personnel, such as physicians, nurses, accountants, lawyers, teachers, psychologists, and home economists. In some social agencies, volunteers are engaged in various activities.

Another element of the agency's organization is the management of offices, buildings, or institutions, procurement, storage, and issuance of supplies. This is particularly important when residential facilities, such as a children's home, a settlement house, a senior

---

[5] Kidneigh, *op. cit.,* pp. 81-82; Robert Dubin, *Human Relations in Administration* (Englewood Cliffs, N. J.: Prentice-Hall, Inc., 1957), pp. 199-211; and, Harleigh B. Trecker, *Group Process in Administration* (New York: Woman's Press, 1950).

citizens' residence, or a correctional institution have to be maintained. Here the proper management of recreational buildings and community centers is essential. Location and equipment of the agency should meet the needs of the people who use its services.

C. Personnel Administration

Competent, reliable, conscientious personnel is the most important factor in social agency administration as it is in other professional services, medicine, nursing, law, and teaching.[6] Only a well-trained staff of adequate size can perform social services as required for the welfare of the people. In this sense "adequate staff" means "economy," because too few or untrained workers cannot perform qualified social work which is necessary to achieve the social agency's objectives. Personnel policy of the social agency demands three basic elements: (1) clearly formulated, written standards of employment for specific positions, based upon competence; (2) provisions for fair-dealing on grievances; and (3) delegation of final authority to the executive in dealing with matters of competence and discipline.

1. *Appointment of Personnel.* For a long time, in public and private social agencies, personnel was employed without legal requirements and without specific qualifications. Frequently, appointments were based upon private connections with influential people, family relations, favoritism, or upon political affiliations. In 1829, President Jackson established political patronage, the so-called "spoils system" under the title of "administrative reform" as a practice of rotation-in-office. This type of unregulated appointment was used in Federal, state, and local government for over fifty years. It was only after the assassination of President Garfield by a rejected applicant for public office, in 1881, that the *Pendleton Act of 1883* changed the spoils system. It created the United States Civil Service Commission composed of three members appointed by the President. Not more than two members of the Commission may belong to the same party. The selection of Federal employees was to be made upon the basis of open competitive examinations. The Pendleton Act estab-

---

[6] R. Clyde White, *Administration of Public Welfare* (New York: American Book, 1950), p. 327; and, Elwood Street, *A Handbook for Social Agency Administration* (New York: Harper, 1947), pp. 210-212.

lished the fundament of *civil service* for the Federal government. Many states and municipalities also enacted civil service systems, but some of them neglected to provide the necessary funds for proper administration.

The main responsibilities of the Civil Service Administration are: classification of positions, establishment of qualifications and of rates of compensation, recruitment of applicants, and preparation and evaluation of examinations. The job classification determines the requirements (age, education, and experience) that must be fulfilled to take the examination. Qualifications are higher for jobs requiring independent work and supervisory responsibility. In social welfare, it is important that supervisors and persons in responsible positions complete two years of graduate studies at a recognized school of social work.

2. *Merit Systems.* Merit systems in personnel practice are designed to promote efficiency through a systematic selection of the best available staff, removing the incompetent and promoting the outstanding. The *Amendment* of the *Social Security Act of 1939* required the introduction of an approved merit system for personnel as a condition for receiving Federal grants-in-aid, and all states complied with this request. The Federal standards require the states to adopt open, competitive examinations as a basis for employment in order to give qualified persons a fair and equal opportunity for an appointment, and to administer a job classification and equitable pay plan. Under the Hatch Act and many state laws, public employees are barred from participating in political activities. Discrimination because of religious, racial, and political affiliations is prohibited. Promotions are based upon length of service and capacity. Where no Civil Service Commissions operate, state merit councils are organized to administer the system.

Under many state merit systems, the state department of public welfare is authorized to determine the qualifications of candidates to be appointed in its administration and in county and city welfare agencies. Frequently a *joint state merit system* is organized, which selects employees for public assistance, child welfare services, public health services, and unemployment insurance administration.

State merit systems have contributed to the employment of competent personnel, have reduced political interference and personal favoritism in social welfare appointments, and have slightly improved the high turnover of staffs, inadequate standards of personnel, substandard compensation, and unfair treatment of personnel.[7] They should encourage education and training of applicants and enable public welfare agencies to adopt good standards of work, salary, and promotions. Above all, merit systems should develop a professional attitude and a spirit of devoted service in welfare administration which is of decisive importance for the public.

Specified examinations are given for certain civil service positions and promotions to secure the recruitment of the best qualified candidates. Some state and local positions, however, are open only to candidates who have lived a certain period (usually one year) in the state or county, and some even limit positions to persons born in the county or city. It is obvious that such requirements are inconsistent with the goal of civil service selection.[8]

Civil service examinations take into consideration education and occupational experience, and consist of written and oral tests which are graded and scored. For positions that require professional skills, graduate education should be a minimum qualification. In practice, there has been a tendency to consider experience as a substitute for graduate education in social work; however, this is incompatible with the professional character of social work.

For leading positions, "unassembled examinations," which set high requirements for experience in responsible assignments, and permit the Civil Service Commission an individual treatment of the candidates, are often preferred.

After civil service examinations are completed, all candidates who passed are "certified" for a given position and arranged in the *Eligible List* in order of their grades. For each position a special eligible list is set up which, according to law, may expire within a certain period, usually two years. Veterans and incumbents may have preferential

---

[7] Marietta Stevenson, *Public Welfare Administration,* (New York: Macmillan, 1938), pp. 326-332; National Resources Planning Board, *Security, Work, and Relief Policies* (Washington: Government Printing Office, 1942), p. 539; and, Louise N. Mumm, "The Personnel of Social Welfare," *Social Work Year Book* (1960), pp. 416-426.

[8] William Brownrigg and Louis F. Kroeger, *Toward Effective Recruiting,* Pamphlet No. 7 (Chicago: Civil Service Assembly of the United States and Canada, 1937), p. 3; and, Harold Silver, "Personnel Standards and Practices," *Social Work Year Book* (1960), pp. 426-432.

rights, and disabled veterans in some instances are placed on the top of the eligible lists, if they pass, with the assistance of their priority treatment. The appointing officer sometimes has to select the person at the top of the list. More frequently, however, he may select one of the first three on the list. Usually, appointments are made for a probationary period, during which time the candidate may be dismissed. In the case of dismissal, the candidate may ask the Civil Service Commission to restore him to the eligible list, but he may not be re-certified to the same agency from which he was discharged.

If a new civil service system is introduced, temporary employees will be appointed and examinations will be given after a certain period. Sometimes, incumbents might be "blanketed in," and will not be required to take the regular examination; this method, as well as preference for incumbents, defeats the principle of appointment according to ability.

3. *Salaries and Tenure.* Under civil service and merit systems, compensations are set up in proportion to the requirements for the positions. The positions are classified, as a rule, as clerical, professional, and administrative. In each class, the compensation scale aims to attract competent personnel. In many agencies, the clerical salaries of certain employees are higher than those of some professional workers, but some professional salaries may exceed those of administrative positions.

Typical salaries in private and public social agencies, in 1959, for caseworkers ranged from $4500 to $6500, up to a maximum of $5700 to $8000. Social group workers were paid from $4500 to $6200 up to a maximum of $7000. Senior caseworkers were offered salaries between $6100 to $8000. Casework supervisors were paid a beginning compensation of $5000 to $6900 up to a maximum $7260. Medical social workers' salaries began at from $4600 to $5000 up to a maximum of $5900 to $7500. Psychiatric social workers' beginning salaries were between $4300 and $7500 with a maximum of $6000 to $9145. Executive positions ranged from $5250 to $7500 up to salaries of $10,000 and more a year.[9]

One of the characteristics of the spoils system was the uncertainty about length of service. Under the merit system, however, an

[9] National Association of Social Workers, *Personnel Information* (July 1959), pp. 1-14; and, William B. Tollen, *Study of Staff Losses in Child Welfare and Family Service Agencies* (Washington: U.S. Children's Bureau, 1959).

employee may be dismissed only "for cause." He is entitled to defend himself against charges and to be heard before an impartial referee, a commission, or a board. For example, the *California State Civil Service Act of 1936* permits the removal of a civil service employee for incompetency, inefficiency, insubordination, dishonesty, intemperance, immorality, profanity, discourteous treatment of the public or other employees, improper political activity, willful disobedience, violation of the Civil Service Act, or of the rules and regulations of the State Personnel Board, for any other failure of good behavior or other acts which are incompatible with, or inimical to, the public service.[10]

Tenure requires that an employee be entitled to appeal to an impartial body when he is dismissed, regardless of the cause. The hearing must permit presentation of evidence and careful consideration and decision by the appeal body with some formal procedure, although no court routine is necessary.

However, tenure should not result in the retention of uninterested, mediocre, inefficient employees. This practice has caused severe criticism of bureaucracy. When reductions in staff because of budget cuts or of legislative changes make separations necessary, seniority alone should not be the decisive factor, but the agency should, rather, retain the employees who are most efficient and best qualified for the job.

4. *Promotion.* To encourage young people to go into public welfare service there must be opportunity for advancement. Promotions should not be based exclusively upon seniority, but also on the service record. This record should evaluate, from an accurate analysis, the specific qualities of the employee's performance. Promotions may also require special examinations. The agency should have an opportunity to hire exceptionally good persons from outside. If there is no competition from outsiders, a close bureaucracy is in danger of becoming self-sufficient, uncritical, indifferent to public opinion, and apathetic in its service to clients. Public welfare personnel should not be recruited solely for the lowest positions and should not be promoted exclusively through the ranks.

5. *Staff Development. In-service-training* serves as an orientation for a new employee to the organization, the technical set-up, the rou-

---

[10] *The Law Governing Civil Service in California* (Sacramento: 1936), p. 19.

tine work, and rules and procedures of the agency. It aims at refreshing the skill and knowledge of the staff with regard to methods of work, new developments, changes in legislation and policy, and new professional points of view. However, it is no substitute for education for social welfare.

In-service-training is carried on at regular staff meetings, either for the entire staff or certain groups of workers or by special courses or at institutes. Institutes should require serious study and permit staff preparation and follow-up conferences. Study courses usually continue over a longer period and should encourage active and critical participation of the staff members.

Staff development intends to improve the capacity and effective work of public welfare personnel. It uses in-service-training and *supervision* as its principal means, but also educational leaves to attend graduate schools, institutes, and conferences. It seeks to secure continued professional growth of all staff members and to strengthen their skill and interest in performing the best possible service for the public. Staff development leads to an improvement of the quality of work performed in the social agency.

Private social agencies do not have to use civil service or merit systems. They establish their own employment practices, which are approved by their governing boards. In most private agencies, personnel standards are equal to or even higher than public service standards. Frequently, standards of recruitment and personnel practice are developed under the auspices of national organizations in which the individual agencies hold membership, such as the Family Service Association of America, and the Child Welfare League of America.

D. Budget and Finance

The financial resources of public welfare agencies are mainly derived from taxes, those of private social agencies from allocations of the local Community Chest, from membership contributions, and from individual donations and bequests.

In order to determine the necessary resources of a social agency, a budget is prepared. This is an estimate of the expenditure required to carry on the services of the agency. The budget contains a detailed analysis of the services of the agency, of expenditures for aid to clients, for personnel who render services, and expenditures for office management, buildings, repair, replacement, or expansion when the services of the agency make such expenses necessary.

In a public welfare agency, the budget serves three functions: (1) it is a financial plan of operations for the next fiscal year (sometimes for two years); (2) it serves as a means of obtaining the necessary funds from the legislature (state assembly, county board of supervisors, and so on); and (3) it renders the basis for control of financial transactions.

In preparing the budget, the agency presents the data for the expenditures of the current year and frequently of preceding years, organized according to the major items of the budget to show the statistical trends.[11]

Public welfare is mainly paid for within the general budget of government agencies by three classes of taxes: (1) property taxes; (2) excise taxes; and (3) income taxes.

(1) *Property taxes* have been, for a long period, the main financial resource of local government, towns, cities, and counties. Property taxes are levied primarily on real estate, buildings, land, and personal property, such as stocks, bonds, and mortgages (liens). Regular household goods and clothes usually are exempt. Property taxes are often classified according to levels of assessed value. For local welfare expenditures property taxes are the primary financial resources, especially where the full burden of general assistance is carried by counties or cities.

(2) *Excise taxes* are domestic taxes on consumption, mainly sales taxes, which are paid directly by the consumer. They include taxes on liquor, tobacco, cigarettes, cosmetics, and theatre and sports tickets. In several states there is a general sales tax which provides part of the revenue for the welfare expenditures of the state.

(3) *Income taxes* are levied primarily on net income of individuals and corporations. They are graduated so that individuals and corporations in higher income brackets pay a higher tax. Because of certain deductions and exemptions, the lowest income group frequently is not taxed. Income taxes provide funds for the Federal and

---

[11] Wayne McMillen, "Financing of Social Welfare Services," *Social Work Year Book* (1957), pp. 260-267.

state governments and finance Federal and state welfare expenditures.

In addition to these three main classes there are other taxes and fees, on deeds and mortgages, that do not play a major role as resources for welfare budgets.[12]

A social worker in a public welfare agency should be well acquainted with the tax structure and the means of raising the resources for the administration of the welfare services in his community and state. He must have an understanding of the reactions of the population toward taxes to be able to discuss intelligently the social and economic factors involved and to interpret the social effects of the agency's services.

E. Trends in Social Welfare Administration

Social workers are showing an increasing interest in welfare administration. This interest is based upon recognition of the fact that welfare administration is a vital element in the quality of services rendered by social agencies and that effective leadership in social agencies under public and private auspices requires full understanding of, and experience in, social work. Social agency administration is beginning to be identified with social work.

Schools of social work are assuming responsibility for teaching social welfare administration and integrating the knowledge of this topic with skills in community organization, casework, and group work. Knowledge of social welfare administration embodies the understanding of: (a) relationship principles applying to individuals and groups, (b) the totality of the process of social agency administration, (c) the program characteristics of social agencies, and (d) advanced skills required for executive and sub-executive positions.[13]

---

[12] For a more detailed analysis of taxation and public welfare revenues, see R. C. White, *op. cit.,* pp. 393-414; Alfred G. Buehler, *Public Finance* (New York: McGraw, 1936), pp. 219-225; and, Ida C. Merriam, "Financing Social Welfare Services," *Social Work Year Book* (1960), pp. 269-272.

[13] John C. Kidneigh, "Social Work Administration: An Area of Social Work Practice?" *Social Work Journal,* Vol. 31, No. 2 (April 1950), pp. 57-61, 79; Eveline M. Burns, "The Role of Government in Social Welfare," *Social Work Journal,* Vol. 35, No. 3 (July 1954), pp. 95-102, 124-125; and, Sue Spencer, *op. cit.,* pp. 33-52.

Theoretical formulations and practical principles of social welfare administration need further clarification and scientific analysis. The interest of social workers seems to go beyond the questions of external organization and structure of agencies to an exploration of the dynamics of effective social welfare administration.

The responsibility for the administration of public welfare functions in our country rests primarily with the states, counties, and cities. The Federal government aids state and local governments in providing the funds for adequate welfare services, in equalizing the financial base for public welfare so that the poorer states carry on satisfactory programs, and in developing national standards and goals.

Personnel in social welfare is being selected, promoted, and retained increasingly on a basis of merit both in public and private agencies. Workers in social welfare administration are qualified by professional education and social work skills, by their human convictions, and by a sense of responsibility toward the clients and toward those who finance welfare services.

In personnel administration, progress is evident in greater job security, sometimes in collective bargaining agreements with unions in social work or as part of civil service and merit rating systems. The increasing number of retirement annuity provisions in public welfare agencies and the partial inclusion of social workers on a voluntary basis in Federal old-age and survivors' insurance are signs of this trend. The National Health and Welfare Retirement Association also has developed private retirement plans for the security of social workers.

Social workers are becoming increasingly aware that public welfare owes to the people and to its representatives a full account of the purposes, policies, methods of operation, and a breakdown of the expenditures. However, such information must protect the privacy of individuals who receive public welfare services.

The development of higher standards of social agency administration is being furthered by national, state, and local agencies of both public and private character, and by constructive teamwork with members of other professional disciplines.

Public welfare has assumed the responsibility for promoting research. Social research is designed also to improve the quality and the effect of social welfare administration, and to help to alleviate or prevent conditions which result in the need for social services.[14]

II. SOCIAL WELFARE RESEARCH

Research in social work is the critical inquiry into and the scientific testing of the validity of social work organization, function, and methods in order to verify, generalize, and extend social work knowledge, skill, concepts and theory.

With the growth of social welfare services organized by both government and private societies, with increasing numbers of persons benefiting from these services, and because of the greater number of workers being employed in these agencies, questions are being raised about the efficiency and cost of the methods of social welfare. Professional social workers showed serious interest in the development of social work research, but there is still, among rank-and-file workers, some hesitation because of the time consumed for research investigation and because of doubts over whether or not it would produce tangible results.

At the 1948 National Conference of Social Work, Professor Philip Klein suggested five types of social research studies: (1) to establish, identify, and measure the need for social service; (2) to measure the services offered; (3) to test, gauge, and evaluate results of social work operation; (4) to test the efficacy of specific social work techniques; and (5) to develop a methodology of social work research.[15]

Professional organizations of social work, the schools of social work, and public and private welfare organizations have recently shown the desire to provide reliable data in order to carry on the necessary research studies and to overcome the reluctance of agencies

---

[14] "Essentials of Public Welfare," A Statement of Principles Prepared by the Welfare Policy Committee of the American Public Welfare Association, *Public Welfare,* Vol. II, No. 1 (January 1953), pp. 5-6; and, Corinne H. Wolfe, *Competent Staff, A Responsibility of Public Welfare Administration* (Chicago: American Public Welfare Association, 1959).

[15] Philip Klein and Ida E. Merriam, *The Contribution of Research to Social Work* (New York: American Association of Social Workers, 1948); William E. Gordon, "Social Work Research in the Future" (Charles I. Schottland, *et al.,* editors), *Community Organization 1958* (New York: Columbia University Press, 1958), pp. 109-124; and, Mary E. Macdonald, "Research in Social Work," *Social Work Year Book* (1960), pp. 507-517.

and individuals to support research. There is an increasing number of research workers in Federal agencies, state departments of social welfare, in many national and regional private organizations, universities, and in advanced public and voluntary agencies.

Social surveys are conducted in order to explore the social needs of the population, how adequately these needs are met, and, if they are not being met, what changes are necessary in order to do so. The first major social research project of comprehensive nature in the United States was the Pittsburgh Survey directed by Paul U. Kellogg, in 1909, financed by the Russell Sage Foundation, which was followed up later by Philip Klein and his associates.[16] Other investigations of health, housing, nutrition, and other social problems of various selected groups of the people, such as migratory workers, children and women in agriculture and in certain other industries, were conducted by Federal organizations, the Social Security Administration, the Children's Bureau, and the U.S. Department of Labor, and by councils of social agencies and community chests.

Social research (into the *adequacy of social services*) reflects the major social problems, as well as the measures taken to meet those needs of the changing historical scene: health and child welfare problems; mass unemployment; economic distress; special needs of the aged, the blind, the crippled, and other handicapped groups; the quest for social and economic security and recreation and leisure time activities. Topics of research have been the history and structure of social welfare systems, the changing principles applied in social work, statistical studies describing operations and cost of social welfare, the methods of social work education, and the professional characteristics of social work.

Social welfare research adapts its concepts from the related social sciences, particularly sociology and psychology, but it also needs to develop its own special tools. Among social science concepts, for instance, human need, cultural values, social stratification, social class, the satisfaction of human needs by social institutions, social process, and social role are important points to be considered. Other concepts of personality theory such as individual stress, situational

---

[16] Paul U. Kellogg (editor), *The Pittsburgh Survey* (New York: Russell Sage Foundation, 1909-1914); and, Philip Klein *et al., A Social Study of Pittsburgh: Community Problems and Social Services of Allegheny County* (New York: Columbia University Press, 1938).

change, personality adjustment, social problems caused by unmet needs, and milieu therapy are equally valuable for social welfare research, but all of these concepts require further clarification and refinement.[17]

Some of the research studies on the objectives of social welfare have covered the history, structure, and organization of welfare programs. Because the number of social agencies is increasing, people involved with legislation, fund-raising, budgeting, and public information desire statistical research in order to obtain uniform, comparable data on social welfare agencies.

Studies attempt to *test and to evaluate the results* of the operation of public and private social agencies and use records of these agencies or interviews to measure the accomplishments against social needs in the community. United Community Funds and Councils publish annually a list of local research projects that during recent years amounted to about two hundred studies.

As another new trend in social work research, studies of international character are being made. Stimulated by the statistical efforts of the U.S. Children's Bureau and of the United Nations Relief and Rehabilitation Administration (UNRRA), research studies abroad are being undertaken by the Economic and Social Council of the United Nations, the Department of Social Affairs of the United Nations Secretariat, the International Labor Organization (ILO), and the World Health Organization. The field of international comparative research has been stimulated by the International Conference of Social Work and by the World Congress of Mental Health. Research studies by social workers and students in foreign countries are encouraged by fellowships under the United Nations exchange program and in the United States through the Fulbright Act of 1946.

Research on social work skills in casework, group work, and community organization are the subjects recently considered for research. Statistical methods, in order to measure the efficacy of the casework process, were first applied by the Institute of Welfare Research of the Community Service Society of New York under John McVicker

---

[17] Henry S. Maas and Martin Wolins, "Concepts and Methods of Social Work Research," in Cora Kasius (editor), *New Directions in Social Work* (New York: Harper, 1954), pp. 215 ff.; and, Ann W. Shyne (editor), *Use of Judgments as Data in Social Work Research* (New York: National Association of Social Workers, 1959).

Hunt and his associates. As criteria for "movement in casework," changes in efficiency of the client, in disabling habits, in attitude or understanding, and in the environment are used. There is, among social workers, some question whether it might be possible to find criteria that could not only be rated but also really measured. Studies in related fields, in social group work, and community organization methods are also being conducted in greater numbers.

The study of *research methodology* in social work has found attention in professional associations and in the literature of social welfare. During the last years, social welfare research included social theory, diagnostic and therapy typologies, theory of measurement and sampling, interpretative theory, social work practice theory, operational research, exploration of new areas for social work practice, identification of relationships between clients, social groups, communities, and social workers, and the creation of continuity in empirical research.[18]

In the area of research methodology, community welfare studies have been carried out mainly with four orientations: (1) as general social surveys with the goal of orientating the public, using random samples of the population, in order to determine essential unmet social needs, (2) studies for the investigation and appraisal of the demand of the community for new health and social services, (3) social breakdown studies for the exploration of poverty, dependency, disease, delinquency, and crime, and the possibilities of preventing and correcting these social evils, and (4) studies with a standard setting orientation for the establishment of effective patterns of social adjustment and accurate evaluation of the effect of social services. Professor Henry Maas and Professor Martin Wolins, however, have shown that these methods are still deficient in their methodology and need further careful refinement and conceptualization to improve the reliability and accuracy of the findings and conclusions of social welfare research. For this reason, a new theoretical framework and an empirical evaluation of social welfare research will have to be developed.[19]

---

[18] Ernest Greenwood, "Social Science and Social Work: A Theory of Their Relationship," *Social Service Review,* Vol. 29, No. 1 (March 1955), pp. 20-33; and, Walter Friedlander, *et al., Concepts and Methods of Social Work* (Englewood Cliffs, N.J.: Prentice-Hall, Inc., 1958), pp. 292-294.

[19] Maas and Wolins, *op. cit.,* pp. 222-225, 233.

Social welfare research procedure does not follow definite or rigid rules of execution. But, typical research might follow this sequence:

(1) Selection of the research subject, as suggested by experience and data from social work practice established in the past by working with individuals, groups, or communities in order to define and formulate the social problem. The project aims to clarify the problem through application of social theory, or to systematize its various aspects.

(2) Formulation of hypotheses to clarify the problems selected for the research.

(3) Construction of a research design that is suited to test the validity of the hypotheses by empirical verification, or by rejection.

(4) Fact-finding through observations, interviews, and inquiries in order to obtain the data and facts that are required by the research design.

(5) Analysis of the collected facts and data in order to determine whether they logically support or refute the hypotheses of the project.

(6) Interpretation and evaluation of the findings and their conclusions; whether or not they present a convincing answer to the problem or whether they may serve as the basis for further research.[20]

III. SOCIAL ACTION

Social action is an individual, group, or community effort, within the framework of social work philosophy and practice, that aims to achieve social progress, to modify social policies, and to improve social legislation and health and welfare services.

Kenneth Pray defined social action as "the systematic, conscientious effort directly to influence the basic social conditions and policies

---

[20] Margaret Blenkner, et al., The Function and Practice of Research in Social Work (New York: Social Work Research Group, 1955), p. 6; Friedlander, et al., op. cit., pp. 294-295; John Frings et al., An Assessment of Social Case Recording (New York: Family Service Association of America, 1958); and, Dorothy F. Beck, "Potential Approaches to Research in the Family Service Field," Social Casework, Vol. XI, No. 7 (July 1959).

out of which arise the problems of social adjustment and maladjustment to which our services as social workers are addressed." [21]

Casework and group work, as their primary objective, help individuals and groups in their social adjustment. Social workers also
study social phenomena which cause general health and welfare
problems. As a result, they recognize the need for social change.
Their knowledge qualifies them to participate in social action in
cooperation with civic leaders and organizations, churches, city
planners, public health officers, and labor groups. Their special
competence is based upon their value orientation and sense of social
responsibility, their commitment to social progress, their awareness
of social problems and conditions and the possibilities of their solution, their training in objective observation, analysis and planning,
and their skill in organizing people for social progress.[22] For these
reasons, social action is an essential part of professional social work
and is the responsibility of every social worker.

There are theoretical questions whether or not social action should
be classified as a separate process of social work,[23] but there is no
doubt that social workers need to feel responsible for their participation in social action. Essential elements of social action are that
group action is necessary, though the initiative may be taken by one
or a few individuals; the movement must be concerted; the movement should attempt to achieve social changes in the interest of the
people; and the action should be taken in accordance with law.

Social action involves influencing public opinion through information or educational publicity. The promotion of social legislation by
pressure upon the legislators is another form of social action. A
typical form of social action is the "legislative council," an organization formed by representatives of various civic and church groups,
labor unions, and social workers. These councils serve as a clearing
house for all groups concerned with social legislation, and they organize citizens and organizations for the support of essential measures
of social legislation. The public, as well as social workers, often

---

21 Kenneth Pray, "Social Work and Social Action," *National Conference of
Social Work, Proceedings 1945,* p. 346; and, Eveline M. Burns, "Social Action
and the Professional Social Worker," *The Compass* (May 1947), pp. 37-40.
22 Sanford Solender, "Social Action," *Social Work Year Book* (1957), pp.
517-519; and, Elizabeth Wickenden, "Social Action," *ibid.* (1960), pp. 529-535.
23 Harry L. Lurie, "Social Action—A Motive Force in Democracy," *Natio-
Conference of Social Work Proceedings* (1941), pp. 631-641.

fear social action because they are afraid that "radicals" or "communists" might be pulling the wires. In fact, however, such social reform movements frequently have been begun by rather conservative groups.

The aims of social action include social advance in the practice or interpretation of social work and improvement of conditions of child and woman labor, housing, and slum clearance. It attempts, through social change, to prevent social maladjustment, illness, and social disorganization. At the same time, it is concerned for the well-being, the self-respect, and the dignity of the individual as are casework and group work.

Social workers have, for a long time, considered participation in social action to be one of their professional duties because they have intimate knowledge of those social conditions which require reform. Many social workers have been pioneers in social action in the period of social reform and during the Depression (1930 to 1935). Social workers as a profession have been frequently accused of not exercising the influence in social policy and social reform which could be expected from them on the basis of their experiences, because they are exclusively interested in individualized treatment.[24] Social workers who are actively engaged in social action, on the other hand, have been criticized for confusing their civic and professional obligations.

These criticisms suggest that a careful rethinking of the social worker's role in social action and social reform, based upon his experiences and his professional philosophy and responsibility, is necessary.

Selected Bibliography

A. Social Welfare Administration

Appleby, Paul H., *Policy and Administration*. University, Ala.: University of Alabama Press, 1949.

---

[24] Charles I. Schottland, "Social Work Issues in the Political Arena," *Social Welfare Forum* (1953), pp. 20-21; Mary Antoinette Cannon, "Guiding Motives in Social Work," in Cora Kasius (editor), *op. cit.*, pp. 27-29; and, Eveline Burns, "Social Welfare is Our Commitment," *Social Welfare Forum* (1958), pp. 3-19.

*Atwater, Pierce, *Problems of Administration in Social Work.* Minneapolis: University of Minnesota Press, 1940.

Baker, Helen, and Mary S. Routzahn, *How to Interpret Social Welfare.* New York: Russell Sage Foundation, 1946.

*Barnard, Chester I., *The Function of the Executive.* Cambridge: Harvard University Press, 1950.

Blau, Peter M., *The Dynamics of Bureaucracy.* Chicago: University of Chicago Press, 1955.

————, *Bureaucracy in Modern Society.* New York: Random, 1956.

Blumenthal, Louis H., *Administration of Group Work.* New York: Association Press, 1948.

Breckinridge, Sophonisba P., *Public Welfare Administration in the United States, Select Documents,* 2nd ed. Chicago: University of Chicago Press, 1938.

Brownrigg, William, *The Human Enterprise Process and Its Administration.* University, Ala.: University of Alabama Press, 1954.

Burling, Temple, *et al., Give and Take in Hospitals.* New York: Putnam, 1956.

Cohen, Wilbur J., and Fedele F. Fauri, *The Objectives of Public Welfare Administration.* Chicago: American Public Welfare Association, 1958.

*Cohn, Martin, and Elizabeth Wallace, *Some Problems of Administration in Social Work.* Toronto: University of Toronto Press, 1944.

*de Schweinitz, Karl, *People and Process in Social Security.* Washington, D.C.: American Council on Education, 1948.

Dimock, Marshall E., *The Executive in Action.* New York: Harper, 1945.

Dimock, Marshall E., and Gladys O. Dimock, *Public Administration.* New York: Rinehart, 1953.

Drucker, Peter F., *Practice of Management.* New York: Harper, 1954.

*Dubin, Robert, *Human Relations in Administration.* Englewood Cliffs, N.J.: Prentice-Hall, Inc., 1957.

Follett, Mary P., *Dynamic Administration: Collected Papers.* New York: Harper, 1942.

Francis, Roy G., and Robert C. Stone, *Service and Procedure in Bureaucracy.* Minneapolis: University of Minnesota Press, 1956.

Gardiner, Robert K., and Helen O. Judd, *The Development of Social Administration.* London: Oxford University Press, 1954.

*Gulick, Luther, and Lyndall Urwick (editors), *Papers on the Science of Administration.* New York: Institute of Public Administration, Columbia University, 1937.

*Hanchette, Helen W., *et al.*, *Some Dynamics of Social Agency Administration*. New York: Family Service Association of America, 1946.

Hunter, Floyd, *Community Power Structure—A Study of Decision Makers*. Chapel Hill, N.C.: University of North Carolina Press, 1953.

Johns, Ray, *Executive Responsibility*. New York: Association Press, 1954.

*Johnson, Arlien, "The Administrative Process in Social Work," *National Conference of Social Work, Proceedings* (1946), pp. 249-258.

Keith-Lucas, Alan, *Decisions About People in Need*. Chapel Hill, N. C.: University of North Carolina Press, 1957.

*Kidneigh, John C., "Social Work Administration; An Area of Social Work Practice," *Social Work Journal*, Vol. 31, No. 2 (April 1950), pp. 57-61, 79.

*———, "The Quest for Competence in Welfare Administration," *Social Service Review*, Vol. 24, No. 2 (June 1950), pp. 173-180.

———, "Simplification in Administration—A Point of View," *Social Service Review*, Vol. 28, No. 2 (June 1954), pp. 137-145.

*———, "Administration of Social Agencies," *Social Work Year Book* (1957), pp. 75-82.

King, Clarence, *Social Agency Boards*. New York: Harper, 1938.

Leirfallom, Jarl, and Russell P. Drake, *Organization and Administration of Local Public Welfare Services*. Chicago: American Public Welfare Association, 1943.

*Lepawsky, Albert, *The Art and Science of Organization and Management*. New York: Knopf, 1949.

McLean, F. H., and Ralph Ormsby, *Organizing a Family Agency*. New York: Family Welfare Association of America (now Family Service Association of America), 1944.

Marcus, Grace F., *The Nature of Service in Public Assistance Administration*, Public Assistance Report No. 10. Washington, D.C.: Social Security Administration, 1946.

Martz, Helen E., *Citizen Participation in Government; A Study of County Welfare Boards*. Washington: Public Affairs Press, 1948.

Miles, Arthur P., *An Introduction to Public Welfare*. Boston: Heath, 1949.

Morstein-Marx, Fritz (editor), *Elements of Public Administration*. Englewood Cliffs, N.J.: Prentice-Hall, Inc., 1946.

Mosher, W. E., and J. D. Kingsley, *Public Personnel Administration*, 3rd rev. ed. New York: Harper, 1950.

Moss, Celia R., *Administering a Hospital Social Service Department*. Washington: American Association of Medical Social Workers, 1955.

Pfiffner, John M., and Robert V. Presthus, *Public Administration.* New York: Ronald, 1953.

*Ross, Murray G., and Charles E. Hendry, *New Understandings of Leadership.* New York: Association Press, 1957.

Routzahn, Evart G., and Mary S. Routzahn, *A Study in Public Relations.* New York: Russell Sage Foundation, 1943.

Sears, Jesse B., *The Nature of the Administrative Process.* New York: McGraw, 1950.

Shartle, Carroll L., *Executive Performance and Leadership.* Englewood Cliffs, N.J.: Prentice-Hall, Inc., 1956.

Simon, Herbert A., *et al., Determining Work Loads for Professional Staff in a Public Welfare Agency.* Berkeley: University of California Press, 1941.

*———, *Administrative Behavior.* New York: Macmillan, 1957.

*Stevenson, Marietta, *et al., Public Welfare Administration.* New York: Macmillan, 1938.

*Street, Elwood, *A Handbook for Social Agency Administration.* New York: Harper, 1947.

Tead, Ordway, *Democratic Administration.* New York: Association Press, 1945.

*Trecker, Harleigh B., *Group Process in Administration.* New York: Womans Press, 1946.

———, Frank Glick, and John C. Kidneigh, *Education for Social Work Administration.* New York: American Association of Social Workers, 1952.

Vasey, Wayne. *Government and Social Welfare.* Part III. New York: Holt, 1958.

White, Leonard D., *Introduction to the Study of Public Administration,* 3rd ed. New York: Macmillan, 1948.

*White, R. Clyde, *Administration of Public Welfare,* 2nd ed. New York: American Book, 1950.

White, William H., *The Organization Man.* New York: Simon & Schuster, 1956.

B. Social Welfare Research

Ackoff, Russell L., *The Design of Social Research.* Chicago: University of Chicago Press, 1953.

American Association of Schools of Social Work, *Research in Social Work.* New York: 1950.

Blenkner, Margaret, *et al., The Function and Practice of Research in Social Work.* New York: Social Work Research Group, 1955.

*Brown, Esther Lucile, *Use of Research by Professional Associations in Determining Program and Policy*. New York: Russell Sage Foundation, 1946.

*Chapin, F. Stuart, *Social Science Research; Its Expanding Horizons*. Minneapolis: University of Minnesota Press, 1953.

Cockerill, Eleanor E., Louis F. Lehrman, Patricia Sacks, and Isabel Stamm, *A Conceptual Framework for Social Casework*. Pittsburgh: University of Pittsburgh, 1953.

*French, David G., *An Approach to Measuring Results in Social Work*. New York: Columbia University Press, 1952.

Goode, William J., and Paul K. Hart, *Methods of Social Research*. New York: McGraw, 1952.

*————, *Toward Basic Research in Social Work*. St. Louis, Mo.: Washington University Press, 1951.

Gordon, William E., "The Research Project: Its Educational Value and its Contribution to Social Work Knowledge," *Social Work Journal*, Vol. XXXI, No. 3 (July 1950), pp. 110-116.

————, "Social Work Research in the Future," in Charles I. Schottland (editor), *Community Organization 1958* (New York: Columbia University Press, 1958), pp. 104-124.

*Greenwood, Ernest, "Social Science and Social Work: A Theory of Their Relationships," *Social Service Review*, Vol. 29, No. 1 (March 1955), pp. 20-33.

*————, "Social Work Research: A Decade of Reappraisal," *Social Service Review*, Vol. 31, No. 3 (September 1957), pp. 311-320.

Herzog, Elizabeth, "An Approach to Family Agency Research," *The Social Welfare Forum 1952*, pp. 152-160.

————, *Some Guide Lines for Evaluative Research*. Washington: U. S. Children's Bureau, 1959.

Hoffman, Isaac L., *Toward A Logic for Social Work Research*. St. Paul, Minn.: Amherst H. Wilder, 1952.

Klein, Philip, and Ida E. Merriam, *The Contribution of Research to Social Work*. New York: American Association of Social Workers, 1948.

Lundberg, George A., *Social Research: A Study in Methods Gathering Data*. New York: Longmans, 1951.

Luszki, Margaret B., *Interdisciplinary Team Research: Methods and Problems*. New York: New York University Press, 1958.

*Macdonald, Mary E., "Research in Social Work," *Social Work Year Book* (1960), pp. 507-517.

McMillen, Wayne, *Statistical Methods for Social Workers*. Chicago: University of Chicago Press, 1952.

Maas, Henry S., and Edith Varon, "The Caseworker in Clinical and

Sociopsychological Research," *Social Service Review,* Vol. 23, No. 3 (September 1949), pp. 302-314.

*Maas, Henry S., and Martin Wolins, "Concepts and Methods of Social Work Research," in Cora Kasius (editor), *New Directions in Social Work.* New York: Harper, 1954, pp. 215-237.

*Morgan, John S., "Research in Social Work: A Frame of Reference," *Social Work Journal,* Vol. XXX, No. 4 (October 1949), pp. 148-154.

Queen, Stuart A., "Research and Social Work," *Social Service Review,* Vol. XXVI, No. 1 (March 1952), pp. 1-14.

Schwartz, Edward E., "Social Work Research," *Social Work Year Book 1952,* pp. 500-512.

*Towle, Charlotte, "Some Basic Principles of Social Research in Social Casework," *Social Service Review,* Vol. XXV, No. 1 (March 1951), pp. 66-80.

Turner, Ralph H., "Statistical Logic in Social Research," *Sociology and Social Research* (January-February 1948), pp. 697-704.

*Witmer, Helen L., "Basic Conceptions in Social Work Research," *Mental Hygiene,* Vol. 33 (January 1949), pp. 108-114.

*Young, Pauline V., *Scientific Social Surveys and Research: An Introduction to the Background, Content, Methods, and Analysis of Social Studies,* 3rd rev. ed., Englewood Cliffs, N.J.: Prentice-Hall, Inc., 1956.

C. Social Action

Altmeyer, Arthur J., "The Dynamics of Social Work," *Social Welfare Forum* (1955), pp. 98-111.

Benjamin, Paul, "Techniques of Social Action: Securing Social Legislation," *National Conference of Social Work, Proceedings* (1945), pp. 326-366.

*Bisno, Herbert, *The Philosophy of Social Work,* Chapter VI. Washington, D.C.: Public Affairs Press, 1952.

de Schweinitz, Karl, "Social Values and Social Action—The Intellectual Base," in Ernest Witte (editor), *Education for Social Work.* New York: Council on Social Work Education, 1956, pp. 55-68.

Dewey, John, *Liberalism and Social Action.* New York: Putnam, 1935.

*Eldridge, Seba, *The Dynamics of Social Action.* Washington: Public Affairs Press, 1952.

Greer, Thomas H., *American Social Reform Movements: Their Pattern Since 1865.* Englewood Cliffs, N.J.: Prentice-Hall, Inc., 1949.

*Howard, Donald S., "Social Work and Social Reform," in Cora Kasius (editor), *New Directions in Social Work.* New York: Harper, 1954, pp. 159-175.

King, Clarence, *Organizing for Community Action*. New York: Harper. 1948.

Leys, Wayne P. R., *Ethics for Policy Decisions*. Englewood Cliffs, N.J.: Prentice-Hall, Inc., 1952.

*Lurie, Harry L., "Social Action; A Motive Force in Democracy," *National Conference of Social Work, Proceedings* (1941), pp. 631-641.

Ohlin, Lloyd E., "The Development of Social Action Theories," in Ernest Witte (editor), *Education for Social Work, 1958*. New York: Council on Social Work Education, 1958, pp. 77-87.

Parsons, Talcott, *The Structure of Social Action*. Glencoe, Ill.: The Free Press, 1952.

Pray, Kenneth L. M., "Social Work and Social Action," *National Conference of Social Work, Proceedings* (1941), pp. 348-359.

Reid, Ira De A., *Minority Groups: Segregation and Integration*. New York: Columbia University Press, 1955.

*Schottland, Charles I., "Social Work Issues in the Political Arena," *Social Welfare Forum* (1953), pp. 18-33.

Solender, Sanford, "Social Action," *Social Work Year Book* (1957), pp. 517-525.

Trecker, Harleigh B. (editor), *Group Work—Foundations and Frontiers*. New York: Whiteside, 1955.

Wickenden, Elizabeth, *How To Influence Public Policy—A Short Manual on Social Action*. New York: American Association of Social Workers, 1954.

———, "Social Action," *Social Work Year Book* (1960), pp. 529-535.

*Youngdahl, Benjamin, "The Role of Social Agencies in Social Action," *Social Work Journal*, Vol. 33, No. 3 (July 1952), pp. 146-148.

III.

Social Welfare Programs and Practice

8.

Social Welfare Agencies:
General Patterns
of Community Services

ORGANIZATIONS THAT PROVIDE SOCIAL SERVICES may be classified into four main groups: (1) agencies designed primarily to give social services to clients, either as individuals or in groups (for example, social welfare departments, family and children's societies, adoption agencies, YWCA, YMCA, Girl Scouts, Boy Scouts); (2) organizations which offer social services as well as other services (for example, American Red Cross, settlement houses, recreation and park departments, International Institutes, Girls' Service Leagues, Salvation Army, Urban League); (3) organizations which are basically designed to offer other services, but which maintain an auxiliary department of social work (for example, hospitals, clinics, schools, juvenile courts, public housing authorities, vocational rehabilitation services, research foundations); and (4) organizations that are not rendering direct services to individuals or groups but are set up to assist other social agencies (for example, Community Welfare Councils, Community Chests).[1]

The structure of welfare organizations differs in those agencies

---

[1] Helen L. Witmer, *Social Work* (New York: Farrar & Rinehart, 1942), pp. 184-186 ff.; and, Harry M. Cassidy, *Social Security and Reconstruction in Canada* (Boston: Humphries, 1943), pp. 13-17. See also Ellen Winston, "Public Welfare," *Social Work Year Book* (1960), pp. 490-498.

established under public auspices from those which are of voluntary or private nature. Public agencies are based upon law or statute, administered within the framework of local, state, or Federal government, and financed by taxation. Private agencies are established by individuals or philanthropic, religious, fraternal, or humanitarian groups; their management is the responsibility of a board of directors, and they are supported mainly by contributions, donations, endowments, trust funds, and often by participation in the distributions of the Community Chest.

I. PUBLIC SOCIAL AGENCIES

Our historical survey has shown that government has gradually assumed the basic responsibility for the maintenance of the social welfare of the people. For a long time in the United States, this responsibility had been assumed by voluntary charitable organizations. But the Depression of the 1930's brought evidence that government could no longer avoid its fundamental obligation to protect the social welfare of the citizens. This change occurred on all three levels of government—local, state, and Federal.

The strength of public welfare agencies lies in their structure. They are established by law; they must provide designated services for all needy people (who are eligible according to legal conditions) and without discrimination against race, faith, and color.

Because public welfare agencies are government institutions, their programs and services need to be understood and appreciated by the public. Public welfare agencies need the approval and support of the citizens, because they depend upon legislation to appropriate the funds for their services and their administration.[2]

A. Local Public Welfare Agencies

The largest number of public social agencies operate on a county, city, and township basis. Their structure differs according to state and local statutes. Frequently, a county or city welfare department is directed by a board of commissioners or board of supervisors. In

---

[2] Wayne McMillen, *Community Organization for Social Welfare* (Chicago: University of Chicago Press, 1949), pp. 75-76; and, Wayne Vasey, *Government and Social Welfare* (New York: Holt, 1958).

rural counties, the elected officials sometimes administer public welfare services themselves, or they appoint a director or commissioner to be responsible for the administration. In other instances, a city or county welfare department may be managed by a board or a commission of lay citizens appointed by county or state officials; one or several members of the county board of commissioners or supervisors may be members and one of them chairman of the welfare board. This board appoints an executive and controls the operation of the public agency. Although the functions of the public welfare agencies differ widely, there is a trend to consolidate the various activities in one local welfare agency and to coordinate the different assistance and child welfare programs. Other local public agencies which deal with programs of influence to social welfare are the public health department, the board of education, the juvenile court, the park and recreation commission, the police department, the city planning commission, and the housing authority. An example of the organization of a typical public welfare department is presented in Chart 3.

B. State Departments of Public Welfare

Among the states, there are substantial differences in the organizational setup of their public welfare organization. The large majority of states has concentrated most, or all, of their public welfare programs in a single agency (department of public welfare, of social welfare, of social security).

As a rule, the state department of public welfare is administered by a board whose members are appointed by the governor, and by a "director" or "commissioner," who also is appointed by the governor. The majority of states leaves the immediate administration of general assistance (indigent aid), of the categorical public assistance programs, and of child welfare and health services to counties, cities, townships, and towns. Some states, however, have assumed the entire responsibility for the direct administration of these programs through local state offices. All state departments of public welfare are responsible for the administration of categorical public assistance and child welfare services for which they receive Federal grants-in-aid; but, in several states, the administration or the supervision of other state institutions, such as mental hospitals, training schools, schools for the blind and deaf, or correctional programs, probation, and

Chart 3.   *Organizational Structure of a Public Welfare Department.*

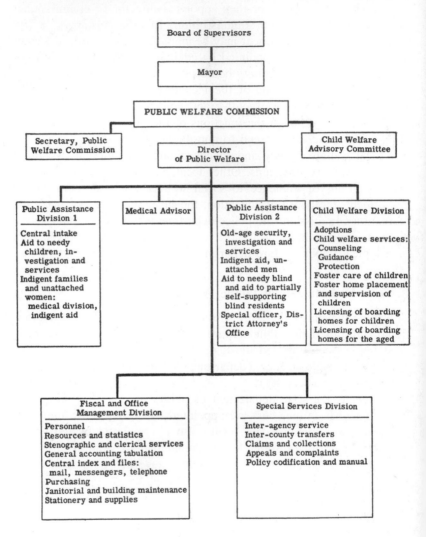

parole services, also falls under their jurisdiction. The question of
whether or not it is desirable to combine all public welfare services
under one single department depends upon the size and the population of the state, and the number of its institutions. We favor such
a coordination, but some students of public administration believe

Chart 4. *Organization of the California State Department of Social Welfare.*

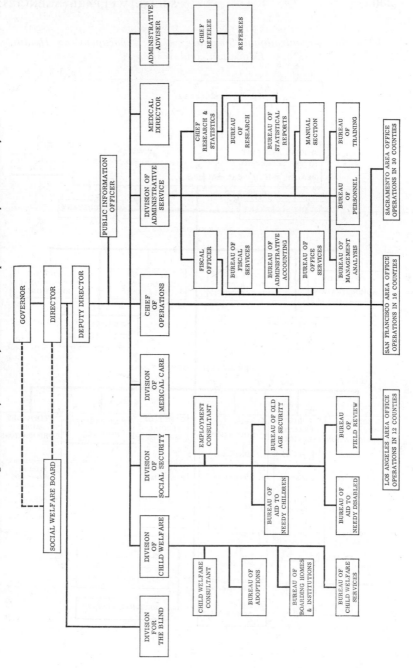

235

Chart 5. *Organizational Structure: U.S. Department of Health, Education, and Welfare.*

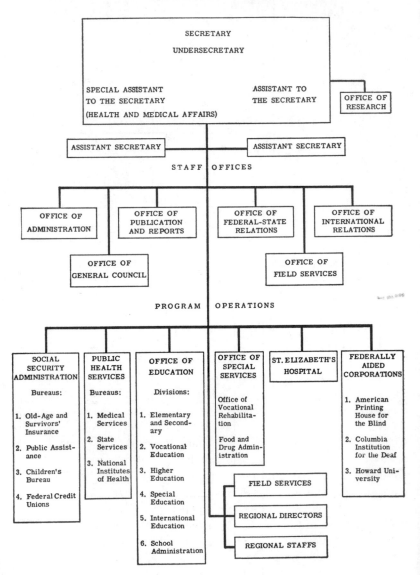

that in a large state such a department may be unwieldy. Delegation of authority to qualified division heads and the setup of area offices would secure effective administration (see Chart 4).

C. Federal Public Welfare Agencies

The main federal agency in the field of public welfare is the Department of Health, Education and Welfare. The Secretary of the Department has full Cabinet rank. An Undersecretary and two Assistant Secretaries of Health, Education and Welfare share with the Secretary the responsibility for the entire area of work, but another Special Assistant Secretary is in charge of health and medical affairs. As in the former Federal Security Agency, a Commissioner of Social Security, a Surgeon General, and a Commissioner of Education are the head executive officers of the three operating branches of the new Department. All these leading officials of the Department are appointed by the President with the confirmation of the Senate (see Chart 5).

Among the social welfare programs, only Old-Age and Survivors' Insurance is directly administered by the Department of Health, Education and Welfare. In other instances, the Federal government only approves state plans, establishes rules and standards (based upon Federal legislation), supervises the operation of the programs in the states, and shares the expenses of the operation by grants-in-aid according to statutory provisions.

There are, however, important phases of social services administered or supervised by other Federal agencies. The Veterans Administration, an independent organization under the President, administers veterans' services directly, throughout the country (see Chapter 15). The Department of Labor is in charge of the United States Employment Service and of the Bureau of Employment Security that cooperate with the states in the administration of employment services and unemployment compensation (see Chapter 9) and in the protection of child labor (see Chapter 11).

The Bureau of Indian Affairs, United States Department of the Interior, provides educational and medical services as well as land rehabilitation aid, hospitals, schools and clinics for Indians on the Reservations. Immigration and naturalization services for newcomers to our country are administered by the United States Department of Justice. The Women's Bureau of the United States Department of Labor conducts research and disseminates information on working conditions.

II. PRIVATE SOCIAL AGENCIES

Private or voluntary social agencies have been the pioneers in creating modern social services. In contrast to public social welfare departments, which serve all parts of the states, including the rural regions, private social agencies operate mainly in urban areas. Often, they also serve the territory which immediately surrounds the cities, but they are rare in remote rural communities. As we have seen, the Charity Organization Societies have helped to integrate and to improve the organization and working methods of private social agencies and the quality of services to the public, whether to individuals or to groups. The efficiency and the standards of private social agencies have been enhanced by the formation of national organizations of either sectarian or functional character, such as the National Lutheran Council, the National Council of the Protestant Episcopal Church, the Presbyterian Church, the National Conference of Catholic Charities, the National Catholic Welfare Conference, the National Conference of Jewish Communal Service, the Child Welfare League of America, the Family Service Association of America, the National Committee for Mental Hygiene, the National Travelers Aid Association, the National Board of the YWCA, the National Council of YMCA, and the Salvation Army. These national organizations, which are themselves members of the National Social Welfare Assembly as a coordinating body, assist their member agencies in planning, organizing, and budgeting; in the development of professional standards of work and personnel; and in research and participation in the total program of health and welfare services in their community. They share the experiences of other local and regional organizations with their member agencies through conferences, institutes, workshops, consultation, and field services.[3]

The foundation of private social agencies and the continuation of their activities is based upon the recognition of the need for this

---

[3] Leonard W. Mayo and Robert M. Webb, "National Organizations in Social Welfare," *Social Work Year Book* (1960), pp. 408-416.

service in the local community. Originally, philanthropists, a group of interested citizens, or a church society became aware of the need for some type of social service, such as a family welfare agency, a children's protective society, or an organization to aid unmarried mothers or crippled children. Currently, the social and health needs of the various groups of the population are considered by the Council of Social Agencies or Community Welfare Council. There is a careful investigation into what resources exist in the community and what institutions or facilities are missing before the establishment of a new social agency is encouraged and supported. But still, individuals or groups of citizens concerned with social and health conditions in the community may take the initiative, if they are able to secure the necessary moral and financial support, for a new enterprise in health and welfare work, such as a mental hygiene association or a vocational guidance clinic.

A. Nonsectarian Private Agencies

According to the variety of social and health needs, voluntary organizations have been organized to meet particular problems of family disorganization, juvenile delinquency and truancy, child and adult recreational needs, and diseases such as tuberculosis and poliomyelitis. They have also aided in caring for orphans and neglected children, crippled children, unwed mothers, and the aged and handicapped. As a rule, the interest of one, or a few persons, is the motivating factor for the establishment of such an organization. After funds have been donated or collected, a constitution and bylaws are usually set up which determine the goal and the place of operation of the agency. It may be incorporated according to statutory provisions of the state where it is organized. In general, the approval of the project is asked from the Community Welfare Council and the Community Chest if their support is expected.

The responsibility for the management of the agency is entrusted to a board of directors. It is usually composed of persons who had taken the initiative for the foundation of the organization or who had helped in gaining the financial support for it. Typical members of the board of directors are bankers, well-to-do businessmen, physicians, lawyers, a representative of the local welfare and health department, a member of the board of education, and one or two representatives of organized labor and consumers groups. The board also should represent, in a nonsectarian agency, the major religious groups in the community and the larger racial minorities. In most social agencies women form a substantial proportion of the board. It is important to include some women who represent influential women's organizations, such as the League of Women Voters, the Federation of University Women, the Junior League, and business women's clubs. Similarly, the board should have prominent members of men's service clubs and fraternal societies, such as the Masons, Rotary, Shriners, Kiwanis, Elks, American Legion, and Chamber of Commerce. The representation of these different groups in the community is essential in order to demonstrate to the public and the authorities the broad interest in the goals of the agency and to testify to its integrity and responsibility in carrying out its purpose. Agencies which receive part of their support from the annual drive of the Community Chest are under some obligation to have representatives of different economic levels on their board of directors that formulates the policies of the agency and controls its work and expenditures.

The board of directors appoints committees which take charge of different administrative functions, because the board usually limits its own tasks to the establishment of the general policy of the organization, the appointment of the executve, and the control of the total agency operation. The *executive committee* supervises the current activities and represents the board of directors during the time when the board is not in session. A *nominating committee* prepares suggestions for the election of new board members; sometimes it also proposes suitable persons for appointments as executive, assistant-director, legal counsel, medical consultant, or similar responsible positions in the agency in cooperation with the executive secretary or director.

The *financial or budget committee* controls the expenditures of the agency, prepares the budget for the approval of the executive committee and for the board of directors, and often develops plans for raising additional funds or enlisting bequests and donations for the agency. If the agency owns real estate property, such as a school, a hospital, or an administrative building, a *committee of buildings and maintenance* assists the executive in its management. Frequently, there are other *standing committees* on which members of the board, representatives of the professional staff, and lay persons of the community serve. They include a *committee on personnel practice,* which determines the salaries of the staff, recruitment, promotion and vacation policy, regulations and working conditions. By cooperating with newspapers, radio, television, and civic and religious societies in the community, a *public relations committee* informs the public about the activities of the agency. Some agencies, that provide services to children, families, unmarried mothers, and handicapped or aged people, have a *case committee* with which the professional staff discusses experiences, in particularly significant cases, in order to keep the board aware of the specific problems which the agency faces, of the methods and changing aspects of the professional work, and of the needs for innovations in policy or practice which seem necessary.

The task of interpreting the agency's work to the citizens is not limited to the committee on public relations; in fact, it is an essential function of all members of the board of directors, of the other committees, and of the entire staff of the agency. Because most private social agencies depend financially upon the current contributions to the Community Chest, continuous information should be given to the public about the necessity and the value of the agency's activities in order to convince the citizens that its services are needed and worthy of their contributions.

The immediate services of a social agency to individuals or to groups are under the control of the executive-director, appointed by the board of directors, and are carried out by the professional and clerical staff. The social work staff may need special assistance by other professional persons, such as a physician, psychiatrist, lawyer, dietitian or home economist, nurse, psychologist, an accountant, and engineer. In casework and recreation agencies of large size, territorial districts are set up under the direction of an assistant executive, and most of them employ one or more supervisors who have the responsibility of working with several caseworkers or group workers and helping them carry out their assignments. This practice of working under a supervisor, rather than as an independent professional practitioner such as a doctor, teacher, or lawyer, has its basis in several facts. The core of social work is the relation of the worker with human beings which is based upon subjective understanding, individual values, and moral judgments. The professional training in schools of social work provides the beginning worker with the basic

professional knowledge and skills, but the introduction of a supervisor in the practical process of operation of the specific agency is
still considered desirable. Even more indispensable is the skilled
supervision of workers without professional social work education,
hired under the so-called "apprenticeship method" of on-the-job
training.[4]

In contrast to public agencies, which according to statutory provision have to accept every client who meets the legal requirements
for eligibility, voluntary agencies are not under obligation to serve
every applicant. Social workers in private agencies have become
convinced that their work will be most effective if the persons who
come to the agency fully understand the conditions under which the
agency can serve them, what the nature and limitations of the services are, and if the applicant himself decides whether or not he
wishes to use these facilities. Where there is conflict between members
of a family, as in cases of marital discord, or neglect of, or cruelty
against children, social agencies attempt to find measures of protection which are acceptable to the other side; only as a last resort is
a court order asked for.

The possibility of the private social agency limiting its services to
special groups, such as to persons suffering from handicaps, particular diseases, or the psychological effects of racial discrimination,
enables the organization to offer intensive methods of aid and to
interpret the importance of its program to the public.

B. Sectarian Social Agencies

In the Colonial period of our country, religious charities played a
minor role in social welfare because the settlers brought over from
England the tradition of public parish poor relief. The parish, however, was often almost identical with its church. Thus, it was not
felt necessary to organize separate church charity activities. Not until
the nineteenth century were denominational charities founded by the
different religious congregations, primarily in order to care for
orphans and deserted children, but also to provide recreational and
educational activities for young people. In addition to welfare aims,

---

[4] H. Witmer, *op. cit.,* p. 190; Charlotte Towle, *Common Human Needs*
(Chicago: University of Chicago Press, 1945), pp. 95-122; and, Harold L.
Wilensky and Charles N. Lebeaux, *Industrial Society and Social Welfare*
(New York: Russell Sage Foundation, 1958), pp. 231-247.

these charities pursued those of culture, religion and education. Religious social agencies are usually supported as though they are non-sectarian voluntary welfare services through Community Chests. However, they also receive contributions, donations, and funds from their own membership, from churches, and from special campaigns since they often extend their charity work beyond the boundaries of the local community within the territory of a larger ecclesiastical unit, such as a bishopric, a diocese, or synod.

One type of sectarian social agency limits its services to the members of the founding denominational group as a part of an extension of its religious training and education. Another type offers welfare service to the entire community without this being thought of as part of the religious education program. However, the activities of the agency are still sectarian. A third type is the interdenominational agency serving more than one denomination and transcending the narrow concepts of sectarianism.

Protestant Social Work. As the dominant religious group in this country, Protestant churches have never been concerned about discrimination against their members by public institutions. Numerous humanitarian and philanthropic charities have been created and maintained by Protestants and their congregations. In addition to such services for the entire community, the individual Protestant denominations have established such religious charities as orphanages, hospitals, homes for the aged and handicapped, settlement houses, reform schools for boys and girls, and agencies for the aid of prisoners and their families, and destitute, runaway children. Some of these services were founded as expressions of religious concern for the fate of the underprivileged and needy and were not closely attached to a particular Protestant denomination; but often some contact with one or several church groups was maintained. The social consciousness of the Protestant church was represented by such personalities as Washington Gladden, Josiah Strong, Lyman Abbott, Vida D. Scudder, George Davis Herron, John Graham Brooks, Walter Rauschenbusch, Francis Peabody, Charles R. Henderson, Bishop Scarlett, Bishop Francis McConnell, and Harry Emerson Fosdick.[5]

---

[5] Wade C. Barclay, *The Church and a Christian Society* (New York: Abingdon Press, 1939), p. 56; Dores R. Sharpe, *Walter Rauschenbusch* (New York: Macmillan, 1942), p. 12; and, F. Ernest Johnson and William J. Villaume, "Protestant Social Services," *Social Work Year Book* (1960), pp. 441-451.

Lutheran, Episcopal, Baptist, and Methodist churches have organized home missions or city missions in New York and other large cities which led to the establishment of "houses of refuge" and temporary shelters for children and adolescents as well as industrial workshops, settlement houses, summer camps, immigrant services, and various health facilities. The Salvation Army and the Methodist Church have been prominent in the development of "goodwill industries" for the employment and training of the handicapped who are able to earn their living in these "sheltered workshops." Episcopal and Lutheran seamen's missions and reception centers are available in several ports for seamen, transients, and migrants. Over 700 old-age homes are in operation under the auspices of Protestant denominations and more than 600 Protestant hospitals.[6]

In Protestant social agencies emphasis is laid upon the postulate that religious life be nurtured, that religious ethics be integrated into the basic principles of social work by pastoral services, and that the members of the Protestant churches, as volunteers, have a good deal to contribute to service for the community. Protestant social agencies are operating either under one of the denominations—a local church or a regional, diocesan, or synodical authority—or under a national mission board of the church. Coordinating bodies of Protestant churches for the entire country are, for instance, the Division of Welfare of the National Lutheran Council, the Board of Hospitals and Homes of the Methodist Church, the Department of Christian Social Relations of the National Council of the Protestant Episcopal Church, the Council on Christian Social Progress of the Northern Baptist Convention, and the Division of Social Education and Action of the Board of Christian Education of the Presbyterian Church. Metropolitan and state councils of churches combine the social welfare activities of the various Protestant denominations, and the Federal Council of Churches attempts to coordinate the national program of Protestant social work through its Department of Christian Social Relations and the Church Conference of Social Work which has its annual convention at the time of the National Conference of Social Work. For rural social work, the Home Missions Council acts as coordinating body.

---

[6] Johnson and Villaume, *op. cit.*, pp. 444-445; and, Charles G. Chakerian (editor), *The Churches and Social Welfare* (Hartford, Conn.: Seminary Foundation, 1955).

The Young Men's Christian Association (YMCA), the Young Women's Christian Association (YWCA), and the Salvation Army are not church organizations in a sectarian sense, but have been founded upon religious principles, and most of their members are active in Protestant churches; they are not controlled by any Protestant denomination. Some YWCA and YMCA centers have accepted young people of various creeds to their membership and have thus assumed intersectarian character. But there is controversy in the YWCA and YMCA over the amount of Christianity that is necessary and desirable in their work.[7]

The Salvation Army has been active in the United States since 1880. Its main interest is the religious needs of people. Its family and child welfare services are less important than its work with groups of people who are reached less by other churches or social agencies. Such work includes providing shelters for alcoholics and the homeless and derelict, and maternity homes and placement services for unmarried mothers. Other activities of the Salvation Army include employment service for the handicapped, prison work, and the establishment of social settlements, boys' clubs, and children's institutions.

The American Friends Service Committee, founded in 1917, and the Unitarian Service Committee, established in 1939, have been active in international peace work, social services for foreign relief and rehabilitation, interracial cooperation and also in domestic services for the mentally ill, young and adult prisoners, and community work camps.

For the victims of Nazi persecution, the American Christian Committee for Refugees was organized by the Federal Council of Churches in 1934, and in 1947 the Church World Service developed an extensive program of aid to displaced persons and refugees under its Committee on Displaced Persons. The Church World Service also carries on foreign relief and religious education abroad.

Protestant hospitals, sanatoriums, and institutions for the chronic sick maintain the American Protestant Hospital Association with

---

[7] Paul Limbert, *Christian Emphasis in Y.M.C.A. Program* (New York: Association Press, 1951), p. 32; Shelby M. Harrison, *Religion and Social Work— Perspectives and Common Denominators* (New York: National Council of Churches, 1950); Harvey Seifert, *The Church in Community Action* (New York: Abingdon-Cokesbury, 1952); and, Margaret E. Kuhn, *Houses and People* (New York: National Council of Churches, 1957).

over three hundred institutions as members, and conferences on Protestant Homes for the Aged are held in order to exchange experiences.

Catholic Social Work. The social services under the auspices of the Roman Catholic Church are inspired by the religious concepts of the Catholic faith, particularly the virtue of charity. Their main objective is the salvation of the human soul. Catholic social work primarily serves communicants of the Catholic Church, but other clients are not rigorously excluded from the aid of Catholic agencies if their funds and facilities permit caring for such persons without offense to religion or any disadvantage to Catholic applicants. Catholic social workers consider the supernatural element of "charity" as an expression of divine grace, as love of man for the love of God; their religious philosophy is primarily based upon the teaching of Thomas Aquinas in the thirteenth century.

The structure of Catholic social work follows that of the church organization. The main unit of its services is the diocese. In most of the 112 dioceses of the United States, a director of charities, appointed by the bishop ordinary, coordinates all Catholic welfare activities. As a rule, he is a priest with training in social work. In metropolitan districts the heads of the various departments of the Diocesan Bureau of Social Services or The Associated Catholic Charities are also priests who have received training in social work. The diocesan charities are responsible for the establishment, planning, and financing of all Catholic charitable activities and for cooperation with other voluntary and public social agencies in the area. They are interested in the maintenance of high standards of service and in professional training of young workers in schools of social work. The program of the diocesan charities, in general, emphasizes child care in foster homes and children's institutions; family casework; cultural, educational, and recreational activities for children and young people; work with juvenile delinquents and endangered youth; and care of the aged and chronically ill.[8]

---

[8] Mary J. McCormick, *Thomistic Philosophy in Social Casework* (New York: Columbia University Press, 1948); Katharine E. Griffith, "Developments in Casework Programs Under Religious Auspices," *The Social Welfare Forum* (1951), pp. 224-235; Daniel McColgan, *A Century of Charity* (Milwaukee: Bruce, 1951); John J. Lennon, "Catholic Social Services," *Social Work Year Book* (1957), pp. 139-146; and, Raymond J. Gallagher, "Catholic Social Services," *ibid.* (1960), pp. 136-141.

The national agency representing Catholic social work is the National Conference of Catholic Charities, which was founded in 1910. Its main task is the coordination of all organizations active in Catholic charitable programs and their cooperation with other private and public social agencies. The Conference arranges national and regional meetings for the exchange of points of view and experiences, conducts research, and encourages the publication of books and studies. It also issues a monthly journal, the *Catholic Charities Review,* in Washington, D.C. In the field of social philosophy and social action, another organization, the National Catholic Welfare Conference, has been established under which the Family Life Bureau and the National Catholic Rural Life Conference operate for the interpretation of their philosophy. The National Catholic Resettlement Council and the Catholic Committee for Refugees provide immigration services for Catholic refugees and displaced persons with resettlement, placement, vocational training, legal advice, and emergency relief. In the United States, six Catholic graduate schools of social work and three in Canada are accredited for professional education.

Volunteer organizations play an essential role in Catholic charitable work in the dioceses. Prominent societies among them are the Society of St. Vincent de Paul, the Ladies of Charity, the Sisters of the Good Shepherd, and the Knights of Columbus. Volunteer work is mainly devoted to the sick and poor in the parish; to the inmates of hospitals, mental institutions, and prisons; to child care and employment services; and to the maintenance of rest homes and residence clubs for young people and the aged, and shelters for transients and homeless.

Jewish Social Work. From ancient times, Jewish laws and traditions have made aid to the poor a fundamental religious obligation for the individual and the community. The Bible and Scriptures emphasized the duty of caring for widows and orphans, the blind and the lame, and of feeding the hungry and sheltering the homeless. Slaves were freed after seven years of service. The consciousness of the need of solidarity grew during the Middle Ages when Jews suffered from cruel persecutions, mass murder, and expulsions. In the Jewish religion, charity is called "justice" and has always been an essential part of Jewish ethics.

Jewish social work is religious in origin, but its agencies are secular; it is not administered by synagogues and congregations.

It is mainly financed by the local religious community. United Jewish Charities were founded in New York, Chicago, Cincinnati, Cleveland, and a few other large cities where the bulk of the Jewish population lived. Homes for the aged, community centers, and group work agencies followed later. In 1895, Boston and Cincinnati organized the first "federations," which were later accepted by most larger Jewish communities and which became characteristic of the form of community organization of Jewish social welfare. Their function was to conduct a unified financial campaign for all Jewish institutions and agencies. They provided central budgeting for all social agencies according to their need, and coordinated social work concerning family welfare and children's services, health and tuberculosis work, hospitals, clinics, group work, and educational and recreational activities.[9]

The Jewish Welfare Funds raise contributions by a unified central drive and provide budgeting for domestic and foreign relief needs. They appeal for contributions to maintain the various Jewish welfare and health services, particularly for Israel and foreign aid programs, and for such local services as religious education, vocational training, and special employment services which cannot obtain Community Chest support. In larger communities the Jewish Community Council coordinates religious, cultural, fraternal, and social service activities, including the relations with other organizations.

Until the Depression of the 1930's, Jewish family societies assumed major responsibility for Jewish people in need, particularly for immigrants who were not eligible for public assistance. Since the change of public welfare policies under the influence of the Social Security Act, Jewish family and child welfare services continue to aid Jews for whom government aid is not available or whose special religious needs require particular help.

Services for immigrants and refugees were organized, since 1884, by HIAS (Hebrew Immigrant Aid Society), to give emergency shelter and transportation aid. These services have been rendered by other Jewish welfare agencies, on a large scale, since 1935. Resettlement work for Jewish refugees and displaced persons and their adjustment

---

[9] Maurice J. Karpf, *Jewish Community Organization in the United States* (New York: Block, 1938); George W. Rabinoff, "Jewish Social Work," *Social Work Year Book* (1945), pp. 203-214; and, William Avrunin, "Jewish Social Services," *ibid.* (1960), pp. 338-344.

in American communities, since this period, is a major task of Jewish agencies, particularly USNA (United Service for New Americans), now united with HIAS. Local family welfare agencies, children's bureaus, vocational services, and women's organizations share the responsibility for the resettlement of newcomers.

The National Jewish Welfare Board was the representative of Jewish social work in the United Service Organizations (USO) and has charge of recreational and group work services for the members of the armed forces. It coordinates and develops the policies for the Jewish Community Centers and the Young Men's and Young Women's Hebrew Associations (YMHA and YWHA) and arranges for recruitment and training of personnel for these recreational agencies.

The largest national organization of Jewish social work is the Council of Jewish Federations and Welfare Funds, with headquarters in New York and eight regional offices. It coordinates Jewish community resources in cooperation with local agencies. The National Conference of Jewish Communal Services serves as a forum for the discussion of problems and experiences and publishes a periodical, *The Journal of Jewish Communal Service*. The Jewish Occupational Council is the clearing house for vocational guidance and placement services and formulates programs regarding Jewish economic problems.

Most national and larger local Jewish agencies employ a professionally trained staff, educated in schools of social work.

III. SOCIAL SERVICES IN RURAL AREAS

The rural population of the United States includes persons living on farms, in villages and towns with less than 2,500 inhabitants, and in the open country; it still comprises about 36 per cent of the total population.[10] Although the average income of farmers had substantially increased during World War II and the postwar years, there was a decline beginning in 1949. The problems of insufficient income from submarginal land, of difficulties in marketing farm products, and of long-term unemployment, low wages, and insecurity among the migratory farm workers created special needs in certain sections

---

[10] *U.S. Census of Population, Current Population Reports* (1955).

of the rural population. These problems differ in the various agricultural areas of our country, but are most urgent in those states where economic and health conditions are less favorable than in New England, the Middle West and the far West.[11]

Under these circumstances, a strong national leadership has developed in order to improve social conditions in rural communities and to develop social services which have long been taken for granted in urban settings. The U.S. Children's Bureau, now under the Federal Department of Health, Education and Welfare, is the oldest Federal agency particularly concerned, in its maternal and child health services, with rural welfare and health. The Bureau of Indian Affairs in the U.S. Department of the Interior is another agency which has been concerned for a long time with rural welfare and health in the Indian reservations. In the U.S. Department of Agriculture, the most important programs for rural communities are administered through the Extension Service in the form of free consultation and demonstrations of scientific methods in farming and home economics. A broad adult education program, 4-H Clubs for teen-age boys and girls, and clubs for older rural youth, develop agricultural and home economics skills and an appreciation for rural life, as well as an understanding of child care and health preservation. The Extension Service is supported by the Bureau of Home Nutrition and Home Economics, the Bureau of Agricultural Economics, and the Farmers Home Administration, which provides loans, a farm housing plan, and a limited medical care program.

Aid to rural communities in recreation, adult education, and rural health protection is stimulated by the American Country Life Association, the Farm Foundation, the National Education Association, and several farm organizations, such as the National Grange of the Order of Patrons of Husbandry, the American Farm Bureau Federation, and the Farmers' Union.

Prior to the Depression of the 1930's, needy persons in rural communities depended upon uncertain neighborly help or meager, local

---

[11] Grace Browning, "Rural Social Programs," *Social Work Year Book* (1949), pp. 446; Marjorie J. Smith, *Rural Case Work Service* (New York: Family Welfare Association, 1943); Charles P. Loomis and J. Allan Beegle, *Rural Sociology* (Englewood Cliffs, N. J.: Prentice-Hall, Inc., 1957), pp. 388-395; and, Clyde W. Linville, Jr., "Rural Social Programs," *Social Work Year Book* (1957), pp. 500-505.

poor relief. The inadequacy of this relief became evident when, in the Depression years, mass unemployment made it difficult to sell agricultural products, and droughts and floods increased the suffering of the rural population in many states. The Federal Emergency Relief Administration and the Farm Security Administration provided financial aid and special measures of assistance in rural communities.

In this period, the rural county public welfare departments developed, for the first time, an effective program of financial assistance. With the support of Federal and state funds, under the *Social Security Act,* rural welfare departments give more adequate economic aid to the needy aged, the needy blind, to dependent children, and to disabled persons. Family and child welfare services, also, were made possible through federal grants-in-aid. Professionally trained child welfare workers, supervisors, and consultants are now employed in rural regions for maternal and child care services, for crippled children, and for casework and group work with difficult, endangered, and delinquent children. In the rural communities where these services are not yet available, there are few qualified, trained social workers. Often, the county welfare department is the only social agency in such a region. A number of state departments of public welfare supplement the forces of the local county welfare agency by sending field supervisors, consultants, and itinerant clinics to provide medical and psychiatric examinations, guidance, and services to the aging.

Among voluntary social agencies, the local chapter of the American National Red Cross is best known to rural communities. A limited number of other private agencies, including religious organizations, the Salvation Army, the National Tuberculosis Association, the National Travelers Aid, the National Foundation (for Infantile Paralysis), and some child-placing and adoption agencies, have field services which serve rural regions.[12]

Social services in the rural community are influenced by its cultural pattern, particular customs, and traditions. The comparative simplicity of the rural village has its bearing upon attitudes toward assistance expenditures and restricts allowances for education and recreation. Rural relief applicants frequently are accustomed to living on a low economic scale, are shy or apathetic about presenting their

---

[12] G. Browning, *Rural Public Welfare* (Chicago: University of Chicago Press, 1941), pp. 95-98; and, Arthur Hillman, *Community Organization and Planning* (New York: Macmillan, 1950), pp. 38-55.

requests, and are seemingly grateful to accept meager relief. Relationship between the client and the visiting social worker is more intimate than in the city—more informal and less professional. This is
particularly true if the social worker is employed in her home county.
If the social worker is not familiar with the rural county, she is forced,
first, to become thoroughly acquainted with its form of government
and its health, recreational, and community facilities.

The rural white population in the Northeast and Middle West
often is rigid in its moral values and attitudes toward illegitimacy,
desertion, birth control, divorce, and sometimes toward drinking and
gambling. Social work with the unmarried mother, a nonsupporting
husband or father, or an alcoholic is made more difficult in a rural
setting because of these rigid attitudes and the closeness of relationships. The high value placed upon thrift and frugality encourages the
rural population to refuse aid to families who do not fully conform to
the moral standards of the community. The social worker has more
difficulty in obtaining information and keeping it confidential due
to the curiosity of the neighborhood. Different customs, however, are
found among minority groups, particularly Negroes, in the South.

Medical care, hospitals, and public health services in rural counties
are poor compared with those in urban regions. There is no complete,
paid public health staff, with a medical officer, sanitary engineer,
laboratory assistant, public health nurse, and medical social worker
in about one-half of the rural counties, and many do not even employ
a public health nurse. Most public health nursing in rural sections
is carried on through maternal and child health centers. With the
aid of Federal funds, granted under the *Hospital Survey and Construction Act of 1946* (Hill-Burton Act), new hospitals in rural areas
have been built, but preventive mental health services are still almost
nonexistent in rural counties. Medical care in isolated areas is very
expensive, so that the inhabitants call a doctor only in severe cases,
preventing early and quick cure. Dental care and lack of proper
diets are sometimes special problems for the social worker in a
rural community.

Recreational activities and sports in rural regions are conducted
under the auspices of high schools, church groups, the 4-H Clubs,
the Extension Service of the Federal Department of Agriculture, and
often, also, through the YWCA, YMCA, Boy Scouts, and Girl Scouts.

Selected Bibliography

Abbe, L. M., and A. M. Baney, *The Nation's Health Facilities: Ten Years of the Hill-Burton Hospital and Medical Facilities Program, 1946-1956.* Washington: Public Health Service Publication No. 66, 1958.

Abts, Dorothy M., *Some Religious and Ethical Problems in the Practice of Catholic Social Workers.* Washington: Catholic University of America Press, 1945.

*Avrunin, William, "Jewish Social Services," *Social Work Year Book* (1960), pp. 338-344.

*Bachmann, Ernst, *The Emerging Perspective.* New York: National Council of Churches, 1956.

Biestek, Felix P., *The Principle of Client Self-Determination in Social Case Work.* Washington: Catholic University of America Press, 1951.

*Bowers, Swithun, *The Nature and Definition of Social Case Work.* New York: Family Service Association of America, 1949.

*Boylan, Marguerite T., *Social Welfare in the Catholic Church.* New York: Columbia University Press, 1941.

Braceland, Francis J. (editor), *Faith, Reason, and Modern Psychiatry.* New York: P. J. Kenedy, 1955.

Brown, Josephine C., *Rural Community and Social Case Work.* New York: Little & Ives, 1933.

Browning, Grace, *Rural Public Welfare: Selected Records.* Chicago: University of Chicago Press, 1941.

Cayton, H., and S. Nishi, *The Changing Scene.* New York: National Council of Churches, 1955.

Cooke, Terence J., *Thomistic Philosophy and the Principles of Social Group Work.* Washington: Catholic University of America Press, 1951.

Crystal, David, *The Displaced Person and the Social Agency.* New York: United HIAS Service, 1958.

Dicks, Russell L., *Pastoral Work and Personal Counseling.* New York: Macmillan, 1945.

*Gallagher, Raymond J., "Catholic Social Services," *Social Work Year Book* (1960), pp. 136-141.

Harrison, Shelby M., *Religion and Social Work.* New York: National Council of Churches, 1950.

Hiltner, Seward, *Religion and Health.* New York: Macmillan, 1943.

Johnson, F. Ernest (editor), *The Social Work of the Churches.* New

York: Federal Council of the Churches of Christ in America, 1930.

———, (editor), *Religion and Social Work.* New York: National Council of Churches, 1956.

*———, and William J. Villaume, "Protestant Social Services," *Social Work Year Book* (1960), pp. 441-451.

Johnston, Helen L., *Rural Health Cooperatives.* Washington: U. S. Public Health Service, 1950.

Jorns, Auguste, *The Quakers As Pioneers in Social Work.* New York: Macmillan, 1931.

Landis, Benson Y., *Rural Welfare Services.* New York: Columbia University Press, 1949.

Landis, Paul H., *Rural Life in Process.* New York: McGraw, 1948.

*Lauerman, Lucian L., *Catholic Education for Social Work.* Washington: Catholic University of America Press, 1943.

*Linville, Clyde W., "Rural Social Programs," *Social Work Year Book* (1957), pp. 500-505.

Loomis, Charles P., and J. Allan Beegle, *Rural Sociology. The Strategy of Change.* Englewood Cliffs, N.J.: Prentice-Hall, Inc., 1957.

Lund, Henriette, *Lutheran Services for Older People.* New York: National Lutheran Council, 1951.

Lurie, Harry L., "The Approach and Philosophy of Jewish Social Welfare," *Jewish Social Service Quarterly,* Vol. 19, No. 3 (March 1953).

McCormick, Mary J., *Thomistic Philosophy in Social Casework.* New York: Columbia University Press, 1948.

Mott, Frederick D., and Milton I. Roemer, *Rural Health and Medical Care.* New York: McGraw, 1948.

*Niebuhr, Reinhold, *The Contribution of Religion to Social Work.* New York: Columbia University Press, 1932.

O'Grady, John, *Catholic Charities in the United States.* Washington: National Conference of Catholic Charities, 1930.

*Oxnam, G. Bromley, "Goals for Social Work in a Contemporary Society," *National Conference of Social Work, Proceedings* 1948, pp. 89-100.

*Pickett, Clarence, E., *For More Than Bread.* Boston: Little, 1953.

Purdie, Arnold, *Episcopal Social Welfare Today.* New York: National Council, Protestant Episcopal Church, 1950.

Roemer, Milton I., and Ethel A. Wilson, *Organized Health Services in a County of the United States.* Washington: U. S. Public Health Service, 1952.

Smith, Marjorie J., *Rural Casework Service*. New York: Family Welfare Association of America, 1943.

Stidley, Leonard A., *Sectarian Welfare Federation Among Protestants*. New York: Association Press, 1944.

Thomas, J. L., *The American Catholic Family*. Englewood Cliffs, N.J.: Prentice-Hall, Inc., 1956.

Villeneuve, Rudolph, *Catholic Social Work*. Montreal: Grand Seminary, 1955.

Webb, Muriel S., *The Social Ministry of the Local Church*. New York: National Council of Churches, 1956.

William, Meloin J., *Catholic Social Thought*. New York: Ronald, 1950.

Withers, Gertrude V., *Effective Rural Social Work Through Community Organization*. Chicago: American Public Welfare Association, 1942.

9.

Income Security: Public Assistance and Social Insurance

I. PUBLIC ASSISTANCE

A. Principles of Income Security

In modern industrial society, the majority of the population is dependent for their livelihood upon their current wages as laborers, workers, and employees, or upon their income as self-employed persons. Whenever the breadwinner is unable to work, when he cannot obtain work, or when his death leaves the family in need, outside help is necessary to provide economic protection. In the industrial countries, we no longer can rely upon relatives, friends, or neighbors to support people in need of financial aid, or upon religious or philanthropic voluntary charities to assume the responsibility to supply the funds for maintaining the indigent and their families. There are two main systems of achieving this goal of economic security: (1) a program of *public assistance* (or social assistance), which is financed by taxation, and (2) a program of *social insurance,* financed by contributions of the beneficiary and of his employer. Public assistance may be provided by payments based upon the economic and social needs of the applicant, "which are determined by a means test," or they may be granted as a "flat-rate

256

allowance" legally fixed with regard to recognized average needs of families of a specific size. Assistance usually is rendered in money so that the recipient is able to purchase the necessities of life, or in kind, such as food, clothing, fuel, and medical supplies. Public assistance may be offered either by accepting the destitute into an institution or by granting aid to the applicant in his own home. Because public assistance is granted only to individuals who are in economic need, this fact must be established through some kind of a means test. Modern programs of public assistance characterize the receipt of the payment as a right of the applicant, provided that its legal requirements are fulfilled. The amount of assistance is usually limited by statute and adjusted to the recipient's social and economic conditions whereby his income, resources, and property are taken into consideration. The administration of public assistance determines the extent of need, and the amount of assistance often cannot be predicted in advance.

In contrast, social insurance benefits are fully predictable. They are based upon legal provisions which provide statutory benefits either on a flat-rate system or in relation to earned wages, or income, length of work, or loss of working capacity in cases of industrial injuries. Insurance benefits are not dependent upon the financial status or the economic need of the insured person. They are provided to the insured who has a legal claim to receive these benefits without arbitrary interference of government authorities. Insurance benefits are financed by contributions from employers, self-employed persons, and from workers. In other countries, often, the government shares contributions for social insurance with the insured and their employers.

Between these two main methods of providing economic security, there is a *third approach* to income security: a *pension system* based upon statute. In our country, veterans' pensions to disabled veterans, to survivors of veterans, retirement annuities, and allowances to dependents of military personnel are examples of such pensions which are granted as a matter of legal right to the claimant. Foreign countries have other programs of this nature such as family allowances, pensions to persons over sixty-five or seventy years of age, or to certain qualified handicapped groups.

In order to provide economic protection, we use, in the United States, a dual system, consisting of public assistance on the basis of individual need, and of social insurance programs in which

benefits are paid to the insured persons as their legal claim in pre-
determined, specific contingencies of life (old age, death of breadwinner, unemployment, industrial accident). These two main programs of economic security are supplemented by a system of health
and welfare services which provides social services, protective and
preventive measures, such as child welfare services, recreation, medical and psychiatric care, occupational guidance, and vocational
rehabilitation, which are of vital importance for the welfare of the
population.

Other public programs, such as public employment services and
correctional treatment of juvenile and adult offenders, may be classified as public welfare measures in a broader sense.

These public activities are often strengthened and augmented by
the work of private social agencies, which contribute to the economic
security of the population. This work is carried on under the auspices of religious or nonsectarian philanthropic organizations or of
industries and labor unions.

The system of public welfare in the United States has its principal
legal foundation in the *Social Security Act of 1935* and its subsequent amendments which deal with all three programs: social
insurance, public assistance, and health and welfare services. It
provides Federal funds for the development and the improvement of
standards in specific programs of public assistance and health and
welfare services. However, the *Social Security Act* does not establish
a comprehensive Federal system; rather, it sets up programs for
Federal aid in selected and specified types of assistance and welfare
services. The social insurance programs of the Old-Age and Survivors Insurance and Unemployment Compensation are financed exclusively by contributions of employers and the insured persons.

B. Characteristics of Public Assistance

The cost of public welfare is shared by the Federal government,
the states, counties, and cities. This circumstance has contributed to
the fact that the importance of public welfare has been recognized
by an increasing proportion of the population. The public is, at the
same time, more critical of the expenditure of huge sums of money,
which necessitate higher taxes, and has become conscious of the
marked differences in the amount of benefits received under the

various programs in states and counties, and in the standards and methods of their administration. In general, it is now accepted that government, on its various levels, has to assume responsibility of caring for the people who have no means of support. But there is, so far, no unanimity of social philosophy as to how this responsibility should be met, what seems an adequate aid to persons in need, and what government agencies should administer the public welfare services.

An application of a person in need of material assistance is, as a rule, made at the local department of public welfare. A blind or disabled person may send a relative or friend to submit the request for assistance to the agency. If the application is made in person, the social worker explains how the application form is to be filled out and what information is needed. The applicant may have to include documents for proof of age, data regarding his income and property, or medical certificates about blindness or disability. If the applicant has not come to the welfare office but has written or phoned, a social worker visits the home and gives the necessary explanation. The social worker also checks the facts presented in the application and attempts to make certain that the applicant is eligible for the assistance he is asking for. If further investigations are necessary (for example, about relatives who may support the applicant, or about income and property), these are made within a reasonable time and a notice is sent to the applicant telling him whether or not he has been accepted for public assistance and how much he will receive monthly. The amount of aid is based upon the applicant's individual needs and resources and is often limited by rules of state or local authorities. In the determination of need, all resources of the applicant are considered, especially all insurance benefits under old-age, survivors and disability insurance, unemployment compensation, workmen's compensation, and the *Railroad Retirement Act*. Other income considered is interest from real or personal property, rents, veterans' and servicemen's benefits, support from relatives, and payments from private life insurance and pension plans and union welfare funds. If the applicant is eligible, he receives a check at regular intervals, usually once a month. If assistance is denied, the applicant is informed about his right to ask for a hearing or to appeal to another authority, insofar as the categorical types of public assistance are concerned. In indigent aid, it is possible, as a rule, only to request, informally, a reconsideration through the county board of supervisors or the city council.

Decisions of the public welfare department must be given in writing so that misunderstandings may be avoided, and so that the applicant is able to make an appeal within the period legally provided for.

In all forms of public assistance, the applicant is required to report promptly to the public welfare department any change in income, economic conditions, address, or other important facts which are essential for granting assistance. The social worker often may be able to help the applicant in other matters regarding his living conditions, health problems, personal questions, and plans for change of his dependent situation.

C. Categorical Assistance

The goal of public assistance is to provide minimum economic aid to persons who have no other means of supporting themselves. Public assistance is granted only to such people as these, in contrast to social insurance benefits which are not dependent upon economic need.[1] Before the enactment of the *Social Security Act* in 1935 less than half of the states had special relief systems which provided more adequate care than general poor relief for the aged, for blind persons, or for children. Under the *Social Security Act* the Federal government shares in the expenses of four major types of *categorical assistance:* old-age assistance, aid to the blind, aid to dependent children, and aid to the permanently and totally disabled.[2] For the residual part of public assistance, which is called *general assistance* (or indigent aid), no Federal standards exist, and no Federal money is provided, so that this field remains the sole responsibility of state or local governments. We shall discuss, first, the categorical forms of public assistance, and then the field of general assistance.

The question whether public assistance should bear a major burden in providing income security to persons who need such protection is controversial. Whereas, public relief before the enactment of social insurance legislation into the *Social Security Act* was the only means

---

[1] Public welfare agencies provide, in addition to financial aid, other services, such as casework and medical care.

[2] The last category was created by the *Amendment of 1950*.

of public aid to people in distress, it is now only one, but no longer the largest, program within the framework of social security. The number of people protected by the categorical forms of public assistance are now, by far, more numerous than the recipients of general assistance. For example, in March 1959, there were 2,433,412 persons receiving old-age assistance, 109,261 needy blind, 331,304 permanently disabled, and 2,916,799 dependent children—altogether 5,790,766 persons receiving aid. 480,000 were supported by general assistance.[3]

Under the amendments of the *Social Security Act of 1950,* Congress decided to emphasize that the old-age and survivors' insurance program shall become the main bulwark against destitution in our country and that, therefore, public assistance will play a less important role in the maintenance of income security for the entire population.[4]

The Federal government shares the cost of categorical assistance, but it does not administer these programs. It pays one-half of all state expenditures for the proper and efficient administration of approved categorical public assistance programs. The *Social Security Act* allows the states wide latitude in the legal provisions and administrative setup of the categorical assistance plans. Only the following conditions must be met by all state plans in order to meet with the approval of the Department of Health, Education and Welfare.

The program must be statewide; it must be effective in all political subdivisions of the state, such as counties and townships.

The state must participate in the financing of the categorical assistance plans. The law does not specify how large the state's contribution has to be, which is regulated in the state's statute, but the state is not permitted to transfer all financial responsibility beyond the Federal grant-in-aid to the county, town, or township.

The state must secure methods of administration which guarantee proper and efficient operation of the categorical assistance plan and which include the establishment and maintenance of a *merit system* of personnel standards. This is of particular importance because only

---

[3] *Social Security Bulletin,* Vol. 22, No. 6 (June 1959), p. 35.

[4] U.S. Senate: *Recommendations for Social Security Legislation.* Reports of the Advisory Council on Social Security to the Senate Committee on Finance, Document No. 208, 80th Congress, 2nd Session, 1949.

competent personnel enables the public welfare department to effectively aid people in need.

The state has to administer the program directly or to supervise it by a single state agency, usually the state department of social welfare.

The state agency has to submit all required reports to the U.S. Department of Health, Education and Welfare.

The state has to give an opportunity for filing of applications for categorical assistance with the provision that action will be taken with reasonable promptness. The specific regulations have to be made in each state.

The state must provide opportunity for a *fair hearing* for a claimant whose application is fully or partially denied or not acted upon with reasonable promptness, as well as the right of *appeal* to the state agency.

The state must take into consideration all income and resources of the recipient in determination of his need and of the amount of the assistance payment. An exception is made for earned income of blind persons, which is disregarded up to $50 a month in order to encourage the blind to maintain themselves as far as possible. For other needy persons, however, income may not be ignored.

A state agency, frequently the State Department of Public Health, must be designated as responsible for the establishment and maintenance of standards for public and private institutions (such as hospitals, nursing homes, infirmaries), in which residents may receive categorical public assistance payments.

It is prohibited to receive concurrently more than one form of public categorical assistance under the state plan.

The state plan must provide safeguards which restrict the use or disclosure of information, concerning applicants and recipients, to purposes directly connected with the administration of public assistance. This provision requiring confidential treatment of categorical assistance records was added by Congress in the *Amendment of 1939*.

The so-called *Jenner Amendment* under the *Federal Revenue Act of 1951* prevents the Department of Health, Education and Welfare from withholding Federal grants-in-aid from a state (or territory) which enacts legislation giving public access to information concerning assistance disbursements, providing such legislation prohibits the use of any list of names obtained for commercial or political purposes.

Thus, the requirement of the *Social Security Act* to keep public assistance records confidential is, as a rule, maintained, but the states are now entitled by statutory measures to give access to people who seek information on assistance disbursements.

In addition to the eleven requirements which have to be met in each state plan in order to get it approved, the plan may not include:

(1) any residence requirement specifying more than five years of state residence in the last nine years and one year preceding application, and in the case of aid to dependent children more than one year residence; and (2) any citizenship requirement barring a citizen of the United States who is otherwise eligible for aid. This does not, however, force the state to require citizenship as a condition to receive categorical assistance; non-citizens may be included in the state provisions.[5]

Categorical assistance is rendered in the form of money to needy persons or as payment for medical or remedial treatment. Categorical assistance usually does not issue vouchers or supply food, clothes, or fuel in kind to needy persons as was frequently the case in the past. It may pay the medical expenses for an individual or for all recipients of public assistance through local or statewide prepayment medical care plans. The categorical assistance plans with Federal grants-in-aid, favor and encourage applicants to live in their own homes. But, since 1950, Federal payments are also made to share the expenses of medical and remedial care of needy persons in public medical institutions (hospitals and sanatoriums), except for psychotic or tubercular patients. Federal grants, in addition to the share in money payments, are given on a 50-50 basis for medical care of recipients of categorical assistance, up to a maximum of $6 per month for all adult recipients and $3 per month for all children. The states decide in what manner medical care is to be provided— by the use of prepaid medical care plans with medical societies, non-profit health service plans or by agreements with hospitals, clinics, physicians, and dentists, to mention a few.

---

[5] Jay L. Roney, "Public Assistance," *Social Work Year Book* (1960), pp. 460-470; and, Elizabeth Wickenden, "Confidentiality of Assistance Records," *Social Work Journal,* Vol. 33, No. 2 (April 1952), pp. 88-93. The important amendments of 1956 and 1958 are discussed by Charles I. Schottland, *Social Security Bulletin* (September 1956), pp. 3-15, and 31; and (October 1958), pp. 3-14.

The Federal share in the expenses for categorical public assistance, until 1958, was based upon the individual payments to the recipients. Since 1958, Federal grants have been allocated on the basis of statewide average payments, considering the state's per capita income, compared with the nation's per capita income, so that the poorer states receive a larger Federal grant (equalization principle). For adult recipients, the Federal grant amounts to four-fifths of the first montly $30 payment, and, according to the state's average per capita income, an additional grant of between 50 and 65 per cent of the monthly payment up to $35 beyond the first $30. The Federal grants for this amount are, for example, 50 per cent for New York, California, District of Columbia, Pennsylvania, Connecticut, Illinois, Michigan, New Jersey, Washington, 52.58 per cent for Oregon, 61.36 per cent for Texas, and 65 per cent for Arkansas, Georgia, Louisiana, South Carolina, Tennessee, Utah, Mississippi, New Mexico, Oklahoma, and Virginia. When the state's per capita income is equal to or greater than the national average, the Federal share in the amount paid, beyond $30 a month, is 50 per cent. This applies as well in Alaska and Hawaii. Special grants for Puerto Rico, Virgin Islands and Guam were ruled. Under the Aid to Dependent Children Program, Federal grants differ for the first child and the mother, or other caretaker, and for subsequent children in the family (see pages 275-279).

The establishment of these ceilings for Federal grants-in-aid, means that the Federal government covers only a part of the actual assistance payments in those states which have higher standards of assistance. They cover a greater part of the assistance cost in the states whose assistance standards are low. The Federal share in the costs of medical care for public assistance recipients has improved the health services for the needy population. However, the maximum amounts payable still leave the main burden for medical and dental treatment, operations, and hospitalization on the states, counties, and cities.

The purpose of public assistance is to help dependent families to obtain, in accordance with their capacities, maximum personal and economic independence, a strengthened family life, and opportunities for their participation in community life. The *Amendment* of the *Social Security Act of 1956* restated the objectives of public assistance with emphasis on social casework, so that the aged are encouraged to care for themselves, and the blind and the disabled are able to support themselves. Family life is maintained and strengthened in order to benefit the dependent children and to help their mothers or caretakers to support and care for themselves without interfering with their parental roles.

The *Social Security Act* does not define the concept of "need" as a prerequisite for the receipt of public assistance. Each state, therefore, determines what resources and property an individual or a family may have and still be eligible for public assistance. Statutes and regulations of the states on home ownership, savings, cash, and insurance policies, to exclude an applicant from eligibility, vary greatly. Many states, counties, and cities impose liens on the real estate of applicants to secure the refund of assistance payments after the death of the recipient or when he becomes financially able to repay. To avoid hardship, some regulations require the refund to be made only after the death of the recipient's spouse.

The establishment of these policies means that an applicant for public assistance first must use up his reserves, income, and property (except a limited amount) before he is granted public assistance. This is often hard for an honest applicant, who has saved for a "rainy day," to understand.

Most state laws require that not only must the applicant exhaust his resources before he may receive assistance, but that, also, his close relatives must support him. Assistance can be given only when the applicant does not receive such support. This "relatives' responsibility" is limited to the spouse, parents toward their minor children, and adult children toward their parents, but the state laws show differences in their approach. In some states, the requirement of the support of family members is limited according to sliding scales, which are classified according to income and number of dependents of the responsible relative.

The effect of family responsibility is disputed. Some statutes base these provisions on the assumption that by requiring the support of close relatives the family ties are strengthened. In fact, however, the demand for support often is a serious strain on the budget of relatives with modest income, and leads to a hostile attitude towards those in need that may cause a breakup of friendly relations and serious emotional suffering. In some states, the contribution which relatives owe to the applicant for assistance is deducted from the assistance payment, even if it is not given. This policy leads to hardship for the poor, and most states deduct the relative's support only if it is in fact rendered.

The amount of public assistance which is given to the individual person or to the family is, as a rule, determined upon a budget consisting of the cost figures for food, shelter, fuel, utilities, and clothing. Most states have standard budgets which include several of these items, but leave consideration of rent, nursing, and medical cost to the county or city. For the categorical forms of public assistance, frequently a flat sum is given which represents the average budgetary needs. From this, the income of the recipient is deducted. Special expenses for medical care, appliances, and medicines may be considered. The financial situation of a number of states sometimes makes it difficult to fulfill the full budgetary needs, so that payments are cut.

Although mobility of labor has been a characteristic of American life, and migrations enable agricultural and industrial development, communities and states have refused to support "strangers" in need of financial help. "Settlement" is a term used when a resident requirement is made for eligibility for public assistance. In most states, settlement laws limit the responsibility of local or state government to support only needy persons who have resided a specified period in the city, county, or state. Nonresidents may be refused aid and may be returned to their former place of residence.

The length of residence required to obtain "legal settlement right" varies from a period of one year, in most states, to a maximum of five years, frequently with different provisions for categorical and general assistance. Rhode Island was the first state to abolish all settlement requirements in 1943. New York followed in 1946, requiring only presence in the state at the time of application. Pennsylvania refuses public assistance to nonresidents, except those who come from states which have no settlement requirements. The majority of states, however, still maintain their settlement laws. Often, a family moving to another state loses its settlement rights in the original residence without gaining new settlement status in the second state. Usually settlement cannot be gained while a person lives in a public institution (county farm, hospital, and so on), nor if he receives private or public relief. The hardships which migrants and their families have suffered under these conditions has led to a more liberal policy in some states, which now permit residents to receive public assistance payments outside of the state; some reciprocal agreements between states permit mutual assistance to their residents. The Social Security Administration and the principal professional organizations in social work are in favor of abolishing these anachronistic settlement laws, but have found little response in the majority of states. Other proposals for remedy are the enactment of uniform settlement legislation in all states, general reciprocal interstate agreements, or a Federal program for the financial support of needy nonresidents, but none seems to offer much hope for realization. Therefore, the establishment of a new general assistance category with Federal grants-in-aid which would give special consideration to aid for nonresidents might be the best possible solution to this problem.

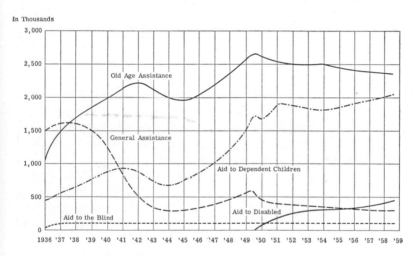

Chart 6. *Recipients of Public Assistance, 1936-1959.*

The development of the public assistance categories since the enactment of the *Social Security Act of 1935* is shown in Chart 6. Until this time, general assistance was the common form of public relief, and under the impact of the Depression, during the years 1936 and 1937 especially, it still served the largest numbers. In 1937, the new category of old-age assistance reached the same level as general assistance and, since then, has been increasing in importance.

After World War II, the number of old-age assistance recipients has steadily grown, while the number of recipients of general assistance declined since 1950.

That financial payments, under the Aid to Dependent Children, became increasingly important, is made evident in Chart 6. During the war years, aid was decreasing because many mothers and adolescents were employed. But, in the subsequent years, the number of dependent children has steadily increased. Supplementary aid to mothers and caretakers, which began in 1950, has made this program still more effective. Compared to these large programs, the number of persons supported under the aid to the blind, and aid to the permanently and totally disabled, is small, but the social significance of aid to these persons should not be underrated.

D. Medical Care in Public Assistance

The provision of medical care for public assistance recipients who are ill has been recognized as a basic need for a long time. Since 1950, an amendment to the *Social Security Act* permitted the Social Security Administration to participate in the payment of the costs of medical treatment that public assistance recipients required by sharing the costs paid to those who provide the medical care. It limited the amount of the monthly payments to individual recipients. The *Amendment of 1956* established a new basis upon which the Federal government shares in state expenditures for medical care on behalf of public assistance recipients. For the first time, the Federal government's payments for this purpose are rendered in addition to the other Federal grants-in-aid to public assistance recipients. The purpose of this change was to help the states to intensify, extend, and broaden their medical care programs for the recipients of public assistance.[6] It enabled the states, effective July 1, 1957, to pay directly to doctors, hospitals, medical societies, and insurance agencies, that provided medical care. The Federal government shares, on a 50-50 basis, payments, up to a monthly maximum of $15, for each recipient of old-age assistance, blind aid, and disabled aid. The govern-

[6] Edward S. Rogers, "Medical Care," *Social Work Year Book* (1960), pp. 365-375; Margaret Greenfield, *Medical Care for Welfare Recipients—Basic Problems* (Berkeley: University of California Press, 1957), pp. 1-39; and, Eveline M. Burns, *Social Security and Public Policy,* Chapter 8 (New York: McGraw, 1956).

ment pays up to $6 for adult relatives and $3 for each child, as its share in the aid to dependent children. The states now may average their medical expenses for public assistance recipients and receive one-half from Federal funds for these expenditures, within the specified limits.

The Federal financial participation in medical care expenditures is based upon the total amount expended in each month and is unrelated to the maximum payment made to an individual recipient.

State public assistance agencies may maintain a pooled fund in order to make prepayment arrangements to meet the cost of medical services for public assistance recipients. Fixed payments may be made into the pooled fund each month, in behalf of each public assistance recipient, which are recognized as assistance expenditure for medical care. Premium payments into a pooled fund are still recognized as assistance payments, and will be shared by the Federal government, subject to the $15 or $3 maximum limitation. Pooled fund coverage, or other payment of medical care, may be provided, also, to the "medically needy" who receive no other money payments than that for medical care.

Medical care includes diagnosis or therapy performed by a physician, surgeon, or dentist, nursing services in the home or elsewhere, drugs, medical supplies, appliances, and laboratory fees, which are provided or prescribed by persons authorized by state law to give such services. Of particular importance is medical care for the aged, because the highest rates of chronic disease and disability occur in this group.

E. Old-Age Assistance

The old-age assistance program is an important source of income to retired or unemployable old people over sixty-five years of age. It is in effect in all states, and the District of Columbia. But, the proportion of the aged population assisted by this categorical program varies widely among the states.

In December 1958, the population, aged sixty-five or over, in the United States was estimated at 15,380,000. Of these aged persons, 2,510,000, or 16.3 per cent, received public assistance payments, while 9,230,000 or 60 per cent were paid old-age and survivors insurance benefits. Frequently, old-age assistance payments served to supplement insurance benefits that do not adequately meet the economic needs of the aged.[7]

The average payment of old-age assistance varies substantially among the states. In March 1959, the national average was $64.34 per month, with $108.41, paid by Connecticut, as the highest, and $33.36, by West Virginia, as the lowest average assistance. The largest numbers of old-age assistance recipients, at the same time, were found to be living in California, with 263,366, and Texas, with 222,830; the smallest number were in Delaware, with 1,477.[8]

Federal grants-in-aid have not been able to raise the level of assistance in some low income states to a really adequate standard. In the majority of states, however, the payments are securing a modest subsistence on a "health and decency level." Many states have monthly maximum payments with limited supplements in case of special needs. In nineteen jurisdictions, citizenship is necessary to apply for categorical assistance, but thirty-four jurisdictions don't have this requirement. In some states, persons are not eligible if they are found begging, have failed to support their minor children, or have committed a felony within the past ten years.

Old-age assistance makes it possible, in general, for aged men and women to go on living in their own homes, either alone or with their families, and to receive regular monthly cash allowances for their maintenance. If they are unable to manage their own households, they may live in boarding homes or in private homes for the aged. Most states provide that old-age assistance is paid to aged persons residing in nonprofit homes for old people, many of them under the auspices of religious or philanthropic charities or fraternal orders or lodges, if the residents have not paid for their maintenance for life, or if the standards of the home are not luxurious. Federal grants are denied to old people in such public institutions, as almshouses or county farms, but a necessary period of treatment in a hospital does not interrupt the receipt of old-age assistance. During recent years, a good many county almshouses were converted into hospitals for the chronically ill, and patients over sixty-five may therefore receive old-age assistance in these medical institutions.

---

[7] Leonore A. Epstein, "Money Income of Aged Persons," *Social Security Bulletin,* Vol. 22, No. 6 (June 1959), pp. 3-11.

[8] *Social Security Bulletin* (June 1959), p. 38, Table 17.

Special needs, that are considered in the public assistance payment, frequently arise because of infirmities, special diets required by a physician, the necessity to eat in restaurants, moving and storage expenses caused by an eviction, and housekeeping and laundry service for persons unable to do this themselves.

The state laws determine how much property and other resources an applicant for old-age assistance may have and still receive aid.[9] The amounts of property vary in the states. For example, California, which calls old-age assistance "Old-Age Security," grants this aid to needy aged who own real property up to an assessed value of $5,000, and personal property of $1,200 for one person and $2,000 for a couple. Usually, transfer or assignment of property in order to qualify for old-age assistance makes such old persons ineligible for aid. Frequently, residence of the last year before application and of five years within the last nine years is required.

At the local welfare department, the applicant receives help in filling out the required application forms and signs his statements under oath. Then a social investigation at his home is made in which the resources of the applicant and the ability of his relatives to contribute to his support are explored. Emergency aid is given during this investigation if absolutely necessary. The decision by the county or city authorities is made in writing so that the applicant may request a hearing and reconsideration if he is not satisfied. He is entitled to attend the hearing and to be represented by an attorney, and he may appeal to a commission or board of the state department of social welfare for another hearing and a final decision. Court suit is usually possible only if the applicant feels himself aggrieved by misinterpretation of the law.

Old-age assistance payments, beyond the Federal share, are paid either by the states in full or partly by counties and cities. Payments are made without discrimination. The Federal and state administrations encourage the preservation of the client's self-respect, dignity, self-reliance, and of his feeling of being a useful "senior citizen"—at

---

[9] For an analysis of the specific features in the states, see "Characteristics of State Public Assistance Plans Under the Social Security Act," *Report No. 27* (Social Security Administration, Bureau of Public Assistance, 1956). The territories—particularly Puerto Rico and the Virgin Islands—are not discussed because social conditions vary widely from those of the continent. See also Wilbur F. Cohen, "Needed Changes in Social Welfare Programs and Objectives," *Social Service Review,* Vol. XXXIII, No. 1 (March 1959).

least in theory—but, the lack of well-trained personnel sometimes makes it difficult to live up to these principles.

Each state designates an authority which has to establish and maintain standards for the types of public and private institutions in which recipients of old-age assistance may live. This supervision discourages such inadequate conditions in nursing and convalescent homes as poor service, untrained personnel, fire hazards, and lack of proper medical and dietary care.

F. Aid to the Blind

The second categorical assistance program for which the Federal government shares expenses with the states is aid to the needy blind. State laws determine which persons are considered "blind," and the designation is usually totally blind or with an impairment of sight which prevents competitive industrial work. A practical definition of "needy blind" is presented in an Oregon statute: "an individual whose vision is so defective as to prevent the performance of ordinary activities for which eyesight is essential." The states also decide whether this category shall be limited to a minimum and maximum age, for example, over sixteen years, and sometimes under sixty-five. In the beginning of 1960, over 109,000 needy blind received aid in the United States. The average monthly payments differed from a maximum of $117.69 in Massachusetts to a minimum of $37.41 in West Virginia, with a total national average of $69.05 per month.[10] Some states require citizenship, but a number require residence, as in old-age assistance, for persons who became blind outside of the state. In order to receive Federal grants, states may not specify more stringent residence requirements than five years out of the last nine in the state, of which the year immediately preceding the application is one. The procedure of application is the same as in old-age assistance. The states decide in their legislation how much property and other resources a person may have in order to receive aid to the blind. Fifty dollars monthly earned income is disregarded in determining the need of the blind person. An applicant for aid to the blind is examined by a medical eye specialist (ophthalmologist) or an optometrist, and Federal grants are used for the remuneration for their services to the blind.

[10] *Social Security Bulletin,* Vol. 23, No. 1 (January 1960), p. 30, Table 12.

California, Missouri, Nevada, and Pennsylvania have set up special state-financed programs in order to encourage blind persons to become self-supporting. An example is the California program of Aid to Partially Self-Supporting Blind Residents which encourages blind persons to achieve self-support by establishing themselves in business, farming, regular trade, employment in industry or commerce, or the operation of a vending stand. This is done by permitting them to keep $1,000 plus one-half of the exceeding gainful income a year without considering this income in the determination for their monthly assistance payment.

Additional services provided by many states for the blind are such as free medical examination and treatment, special education of children in schools for the blind, or classes for visually handicapped children, conducted usually under the auspices of the state department of education. Rehabilitation services render occupational counseling, vocational guidance, and training for employment or special trades, such as for piano tuning, broom making, handicrafts, or professional work. They are administered by a State Bureau of Vocational Rehabilitation, which serves the blind as well as other handicapped people.

Federal grants-in-aid for rehabilitation work are allocated by the Department of Health, Education and Welfare, Office of Vocational Rehabilitation. The Federal government provides, as a part of the rehabilitation effort, grants for medical treatment, surgery, hospital care, artificial appliances, adult training centers, placement services, and assistance in providing occupational equipment. Federal grants-in-aid for the needy blind may be used for medical care to remove cataracts by surgery or to conserve vision in cases of glaucoma. Earlier and more effective medical treatment, including eye surgery, is unfortunately still a goal far from being generally achieved for persons with limited means who might be saved from blindness.

Private organizations play an important role in supplementing the services for the blind offered under public auspices. Some of them strengthen educational and rehabilitation work for the blind. Since 1921, the American Foundation for the Blind in New York has served as coordinating agency for all nationwide interests of the blind. In all states, local private groups of the blind and organizations interested in helping the blind are making valuable contributions in the field of social and recreational life of the blind. They assist them in finding employment and organizing cultural and recreational activities, and pioneering in new adventures for the blind. They promote a better understanding of the public for the needs of the blind and of the importance of more adequate services and legislation for them.

G. Aid to the Permanently and Totally Disabled

The Amendment to the Social Security Act of 1950 added a public assistance category for permanently, totally disabled persons in economic need. Until this time, many of them had been meagerly supported by counties and cities under general relief provisions without help from state or federal funds. This category includes adults over eighteen years who have serious physical or mental handicaps. The *Social Security Act* does not give a definition of "permanently and totally disabled" but allows the states to define the terms and the conditions of need which entitle one to apply for this categorical aid. The program provides either money payments to adult, invalid persons under sixty-five who are not eligible for old-age assistance, or medical and remedial care for them. In 1960, this categorical aid was in operation in all states except Arizona, Indiana, Iowa, and Nevada.

The group of persons under this category consists mainly of people who suffer from physical or mental impairment, which, in medical judgment, offers no indication of a substantial improvement, and which prevents the invalid person from being gainfully employed or from normal homemaking, such as heart diseases, arthritis, or paralysis. The program, however, is not limited to completely helpless people. Economic assistance to these disabled persons resembles the aid to needy blind people. Standards of assistance and special requirements in the states vary. In general, the administration is carried out by the state and local agencies, such as the department of social welfare, which also are in charge of the other categorical assistance programs. The average payment, in October 1959, in this category of 346,783 recipients was $64.12 per month per person, slightly less than the average aid for the needy blind.[11] It is hoped that medical care and rehabilitation for these invalids will be intensified by more adequate financial support with the help of Federal grants-in-aid for this group. At present, the categorical assistance may be used for

---

[11] *Social Security Bulletin,* Vol. 23, No. 1 (January 1960), p. 32, Table 14.

cash payments, remedial care, hospitalization, and medical treatment. The physicians and hospitals may be paid directly by the welfare authorities in behalf of the patients.

Categorical assistance is given on the basis of the medical findings and upon the applicant's social and emotional ability to carry out his responsibilities as a wage-earner or homemaker. A permanent physiological or mental impairment may exist from birth or may be caused by illness or accident. It must be a permanent condition, likely to last for life or not to improve or disappear spontaneously. The possibility of improvement or recovery by remedial or therapeutic treatment and vocational rehabilitation, however, does not prohibit the assistance payment. The Federal grant to the states is based upon: (1) expenditures for assistance, as money payments, to the recipients for expenses incurred from medical and remedial treatment, and (2) one-half of the costs of proper, efficient administration of the program.

Among the 2,000,000 physically handicapped persons in the United States, in need of rehabilitation, are many permanently and totally disabled. New York supports the largest number of the needy disabled. The expansion of the Federal old-age and survivors insurance system to include disabled insured workers fifty to sixty-five years of age, also helps a group of the disabled by social insurance benefits. But, due to the limited scope of the Disability Insurance Plan, public assistance to the permanently, totally disabled still remains a major source of support to the severely handicapped.

H. Aid to Dependent Children

Destitute children have always constituted a large proportion of the poor. In Colonial times, they were indentured, or sold outright, to foster families; during the nineteenth century they were placed in almshouses and, later, in orphan asylums, until criticism of the damage of institutional care again led to the use of boarding homes, particularly in rural families. The first White House Conference, in 1909, advocated that children should remain in their own homes whenever possible and not be removed for economic reasons. Their mothers should receive "mothers' allowances" so that they would not be forced to give their children away while they worked as domestics or in factories. From this concept, grew a program of Aid to Dependent Children as a categorical form of public assistance under the *Social Security Act*. Its definition of a dependent child is, "a needy child under eighteen years of age, who has been deprived of parental support or care by reason of the death, continued absence from the home, or physical or mental incapacity of a parent, and who is living with his father, mother, grandmother, grandfather, brother, sister, step-mother, step-father, step-brother, step-sister, uncle, aunt, first cousin, nephew, or niece in a place of residence maintained by one or more of such relatives as his own and their own home." This does not include all needy children, such as orphans, who have no close relatives and, therefore, cannot live with them, or children who must be placed in foster families or children's institutions.[12] The payment is made to the mother or to the relative who takes care of the child. Upon application, aid has to be given with reasonable promptness. The time which elapses between application and payment of aid differs among the states.

In order to receive Federal grants, the states cannot impose a residence requirement of more than one year or any special county residence for aid to dependent children. The states determine, in their laws and regulations, the requirements for eligibility to receive ADC (Aid to Dependent Children) and how much shall be paid. Frequently, the need of the child is caused by the desertion of the father; many statutes require a certain period of absence. Usually, aid is given on a standard budget basis which considers the elementary needs of the child and of the mother or the caretaker with regard to local conditions. In March 1959 the average payment was $107.86 per family and $28.68 per recipient, but these payments varied greatly between the states. The lowest average payment per family, in Mississippi with $40.75 per month, contrasted with the highest average of $166.33 in Wisconsin. The lowest monthly average payment per recipient of $7.03 in Missouri differed substantially from the highest average of $48.16 in Connecticut.[13] The proportion of the entire child population receiving aid also varies between 1.1 per

---

[12] The number of full orphans is rather small, since many are adopted either by relatives or other persons, and they are only an insignificant proportion of all children in financial need. See Ernest F. Witte, "Children in the Public Assistance Family," *Child Welfare*, Vol. XXXVIII, No. 1 (January 1959).

[13] *Social Security Bulletin* (June 1959), p. 39, Table 19.

cent in New Jersey to 7.8 per cent in Louisiana. Only one-fifth of the children receiving help under this program, in 1951, lost their fathers through death; in about one-fourth of the cases the fathers were insane, crippled, chronically ill, or committed to prison; and in the cases of more than one-half of these dependent children, the father had deserted the family, or was divorced and did not support the child.

Aid to dependent children is not the only social security program to help needy children. An increasing number of children receive support under Old-Age and Survivors Insurance and some under Workmen's Compensation laws, but, at present, ADC supports a larger number than all other measures which provide children economic aid.[14]

Whenever aid to dependent children is given to a child who has been abandoned by a parent, the state agency has to report the case promptly to the law enforcement authority—usually the district attorney. The purpose of this so-called *"NOLEO"-Amendment of 1950* (notice to law enforcement officials), is to facilitate legal action against the deserting father, to force him to assume his financial responsibility for the support of his child. Nearly all states enacted reciprocal legislation to enforce the support of dependents; but, still, many difficulties exist in legal procedure against parents in other parts of the country. Mothers sometimes are afraid that court action may prevent their husbands from returning to the family, making them hostile and desiring divorce rather than reconciliation. However, the public resents deserting fathers relinquishing their moral and legal responsibility for the support of their children, and insists that they should be discouraged from unburdening their own obligations upon public welfare agencies.

Violent accusations are made, again and again, in newspapers and journals that the public is exploited through the abuse of ADC, which the public supports, by shiftless, irresponsible people unwilling to work, particularly women, who live with various men and have numerous illegitimate children. But, even these critics usually admit that cases of abuse are only exceptions, and that the maintenance of family life for the children in economic need, which is made possible

---

[14] In March 1959, 2,235,435 children were supported by ADC while 1,695,-411 children received insurance benefits under Old-Age and Survivors Insurance. *Social Security Bulletin* (June 1959), p. 29, Table 6, and p. 39, Table 19.

by ADC, will protect the vast majority against the dangers of maladjustment, delinquency, and crime.

The Federal government shares the expenses for aid to dependent children, and pays one-half of the administrative cost of the program. The Federal share amounts to 14/17 of $17 for the first dependent child and the same amount for his mother or care-taker, plus one half to 65 per cent of the balance, up to $32 monthly, for child and care-taker. The Federal government's share has been established in accordance with the principle of equalization in favor of the poorer states, on the basis of the state's per capita income during the last three years compared with the national income. For the second, and all subsequent children in the same family, the Federal share for ADC is 14/17 of the first $17 of the state's average monthly payment, plus 50 to 65 per cent of the payment over $17 but not exceeding $23.

The states either meet the entire residual cost for ADC or divide it among the state and local units of government (counties, cities, and townships).

Since some children in economic need cannot live with relatives and have to be placed in foster families, or in orphanages or other children's institutions for which Federal grants-in-aid are not available, the states support these children either in the same way as "dependent children" or under their general assistance plans. For example, California administers categorical assistance under the title "needy children" to all children who are deprived of parental support. These children in foster families or children's institutions are supported, from state and local funds; but, less than 7 per cent of needy children live outside of their own families.

The American Public Welfare Association conducted an interesting study to determine whether the program of aid to dependent children is successful in conserving the human resources of our nation upon which its future depends.[15] The results of this research show that it is necessary to expand and to improve financial assistance and

---

[15] Gordon M. Blackwell and Raymond F. Gould, *Future Citizens All* (Chicago: American Public Welfare Association, 1952); Maude Von P. Kemp, *et al.*, *"Casework Services in ADC,"* (Chicago: American Public Welfare Association, 1957); and, Helen B. Foster, "Family-Centered Services Through ADC," *Social Welfare Forum* (1958), pp. 154-165.

social services to children and young people deprived of sufficient support by their parents. One of the most important achievements of ADC is that it has encouraged keeping families together. Through this program, child neglect, illegitimate births, delinquency, and crime have occurred less frequently than might have been expected in this endangered and stress-ridden group without such aid. It was found that one-fourth of the families were still in economic need when the assistance under this program had to be terminated because of its legal restrictions about the age of the children, other income, and return of an absent father. But, the study also proved that the assistance payments in many parts of the country are still so low that they barely reach minimum subsistence standards.

I. General Assistance

General assistance is public relief to needy persons who are not eligible for one of the four categorical public assistance programs. The rigid limitations of our public assistance categories explain why numerous persons are not encompassed by this categorical approach; general assistance, as a rule, is their only recourse. The requirements for public assistance, such as legal settlement, no family to assume support, and exhaustion of all resources and savings, which we have discussed, apply to general assistance even more rigidly than to the categories of public assistance. One reason for this practice is the fact that general assistance is financed, more than any other economic relief program, by the cities, townships, or counties which have the weakest tax power. In some states, the cost of general assistance is shared between the state and the community or county, with the state frequently paying one-half or more of the expenses. In only ten states, was the entire financial burden of general assistance in 1960 met by the state without a contribution from the communities and counties. Since the Federal government does not share the cost of general assistance, the poorer states and communities are inclined to spend as little as possible for general assistance.

The uneven treatment of the persons in need under general assistance in the various states is characterized by the following facts: In October 1959, 403,000 persons were supported by general assistance with an average aid of $70.97 monthly per person. Here again, the average monthly payment varied widely between the states, from $12.63 in Alabama to $102.16 in New Jersey.[16]

"Work-relief" may sometimes be required as a condition for the receipt of general assistance, although it is seldom applied even when state and local statutes authorize this method of determining the willingness of an applicant to work. The assignment of "relief clients" to useless types of work, such as leaf-raking and wood-piling, is rare today.

In some states, the administration of general assistance is integrated into the public assistance program at the local level; in other states, it is still administered separately. Whenever the state pays the entire cost or shares the expenses for general assistance, the state welfare agency sets the standards of the program, supervises the administration, or carries it out itself. Where no financial aid for general assistance is given to community or county, the local authority determines the methods and form of general assistance, sometimes still granting relief in kind, by vouchers or tickets, which is no longer permitted in categorical assistance. Frequently, persons who seem employable are denied relief in order to force them to work regardless of whether or not a job is, in fact, available. Furthermore, the county or township will not give general assistance until the person has spent his last penny.

General assistance has been called "a patchwork" because each state handles it in a different way. Principles, standards, administration, and financing vary even within the counties and cities of the same state. Frequently, the treatment of needy persons depends upon the local community in which they fall sick or find themselves unemployed. Professional associations in social work have advocated that the Federal government share the expenses for general assistance as a special category or combine all public assistance categories into one which would be supported by grants-in-aid from the Federal government. But, Congress and the conscience of the people have not, as yet, been ready to translate this proposal into reality. There is still too much suspicion that an unemployed, able-bodied person asks for relief because of willful idleness, whereas he could find a job and support himself and his family. The public is afraid that public

---

[16] *Social Security Bulletin,* Vol. 23, No. 1 (January 1960), p. 32, Table 15.

assistance might be made too easy, and too generous, and the anxiety of the taxpayers that their burden might be still heavier is understandable in a time of high taxes. Despite these facts, however, the need for integration of all types of public assistance into one unified program, administered by the same agency, and staffed with trained social workers remains an essential goal.

J. Training and Research

Training of Public Welfare Personnel. Congress authorized, in 1956, Federal appropriations to the states to help them to increase trained personnel for public welfare programs. A Federal share of 80 per cent of the total expenses for a period of five years, with an initial appropriation of $5,000,000, was scheduled. The funds were to be used for grants to public or private institutions of higher learning for the education of public welfare personnel and for fellowships, traineeships, study courses, and seminars.

Research and Demonstration Projects. To learn more about the causes of dependency in our present society, and to find the most effective means of preventing and eliminating dependency, the *Amendment of 1956* introduced, under Title XI, of *the Social Security Act,* a new program of cooperative research and demonstration projects. It authorized Federal grants to the states, jointly financed cooperative arrangements with the states and with public and non-profit organizations for sharing the expenses of research and demonstration projects. They were to be related to the prevention or reduction of dependency, to the coordination of planning between private and public welfare agencies, or the improvement of the administration and the effectiveness of programs under the *Social Security Act* and related measures.

Unfortunately, the *Amendment of 1956,* calling for Federal grants to the states for training of public welfare personnel and for research and demonstration projects, was not followed by actual appropriations of Congress. The Senate Appropriations Committee, in June 1959, disallowed the requested funds with the argument that states have made little use for Federal funds for educational purposes. It is necessary that Congress finally implement its own policy by securing the funds for education and research.

K. Casework in Public Assistance

Prior to the Great Depression of 1929, most townships and counties limited their poor relief to meagre financial assistance in kind or money, while private charities in urban communities helped a large proportion of the needy and tried to rehabilitate them through casework services based upon an understanding of the cause of their poverty. At that time, most poor law authorities employed untrained personnel, although supervisors were partly professional workers. The changes made during the Depression and under the New Deal, transferred the main responsibility for the care of persons in need to the public welfare agencies where many professional social workers from private charities were employed. They applied their belief that the cause of destitution needed to be explored in each individual case in order to cure it and to prevent its recurrence. Since the enactment of the *Social Security Act of 1935* and the creation of public assistance categories (the aged, the blind, the dependent children, and, later, the disabled), the objective of public welfare is undergoing progressive change. Assistance is no longer a "handout," but is rendered to persons in need as a "right." The applicant must be considered in his social, economic, and personal condition, his feelings about relief, and his fear of humiliation.[17] Casework in public assistance agencies, with large case loads and pressure of work, requires different approaches from those applied in private family and children agencies. The *Amendment of the Social Security Act of 1956* broadened the purpose of public assistance beyond giving financial aid to provide personal services to the recipients, in order to help them toward independent living. Casework with aged people is directed toward self-care, and in work with the blind and disabled toward self-care and self-support after rehabilitation or training. Casework in the aid to dependent children program aims to keep the children in their own homes and to maintain and to strengthen family life, whereby co-operation with other public and private social and health agencies shall be secured. The purpose of public assistance, therefore, is to

---

[17] An interpretation of the need of casework skills in public welfare is presented by Professor Charlotte Towle, *Common Human Needs* (Chicago: University of Chicago Press, 1945); and, Kermit T. Wiltse, *Public Assistance Personnel: Educational Requirements and Training Facilities* (Berkeley: University of California Press, 1959).

assure adequate economic help, keeping in mind the self-respect, the dignity, and the legal rights of recipients. Furthermore, in order to achieve its purpose public assistance must be provided with consideration of the goal of financial and personal independence, so that the recipients will be able to live in the community in the same way as other individuals.

The caseworker in a public welfare agency has to be sincerely convinced of the fact that an individual in economic need has a rightful claim on society for public assistance. By explaining clearly legal requirements and the policy of the agency, the worker will be able to help the client present the necessary data and facts for establishing "eligibility" for public assistance. This has to be done in a way which expresses the confidence of the worker in the client and her respect for him, rather than using a hostile attitude which tries to prevent the client from getting aid. The worker has to understand how vitally important money is for everyone in financial stress in our society. In general, clients come to social agencies in times of want and anxiety, and they often are emotionally disturbed. They naturally are more sensitive to their treatment than the average citizen, and they react differently to the kind of approach used by the caseworker.

Casework in public welfare, therefore, requires professional skills. The caseworker in his job must have: skill in personal interviewing; skill in establishing a positive, constructive relationship with the client; training in perception and observation of human beings and in interpreting documents; ability to distinguish between pertinent facts that are essential for the application and personal information not needed for the decision on assistance or service in which the client is interested; skill in recognizing distress and emotional imbalance, which requires help from such other sources as a mental hygiene clinic; skill in administration, communication, recording, and reporting; ability to comply with the prescribed policy and procedure of the agency; awareness of the client's social, health, and personal needs and ability to encourage the client to use other community resources; ability to plan and organize his own work load efficiently; and ability to accept and use supervision with intelligence in the interest of the client.

In rural areas there usually are no private social agencies available for casework services, so that the county welfare department is the only source of help for the client. The caseworker in the urban public agency needs to have accurate knowledge of the services and policies of other agencies in the community, in order to refer clients who will receive more effective aid to another social agency. The caseworker in public assistance has to be careful not to use the client's economic helplessness to force upon him an undesired change in attitude or way of life, even if the worker is convinced that such change is in the interest of the client or of his family. If the caseworker acts upon request of an authoritative agency, such as a court, a parole board, or a youth authority, the source of any specific request has to be clearly explained to the client.

The following case may illustrate casework in public assistance:

The Case of Mary [18]

The worker was frankly intrigued by this small, pleasant girl who was declining her offer of help with planning for her unborn child. Mary, just 20, unmarried, and pregnant with her third illegitimate child, had come to apply for ADC for Jack, her 18-month-old son, until she would be able to return to work. Because she was undecided about plans for her coming child, she had been referred to "child welfare." By now the worker was grasping rather quickly that Mary was making her own plans and was only asking for help in carrying them out; also, that she meant the decision about the baby to be her own decision.

The application for ADC was soon approved, and the child welfare worker began seeing Mary regularly. She had learned a little about Mary by the time the baby was born. Mary wouldn't talk much about her first child, born in a maternity home when she was only fifteen. This baby had been released to an agency for adoption. Two years later, when Jack was born, Mary had not sought agency service. Instead, she had prevailed upon her mother to keep Jack for her while she worked. Mary, in turn, had taken a job as waitress to support the entire family, which included a sister, just out of the TB hospital, and an unemployed thirty-three-year-old brother who was not looking for a job. Later another sister, dying of TB, moved into the home with her husband and six children.

---

[18] The author is indebted to the *Tennessee Public Welfare Record*, Vol. XII, No. 5 (October 1958), pp. 91-93, for permission to use this case study.

Mary's whole background was one of poverty and disease, especially TB. Her father had died when she was thirteen, the youngest of six children. Mrs. James, who did not object to Mary's working to support the entire family, reported that Mary wasn't bright, and that she wasn't capable of caring for a child. Mary was reported as being a "crackpot," "immoral," and "one who could not stand up under a mental test."

When Mary's baby was born, the worker visited her in the hospital. They walked down to the nursery together to see Becky, her baby girl. Mary was still undecided about what she wanted for Becky. She knew she didn't want to take her home. She had had enough experience with TB to realize what a hazard it would be for Becky. She asked for temporary boarding care and time to work out other plans. Recognizing that Becky needed to be with her permanent family soon, they set up a plan for regular interviews in order to think about Becky's future, and Mary understood that as Becky's mother the decision must be hers.

As Mary grew to trust the worker, she let her see what she was really like. Mary was not stupid. She was intelligent and ambitious. She told how badly she wanted to get a factory job, go to night school, complete her education, and get a job in an office. She did not want to be a waitress. As Mary talked about her mother, the worker realized that a strange attachment was all mixed up with anger and resentment. She was helped to tell how she really felt about the burden of supporting her brother. Mary felt that her mother had taken over Jack completely and had made him her child rather than Mary's. The worker realized that this girl who had had three babies, never really had a child that she could call her own. She knew that her job was to help Mary to become a person in her own right and to feel and function as a parent.

When Becky was a few weeks old, Mary called to say that she was now working and the ADC grant could be discontinued. She did have to return to waitress work because it was all she knew how to do, but it allowed no time for night school. She still had to support her family, but the Department paid the total cost of Becky's care in a foster boarding home. There were times when Mary could easily have been led into surrendering Becky for adoption or taking her back to her mother, but the worker knew she was not ready. She visited Becky in the office, and inquired regularly about her progress.

When Becky was about eight months old, Mary came to the office with a plan and a request: Would the agency continue to board the baby for an additional six to eight months? Mary had enrolled in a training course for licensed practical nurses. When she completed the course she would be eligible for a really good job and could take the baby. When asked how she was going to finance herself and the family during this period, she explained that for most of the time, until the training involved night duty, she would continue to work as a waitress from 4 P.M. until midnight and on weekends. The worker wondered whether Mary's ambition would last through this sort of schedule and whether she could stand it physically. She thought she could do it. The worker agreed to continue to keep the baby. Mary was introduced to the foster mother who gladly gave permission for her to visit the baby on Sundays.

Mary did it, too! Although her schedule made it difficult for the worker to see her, she kept in touch to report her progress and her problems. She was enjoying the work and was able to stand the long hours, although she lost some weight. The home situation did not improve, and the family continued to criticize her. Mary found the courage to tell her brother that he would have to go to work or leave home, or she would. And she did. She moved into a room of her own across town. She continued to support her mother and Jack and spent part of each Sunday with him. Mary said she was tired of living as she had always done, as the family had always done! She intended to BE somebody! There was an obvious improvement in her grooming, her manners and her speech.

When Mary finished her course, she took over financial responsibility for Becky. Her first nursing job was in a small infirmary where she had to "live in." Although she changed the Miss to Mrs. in front of her name, she was completely frank with her employer about her status as an unwed mother. This woman took a special interest in Mary and helped her arrange a correspondence course to complete her high school work. Mary spent her days off visiting Jack and Becky. She began to face the reality of living away from her children and supporting the two of them on her small salary. She reckoned with the fact that, as long as she had to be away ministering to others, she could not give her own children the kind of mothering she wanted them to have. Realizing too, that as the months flew by Becky was growing up, she finally decided to release her for adoption.

Mary later told the worker about a young man she began dating. They eventually became engaged. Occasionally she would ask the worker's advice about various problems: What did the worker think of her taking a trip to the mountains with him—with her mother as chaperone? She shared with the worker some of the plans they began to make for their life together. She would continue working until they could start buying a home, and then she would give up her job and spend all her time taking good care of her husband and Jack, who was to live with them.

After her marriage Mary's calls grew further apart. It has been a long time since we have heard from her. We really don't know how things worked out. But Mary had a way of seeing things through. Perhaps she doesn't need us any more.

In concluding our discussion of public assistance, we might well look at the two conflicting philosophies about the best method of aiding people in financial need which we have observed in the development of public relief and in the new modern concept of public assistance. The old, traditional policy was the "punitive approach." In England, and, during the two first centuries of American history, under the impact of Puritan theory, this practice made the receipt of poor relief as unbearable and intolerable as possible. It was hoped that these conditions would induce people in need to avoid asking for support. The humiliations connected with poor relief, the swearing of the pauper oath, and the posting of pauper lists on the market place, in church, and at the city hall were devised to deter most indigent people from applying for poor relief. One expected they would seek other sources for relief, such as asking relatives and neighbors for help, accepting underpaid work and substandard labor conditions, or even begging, to sustain themselves. Recently, some inclination to revive this punitive method has shown itself in the *Jenner Amendment,* and legislation in twenty-three states desires to deter people in economic need from asking for assistance by opening the assistance rolls for public inspection. The experience in those states has not led, so far, to any larger reduction in public assistance cases than in other states which continue to keep the names of recipients of public assistance confidential. This is evidence of the fact that the number of chiselers and swindlers of public assistance is small, and that the vast majority of recipients are in such urgent need of economic help that at the cost of their self-respect and pride they must apply for assistance, even if their name is exposed to public humiliation. There are some exceptions, such as an old, respectable man who committed suicide a few days after it had been announced that the names of all assistance recipients would be made public. Not only social workers are convinced that this punitive approach is placing an unwarranted humiliation upon human beings who are mostly in need without a personal fault, and that it will not really reduce the expense of public assistance.

Other reflections of this punitive approach can be seen in the measures taken by some states in denying aid to dependent children of a mother whose husband has deserted her and the children, before she has exhausted all legal efforts to force support from the father. Because these measures disregard hope for the return of the father to the family, a reconciliation of the parents may be discouraged in enforcing them. Certainly, desertion should not be encouraged, in the interest of the family, the mother, and the children; but careful, conscientious counseling of the mother is needed in order to advise her about the proper efforts she should make to induce her husband to support the children. The same efforts have often been made with unmarried mothers who did not want to destroy the chance of a marriage by hostile enforcement of support from the father of the illegitimate child.

In regard to the treatment of unmarried mothers, some have suggested another punitive measure: demanding the denial of economic aid to children in order to discourage the mother from promiscuous behavior. Advocates of this method seem to believe that women have become pregnant and bear illegitimate children in hope of getting from $10 to $28 a month from ADC which states pay on an average. Social workers have found little evidence of this claim. In fact, vital statistics prove that only 3 to 4 per cent of births in our country occur out of wedlock, and about one-half of these babies are born to teen-age girls who seldom, in their adolescent status, speculate about such a doubtful financial basis for their lives. Most of those women who have several illegitimate children are retarded, feeble-minded, or disturbed persons with serious personal mental problems. It also should not be overlooked that in depriving the mother of an illegitimate child of public aid, the child is hurt most.

Another punitive treatment of parents is found in the attitude of some social agencies to refuse aid because housing is not considered adequate. It is true that child welfare workers will insist that children should not be endangered by living in vermin-infested, unsanitary places whenever the parents can get better, healthier quarters. But the size of the payments made by ADC, in many states, is still so low that it would be difficult for widows or unmarried mothers to avoid living in substandard housing conditions. Judges and social workers, aware of the findings of child psychology, do not want to take the responsibility for separating children from their mother as long as she loves the children and does not endanger them. However, the denial of public aid leads to hunger, sickness, and suffering of the children, and to a delinquent behavior which is destructive to them, and a burden to society.

Thus, the punitive approach with its restrictive, harsh treatment does not produce substantial savings of assistance funds and creates human suffering, bitterness, delinquency, and humiliation as well. In contrast to this attitude, stands the *philosophy of rehabilitation,* or *constructive aid.* Practice of this approach has been given less attention in newspapers, radio, and public discussions than the rare incidences of chiseling, abuse of public aid, and the demands for harsh treatment. Particularly important have been measures of rehabilitation for persons with physical handicaps who have been helped by vocational training, placement, and equipment to become financially self-supporting. Rehabilitation services make it possible for these families not only to be removed from public assistance rolls, but also to gain the satisfaction of becoming respected members of their community. Often, some hundred dollars spent on rehabilitation save, in the long run, thousands on relief, and transform the former relief clients into happy, proud, self-supporting citizens. The same approach has been encouraged by Congress in the establishment of the categorical assistance program for disabled adults, financed by Federal grants-in-aid. As a result, more adequate and effective medical and orthopedic treatment, vocational guidance, occupational training, and psychological and social casework help may be applied to assist them to take care of themselves and of their families again.

In this rehabilitative approach, preventive services play an important role. They protect vulnerable groups so that they do not become destitute, desperate, or hostile toward society. Such a concept includes the establishment of reasonable standards of public aid.

This permits the underprivileged to live on a level of decency so that they are not threatened by hunger and cold, contagious diseases, and emotional upset; and may rear their children to become responsible citizens.

The future trends in public assistance depend upon two major factors: the social and economic conditions of our country, and the amount of economic security granted the population under the expanded system of social insurance. In times of depression and unemployment, both general and categorical assistance will have to assume greater responsibility for those persons and families who find insufficient protection, or none at all, from unemployment insurance benefits. There are still many people who are not covered by insurance schemes—casual workers, migratory labor, and other unprotected groups. Thus, a substantial responsibility remains with the public assistance program to protect people against destitution and to help them to become self-supporting again, as much as their health and capacities permit.

II. SOCIAL INSURANCE

Social security in our American form of democratic government is based upon three types of services: (1) a program of *social insurance*, which primarily aims to establish a minimum standard of health and decency by providing insurance against the loss of earning capacity; (2) a program of *public assistance* to aid persons in individual economic need; and (3) a program of *welfare and health services* devised to prevent ill health and maladjustment and to meet individual and social needs.

The historical background of social insurance begins in the functions of the medieval craft and merchant guilds, in the twelfth century. Each organized, among their own members, mutual aid societies which provided benefits in cases of severe sickness and invalidity, burial expenses, and pensions to widows and orphans after the member's death, in return for regular contributions to the fund. What the required contributions lacked in accuracy of actuarial precision, was compensated for by the warm and sympathetic spirit in the benevolent administration of the funds by fellow members in small, closely knit societies.

At the time of the Industrial Revolution, a more comprehensive system of governmental social insurance was first established in Germany under Chancellor Bismarck. The program included sickness and maternity insurance (1883), workmen's compensation (1884), and old-age and invalidity insurance (1889). In England, workmen's compensation was enacted in 1897, and unemployment and health insurance was established by the *National Insurance Act of 1911.*

A. The Nature of Social Insurance

The mutual aid societies of the guilds protected their members from destitution and from the humiliation of pauper relief. Modern programs of social insurance were established in order to protect the insured workers against the many more contingencies of life in an industrial society: unemployment, old-age dependency, industrial accidents, sickness, disability, and death of the breadwinner. Social insurance protection is based upon statutory provisions which determine precisely which persons are eligible, the conditions under which benefits are to be paid as a matter of legal right, and the amount and nature of these benefits. As in the practice of commercial insurance, the risk of loss of income or of incurring catastrophic expenses is spread by social insurance over large groups of people and over long periods of time. The few persons who suffer these losses, in a given year, could not meet this risk from their own means or providence. Social insurance benefits are financed either entirely or in part by contributions of the insured persons, by their employers in their behalf, or by both. Thus, the beneficiaries have a legal as well as an economic and moral claim to the benefits when the contingency occurs. Eligibility and benefits are predictable. Social insurance benefits are a legal right of the insured person without regard to his personal economic need or financial situation; no means test may be required in order to qualify the insured for benefits. The claim for social insurance is based upon the former occupation of the insured person, whether independent or employed, and not upon individual financial indigence. The insured, or his survivors, may use the benefits as they please. This fact implies that the claimants of social insurance benefits are less subject to the discretion of the agencies which administer the social insurance plan than are the applicants for public assistance. As a social institution, social insurance provides income security on the basis of presumptive need, not of demonstrated want, and its benefits are determined by the principle of average, common necessities of life rather than individual poverty. In cases of special, increased personal needs, social insurance benefits may have to be supplemented by public assistance payments.

Another difference between social insurance and public assistance is the method of financing. In the United States, social insurance is financed exclusively by the insured persons and their employers, whereas public assistance is financed by taxes. In many foreign systems, taxes supplement these contributions. Social insurance uses an actuarial base for determining contributions and benefits, but the operational principles of private, commercial insurance and nonprofit social insurance in this respect are not the same. Social insurance benefits in the United States, and in other countries which do not apply a flat-rate system, are related to the previous work and earnings of the insured. In public assistance, this element is without importance; merely the individual want of the applicant is considered.

Social insurance has been preferred to public assistance because social insurance recipients maintain a feeling of self-earned rights, independence, and self-reliance; they have built up social insurance funds by their own work; no connection with charity or poor relief exists; and the receipt of social insurance benefits does not impair their social status, the respect of their neighbors, nor any citizen's rights. From the standpoint of administration, social insurance provides income security by means of simple procedure. Detailed, individual social-economic investigation is not required, because the benefits are not dependent upon personal want of the insured. It reduces the number of people who are in poverty and have to depend upon public assistance payments. In general, the principle of social insurance, as a sound system of necessary basic economic protection against the dangers inherent in an industrial society, is recognized in most countries of the world.

In the United States, the ideals of private enterprise and individual initiative, as well as the fear of government interference and of the financial burden of higher taxes, have long delayed the introduction of social insurance. The first social insurance legislation, which started on a state basis in 1910 in our country, was workmen's compensation for the protection of workers, and their families, who were injured or killed by industrial accidents. The *Social Security Act of 1935* established old-age insurance as a Federal social insurance program and unemployment compensation as a Federal-state program. Special social insurance systems have been created for railroad workers and employees, including unemployment, disability, maternity, and retirement insurance benefits. No compulsory health insurance and maternity insurance program has been enacted in the United States.

The basic principle of social security itself, however, has been fully accepted with the enactment of the *Social Security Act* and its amendments by both political parties in our country.

We shall discuss, first, the existing three types of social insurance in our country: old-age survivors' and disability insurance, unemployment compensation (both based upon the provisions of the Social Security Act), and workmen's compensation established by state legislation. We shall then take up the question of health insurance and family allowances.

B. Old-Age, Survivors, and Disability Insurance

The Old-Age and Survivors Insurance Program, created by the *Social Security Act of 1935,* is the only Federal program, and the most comprehensive social insurance system in the United States. About 90 per cent of our working population are covered, and nearly thirteen million people already receive monthly benefits under its provisions. The purpose of the system is to protect workers and self-employed persons and their families from the economic hazards of old age and death. The law provides for compulsory contributions from workers, their employers, and self-employed people throughout the period of their gainful employment; and for benefits related to prior earnings to the retired, their families, and the dependent survivors after the death of the breadwinner. The original *Social Security Act of 1935* protected the workers, but the *Amendments of 1939* and *1950* changed the emphasis to a family basis. The groups covered were increased and benefits were made more adequate in the *Amendments of 1950, 1952, 1954, 1956,* and *1958,* to compensate the family of the insured for a portion of the loss in income sustained after retirement or through the death of the breadwinner.

C. Coverage

Insured under old-age, survivors' and disability insurance are workers in "covered employment," in industry, commerce, agriculture, domestic employment, Federal employment not covered by special retirement systems, and self-employed persons, including farm operators with yearly earnings of $400 or more. For employees and self-employed persons, earnings are considered up to $4,800 a year.

The insurance coverage includes now, as a rule, most farm and domestic workers, and self-employed people, such as artisans, craftsmen, artists, store owners, businessmen, fishermen, persons employed in American firms abroad, life insurance and traveling salesmen, agent drivers, commission drivers, homeworkers, and farmers.

Excluded from coverage are (1) railroad employees who receive benefits under a special plan; (2) independent farmers with net cash incomes of less than $400 a year; (3) other self-employed persons with annual incomes of less than $400; (4) specified agricultural workers, such as those employed in crude gum processing, and farm hands who are not regularly employed; (5) domestic workers who are not regularly employed; (6) physicians; (7) policemen and firemen covered by local or state retirement systems; (8) Federal civilian employees covered by staff retirement plans, and (9) employees of subversive organizations.

Agricultural workers are covered only in regular employment, when they earn at least $150 a year for their labor, or work 20 days for cash for one employer. If the farm worker changes employers frequently, he thereby loses his status as being regularly employed. The employer has to report cash wages, to withhold the worker's tax, and to pay the entire tax. Board, lodging, meals and pay in kind are disregarded however. Crew leaders are treated as self-employed people.

Domestic servants are covered if they are paid cash wages of $50 or more by one single employer during one calendar quarter. Thus, a cleaning woman who works for a number of employers is only protected if she receives from one employer at least $50 in a calendar quarter. For those domestic servants who are covered, the law permits that the husband of the employing couple add the domestic servant in his home to the social security report for his commercial employees in his business. Otherwise, the housewife reports the income of the domestic worker on a simple form to the Director of Internal Revenue. Casual domestic work is not included.

Voluntary Insurance. Ministers and members of religious orders, public servants in state and local government, and employees of nonprofit organizations are not compulsorily insured but may be covered by voluntary arrangements. Agreements have to be made with the Department of Health, Education and Welfare.

(1) Ordained ministers of all creeds and members of religious orders employed by nonprofit organizations may be insured under old-age and survivors' insurance if they elect to be covered. The ministers have self-employed status and pay contributions of one and one-half times the rate of an employee.

(2) State, county, and city employees (other than policemen and firemen) may be insured under old-age and survivors' insurance through voluntary agreements between the state and the Federal government, if a majority of the employees vote in a referendum and a majority of the voting members favor coverage under social insurance. No referendum is required by public servants not covered by a retirement plan.

(3) Other employees of nonprofit organizations, such as schools, hospitals, churches, social agencies, foundations for scientific, literary, educational or charitable purposes, who earn at least $50 a calendar quarter, may be insured under the following conditions: The employing organization voluntarily elects to insure its employees, to pay its portion of the contribution, to deduct the employees' share of the tax, and to pay the entire contribution; and at least two-thirds of the employees vote in favor of coverage. Only those members of the present staff who voted in favor of the insurance at an election are insured, but new workers engaged by the nonprofit organization are covered on a compulsory basis after the coverage of the employees has been certified.

Social workers are not protected if they work for a social agency which does not wish to pay taxes, but they are covered if the agency is willing to do so and two-thirds of the staff members desire to be insured. They are not covered by old-age insurance if a two-thirds majority is not obtained or if they belong to a minority that voted against coverage. Social workers are insured if they join the staff of an agency which has already secured coverage for its employees. If they work for a public welfare agency which does not want to insure its staff, they are not covered. But they are insured, if the public welfare agency is willing to insure its staff and secure a state agreement to this end.[19] Workers engaged in private social work practice are covered as self-employed persons if earning over $400 a year.

D. Eligibility

Workers are insured after they have worked a certain length of time, and received more than a minimum income. Employed and self-employed workers are classified according to the length of their work into two groups—the fully insured and the currently insured. A worker is considered to be "fully insured" who, upon retirement at sixty-five years of age or later, or at the time of his death or total disablement, had worked either one-half of the calendar quarters since December 31, 1950, or, since he reached the age of twenty-one, whichever is later, but had at least six quarters of coverage, earning a minimum of $50 in each quarter. The quarters required for fully insured status increase from 18 in 1960 to 40 in 1971. Self-employed persons, under the same conditions, must have had a minimum income of $400 a year, to be counted for fully insured status. If the worker has been covered for forty quarters, whether self-employed or otherwise, he is "fully insured" for life. A person who has been covered for at least six quarters out of the thirteen preceding his death or total disability, is considered to be "currently insured." This provision secures for the widow and children of a deceased worker, the receipt of survivors benefits even if the worker was not fully insured. It also permits the totally disabled breadwinner to retain his insurance status.

The following are examples.

George Brass retired April 1, 1954 at the age of 67. He worked as an auto mechanic most of his adult life, without any long interruption due to illness. He earned, each month, more than $200. He is eligible for retirement benefit because he has been employed more than one-half the calendar quarters since December 31, 1950.

Glenn Sannon, a mill worker, died June 17, 1954 at the age of twenty-four, in an automobile accident. After working as a farm

---

[19] Eveline M. Burns, "Further Needs in the Social Insurances," *The Social Welfare Forum* (1951), p. 183.

hand with various employers, he had been employed at the mill since February 1, 1952, earning over $50 every quarter. Glenn was born August 10, 1930, and was twenty-one in 1951. His widow and his child, age fourteen months, are eligible for survivors' insurance because Glenn was currently insured by working in covered employment more than six calendar quarters during the last thirteen quarters before his death.

Eligible for insurance payments after retirement age (65 for men, and 62 for women) are: (1) the insured person, (2) his wife if she is herself sixty-two years of age, or (3) if she is younger but has in her care a child, under eighteen years, of the insured husband, and (4) a child of the insured wage earner under eighteen years of age. If the insured person is a woman, she is entitled to her own primary insurance amount, and her husband may claim benefits if he is over sixty-five, lives with his wife, and is at least half-supported by her, provided he is either not himself entitled to a primary benefit or only to one that is less than one-half of his wife's benefit.

After the death of the insured worker, the following survivors may be entitled to insurance benefits: (1) his widow, aged sixty-two, or (2) his widow, who is younger but taking care of his child; (3) a divorced wife caring for his child if he is not yet eighteen; (4) unmarried children under eighteen years of age; (5) a dependent widower of sixty-five years of age; and (6) dependent parents (father 65, mother 62).

The beneficiary may earn, in covered employment or as a self-employed person, $1,200 a year and still receive his full benefit. One month's benefit is withheld for each $100 he earns in excess of $1,200 a year. But he is entitled to his benefit for any month in which he earns less than $100. Some beneficiaries with earnings up to $2,080 a year still receive some benefits. Beneficiaries over seventy-two years of age receive their full benefit even if they have higher earnings.

The same principles apply for self-employed persons who render substantial services in the operation of their own business or trade. A wife or widow under sixty-two loses the right to receive benefit if she is divorced or remarried, or no longer caring for a child under eighteen. A child under eighteen loses his benefit rights by marriage.

Disability Insurance. In 1954, Congress enacted provisions to freeze the benefit rights of workers who were totally disabled for long periods during their working life. This is similar to a "waiver of premium" in commercial life insurance policies, to prevent the loss of retirement rights of the stricken person. In 1956, cash benefits for severely disabled insured workers, between the ages of fifty and sixty-five, were provided which are financed through a tax increase on employees, employers and the self-employed. To qualify for disability insurance benefits or for the disability freeze, if the insured worker is under fifty years of age, he must be so severely physically or mentally impaired that he cannot engage in any substantial gainful activity. Furthermore, he must have been working five years out of the ten years before the disability occurred and one and one-half years in the three years preceding his disability. The disability must have lasted at least six months, must be expected to continue indefinitely, and must be certified by medical evidence. The determination of disability usually is made by the state vocational rehabilitation agency, whereby age, education, work experience, and vocational prospects are considered. Causes of disability are mainly circulatory and nervous diseases, cancer, mental, psychosomatic and personality disorders, injuries, tuberculosis, and other infective diseases. The amount of disability benefits is the same as in old-age insurance and depends upon the average earnings of the insured person. Disability benefits are paid in addition to workmen's compensation or other Federal disability benefits. In 1958, Congress provided benefits to the dependents of the disabled worker of the same amount as in old-age insurance.

Children whose disability began before they reached age eighteen, are entitled to receive child's benefits as long as either parent receives old-age insurance payments and after the death of the parents as long as they remain disabled.

The vocational rehabilitation bureau provides vocational and medical services to disabled adults and children to prepare them for suitable work and to find employment for them. Disability insurance benefits may be withheld from individuals who refuse to accept rehabilitation services without any special reason.[20]

---

[20] Charles I. Schottland, "Social Security Amendments of 1958, A Summary and Legislative History," *Social Security Bulletin,* Vol. 21, No. 10 (1958), pp. 3-12.

E. Benefits

The benefits to the insured person, his family, and his survivors are defined as percentages of the monthly "primary insurance amount" to which the insured person is entitled under the law. This amount may be found by two different methods. It may be determined by the average wages earned since January 1, 1937 until retirement or death, or by counting only the wages he earned since January 1, 1951. The latter method, as a rule, is more advantageous because wages after 1950 were higher than those in the earlier years. This latter method is used for persons who have reached the age of twenty-two after 1950. Earnings before the insured person reached this age may be omitted. All other income, earned in covered employment, is added and divided by the total number of months since 1937, or 1950, or the attainment of the age of twenty-two. In order to raise the average of wages or income, the four years of lowest earnings may be eliminated from the computation. If the insured has twenty quarters of coverage, a "drop-out" of the five lowest income years is permitted. Thus, the average income becomes higher, and retired workers receive higher benefits.

The minimum primary benefit is $40 a month, the maximum benefit $127 a month for an insured individual. The benefit is based upon a formula by which 58.85 per cent of the first $110 of the average monthly wage is taken and 21.4 per cent of the exceeding average income is included, up to $290, rounded to the nearest dollar and increased slightly for average wages under $85.

The benefit paid to a wife or dependent husband is one-half of the primary benefit. The minimum benefit one survivor can receive is $33. A single child under eighteen is entitled to three-quarters of the father's primary insurance amount, several children to an amount based upon this sum. The insurance benefits a widow of sixty-two years can receive, or a widow with a child under eighteen, or a dependent widower and a dependent parent, are, for each, three-quarters of the primary insurance amount. However, the total monthly payment to the family cannot be more than 80 per cent of the retired person's previous average earnings, and the total family benefits shall not be reduced below one and one-half times the insured worker's primary insurance amount or $50, whichever is the greater, and no more than $254 a month as a maximum. If the percentages of the primary insurance amount exceed these limits, each dependent's payment is reduced to bring the total down to the maximum allowed. The monthly minimum payment to a family is $49, but if the wife already retired at sixty-two, $45. A woman retiring at sixty-two would receive a minimum benefit of $26 a month. The *Amendment of 1958* increased the insurance benefits by an average amount of 7 per cent.

F. Financing Old-Age and Survivors Insurance

The insurance plan is paid for by a contribution of the employee's wages and the self-employed person's earnings up to $4,800 a year. The employer and the employee each pay 3 per cent of the wage; the worker's part is deducted from his wage and sent together with the employer's share to the Bureau of Internal Revenue. The self-employed persons pay 75 per cent of the combined rate of 6 per cent, for 1960 to 1962, that is 4½ per cent of the monthly earnings up to $400 a month.

These tax rates are scheduled to increase:

Calendar year	Total	Worker	Employer	Self-employed
1960-1962 ...	6 %	3 %	3 %	4½ %
1963-1965 ...	7	3.5	3.5	5¼
1966-1968 ...	8	4	4	6
1969 and after .	9	4.5	4.5	6¾

The taxes are deposited in the Federal Old-Age and Survivors Insurance Trust Fund and the Federal Disability Insurance Trust Fund whose managing trustee is the Secretary of the Treasury.

G. Administration

The Old-Age, Survivors and Disability Insurance Program is administered by the regional offices of the Bureau of Old-Age and Survivors Insurance of the Social Security Administration, Department of Health, Education and Welfare. The central office of the Bureau, in Washington, D.C. and Baltimore, maintains wage records of all insured persons, issues rules and regulations, and carries on research. The Field Operations Division of the Bureau is part of the Department, with six area offices, several hundred field offices, and over 2,000 field stations.

H. Procedure

Everyone who is employed or self-employed in work covered by the *Social Security Act* receives a social security card. This card shows an account number under which the record of the worker's earnings is kept. No one should have more than one such card. It permits the insured person to check on his earnings and his insurance rights. The card should be shown to each employer at the beginning of a job.

Before benefits can be paid, the persons entitled to them must file an application with the nearest social security field office, the address of which may be obtained from the post office. If the claim is denied or the applicant is dissatisfied with the benefit award, he may ask for reconsideration, or a hearing before a referee. If the applicant is still dissatisfied, he may request a review by the Appeals Council of the Social Security Administration. The decision of the Appeals Council may be contested by an action in the U.S. District Court.

I. Unsolved Problems

For older people, obviously, hospitalization is more frequently needed than for other age groups. The benefits under old-age and survivors' insurance are not high enough to allow the recipients to pay substantial hospital costs, and they badly need financial protection when they have to go to a hospital. Since 1951, the Administration and several bills in Congress, such as the Forand Bill of 1958 (HR 4700) recommended the introduction of hospitalization insurance to cover up to sixty days a year for the recipients of old-age and survivors' benefits, including dependents of deceased insured people. Hospital benefits would be paid from the current contributions to the insurance plan without the use of general tax funds. Hospital and surgery insurance, within the framework of old-age and survivors' insurance, would be particularly important because the recipients cannot obtain medical and hospital insurance by private insurance companies, which do not accept people of such age or such physical conditions. Inclusion of health and hospital insurance would greatly enhance the emotional and social security of this group. Its costs could be met by a modest increase of the regular old-age and survivors' insurance contributions.

The development of old-age and survivors' insurance has brought us a long way to the goal of this program: to provide protection against destitution and want for people working for a living when their income is cut off by major catastrophes in their lives. But certain aspects of this goal for all citizens have not been considered yet. The most critical deficiency is the lack of a social insurance program for meeting medical and maternity care costs, particularly the expenses for hospitalization.

III. UNEMPLOYMENT INSURANCE

A. Concept and Organization

Unemployment has been called the scourge of modern industrial society. Enforced idleness of millions of citizens has caused widespread deprivation. The idea of unemployment insurance is to secure an income to replace wages when they are interrupted by loss of employment. Insurance payment is secured for a defined period only, and in instances where loss of employment has occurred through no fault of the worker. At the same time, unemployment insurance attempts to reduce the period of unemployment by the procurement of jobs through public employment services.

When the *Social Security Act* established unemployment insurance in 1935, our country had just passed through an economic depression with its high rates of unemployment and severe suffering. Different than the Federal program of old-age and survivors' insurance, "unemployment insurance" or "unemployment compensation" was established as a Federal-state system. The Federal law induced all states to adopt unemployment compensation laws by the so-called "tax offset device." This means that the *Social Security Act* levied everywhere a tax of 3 per cent on the payroll of all persons who employed eight or more people, for more than twenty weeks a year, and paid them up to $3,000 a year. (Certain types of employment were excluded.) The *Amendment* of the *Social Insurance Act of 1954* extended the coverage to firms hiring four or more workers. Whenever a state employment insurance law has been approved, 90 per cent of the Federal unemployment tax is credited to the state unemployment insurance fund, and becomes available for unemployment benefits in that state. Under these circumstances, all states enacted unemployment compensation laws because, without a law, employers would have had to pay the Federal tax, without possibility of a tax reduction, and the unemployed in their state would not have benefited. For the approval of a state unemployment compensation law, the following requirements have to be met: (1) All benefits must be paid through public employment offices; (2) taxes must be deposited into the Unemployment Trust Fund, which is administered by the Secretary of the Treasury; (3) the funds must be used only for unemployment compensation; (4) benefits must not be denied for refusal to accept work made available by a strike, lockout, or labor dispute, or because substandard wages are paid; and (5) nobody must be forced to join a company union or to join or to resign from a labor union.

B. Legislation and Administration

All states and the District of Columbia passed unemployment compensation laws that meet the Federal requirements; all provide that unemployed workers be registered by the public employment service, which tries to help them find suitable jobs. Each state administers its own unemployment compensation law, but the entire cost of administration is paid by the Federal government out of the 10 per cent of the payroll tax that is reserved for this purpose and not credited to the state fund. It amounts to 0.3 per cent of the payroll, while the remaining 2.7 per cent are credited to the state. The states have to guarantee correct administration. They must provide, in case of grievance, a fair hearing before an impartial tribunal, and employment of personnel on a merit basis.

Since July, 1954 the excess of the Federal unemployment insurance tax over expenses has been used for a $200 million reserve, available for interest free loans to the states with depleted reserve accounts. The remainder of the excess is returned to the states for unemployment compensation benefits and administration of the program.

The Federal administration is the responsibility of the Bureau of Employment Security in the U.S. Department of Labor. In the states, either a special department or commission, or an agency in charge of administration of other labor laws is responsible for the administration of unemployment insurance. There are questions whether the arrangement is fortunate in that the Federal government pays the entire administrative expenses but has little control over the laws which are administered.

C. Covered Employment

In general, all labor except agricultural, domestic, and homemaking, and service with religious, charitable, scientific, and educational organizations, falls under state laws. Several states, however, have covered one or the other of these groups, and many state laws protect employees in firms with fewer than four workers; seventeen states even include employment where only one worker is involved. The *Amendment of 1954* added also about two and one-half million federal government employees to the groups covered by unemployment compensation laws.

About 20 per cent of wage and salary workers are not covered, especially public employees, social workers, employees of charitable and non-profit institutions, domestic, and agricultural workers.

The payroll tax is, in most states, paid by employers only, but Alabama requires, also, contributions from employees, and Rhode Island, California, New Jersey, and New York require such contributions for special temporary disability insurance benefits.

Contributions and benefits are related to wages, with limits on minimum and maximum benefits. The large majority of states determines the duration of unemployment compensation according to past earnings or employment. Weekly maximum benefits and the minimum period for which benefits may be paid differ within the various states, from sixteen to twenty-six weeks, in one year, based upon the statutes and special provisions. These provisions have resulted in a condition in which substantially less than about 50 per cent of the average wage received before the loss of the job is paid to the beneficiaries. This has raised criticism from organized labor that the protection offered by unemployment compensation is not sufficient.

D. Benefits

Compensation is paid to workers who are able to work and are available for work. Before an unemployed worker may file a claim for unemployment compensation, he has to be registered with the public employment service. Usually, the claim for compensation may be based upon loss of the job, for example, the closing down of a factory or dismissal of workers due to lack of orders, or partial loss of work. After filing his claim, the worker has to wait, usually for one week, during which time he does not receive unemployment compensation ("waiting period").

According to unemployment compensation laws, a worker who loses his job is entitled to receive compensation, provided he has earned a certain amount of wages or worked a certain number of weeks, or both, during a so-called "base period"—usually one year preceding his loss of the job with a one-calendar-quarter interval. These requirements aim to limit unemployment compensation to fairly regularly employed workers, but they discriminate against low-paid and migratory workers who may not earn enough during the base period to qualify for benefits.

In some states, the minimum benefit is as low as $10 per week, while the maximum varies between $20 and $55 a week. Many state laws also determine a maximum amount which, during a given year, may be paid to an unemployed worker. In July 1958, the average weekly compensation amount in the United States was $30.62. As unemployment compensation is limited to a short period, it does not provide continuous economic security to workers who exhaust the unemployment benefits without finding a new job. For this reason, an extension of benefits by 50 per cent was allowed by a legal amendment in 1958, which provided an average additional payment of up to $29 for eight weeks. This payment is financed by Federal loans to the states. It benefits workers who had exhausted unemployment compensation or who had not been covered before under unemployment insurance.

An unemployed worker may be disqualified for unemployment insurance benefit if he lost his job in a labor dispute, if he was discharged for misconduct on the job, if he left his work voluntarily without good cause, and if he refused suitable work without valid reason. Many states disqualify a worker who has not been "actively seeking work" beyond registering with the employment service. In the majority of states, disqualification postpones unemployment compensation for a certain number of weeks, but, in others, it reduces benefits or even cancels them entirely.

Dependents. In eleven programs, unemployment insurance benefits are supplemented by additional allowances for dependents, ranging from $1 to $3 weekly per dependent, with maximum weekly benefit for the insured and dependents ranging between $20 and $70.

Interstate Benefit Payment Plan. For workers who move from one state to another, reciprocal agreements between forty-five states make it possible that wages earned in several states may be combined in order to establish eligibility for unemployment compensation.

E. Experience Rating

The payroll tax of 3 per cent for unemployment compensation may be reduced for employers who were able to maintain regular employment, so that few workers in these firms claimed compensation. The reduction is determined by means of an "experience rating" or "merit rating" according to which, the employer's tax can be reduced by the state from the 2.7 per cent of the payroll (up to $3,000 a year) to a smaller percentage or even to nothing. The amount paid is dependent upon the ratio of benefits paid to his former workers during a "base period" of one year preceding the year of taxation. The Federal proportion of the contribution of 0.3 per cent of the payroll is not involved in this reduction.

Students of economics have objected to this method of experience rating on the ground that it defeats the principle of collective responsibility. Stabilization of employment is not an achievement of the individual employer, but depends upon the type of industry and production methods. As a result, experience rating favors large firms over small ones. It also drives employers to attempt to defy claims of discharged workers, and it increases administrative cost of unemployment insurance.[21] But the advantages of reduced taxes have induced all states to adopt "experience rating." The specific forms of "merit rating" have led to inequities among the states. They might require an increase of the contribution rates at times of higher

---

[21] E. Burns, *The American Social Security System* (Boston: Houghton, 1951), pp. 162-169, and for details about the various types of "experience rating," pp. 156-159; and, Charles A. Myers, "Experience Rating in Unemployment Compensation," in W. Haber and W. Cohen (editors), *Readings in Social Security* (Englewood Cliffs, N.J.: Prentice-Hall, Inc., 1948), pp. 199-200. The question of fraud is discussed by Joseph M. Becker, *The Problem of Abuse in Unemployment Benefits* (New York: Columbia University Press, 1953); and, Alfred M. Skolnik, "Temporary Disability Insurance Laws in the United States," *Social Security Bulletin*, Vol. 15, No. 10 (October 1953), pp. 11-22.

unemployment and economic depression when business will be less able to pay higher taxes. Provisions are made that Federal advances may be paid when a state unemployment insurance fund approaches insolvency. This provision has not been relied upon as yet.

F. Disability Insurance Benefits

In four states (California, New Jersey, New York, and Rhode Island) *Temporary Disability Insurance Laws,* combined with unemployment compensation, provide insurance benefits, also, for a specified period for wage loss due to unemployment caused by illness or disability (other than industrial accidents). Disability insurance benefits are paid according to the same scale as that provided under unemployment compensation and to the same workers. Temporary disability insurance is administered by the unemployment insurance agency in three states (for example, by the Employment Stabilization Commission in California). In New York it is administered by the Workmen's Compensation Board. Benefits are the same cash payment as unemployment compensation, but, in California, an additional hospitalization benefit for a maximum of $10 a day, for twelve days in one year, is also paid by the Disability Insurance Division. The contributions for disability insurance in California and Rhode Island, are made exclusively by 1 per cent of the payroll tax paid by the workers (not by the employers!). It is deducted from their wages; in New Jersey and New York both employer and worker contribute. Except in Rhode Island, employers may be insured under an approved "private plan."

IV. RAILROAD WORKERS INSURANCE

Two separate Federal social insurance programs protect railroad workers with a unique, comprehensive system. These programs provide benefits for retired workers and their survivors, and for unemployed and disabled railroad men.

A. The Railroad Retirement System

This system has its legal foundation in the *Railroad Retirement Act of 1937* and its amendments (particularly the *Crosser Act of 1946*). It covers over 8,000,000 employees of railroad companies and related associations and provides the following types of benefits: (1) pensions to retired railroad employees; (2) age annuities to retired workers at sixty-five, or at sixty years of age after thirty years of service; (3) permanent disability annuities; (4) survivors' insurance annuities to widows, orphans, and aged dependent parents; (5) lump-sum death insurance benefits for burial expenses; and (6) residual payments guaranteeing the full return of the worker's own tax payments plus an allowance in lieu of interest.

The retirement and disability benefits include a monthly compensation computed on the basis of the worker's wage, within certain limits, and survivors' insurance annuities related to the last monthly remuneration of the worker. The program is financed by equal contributions from employers and workers of $6\frac{1}{4}$ per cent of the payroll up to $3,600 a year. The contributions are placed into a Railroad Retirement Trust Account.

B. The Railroad Unemployment and Temporary Disability System

This system is based upon the *Railroad Unemployment Insurance Act of 1938* with several amendments. It covers railroad employees who received at least $150 in wages in the base year preceding the fiscal year in which unemployment or disability occurred. There is a waiting period of seven days for unemployment and disability benefits, both of which are divided into nine classes depending upon the amount of annual earnings. All the costs for this system are met by the employers. Their annual contribution rate is determined by their balance in the Railroad Unemployment Insurance Account.

C. Administration of Railroad Insurance

Both of the railroad insurance programs just described are administered by the Railroad Retirement Board. It is composed of three members appointed by the President, with consent of the Senate, for five years with overlapping terms. One member is appointed upon recommendation of the railroad carriers, the second upon that of the railroad employees; the chairman is neutral, being recommended by the Railroad Carriers and the union. The staff is employed under civil service. Nine regional offices and ninety-five branch and district offices receive the claims for the various benefits, determine eligibility, and pay the benefits.

V. WORKMEN'S COMPENSATION

Workmen's compensation was the first system of social insurance enacted in England and in the United States. With the development of modern industry, the provisions of the common law on work injuries proved to be wholly inadequate. They were based upon old master-servant relations when injuries were rare, and they limited the claim for damage made by the injured worker to cases in which the employer had neglected to provide reasonable protection for the safety of the worker. Worse than that, the employer was able to refuse damage recovery on the basis of three "common law defenses": (1) that the worker had assumed the risk of accidents at work, and (2) also the risk of injuries caused by fellow-workers, and (3) that he must prove that he was not negligent when the injury occurred. The worker, or his survivors, had to sue before civil courts, had to pay court and attorney fees, and, usually, had to wait for years until a decision was reached. Thus, many never went to court as they had no means, or accepted whatever poor settlement was offered them. These legal provisions made an injured worker, or his widow and orphans helpless victims. The condition was so appalling that many states introduced employers' liability laws, which prohibited the use of the common law defenses, particularly for the mining industry, the railroads, and the merchant marine where accidents were most frequent. But these laws still offered no adequate protection to injured workers.

The movement for the enactment of legislation to eliminate this social injustice in our country, to clarify the question of fault, and to prevent demoralization was started by social reformers, economists, and the American Association for Labor Legislation. In 1908, the first workmen's compensation law for Federal employees was passed, and, in 1911, a large number of states enacted this legislation, with the others following soon after. Now, all states have workmen's compensation laws.

A. Principles and Coverage

Workmen's compensation is based upon the principle that the risk of work injuries is an element of industry and that the cost of such injuries is to be considered a part of the cost of production. It should not be blamed on either employer or injured worker. The aim of this program is to assure prompt medical aid, rehabilitation, and cash benefit to the injured worker and to his dependents, regardless of who is at fault. But, there are still many differences among the state laws.[22] Only about 78 per cent of all workers are covered; certain groups of workers are excluded because they are not employed in "hazardous occupations," or because they work in agriculture, domestic service, or casual jobs. About one-half of the states have elective systems of workmen's compensation where the employer is permitted to refuse insurance for his workers if he prefers the risk of being sued for damage by an injured worker or his survivors. Thirty-one of the states cover all occupational diseases as well as industrial accidents; the other states, only some of these diseases. Eight states do not cover the damage caused by occupational diseases, such as lead poisoning and silicosis, but other systems treat occupational diseases like industrial accidents.

Because workmen's compensation was the first social insurance in our country, this legislation was enacted under a great variety of patterns in the different states. Furthermore, no specific type of workmen's compensation has found adoption as the most effective system. In some states, the "compulsory," and in others, the "elective," method of covering workers and employment is used. Considering organization, there are many states where private insurance companies compete with a public compensation fund. In a minority of states, exclusive private insurance or exclusive public insurance is in operation. "Self-insurance" gives the employer the right not to insure his employees, provided he is able to deposit securities, giving proof of his financial ability to carry his own risk. In the majority of the states, the employer can choose whether or not he wants to: (1) insure with a private insurance company, (2) insure with a state

---

[22] Herman M. Somers and Anne R. Somers, *Workmen's Compensation: Prevention, Insurance and Rehabilitation of Occupational Disability* (New York: Wiley, 1954), pp. 15-37.

workmen's compensation fund, or (3) apply for self-insurance permission.

Usually, injuries that have occurred because of the injured worker's willful misconduct, gross negligence, intoxication, or by intentional self-infliction, are not granted compensation.

B. Compensation Benefits

Workmen's compensation laws provide two types of benefits—medical treatment and cash indemnities—as compensation for loss of earning. Cash benefits provide for temporary disability, for total or partial permanent disability, and for the survivors in case of death of the injured worker.

Medical Benefits. In the majority of states, full medical care, including first aid, medical and surgical treatment, hospitalization, medicines, and medical and surgical appliances, are provided free to the injured worker. This medical aid, however, is limited in nineteen states either to a certain time or to a maximum amount of expenses. Thirty-one states, however, impose no limit, either in the period of medical treatment or as to the amount of medical expenses.

As a rule, the employer or the insurance carrier arranges for medical care and hospitalization. But, in some instances, the injured worker can choose the physician and hospital. The quality of medical service, nursing care, and rehabilitation service differs widely among the states. Where medical treatment is limited to a certain period or to a definite expense maximum, extensions may sometimes be granted.

Indemnity Payments. After a waiting period, usually of seven days, the injured worker who had to leave his work, due to the accident or the occupational disease, is entitled to an indemnity payment. The amount of this indemnity is, as a rule, different for temporary disabilities and permanent impairments.

Temporary Disability. This is compensated for by a payment based on a percentage of the last wage, which may vary from 50 to 80 per cent—frequently it is 66⅔ per cent. The worker who receives compensation based on a percentage of his regular wage, usually has difficulty meeting high living costs. In a few states, the rate of compensation is higher for married workers, and increased according to the number of dependent children.

There is usually, also, a maximum period for which temporary disability indemnity is paid (frequently five years) or a maximum sum, which amounts to the same limitation.

Permanent Disability. In all states compensation is provided for permanent disabilities caused by industrial accidents, and different rates are scheduled for permanent total or partial disability.

Permanent partial disabilities. These are either classified as specific injuries, such as loss of an eye, a hand, or a foot, or as of general nature, such as disability caused by injury to the head or back. For such partial disability compensation is limited in the majority of states to a stated number of weeks, but in several states the weekly payments are fixed sums. In California compensation is rated upon degrees of total disability as classified in a Rating Schedule in relation to nature of injury, occupation, and age of injured worker.

The periods of compensation for specific injuries vary from state to state, which certainly is not logical; they are sometimes paid in addition to the indemnities during temporary disability.

Permanent total disability. If the injured worker is totally disabled by the injury, often defined as having lost 70 per cent or more of his working capacity, he receives an indemnity as a smaller proportion of his last wage with weekly and total maximum amounts. The periods range from 250 to 1,000 weeks, and the money maximum amounts from $5,000 to $15,000.

The Federal compensation systems for civil employees and longshoremen, and the laws of eighteen states provide for lifelong benefits in case of permanent total disability, but often with reduced rates and dependent upon the severity of the disability. In some states, different rates are paid with regard to dependents.

Subsequent Injuries. The majority of compensation laws contain provisions to secure benefits for workers who have been injured before, or lost a member of the body, but who suffer another injury which may involve total, permanent disability. Without legal provisions, handicapped persons might be refused employment because an employer or the insurance carrier would not take the risk of another injury occurring. In order to counter this, "second-injury" or "subsequent injuries" funds have been established which, as a rule, secure full compensation for the actual disability to the injured worker without placing undue burden on the new employer.

Death Benefits. If the injured worker dies, the economic security of his wife and his children often depends upon the death awards under workmen's compensation. In general, they are based upon the average weekly wages of the deceased breadwinner, but some states grant a flat pension. Only seven systems provide that death benefits be paid to the widow for life or until remarriage. In the majority of compensation plans, death benefits, again, are limited to payments for a specific period—ranging from 260 to 600 weeks, or up to a maximum amount ranging from $3,500 to $15,000. Weekly minimum and maximum payments usually are similar to those of permanent disability benefits. These laws do not provide adequate economic security for survivors of an injured worker because of the limitations set on the number of weeks and the maximum sums which may be paid. In addition to survivors' benefits, funeral expenses are paid in many systems.

Not all state laws require that reports be made of all industrial accidents and occupational diseases. Therefore no reliable statistics are available. It is estimated that approximately 17,000 workers die from industrial injuries annually throughout the country, that about 100,000 workers suffer permanent total or partial disablement, and that about 1,700,000 persons are temporarily disabled by accidents and occupational diseases at work. But it is correct to state that workmen's compensation has encouraged the prevention of accidents through safety measures and has improved the conditions of the victims of occupational accidents and diseases, as well as the social conditions of their families.

C. Administration of Workmen's Compensation

The main objective of the system is to guarantee a simple, fair, convenient, and inexpensive method of settling the claims of injured workers and their dependents. For this reason, in most states, an administrative commission (for example, the Industrial Accident Commission) or board administers the program. Five states, however, still rely upon court administration.

State Compensation Insurance Funds are, as a rule, administered by a board of directors, which is independent, and separated from, the industrial accident commission. State funds are a nonprofit, self-supporting organization. Although the organization does not operate as a private organization (though in some states commercial insurance companies do carry workmen's compensation insurance), it must comply with the rates and classifications ordered for all insurance companies under state laws. The prevention of industrial accidents and occupational diseases, by improving safety devices and instructing workers, is an important function of workmen's compensation, but not yet equally achieved in the various systems. Workmen's compensation is financed by the employers because industrial accidents are recognized as part of the cost of production. Oregon requires a one-cent-a-day contribution from the workers. A few other states, as well, require contributions toward medical care.

The Federal programs of workmen's compensation for Federal civil employees and for longshoremen are administered by the Bureau of Employees' Compensation, U. S. Department of Labor. The Bureau has twelve branch offices spread about the country.

VI. PERSONNEL IN SOCIAL INSURANCE ADMINISTRATION

The competence of personnel in social insurance administration is, in many respects, related to the skill required in other fields of social welfare administration.[23] The personnel must have a good, general education in order to understand laws, rules, and regulations and to explain them clearly and with sympathetic attitude to the public. They must maintain an objective approach as the representatives of a public agency, impartial and polite consideration for the applicants, and an awareness of the personality of the person for whom the social insurance program has been established. Beyond these general requirements, and the skills connected with technical problems of legal and financial nature, accounting, and computation, the question has been frequently raised whether specific professional social work skills are required in the administration of social insurance. Under present conditions, it is certain that the administration of the various social insurance systems does not require trained professional social workers for most of its functions.

---

[23] For a discussion of the question of personnel in social insurance administration, see Karl de Schweinitz, *People and Process in Social Security* (Washington, D. C.: American Council of Education, 1948), pp. 62-93; and, Neota Larsen, "OASI and the Social Services," *Social Work,* Vol. 1, No. 3 (July 1956), pp. 12-17.

The people who come to the social insurance offices in order to file their claims often incidentally express personal, emotional, or health problems. In our present setup of the social insurance administrations no one is prepared to cope with those needs which are not met by the cash benefits and medical care offered under the social insurance program. When claimants reveal psychological problems indicating health or emotional disturbance, anxieties, and fear, personnel not trained professionally to handle these problems, cannot recognize their needs and refer them to social agencies which are equipped to help. It is to meet these problems of great importance that the various social insurance programs employ social workers as consultants who are fully acquainted with the social agencies of the community and their special facilities and services. These workers would be available for the insurance benefit recipients who need to be counseled regarding the facilities of other health and welfare services, family and children's agencies, child guidance and mental hygiene clinics, and recreational facilities. In interviews and discussions, they could bring the resources of the community to the attention of the recipients of insurance benefits, who would benefit accordingly.

It might be worth mentioning, that in other countries, particularly France, Belgium, and England, a much closer integration of social insurance and family allowance benefits with the general system of welfare services has been highly beneficial and is accepted by the population.[24] The establishment of social work consultants in the field offices of the Social Security Administration, the state unemployment compensation, and workmen's compensation programs would be valuable progress in the interest of the public.

VII. GAPS IN OUR INSURANCE PROGRAM

A. Health Insurance

The most flagrant gap in our system of social insurance is the lack of health insurance. Insurance against the hazard of ill health, by the provision of medical care and cash allowances during the time of illness, was the earliest type of compulsory, public social insurance in many other countries. In fact, the United States is the

---

[24] Walter A. Friedlander, "Coordination of Family Welfare Services in France," *Social Service Review,* Vol. XXVII, No. 1 (March 1953), pp. 62-66.

only great nation which has no public health insurance program today. Under auspices of the Federal government, medical care is given to members of the armed forces, veterans, Indians, and seamen. Under state systems of workmen's compensation, medical care and cash indemnity are provided for workers injured in industrial accidents and occupational diseases. In four states, unemployment insurance in the form of disability benefits, but no medical care, is given to insured workers who are unable to work due to illness over a short time. Persons who receive various forms of public assistance also, as a rule, receive a certain amount of medical care. Federal grants-in-aid are made for the payment of doctors and hospitals. This program provides medical care for the recipients of public categorical assistance, but it does not protect the other population.

The idea of a compulsory health insurance program has been vigorously opposed in our country. The main objections to such a program are presented by representatives of the medical profession, by some of the commercial insurance companies, by the Christian Science churches, and drug manufacturing companies. Medical societies fear that compulsory health insurance would lead to a lowering of standards of medical care which would result from overloading doctors, clinics, and hospitals. They claim it would subject the medical profession to bureaucratic control, red-tape, and would decrease their income. Some commercial insurance companies are afraid that their own accident, hospitalization, and medical care policies would be cancelled and their profits might be lowered. Drug manufacturing firms which sell patent medicines, feel that their products would no longer be bought by health insurance administrators and patients under a health insurance program which would standardize medicines and drugs. The Christian Science churches do not want health insurance because their members believe in cure through prayer, not through medical service. In public discussion, health insurance is often confused with socialized medicine, a system under which doctors and nurses are government employees, and patients have no free choice in selecting doctor, pharmacist, clinic, or hospital. None of these characteristics applies, however, to the concept of health insurance as it operates in other democratic countries.

The need of a large proportion of our population to protect themselves against the heavy cost of serious illnesses, which make, every year, about 4,000,000 people ill for longer than six months, is obvious. Many families attempt to solve this need by selecting a "medical care prepayment plan"—a voluntary health insurance program. Such plans are established either by nonprofit organizations, such as the "Blue Cross," and the "Blue Shield," which are closely connected with the state medical societies, by some private foundations, labor councils, unions, fraternal societies, and business concerns, or by commercial insurance companies.

Approximately 70 per cent of the population has some form of hospital insurance, the majority under commercial plans and about 45 per cent under "Blue Cross" plans.

The benefits under these plans vary considerably. Most of them offer either only hospitalization, or only medical care in the doctor's office, or a cash allowance for the patient to compensate for the loss of earnings—frequently, only a part payment toward the various expenses. Membership is often limited to persons of low income or to people within specific age limits, and some plans exclude persons who are suffering from various diseases. An analysis of the effect of voluntary insurance plans demonstrated that, in 1951, under such arrangements for the insured persons, 36.3 per cent of hospital costs and 17 per cent of costs of hospital, physician, and loss of income were provided; and for 17 per cent, medical expenses alone were covered.[25] Only a small proportion of our population has comprehensive insurance in case of sickness, including medical care at home, in the doctor's office, in the hospital, and the necessary operations, medicines, and medical appliances. The premiums for comprehensive health insurance coverage are frequently too high for persons in the low income groups, so that patients most in need of this protection are not able to become members of voluntary plans.

In the discussion of comprehensive compulsory health insurance legislation, the question has come up whether or not a general public health service, such as that in Great Britain, New Zealand, Australia

[25] "Voluntary Insurance Against Sickness: 1948-1951 Estimates," *Social Security Bulletin* (December 1952), pp. 3-7; George W. Cooley, "The Potentials of Voluntary Health Insurance," *Building America's Health*, Vol. 4 (1952), pp. 76-82; and, Edward S. Rogers, "Medical Care," *Social Work Year Book* (1960), pp. 370-374.

and Chile, may be preferable to a health insurance plan. It should be seriously considered by Congress.[26]

B. Maternity Insurance

In many nations, maternity insurance provides for insured women workers and for wives of insured men, medical and maternity ward care, midwife aid, nursing, and medicines at the time of childbirth. Cash allowances of one-half of the actual or average wage are paid for periods from about four weeks before, to six weeks after, confinement. This insurance proves of considerable help to mothers and infants. No public insurance of this type is available in the United States, except to railroad workers.

C. Family Allowances

Family allowances were first introduced in France and Belgium, on a voluntary basis, by employers for families with several children. Their goal was to alleviate the financial burden, especially of the mother, of rearing more than one young child and to secure a living standard of health and decency which could not be obtained from the normal wage alone. The individual and health needs of the worker and his family are not considered in the determination of wages and salary. A young bachelor may get along on his wage without difficulty, but his married fellow worker with five young children at home will have a hard time to make ends meet with the same wage. Organized labor, originally, was opposed to family allowances; but, later, it favored legislation which made the family allowances compulsory so that their payment is no longer dependent upon the discretion of the employer. At present, a large number of countries, including Canada and England, have enacted family allowance legislation. There seems, however, no indication that Federal or state legislatures in our country are inclined to pass a compulsory family allowance law.

---

[26] E. Burns, "Further Needs in the Social Insurances," *op. cit.,* p. 188; I. S. Falk, "The Need, Potential and Implications of Compulsory Health Insurance," *Building America's Health,* Vol. 4 (1952), pp. 66-75; and, Michael M. Davis, "Needs and Problems of Medical Care," in Cora Kasius (editor), *New Directions in Social Work* (New York: Harper, 1954), pp. 110-130.

Selected Bibliography

I. Public Assistance

*Abbott, Edith, *Public Assistance,* Vol. I. Chicago: University of Chicago Press, 1940.

*Abbott, Grace, *From Relief to Social Security.* Chicago: University of Chicago Press, 1941.

Cohen, Wilbur J., "Social Security Act Amendments of 1952," Social Security Bulletin, Vol. 15 (September 1952), pp. 3-9.

Corson, John J., and John W. McConnell, *Economic Needs of Older People.* New York: Twentieth Century Fund, 1956.

Elmore, Edith B., "The Public Assistance Job," *Tennessee Public Welfare Record,* Vol. XIV, No. 3 (March 1951), pp. 43-46.

Fauri, F. F., "Public Assistance," *Social Work Year Book* (1949), pp. 370-381.

Geddes, Anne E., "The Changing Role of Old-Age Assistance," *The Social Welfare Forum* (1953), pp. 238-249.

Greenfield, Margaret, *Permanent and Total Disability Aid.* Berkeley: University of California, Bureau of Public Administration, 1953.

*———, *Medical Care for Welfare Recipients—Basic Problems.* Berkeley: University of California Press, 1957.

Keith-Lucas, Alan, *Decisions About People in Need.* Chapel Hill: University of South Carolina Press, 1957.

Kurtz, Russell H. (editor), *The Public Assistance Worker; His Responsibility to the Applicant, the Community, and Himself.* New York: Russell Sage Foundation, 1938.

Leyendecker, Hilary M., *Problems and Policy in Public Assistance.* New York: Harper, 1955.

Linford, Alton A., "Public Assistance Categories, Yes or No?" *Social Service Review,* Vol. XXII, No. 2 (June 1948), pp. 199-210.

Marcus, Grace F., "The Nature of Service in Public Assistance Administration," *Public Assistance Report No. 10.* Washington, D.C.: The Federal Security Agency, 1946.

Perlman, Helen H., "Are We Creating Dependency Through Our Public Assistance Programs"? Madison: Wisconsin Welfare Council, 1951.

Presley, Betty, *et al.,* "A Study of Marin County," *Building Societies into a Public Assistance Program Can Pay Off.* Sacramento: California State Department of Social Welfare, 1958.

Russell, Elizabeth, *Professional Growth on the Job: A Guide for the Public Assistance Worker.* New York: Family Service Association of America, 1947.

Schottland, Charles I., "Social Security Act Amendments of 1956," *Social Security Bulletin,* Vol. 19 (September 1956), pp. 3-15, 31.

*————, "Social Security Act Amendments of 1958," *ibid.,* Vol. 21, No. 10 (October 1958), pp. 3-14.

Smalley, Ruth, *et al., Meaning and Use of Relief in Case Work Treatment.* New York: Family Welfare Association of America, 1941.

Taylor, Alice L., *Case Recording in the Administration of Public Assistance.* Washington, D.C.: Federal Security Agency, 1950.

*Towle, Charlotte, *Common Human Needs. An Interpretation for Staff in Public Assistance Agencies.* Chicago: University of Chicago Press, 1945.

Wessel, Rosa (editor), "Method and Skill in Public Assistance," *Journal of Social Work Process,* December, 1938.

Wickenden, Elizabeth, *The Needs of Older People and Public Welfare Services to Meet Them.* Chicago: American Public Welfare Association, 1953.

Wiltse, Kermit T., *Social Casework in Public Assistance: Testing Method and Skill Applied to a Selected Case Load.* Sacramento: California Department of Social Welfare, 1952.

————, *Public Assistance Personnel: Educational Requirements and Training Facilities.* Berkeley: University of California, 1959.

*Witmer, Helen Leland, *Social Work: An Analysis of a Social Institution.* New York: Farrar & Rinehart, 1942.

Witte, Ernest F., "Who Speaks Now for the Child on Public Assistance," *Child Welfare* (March 1954).

II. *Social Insurance*

Altmeyer, Arthur J., *Your Stake in Social Security.* New York: Public Affairs Committee, 1954.

Atkinson, Raymond C., *The Federal Role in Unemployment Compensation Administration.* Washington, D.C.: Social Science Research Council, 1941.

Bachman, George W., and Lewis Meriam, *The Issue of Compulsory Health Insurance.* Washington, D.C.: Brookings Institution, 1948.

Becker, Joseph M., *The Problem of Abuse in Unemployment Benefits.* New York: Columbia University Press, 1953.

Breul, Frank R., "The Genesis of Family Allowances in Canada," *Social Service Review,* Vol. 27, No. 3 (September 1953), pp. 269-280.

*Burns, Eveline M., *Social Security and Public Policy.* New York: McGraw, 1956.

————, *The American Social Security System.* Boston: Houghton, 1949, and Appendix, 1951.

Cohen, Wilbur F., "Social Insurance," *Social Work Year Book* (1954), pp. 486-495.

Davis, Michael M., *America Organizes Medicine*. New York: Harper, 1941.

————, and Dewey Anderson, *Medical Care for the Individual and the Issue of Compulsory Health Insurance*. Washington, D.C.: Brookings Institution, 1948.

Dawson, Marshall, "Problems of Workmen's Compensation Administration," Bulletin No. 672. Washington: U.S. Department of Labor, 1940.

*de Schweinitz, Karl, *People and Process in Social Security*. Washington, D.C.: American Council on Education, 1948.

*Dodd, Walter F., *Administration of Workmen's Compensation*. New York: Commonwealth Fund, 1937.

Epstein, Abraham, *Insecurity: A Challenge to America*, rev. ed. New York: Random House, Inc., 1938.

*Ewing, Oscar R., *The Nation's Health*. Washington: Federal Security Agency, 1948.

Falk, I. S., *Security Against Sickness: A Study of Health Insurance*. New York: Doubleday, 1936.

Gagliardo, Domenico, *American Social Insurance*, rev. ed. New York: Harper, 1955.

*Goldmann, Franz, *Voluntary Medical Care Insurance in the United States*. New York: Columbia University Press, 1948.

*Haber, William, and Wilbur J. Cohen, *Readings in Social Security*. Englewood Cliffs, N.J.: Prentice-Hall, Inc., 1948.

Hamilton, James A., and Dorrance C. Bronson, *Pensions*. New York: McGraw, 1958.

Hamovitch, Maurice B., "History of the Movement for Compulsory Health Insurance in the United States," *Social Service Review*, Vol. 27, No. 3 (September 1953), pp. 281-299.

Huntington, Emily H., *Cost of Medical Care*. Berkeley: University of California Press, 1951.

Kingsbury, John A., *Health in Handcuffs*. New York: Modern Age Books, 1939.

Mathiasen, Geneva, *Flexible Retirement*. New York: Putnam, 1957.

Means, James H., *Doctors, People and Government*. Boston: Atlantic, 1953.

Meriam, Lewis, *Relief and Social Security*. Washington, D.C.: Brookings Institution, 1946.

Moore, Elon H., *The Nature of Retirement*. New York: Macmillan, 1959.

Mott, Frederick D., and Milton I. Roemer, *Rural Health and Medical Care*. New York: McGraw, 1948.

National Resources Planning Board, *Security, Work and Relief Policies*. Washington: Government Printing Office, 1943.

Osborn, Grant, *Compulsory Temporary Disability Insurance in the United States*. Homewood, Illinois: R. Irwin, 1958.

*President's Committee on the Health Needs of the Nation, *Building America's Health*, 5 vols., Washington: U.S. Government Printing Office, 1952.

Rathbone, Eleanor F., *The Case for Family Allowances*. London: Penguin Books, 1940.

Reede, Arthur H., *Adequacy of Workmen's Compensation*. Cambridge: Harvard University Press, 1947.

Robbins, Rainard, *Railroad Social Insurance*. New York: American Enterprise Association, 1947.

Simpson, Herbert, *Compulsory Health Insurance in the United States*. Evanston: Northwestern University Press, 1943.

Sinai, Nathan, *Disability Compensation*. Ann Arbor: University of Michigan Press, 1949.

*Somers, Herman M., and Anne R. Somers, *Workmen's Compensation: Prevention, Insurance and Rehabilitation*. New York: Wiley, 1954.

———, "Private Health Insurance," *California Law Review* (August and October 1958).

Steiner, Peter O., and Robert Dorfman, *The Economic Status of the Aged*. Berkeley: University of California Press, 1957.

Stern, Bernhard J., *Medical Services by Government—Local, State and Federal*. New York: Commonwealth Fund, 1946.

Stewart, Maxwell, *Social Security*. New York: Norton, 1939.

Tibbitts, Clark (editor), *Aging and Society*. Chicago: University of Chicago Press, 1960.

10.

Family Social Services

THE FAMILY IS the basic unit of our society. In the family individuals receive most of their personal satisfactions, and perhaps most important the personality of the child is formed. It is within the family that sexual relations are regularized; children are given nurture and education; and food, clothing, and the dwelling place for its members are provided. In illness the family renders care. It is the center of warm affection for its members (as long as normal, healthy conditions prevail). Regardless of the social changes of modern, industrial society, family life has values for most individuals that cannot be found elsewhere. It is desirable, in terms of these values, to the individual members of the family as well as to society, that family life be protected and strengthened.[1] Family service of social agencies has the purpose of preserving healthy family life; the aim of family casework is to assist the individuals in the family to develop their capacities in order to lead personally satisfying and socially useful lives.

Social anthropology has described the influence of tradition, habits, customs, and the pattern of social organization upon the behavior of human beings. Sociology recognizes these factors as essential determinants in human values, ambitions, and reactions. Knowledge of the

---

[1] James S. Plant, *Personality and the Cultural Pattern* (New York: Commonwealth Fund, 1937); Andrew G. Truxal and Francis E. Merrill, *Marriage and The Family in American Culture* (Englewood Cliffs, N.J.: Prentice-Hall, Inc., 1953), pp. 29-51, 349-374; and, John and Mavis Biesanz, *Modern Society* (Englewood Cliffs, N.J.: Prentice-Hall, Inc., 1956), pp. 203-247.

decisive role of culture in the formation of the human personality is essential in family casework, because the individual may be understood at times in terms of his environment. The role of the family in society, however, is not static. In our predominantly industrial, urban society, many features of the earlier rural family have changed. Margaret Mead went as far as to characterize the new pattern of the American family as follows:

The typical American couple is composed of two people with no common childhood associations or traditions, living apart from the relatives of either, without responsibilities for their family shared as in other countries and in earlier American society with other relatives and neighbors. Divorce has increased to its present rate for a variety of reasons related to the complexities of modern society, and is self-increasing in that prospective partners approach marriage with the tacit—often explicit —understanding that divorce is an acceptable way of "resolving" marital difficulties. The role of women is particularly demanding and unrewarding. The increased social and political freedom of women has led to the desire and expectation for a professional career relatively independent of their husbands, yet the desire for marriage and the demands of the household make this difficult or impossible despite technical facilities. If the woman tries to have both home and career, both are likely to suffer. If she gives up the career, she is constantly reminded of what she might have made of herself if she had not. If she fails to prepare for a career, she faces the likelihood that her marriage might fail and she will have to support herself and her children because of divorce without being equipped for earning sufficient money. The rewards of maintaining the household are less tangible than formerly. Schools, nurseries, and kindergartens have largely taken over the training of children. Canneries, bakeries, and factories have taken over the production of food and clothing. The complexities of keeping a home intact have increased in rough proportion to the decrease of visible achievement in accomplishing this.[2]

Whether we consider the changes of our pattern of family life either a "progress" or a "decline," compared with the quiet satisfaction of earlier rural family life, these changes undoubtedly have created many serious problems which afflict the members of the families concerned. Margaret Mead explains: "To the extent that we continue to act as if the family were what it used to be, we

---

[2] Margaret Mead, "What Is Happening to the American Family?" *Journal of Social Casework* (now *Social Casework*) (November 1947), pp. 322-323; quoted by permission of the Family Service Association of America. See also, A. Truxal and F. Merrill, *op. cit.,* pp. 583-603.

compromise our capacity to understand its limitations, and also we delay the development of the community services, the education, and the counseling we need." [3] The community services which Mrs. Mead mentions are primarily family welfare services.

Our present "conjugal family" or "family of procreation" consists of the two marriage partners and their children. There is no strong connection with the parental families of both partners, their "families of orientation," nor with other relatives which frequently causes an isolation of the family.

The difficulties which arise in the life of the family are of great variety. There may be lack of harmony between husband and wife, emotional instability of either, economic problems caused by failure of good home management, or small income; or they may be caused by unemployment, sickness, accidents, health problems, lack of support, or desertion of the breadwinner. We find problems, in relations of parents, or adults, with children, sometimes leading to neglect or cruelty, housing problems, financial need for the mother to obtain work and to place the children, or delinquency or other maladjustment of the children. Personal and family difficulties are usually caused by a combination of various elements, frequently involving several members of the family and based upon social, economic, emotional, and physical factors. Therefore, an improvement in unsatisfactory family situations may be obtained by explaining to the members of the family the reasons for their difficulties and the need for changing their emotional reactions and behavior. Changes in the environment or in the economic conditions in which the family lives may help to improve relationships between its members.

In former times, family casework depended mainly upon the overt behavior of the people for both social diagnosis and cure. If a husband neglected his wife and children because he was devoted to drink, the social worker advised him to stop drinking and threatened him with legal measures or jail. At present, family casework attempts to explore the motives for his drinking and to find ways to convince him, by insight into his personality, of the necessity for his changing his habits and of going to a clinic for therapy.

---

[3] M. Mead, *op. cit.*, p. 327; see also, A. Truxal and F. Merrill, *op. cit.*, pp. 267-272; and, Talcott Parsons, "The Kinship System of the Contemporary United States," in Herman D. Stein and Richard A. Cloward (editors), *Social Perspectives on Behavior* (Glencoe, Ill.: Free Press, 1958), pp. 7-19.

Some characteristics of the present form of American family life may be called "democratic"; husband and wife have a larger amount of equality than did former generations and are aware of their equality. In the choice of the mate, greater freedom is granted the young couple than in other cultures. After marriage, the young couple seeks to obtain independence from the families of each partner and rejects interference from parents and relatives. The "conjugal," or "nuclear family," however, lacks the moral, economic, and social status support which the "extended" or "joint family" offers. This is typical for Asian and most European countries. In principle, decisions on their way of life here are reached between the couple, sometimes with participation of adolescent children. The changes in the family pattern of the past to new forms of family living, sometimes lead to conflicts for those who cannot accept new customs, and require aid for adjustment. Progress in psychology and psychiatry, as well as in natural sciences, enables the caseworker to recognize difficulties in family life which formerly were not detected. The ability to diagnose the nature of each member of the family helps to find a solution for them if they have problems.

I. FAMILY SERVICE AGENCIES

Both public and private social agencies frequently offer family services. In public welfare agencies, family casework, as a rule, is offered in connection with the granting of public assistance, particularly in the program of aid to dependent children. But only a few, well-organized public welfare departments have introduced a special family casework unit to aid applicants independent of any consideration of their economic need.[4] Financial help for the maintenance of a family in need is an accepted function of the public welfare department, provided that the family meets the legal eligibility requirements for assistance. Private family welfare agencies, therefore, frequently refer applicants who ask mainly for financial support to the public assistance agency. Private family service agencies are

---

[4] Clark W. Blackburn, "Family Social Work," *Social Work Year Book* (1957), pp. 244-250; Gunnar Dybwad, "Family Life Education," *ibid.*, pp. 239-244; and, Robert H. MacRae, "Prerequisites for Strong Family Life," *Social Welfare Forum* (1958), pp. 114-121.

primarily concerned with personal problems and the emotional maladjustment of members of the family. Their casework attempts to help in the solution of such problems, by counseling in health, educational, and adjustment questions, and to overcome disturbances to normal, healthy family living. Counseling may include giving advice on family budget and home management, and on vocational opportunities by referring the client to employment services and occupational guidance centers. Often, family casework includes premarital counseling when the social worker is consulted by the young couple or the parents. It is concerned with marital disturbances—helping the couple to gain better mutual understanding and satisfaction— and with the adjustment of difficulties which have arisen between parents and children.

Most family welfare agencies are situated in urban areas, but surrounding rural communities are often included in their activities. Little family welfare service is available in most rural areas, which are remote from cities, except for social work rendered by the county welfare department to persons receiving financial assistance, and occasionally by Red Cross chapters.

Many private family service agencies are nonsectarian and help families regardless of their creed and ethnic background. Family service agencies of high standards are organized in the Family Service Association of America. The Association accepts only such agencies that guarantee the clients a well-developed program of services, employ a qualified professional staff and maintain an adequate agency structure and a sound financial policy.[5] In 1960 the Family Service Association had 284 agency members; most of them are private social agencies, but a number of public welfare departments which provide family services and meet the requirements of the Association have also been accepted as members.

The staff of the family service agency depends upon the size and resources of the community. It consists, usually, of an executive director, one or more supervisors, and a group of caseworkers competently trained for family work. In private agencies, a board of directors must be active and responsible; a public agency needs an advisory

---

[5] The Association formerly was named "Family Welfare Association of America," and its noted monthly journal, *The Family,* now is called *Social Casework.*

board on family work in order to be accepted as a member of the Family Service Association. The executive is in charge of the organization, administration, and liaison work with the board and other agencies, but in a small community he also may serve as casework supervisor or even carry a case load himself. Funds for the private family service agency are provided from the annual campaign of the Community Chest, from contributions of members, interest on endowments, and other donations. Persons may come to the family service agency on their own initiative, informed by the radio or the press, on advice of friends, a minister, or neighbors. They may also come on referral by other social agencies, public or private.

The first interview usually takes place at the office of the agency. The applicant explains why he came to the agency, which difficulties have induced him to ask for help or advice, and what he expects from the agency. The caseworker listens to the story of the applicant and helps him by friendly encouragement and sympathy to present his explanation. She will frequently discover that the reasons which the applicant presents are not the real core of his troubles and that he, in fact, wants help concerning other problems than he discusses first— such as legal advice, employment, and vocational training. The caseworker will clearly explain to the client what services the agency is able to offer, and under what conditions. She will leave him free to decide whether or not he wishes to use these services, but she may well help him in making a decision which lies in his interest and in that of his family. After the interview the caseworker records the client's description of his problems and of their causes in a "case history." If the client decides to make use of agency services, the caseworker attempts to help the client solve his problems by applying his capacities, as well as by relying upon facilities in the community. The length of contact, the frequency of interviews, and the intensity of the helping relationship of the caseworker vary according to the circumstances.

Although private family service agencies are mainly asked for help in personal and emotional problems, request for financial assistance also is frequently made. Sometimes financial aid is given to clients where it is necessary to implement other services given by the agency (casework, counseling, legal advice), and where financial assistance is an integral part of the family casework process. Such support may be necessary for clients who feel they cannot apply for public relief, who are not eligible for it, or who need it while their case is being investigated by the public welfare department. Financial help is given in emergencies for the maintenance of the household before public assistance can be obtained, and for recreational or educational purposes for which public funds might not be available. Among the clients who need material help, particularly, are non-residents, families who have not gained settlement rights and therefore are not eligible for public assistance. In this category might be new immigrants who cannot apply for material assistance to public welfare agencies unless their economic need has been caused by events which could not be anticipated at the time of their immigration to the United States.

The following case will illustrate the approach of family welfare casework:

Case of the Webb Family

Mr. and Mrs. W, a couple in their forties with three children, were referred by their minister because they had reached an impasse in their management of money. There was no real financial need. Just prior to the referral, Mrs. W had suddenly bought a new washing machine. This had upset Mr. W and he had threatened to leave home. The minister indicated that Mr. W was extremely thrifty, was a good workman, and had held his job for years. To the community, the church, and friends they appeared to be a substantial family.

Mr. and Mrs. W were interviewed separately. Mr. W stressed the need to save as much as possible for the family's future; he wanted his family to have more security than he had had as a child. Mr. W's preoccupation with money, his stubbornness, and his orderliness were all traits suggestive of a rigid personality pattern. Mrs. W was more anxious than her husband. She had been having various aches and pains which she attributed to her approaching menopause. She expressed a desire for outside activities and for a more attractive home.

Psychiatric consultation confirmed the caseworker's impression that Mr. W's capacity for change was limited. His defenses seemed effective and his activities, such as hoarding money, fishing, and hunting, were socially acceptable. Mrs. W, also controlling, used money as a tool to express aggression against her husband. Each capitalized on the other's vulnerability and used similar defenses of projection, denial, and rationalization.

Casework treatment was directed toward fortifying Mr. and Mrs. W's defenses and toward helping Mrs. W relate to her husband in a less aggressive way.

Because of Mr. W's absorption with his own needs, he did not realize that he was not providing some of the things that were important to his wife and to the management of the home. The caseworker pointed out that he could continue to manage the finances, but that he could also afford to spend more for certain items for the home; that this would enable his family to manage better and his children to get more enjoyment, and would be an investment for himself and his family.

Mrs. W was helped to realize that her earlier acceptance of her husband's ways of doing things made it difficult for him to accept her change of attitude and behavior.

The caseworker's acceptance of Mrs. W helped her to discuss the day-by-day events in order to see why she was now acting differently. She could bring out her need for more money than she was getting and was helped to realize that it was important for her to let her husband know what she wanted so that he could have a part in planning expenditures for things that were needed. Both Mr. and Mrs. W were able to make some modifications in their behavior. Through this treatment, the marital balance was restored and the marital relationship improved.

The caseworker, in this type of treatment, attempts to help the marital partners clarify factors in the current situation and their reactions to them, with the aim of helping them achieve greater ability to meet social responsibilities. The aims of this method are to support existing strengths and to produce modification of adaptive patterns, but not to help the client achieve basic personality change.[6]

II. FEE CHARGING IN FAMILY SERVICE AGENCIES

Family welfare agencies, in general, provide their service to the clients without charge. It has been known for some time, however, that some clients want to pay for casework service and counseling. They feel that they can afford to pay for such professional service in the same way as they pay their doctor or lawyer, and they express their preference to pay for casework, rather than to have to ask for free service. Family service agencies which offer such paid service use a graduated scale so that the client pays a fee according to his financial ability. The agencies have made it possible, thereby, for a type of client to use casework who, otherwise, never would have been willing to seek counsel from any charity agency. This type of client includes bankers, merchants, factory workers, engineers, teachers, white-collar employees, artists, and craftsmen.

---

[6] This case illustration is quoted from Eleanor A. Moore, "Casework Skills in Marriage Counseling," *Social Casework,* Vol. XXXIV, No. 6 (June 1953), pp. 255-258, by permission of the Family Service Association of America.

There are about 273 fee-charging family service agencies in the country, most of them in large cities. Casework with paying clients includes all aspects of social problems, personal, emotional, and family difficulties, employment questions, placement of children in summer camps or in schools and of adults in rest homes, sanatoriums, old-age homes, and mental institutions. Most family service agencies are satisfied with their clients' reactions about fee charging and consider this form of service a real contribution to the needs of the public.[7] In a few large cities, some individual social workers, usually well-experienced and trained, are engaged in casework as a personal, professional activity without connection with a social agency, sometimes under the title of "personal relations counselor."

III. PRINCIPLES OF FAMILY SERVICE

The goal of family casework in social agencies is to aid the individual client and the members of his family in achieving harmonious relationships in their family life. In recent years, there has been a growing emphasis on education as a process for strengthening the relationships of the members of the family, their mutual affection, and cooperation. Some of these activities have been called "family life education" [8] and have been carried on by social workers in family service agencies. These agencies share, however, the effort for family protection with programs of adult education, parent-teachers associations, discussion groups of young married couples, and church and mothers' clubs. The Family Service Association defines it as a "process by which people are helped, through group discussion, to broaden their understanding of family relationships." The specific role of the caseworker here is to devote full interest to the individual who is in anxiety or trouble, and to be aware of the resources of the community which may help in this process.

---

[7] Alice D. Taggart, *et al., Fee Charging in a Family Agency* (New York: Family Welfare Association of America, 1944); Saul Hofstein, "Fee Payment in Social Work Counseling," *Social Casework*, Vol. XXXVI, No. 7 (July 1955); and, Rae C. Weil, "Family Social Work," *Social Work Year Book* (1960), pp. 251-257.

[8] Helen L. Witmer, *Social Work: An Analysis of a Social Institution* (New York: Farrar & Rinehart, 1942), pp. 246-247; and, Gertrude K. Pollak, "Family Life Education: Its Focus and Techniques," *Social Casework* (May 1953), pp. 198-203.

In our urban-industrial civilization, the family has assumed a highly individualistic pattern which often has not been conducive to the happiness of all its members. Marriage counseling is, in most family service agencies, one of the essential activities of the caseworkers' assignment. It regularly includes premarital guidance, wherein the caseworker helps the two marriage partners to decide whether or not their plan promises happiness to both of them in their social, sexual, and cultural relationship, especially with regard to economic and occupational conditions, employment of the wife, relationship to parents and relatives of both partners, and health and behavior problems.[9] In both premarital and marital counseling, regarding conflicts of husband and wife, the caseworker may advise them to consult clinics and physicians, whenever medical and psychiatric problems seem to be important for their decisions. She suggests the use of a mental hygiene clinic or a psychiatrist if sexual maladjustment and behavior patterns make it advisable to explore the chances of successful therapy. Family casework attempts to settle conflicts between parents and children in which the rights of children to their own choice of play, companionship, and activities are recognized in accordance with their age. In some instances, the family service agency shares the responsibility of premarital, marital, and child counseling with other community facilities engaged in this work.

The main element in family casework is the counseling of all members of the family in order to prevent individual and family disorganization, mutual hostility, unhappiness, and breakdown. If differences of opinion, apathy, or anxieties develop, the family caseworker tries to help the members of the family understand one another better and to create among them the desire of mutual assistance to overcome these threats to their successful family life. This service is given to people who are willing to use it constructively, whether or not they are in economic need.

Modern family service is convinced that most clients will make real use of a plan of rehabilitation only when they themselves share in the planning, and when their desire for self-support and respon-

---

9 Judson T., and Mary G. Landis, *Building a Successful Marriage,* 2nd ed. (Englewood Cliffs, N. J.: Prentice-Hall, Inc., 1953); *Personal Adjustment, Marriage, and Family Living* (Englewood Cliffs, N. J.: Prentice-Hall, Inc., 1956); and Ethel Kawin, *Parenthood in a Free Nation* (Chicago: University of Chicago Press, 1954).

sibility for their life is fully considered. In order to carry on such a plan, the social caseworker frequently helps to straighten out differences and tensions within the family, and to change the environmental or health situation by arranging financial assistance, finding housing at reasonable cost, a satisfactory job, and securing necessary medical or psychiatric treatment through the use of community facilities, hospitals, and clinics.

This type of social casework includes so-called "supportive work" —encouragement and supervision rendered to parents in order to secure constructive relations to the children or other members of the family. Family casework requires that the social worker possess a full understanding of the client's personality, motivations, behavior, and his situation within the family. On this basis she [10] assists the client in developing his plans to meet his difficulties. The caseworker's task is to inform the client which social institutions are available that may be helpful in the solution of his problems, and she explains the nature and conditions of these services. If the client desires to use some of these facilities, the caseworker arranges for the necessary contact and referral. But the client himself makes his final decision; he exercises his right of self-determination.

In her relationship with the client and with his family, the caseworker encourages all members of the family to use their thoughts and resources, thus preserving and strengthening their energy and desire of independence. She helps the client to overcome his anxieties and confusions, which are a barrier to finding a way out of his difficulties. In enabling the client to make his own decision in his affairs, she strengthens his self-reliance and self-respect. She clearly explains to the client what the facilities and limitations of the family service organization are, so that he knows what to expect from the agency according to its policies and resources, and what his own role has to be.

The characteristic problems which families face today are based upon economic, environmental, health, and psychological conditions. Economic suffering is very often caused by illness in the family which as a result, also causes great anxiety and personal difficulties. It is especially unfortunate that the achievements of medical science are

---

[10] Lola Selby, "Supportive Treatment: The Development of a Concept and a Helping Method," *Social Service Review,* Vol. XXX, No. 4 (December 1956).

not always readily available to patients of modest means or low income. Unemployment, change of jobs, and low wages also may impair a normal, happy family life. After World War II, adequate housing was, in many areas, difficult to obtain, particularly for families of minority groups and families with several children and low income. Young couples sometimes were forced to live with parents and in-laws, and to give up their independence and privacy. The expectations and dreams of other families for a fine house, garden, car, and television set were frustrated, and contributed to dissatisfaction and emotional disturbance.

Psychological influences on family discord are sometimes caused by hasty marriages of young couples who are driven together by a short-lived passion and use marriage as a device to create a semblance of love and security. Counseling, alone, may not produce sincere affection, patience, and the tolerance necessary for successful adjustment to married life; but it may well serve as a medium gaining mutual understanding to serve as a background to strive for such an adjustment.

We discussed in the preceding chapters the fact that basic financial needs of families without income or resources are increasingly met by public assistance and social insurance payments. The role of the private family service agency under sectarian or humanitarian auspices has primarily helped in emotional and personal troubles. However, families in financial distress frequently suffer from dissatisfaction, frictions, and hostilities, and need help in these problems as well. For this reason, private family service agencies give temporary financial aid or supplement public assistance payments in order to make it possible for the client to re-establish normal family life.

IV. SPECIAL SERVICES IN THE FAMILY WELFARE FIELD

We shall discuss now a few activities of family service agencies which deal with special problems of clients who have particular needs.

A. Services to the Aged

The number of aged people, in relation to the entire population, is steadily increasing in all countries. This condition has called attention to their specific needs. In 1850, only 2.6 per cent of the population was sixty-five years of age or older; in 1950, 7.7 per cent and in 1958, 8.6 per cent had reached this age. The average life expectancy has advanced from forty years in 1850, to forty-nine years in 1900, to sixty years in 1930, to sixty-three years in 1940, and to seventy years in 1959. Improved living conditions and sanitation, easier work and shorter hours due to machinery, and advances in medical science, nutrition, and health education have contributed to these longer life spans. But, our society has not yet succeeded in filling, sufficiently, the lengthened life of older persons with useful activities and cultural satisfaction.

Our methods of public assistance and social insurance, industrial pension plans, and private insurance provisions have emphasized securing economic protection for older people who cannot work any longer. But, social workers have become aware of the fact that the "senior citizens," living in enforced retirement, often, not only suffer from chronic diseases and frailties of their age, but also from the unhappiness caused by their feeling of uselessness, loneliness, or despair. In addition, family welfare and social group work agencies are in full agreement that the communities have to pool all their resources in order to offer older persons more than the bare necessities of life— food, clothing, shelter, and medical care. "Senior citizens" need understanding, sympathy, companionship, and acceptance in the community in order to continue a way of life that gives them some amount of satisfaction.[11] When an old person loses the ability to take care of himself, and his own family is not able to care for and nurse him, a protective environment has to be found for him. The services of the community must be mobilized for helping the aged to meet their personal, economic, medical, and social needs, and to offer cultural, educational, recreational and vocational projects for the lonely and unemployed.

In the past, a "home for the aged" was considered the traditional place where an older person could find shelter when he could not live in his own home or with his family. At present, social agencies

---

[11] Clark Tibbitts, "The Aging," *Social Work Year Book* (1957), pp. 93-100; Geneva Mathiasen, "The Aging," *ibid.* (1960), pp. 95-102; and, Senator Thomas C. Desmond, *Enriching the Years* (Albany: New York Joint Legislative Committee on Problems of the Aging, 1953), with many practical illustrations of services to the aged.

consider institutions only one of several possibilities to care for old people. For the chronically sick, hospitals, special institutions, homes for the aged, and family foster care with the support of medical and nursing services are beginning to be used. Other programs for the aged are special housing units or apartment projects equipped with easy housekeeping facilities and arrangements for collective use of kitchens, laundries, living rooms, library, or music room. The units provide medical and nursing supervision and special recreational centers for older citizens.

Family welfare agencies have noted that older people express the desire to be counseled by caseworkers with special experience, sympathy and skill in working with the aged and their families. If housekeepers are provided for older people, the family welfare agency prepares them for a longer period of service than is customary with other age groups, and for taking care of the shopping, cleaning, and cooking, as well as giving some personal aid.

Family welfare agencies develop placement services to board older people with private families, and supervise boarding homes for older people, who either pay the monthly board themselves or receive aid from relatives, public assistance, or the family agency. They assist older people in finding convalescent and nursing homes, sometimes supplementing private resources or old-age assistance payments in order to secure adequate medical and nursing care.

Clubs and community centers for the aged have been established recently in order to give older citizens the feeling that they are not unwanted, and to offer them opportunities to apply their experience and creative abilities, or to learn new skills, in order to gain the satisfaction of accomplishment.[12] Recreational activities of the aged are not limited to clubs and centers, but are included in modern homes for the aged, in hospitals and homes for the chronically ill.

Private homes for the aged, frequently maintained by charitable organizations, sectarian agencies, and fraternal orders, are applying, more and more, the payments of social insurance and public assistance benefits of their residents for their care and maintenance. Since, in old-age assistance, the need of the individual has to be proved, most

---

[12] Wilma Donahue (editor), *Education for Later Maturity* (New York: Whiteside, 1955); Jerome Kaplan, *A Social Program for Older People* (Minneapolis: University of Minnesota Press, 1953); and, George Soule, *Longer Life* (New York: Viking, 1958).

old-age homes have changed their former policies of requesting, when a resident is admitted, the payment of a lump sum in order to secure life-time care. Instead, they have introduced boarding contracts which include provision for monthly payments for the services rendered by the home. Advantages of this policy are that the institution is no longer compelled to keep a resident who cannot adjust to congregate living, and that the resident himself is not compelled to stay on, if he does not like the conditions of the home. Furthermore, in periods of inflation the home is not obliged to continue care because the money paid has lost part of its value, and those residents who at the time of admission were able to pay their board may then become eligible for public assistance after their financial means have been used up.

B. Homemaker Services

In families, problems arise if the mother is absent or sick and no adult member of the family nor any relatives and friends are available to care for the children and the working father. Family service and child care agencies have found that in such instances the temporary break-up of the family may be avoided by providing the family with a "housekeeper" or "homemaker." Homemakers are carefully selected and trained in advance by social agencies which provide this type of service. When a family asks for homemaker service, the agency decides whether that family may receive this aid under the rules of the agency. The social worker explains the relationship and duties of the homemaker in the family and makes arrangements for the family's contribution to the salary of the homemaker. If circumstances allow, an interview between the mother and the homemaker is arranged so that the mother may explain her wishes for the care of the family and the special duties which the home management entails. This contact usually eliminates the mother's anxiety and feeling of jealousy.

In general, the homemaker is sent to a home only for limited periods of time. She tries to continue the regular routine of home management, diets, and child care. The children have the advantage of remaining with their father in their own home with little change is their accustomed life. If the family has no means for paying the homemaker, the social agency's budget often provides funds for assuming this expense. As a rule, the agency guarantees the payment of the salary to the homemaker and collects from the family according to its ability to pay. In 1958, 145 family and child care agencies offered homemaker service, among them thirty-four public welfare agencies. Most homemakers are employed on a full-time basis. The social agencies assume training and supervision of the homemakers, frequently by their own supervisors and caseworkers.[13]

C. Services to Travelers and Migrants

Travelers and migrants (or immigrants) often encounter serious difficulties en route. They become stranded without means, are without funds for food or shelter, or need medical care. They face these difficulties in a strange environment where they do not know anyone and do not know what means of help may be available. Family welfare agencies, therefore, have been giving aid to transients for many years, but since they are often limited by policy to serve the resident population, specialized services are necessary.

These services are rendered, primarily, by the Travelers Aid Association. This agency, through its branches, usually located in railroad stations, bus terminals, and piers, is prepared to assist travelers and transients in need on a "short-contact" basis. The problems the agency handles vary from giving information on trains, buses, and planes, and hotel accommodations, to locating families and friends, and providing information on vocational and employment opportunities, as well as financial aid, and medical or hospital assistance.

Runaway children and adolescents, without realistic plans, are among the groups which frequently become charges of the Travelers Aid Societies. Wayward children may be cared for by a children's agency until the return to their own home is arranged. Then they might be put on a train or bus and agreements made with other social agencies en route to help in the safe return of the child, unless his problems require that a social worker or an attendant accompany him all the way home. Other help might be necessary for aged or invalid, crippled, blind, or mentally disturbed people who have tried to travel alone but are found in need of direction.

---

[13] Maud Morlock, "Homemaker Service," *Social Work Year Book* (1951), pp. 225-229; U. S. Children's Bureau, *Homemaker Service; A Method of Child Care,* Publication No. 296 (Washington, D.C.: 1946); and, Adelaide A. Werner, "Homemaker Service," *Social Work Year Book* (1960), pp. 297-302.

The need for travelers aid is particularly great in periods of war, defense, or economic distress when many people are on the move. Again, as in peacetime, the Societies assist not only travelers who are just on their way, but also migrants looking for a new home and refugees and displaced persons who have not received help in settlement and adjustment by other social agencies. Since 1917, the National Travelers Aid Association has coordinated local Travelers Aid Societies, established in 103 places, with enough representatives in other communities to allow about 2,900 cities to use their services.[14]

Travelers Aid Societies, public welfare departments, and private family service agencies are engaged in helping migratory agricultural workers who frequently face serious problems. Our production, particularly at harvest time, relies partly upon seasonal labor. Most workers cannot make a living in one place due to crop specialization and changes in the sharecropper system. They are often unskilled, earn their principal income from temporary employment, and move several times a year. Their total number is estimated at 1,300,000, of whom about 473,000 are foreign workers, mainly Mexicans. Housing outside of labor camps is frequently inadequate and improvement of sanitary conditions necessary. Communicable diseases are widespread, and often migratory workers are denied public health service and economic assistance. Their children work to supplement the low wages of the parents, and communities sometimes do not enforce school attendance laws for migratory children to avoid overcrowding of classrooms and higher costs. Local recreation services do not encourage migratory children to participate so that their mothers have to take them into the fields.

The casework in each Travelers Aid Society requires a thorough knowledge of all community resources within the city where the agency is located, special contact with facilities in other cities, and the ability to refer the client to places where his needs really will be met.

D. Legal Aid Service

Another service which is sometimes connected with family welfare agencies is called Legal Aid. It renders persons without sufficient money, free, or for a nominal charge, legal advice and representa-

---

[14] *Social Work Year Book* (1957), pp. 701-702.

tion before a court. Caseworkers may have some knowledge of certain legal questions, but are not equipped to give responsible legal advice on a professional basis. The provision of special legal service developed first in New York, in 1876, and in Chicago, in 1886. It was established primarily for large immigrant groups frequently victimized by swindlers, extortionists, and ruthless exploiters who refused to pay their wages. Arthur von Briesen, a New York lawyer, established the New York Legal Aid Society for German immigrants, and in Chicago the Protective Society for Women and Children was organized to aid immigrant women. Both agencies broadened their scope and developed into organizations which assisted persons without regard to origin, race, and creed. Among the pioneers of this movement Reginald Heber Smith (Boston), John S. Bradway (Duke University), and Harrison Tweed (New York) should be mentioned.

In many small communities, lawyers give their services freely to people who have no funds to pay for their professional counsel. In large cities, the needs of the poor cannot be met by casual arrangements, since most lawyers are too busy to serve clients without a charge. Thus, branches of the Legal Aid Society in larger cities are necessary in order to allow the people without means the protection of the law, which would be denied to them if they had to miss professional counsel and representation in legal matters.[15] In 1949, the Legal Aid Societies established the National Legal Aid Association in Washington, D.C. as their coordinating body. It develops standards and promotes the general aims of legal aid.

Local Legal Aid Societies are organized, as a rule, in one of the following six types of organization: (1) as a division or branch of a *family welfare agency,* such as the Legal Aid Bureau of the United Charities of Chicago; (2) as an *independent legal aid society* under its own board of directors, supported by the Community Chest, and, often, with prominent lawyers as members of the board; (3) as a *bar association office* which employs paid personnel; (4) as a *law school clinic* of a university, where advanced law students provide legal service under supervision of faculty members; (5) as a government *legal aid bureau* where a lawyer is employed from tax funds,

---

[15] Junius L. Allison, "Legal Aid," *Social Work Year Book* (1960), pp. 362-364; and, Emery A. Brownell, "Availability of Low Cost Legal Service," *The Annals* (May 1953).

usually under the city authorities; or (6) as a *public defender office* where in a criminal case the accused receives free counsel when he is unable to pay an attorney.

To engage a lawyer they can afford, people are referred by Legal Aid Societies to a list supplied by the local bar association. In cooperation with the bar association, the Societies often make special financial arrangements for clients with moderate means. The problems brought before Legal Aid Societies include family and personal legal questions (family discord, divorce, separation, adoption), which are the largest group, economic legal problems (eviction, debts, mortgages, sick pay, wage difficulties, budget collection, compensations, and insurance benefits), some litigation on real estate or personal property, and other legal matters.

Selected Bibliography

Beattie, Anna B., and Florence Hollis, *Family Case Work: A Good Profession to Choose.* New York: Family Welfare Association of America, 1945.

Berkowitz, Sidney J., *et al., Diagnosis and Treatment of Marital Problems.* New York: Family Service Association of America, 1949.

Bradway, John S., *Law and Social Work.* Chicago: University of Chicago Press, 1929.

Breckrinridge, Elizabeth, *Effective Use of Older Workers.* Chicago: Wilcox and Follett, 1953.

*Brownell, Emery A., *Legal Aid in the United States.* Rochester, New York: Lawyers' Cooperative Publ. Co., 1956.

Burgess, Ernest W., and Harvey J. Locke, *The Family: From Institution to Companionship.* New York: American Book, 1945.

———, and Paul Wallin, *Engagement and Marriage.* Chicago: Lippincott, 1953.

Creech, Margaret, "Migrants, Transients, and Travelers," *Social Work Year Book* (1954), pp. 355-360.

Cuber, John E., *Marriage Counseling Practice.* New York: Appleton-Century-Crofts, Inc., 1948.

Davis, Allison, and R. J. Havighurst, *Father of the Man.* Boston: Houghton, 1947.

Desmond, Thomas C., *Age Is No Barrier.* New York State Joint Legislative Committee on Problems of the Aging, 1952.

———, *Enriching the Years.* New York State Joint Legislative Committee on Problems of the Aging, 1953.

*Feldman, Frances L., *The Family in a Money World*. New York: Family Service Association of America, 1957.

French, Thomas M., "Personal Interaction and Growth in Family Life," *The Family in a Democratic Society*, pp. 29-40. New York: Columbia University Press, 1949.

Gilbert, Jeanne G., *Understanding Old Age*. New York: Ronald, 1952.

Gomberg, M. Robert, and Frances T. Levinson, *Diagnosis and Process in Family Counseling*. New York: Family Service Association of America, 1951.

Groves, Ernest R., *Conserving Marriage and the Family*. New York: Macmillan, 1944.

Gruenberg, Sidonic, *Our Children Today*. New York: Viking Press, Inc., 1952.

Hertel, Frank J., "Family Social Work," *Social Work Year Book* (1951), pp. 183-190.

*Hess, Robert D., and Gerald Handel, *Family Worlds: A Psychosocial Approach to Family Life*. Chicago: University of Chicago Press, 1959.

*Hollis, Florence, *Women in Marital Conflict: A Casework Study*. New York: Family Service Association of America, 1949.

Kaplan, Jerome, *A Social Program for Older People*. Minneapolis: University of Minnesota Press, 1953.

Karpf, Maurice J., *The Scientific Basis of Social Work: A Study in Family Case Work*. New York: Columbia University Press, 1931.

*Kasius, Cora (editor), *A Comparison of Diagnostic and Functional Casework Concepts*. New York: Family Service Association of America, 1950.

Kimble, Grace E., *Social Work with Travelers and Transients: A Study of Travelers Aid Work in the United States*. Chicago: University of Chicago Press, 1935.

Kimmel, Dorothy D., *Homemaker Service for Older People*. Chicago: American Public Welfare Association, 1955.

Kluckhohn, Clyde, "Variations in the Human Family," *The Family in a Democratic Society*. New York: Columbia University Press, 1949, pp. 3-11.

*Landis, Judson T., and Mary G. Landis, *Building a Successful Marriage*, 2nd ed. Englewood Cliffs, N.J.: Prentice-Hall, Inc., 1953.

———, *Readings in Marriage and the Family*. Englewood Cliffs, N.J.: Prentice-Hall, Inc., 1952.

Lawton, George, *Aging Successfully*. New York: Columbia University Press, 1946.

Levy, John, and Ruth Monroe, Jr., *The Happy Family*. New York: Knopf, 1938.

Loomis, Charles P., and Allan Beegle, *Rural Social Systems*. Englewood Cliffs, N.J.: Prentice-Hall, Inc., 1950.

Maclachlan, John M. (editor), *Health in the Later Years*. Gainesville: University of Florida Press, 1953.

Mead, Margaret, "What Is Happening to the American Family?" *Journal of Social Casework* (November 1947), pp. 322-329.

Miller, Daniel R., and Guy E. Swanson, *The Changing American Parent*. New York: Wiley, 1958.

*Plant, James S., *Personality and the Cultural Pattern*. New York: Commonwealth Club, 1937.

*Rich, Margaret, *A Belief in People*. New York: Family Service Association, 1956.

Rogers, Carl R., *Counseling and Psychotherapy: Newer Concepts in Practice*. Boston: Houghton, 1942.

Smith, Reginald Heber, "Growth of Legal Aid Work in the United States," rev. ed., *Bulletin No. 607*, Washington: Bureau of Labor Statistics, 1936.

Stein, Herman D., *Careers for Men in Family Social Work*. New York: Family Service Association of America, 1946.

*Taft, Jessie (editor), *Family Casework and Counseling*. Philadelphia: University of Pennsylvania Press, 1948.

Taggart, Alice D., et al., *Fee Charging in a Family Agency*. New York: Family Welfare Association of America, 1944.

Tibbitts, Clark (editor), "Social Contribution by the Aging," *The Annals* (January 1952).

Truxal, Andrew G., and Francis E. Merrill, *Marriage and the Family in American Culture*. Englewood Cliffs, N.J.: Prentice-Hall, Inc., 1953.

Werner, Adelaide, "Homemaker Service," *Social Work Year Book* (1960), pp. 297-302.

Woods, James H., *Helping Older People Enjoy Life*. New York: Harper, 1953.

Young, Leontine, *Out of Wedlock*. New York: McGraw, 1954.

11.

Child Welfare

I. CHILDREN'S NEEDS FOR SPECIAL SERVICES

Care for orphans and abandoned children, is one of the oldest forms of charity. It was originally carried out by the church. Recognition that children are in need of a different type of care from adults is only a recent development, and the modern term of "child welfare" has assumed a broader meaning. It is not only concerned with the care for destitute, neglected, deserted, sick, handicapped, or maladjusted and delinquent children. It is understood that "child welfare" also incorporates the social, economic, and health activities of public and private welfare agencies, which secure and protect the well-being of all children in their physical, intellectual, and emotional development.[1]

Scientific progress in the fields of anthropology, biology, medicine, psychology, and social research during the past hundred years has changed the attitude of society toward the child. He no longer is treated as an adult person, of smaller stature, but as a human being with his own, different rhythm of life, and with his own laws of biological and mental growth. We are aware that the child is following drives, social forces, and motivations which are basically different from those which govern adult behavior. In the child's mind, the

---

[1] Hazel Fredericksen, *The Child and His Welfare*, 2nd ed. (San Francisco: Freeman, 1957), p. 1; and, Helen L. Witmer and Ruth Kotinsky, *Personality in the Making—The Fact Finding Report of the Midcentury White House Conference on Children and Youth* (New York: Harper, 1952).

world is identical with his own personality; fantasy and reality are not yet separated. Only in the period of adolescence do reality and fantasy begin to part.

As we have seen, during the Colonial period in the United States dependent children were indentured for many years and served as cheap labor. Young children were boarded out to foster families or were later placed in the almshouses. The large stream of immigrants from many countries and the high rate of mortality among indentured servants left numerous children alone and destitute. The Colonies were ill prepared for their care. Relatives, neighbors, church members, and a few national groups or religious societies took care of some dependent children. But, usually, the overseer of the poor chose indiscriminately to place them out—which was cheapest for the community.

During the nineteenth century more and more children were brought into the almshouses. They lived in dark, overcrowded, filthy rooms, without adequate food and clothing, herded together with adults suffering from various physical and mental diseases. The typical conditions in these almshouses were revealed in an investigation in New York in 1857.[2] The committee described the poorhouses as the most disgraceful memorials of public charity, "where the misfortune of poverty is visited with greater deprivations of comfortable food, lodging, clothing, warmth, and ventilation than constitute the usual penalty of crime." Children should never have been permitted to enter the poorhouses. Young children were forced to pass their most impressionable years in the midst of such "vicious associations as will stamp them for a life of future infamy and crime." The committee recommended that children should be removed from the poorhouses and be placed in orphanages or asylums in which they would be educated according to the needs of their age. The idea of saving destitute children from the dangers of the "mixed almshouse" was the first, but not the only, cause for the rapid growth of orphan asylums during the twentieth century. There was also the need to find a place for

---

[2] State Board of Charities of New York, *Annual Report*, Part I (1903), pp. 795-820; Sophonisba P. Breckinridge, *Public Welfare Administration in the United States* (Select Documents) (Chicago: University of Chicago Press, 1935), pp. 149-158; Grace Abbott, *The Child and the State*, Vol. II (Chicago: University of Chicago Press, 1938), pp. 3-9, 51-54; and, Dorothy Zietz, *Child Welfare: Principles and Methods* (New York: Wiley, 1959), pp. 17-52.

other children whose health and morale were endangered by conditions in their own families, who were neglected, and who were roaming the streets in large cities. A special problem existed for Negro children for whom no care at all could be found. Religious societies wanted children to be placed in orphanages where they would be brought up in the faith of their parents.[3]

Before the nineteenth century, only a few orphanages had been established in this country. The first was built by the French Ursuline Sisters in New Orleans, in 1729, to place homeless orphans whose parents had been killed by Indian massacres, and the first public children's asylum was the Charleston Orphan House, founded in 1790 in South Carolina. In the large cities, private orphanages and children's branches of public almshouses, or asylums, took care of an increasing number of dependent and neglected children. In smaller communities and rural counties, the segregation of children from adults took a long time, and children remained exposed to the undesirable influence of adult rogues and vagabonds who, as inmates, still were used to care for the children in almshouses and even some public orphan asylums. The Congress of State Boards of Charities, in 1875, challenged the legislatures in the states to remove all children from county poorhouses, city almshouses, jails, and from all associations with adult paupers and criminals, and to place them in families, asylums, reformatories, or other children's institutions.

Child placement in families in the form of indenture, which had been customary in the Colonial period, lead, in most instances, to neglect of the child's needs for affection and education and to his being overworked and exploited as cheap domestic labor. In fact, the almshouse, at first, seemed to promise better treatment and education when it was proposed as a method of relief in the 1820's. The disadvantages of bringing up of children in almshouses, asylums, and orphanages, however, were recognized fairly early. Children reared in institutions became dull, without vigor and initiative.

Around 1850 run-away, wayward children became a problem in some metropolitan areas. At this period, hundreds of thousands of immigrants landed each year in New York, and the police complained that over 10,000 vagrant children were running loose in the streets,

---

[3] Henry W. Thurston, *The Dependent Child* (New York: Columbia University Press, 1930), pp. 40, 90; and, Maurice O. Hunt, "Child Welfare," *Social Work Year Book* (1960), pp. 141-157.

begging and stealing. Due to the initiative of Charles Loring Brace, the New York Children's Aid Society was founded in 1853 which located rural foster homes for neglected children.[4] The main activity of the newly founded Society became the organization of a "mass deportation" of underprivileged or homeless children to farmers and mechanics in rural communities of the midwestern states. Many children found homes in the rural families where they were placed, but others did not adjust to the unfamiliar country life and agricultural work. The majority of the farmers who asked for children were poor and wanted cheap labor, without being too deeply interested in rehabilitating them.

In Baltimore, Boston, Brooklyn, and Philadelphia, Children's Aid Societies followed the New York example. In Chicago, Martin Van Buren Van Arsdale founded in 1883 the American Educational Society, the first statewide child placing agency for Illinois, which later expanded its services as the National Children's Home Society with charters in other states. Several states began to place children in foster homes under the auspices of state boards of charities, later departments of social welfare. They tried to select foster homes in which the children would not be treated only as an economic asset. Their inspectors provided a certain amount of supervision by visiting the families from time to time. Since the Children's Aid Societies, however, did not pay board to the foster parents, they felt they could not require higher standards of care which were desirable for the children. Placement in rural regions in other states, frequently far away from the former residence of the child, usually led to a permanent breakup of the child's ties with his family and made it difficult for the family to maintain contact or to take back the child.

Foster care was a forward step compared with the shortcomings of orphanages and other children's Homes which existed in that period. Children's asylums did not meet any individual needs of the children. They were mostly mass institutions with huge dormitories. The children lacked personal attention and understanding, received treatment in groups rather than as individuals, and missed the

---

[4] Emma Brace, *The Life and Letters of Charles Loring Brace* (New York: Scribner, 1894); and Edith Abbott, *Some American Pioneers in Social Welfare* (Select Documents) (Chicago: University of Chicago Press, 1937). For recent developments in foster care, see Henry S. Maas and Richard E. Engler, *Children in Need of Parents* (New York: Columbia University Press, 1959).

feeling of belonging and the love of parents and family. It was only toward the end of the nineteenth century, that some children's institutions recognized these deficiencies and introduced the "cottage plan." Large dormitories were replaced by small family-like groups living in a separate building with a housemother and a housefather who were to function as a substitute for a real family. Even with such improvements, care of children in institutions deprived them of growing up in the normal setting of the community, playing with the neighbors, going to school, and returning to "their home." This fact explains why the introduction of carefully selected and supervised foster homes seemed a better solution to the problem.

The latest idea in the development of methods for child protection is that, whenever possible, the child should be left in his own family. We have already noted that, until the end of the nineteenth century, many children were taken away from their parents because of their poverty, and because it was thought that a pauper family could not properly bring up a child. The findings of modern psychology and psychoanalysis, as well as the observations of the juvenile courts and social agencies dealing with difficult and maladjusted children, proved, however, that it would be advisable to enable children to remain at home with their mothers and their siblings. Economic aid granted to the mother would allow her to rear her children instead of forcing her to give the children away and work in a factory, on the farm, or as a domestic worker. It was the first White House Conference on the Care of Dependent Children, in 1909, which emphasized the need of financial help to mothers in order to preserve the family.

Originally, private agencies carried a major share of responsibility for maintaining the family in cases of death of the father, divorce, and desertion, but more and more public funds were made available for this purpose. As we discussed before, the function of aid to dependent children with the support of Federal and state funds is, at present, the main factor in overcoming the problems of financial maintenance of needy children in their families in the United States. This support enables these families to provide shelter, food, clothing, medical care, education, and recreation for their children. Our public social welfare services thus contribute to the maintenance of family life for the entire population. Other institutions and measures, such as public health services, schools, minimum wages and

hours, agricultural subsidies, low-rent housing, social insurance benefits, and recreation facilities, also play an important role to this effect.

Dangerous as economic deficiencies are for the development of
the child in his family, they are not the only problems which require
child welfare activities. Children are often endangered not only by
poverty, insufficient income, or sickness in the family, but also by
neglect or rejection, lack of understanding or love, or because the
parents are unable to educate the child. For these reasons, casework
for children is a vital necessity, and private family and child care
agencies as well as the child welfare divisions of city and county
welfare departments have developed casework for children as an integral part of their programs.

Child welfare services are rendered by providing (1) economic
and personal aid to children living in their own homes, (2) substitute
families or an adoptive home for children who have no home or cannot remain with their own families, and (3) institutional care in children's homes and orphanages when children, for particular reasons,
cannot be left in their own homes or in foster families. Casework for
the child in his own home considers the individual needs of the child
for well-being and health. It uses such facilities of the community as
day nurseries, recreation, organized children's and youth activities,
and clinics. In general, casework with the parents or the foster parents
is indispensable in the interest of the child. Still more vital is individual
service to children who cannot remain in their own families and for
whom, therefore, substitute care has to be provided, either in a foster
home or in a children's institution.

II. WELFARE AND HEALTH SERVICES FOR CHILDREN

Public child welfare services in the states are supported by Federal
grants-in-aid, when approved by the United States Children's Bureau.
They include maternal and child health, crippled children services,
and "child welfare services for the protection of homeless, dependent,
neglected and endangered children in urban and rural areas." [5] An
Advisory Council on Child Welfare Services is composed of twelve

---

[5] "Child welfare services" is a technical term used in the *Social Security Act*
to designate preventive and protective activities as distinguished from material
aid under public assistance.

members appointed by the Secretary of the Department of Health, Education and Welfare who represent public, voluntary, civic, religious, and professional welfare organizations. The Council reports findings and recommendations to the Secretary and Congress. Private social agencies continue to supplement public child welfare services. The Federal grants are in direct proportion to the total child population and in inverse proportion to state per capita income. State and local funds must match Federal grants.

A. Maternal and Child-Health Services

For the promotion of the health of mothers and young children, services are supported by annual Federal grants of $21,500,000. The states share the expenses and administer the program through the state health agency. Rating personnel on a merit basis, and proper efficient administration are required; reports must be rendered, and the funds must be used for improvement of local services. Cooperation with medical, nursing, and private welfare organizations is required, and demonstration services in deprived areas and for groups in particular need have to be arranged. The Federal allotment is composed of a uniform rate to all states—a sum based upon the ratio of live births in the state to the total in the United States, and an amount based upon the individual need of the state for financial assistance in order to carry out its maternal and child-health program. The services include well-baby clinics for regular medical examinations of young children and advice to their mothers, and prenatal clinics; home delivery nursing; infant and child health conferences; school, dental, and mental health services; advisory and consultation services; and training programs for pediatricians, dentists, nurses, nutritionists, and social workers. The necessity for further improvement of specialized medical care for young children and school children in rural areas is generally recognized.

During World War II, the Federal government provided free "emergency maternity and infant care" to wives of service men of the lower ranks, including medical care for infants during their first year. The costs of this program were entirely met by Federal funds, and its remarkable success showed the value of comprehensive medical care. During the period 1939 to 1948, the mortality rate of infants under one month has decreased by 24 per cent, that of children under one year by 48 per cent, from one to four years by 50 per cent, and maternal mortality by 71 per cent.[6]

B. Services for Crippled Children

These services are also administered, at the Federal level, by the Division of Health Services of the Children's Bureau in the Department of Health, Education and Welfare. The *Social Security Act* defines these services as locating crippled children; providing medical, surgical, corrective, and other services and care; and facilities for diagnosis, hospitalization, and after care. They include provision of aids and prosthetic appliances, physiotherapy, medical social services, and maintenance of a state crippled children's registry. The Federal grant of $15,000,000 annually is allocated by a uniform grant of $60,000 to each state, and a portion of $4,320,000 on the basis of the state's particular need for this program in relation to the number of crippled children; this amount must be matched by state, local, or private funds. The remaining $7,500,000 are allotted according to each state's need and in proportion to urban and rural child population without the requirement of matching funds. The state relies upon local public and private social agencies, public health nurses, physicians, midwives, hospitals, and nursery and kindergarten teachers, as well as elementary school teachers to locate crippled children. In all states, diagnosis and treatment cover children with severe crippling conditions, such as clubfoot, harelip, and cleft palate. Other diseases, such as rheumatic fever, heart diseases, cerebral palsy, eye and speech defects, ear diseases, epilepsy, and dental defects requiring orthodontia, are covered in some state programs (at present, frequently only on a demonstration basis). Usually, the program is administered by the state and local health departments. In the urban areas of most states, special classes for the instruction of crippled, deaf, and blind children are organized.

Private crippled children's agencies, established and supported by such fraternal orders as the Shriners, the Elks, and the Rotary Clubs, and also by religious and nonsectarian societies, have been the pioneers in this field. They built the first orthopedic hospitals and

---

[6] Children's Bureau, "Changes in Infant, Childhood, and Maternal Mortality Over the Decade 1939-1948," *Statistical Series, No. 6* (1950); and, Betty M. Flint, *The Security of Infants* (Chicago: University of Chicago Press, 1959).

clinics and encouraged state legislation for crippled children preceding the *Social Security Act of 1935*. Despite the more generous federal and state appropriations granted recently for crippled children, supplementation by private social agencies is still urgently needed, since most states do not yet provide adequate diagnostic services, and particularly, the expensive treatment for many crippling diseases.[7]

C. Child Welfare Services

When the *Social Security Act of 1935* was passed, nearly 7,500,000 boys and girls were "on relief," 300,000 children were dependent or neglected, and about 200,000 children annually came before the juvenile courts. Help and protection for these children was mainly left to private social agencies and to the inadequate powers of local communities. With the support of Federal grants-in-aid, public services for the protection of the unfortunate homeless, orphaned, abandoned, dependent, or neglected children, and for children in danger of delinquency, have been greatly strengthened. The *Amendment of the Social Security Act of 1958,* no longer limited Federal grants to rural and special emergency areas. Every state now has a child welfare division in its public welfare department, and local child welfare departments are more efficiently operated. These public services include casework with parents and relatives for the improvement of unsatisfactory family and personal relationships of the child, and help in economic and social difficulties. Children with physical, mental, and emotional handicaps receive aid. Special attention is given to children born out of wedlock, and foster families or institutional care are provided for children who need to live away from their own homes. Public child welfare authorities are responsible for the supervision of foster homes and children's institutions. These child welfare services also provide assistance to courts which handle children's cases, to schools, to child guidance and mental hygiene clinics, and other health agencies concerned with individual children.[8] Fre-

---

[7] Dean W. Roberts *et al.,* "The Physically Handicapped," *Social Work Year Book* (1960), pp. 432-440; U. S. Children's Bureau, *Services for Crippled Children* (1952); William M. Cruickshank, *Psychology of Exceptional Children and Youth* (Englewood Cliffs, N. J.: Prentice-Hall, Inc., 1955); and, Dorothy Zietz, *op. cit.,* pp. 205-240.

[8] Fred Delli Quadri, "Child Welfare," *Social Work Year Book* (1957), pp. 146-157; and Wayne Vasey, *Government and Social Welfare* (New York: Holt, 1958), pp. 186-202.

quently, they cooperate with group work agencies for the protection of children. The child caseworker also is concerned with the promotion of an understanding of the needs of children in the community, and with the encouragement and development of such public or private facilities as day care centers, nursery schools, group work agencies, community centers, and recreation places for children and adolescents.

The annual Federal grant-in-aid for child welfare services has been increased from $1,500,000 in 1936 to $17,000,000 in 1958. Each state receives a flat amount of $60,000 and shares in the balance according to the proportion of its population under eighteen years to the total population in the United States under such age.[9] The Federal grants may be used by returning a runaway child under the age of eighteen to his home community when his parents or relatives, a social agency or institution cannot meet the expense. The principal advantage of these child welfare services is that they employ trained child welfare workers and consultants to improve the work of local welfare departments, institutions, public and private child and family welfare agencies, clinics, and community centers. The facilities and the experience of voluntary organizations may be utilized as well. The states may authorize coordinated programs for child care and protection with private social agencies in the field of group work and casework, and cooperate with probation departments of juvenile courts and police juvenile aid bureaus. Child welfare work is devoted to strengthening family life and permitting the child to grow up in his own family. Children shall not be deprived of this emotional security based upon life with their own family because of economic need. In case of personal or emotional difficulties within the family, the child welfare worker will try to help in an adjustment by counseling the child and parents. She will assist in making available other facilities, such as participation in a children's or youth group, in recreational activities, or the use of a mental hygiene or child guidance clinic. Only if a child cannot remain in his own family for reasons of health, education, or adjustment, will he be placed in a foster home or in a Children's Home.

The functions of child welfare divisions of each state depart-

---

[9] The *Social Security Act of 1935* considered the entire rural population ratio, but the *Amendment of 1950* replaced this factor by the ratio of rural children and youth under eighteen years of age.

ment of public welfare include the development of standards for child care and for adoption procedure, licensing and inspection of children's institutions and foster families, and the promotion of legislation for child protection. In some states, the child welfare division also administers state institutions for delinquent and mentally and physically handicapped children. In other states, a separate state agency, such as the California Youth Authority, is in charge of all institutions, or assumes the responsibility for prevention and treatment of juvenile delinquency.

III. FOSTER FAMILY CARE

There are children who cannot live with their families; children who are orphans without relatives; abandoned children whose parents are unknown; children who have been deserted by their parents; and children whose parents are unable to keep them because of illness or who have been committed to a prison. Some parents also may be a direct threat to their children. For such children, as a rule, placement in a foster home is considered. The social agency, which handles foster family placement, needs to know the child well enough to find the proper home for him. The caseworker helps the child to accept the necessity for placement and to share, as much as his age permits, the plans for his foster family. The caseworker also sustains the child in this inescapably anxious period. The child receives medical and psychological examinations, and the child placing agency considers his social and cultural background; his relation to all members of the family, the neighborhood, and school; his behavior, attitudes, and personal preferences, as well as the wishes of his parents (whenever this is possible). Working together with the parents, the child, and the foster parents in order to secure a mutually satisfactory solution for all persons concerned, the social agency attempts to find the foster home best suited to the individual child's needs.

In the selection of foster families, the social agency considers whether the family will provide the right home for a healthy and normal development of the particular child, but it also gives attention to the financial situation, housing conditions, neighborhood, and housekeeping standards. The educational, spiritual, and religious background of the foster parents deserves serious thought as well. Professional skill in foster placement is needed for fitting together the child's emotional, intellectual, and physical needs with the abilities of foster parents, to achieve the best possible adjustment and satisfaction for both child and foster family.

In the foster family, a normal and harmonious relationship between the parents is necessary, and, if there are children or other relatives, the entire family group should be congenial. They also must have (particularly the foster mother) a sincere interest in children, because a child in a foster home requires, above all, love and understanding in order to adjust to a new family environment. The main motivation of families applying for a foster child should be their desire to rear such a child as if he were their own. Families who apply merely for financial reasons, or who want to get a child primarily for their own emotional satisfaction, without being able to give the child warmth and understanding, should not be accepted. It is often difficult for the child welfare worker to refuse applicants who want to be foster parents badly; sometimes it is necessary to refer such applicants to a family service agency in order to help them in their own personal problems.[10] As a rule, it is desirable that the foster parents be of about the same age as the natural parents of the child. However, practical experience shows that older, well-suited foster parents often establish an excellent relationship with the child if he responds to their affection and understanding. Foster parents need to accept the fact that the child's ultimate security is with his own family, that he will return to them, and that his ties to his parents or other close relatives are not to be weakened or destroyed.

In general, the child placing agency assumes the supervision of the foster home after the child has been placed. Of course, the foster family has responsibility for the physical care of the child, and his education. The child caseworker helps the child and the foster parents to adjust in their mutual relations, and to solve the difficulties and

---

[10] Dorothy Hutchinson, *In Quest of Foster Parents: A Point of View on Homefinding* (New York: Columbia University Press, 1943), pp. 13-15; Jean Charnley, *The Art of Child Placement* (Minneapolis: University of Minnesota Press, 1955); and, Henrietta L. Gordon, *Casework Services for Children* (Boston: Houghton, 1956).

disappointments which are rarely missing in any family. The child frequently brings into the foster home his suspicions, anxieties, resistance, or hostility. The caseworker aids the foster parents in their effort to overcome these problems and to give the child the security he longs for. Whenever possible, the caseworker attempts to preserve the child's interest in his natural family, and to keep alive the family's feeling of responsibility for the child, because, in the majority of cases, the child finally will return to it. Sometimes, visits of the parents with the foster family, or of the child with the mother or siblings are arranged, but this has to be done with the full cooperation of the foster family. In cases of conflict, the caseworker will consider the welfare and happiness of the child as the decisive factor in such arrangements.

Some child welfare and family service agencies use temporary foster homes in order to place children in emergencies until they have enough time to find a more permanent family home in which the child will feel accepted and secure. During this period, the child himself, who in his own family has experienced the neglect and domestic discord that leads to running away, stealing, or other expressions of maladjustment, has time to adapt himself to the idea of living with another normal and understanding family.

Among the various types of foster homes, only one plays a major role in present child care practice: the boarding home. Here, the foster parents receive payment for their service, either by the parents, relatives, guardian of the child, juvenile court, or by the social agency which places the child. Free foster homes, in which the foster parents do not receive any remuneration, are rare today, because such families usually are not willing to submit to the standards, conditions, and supervision of the social agency or to the special needs of the child. There are sectarian agencies which still find free homes in a few instances. Wage homes, or work homes, in which the older child is maintained in exchange for the work he does for the foster family, are infrequently relied upon for placing children.

The adoption home provides a different type of care. The child is placed without payment of board and with the understanding that the adoptive parents will accept the child as a permanent member of the family if the placement of the child proves to be mutually satisfactory.

IV. ADOPTION

Adoption is the legal, social, and psychological method of providing a family for children who have lost their natural parents or who cannot be reared by them under sound conditions. Adoption, as a legal proceeding of the courts, establishes the relationship of parent and child between persons who are not related by nature. Through adoption, the child, in effect, becomes a permanent member of the adopting family. Often, children are adopted by relatives or by a stepparent, but the legal and social safeguards of present adoption laws are basically designed to protect children who are not related to the adopting family.[11]

Adoption was widely used in Roman law and was brought from France and Spain to Louisiana and Texas in the seventeenth century. The first state to introduce adoption legislation under common law was Massachusetts (1851). At present, every state has an adoption statute, though it varies widely from one to another. One objective of adoption laws is *to protect the child* from unnecessary separation from his natural parents; from adoption by unfit parents; and from interference by his natural parents after a successful adoption has been arranged. Another objective is to protect *the natural parents,* particularly the unmarried mother, from unwise, hurried decisions made under emotional stress or economic pressure, which they might greatly regret later. Still another is *to protect the adopting parents* from taking a permanent responsibility for children whose health, heredity, or physical and mental capacities might lead to their disappointment, and also to protect them from disturbance of their relationship with the adopted child by threats or blackmail from the natural parents.

More than one-half of adoptions concern illegitimate children. Others involve pre-marital, extra-marital, and unwanted children. Nearly 98 per cent of children placed for adoption are under one year of age. In some states, a trend exists to limit the adoption placements to licensed social agencies, but it is questionable whether one should attempt to prevent parents from placing their own child,

---

[11] Clyde Getz, "Adoption," *Social Work Year Book* (1957), pp. 82-88; Florence G. Brown, "Adoption," *ibid.* (1960), pp. 85-90; and, Michael Schapiro, *A Study of Adoption Practice,* 2 vols. (New York: Child Welfare League of America, 1956).

particularly with relatives or friends. In adoptions, carried out under agency auspices, the natural parents (or the unmarried mother) "relinquish" the child to a licensed social agency which then takes full responsibility for the placement of the child in an adoptive home, not known to the natural parents. This decision is made only after careful interviews. Many an unmarried girl comes to the agency during her pregnancy and wants to relinquish her baby immediately. Frequently, she is motivated by fear, shame, or feeling of guilt, and might be very unhappy later about a hasty decision. She is counseled about all the possibilities which exist, such as aid to dependent children, foster care, and other temporary arrangements, which help her keep her child for a time before making her decision over whether or not to rear him. Adoption should be a free, well-considered plan, not a hasty decision of the mother under emotional and economic pressure.

Typical features of adoption laws are that adult persons may adopt a child only with the consent of the natural parents or of the unmarried mother, that the adoptive parents must be at least ten years older than the child, and that the child has to give his consent to the adoption if he is twelve or fourteen years or older. The consent of the natural parent or parents has to be given before the court (frequently the juvenile court or the probate court), or before the state department of social welfare or a licensed adoption agency. In general, a social investigation by a public or private welfare agency is required so that the court can be fully informed of all essential factors before it makes a decision on the petition. As a rule, the child is placed in the adoption home for a trial period from six months to one year under supervision of a social agency until the final decision of the court on adoption is rendered. During this time, the development of the child in his new environment is observed by the social worker, and the adoptive parents have an opportunity to find out whether they really want to have this child as a member of their family.[12]

Throughout the United States, there is a great demand from child-

---

[12] American adoption laws of today do not, in general, limit adoption to a married couple, or a couple that cannot have children. But, the practice of social agencies and courts has been to place children for adoption into "full families" to give the child the opportunity for normal development. Georgia, alone, of all states, legally limits adoptions to married couples.

less couples for children to adopt, particularly babies. There are, however, not nearly enough children available for adoption to meet this demand. This discrepancy explains the public criticism that adoption agencies are too strict in their postulations, preventing people who wish to adopt a child from getting the desired child, and that a family is denied to homeless children. Social agencies are conscious of this widespread criticism and are trying to find ways to improve their service and to curtail the long waiting period preceding adoption. They also are anxious to create better public understanding of the reasons for the time involved in this process. These conditions have encouraged the "black market in babies" in which unscrupulous employees of maternity wards, together with other "middle-men," abuse the anxiety of unmarried girls and the sentimental attitude of well-to-do childless couples desirous of receiving a baby. Arrangement is made for adoption placement before, or immediately after, the birth of the child in exchange for the payment of substantial amounts of money (sometimes from both parties), called a "gratitude donation." This "selling of babies" results in handsome profits for the managers of this business, and no questions or investigations delay the placement of such a baby. However, unhappiness for the child and the adopting parents often results.

Similar manipulations, which are not exclusively based upon greed, are called "the gray market in babies." They are carried on by those people who attempt to please a couple, wishing to have a child, by persuading fearful unmarried mothers to give up the child immediately after birth. There is no competent method of determining whether this action really will be in the interest of the child and the mother. Trained workers of an adoption agency are the only ones professionally qualified to counsel with the mother, to acquaint her with alternatives to adoption placement, and to proceed with skillful study of the child's parental background and potentialities to suit him to the adopted home. Although child placements by unauthorized persons are prohibited in some states, these "independent adoptions" are still very frequent, and the unmarried mother or the natural parents are usually entitled to place their child in a family of their choice. The danger in these "independent adoptions" is that the mother may not have time or insight to form a clear opinion of whether or not she really wants to give away her child. She may be unable to assess the qualities of the adoptive family. The child may unnecessarily lose his natural mother. This method also involves the risk for the adopting parents that the child in his mental and physical health, temperament, and personality may not fit into their family. For these reasons, agency adoption offers greater security to the three parties concerned—the child, the natural parents, and the adoptive parents.

If the parents or the unmarried mother are determined to relinquish the child, the social agency makes a thorough study of the child with medical examination, psychological tests, and information about the social and health background of the child's mother and father. Also, their hereditary, racial, and constitutional type is studied. The agency attempts to find an adoptive home in which these factors are similar. This explains why outsiders frequently comment on the resemblance of adopted children to their adoptive parents. Relinquishing the child to the agency also assures the parents that their identity and that of the adoptive parents are concealed from each other so that embarrassment, jealousy, friction, interference, and blackmail are avoided.

Recently, however, some adoption agencies have begun to place newborn babies in their first months of life in adoption homes because they have become convinced that the child's stay in a new permanent home without any change of environment offers the best chances for his emotional development. Agencies investigate and select suitable adoption families from their applicants before a child is available for adoption. More adoptive couples are willing, at present, to take the risks involved in adopting a very young child than in former times. The so-called "intelligence test" of the infant to check the probability of his normal mental growth is, as a rule, no longer considered necessary. Only a medical statement is required by the adoption agency that the baby has not suffered injury or damage in his delivery. In these early adoptions as in others, the mother of the child is counseled by the caseworker of the agency so that she is able to weigh the reasons for or against the relinquishment of the child before she decides whether or not to have him adopted.

The role of the adoption worker is a very responsible one. She must be well aware of her own feelings and attitudes in order to give an objective, but warm-hearted understanding to the needs of the three parties in the adoption process, and to perform a service satisfactory to the community.

In the selection of the adopting parents, the social agency looks for families who are in good physical and mental health and are emotionally and economically able to rear the child. After the child is placed with the selected family, the social agency generally maintains contact with the child and the new parents for one year. This is done to give help in whatever adjustment difficulties might arise, and to observe whether the child satisfactorily takes roots in the new family. If the adjustment is satisfactory, the social agency recommends that the court grant the adoption.[13] In general, the courts follow the social agency's suggestion, which is based upon its work with natural parents, child, and adopting parents. In many states, court hearings are not open to the public, but the older child is usually present in order to give his consent. The decree of adoption declares that the child is the child and legal heir of the adopting parents and acquires the same rights, privileges, and obligations as a child born to them.

There are two other types of adoption: the stepparent adoption, and adoption of an illegitimate child by his natural father. Under stepparent adoption, the child remains with his mother, whether she was not married before, widowed, or divorced. The petition for adoption is filed with the court by the stepfather, and requires the formal consent of the mother. It is done so that the child has the same legal status and name as other children in the family. In these cases, social investigations are often carried out by the probation officer of the court. A father who wants to adopt his own natural child has to undergo different procedures in the various states. For instance, in California he has to acknowledge the child as his own before the court, has to receive him into his family, and treat him like a legitimate child. He needs the formal consent of the natural mother if she is alive, and also of his own wife if he is married.

V. CHILDREN OF UNMARRIED PARENTS

Programs to meet the needs of the unmarried mother and to offer care and protection to her child are among the most important serv-

---

[13] If the child does not adjust well, the social agency removes him and makes another arrangement, but, because careful selection is made, such cases are rare.

ices organized by family and children's agencies. The unmarried mother often moves away from her home community in order to avoid the embarrassment and disdain which, even today, frequently is connected with this situation. The social agency may have to assist in arrangements for the confinement and for the care of the child. Obviously, the illegitimate child needs just as much affection and feeling of belonging as any other child, and, for this reason, children's agencies usually attempt to permit the mother to stay with the baby until she decides what she wants done with the child. The child born out of wedlock, fundamentally, should not be treated differently than other children in providing for his needs of protection and care. His mother, as well, frequently, needs intensive help and counseling by the caseworker in order to avoid unwise plans for herself and for the child. The unmarried father, also, should be included in the work of the social agency, in order to help and encourage him to meet his moral and financial responsibilities for the child.[14]

VI. GUARDIANSHIP

Guardianship is the establishment of legal protection for children when the parents are dead, incapacitated, incompetent, or have failed in their duty toward the children.[15] The guardian is a substitute for the parent, but he is not liable for the child's support. The guardianship ends with the child's majority or with his marriage. In case of death of the father, the mother is the *natural guardian* of the children, and the unmarried mother is the *sole guardian* of her child. *Testamentary guardians* are named in the will of the deceased parents, and often are relatives or friends of the family; *public guardians,* as a rule county officials, are provided in ten states for the protection of children; there are *guardians of estate* to manage property rights of the ward, and *guardians ad litem* who are appointed by the court

14 Some states have adopted the *Uniform Illegitimacy Law* drafted by the National Conference of Commissioners on Uniform State Laws in 1922, by which both the mother and the unmarried father are responsible for support, maintenance, and education of the illegitimate child.

15 Irving Weissman *et al.,* "Guardianship for Children," *Publication No. 330* (Washington: U. S. Children's Bureau, 1949), p. 19; Leontine Young, *Out of Wedlock* (New York: McGraw, 1954); and, Ruth L. Butcher and Marion O. Robinson, *The Unmarried Mother* (New York: Public Affairs Committee, 1959).

for special purposes, mainly legal proceedings. The legal provisions for guardianship in most states are enacted in the laws on infancy and guardianship, but too much emphasis still is placed upon the management of estate rather than upon the protection of the child's healthful placement, education, and guidance. In addition to testamentary guardians, guardians are appointed by various courts, such as the probate court, the juvenile court, orphans', or surrogate court. In some states the probation officer of a rural juvenile court is guardian for the wards of the court. The investigation of the fitness of guardians before their appointment and supervision of the activities of guardians are necessary for the protection of children, but these measures unfortunately are seldom carried out.[16]

VII. CHILDREN IN INSTITUTIONS

In the nineteenth century, destitute and orphaned children were customarily cared for in orphanages and asylums. The trend since then has been away from institutional care. The main reason is that children's homes require from the child an adjustment to a large number of other children, educators, staff members of the institution, in at atmosphere unlike home. That children become "institutionalized," that they lose their personality in conforming to strict, general regulations, and that they have no opportunity to develop their individuality, their mental, physical and creative abilities, and are apt to become docile and dull have been the main arguments against institutional care. Life in an institution makes a certain routine necessary that often limits warm personal relationships with the personnel and other children in the home and easily inhibits the development of initiative in the child. However, the modern children's institution offers an opportunity for an experience in more constructive group living, regular physical care, a healthy diet, an atmosphere provided by friendly, interested, trained educators concerned with the well-being of the child, and medical (often psychiatric) aid and trained social work service.

---

[16] Hazeltine Byrd Taylor, *Law of Guardian and Ward* (Chicago: University of Chicago Press, 1935), p. 5; and, Mary Stanton, "The Administration of Guardianship by a Local Probate Court," *The Social Service Review,* Vol. XIV, No. 4 (December 1945), pp. 495-505.

Modern children's institutions have tried to overcome the problems presented by mass education and living in large dormitories by the establishment of the "cottage plan." The institution is decentralized into a number of cottages, usually accommodating a group of about twenty girls and boys with a couple of cottage parents. Instead of dormitories, small sleeping rooms for two to four children, and living and dining rooms are used in which the children feel more like they are "at home." [17]

Which children need institutional care? Infants and preschool-age children who cannot remain with their own families are rarely placed in institutions, but into foster families. It also is an accepted principle that institutional care for children should be a temporary placement, and not planned until the child has fully grown up. The following groups usually seem to need institutional care: (1) children who, because of severe illness or injury of the parents, have to leave their home and who are so strongly emotionally tied to the parents that they or the parents feel threatened by a placement in another family; (2) children who because of family disturbances, tensions, or divorce have become so difficult that they cannot remain in their family, but who also are unable to establish sound emotional relationship with a foster family; (3) children who have been so badly disappointed or so deeply hurt by previous foster placement that they are unfit to become, at this point, an integral part of a new family; (4) children presenting such difficult health or behavior problems that they are not acceptable to foster families, and are in need of professional observation and guidance, as well as medical or psychiatric treatment in a controlled environment; (5) large family groups of siblings who do not want to be separated, but who, otherwise, would have to be split up among several foster families; (6) older children and adolescents who are breaking away from their own families and would tend to break away from the foster family as well; and (7) adolescents who for various reasons arising from within their own families need only short-term care and would profit more from the experience of group living during such a period.[18]

---

[17] Examples of various types of children's homes and of the life of the children in such institutions are found in Howard W. Hopkirk, *Institutions Serving Children* (New York: Russell Sage Foundation, 1944).

[18] Helen R. Hagan, "Foster Care of Children," *Social Work Year Book* (1957), pp. 267-274; Elizabeth G. Meier, "Foster Care for Children," *ibid.*

Placement of a child in an institution often seems easier for parents to accept than placement in a foster family because it does not endanger their social prestige in the community, which often interprets foster home placement of children as a failure of the parents. Effective treatment of children in an institution requires that the children receive a friendly, homelike reception in a small group according to the cottage system; that medical and, if necessary, psychiatric examination and service be available; and that the individual needs of the children be met by trained casework service. It is also necessary that educational, recreational, and vocational facilities be of a high standard, and that the work in the institution be fully devoted to the development of the children into useful and happy members of the community.

Under such circumstances, the institution is able to care more successfully for children than their own home or a foster family. Recently, the special merits of children's institutions have been recognized for certain types of difficult, disturbed, predelinquent children. Institutions have been used for a long time for the care of feeble-minded, blind, deaf, deaf-mute, epileptic, and crippled children in need of special education, and also for delinquent children who are so dangerous to the community and to themselves that placement in a family does not promise success. There is a new trend toward keeping blind and deaf children in their own or in foster families and to encourage them to take part in normal activities as much as possible. Furthermore, special classes for handicapped children in public schools are limited to subjects in which their health makes it impossible to learn together with normal children. These developments were made necessary because the number of institutions for seriously disturbed children and adolescents that offer intensive treatment with psychotherapy and skillful therapeutic group living experience is not sufficient.[19]

The number of children placed in public and private institutions is still large. The U.S. Children's Bureau estimated, that in 1950, the number of children living in public institutions was 37,000, and it is

---

(1960), pp. 277-280; and Joseph F. Meisels and Martin B. Loeb, "Unanswered Questions about Foster Care," *Social Service Review,* Vol. XXX, No. 3 (September 1956).

[19] Susanne Schulze, *Creative Group Living in a Children's Institution* (New York: Association Press, 1951), pp. 158-186.

assumed that about the same number reside in private children's institutions. The median number of children in homes for neglected and dependent children was forty-six, and the number in institutions for delinquent children was 110.[20] The establishment of small, well-staffed institutions which give individualized, personal care to each child and provide understanding for young and disturbed children seems most desirable.

A special type of care, which lies between that given in an institution and a foster family is that provided in a "group home." The group home accommodates between six and ten children or adolescents in a house or spacious apartment. The housemother or the houseparents are in a position to let the children participate in home management in the same manner they would be required to in a large family, and the personal contact between the foster parents and children is the same as it is in a family of substantial size. This type of care might well be used as a transition from institutional placement to a foster family or to the return of the child or adolescent to his own family.[21]

VIII. DAY NURSERIES AND CHILD CARE CENTERS

Day nurseries provide care for young children (between two and five years of age) during the day while their mothers are at work. These nurseries have become necessary because of the increasing employment of women in industry. At first, only custodial care was offered. More recently, however, day nurseries have assumed broader responsibilities for the health and education of the children. These include social casework with parents and relatives, mothers' study groups, and cooperation with children's and family service agencies whenever the children require additional services or special treatment.

Nursery schools are educational institutions for preschool children, age two to five, which attempt to develop the mental, physical,

---

[20] I. Richard Pearlman and Jack Wiener, *Children Living in Selected Public Institutions* (Washington: Children's Bureau, May, 1950); and, Joseph H. Reid and Helen R. Hagan, *Residential Treatment of Emotionally Disturbed Children* (New York: Child Welfare League of America, 1952).

[21] Helen R. Hagan, *op. cit.*, p. 270; and F. Fischer, *The Group Home: An Innovation in Child Placement* (New York: Child Welfare League of America, 1952).

social, and emotional capacities of the children, and to help in the formation of desirable habits and behavior patterns. These schools are not limited to caring for children, but, like the day nurseries, may devote considerable effort to parent education through conferences, study groups, and mothers' participation in the nursery school activities and in discussions with the nursery school staff.

When numerous women went into industrial work during World War II, the establishment of day care centers for school children became imperative. Funds were provided by the *Lanham Act* for their organization and operation during the war, and, after the war, state subsidies in several states have made the continuation of day care centers possible. Their number has decreased during recent years because children are accepted in the centers, now, only if the income of their parents does not exceed certain limits, or if their parents are veterans. It seems desirable that day care centers be made a permanent part of child welfare services. They function as valuable substitutes for family care during the time when the mother is not available at home, improve the health, education, and social attitudes of the children, give them a healthy outlet for their energies in play, games, and leisure time activities, and, above all, an experience in group living (aside from that gained in school) with other children of the same age. The potentialities of day care centers could be increased if trained social caseworkers would be employed to serve as intake workers and to establish the individual contacts with the children and their families which prove to be constructive in such relationships. Until now, few of the day care centers have been able to use caseworkers for this service, but, some have made arrangements with family welfare or children's agencies for members of their staff to establish liaison work as "outposts" in the centers.

IX. SCHOOL LUNCHES

During the Depression and, later, during World War II, school lunches were provided in many schools in order to safeguard the health of children who were fed no breakfast at home. The program was partly financed by the parents, partly by local communities and private social organizations, and was supported by *Lanham Act* funds. In 1946, the *National School Lunch Act* appropriated Federal funds to be administered by the Department of Agriculture, to encourage the proper nutrition of children and, at the same time, to increase domestic consumption of farm products on a permanent basis. Under supervision of the various state departments of educations, which finance an increasing proportion of the program as well, the schools make the lunch available to children regardless of their race, religion, and ability of their parents to pay.[22]

X. SCHOOL SOCIAL WORK

Until the end of the nineteenth century, the concept prevailed that children with reasonable physical care would grow into normal, happy adulthood. But scientific investigation of psychological, sociological, and psychiatric principles regarding personality development has discovered the greater importance of the growing-up process and its lasting effects on the total human personality. The introduction of programs of social work in schools was felt to be necessary, almost at the same time, in Boston, Hartford, Connecticut, and New York City in 1906 and 1907. They were established under the title "visiting teachers' work," because the difficulties which children had in schools frequently were due to faulty relationships within the family or environment, or by the child's personal problems which could not be well handled by the teachers in school.

In Boston, the West End Neighborhood Association, a social settlement, and the Women's Education Association, a parent-teachers group, each engaged a social worker, called a "home and school visitor," in order to assist the schools in overcoming misunderstanding between the families and the schools. In Hartford the director of the Henry Barnard School Clinic, a psychological clinic, requested the employment of a "visiting teacher" in order to coordinate the work in school, family, and clinic and to prevent serious maladjustment of children.

In New York, two settlement houses, Hartley House and Greenwich Neighborhood House, each assigned a social worker to assist in the home-school relationships of children and to meet the social problems which seemed to cause trouble for children in schools.

---

[22] Charles C. Wilson, "School Health Services," *Social Work Year Book* (1949), p. 455.

Other cities followed these examples, and in 1913, Rochester, New York, established the first public, municipal system of visiting teachers with the requirement that they have social work training.[23]

The program of school social work was greatly strengthened by funds granted by the Commonwealth Fund in New York, in 1921, to serve in the prevention of juvenile delinquency. The program was designed to develop four different, but coordinated, programs: (1) demonstration projects for visiting teachers in thirty communities; (2) child guidance clinics established with the advice of the National Committee of Mental Hygiene; (3) psychiatric studies of difficult, pre-delinquent, and delinquent children in connection with schools and juvenile courts; and (4) the training of social workers, visiting teachers, and psychologists for competent work in the field of delinquency prevention.

The Commonwealth Fund insisted that the communities, which received allocations for visiting teacher work, share one-third of the expenses during a demonstration period of five years and, after that helped, for another three years, train personnel to understand behavior problems. After this experience, many cities, including smaller and rural towns, developed school social work programs. The American Association of Visiting Teachers was organized in 1916 and renamed the National Association of School Social Workers in 1945. In some states, the employment of at least one school social worker in each community is required; in others, such as Michigan and California, state funds support the school districts or communities in school social work. In 1950, 450 cities were estimated to have full-time school social workers, but many more have part-time service.[24]

The school social worker helps individual children who have difficulties in making a satisfactory school adjustment. These difficulties may be expressed in truancy, failure in school subjects and in timid, fearful, withdrawing, or overaggressive behavior. Other indica-

---

[23] Helen L. Witmer, *Social Work* (New York: Farrar & Rinehart, 1942), pp. 359-360.

[24] Mildred Sikkema, "School Social Services," *Social Work Year Book* (1951), p. 448; Florence Poole, "School Social Services," *ibid.* (1954), pp. 467-469; Theodore L. Reller, *et al.,* "The Public School and Other Community Services," *The Annals,* Vol. 302 (November 1955), pp. 1-73; and, Grace Lee (editor), *Helping the Troubled School Child* (New York: National Association of Social Workers, 1959).

tions may be stealing, fighting, sullenness, resentfulness, inability to get along with other children, to accept the authority of the teacher, or demand for special attention. The classroom teacher will ask for the help of the school social worker for such children. The social worker usually observes the child in class first, and then discusses his problems with the teacher and principal. She learns more about the child's difficulties from school records, the school nurse, the attendance or truant officer, and, above all, from the child himself. Sometimes, a discussion with the child changes his attitude. The school social worker, in most instances, contacts the parents after the interview with the child in order to understand his difficulties and to ask for the parents' help to improve the child's adjustment in school.

The school social worker will also interpret the methods and philosophy of the school to the parents in order to enlist their active cooperation. In this way, she helps the school to establish constructive parent-school relationships. She interprets the school program to parent-teachers associations, civic groups and to the community, and participates in faculty meetings, school committees, and group projects. The school social worker maintains an independent role in the interest of the child, so that the child trusts her and does not identify her fully with the school authority. She works with four parties: (1) the child, (2) the family, (3) the school staff, and (4) the community. She attempts to change attitudes of the child, the parents, teachers, and community groups which are detrimental to the adjustment of the child and to the requirements of the school. The maladjusted child is often a serious handicap to other children in his class.

The social worker's functions vary in different communities. Whether she should also serve as a truant or attendance officer is questionable, but the execution of the compulsory school attendance laws is not limited to police, or legal means. It is also debatable how much a school social worker may effectively prevent the development of mental disorders. Practical experience has shown that the school social worker is frequently successful in solving behavior problems and disciplinary questions. Sometimes, she is able, through the use of other community resources, group work agencies, and family welfare services, to improve the conditions in the family which caused the child's failure or maladjustment in school and thus change the child's behavior.

The school social worker should have professional training in social work and understanding of the educational process of the school, possess the ability to work with children and adults, and be able to operate in a team relationship with the school faculty. She needs humor, imagination, flexibility, and a good knowledge of the resources of the community.

XI. CHILD LABOR PROTECTION

Children worked in the fields and the trades since the first settlements in our country were established. They were cheap, willing, useful workers in a time when labor was scarce. Children represented a large proportion (more than half) of the labor force in this period. The philosophy of the Puritans and Quakers taught that labor was the right way for children to learn farming or craftwork and to become thrifty and industrious as well. During the seventeenth and eighteenth centuries, children were apprenticed to a farmer, craftsman, or merchant, and lived in the master's family. When the factory system developed in the nineteenth century, parents no longer apprenticed their children but sent them to factories where they earned higher wages.[25]

The first laws limiting daily working hours of young children to ten hours were enacted in some of the northern industrial states, beginning in Massachusetts and Connecticut. At first, child labor laws passed by the states applied to manufacturing shops and textile mills only. The maximum age of the children, covered by these laws, differed from twelve to sixteen years. None of these statutes, however, required proof of age from working children, nor did they provide for inspectors to enforce the observation of the laws,[26] so they were not effective. Children continued to be employed for long hours, at night, at dangerous work, and even in occupations

---

[25] Grace Abbott, *The Child and the State,* Vol. I (Chicago: University of Chicago Press, 1938), pp. 189-191.

[26] *Ibid.,* pp. 260, 405. These laws were widely disregarded, since children, parents, and employers were interested in child labor for profit, and fellow employees were either indifferent or scared to report violations of the laws.

in restaurants, music halls, bar rooms, and dance halls which damaged their morale.

The early trade unions complained of the excessive hours children had to work, and began, before 1860, to demand universal education for them, but they were fighting for their members' benefit as well as for that of children when they attempted to secure a shorter working day.

When industries expanded and the use of machine power increased, after the War between the States, the number of children working in factories and mines grew larger, and the demand for child labor legislation and means to enforce the statutes became stronger. The main arguments were the health damage to the child, interference with the child's education, and the depressing effect of children's work on the wages of adult workers. Another reason the demand was made to restrict child labor in factories was that they took the places of adults, a complaint which was raised particularly in periods of large-scale unemployment during the last two decades of the nineteenth century.

Following the example set by Massachusetts in 1836, the states enacted compulsory school attendance laws, but progress was slow in the face of stubborn opposition both from parents who did not want to lose the income from the labor of their children and from employers who preferred to use cheap child labor. The industrial states began to introduce factory inspectors in order to supervise and to enforce child labor statutes after social reformers, educators, and social workers showed their concern for the damage which excessive child labor did to the health and education of the children. Among the leaders of the movement for the protection of children were Jane Addams, Florence Kelley (she became the first factory inspector in the state of Illinois), Julia Lathrop, Edith and Grace Abbott, and Sophonisba P. Breckinridge. But public opinion was sharply divided over the question of child labor laws, and the influential groups, which had opposed this legislation earlier, continued to do so for a long time afterwards. By the end of the nineteencth century, most industrial states had enacted child labor legislation which limited the daily hours of work of children and young persons to nine or ten hours, and prohibited work of children during school hours and at night between 10 P.M and 6 A.M. This usually applied to children employed in manufacturing, mining, and industry. Employment in particularly dangerous occupations was, as a rule, prohibited for children and adolescents under sixteen years of age, whereas child labor laws, in general, applied to children only up to twelve, thirteen, or fourteen years. Children working in agriculture and as domestic servants were not protected at all.

The provisions of these state laws were not well enforced throughout the country, because the staff of factory inspectors was insufficient, and many judges were not disposed to fine parents or employers for violating the laws. Conditions in most southern states were far worse, for they had almost no child labor legislation at all. In several states, children could be legally employed in the cotton mills as young as twelve years of age. The exploitation of these children, their poor health, and lack of school attendance, led to the organization of the National Child Labor Committee in 1904, under the leadership of the Reverend Edgar Gardner Murphy and Reverend Alexander J. McKelway. The committee urged that the employment of the "poor white children" in the southern states be restricted, as it was in the industrial states, to a minimum age of fourteen years. The southern millowners denounced the campaign for a federal child labor law as "the effort of northern agitators to kill the infant industries of the South" and argued that due to the widespread poverty of the southern states the children were much better off in the mills than in their own homes.

Proposals for a Federal child labor law, dating from 1906, either failed to pass both houses of Congress, or were declared unconstitutional. A constitutional amendment was introduced in 1924, and was passed by both houses of Congress. However, it failed to gain ratification by the necessary number of states.[27] Since that date no further ratification has taken place so that the amendment has not become effective.

The application of two Federal laws, before they were declared unconstitutional, and the campaigns for the child labor amendment, however, had the effect of clarifying in the minds of the public the necessity for protection of children against excessive and damaging labor. Thus, they led indirectly to important improvements in the

---

[27] The reader will find the decision of the U. S. Supreme Court in *Hammer* vs. *Dagenhart* of June 3, 1918 which declared the child labor law unconstitutional and the famous dissenting opinion of Chief Justice Oliver Wendell Holmes in Grace Abbott, *op. cit.*, Vol. I, pp. 493, 495 ff., and 502-506.

child labor laws of most states and in raising the standards and methods of their operations.

Other social forces that contributed to a decline in child labor were the growth of union strength, a rise in the level of the national income which made education for more children possible, and then the Depression of 1930-1932 which encouraged factory owners to dismiss children in order to employ adults who had lost their jobs.

In 1932, industry, again, started to employ children because they were cheaper labor than adults. After the *National Industrial Recovery Act of 1933,* which limited the employment of children younger than sixteen, was declared unconstitutional, the number of young children employed rose higher.[28] The *Fair Labor Standards Act* (so-called "Wage Hours Act") of 1938 prohibited the employment (during school hours) of children under sixteen years of age in industries engaged in interstate commerce and producing goods for shipment to other states, and (at any time) in mining, manufacturing, and processing industries. Agricultural work outside of school hours is not included in this law.

The Child Labor Branch of the Department of Labor enforces the provisions of the Fair Labor Standards Act. Its small staff of inspectors, however, can only make sample inspections and on special complaint, so that relatively few industries employing child labor are visited. Inspections reveal that a tendency toward disregard of the Federal child labor provisions is prevalent. The great majority of the violations consists in the employment of children under sixteen without special permit.

Certain progress in state child labor legislation has led to the enactment, in twenty-three states, of a basic sixteen-year minimum age for work in factories and to the prohibition of employment of young people during school hours. Twenty-two states do not permit gainful employment for children under fourteen years during school hours. But only six states protect agricultural labor and domestic services under these provisions.

---

[28] Other federal laws affecting child labor were the *Walsh-Healy Act* of 1936, establishing a minimum age of sixteen years for boys and eighteen years for girls for employment in production under federal contract, and the *Sugar Act* of 1937, which prohibited federal subsidies to sugar growers employing children under fourteen—or children under sixteen longer than eight hours daily.

In Thousands

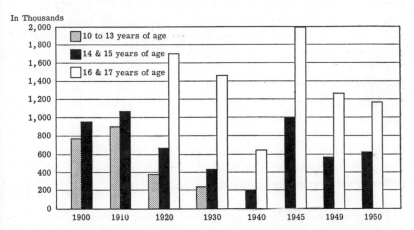

Chart 7. *Employed Children and Minors in the U.S., 1900-1950.*

The present standards of child labor regulation in the states are the following:

(1) *Employment during school hours.* A minimum age of sixteen years has been adopted by twenty-three states, a minimum of fifteen by two states, and a minimum of fourteen years by twenty-two states. Exceptions for agriculture and domestic service are frequent, and some states provide special permits for children in economic need.

(2) *Employment outside of school hours and during summer vacations.* Minimum of fourteen years of age has been adopted by one-half of the states, with wide exemption of agriculture, domestic service, and street trades. Certain states have no minimum age limit for this type of employment.

(3) *Working hours for children and young persons.* In forty-two states an eight-hour day has been set as maximum for most occupations, but twenty-seven states limit this rule to adolescents under sixteen years.

(4) *Part-time employment during school.* No regulation exists in thirty-four states; sixteen states have limited the hours for children under sixteen, frequently to three or four hours a day, or to a combined school and work period of eight hours daily. Most school attendance laws contain exemptions permitting children to work after

completion of the eighth grade, or because of family poverty.

(5) *Prohibition of night work.* Most states prohibit night work for children under sixteen, but only twelve states require a rest of thirteen consecutive hours from 6 P.M. to 7 A.M.

(6) *Work permits.* Forty-four states require a work permit for the employment of adolescents under sixteen years of age; twenty-two states also for the employment of young workers under eighteen, but not for all occupations.

(7) *Hazardous occupations.* In most states, the employment of children under sixteen years of age for a substantial number of hazardous occupations is prohibited, but this protection is extended to young workers under eighteen in only a few states.

Eighteen states have not yet enacted adequate child labor legislation, and the extension of the sixteen-year minimum age to these states is one of the urgent tasks for future legislation.[29] Another essential problem which has not been solved is the extension of child labor protection to agriculture, domestic services, street trades, and industrial homework. Agriculture still relies most extensively on the employment of children. In California, New Jersey, New York, Connecticut, and Hawaii special laws for the control of child labor in agriculture have been established, but in the other states much remains to be done.

The exemption of agricultural work from the child labor provisions of most states causes children of sharecroppers and low-income farm families to be kept from school by farm work in rural areas and permits six-year-old children to work as cotton pickers. The enforcement of school attendance laws often is inadequate. The Federal child labor law does not protect children employed in agricultural work, neither during the long summer vacation nor after school hours. These children may have to work at an early age, sometimes for long hours under the hot sun and occasionally in backbreaking, monotonous labor. This is true not only for children of migratory farm workers whose miserable conditions frequently arouse

---

[29] Since the *Fair Labor Standards Act* does not cover intrastate industries, children under sixteen are frequently employed in retail stores, bakeries, garages, beauty parlors, repair shops, hotels, restaurants, motels, bowling alleys, theaters, on merry-go-rounds, in offices, and domestic services without Federal protection and often without state protection.

public concern, but also for other children of farm families, though their exploitation may be less known.

The selling and distribution of newspapers by small boys, classified as "independent little merchants," is of questionable value as business experience. Twenty-seven states have no regulations of hours and working conditions for newsboys, and only four have adequate protective legislation. The usual standards permit the employment of ten-year-old boys for newspaper delivery and of twelve-year-old children for street selling; they may begin their work at five o'clock in the morning and work until eight or nine o'clock at night in most of the states. The newspapers profit from the "little merchant system" by making the children responsible for uncollectible subscription rates and by escaping the payment of workmen's compensation contributions which would be due if the children were employed. Thus the children are not protected if they are injured on their jobs.

Changing economic conditions and technical progress induce employers to prefer high school graduates when there is no shortage of workers. Children who leave school early have little chance for satisfactory jobs and advancement. Uniform protection of children against damaging child labor, enforcement of compulsory education laws, federal aid to elementary and secondary schools, and scholarships to aid students in completing their secondary education will assist in educating children to become healthy, responsible citizens.

Selected Bibliography

*Abbott, Grace, *The Child and the State,* Vol. I. Chicago: University of Chicago Press, 1938.

Addams, Jane, *Spirit of Youth and the City Streets.* New York: Macmillan, 1900.

Allen, Clara M., *Day Care Centers for School Children; Planning and Administration.* New York: Child Welfare League of America, 1947.

*Baylor, E. M., and E. D. Monachesi, *Rehabilitation of Children: The Theory and Practice of Child Placement.* New York: Harper, 1939.

Beer, Ethel S., *The Day Nursery.* New York: Dutton, 1942.

Bierman, Jessie M., "Maternal and Child Health," *Social Work Year Book* (1954), pp. 323-327.

Bossard, James H. S., *Parent and Child.* Philadelphia: University of Pennsylvania Press, 1953.

Branscombe, Martha, "Basic Policies and Principles of Public Child Care Services," *Social Welfare Forum* (1951), pp. 335-348.

Brooks, Lee M., and Evelyn C. Brooks, *Adventuring in Adoption.* Chapel Hill: University of North Carolina Press, 1939.

Burmeister, Eva, *Forty-five in the Family: The History of a Home for Children.* New York: Columbia University Press, 1949.

Cady, Ernest, and Frances Cady, *How to Adopt a Child.* New York: Whiteside, 1956.

Carson, Ruth, *So You Want to Adopt a Baby.* New York: Public Affairs Committee, 1951.

Cruze, Wendell W., *Adolescent Psychology and Development.* New York: Ronald, 1953.

Fiedler, Miriam F., *Deaf Children in a Hearing World.* New York: Ronald, 1952.

Fredericksen, Hazel, *The Child and His Welfare,* 2nd ed. San Francisco: Freeman, 1957.

Freud, Anna, and Dorothy I. Burlingham, *Infants Without Families; The Case For and Against Residential Nurseries.* New York: International Universities Press, 1944.

Friedlander, Walter, and Earl Dewey Myers, *Child Welfare in Germany Before and After Naziism.* Chicago: University of Chicago Press, 1940.

Fuller, Raymond Garfield, *The Meaning of Child Labor.* Chicago: McClurg, 1922.

*Gordon, Henrietta L., *Casework Services for Children.* Boston: Houghton, 1956.

Hagan, Helen R., "Foster Care for Children," *Social Work Year Book* (1957), pp. 267-274.

Hallowitz, David, and William Singer, *Discipline in the Child Care Institution.* New York: Child Welfare League of America, 1950.

Healy, William, Augusta F. Bronner, E. M. H. Baylor, and J. P. Murphy, *Reconstructing Behavior in Youth.* New York: Knopf, 1929.

Hopkirk, Howard W., *Institutions Serving Children.* New York: Russell Sage Foundation, 1944.

*Hutchinson, Dorothy, *In Quest of Foster Parents.* New York: Columbia University Press, 1940.

Ireland, Tom, *Child Labor: As a Relic of the Dark Ages.* New York: Putnam, 1937.

*Konopka, Gisela, *Therapeutic Group Work with Children.* Minneapolis: University of Minnesota Press, 1949.

Landreth, Catherine, *The Psychology of Early Childhood.* New York: Knopf, 1958.

Lesser, Arthur J., "Services for the Child Who Is Hard of Hearing," *Publication No. 334*. Washington: U.S. Children's Bureau, 1950.

Lockridge, Frances, *Adopting a Child*. New York: Greenberg, 1947.

Lumpkin, Katharine DuPre, and Dorothy Douglas Wolff, *Child Workers in America*. New York: McBride, 1937.

*Lundberg, Emma O., *Unto the Least of These*. New York: Appleton-Century-Crofts, Inc., 1947.

*Maas, Henry S., and Richard E. Engler Jr., *Children in Need of Parents*. New York: Columbia University Press, 1959.

McWilliams, Carey, *Factories in the Field*. Boston: Little, 1939.

Mangold, George B., *Problems of Child Welfare*, 3rd ed. New York: Macmillan, 1936.

Prentice, Carol S., *An Adopted Child Looks at Adoption*. New York: Appleton-Century-Crofts, Inc., 1940.

Raymond, Louise, *Adoption and After*. New York: Harper, 1955.

*Reid, Joseph H., and Helen R. Hagan, *Residential Treatment of Emotionally Disturbed Children*. New York: Child Welfare League of America, 1952.

Sayles, Mary Buell, *Substitute Parents: A Study of Foster Families*. New York: Commonwealth Fund, 1936.

*Schulze, Susanne, *Creative Group Living in Children's Institutions*. New York: Association Press, 1951.

Slingerland, William Henry, *Child Placing in Families*. New York: Russell Sage Foundation, 1919.

Smith, William Carlson, *The Stepchild*. Chicago: University of Chicago Press, 1953.

Taft, Jessie (editor), *Day Nursery Care as a Social Service*. Philadelphia: Pennsylvania School of Social Work, 1943.

Taylor, Florence, "Child Labor Fact Book, 1900-1950," *Publication No. 403*. New York: National Child Labor Committee, 1950.

*Thurston, Henry W., *The Dependent Child*. New York: Columbia University Pres, 1930.

Truxal, Andrew G., and Francis E. Merrill, *Marriage and the Family in American Culture*. Englewood Cliffs, N.J.: Prentice-Hall, Inc., 1953.

Walker, Wilma (editor), *Child Welfare Case Records*. Chicago: University of Chicago Press, 1937.

*Weissman, Irving, *et al.*, "Guardianship: A Way of Fulfilling Public Responsibility for Children," *Publication No. 330*. Washington: U.S. Children's Bureau, 1949.

*Witmer, Helen Leland, and Ruth Kotinsky, *Personality in the Making*. New York: Harper, 1953.

*Young, Leontine, *Out of Wedlock*. New York: McGraw, 1954.

*Zietz, Dorothy, *Child Welfare—Principles and Methods*. New York: Wiley, 1959.

Zimand, Gertrude F., "Child Labor Facts, 1939-1940," *Publication No. 379*. Washington, D.C.: Child Labor Committee, 1939.

12.

Social Work in Medical
and Psychiatric Settings

I. HEALTH AND MEDICAL CARE

A. Medical Institutions and Health Services

One of the most important aspects of social welfare is the maintenance of health. Health is the most precious asset in our society, and its preservation and restoration is one of the main goals of social welfare. Private physicians have been available to the individual patient in the larger communities since Colonial times. For sick people, who could not afford to pay a physician, the Colonies ordered the towns to provide medical treatment. Indigent patients who were too sick to remain in their homes were placed in the infirmary of the poorhouse or of the house of correction. These were the forerunners of the hospitals of the United States, together with the "pest-house" where patients with communicable diseases were confined in order to protect the citizens from contagious infection. Patients were treated by physicians under contract or engaged for the individual case of illness. Sick wards were poorly equipped and gave mainly custodial care.[1]

With the development of medical science and skills, the need

---

[1] Edith Abbott, *Public Assistance* (Chicago: University of Chicago Press, 1940), p. 349; and, Bernhard J. Stern, *Medical Services by Government* (New York: Commonwealth Fund, 1946), pp. 15-16.

grew for specialized hospitals for the various types of diseases. At the same time, the trend developed to replace small hospitals by larger institutions with better diagnostic equipment and with general surgical treatment as well as special medical facilities. In 1956, 6,966 hospitals with 1,607,692 beds were registered with the American Hospital Association. Other beds were available in rest homes, convalescent homes, and old-age institutions.[2] Still, there are not enough hospitals to meet the need of all patients who should be hospitalized. Most of the hospitals with high standards have been set up in large cities in the industrial states, whereas rural areas are still short of hospitals and physicians. In order to assist in the provision of adequate hospital care for rural districts, the Federal government is granting annual funds to the states under the "Hospital Survey and Construction Act" (*Hill-Burton Act*) of 1946. Programs have to be approved by the Surgeon General of the U.S. Public Health Service, and the funds are used for the construction of public or private nonprofit hospitals, but not for their maintenance. The difficulty is that communities and counties which cannot afford to build a hospital will later not be able to pay the maintenance costs either.

Hospitals are classified according to their *type of administration:* (1) governmental hospitals (federal, such as veterans hospitals and army hospitals; state; county; and city hospitals); (2) voluntary nonprofit hospitals (such as hospitals maintained by social agencies and charities, churches, fraternal orders); and (3) private proprietary hospitals which are financially self-maintaining, frequently owned by a group of physicians or a business concern. According to *type of service,* hospitals are classified as (1) *general hospitals* for general medical care and surgery; (2) *specialized hospitals* either for certain groups of patients (such as veterans, military personnel, and members of a religious sect or of a fraternal order) or for special diseases (such as heart, eye, ear, nose and throat, communicable diseases, cancer, maternity hospitals, drug addiction, and children's diseases); (3) *tuberculosis sanatoria;* (4) *mental hospitals,* including hospitals

---

[2] Edward S. Rogers, "Medical Care," *Social Work Year Book* (1960), pp. 365-375; Roger I. Lee and Lewis W. Jones, *The Fundamentals of Good Medical Care* (Chicago: University of Chicago Press, 1933); and, Elizabeth P. Rice, "Social Work in Public Health," *Social Work,* Vol. 4, No. 1 (January 1959).

for the insane and for the mentally deficient; and (5) *hospitals of custodial type* (such as homes for the aged and infirm and convalescent and rest homes). (See Table I.)

It is generally accepted that the most effective form of medical care is provided through group practice by physicians in a hospital or a clinic (as in the Mayo Clinic), and that this form of treatment should become the method of care in the health center of a community, which should also include curative and preventive care. At present, a large proportion of the population cannot pay for long hospitalization or is running into heavy debt for such treatment. It seems necessary to increase Federal appropriations for the construction of hospitals and to extend, also, Federal and state support of their maintenance so that financial limitations will no longer constitute a barrier to medically required hospital care.[3]

TABLE I

HOSPITALS AND HOSPITAL BEDS IN THE UNITED STATES, 1956

Type	Hospitals	Beds	Percentage of Beds
General hospitals	5,506	696,978	43.8
Nervous and mental	569	762,294	46.5
Tuberculosis	342	76,380	5.0
Other institutions .... (including convalescent and rest homes)	549	72,040	4.7
Total	6,966	1,607,692	100

Source: Statistical Abstract of the United States, 1958 (Washington: Government Printing Office, 1959), p. 77, Table 58.

The second type of institutional care is provided by *clinics*. Most clinics are outpatient departments of hospitals which serve as diagnostic and treatment centers for patients who do not need to be hospitalized (ambulatory patients). In rural areas, they also serve sometimes as district health centers. They have become one of the most important means of preventing sickness through early examination, medication, and checkup. Clinics developed from "dispensaries" which usually were connected with hospitals and were mainly devoted

---

[3] Oscar R. Ewing, *The Nation's Health* (Washington: Federal Security Agency, 1948), p. 17. See also Milton Jones, "Medical Care for the Needy and Medically Needy," *Annals,* January 1951.

to the care of the poor. The first was established in New York in 1791.

They provide medical and surgical treatment, medicines, drugs, and appliances free, or at reasonable or nominal cost, to those who cannot afford to pay much, but there are few clinics which provide dental care. The clinics provide care at home only in emergencies.

A number of itinerary clinics, particularly for maternal, well-baby care, and some dental treatment of children have been developed with the aid of Federal grants under the maternal and child health services, which we discussed in Chapter 11.

Public medical services have been extended in recent times to patients who are not indigent in the general sense of the word and who are not supported by public assistance, but who still cannot afford to pay for necessary expensive medical care. This group is called the "medically needy." Some county and city governments assume responsibility for the medical care of these otherwise self-supporting citizens. Several state laws recognize the social need for adequate medical care for this group.

The expenses for medical treatment in time of severe illness are usually so high that numerous *voluntary health insurance plans* have been organized in order to provide either prepaid medical treatment, or hospital care, or cash allowances for the loss of income in case of illness. Thus, at least a part of medical cost and loss of income is defrayed. Voluntary health plans are administered either by commercial insurance companies or by private nonprofit associations. They vary widely in their policies of admission of members and in type and quality of their services. Few of them furnish complete medical and dental care, medicines and hospitalization. The most noted of the voluntary hospital plans is the Blue Cross Plan. Among the medical prepayment programs, the Blue Shield Plan represents nonprofit health services under the auspices of state or local medical societies which permit insured patients to select a physician among a panel of doctors. Most of the plans, however, limit the free medical service under contract to patients with a modest annual maximum income, graduated according to the size of family. Usually, the plan excludes older applicants and requires substantial additional payments for persons of medium income that exceeds a stipulated amount.

The number of so-called "comprehensive or group practice prepayment plans" is still small. They usually offer medical care in a hospital and clinic or require "Blue Cross" coverage for hospitalization. An example of such a comprehensive plan is the "Health Insurance Plan of Greater New York" which, however, does not include dental care, hospital maintenance, and medicines. Comprehensive group care plans are valuable for health education and enable the patients to make early contact with the physician and to receive preventive care.[4]

Another recent type of voluntary health insurance, is the "catastrophic illness" or "major medical expense" insurance. It requires the patient to assume the first $300 to $500 of medical and hospital payments, but covers the rest of the costs up to a fixed limit, usually between $5,000 and $10,000, but with the provision that the patient has to pay 20 to 25 per cent of these expenses.

It is estimated that more than 110 million people have some type of hospital insurance in the United States, and the proportion of the expenses for hospitalization assumed by voluntary health insurance plans and by public assistance payments from medical care funds is increasing. Industrial medical care plans, which we shall discuss in Chapter 15, play an important role in the framework of health insurance protection.

Neither the increase in public medical services nor the present voluntary health plans have solved the problem of medical care for patients not eligible for free public medical treatment. Millions of self-supporting sick persons find themselves in the serious dilemma of having to pay the excessive cost of medical treatment, operations, medicines, drugs, and hospitalization. Since the occurrence of illness and its cost are unpredictable for the individual family, it is usually impossible to budget these expenses. For this reason, it seems necessary that some method be found to distribute the risks of sickness and medical costs among the total population. This can be done by establishing a general system of health insurance, integrating existing effective voluntary prepaid group health plans, or by extending

---

[4] For more detailed information the reader is referred to Franz Goldmann, *Voluntary Medical Care Insurance in the U.S.* (New York: Columbia University Press, 1948); E. Richard Weinerman, "An Appraisal of Medical Care in Group Health Centers," *American Journal of Public Health* (March 1956); and, Herman M. Somers and Anne R. Somers, "Private Health Insurance," *California Law Review* (August and October 1958).

substantially supplementary tax-supported medical services for patients for whom special public responsibility is acknowledged (such as military personnel and veterans) and for those who are not protected by other facilities.[5] The idea of a compulsory system of health insurance has been opposed in varying degrees by commercial insurance companies, the patent medicine and drug industries, the American Medical Association, and the Christian Science movement. It is felt that some program of public health insurance or general public health service will be indispensable, in the long run, in order to secure adequate health protection for the part of the population which is, for reason of cost, now excluded from the full benefits of modern medical science.

An important role in the progress of health services is played by numerous voluntary health agencies. Among them are the National Tuberculosis Association, the National Foundation (for Infantile Paralysis), the American Heart Association, the American Foundation for the Blind, the American Cancer Research Association, the American Hearing Society, the American Rheumatism Association, the United Cerebral Palsy Association, and others with state and local chapters. They emphasize in their work prevention, control, and treatment of such specific diseases as tuberculosis, cancer, and diabetes. Some devote their main efforts to research and health education, others to the development of higher standards of care and the provision of consultant or demonstration services.

Voluntary agencies derive their funds from membership fees, sales of seals, or from special fund raising campaigns. Research often is financed by foundations, private endowments, and public grants. Several voluntary health agencies have encouraged studies by making grants and fellowships to universities and individual scientists. They have done pioneer work in new fields of health education, disease prevention, and treatment and have stimulated the development of public health services. The National Health Council has been operat-

---

[5] For a fuller analysis of this question see Franz Goldmann, *Public Medical Care: Principles and Problems* (New York: Columbia University Press, 1945); Oscar Ewing, *op cit.*, especially pp. 63-114; C.-E.A. Winslow, *Health Care for the Americans* (New York: Public Affairs Pamphlet No. 104, 1945); and, Michael M. Davis and Dewey Anderson, *Medical Care for the Individual and the Issue of Compulsory Health Insurance* (Washington: Government Printing Office, 1948).

ing as a coordinating body for voluntary health organizations since 1921.

B. Public Health Services

Public health services are devoted to the protection and improvement of the health of the entire population. Their main object is prevention of diseases and elimination of environmental health hazards. Public health includes sanitation services, control of epidemics, sanitary disposal, and the protection of water supply and food. The functions of the Federal government, in this field, are mainly the responsibility of the U.S. Public Health Service, under the Department of Health, Education and Welfare, the Veterans Administration, and the U.S. Children's Bureau, and were explained above.[6] The main responsibility in the area of public health lies with the city and county health departments. More recently, district health departments, combining several counties, or city and county health units, have come to be considered the most effective type of administration. A full-time medical officer, a sanitary engineer, some part-time medical specialists, ten public health nurses, a medical social worker, and clerical personnel are recommended as the minimum staff of a public health department. The program includes the compilation of vital statistics, maternal and child health services, laboratory services, and public health education.

In the states, the responsibility for public health usually is embodied in the state departments of public health. The functions of the state health authority are the observation of health needs, coordination and supervision of local health services, preparation and enforcement of legislation and regulations, the establishment of an adequate collection of statistics, and education of the public on health protection.[7]

---

[6] See Chapters 3, 8, and 11—also 15.

[7] For more details, see Haven Emerson and Martha Luginbuhl, *Local Health Units for the Nation* (New York: Commonwealth Fund, 1945); Wilson G. Smillie, *Public Health Administration in the United States* (New York: Macmillan, 1947); Leonard A. Scheele, "Public Health," *Social Work Year Book* (1957), pp. 451-463; and, Berwyn F. Mattison, "Public Health," *ibid.* (1960), pp. 471-481.

C. Cost of Medical Care

The total annual expenditure for medical care of the entire population in the United States during recent years is estimated at $17 billion. Federal, state, and local government paid about 28 per cent of this amount. Families spend a varying part of their income on health expenditures. The average figure is 4 to 5 per cent of all consumption expenditures of the family. But the proportion of medical expenses varies with the level of income. Health surveys show that in low income groups, earning less than $500 a year, the medical expenses averaged 17 per cent, but those in higher income groups, with income over $5,000, had an average medical expense of 3.4 per cent. In the low income group 14.2 per cent of families account for only 4.7 per cent of medical outlays. In the high income group, 0.9 per cent of the families spent 7.1 per cent of funds for medical care. The high income group, therefore, spent 25 times as much for health per family than did the lowest income group.[8]

Various surveys of the distribution of the cost of medical care have not resulted in the same findings. A study by the Health Information Foundation found that physicians' services required 37 per cent of the total expenditures, dentists 16 per cent, hospitals 20 per cent, medicines and drugs 15 per cent, and auxiliary services 13 per cent. Another survey by F. G. Dickinson and J. Raymond under the auspices of the Bureau of Medical Economic Research of the American Medical Association indicated that 28 per cent of the expenses was paid to doctors, 10 per cent to dentists, 26 per cent for hospitalization, 16 per cent for drugs and medicines, and 20 per cent for auxiliary services.[9]

Much of the rise in the cost of medical care seems to have been caused by the increasingly more common practice of treating patients in hospitals. This has come about because many of the voluntary health insurance policies pay only in case of hospitalization, which encourages patients and doctors to choose hospital care rather than

---

[8] Seymour E. Harris, "Medical Care Expenditures in Relation to Family Income and National Income," *Building America's Health,* President's Commission on the Health Needs of the Nation, Vol. 4 (1952), pp. 8 and 12.

[9] F. G. Dickinson and J. Raymond, "The Economic Position of Medical Care, 1929-1953," *Bulletin 99* (Chicago: Bureau of Medical Economic Research, 1955).

ambulatory treatment. It is questionable if this practice is in the best interest of the patients.

The Health Information Foundation research confirmed the assumption that the burden of medical expenses is very unevenly distributed. Only 7 per cent of all families incurred medical expenses of more than $495 a year, but 2 per cent paid more than one-half of their entire income and about 1 per cent had medical bills which were higher than their total earnings during the year.

The low-income groups paid a median of $54 from an income less than $2,000, whereas the group with income over $7,500 paid a median of $238 for medical care. These findings confirm the long-standing knowledge that families with the lowest income are also spending the smallest percentage of their earnings for medical care, are barely receiving even preventive services, and are suffering more frequent and longer lasting disabling illness than the groups which are in better economic conditions.[10]

D. Medical Social Work

Medical social work, as a specialized method of social work, is of recent origin. It involves the practice of social casework, and sometimes, group work in a hospital, a clinic, or another medical setting in order to make it possible for the patient to use the available health services most effectively. Medical social work is characterized by emphasis on help in the social and emotional problems which affect the patient in his illness and his cure.

The development of medical social work is based on four main sources. The first was the recognition in England, in the 1880's, that discharged patients of mental hospitals needed "after-care" in their homes in order to avoid recurrence of their illness. "Visitors" went to the patient's home and advised family and friends about the necessary care of the patient after his discharge. A second source of medical social work were the "lady almoners" in English hospitals; they organized, upon the initiative of Sir Charles S. Loch in

---

[10] Harry Becker (editor), *Financing Hospital Care in the United States* (New York: McGraw, 1955), pp. 11-62; Edward S. Rogers, *op. cit.,* pp. 347-349; Oscar N. Serbein, *Paying for Medical Care in the United States* (New York: Columbia University Press, 1953), pp. 246-254; and, Odin W. Anderson, *National Family Survey of Medical Costs and Voluntary Health Insurance* (New York: Health Information Foundation, 1956).

London, in the 1890's, and served as volunteer receptionists, made social investigations, and decided whether the applicant should be admitted as a free patient to the hospital, and what charity organization might be asked to assume the patient's support.[11] Visiting nurses were the third precursors of medical social workers. In 1893, Lillian Wald and Mary Brewster of the Henry Street Settlement House in New York began to visit the homes of sick people in the neighborhood who were too poor to pay for medical and nursing care. They found many social and personal problems which were caused by the illness of the patients. Some hospitals in New York learned from the experiences of the Henry Street Settlement House that visits in the home might greatly improve the effect of medical treatment; they sent nurses from the hospital staff for "after-care" and supervision of discharged patients. The fourth source of medical social work was medical students trained in social agencies. Dr. Charles P. Emerson of Johns Hopkins University at Baltimore, in 1902, wanted to include the study of social and emotional problems into medical education and requested that his students serve as volunteers with charity agencies in order to gain an understanding of the influence of social, economic, and living conditions on the illness of patients.

On the basis of these experiences, medical social work was established in 1905, at four different places almost at the same time. Social workers became members of the staff at Massachusetts General Hospital in Boston, at Bellevue Hospital in New York, at Johns Hopkins Hospital in Baltimore, and at the Berkeley Infirmary in Boston. The medical specialist is no longer able to be acquainted with the living conditions, income, environment, habits, and personality of the patient as was the old family doctor. Therefore, the medical social worker has had to make the personal contact with patient and family, to investigate social and personal conditions of the patient, and to supply the factual background to the physician in order to help him in diagnosis and treatment. Dr. Richard C. Cabot of Massachusetts General Hospital was the first to recognize the need of a social worker to help the patient after his return from the hospital observe

---

11 Ida M. Cannon, *Social Work in Hospitals: A Contribution to Progressive Medicine* (New York: Russell Sage Foundation, 1930), pp. 5-15; *On the Social Frontier of Medicine* (Cambridge: Harvard University Press, 1952), pp. 46-94; and, Eleanor E. Cockrill, "Medical Social Work," *Social Work Year Book* (1960), pp. 375-382.

the orders of the physician, to instruct the family in diets and administer medical prescriptions. The social worker also interprets the nature of the illness to the family and advises it about specific precautions to take in order to avoid recurrence of the disease.[12]

Medical social work often includes making suggestions about the possibility of convalescent care, the influence of emotional strain upon the patient, the need of medical examination of other family members, and the provision of financial aid through social agencies. Questions concerning the care of children during the mother's illness, arrangements for rest of the patient during convalescence, and finding a suitable job which would not jeopardize the results of medical treatment are among those problems which occupy medical social workers. An increasing emphasis is placed upon the social relationships of the patient, the attitude of spouse and children, and the patient's own reactions and feeling toward his illness.[13] The medical social worker operates in a team with the physician, the nurse, the physical and occupational therapist, and the laboratory technician. Her particular contribution in this teamwork is to enable the patient to help himself to become well again. Although physician and nurse in hospital and clinic represent professional authority, which easily makes the patient dependent upon their orders, the medical social worker strengthens the patient's self-confidence. She respects his natural feelings of worry about his illness and about social, economic, and personal implications for himself and his family and so tries to lessen his concern.

The medical social worker acquires an intimate knowledge of the personal and social situation of the patient, and she assists him in

---

[12] The use of medical social work goes back to an experience of Dr. Cabot with a small boy cured of acute gastric conditions after careful medical treatment. A few days after his release, he was returned by his mother in the old, bad condition. When this happened again and once more, it became evident that observation in the family and instruction of the mother was needed to preserve the health of the child.

[13] Harriett Bartlett, *Medical Social Work: A Study of Current Aims and Methods* (Chicago: American Association of Medical Social Workers, 1934), pp. 98-103; and, Frances Upham, *A Dynamic Approach to Illness* (New York: Family Service Association of America, 1949), pp. 8, 109. Examples for effective social work in a medical setting may be found in Walter Friedlander (editor), *Concepts and Methods of Social Work* (Englewood Cliffs, N. J.: Prentice-Hall, Inc., 1958), pp. 101-114, 154-183.

using the resources in the community which will help him most effectively to regain his health.

Medical social work does not attempt to solve all the patient's problems, but deals with those factors which are directly related to the cause and nature of the patient's illness and its treatment and are called the "social component of illness." Medical social work has shifted its emphasis from attention to the disease to the personality of the patient—his anxieties, attitudes, and feelings. The physician remains the highest authority in the team at the hospital and the clinic; the medical social worker as well as the nurse, laboratory technician, psychologist, and physiotherapist must be able to cooperate wholeheartedly under the doctor's direction in the team relationship. The medical social worker interprets to the patient and his family requests and commendations of the physician. She helps the patient understand his disease and to make the best use of the medical treatment and the doctor's prescriptions. She thus extends the medical service of the hospital into the patient's home and into the community. Her work may be illustrated by the following example:

The Mills Case [14]

After treatment for tuberculosis in the hospital, Mrs. Mills was told that she should go to a sanatorium. She refused to go, however, so that the physician had to plan to continue medical treatment in her home. The doctor could not understand why Mrs. Mills, an intelligent woman, insisted on remaining at home, since she had carefully obeyed all orders in the hospital. The medical social worker after several home visits found that the husband of the patient who had been an excellent father to the two small children and an exemplary husband to the patient until this time had suddenly begun to come home intoxicated, at late hours, and without his salary. The social worker felt that such a change could not happen without some reason, and in a conversation with Mr. Mills learned from him that recently he had felt severe pains in his wrists at work which he had tried to ease by drinking. She persuaded Mr. Mills to go to the hospital for an examination which revealed that the pains were caused by an industrial poisoning which would become worse if he stayed in his job in the factory. The doctor recommended an out-of-door work. The Mills were discouraged because they had started to save money for building a home in the country, and Mr. Mills was sure that he could

---

[14] American Association of Social Workers, *Vocational Aspects of Medical Social Work* (New York: 1927), p. 18.

not continue to save if he left his factory job. With the advice of the medical social worker it was possible, however, to obtain a mortgage on three acres of land which permitted Mr. Mills to work in his trade in out-of-door work, and at the same time to build a small house and to grow a garden. After a period of one year, the city decided to expand the water system to the land of the Mills so that they were able to sell several lots, and with this income to complete the house and to accept work which was not harmful to Mr. Mills' health and which permitted Mrs. Mills to recover fully from her tuberculosis. This successful solution was due mainly to the intelligent cooperation and initiative of the patients, but was also reached through the understanding of the social worker.

The medical settings in which social work is practiced are private and public hospitals and clinics; voluntary health agencies; local, state, and Federal health services; other public and private social welfare agencies; schools of social work, schools of nursing and medical schools. In most instances, medical social work is casework with the individual patient, but it also encompasses administrative, supervisory, and consultant activities and community organization, teaching, group therapy, and research. Particularly essential is the field of vocational rehabilitation in which the medical social worker plays a vital role in helping and encouraging the patient in his important adjustment for his future life and for his family responsibilities.

The medical social worker in a public welfare department is responsible for the authorization of requests for medical care of an applicant, and for the full utilization of other medical facilities in the community. She will help in early hospital discharges whenever possible and in providing aftercare. Medical information on patients is interpreted by the medical social worker to the patient and to the staff of the department, and she may arrange such services as an ambulance, laboratory and X-ray tests, referral to clinic, hospital, or visiting nurse service. The medical social worker helps the patient who must make difficult decisions, such as whether or not to undergo a major operation, and informs the family about the patient.

Medical social work is concerned with social and economic conditions of the patient and his family, and with the interrelation of the physical and the emotional factors in illness. For some time, medical science has recognized that there is an essential mutual influence between psyche and body, between the emotions of the patient and his organic well-being, and between organic disturbances, external factors and the patient's emotions and mental behavior. This is called the "psychosomatic approach." It emphasizes the consequence of the emotions of the patient and of his determination to become well again upon his cure. The many new scientific inventions in pathology, surgery, bacteriology, and biochemistry almost make the doctor forget the patient is a human being. For the final success of medical treatment, medical social workers are aware of the decisive role which is played by the patient's own attitude toward his illness and his desire to regain his health. Medical social workers attempt, therefore, to help the patient understand the nature of his disease, for instance tuberculosis or rheumatism, and the possibilities of its treatment, and to create in him a strong desire to recover. The patient, under such conditions, will adjust his life in a way which makes his cure more probable and complete. Modern medical social work accepts the concept of the functions of the human organism as a whole, not merely as a sum of various parts. Psychiatry, with its emphasis on the patient as a unique personality, and biology and psychology, with their findings that functions of the human body and mind are not localized, have contributed to this concept.[15]

Among recent trends in medical social work is the growing recognition by the medical profession and universities that social and psychological factors greatly influence diagnosis, treatment, and prevention of disease. This interrelationship is now taught in schools of medicine and of public health.[16] Another trend is the continuous expansion of health programs outside of hospitals and clinics. In public school systems, vocational rehabilitation services, in state, county, and municipal health departments, in services for crippled children and for other groups of handicapped patients, medical

---

[15] H. Flanders Dunbar, *Mind and Body: Psychosomatic Medicine* (New York: Random House, Inc., 1947), pp. 65-66, presents characteristic examples for the influence of the patient's will for his recovery; see also Franz Alexander, "Psychosomatic Aspects of Medicine," *Psychosomatic Medicine,* Vol. 1, No. 1 (January 1939), pp. 7-18; *Psychosomatic Medicine* (New York: Norton, 1950); Roy R. Grinker, *Psychosomatic Research* (New York: Norton, 1953); and, Juergen Ruesch, "The Infantile Personality—the Core Problem of Psychosomatic Medicine," *Psychosomatic Medicine,* Vol. 10 (February 1948), p. 134 ff.

[16] Elizabeth P. Rice, "Medical Social Work," *Social Work Year Book* (1957), pp. 356-363; Eleanor E. Cockorill, *ibid.* (1960), pp. 378-382; and, Dora Goldstine, *Readings in the Theory and Practice of Medical Social Work* (Chicago: University of Chicago Press, 1954).

workers find an increasing challenge to contribute their skill of integration in meeting social, emotional, and health needs.

Finally, medical social work is recognized in such community health planning bodies as municipal, county, or regional welfare councils and local health boards, and in coordinated programs of medical, health, and welfare projects. This also applies to the expanding area of health education in connection with schools and adult civic groups and to the use of medical social workers as teachers in medical schools and schools of public health.

II. MENTAL HYGIENE AND PSYCHIATRIC SOCIAL WORK

A. Mental Hygiene Services

The terms "mental health" and "mental hygiene" are sometimes used interchangeably, and there are many definitions of both terms. We want to present mental health as the desirable goal, and mental hygiene as one of the important means to preserve or to achieve the objective of mental health.

Mental hygiene is: (1) a public health movement which has the aim of preventing mental disorders through mental health education and freeing patients from external and internal conflict, anxiety, and emotional strain; (2) a science based upon psychiatry and psychology, applied to help people overcome inner conflicts and maintain or regain mental health, through psychiatric, psychological, and social treatment (frequently provided in mental hygiene or child guidance clinics); (3) a medical and psychiatric treatment in mental hospitals to aid severely disturbed mental patients; (4) a special orientation in education based upon recent developments in psychiatry and the social sciences; and (5) a philosophy of life and a concept of ethics that pursues the goal of healthy living in a democratic society.[17] Mental hygiene societies are groups of interested citizens, frequently including psychiatrists, public health officers, physicians, educators, psychologists, and social workers, that seek

---

[17] Joseph S. Kasanin, "Mental Hygiene," *Social Work Year Book* (1945), pp. 267-268. James V. Lowry uses the definition: "the aggregate of measures designed to preserve mental health" ("Mental Hygiene," *Social Work Year Book* (1951), p. 320); and, Kenneth E. Appel, "Mental Health and Mental Illness," *Social Work Year Book* (1957), pp. 363-370.

to secure adequate psychiatric services in the community and attempt to create the conditions for a healthy emotional climate.

Only recently, man has acquired more knowledge of the origin, treatment, and prevention of mental disease. In ancient times, people of disturbed mind were considered to be possessed by demons who were punishing them for their sins because they had offended the gods. The demented were tortured in order to drive out the evil spirits and were drowned, hanged, or burned at the stake for having allegedly practiced sorcery or witchcraft. In the eighteenth century the idea of treating the mentally deranged humanely and of giving them medical treatment was first conceived of in France by Philip Pinel, in England by William Tuke, and in Italy by Vincento Chiarugi. In the United States, Benjamin Franklin, the Quakers in Pennsylvania, and, particularly, Dr. Benjamin Rush became the pioneers of the movement to grant medical care and humane treatment to the mentally ill.[18] Toward the end of the nineteenth century, scientific discoveries in medicine, psychiatry, biology, physiology, and psychology revealed the interdependence of mind and body and created a new outlook in the approach to mental disorders. Emil Kraepelin and Wilhelm Griesinger classified mental diseases upon their symptoms. Sigmund Freud and his followers studied hysteria and neuroses, found the key to the knowledge of the unconscious and opened up new possibilities of cure through psychoanalysis.

Psychoanalysis caused a revolutionary change in the methods of psychiatry and psychotherapy all over the world. The psychiatric schools of Jung, Adler, and Otto Rank also contributed new methods for the treatment of mental disorders. In the United States, Dr. Adolf Meyer developed the psychobiological theory in psychiatry. The scientific contributions of the pioneers in social psychiatry emphasized that mental disorders and emotional disturbances frequently are not, or not exclusively, caused by biological and organic conditions, but also by social factors in family and environment. Therefore, counseling and therapeutic treatment of the patient are necessary. Diagnosis of mental instability, alone, is not sufficient. Often, social changes in the environment also are indispensable in order to prevent new illness and to help in the cure of the mental patient.

---

[18] Albert Deutsch, *The Mentally Ill in America* (New York: Columbia University Press, 1946), p. 16 ff.; see also Arnold M. Rose, *Mental Health and Mental Disorder* (New York: Norton, 1955).

Until the beginning of this century, most hospitals for mental diseases offered scarcely more than detention and custodial care. Little insight into the personality of the patient was attempted, and limited facilities for treatment were provided. As a patient in several mental hospitals, Clifford Beers had suffered under the usual brutal treatment and devoted his life after his release to the reform of mental institutions. He became the founder of the mental hygiene movement. In 1908, he published his diary, *A Mind That Found Itself,* with an introduction by the famous philosopher and psychologist, William James, and the noted psychiatrist, Adolf Meyer. Widespread public interest led to the foundation of a State Mental Hygiene Society in Connecticut in 1908, and, in the following year, to the establishment of the National Committee for Mental Hygiene, on which Clifford Beers served as its executive.[19]

The mental hygiene movement's first concern was with the improvement of the inhuman methods of treatment in mental hospitals and institutions. There is, at present, a total of more than 1,000 public and private mental hospitals in the United States, in which more than 1,000,000 patients are treated annually. About 70 per cent of these patients are in need of longer residential care. Around most mental hospitals there are well-kept grounds, and an air of quiet peace, but inside frequently we find hundreds of silent, staring human beings who either polish floors or do nothing but sit in rocking chairs and wait endlessly. Sometimes weird screams are heard from the "violent wards." State hospitals are often overcrowded, and new building programs have been delayed. Some states have recently appropriated funds for the expansion and improvement of mental institutions. It is frequently difficult to obtain a qualified staff—psychiatrists, attendants, nurses, psychologists, and psychiatric social workers—because of the isolation of most mental hospitals, lack of cultural facilities, and low salaries.

The incidence of mental diseases is indicated by Table III. As in the case of illness in general, mental disorders have been found more frequent and more severe in the lower income groups according to the surveys conducted during recent years. But, obviously, low

---

[19] The term "mental hygiene" had been the title of a book of Dr. William Sweetser in 1843, but it had been forgotten until the mental hygiene societies brought it again to public attention. Since 1950, the National Association for Mental Health has united various organizations in this field.

TABLE II

DATA FOR PATIENTS IN MENTAL HOSPITALS IN THE UNITED STATES, 1951

	Number	Percentage of Estimated Civilian Population
Average daily patient population	515,108	0.34
First admissions	108,778	0.072
All admissions	146,506	0.097
Discharges	90,260	15% of patients
Deaths in hospital	42,027	6.4% of patients
Patients in mental hospitals at the end of 1951	610,458	
Patients at the end of 1950	598,000	
Maintenance cost per patient	$825.62 per year	$2.26 per day

Source: "Patients in Public Hospitals for the Prolonged Care of the Mentally Ill, 1951" in *Mental Health Statistics, Current Reports* (U.S. Department of Health, Education and Welfare, Public Health Service, National Institute of Mental Health, April 1953).

An interesting analysis of the social structure and functions of mental hospitals is presented in S. Kirson Weinberg, *Society and Personality Disorders* (Englewood Cliffs, N.J.: Prentice-Hall, Inc., 1952), pp. 375-450.

TABLE III

PATIENTS IN MENTAL HOSPITALS IN SELECTED YEARS

Year	In Hospitals for Mental Diseases	Rate per 100,000 Population	In Hospitals for Mental Defectives	Rate per 100,000 Population
1940	461,358	351.0	102,292	77.8
1944	501,751	363.4	118,153	85.6
1949	554,372	375.2	129,402	87.6
1953	609,950	390.9	142,688	91.4
1954	622,849	391.5	147,116	92.5
1955	631,503	389.1	151,087	93.1

Source: *Statistical Abstract of the United States 1952*, p. 83, Table No. 89; and *ibid., 1958*, p. 79, Table No. 90.

income patients are less able to afford rest, vacations, psychiatric consultation, and therapy, so that free or low cost clinics are particularly needed. Among the patients placed, on an average day in American hospitals, more than one-half are treated for mental disorders.[20]

---

[20] Franz Goldmann, "Medical Care," *Social Work Year Book* (1951), pp. 303-305; and, August B. Hollingshead and Fredrick C. Redlich, *Social Class and Mental Illness: A Community Study* (New York: Wiley, 1958).

Besides patients in need of hospital care, there are an estimated total of 8,000,000 persons in our country suffering from some kind of mental disorder, and one in every twenty citizens will require psychiatric care at some time during his life. Because the incidence of mental disease is heavier in old age than in younger age groups, the increasing proportion of our older population carries with it the probability of a further growth of mental illness unless we are able to provide efficient services of prevention, early diagnosis, and treatment. The number of practicing psychiatrists, about 5,000, are not sufficient to diagnose and treat all mental patients, particularly in rural regions and in the southern states, and the number of psychiatric nurses, psychiatric social workers, and clinical psychologists is also insufficient. Over 300,000 more hospital beds for mental patients and improvement in staffs, equipment, and facilities of hospitals as well as clinics are required.[21]

The second concern of the mental hygiene movement is the prevention of mental disorders. To this purpose it pursues the establishment of mental hygiene clinics for diagnosis and therapy.

In 1957, there were thirty-eight state and 500 local mental hygiene societies which conducted programs of education and information about emotional conflicts and disturbances, promoted social legislation for the improvement of prevention and care of mental illness, and cooperated with public and private organizations in the setup of mental hygiene and child guidance clinics.

The main obstacle to the development of effective mental hygiene work was, and still is, presented by the social stigma attached to mental illness, caused by the lack of understanding of the nature of mental disturbances. It discourages mentally ill patients and their families from seeking early professional aid and is a retarding factor in public awareness of the large extent and urgency of the mental health problem. Other obstacles are the lack of financial resources for preventive mental hygiene clinics and the scarcity of well-trained personnel.

---

[21] Paul V. Lemkau, *Mental Hygiene in Public Health* (New York: McGraw, 1955); and, Ruth I. Knee and Warren C. Lamson, "Mental Health and Mental Illness," *Social Work Year Book* (1960), pp. 383-395.

B. Child Guidance Clinics

Psychiatric experience has proved that mental illness of many adult patients has its beginning in childhood, and so it becomes evident that helping children with their emotional problems would minimize serious mental diseases in their later years. The need for psychotherapy of children was particularly felt by juvenile courts. Already in the first years of this century, the juvenile court in Chicago found that it needed to know the causes of the child's troubles in order to decide about his treatment. A gift of Mrs. W. F. Dummer provided funds for the first child guidance clinic in Chicago, in 1909, known as the Juvenile Psychopathic Institute, under Dr. William Healy. Members of this clinic studied the wards of the juvenile court and suggested methods for their mental and social adjustment. The Institute in Chicago was renamed the "Institute for Juvenile Research" in 1917, when it was taken over by the state of Illinois. Other pioneer clinics were set up in Boston, Baltimore, Cleveland, and in Whittier, California.

An important expansion of child guidance therapy was made possible through the demonstration program developed by a grant of the Commonwealth Fund of 1921.[22] The first demonstration child guidance clinic was set up in St. Louis. Since that time, about 700 psychiatric clinics have been opened in our country that provide child guidance services; about 400 operate full time. The first clinic stressed necessary cooperation among psychiatrists, psychologists and social workers. This teamwork became a generally accepted basic principle in these clinics. Also, the experience in the child guidance clinics brought out the importance of social work cooperation in therapy. It proved to be necessary for children's agencies, recreational programs, and school social work to work closely together with the clinics and the juvenile courts in order to prevent further juvenile delinquency. The teaching of mental hygiene principles to physicians, teachers, nurses, and social workers of juvenile courts and welfare agencies was emphasized.

Child guidance clinics have now become part of community serv-

---

[22] Helen L. Witmer, *Psychiatric Clinics for Children* (New York: Commonwealth Fund, 1940), p. 47; and, George E. Gardner, "American Child Psychiatric Clinics," *The Annals*, Vol. 286 (March 1953), pp. 126-135. See also, Maxwell Jones, *The Therapeutic Community* (New York: Basic Books, 1953).

ice in most larger cities. Difficulties which are brought to their attention cover a wide range from behavior problems and habit disturbances to personality maladjustments. Behavior problems include, for example, lying, running away, truancy, stealing, fire-setting, sex aggression, destruction of property, and cruelty to other children or animals. Personality difficulties are often expressed by nightmares, anxiety, withdrawal, shyness, day dreams, and apathy. Under habit disturbances, there are enuresis, excessive masturbation, nail biting, eating difficulties and thumb sucking. Children are referred to the clinic usually by their own parents, or by doctors, social agencies, schools, churches, parent-teacher associations, juvenile courts, or the public.

The procedure of child guidance work starts with an application of both parents or just of the mother. In the "intake interview" they describe the child's difficulties to the social worker and what they expect from the treatment of the child. The social worker explains what services the clinic offers and the arrangements and financial obligations required. If the child is accepted, a medical and psychiatric examination of the child follows, and a clinical psychologist gives the indicated tests for proper diagnosis.

Usually, mother and child come for treatment to the clinic once weekly for one hour. The young child engages in play therapy with the psychiatrist and thus reveals his feelings about his parents, siblings, teachers, and playmates. The psychiatrist gains a comprehension of the child's disturbance and personality. In the interviews with the mother, the social worker attempts to make her understand the causes of the child's difficulties and behavior, her own attitude toward the child, and their relationship. Behavior change in mother and child leads to improvement of the original difficulties. Sometimes, the mother becomes aware of her own emotional disturbance and asks for treatment for herself. There is also growing recognition of the importance of the father's role in the behavior of a difficult child. Several child guidance clinics now include fathers in the treatment process.

In the development of child guidance clinics, emphasis was first laid upon the advice to the parents about the child's education, and later upon the direct treatment of the child. Finally, the concept has been accepted that the child's problems are usually a part of an emotional disturbance in the whole family pattern, and, for this reason, a coordinated treatment of child and parent now is considered the most effective method.[23]

Whenever social workers and clinical psychologists treat the child or his parents, they are working in consultation with a psychiatrist. Psychiatrist, social worker, and psychologist have conferences to co-ordinate their work. Representatives of other social agencies are invited for joint case conferences if they have referred the child to the clinic.

Unquestionably, child guidance clinics are of great value for the early treatment of child behavior problems and for the preven-tion of some mental illness in adulthood. But only the larger cities in the United States have full-time clinical services of this type. In small cities, and in many rural areas, such clinics are either lacking or are only occasionally available as "itinerant clinics." As a result, several states are still without adequate psychiatric preventive fa-cilities. Other community services, such as prenatal and child guid-ance clinics have also incorporated into their work preventive mental hygiene concepts.[24]

B. National Mental Health Act

During World War I, the large number of war neuroses revealed the need for intensive work in the cure of nervous and mental dis-orders. In field stations and neuropsychiatric hospitals, as a result, social workers assisted the medical officers in obtaining information about personal, family, and community background of the patients, to be used in making decisions about dismissal and after-care.

---

[23] Genevieve B. Short, "Psychiatric Social Work in the Child Guidance Clinic," in *Education for Psychiatric Social Work* (New York: American As-sociation of Psychiatric Social Workers, 1950), pp. 12-13; Solomon E. Asch, *Social Psychology* (Englewood Cliffs, N. J.: Prentice-Hall, Inc., 1952), pp. 117 ff., 135 ff.; and, S. Kirson Weinberg, *Social and Personality Disorders* (Englewood Cliffs, N. J.: Prentice-Hall, Inc., 1952), pp. 491-495.

[24] Robert H. Felix, "State Planning for Participation in the National Mental Health Act," *Public Health Reports,* Vol. LXII (August 15, 1947), p. 1,188. The vital importance of team work in mental hygiene and child guidance work is emphasized in *Mental Health and World Citizenship,* a statement prepared for the International Congress on Mental Health in London, 1948. It shows the value of cooperation among psychiatrist, physician, social worker, nurse, clinical psychologist, economist, minister, lawyer, and political scientist in releasing human potentialities for the common good.

World War II greatly aroused public concern over the increase of mental illness. The demand for physicians and psychiatrists was not only heavy in the armed forces, but also in the civilian population where the mental stress of war caused neuroses and exhaustion. The public became alarmed when it was informed that, among 15,000,000 men examined during World War II, 856,200 were rejected for neuropsychiatric disorders. This was by far the largest cause for rejection. This type of disorder was also responsible for the majority of all medical discharges from the armed forces.

It is just as difficult to obtain psychiatric examination, consultation, and treatment for adult patients as for children. Mental hygiene clinics for adults are equally scarce in smaller cities and rural areas. Of all hospital beds which are available in the United States, one-half are used for mental patients. In veterans hospitals, an even larger number —60 per cent—are used for patients suffering from neuropsychiatric diseases. These appalling figures have caused considerable concern among legislators, psychiatrists, social workers, and psychologists.[25] They encouraged the enactment of the *National Mental Health Act of 1946*. Its preamble says:

The purpose of this Act is the improvement of the mental health of the people of the United States through the conducting of researches, investigations, experiments and demonstrations relating to the cause, diagnosis and treatment of psychiatric disorders; assisting and fostering such research activities by public and private agencies, and promoting the coordination of all such results; training personnel in matters relating to mental health; and developing and assisting states in the use of the most effective methods of prevention, diagnosis and treatment of psychiatric disorders.

The Act is administered by the National Institute of Mental Health of the U.S. Public Health Service in the Department of Health, Education and Welfare. Its governing body is the National Mental Health Council. The Surgeon General is chairman. He appoints six members (selected from outstanding authorities in the field of mental health) for three-year terms.

---

[25] Another stirring fact is that since 1880 mental disorders have multiplied twelve times over in our country. (S. Kirson Weinberg, *op. cit.*, pp. 138-159, 160-180, 182-208). See also Milton Wittman, "Education for Community Mental Health Practice: Problems and Prospects," *Social Work*, Vol. 3, No. 4 (October 1958), pp. 64-70.

Three programs have been developed under the National Mental Health Act: (1) research, (2) training of psychiatrists, psychologists, psychiatric nurses, psychiatric social workers, and laboratory technicians, and (3) development of community services for mental health protection and treatment.

Research grants are appropriated to such nonprofit institutions as universities, hospitals, and laboratories, and to qualified individuals engaged in mental health research. The National Institute of Mental Health maintains a hospital for clinical observations and research. Training grants are distributed to psychiatric centers, schools of social work, psychology, and nursing, and to medical schools for premedical studies. Grants-in-aid for the establishment of local diagnostic and treatment facilities and mental hygiene and child guidance clinics are distributed in each state by a State Mental Health Authority. Since the Federal grants-in-aid are allocated to the states on a matching basis, the success of the program depends upon the participation of states, counties, cities, and of such private organizations as mental health societies. These funds cannot be used for services in mental hospitals and institutions or for the building of new institutions and clinics. The construction of hospitals and clinics remains the responsibility of states and local communities.

Important progress is being made in the training of psychiatrists, psychologists, psychiatric social workers, and nurses, with the goal in mind of making earlier diagnosis and more effective treatment available for adults and children. The present shortage of personnel is being slowly alleviated by various grants for studies and research in the field of mental hygiene. Furthermore, psychiatric facilities and well-equipped adult and children's clinics are being established in order to meet the heavy demand for examination, diagnosis, consultation, and treatment. Based upon experiences in military hospitals during World War II, treatment of small, selected groups has been introduced with success, and "group therapy" is now utilized for adults and children. Special attention is being given to the treatment and rehabilitation of alcoholics, drug addicts, epileptics, and intellectually defective patients. The growing number of older people who are disoriented and disturbed, and who require institutional care, presents a serious problem. There are not sufficient facilities available at present for the aged and senile who do not require care in a mental hospital, but rather in a proper foster family or old-age home.

C. Psychiatric Social Work

Psychiatric social work is social casework undertaken in direct and responsible cooperation with psychiatry, practiced in hospitals, clinics, or under psychiatric auspices, with the purpose of helping patients with mental or emotional disturbances.[26] Recently, group work and group therapy have also been applied in psychiatric social work.

Its development is closely linked with the practice of mental hygiene. Psychiatric social work may be traced to four main sources: (1) the need for individual casework and after-care for patients in psychiatric wards and in mental hospitals; (2) casework with children and adolescents brought before juvenile courts and referred to child guidance clinics and social agencies for treatment and adjustment; (3) casework with adult patients in mental hygiene clinics; and (4) casework and group work with psychoneurotic patients in military, veterans, and other hospitals and clinics.

After-care by social workers first was found to be necessary in state hospitals and neurological clinics as being the best way to learn of the economic and environmental conditions of the patient in regard to the therapy plan and to preserve the effect of hospital treatment after the release of the patient. The first specific assignment of a social worker to a neurological clinic was made in 1905, at Massachusetts General Hospital in Boston. Bellevue Hospital, Manhattan State Hospital, and Cornell Clinic in New York employed social workers shortly thereafter.[27]

Of great importance for the development of psychiatric social work were the experiences during and after the two world wars. Because of the large number of patients suffering from war neuroses, psychiatric social work training facilities were extended in 1917, and a joint training project was organized by the National Committee for Mental Hygiene, the Red Cross, and the Smith College School of Social Work.

---

[26] Lois French, *Psychiatric Social Work* (New York: Commonwealth Fund, 1940), p. 12; and, Daniel E. O'Keefe, "Psychiatric Social Work," *Social Work Year Book* (1960), pp. 451-460.

[27] E. E. Southard, *The Kingdom Of Evils* (New York: Macmillan, 1922), p. 521; and, Tessie D. Berkman, *Practice of Social Workers in Psychiatric Hospitals and Clinics* (New York: American Association of Psychiatric Social Workers, 1953). Recent conditions are discussed in George W. Albee, *Mental Health Manpower Trends,* Chapter V (New York: Basic Books, 1959).

Psychiatrists, psychiatric social workers, clinical psychologists, and psychiatric nurses were needed not only for the armed forces and for veterans, but also for the civilian population. Since 1945, psychiatric social workers in the Division of Neuropsychiatry in the Surgeon General's Office of the Army have received officer status. The largest number of psychiatric social workers in the United States is employed by the Veterans Administration in neuropsychiatric hospitals, in mental hygiene clinics in its regional and subregional offices, and in psychiatric wards of many general hospitals.

The function of the psychiatric social worker in child guidance and school clinics is, as a rule, to carry out the intake process and casework with the parents or relatives. The psychiatrist concentrates usually on treating the child. However, this pattern varies and sometimes the psychiatrist assumes the therapy of the more deeply disturbed adult patients—parents, or close relatives—while the psychiatric social worker sees the child. The activities of psychiatric social workers in mental hygiene clinics and out-patient departments of hospitals also include the intake interview and casework treatment with the patient and his family. There is some controversy concerning to what extent the psychiatric social worker should engage in psychotherapy and share the treatment with the psychiatrist.

New trends in psychiatric social work are the use of experienced workers as consultants in family and child welfare agencies, in schools, juvenile courts, hospitals, rehabilitation centers, and personnel divisions of industrial firms. Professional requirements for employment as psychiatric social worker, as a rule, include two years of graduate studies in an accredited school of social work with the specialty of psychiatric social work and the completion of the master's degree. The training must include supervised field work training in a psychiatric setting.

Psychiatric social workers have been active in the development of new therapy techniques, particularly in group therapy with mental patients, the instruction and supervision of volunteers in clinics and hospitals, the expansion of family care for discharged patients of mental hospitals, and in research studies of the results of psychosurgical operations and shock therapy. Psychiatric social workers are teaching courses in medical, public health, and nursing schools, as well as in schools of social work.

Psychiatric social workers recently have given special attention to the placement of mentally deficient patients—children and adults —from state institutions in their own families or other types of family care. They have been able to help in the rehabilitation program for handicapped people, to interpret the necessary treatment to their families, friends, and to their employers, and they assist in the use of clinical out-patient services for the large number of mentally deficient, but not mentally ill (insane) patients.

The following case history may illustrate psychiatric social work in a child guidance clinic.

Case of Bobby [28]

Family's First Contact with the Clinic

Mrs. B, upon suggestion of the elementary school, telephoned the clinic asking for help with her son, Bobby. Upon the admission worker's inquiry she presented a brief picture of the behavior difficulties of the child at home and at school; he is nine years of age and an only child. The father is forty years old, she herself thirty-five. The family is of moderate means. There had been medical care but no previous psychiatric treatment. The admission worker's impression was that the clinic could be of service and informed the mother that she would be called for an appointment. In the meantime, she was asked to have the doctor and school send reports to the clinic directly.

Admission Interview (conducted two weeks later)

Mr. and Mrs. B were seen individually by a psychiatric social worker without the child because the total family constellation and relationships are important in the diagnosis and the therapeutic process.

The parents explained Bobby's difficulty. They told that he was unable to concentrate in school, had a reading and writing block, and that he was rebellious, negativistic, destructive, and overaggressive both at home and at school. He could not get along with his playmates, had been repeatedly transferred from school to school, and now again was faced with exclusion from school, pending the clinic's evaluation. The father, a businessman, described his own very unhappy childhood as an only child. He came from a broken home and had to work at an early age because of financial hardship. He thought of his eleven years marriage with Mrs. B as happy. He was unaware of internal conflicts, but seemed rather tense. He expressed interest in his son, engaged in activities with

---

[28] The author is indebted to the California State Mental Hygiene Clinic in Los Angeles, under the direction of Simon Conrad, M.D., Chief Psychiatrist, and to Mrs. Madeline De Antonio, psychiatric social worker, for the contribution of this case history.

him, but was prone to occasional temper outbursts where he would reprimand Bobby severely. The worker's impression of Mr. B was that he was
a passive man, dominated by his wife.

Mrs. B said she was oldest of four children. She had a sister and two
brothers. She was very close to her mother, but was aloof toward her
father. She felt competitive with her sister whom she described as more
beautiful. She worked five years as a secretary before marrying at the age
of twenty-four. The social worker's impression of Bobby's mother was
that she was a tense, overconcerned woman with a great deal of drive;
that she forced Bobby to do things he disliked or which were beyond
what he could do. Mrs. B seemed to press Bobby toward achievement;
Mr. B was inclined to discount the seriousness of his problem.

The parents described Bobby's infancy and early development as being
normal. The first signs of disturbance apparent to Mr. and Mrs. B was
when Bobby entered school.

Report from Family Doctor

As Bobby had had considerable medical care, the clinic asked for a
medical report upon the written permission of the parents. The doctor
reported that there were no significant medical problems. The patient had
had behavior problems since early infancy (in contrast to the parent's
present report) and he was having steady difficulties in school. He also
told that the boy had been masturbating the past three years. An electro-
encephalogram which was performed six months prior to therapy was
normal for the patient's age.

School Report

A report from the school confirmed that Bobby was in the third grade,
but had already attended four different schools. He was repeating his
grade because his academic accomplishment was below average. A Stan-
ford-Binet test given at the school showed an IQ of 113. School described
Bobby as a nonconformist, as having a short interest span, as not being
able to work up to his ability because of hypertension. They further
stated that he was sweet-natured, accepted socially, but that he gravitated
toward other boys with problems.

Psychiatric Examination

The diagnostic evaluation of the psychiatrist was adjustment reaction
of childhood—conduct disturbances. Psychological tests showed the following results:

Rorschach: This youngster's record indicated considerable anxiety and
a tendency to become disorganized and unrealistic under pressure. He is
able to recover fairly readily.

This is a child who is quite mixed up in his feelings and who seems to
be making some cautious attempts at understanding himself.

He has a lot of dependency needs and wishes, yet is afraid to give in to them. He has the capacity to form satisfying relationships with others, yet is distrustful of others initially and tends to avoid getting close to anyone. He shows increased physical activity and wishful fantasy, is a rather controlling youngster, particularly in his use of negativism and opposition. Much of his behavior is in reaction to his environment, as well as to inner impulses.

The record suggests better than average intelligence, but patient is certainly not functioning up to capacity. He is erratic and inconsistent in both attention and performance and does not seem motivated to try for good achievement.

Bobby seems slightly less threatened by his mother than by his father, though neither relationship is adequate. He seems quite concerned about his masculinity, shows some castration anxiety, and some preoccupation with sexual material.

Drawing of family: This drawing does not contribute much to understanding of this patient. All of the figures seem rather vacuous and empty, as though they have little to give each other. There seems to be little open rejection, but a real inadequacy in both parents under the pleasant exterior. The drawing is quite immature and was done hastily and without particular effort, again showing patient's lack of concern with achievements.

Therapy

A month after the application interview, Mrs. B and Bobby began therapy. Mr. B was not seen for further therapy because he could not arrange to take time from work. Mrs. B and Bobby were treated once a week over a period of nine months with a total of thirty interviews each— the child by a child psychiatrist, the mother by a psychiatric social worker.

Mother's Interviews

The first hour. Mrs. B was upset and said that she did not know where to begin. Words tumbled out rapidly as she described numerous incidents indicating Bobby's destructiveness and ingenuity, hostility and aggressiveness. She seemed to have a great need to "pour out," and probably expected answers to patient's problems in terms of "what to do."

Second through seventh hour. Mother continued to be anxious, overwhelmed and extremely tense during the interviews, recounting many of the patient's activities and episodes with him. It became increasingly clear that she was rigid, punitive, restrictive, and controlling with the child. She was concerned about what was going on in therapy with the boy and what he was doing.

Eighth through twelfth interview. Mrs. B appeared more relaxed and was allowing Bobby to do more things alone. She was beginning to see her role in the difficulty and the implication of rejection in her relationship with the boy. She began to show more awareness of Bobby's behavior pattern rather than preoccupation with each episode. She began to express guilt over failure as a parent; yet at the same time expressed feelings that she had been helped.

Thirteenth through eighteenth interview. She began to report the first signs of improvement in Bobby, initially shown in his newly developed motivation. He still had many behavior problems, but she seemed better able to handle some situations and to maintain this attitude with the continued encouragement and clarification from the worker. Mrs. B was in better spirits, felt more relaxed, and spontaneously began to talk about herself. She ventilated pent-up feelings about the control of the paternal grandmother.

Nineteenth through twenty-second interview. Although Mrs. B was feeling better and there was continued improvement with Bobby, he still had difficulty comprehending his school work and was disturbed about the possibility of not passing again. Bobby had begun to express more of his feelings to his parents and told them, "I'm afraid to read or write, almost as afraid as I am that you and daddy don't love me." It was apparent that part of this problem could be alleviated, because the boy had no orientation in basic school subjects and now seemed more emotionally ready to learn. Therefore, arrangements were made for training in a special school during summer recess.

Twenty-third through thirtieth interview. Mrs. B was surprised that things were going so well. She reported that Bobby was calmer, more relaxed, accepted limitations more easily, was playing with other children more, and had lost some of his fears. He was able to remain in school, where he was making gradual progress. Mrs. B continued to work out some of her own personal problems and conflicts and the difficulties which arise in the home. She was able to give Bobby more freedom and was not as overwhelmed or upset when he acted up, since she understood the cause of his behavior. She seemed encouraged, to have lost her sense of failure, and to be relaxed to the point of handling intelligently provocative situations when they arose. Bobby talked more to his mother about his feelings and was able to gain confidence for her reassurance. Both Bobby and his mother began to express a desire to terminate their contacts. This was agreed upon and the family was given the assurance that they could return to the clinic for help at any time.

Interviews with Patient

Therapy with Bobby was conducted in a playroom which had a variety of toys: a play house, a doll family, a punching bag, blocks, crayons, guns, a blackboard, finger paints, carpentry tools, wood, and a sink (for water play). This allowed Bobby an opportunity to express his feelings and conflicts through the media of play as well as through conversation.

First play interview. Bobby appeared as a tense youngster of slight build who had well-formed features, mildly slanting eyes, giving him a pixie-like expression and demeanor. He seemed friendly and interested and went into the playroom without difficulty. He showed open interest in the therapist. He made tentative explorations of the playroom and listened to the discussion with the therapist of why he was coming to the clinic. He was usually smiling but at times sad and forlorn. He showed no hyperactivity and concentrated on a quiet game of checkers. There were indications of competitiveness and anxiety in the game.

Second through seventh hour. He continued to be somewhat conforming and restricted his activity to checkers. It became apparent that he wished to alter rules to win. He would express hostility toward the therapist playfully. Slight distrust, confusion and suspicion were noted, as well as more frequently frowning and scowling expressions.

Eighth through eighteenth interview. He brought out more of his underlying feelings, conflicts, and true behavior. He became increasingly hyperactive and destructive; at the same time he showed repeated indication of marked attempts to reach out for affection and contact from the therapist. He strongly resisted limitations. He expressed intense and bewildering confusion about himself and deeply ambivalent feelings toward the therapist when saying for instance in rapid succession, "I love you. I hate you."

He appeared to the therapist to be a deeply disturbed boy who was full of tense, anxious hostility, and who was reaching out desperately for a warm, close relationship with an adult, yet was fearful of rejection. Much of his hyperactive and near destructive behavior appeared reactive to the disturbances at home as reported by his mother. It was evident that the environmental stress had to be lessened before Bobby could be helped.

Nineteenth through twenty-fifth interview. Bobby became quieter and began to play more constructively; destructive activity was minimized and at times ceased. Suspiciousness lessened. He was more relaxed. He began to discuss activities he engaged in when away from the clinic. He did not want to leave sessions and could talk about this rather than engaging in angry play. An example of the patient working through his conflicts through play activity was shown as follows: On his own volition, Bobby said, "Let's build something." He built a large tower and knocked it down. He rebuilt the tower and put a man and baby into it and then bombed it The therapist asked where his mother was, and Bobby said that she died in the bombing. He had the father taking care of the baby, but always being bombed and killed. He built and rebuilt the tower several times.

An example of his working out his conflicts through discussion and interpretation was as follows: He told the therapist with pride of his acceptance into the special school. The therapist discussed with Bobby his reading and writing problem this way: "By the end of summer, you will have such a good time in school, you won't be afraid to read any more." Bobby asked "What do you mean?" The therapist then explained that some boys who couldn't read, could not because they were frightened, that it was troublesome for him because he was scared, that when he felt better he would be able to read well. He did not make any comment, but his play became more organized after this.

Twenty-sixth through thirtieth interview: Bobby was more cheerful, smiled freely, and talked easily. He told how well he liked it in his special school and expressed his wish not to continue at the clinic. He could tell the therapist that he was feeling better and that the family was pretty busy. The therapist agreed with Bobby that he need not come in as he was feeling better and assured him that if anything came up, he should tell his mother and arrangements would be made to see him.

Results of Therapy

As a result of Mrs. B's and Bobby's active participation in therapy and the help received from the psychiatric social worker and the psychiatrist, there was a change in both the mother and the patient and in their relationship. Mrs. B became more relaxed, could understand and accept Bobby, could give up pressures, and felt comfortable and secure with her son. Bobby gained greater self-acceptance, was not as tense, angry or frightened, could accept limitations, had a longer span of attention, was more relaxed and happier. He was able to remain in school, improved in his school work, and used special training constructively. He was more secure with his mother and was making strides in his social relationships.

Follow-up

Four months later, a brief contact with Mrs. B and Bobby showed that the improvement had been sustained.

Summary

The picture presented was of a nine year old boy who was extremely fearful and anxious. He had coped with his internal conflicts and continual external pressures with immobilization as shown in his reading and writing block and with disorganization, hyper-aggressivity, and destructiveness as shown by his behavior. He was not able to grow emotionally because of problems in the familial relationships.

His mother was a chronically dissatisfied woman who was working out her needs and unresolved conflicts through her child. Her earlier deprivation, anger and resentment toward having assumed responsibility before she was ready, and the current frustrations in her marriage impeded healthy relationship with her son. Through therapy, she could accept herself more readily and accept Bobby as an individual. As her attitudes changed, the boy could grow and the concurrent improvement in both led toward stability and normal relationships.

Selected Bibliography

I. Health and Medical Care

Allan, W. Scott, *Rehabilitation: A Community Challenge*. New York: Wiley, 1958.

Anderson, Odin W., and Jacob J. Feldman, *Family Medical Costs and Voluntary Health Insurance*. New York: McGraw, 1956.

*Bartlett, Harriett M., *Some Aspects of Social Case Work in a Medical Setting: A Study in the Field of Medical Social Work*, rev. ed. Chicago: American Association of Medical Social Workers, 1952.

Bibring, Greta L., "Psychiatry and Social Work," in Cora Kasius (editor), *Principles and Techniques in Social Casework*, New York: Family Service Association of America, 1950.

Cabot, Richard C., *Social Service and the Art of Healing*, rev. ed. New York: Dodd, 1928.

Cannon, Ida M., *On the Social Frontier of Medicine*. Cambridge: Harvard University Press, 1952.

Cannon, Mary Antoinette, and Harriet M. Bartlett, "Medical Social Work," in New York Academy of Medicine, *Medical Addenda*. New York: Commonwealth Fund, 1947, pp. 38-81.

*Champion, William M., *Medical Information for Social Workers*. Baltimore: Williams & Wilkins, 1938.

*Davis, Michael M., *Medical Care for Tomorrow*. New York: Harper, 1955.

Davis, Michael M., and Dewey Anderson, *Medical Care for the Individual and the Issue of Compulsory Health Insurance*. Washington, D.C.: Government Publishing Office, 1948.

*Dunbar, H. Flanders, *Mind and Body: Psychosomatic Medicine*. New York: Random House, 1947.

Elledge, Caroline H., *The Rehabilitation of the Patient*. Philadelphia: Lippincott, 1948.

Ewing, Oscar R., *The Nation's Health*. Washington, D.C.: Federal Security Agency, 1948.

Falk, I. S., "Health Services, Medical Care Insurance, and Social Security," *The Annals*, Vol. 273 (January 1951), pp. 114-121.

Faxon, Nathaniel W., *The Hospital in Contemporary Life*. Cambridge: Harvard University Press, 1949.

*Goldmann, Franz, *Public Medical Care: Principles and Problems*. New York: Columbia University Press, 1945.

————, *Voluntary Medical Care Insurance in the United States*. New York: Columbia University Press, 1948.

*Goldstine, Dora, *Expanding Horizons in Medical Social Work.* Chicago: University of Chicago Press, 1955.

Greenfield, Margaret, *Medical Care for Welfare Recipients—Basic Problems.* Berkeley: University of California, Bureau of Public Administration, 1957.

Harris, Seymour E., "Medical Care Expenditures in Relation to Family Income and National Income," *Building America's Health,* Vol. 4 (1952), pp. 3-16.

Mattison, Berwyn F., "Public Health," *Social Work Year Book* (1960), pp. 471-481.

*President's Commission on the Health Needs of the Nation, *Building America's Health.* 5 vols. Washington, D.C.: Government Printing Office, 1952.

*Rice, Elizabeth P., "Medical Social Work," *Social Work Year Book* (1957), pp. 356-63.

Rogers, Edward S., "Medical Care," *Social Work Year Book* (1960), pp. 365-375.

Scheele, Leonard A., "Public Health," *Social Work Year Book* (1957), pp. 451-463.

Serbein, Oscar N., *Paying for Medical Care in the United States.* New York: Columbia University Press, 1953.

Stern, Bernhard J., *American Medical Practice in the Perspectives of a Century.* New York: Commonwealth Fund, 1945.

*————, *Medical Services by Government: Local, State, and Federal.* New York: Commonwealth Fund, 1946.

Terris, Milton, "Medical Care for the Needy and Medically Needy," *Annals,* Vol. 273 (January 1951), pp. 84-92.

Thornton, Janet, and Marjorie S. Knauth, *The Social Component in Medical Care.* New York: Columbia University Press, 1937.

Turner, Clair E., "Public Health Education," *Social Work Year Book* (1954), pp. 415-418.

*Upham, Frances, *A Dynamic Approach to Illness: A Social Work Guide.* New York: Family Service Association of America, 1949.

Weiss, Edward, and O. Spurgeon English, *Psychosomatic Medicine.* Philadelphia: Saunders, 1943.

Witmer, Helen L., *Teaching Psychotherapeutic Medicine.* New York: Commonwealth Fund, 1947.

Yost, Edna, and Lillian M. Gilbreth, *Normal Lives for the Disabled.* New York: Macmillan, 1944.

II. Mental Hygiene and Psychiatric Social Work

Aldridge, Gordon J. (editor), *Social Issues and Psychiatric Social Work Practice.* New York: National Association of Social Workers, 1959.

Alexander, Franz, *Our Age of Unreason*. Philadelphia: Lippincott, 1942.

Alexander, Franz, and Thomas French, *Psychoanalytic Therapy: Principles and Applications*. New York: Ronald, 1946.

*Allen, Frederick H., *Psychotherapy with Children*. New York: Norton, 1942.

American Association of Psychiatric Social Workers, *Education for Psychiatric Social Work*, Proceedings of the Dartmouth Conference. New York, 1950.

Asch, Solomon E., *Social Psychology*. Englewood Cliffs, N.J.: Prentice-Hall, Inc., 1952.

Beck, Bertram M., and Lewis L. Robbins, *Short-Term Therapy in an Authoritative Setting*. New York: Family Service Association of America, 1946.

*Beers, Clifford W., *A Mind That Found Itself: An Autobiography*. New York: Doubleday, 1935.

*Bowlby, John, *Maternal Care and Mental Health*. New York: Columbia University Press, 1951.

Brill, Abraham A., *Freud's Contribution to Psychiatry*. New York: Norton, 1944.

Cabot, Richard C., *Social Work: Essays on the Meeting Ground of Doctor and Social Worker*. Boston: Houghton, 1919.

Clifton, Eleanor, and Florence Hollis, *Child Therapy, A Casework Symposium*. New York: Family Service Association of America, 1948.

Crutcher, Hester B., *Foster Home Care for Mental Patients*. New York: Commonwealth Fund, 1944.

Davies, Stanley P., *The Mentally Retarded in Society*. New York: Columbia University Press, 1959.

*Deutsch, Albert, *The Mentally Ill in America: A History of Their Care and Treatment from Colonial Times*. New York: Columbia University Press, 1946.

Dysinger, Robert H., "Mental Health in the United States," *The Annals*, Vol. 286 (March 1953), pp. 1-174.

*English, O. Spurgeon, and Gerald H. J. Pearson, *Emotional Problems of Living: Avoiding the Neurotic Pattern*. New York: Norton, 1946.

Felix, Robert H., and Morton Kramer, "Extent of the Problem of Mental Disorders," *The Annals*, Vol. 286 (March 1953), pp. 5-14.

*French, Lois Meredith, *Psychiatric Social Work*. New York: Commonwealth Fund, 1940.

Fromm, Erich, *The Sane Society*. New York: Rinehart, 1955.

Halliday, James L., *Psychosocial Medicine*. New York: Norton, 1948.

Hamilton, Gordon, *Psychotherapy in Child Guidance.* New York: Columbia University Press, 1947.

Hendrick, Ives, *Facts and Theories of Psychoanalysis.* New York: Knopf, 1946.

*Hollingshead, August B., and Frederick C. Redlich, *Social Class and Mental Illness.* New York: Wiley, 1958.

Horney, Karen, *Our Inner Conflicts.* New York: Norton, 1945.

————, *The Neurotic Personality of Our Time.* New York: Norton, 1937.

*Jahoda, Marie, *Current Concepts of Positive Mental Health.* New York: Basic Books, 1958.

*Jones, Maxwell, *The Therapeutic Community.* New York: Basic Books, 1953.

Knee, Ruth I., "Psychiatric Social Work," *Social Work Year Book* (1957), pp. 431-439.

Kotinsky, Ruth, and Helen L. Witmer, *Community Programs for Mental Health.* Cambridge: Harvard University Press, 1955.

Krech, David, and Richard S. Crutchfield, *Theory and Problems of Social Psychology.* New York: McGraw, 1948.

Lee, Porter R., and Marion E. Kenworthy, *Mental Hygiene and Social Work.* New York: Commonwealth Fund, 1929.

*Lemkau, Paul V., *Mental Hygiene in Public Health.* New York: McGraw-Hill, 1955.

Levy, John, and Ruth Munroe, *The Happy Family.* New York: Knopf, 1938.

*Lowry, Lawson G., *Psychiatry for Social Workers.* New York: Columbia University Press, 1946.

Menninger, Karl A., *Man Against Himself.* New York: Harcourt, 1938.

————, *The Human Mind,* 3rd ed. New York: Knopf, 1946.

*Menninger, William C., *You and Psychiatry.* New York: Scribner, 1948.

Meyers, Jerome K., and Bertram Roberts, *Family and Class Dynamics in Mental Illness.* New York: Wiley, 1959.

Moustakas, Clark E., *Children in Play Therapy: A Key to Understanding Normal and Disturbed Emotions.* New York: McGraw, 1953.

Opler, Marvin K., *Culture, Psychiatry and Human Values.* Springfield, Ill.: Thomas, 1956.

Phelps, Harold A., and David Henderson, *Contemporary Social Problems,* 4th ed. Englewood Cliffs, N.J.: Prentice-Hall, Inc., 1952.

*Plant, James S., *Personality and the Cultural Pattern.* New York: Commonwealth Fund, 1937.

Powdermaker, Florence B., and Jerome Frank, *Group Psychotherapy:*

Studies in Methodology of Research and Therapy. Cambridge: Harvard University Press, 1953.

Preston, George H., *The Substance of Mental Health.* New York: Rinehart, 1943.

Rennie, Thomas A., and Luther E. Woodward, *Mental Health in Modern Society.* New York: Commonwealth Fund, 1948.

Rogers, Carl R., *Counseling and Psychotherapy.* Boston: Houghton, 1942.

Rose, Arnold M., *Mental Health and Mental Disorder.* New York: Norton, 1955.

Saul, Leon J., *Emotional Maturity.* Philadelphia: Lippincott, 1947.

Stern, Edith M., *Mental Illness: A Guide for the Family,* rev. ed. New York: Commonwealth Fund, 1945.

*Stevenson, George S., *Mental Health Planning for Social Action.* New York: McGraw, 1956.

Sullivan, Harry Stack, *Modern Conceptions of Psychiatry.* Washington: W. A. White Psychiatric Foundation, 1945.

*Towle, Charlotte, *Social Case Records from Psychiatric Clinics.* Chicago: University of Chicago Press, 1941.

*Trecker, Harleigh B. (editor), *Group Work in the Psychiatric Setting.* New York: Association Press, 1959.

Weinberg, S. Kirson, *Society and Personality Disorders.* Englewood Cliffs, N.J.: Prentice-Hall, Inc., 1952.

Witmer, Helen Leland, *Pediatrics and the Emotional Needs of the Child.* New York: Commonwealth Fund, 1948.

———, *Psychiatric Clinics for Children.* New York: Commonwealth Fund, 1940.

*———, *Psychiatric Interviews with Children.* New York: Commonwealth Fund, 1946.

13.

Crime, Delinquency, and Correctional Services

I. CAUSES OF DELINQUENCY AND CRIME

Social services for children, youth, and adults who violate laws are an important part of modern social work. These services developed only after the criminal courts already had a long history. Thus, court authorities have been reluctant to recognize the value of the contribution of the services of social workers whose techniques and skills had not yet taken definite form. We shall discuss, first, the social services rendered to children and young persons who have difficulties in abiding by the legal rules of community life, and then proceed to social services for the adult offender.

Maladjustment and delinquent behavior of children and youth are among the most serious problems of our society.[1] From the point of view of social work, it seems necessary to help children and ado-

---

[1] For a full discussion of the topic, the reader is referred to Negley K. Teeters and John Otto Reinemann, *The Challenge of Delinquency: Causation, Treatment, and Prevention of Juvenile Delinquency* (Englewood Cliffs, N. J.: Prentice-Hall, Inc., 1950), Chapter I; and to John R. Ellingston, *Protecting Our Children from Criminal Careers* (Englewood Cliffs, N. J.: Prentice-Hall, Inc., 1948), Chapters 1 and 2.

lescents to avoid asocial behavior, whether or not they are brought before a court or are pronounced delinquent. Social work assists young people in their efforts to abide by the rules of social conduct required by tradition or statute. These efforts include the development of social attitudes and modes of behavior which are not necessarily embodied in legal provisions.[2] Thus, juvenile protection in social work is concerned with maladjusted children and youth whose delinquency brings them before the law, but also with those who, although not violating laws, prove to be difficult to educate in the family or who are endangering others in school and in the streets.

Such deviant behavior cannot be treated alike in all children because of the different circumstances under which it occurs. One difficult child may be accepted or even encouraged in his delinquent behavior by his family and neighbors, according to the mores in a certain area or community; another child under the same conditions may be brought to a social agency or referred to a child guidance clinic; and still another may be denounced to the police, arrested, and cited before the juvenile court. The economic status of the parents, customs of the local community, and cultural patterns of the social group to which the child belongs are essential factors in determining what happens to a delinquent child. The White House Conference of 1930 defined "delinquency" as juvenile misconduct that might be dealt with under the law. But, from the point of view of social work, it is desirable to help the child before he gets in trouble and police authorities and juvenile courts are forced to interfere with his life.

No exact statistical data on the extent of juvenile delinquency in our country are available. But it is estimated that about 1,500,000 children under 18 years are arrested for delinquencies each year and that about the same number are not brought before a juvenile court although they also are involved in crime.[3]

The causes of delinquency are analyzed by different theories.

---

[2] Helen L. Witmer, *Social Work: An Analysis of a Social Institution* (New York: Farrar and Reinhart, 1942), p. 383; and, Joseph S. Roucek (editor), *Juvenile Delinquency* (New York: Philosophical Library, 1959).

[3] Katherine B. Oettinger, "Current Concerns of the Childrens Bureau," *Children*, Vol. 5, No. 4 (July-August 1958), pp. 123-128; Benjamin Fine, *1,000,000 Delinquents* (New York: World Publishing Co., 1955); and, Norman V. Lourie, "Juvenile Delinquency," *Social Work Year Book* (1960), pp. 344-355.

Cesare Lombroso, the noted Italian anthropologist and criminologist, taught that the criminal was born, doomed by certain biological characteristics to lead a life of crime. Today only few scientists adhere to this "constitutional school of criminality." Most students of criminology are convinced that crime and delinquency are not caused through any single source, whether it be heredity, biological structure, or environmental influences, but usually by several factors working together. This school is termed the "Multiple Causation Theory." Among these various factors may be included hereditary and biological influences, such as poor health, physical handicaps, abnormalities, glandular disturbances, various degrees of mental deficiency or even psychosis, emotional instability, insecurity, uncontrolled sexual drives, or neurotic behavior. Other factors may be contributed by environment, neglect or rejection by parents, siblings and friends, detrimental influences of a broken home, criminal attitudes of the family, neighbors, or predatory gangs in a slum area. There may also be poverty in the family, gambling, bad companions, irregular or poor education, lack of healthy recreation, excitement through the radio, television, the newspapers, crime stories, comic books, and movies.

Research studies, particularly those of Sheldon and Eleanor Glueck, and Clifford Shaw, have shown that certain young persons may become delinquent while others remain law-abiding citizens under the same hereditary conditions and in the same environment.[4]

Since human behavior is determined in part by the customs and the culture in which we live, much delinquency is based upon the conflicting values within and between cultural groups. As an example of such a conflict, the difference between the customs of foreign-born parents and their native-born children is frequently mentioned. Children are ashamed of the "strange" habits and values of their parents while they themselves, as a rule, accept those of their play companions and classmates in school. In fact, our present civilization is not ruled

---

[4] Sheldon Glueck and Eleanor Glueck, *One Thousand Delinquents* (Cambridge: Harvard University Press, 1934); Clifford Shaw, *Delinquency Areas* (Chicago: University of Chicago Press, 1929); *Brothers in Crime* (Chicago: University of Chicago Press, 1938); Miriam van Waters, *Youth in Conflict* (New York: Republic Printing Co., 1925); and, Albert K. Cohen, *Delinquent Boys: The Culture of the Gang* (Glencoe, Ill.: Free Press, 1955).

by a single set of cultural and ethical values, but by several conflicting systems. This conflict is more evident in the United States than in other countries due to the wide mobility of its population, its different ethnic background, and the lack of a strict class system.[5]

Cultural anthropology explains the divergence in sexual customs and habits; in approval or disapproval of street fighting, gang rule, stealing of money, food, or automobiles; in fraud, cheating in measures and weights, gambling and betting, riding freight trains, trucks and busses; truancy, and the illicit manufacture of liquor, among various minority groups and underprivileged classes of our population. Whenever youngsters act in conformity to the customs of their own group, but in violation of the written law or the habit of other groups, the lawbreaker and his family and friends often consider it merely an unfortunate accident to be caught by the police and reprimanded by the court.

More general, and not dependent upon the particular customs of minority groups, is the conflict existing between the teaching of religious and moral ethics on one hand, and, on the other, the practical demands of the economic rules of our society. Religious teaching and social philosophy ask the individual to love others, and praise mutual aid and cooperation. In conflict with this humanitarian ideal, the principle of ruthless economic competition and individual achievement in terms of success, wealth, property, and high income, as a measurement of efficiency, urge the child to excel others in school and to aim at economic success, even at the expense of others. It is obvious that many children and youngsters find it difficult to establish a balance between these conflicting theories.[6]

---

[5] H. Witmer, *op. cit.*, p. 385; J. Ellingston, *op. cit.*, pp. 13-27; Fritz Redl and David Wineman, *The Aggressive Child* (Glencoe, Ill.: Free Press, 1957); and, D. W. Winnicott, *The Child and the Outside World* (New York: Basic Books, 1957).

[6] Karen Horney, *The Neurotic Personality of Our Time* (New York: Norton, 1937); Franz Alexander and William Healy, *The Roots of Crime* (New York: Knopf, 1935); Bernard Lander, *Toward an Understanding of Juvenile Delinquency* (New York: Columbia University Press, 1953); Milton L. Barron, *The Juvenile in Delinquent Society* (New York: Knopf, 1954); William McCord *et al.*, *Origins of Crime* (New York: Columbia University Press, 1959); and, Lewis Yablonsky, "The Delinquent Gang as a Near-Group," *Social Problems*, Vol. 7, No. 2 (Fall 1959), pp. 108-117).

II. THE JUVENILE COURT

After the French Penal Code under Napoleon provided for a minimum age at which children could be made responsible for offenses, and for a different treatment of young lawbreakers, the postulate of such differentiation spread in most countries of Western civilization. The English Courts of Chancery already had been protecting the interests of young children under seven years of age who were considered to be incapable of "criminal intent." Children between seven and fourteen years of age could be punished by the courts, provided the prosecutor was able to prove their capacity of entertaining criminal intent. Children over fourteen years of age were punished as adult criminals.

In the United States, the press and charity societies complained that children begging in the streets, or pilfering, needed protection and reformation rather than punishment in the same manner adults received. It became evident that harsh punishment, particularly the death sentence, against children was out of proportion to the child's responsibility, and that children placed in jails or prisons with adult criminals were really becoming trained in crime and vice by the older inmates.

In the 1820's New York, Boston, and Philadelphia established "houses of refuge" for wayward or delinquent children and youngsters in order to separate them from adult criminals.

The first juvenile court was created in Chicago on July 1, 1899. Since 1891, a group of citizens under the leadership of Jane Addams and Judge Harvey B. Hurd, urged the Chicago Bar Association to encourage the state legislature to enact legislation for the protection of children and for their segregation from adult offenders. The law was adopted on April 14, 1899 with the aim of treatment and supervision of dependent, neglected, and delinquent children.[7] The juvenile court judge had to combine legal skill with the knowledge of human behavior in order to help the child in his adjustment.

The law established the jurisdiction of circuit and county courts over children's cases. It based the entire process of investigation, court hearing, and judicial disposition upon the idea of rehabilita-

---

[7] Grace Abbott, *The Child and the State, II* (Chicago: University of Chicago Press, 1938), pp. 303-331.

tion of the juvenile delinquent. The juvenile court is not a criminal court; it does not make charges against the child who, therefore, is not in need of a defense lawyer. There is no jury to determine the guilt or innocence of the child. Rather, the court attempts to understand the causes for the behavior of the child or adolescent and orders measures to be taken for his adjustment and rehabilitation.

In the same year in which the Chicago Juvenile Court was established, 1899, Judge Benjamin B. Lindsay organized a special children's court under the Board of Education in Denver, Colorado, which developed into a juvenile court in 1903. Other states have followed the Illinois example so that at present all states, as well as the Federal government, have juvenile courts.

The operation of the juvenile court may be best characterized by its comparison with the adult criminal court. An adult who has committed an offense is, as a rule, arrested and after a hearing before a magistrate either summarily punished by a fine or jail sentence, or held for trial in jail, or released under bail or upon his pledge to appear in court. After a criminal investigation, the prosecuting attorney submits the evidence to a jury requesting an indictment of the accused. If the jury finds that the evidence does not justify an indictment, the accused is released. If the indictment is pronounced by the jury, the trial proceeds. The defendant is entitled to have an attorney to represent him. At the arraignment he pleads "guilty" or "not guilty"; in the latter case, a trial jury of twelve members brings in, upon examination of the facts and cross-examination of the witnesses by the prosecuting officer and the defense lawyer, a verdict of "guilty" or "not guilty."

Quite different is the procedure of the juvenile court. Its jurisdiction covers, in the majority of states, youth under eighteen years of age. As a rule, neglected and dependent children also are under the jurisdiction of the juvenile court, and in some states are placed under adoption, guardianship, or committed to institutions for handicapped and mentally defective or ill children. The action of the juvenile court usually is initiated by petition; no jury is asked for an indictment.

If a juvenile offender is arrested after violating the law, he should be placed in a detention home, not in a jail with adults. In spite of the knowledge that children and youthful offenders are trained in crime, distrust society, and become more hostile to good citizenship as a result of being kept in jail, prohibition of jail detention varies widely among the states. Often, exceptions are possible for older youth or by order of the juvenile court judge. Frequently, the young offender is heard before a referee or a probation officer at once or the next day, and released upon his promise of good behavior, or held for the juvenile court session in the detention home. Many juvenile courts place the child under the supervision of a probation officer when the youngster is released before the final court hearing.

III. THE DETENTION HOME

The detention home, or "juvenile hall," receives children who may be classified into three main categories: (1) children in need of protection, such as dependent and neglected children without proper care, lost children in need of an emergency shelter, mental defectives awaiting commitment, and habitual truants that are being returned to their parents; (2) children in temporary custody, such as children who are runaways from their own or foster families and from children's institutions, and children who must serve as witnesses in order to secure their presence in court; and (3) children expecting trial before the juvenile court, and children awaiting transfer to a training school or another institution after court decision.

In some detention homes, dependent and neglected children are kept separate from delinquent children. Many children remain only a day or a night in the detention home until they return to their families, but for three types of children frequently a longer placement in the detention home is necessary: (1) children and youngsters beyond the control of their parents, foster parents, and guardians who cannot be prevented from committing new delinquencies, such as serious assault, sexual attacks, burglary, armed robbery; (2) children who are in physical or moral danger in their own families or are without a home; and (3) children whose attendance or uninfluenced testimony at a court hearing or whose placement in an institution can only be assured by detention.[8]

The detention home is administered by either: (1) the juvenile

---

[8] Sherwood and Helen Norman, *Detention for the Juvenile Court: A Discussion of Principles and Practices* (New York: National Probation Association, 1946); Sherwood Norman, "The Detention Home," *The Annals,* Vol. 261 (January 1949), pp. 158-165; and, N. Teeters and J. Reinemann, *op. cit.,* pp. 237-246.

court (sometimes the chief probation officer is superintendent of the home), (2) the county authorities (board of supervisors or commissioners), (3) a local public welfare department, (4) the state's department of social welfare, or (5) a private child welfare agency.

Services to the child in the detention home include good physical and custodial care, medical and dental treatment, recreation, instruction according to the age of the child and the length of his stay, and religious services. Although a certain security against escape is necessary, the detention home should avoid an atmosphere of fear and repression. More recently, the need of professional casework and clinical services for emotionally disturbed children has been acknowledged, as well as stimulating, cheerful group activities in workshops, play, and recreation so that the children are occupied and socially interested. However, many detention homes are still far from meeting these standards, which require employment of trained personnel, a superintendent, teachers, caseworkers, group workers, and supervisors. The observation of the child in the detention home regarding his health, mental abilities, and behavior renders valuable information for the court, the probation staff, and social agencies which may later help the child.

Because most children are held only a few days or weeks in a detention home, little systematic, academic, or technical education and personality adjustment is possible. The children are of different age groups. Most of them are sent home again or are placed in a foster home or another children's institution before they get well acquainted with the detention home staff.

With an accepting, friendly attitude toward the child the staff sometimes is able to break through the fearful or hostile defense which most children bring to the detention home after they have been arrested. The establishment of a contact between the child and the caseworker, group worker, or counselor may be the beginning of a treatment process. An intensive influence on corrective adjustment of the child can seldom be exercised during such a short period. But the child is protected against destructive influences, is well cared for physically, and the family and society are protected against the child's delinquent actions for the period of detention. Whenever the child feels that the staff takes a sincere interest in his well-being and is willing to help him, a start in his treatment may be made in the detention home.

IV. JUVENILE COURT PROCEDURE

A major characteristic of the juvenile court procedure is the social investigation, conducted by the probation officer attached to the juvenile court. It supplies the data for gaining an understanding of the personality of the young offender, his family, social and economic conditions, and the motive of his offense, in order to determine the plan for treatment and rehabilitation.

The probation officer needs knowledge of human behavior and personality for his interview with the child and his family. It is not easy to make contact with delinquent children because they frequently carry over toward the police, the probation officer, and social worker their resentments against their parents or against authority in general. The delinquent child is unable to deal himself with his problems, but also avoids revealing them to adults. He may have been hurt by others and inconsistently treated by his parents or teachers. Then, the child is distrustful and fears being betrayed and punished. To hide this fear, delinquent children give themselves an air of reckless bravery and of callous hardness.

In cases of juvenile delinquents, the probation officer, as a rule, will have to make a home call to see the youngster and his family. He will not wait until the youth comes into his office. He studies the nature and circumstances of the offense, former delinquencies of the child, the family background with an analysis of its personal, educational, and economic conditions, the question of employment, housing, and moral conditions, as well as the health status of the child and of the family. In the child's history, his relation to parents, siblings, and neighbors, personality traits, conduct, and behavior, the physical and emotional effect of illness, his religious and school experiences, his work records, recreational activities, and his outlook for the future need exploration. The probation officer evaluates these data in relation to the cultural and social conditions in which the youngster is living, and presents his recommendations to the court with the aim of finding measures which will be most helpful to the child. Physical, as well as mental, examinations of the young offender are desirable to interpret his personality. Mental tests by a psychologist or a psychiatric diagnosis are dependent upon local facilities available to the juvenile court. Different psychological tests may be used in order to explain the child's intelligence, the areas of his maladjustment, and the possibilities of rehabilitation and adjustment.

Juvenile courts frequently dispose of minor cases of delinquency informally without filing a petition, preparing a court record, or holding a court hearing. The arrangement of such an informal adjustment may be assigned to a probation officer, the chief probation officer, or to a referee by the judge, sometimes even to a juvenile bureau or crime prevention division of the local police department.[9] At the court hearing, often, the child meets the judge of the juvenile court for the first time. The meeting should be dignified, but free from judicial technicalities which frighten the child and his parents. The court hearing is centered around the questions of why the child has become delinquent and what measures may be most effective in preventing further delinquencies and in assisting the child in his readjustment. The establishment of the facts of the specific delinquency is less relevant.

As a rule, the juvenile court hearing is private; the general public and the press are excluded. The presence of spectators is harmful to the youngster because in an open court hearing he either finds himself the center of attraction and is inclined to act as a hero, therefore appearing tough and nonrepentant, or he risks losing the respect of his fellows and neighbors by showing regret of his behavior. The parents of the child, necessary witnesses, and the probation officer are present; representatives of social agencies and of the school authorities may be admitted. The atmosphere of the court hearing should create confidence in the child and his parents that the judge is willing to help them in the solution of the youth's problems.

The disposition of the juvenile court may be one of the following:

(1) The child may be placed, with a reprimand of the judge, under supervision of his parents in his own home.

(2) The child may be placed on probation.

(3) The child may be taken away from his own home and be placed in a foster family, either through a social agency or under the auspices of the juvenile court.

---

[9] J. Ellingston, *op. cit.*, pp. 214-215; Alfred J. Kahn, *A Court for Children* (New York: Columbia University Press, 1953); and Sol Rubin, *Crime and Juvenile Delinquency: A Rational Approach to Penal Problems* (New York: Oceana, 1958).

(4) The judge may order the medical or psychiatric examination of the child and place the child for this purpose in a hospital, a children's institution, or a suitable family.

(5) The judge may order the commitment of the child to the custody and guardianship of a public or private social agency or children's institution, frequently a "training school" or "industrial school."

(6) The judge may order restitution or reparation for damage caused by the child's delinquency.

The adjudication in juvenile court is not a penal conviction of the child and does not constitute a criminal record. However, many juvenile court laws do not yet have statutory provisions to the effect that the disposition of the juvenile court shall not disqualify the young person for any future civil service appointment.

The decision of a criminal court against an adult offender may be changed only by another sentence of an appellate court, but the disposition of the juvenile court may be modified by the judge according to the needs of the child. The right to appeal the decree of the juvenile court to an appellate court is limited in several state laws to questions of law, errors of fact, or certain decisions, such as commitment to a training school or removal from the custody of the parents.

In a few instances, adolescent courts or boys' courts have been established in order to separate the trial and treatment of young persons between seventeen and twenty-one years of age from that of adult offenders.[10] The development of adolescent courts has been hampered by a hostile attitude of the public toward a mild or "sentimental" treatment of nearly adult offenders.

V. PROBATION

"Probation is a process of treatment, prescribed by the court for persons convicted of offenses against the law, during which the individual on probation lives in the community and regulates his own

---

[10] N. Teeters and J. Reinemann, *op. cit.*, pp. 328-333, and 344-354; and Clyde B Vedder, *The Juvenile Offender* (New York: Doubleday, 1954).

life under conditions imposed by the court (or other constituted authority) and is subject to supervision by a probation officer." [11]

Characteristic of probation, therefore, is the postponement of either the final judgment or the postponement of the execution of the sentence combined with certain conditions imposed by the court, under the guidance and supervision of the probation officer. In practice, it is not uncommon that an adult offender is ordered, first, to serve a certain period in jail or prison and then, under suspension of sentence, to live freely in the community on condition of good behavior under supervision. For juvenile delinquents, the probation order of the juvenile court allows the youth to live at liberty in his own home or in the custody of a relative, friend, or foster parents, under supervision of the probation officer, instead of being committed to a correctional institution or training school.

The social elements of probation are threefold: (1) Probation permits the probationer to live a normal life in the community and to readjust to socially acceptable attitudes without being confined, during this period, to a penal or correctional institution; (2) it is granted, on the basis of a social investigation by the court, assuming that the probationer will be able to live a lawful life and may be expected to do so; and (3) it is a process of adjustment with the supervision of a probation officer.

Probation has its legal basis in the authority of the court under common law to suspend sentence and to allow the convicted offender to remain at liberty upon condition of good behavior.[12] As a practical method, probation was introduced in the United States as early as 1841 by John Augustus, a Boston shoemaker. He provided bail for a poor drunkard who was threatened to be sentenced to the house of correction, and assumed his supervision during a period of "probation." John Augustus, encouraged through the success of his first case, continued to bail, supervise, and assist about 2,000 adults and

---

[11] National Commission on Law Observance and Law Enforcement, "Penal Institutions, Probation and Parole," *Report No. 9, Wickersham Report* (1931), p. 184.

[12] John Otto Reinemann, "Probation and the Juvenile Delinquent," *The Annals*, Vol. 261 (January 1949), p. 109. In English common law, probation may be traced to the institution of formal "recognisance," an obligation entered before the court to keep the peace. See also, David Dressler, *Practice and Theory of Probation and Parole* (New York: Columbia University Press, 1959).

juveniles until his death in 1859. He also advocated the establishment of an asylum for the treatment of alcoholics.

The first probation law for adult offenders was enacted in 1878, in Massachusetts, and since 1959, all the states, the Federal government and the District of Columbia have enacted probation laws.

Probation provisions vary among the states and even among the individual courts. Probation is not just leniency. It is an educational measure of treating an offender through supervision while he lives in the community. The cost of probation is only a small fraction of that of institutional commitment. Its advantages are as follows: the probationer remains in his home; his social status is not impaired; he is able to support himself and his family and to pay restitution to the victim of the offense; and he may be rehabilitated with the aid of the probation officer, who can use the resources of the community and take advantage of the fact that the probationer's status discourages him from committing new offenses

Requisite for an effective probation system is the employment of skilled social workers trained in casework, in the use of community resources, in understanding the behavior of juvenile and adult offenders, and in the cooperation with psychiatrists and psychologists. During recent years, standards for probation officers have risen, and in some states civil service requirements and merit systems have been set up. Much remains to be done.

Usually, the probation service is attached to the court, and the appointment of the probation officers is made by the judge. But there have been some recent exceptions made. The Probation service, for example, has been established an an independent agency, in the Los Angeles County Probation Department, the New York City Youth Board, or on a state-wide level, as the California Youth Authority, the Youth Conservation Commission in Minnesota, the Youth Service Commission in Wisconsin, the State Department of Correction in New York, and the State Department of Public Assistance (Division of Child Welfare) in West Virginia.

The probation officer begins with a social investigation in the case of a juvenile court hearing. For the criminal court, the investigation, as a rule, is ordered only after a verdict of guilty is rendered against the adult offender, particularly if the judge is considering not sending the offender to a penal institution. The investigation requires that the probation officer understand the motivations, feelings, and attitudes of the offender, and the influences which the neighborhood gangs and other elements may have had on his behavior. The probation officer cannot apply his own standards of life and morals to the offender; his function is to help a person who has got into trouble with the law. He will consider the offender's personality, his physiological equipment, his mental and intellectual capacities, life experiences, cultural background, and setting.

When the probation officer interviews the young person, he gives him a chance to express his difficulties, and discuss his social and personal situation. The probation officer explores with him possibilities of making changes in work, environment, or social relations, and joining church or group activities which may be helpful in his adjustment. In presenting data on the young delinquent collected in the family, school, and neighborhood, the probation officer has to distinguish between objective facts and his own interpretation of the situation and of the young offender's personality.

For juvenile delinquents, as well as for adult offenders, the probation officer recommends probation to the court only if he is convinced that the offender will be able to use it constructively for his adjustment. If he feels that the offender is not ready to adjust himself in the community, he suggests commitment to an institution.

After the court has placed an adult offender or a juvenile delinquent under probation, the probation officer supervises him as a helping service, but under the authority of the court. Whether it is good practice to have the same probation officer carry out the social investigation and the supervision, or whether these two main activities should be separated and assigned to different groups of probation officers, has been the subject of discussion.[13]

In general, girls' supervision and, often, that of boys under twelve years of age is assigned to women probation officers, and cases of boys over twelve years of age to men. The regional principle, according to which a certain geographical area is assigned to the individual probation officer who supervises the children and young persons in this area, is considered economical and practical.

The probation officer recognizes the positive possibilities of au-

---

[13] Jay Rumnay and Joseph P. Murphy, *Probation and Social Adjustment* (New Brunswick, N. J.: Rutgers University Press, 1952); and, Z. Alexander Aarons, "Some Problems of Delinquency and Their Treatment by a Casework Agency," *Social Casework,* Vol. 40, No. 5 (May 1959), pp. 254-262.

thority and its implications for the probationer. He knows that this authoritative element is a necessary function of the judiciary system and of the probation process. However, he should be free of a feeling of vindictiveness and moral superiority toward the probationer which would prevent him from interpreting the court decision objectively and the meaning of probation to the probationer in a way which is acceptable to him. He will explain that the court's requirements, such as making regular reports to the probation officer or to the court, planning permanent work, and avoiding drugs and excessive drinking, have to be strictly followed. The probation officer will make it clear that the probationer is free to ask for his help, but that the responsibility for complying with these court orders is his own, and that the success of the probation process depends upon his attitude and behavior. During this period, the probation officer assists the probationer in his personal, emotional difficulties as well as in environmental problems, housing, employment, schooling, and group and cultural relations. Despite the authoritative element in probation, the probation officer should not direct the life of the probationer, depriving him of the responsibility for his decisions.

The probationer has to be educated to assume responsibility without shifting it back to the probation officer, who will not always supervise his life. The relationship between probation officer and probationer must be based upon understanding, respect, sincerity, and confidence, in the sphere of authority that is a part of the court's jurisdiction. Revocation of probation will be recommended by the probation officer if he is convinced that the probationer cannot profit from a continuation of the probation service, and if he violates the rules of probation so flagrantly that institutional treatment seems necessary. However, the probation officer should be well aware of the fact that failure of probation might be due to his own inability to find the right contact with the probationer or to mobilize other resources of the community. Such reasons would not justify the revocation of probation.

VI. TRAINING SCHOOLS

Children and adolescents who are not granted probation by a juvenile court because their rehabilitation cannot be achieved in their own home or in a foster family are committed to a "training school," frequently called "industrial school" or "reform school." [14] The first local school of this type founded in the United States was the New York City House of Refuge, founded in 1825 by the Society for Reformation of Juvenile Delinquents, in order to save neglected, and vagrant children from the vicious influence of the adult prisons. Other schools in Boston, Philadelphia, and New Orleans followed, but it was only in 1847 that the first state reform school was established in Massachusetts. There were, in 1959, 130 state industrial schools, a number of county and municipal schools, and about as many private training schools providing care for dependent, neglected, truant and delinquent children and youths ranging from six to twenty-one years of age.

Some of these institutions have maintained practices of mass treatment, a repressive attitude, and even corporal punishment. Others offer little more than physical and custodial care; they accept the policy that the school is the place where troublesome and disturbing children may be placed primarily for the safety of the population of their home community, and that such children and adolescents should be controlled in the school by the denial of their liberty, enforcement of some general education and vocational training, and strict regulation of their activities. A third type of training school, however, has developed an integrated program of rehabilitation for these children and youths by providing a positive plan for group living under educational guidance. They offer medical and mental health supervision, spiritual, religious, academic and vocational training, recreation, and leisure-time activities, permitting as much freedom and choice as possible. This type of school still represents a controlled environment in which the children have to accept limitations on their freedom and have to conform to the rules of group living, but they contribute to a constructive development of the children and prepare them for the return to life with their family or in their home community.

Only the last type of training school will achieve a positive change of personality, readjustment and rehabilitation in children and ado-

---

[14] Though the terminology is not unanimously accepted, we want to speak of "reformatories" only as penal institutions for young offenders sentenced by the criminal court, or for adult offenders sentenced for the first time. Some schools for truant children are called "parental schools."

lescents committed to the school. Many schools suffer from their geographical isolation, which makes it difficult to teach the children how to live in a normal community, how to get along with other groups, how to participate in community activities, and how to use services outside the school. The isolation makes it difficult to find competent personnel interested in professional growth and in the adjustment of young persons. Despite these facts, often there is pressure by the population to remove training schools, particularly for older, aggressive boys, from the metropolitan centers in order to protect themselves from them. In the interest of the readjustment of difficult and disturbed children, the purpose of protection of the community should be considered only of secondary importance, and the construction of new schools in isolated regions should be abandoned.

One of the main obstacles to the successful rehabilitation of difficult and disturbed children is the lack of trained and competent personnel. There are, in many institutions, employees who have no proper training for their challenging job—former guards in jails or custodians without educational background or skill. Others, however, are well prepared by education, studies, and experience in child development, social work, and psychology to work with children in need of understanding and readjustment. There is in many training schools a trend toward the selection of a really qualified superintendent and staff who, as a team, will be able to help the children to overcome the difficulties in personality and behavior which brought them into the training school.

After-care (or post-institutional care, or parole) is an important factor for securing the effect of the institutional treatment of children and adolescents in training schools. As a rule, the children return to homes and neighborhoods which are far from ideal. There is no complete agreement as to who should be responsible for after-care, what the content and procedure of after-care should be, and what training is necessary for this service, nor are there, in general, sufficient funds available. After-care might be carried on by a parole officer of the training school, or by a state-wide central after-care agency for released children and adolescents, or by a child or family casework agency in the local community. Of utmost importance is the employment of well-trained personnel, which is possible only if adequate salaries, professional in-service training, and possibilities of promotion are secured.[15]

VII. YOUTH CORRECTION AUTHORITIES

After World War I, widespread juvenile delinquency had aroused the interest and concern of many legislators, judges, social workers, and sociologists. In New York, a study by Leonard V. Harrison and Pryor McNeill Grant, *Youth in the Toils,* published in 1938, criticized the destructive effect of committing adolescent youth to reformatories and prisons with hardened adult criminals. In lieu of retributive punishment, which had failed, the American Law Institute, composed of outstanding lawyers, criminologists, and judges, suggested a new approach to educating and treating youthful offenders. It published, in 1940, a model *Youth Correction Authority Act,* proposing that the state legislatures establish preventive protection and correctional treatment of young offenders. The America Law Institute suggested that a Youth Correction Authority in the state should coordinate all facilities in educational, medical, and rehabilitation work for juvenile delinquents carried on in social agencies, children's institutions, training schools, clinics, and hospitals. Whenever necessary, the authority itself should establish and operate detention homes, observation clinics, and corrective institutions.

The first state to write the suggestion of the American Law Institute into law was California.[16] In 1941, the *Youth Correction Authority Act* embodied all essential features of the model act. (In 1943, the name of the organization was changed to "Youth Authority.") Professor August Vollmer of the University of California, president of the California Prison Association, was mainly responsible for this legislative action. The Authority was authorized to offer consultation services to local communities, conduct research on the causes of

[15] Richard Clendenen, *After the Training School—What?* (Washington, D.C.: U.S. Children's Bureau, 1950). See also, Rudolph M. Wittenberg, *Adolescence and Discipline* (New York: Association Press, 1959).

[16] An analysis of the development of the California Youth Authority and its operation is presented in J. Ellingston, *op. cit.,* pp. 55-345; N. Teeters and J. Reinemann, *op. cit.,* pp. 354-368; and the valuable, recent practice in the New York City Youth Board, "How They Were Reached," *Monograph No. 2* (1954).

juvenile delinquency, and develop preventive services, diagnostic and treatment facilities.

One of the Youth Authority's major objectives is to protect society more effectively against the danger of crime by substituting for the old unsuccessful methods of retribution and punishment measures of education, correction, and rehabilitation of young offenders. The other major objective is prevention of delinquency.

The first step in rehabilitation of young offenders referred to the Youth Authority by the juvenile courts, is a clinical diagnosis in reception centers. Studies by a physician, psychiatrist, psychologist, social worker, and teacher secure an understanding of the personality and motives of the adolescent, and of the factors which brought the young person to his antisocial action. On the basis of clinical observation, the youngster then is classified according to his age, sex, mental capacities, emotional stability, aptitudes, and personal interests, and the treatment is determined upon these factors. The subsequent therapy and adjustment is carried on under a program of re-education and work assignments formulated to meet the individual needs and capacities of the youth. After adjustment of the young person in a selected institution is achieved, parole supervision is provided with careful preparation of the adolescent's return to his family or to the community. Before the release of the young offender, the Youth Authority contacts his family, his employer, and sometimes other people in the community to insure his acceptance when he returns. Parole service offers guidance for the young offender in the beginning of his new life in the community.

The second objective, delinquency prevention, is partly pursued by the systematic development of facilities for sports, recreation, and leisure-time activities for children and young persons in the community. The program includes the establishment or improvement of probation departments, police juvenile bureaus, and detention homes (in California called "juvenile halls") to secure better services for children and adolescents who get into trouble. Another aspect of the preventive activities is the creation of community councils for the coordination of the various social services to youth. Youth groups are invited to participate in recreation work in community and youth centers and other constructive cultural group action.

The Youth Authority succeeded in establishing smaller schools and forestry camps for the different age groups, with consideration of their character and behavior problems. Classification considers maturity, behavior, and vocational and personal aptitudes of the children. The necessary isolation of children in correctional schools is alleviated through contacts with the surrounding communities so that the children are prepared for their return to the family. Forestry camps for older boys acquaint the youngster with normal work habits in forestry projects, forest fire and blister rust control, road construction, and lumber mill work. Younger boys are placed in several ranch schools whose program is applied to the abilities of their age, including instruction in farming and animal husbandry.

The number of girls with delinquency records is much smaller. In the schools, the girls are divided according to age groups; special techniques are used for adjusting mentally retarded children. Recreation, art, craft, and hobby programs supplement vocational and social adjustment in class work. Home making, garden work, and housekeeping instruction is provided, but gifted girls are encouraged to prepare themselves for higher education.

The Delinquency Prevention Section assists the communities in their efforts to prevent and to reduce juvenile delinquency. Preventive work is more effective than punishment, but it has to be done on the local level in the community and neighborhood. The Youth Authority encourages community programs of social agencies, civic groups, youth groups, and individuals for sports and recreation, which divert youth from criminal actions. Consultants are sent to the counties to help in the coordination of recreational facilities with detention homes and juvenile control.

The Youth Authority Board has the final decision for the release of the youngster, but the Parole Section prepares his return to the community by securing, in advance, a job in business, industry, or agriculture, an apprentice position, or the possibility of entering school. If the family is not able to take the youth back, a foster home might be necessary. After the return of the adolescent, the parole officer is responsible for counsel, advice, and supervision until discharge of the youth from parole. Sometimes, a return to one of the institutions of the Youth Authority for further education and training is necessary.

The integrated program of the Youth Authority has resulted in broader public understanding of the modern concept of rehabilitation of maladjusted youth. It has encouraged a coordination of correctional facilities in the communities, the counties, and the state, and a working relationship between the Youth Authority, and other judicial, civic and social institutions.

Similar arrangements have been made in Minnesota which formed the Youth Conservation Commission, and in Wisconsin which established a Youth Service Commission under the Department of Public Welfare. New York has set up a City Youth Board which has engaged numerous citizens' groups and social agencies in co-ordinated action for prevention of juvenile delinquency in particularly endangered areas. In Massachusetts, the Youth Service Board deals with offenders of juvenile court age, and Texas formed a State Youth Development Council to conduct research and administer state institutions for delinquent children. It seems that the advantages of a united state authority in the field of juvenile delinquency are becoming recognized. But it might be seriously considered whether such state agencies would not be even more effective if they were coordinated under the Child Welfare Division of the state's department of public welfare. Such an organization could use all the facilities in the field of child welfare and maintain the contact with counties and com-· munities without being limited to the specific field of juvenile delinquency.

VIII. DELINQUENCY PREVENTION AND CONTROL

During the past decades, knowledge of delinquency and some of its causes has grown and proved the necessity that people in the community must understand that children are not "born to become criminals." We have seen that the causes of delinquency are complex and variable. They may be classified into three groups: individual factors, home factors, and neighborhood factors.[17]

Among the individual factors which lead a child into difficulties are biological conditions, such as glandular disorders, physical handicaps, and biological weakness, conducive to abnormal development or behavior. Mentally retarded children and youth below average

---

[17] Charlotte Elmott, *Aspects of a Community Program for Delinquency Control and Youth Protection* (Sacramento: California Youth Authority, 1945); J. Ellingston, *op. cit.*, pp. 337-342; and Gisela Konopka, "Co-ordination of Services as a Means of Delinquency Prevention," *The Annals* (March 1959), pp. 30-37.

intelligence, as well as psychopathic, nervous, unpredictable, and irresponsible adolescents easily fall prey to asocial actions. The mentally ill may endanger themselves and others. A third set of individual factors leading to delinquent behavior includes emotional instabilities caused by inferiority complexes, inner conflicts, temperamental disorders, and sex abnormalities. A fourth cause of delinquency is early childhood habits which create anxieties, truancy, run-away tendencies, and the abuse of alcohol or narcotic drugs.

Destructive influences of home life are a second group of factors leading to crime. The disorganized, divorced, or separated family in which children are mistreated or neglected causes delinquency; illegitimate children growing up without love and proper care are a part of this group. Families with quarreling, disunited parents who are in disagreement about education and discipline; living in inadequate housing without sufficient privacy for the members of the family. The lack of leisure time and recreation, and too heavy work responsibilities make children tired or rebellious and drive them into the streets. Other causes of conflict in the family may be differences of values and customs between the generations, particularly of parents of foreign descent, or the lack of spiritual and religious attachment to a church or an ethical philosophy.

The third group of neighborhood factors is particularly dangerous in "blighted areas" where the "gang leader" easily becomes the hero for young children and where "street corner associations" are the rule. The examples of drunkenness, vice, and adult crime influence the young. In rural regions, the lack of healthy recreation and of a community center may induce youths to make the "highway night spot" their gathering place with gamblers, prostitutes, and other dubious acquaintances. In such neighborhoods, schools and churches should open their meeting halls and playgrounds for sports, recreational, and cultural activities; youth organizations and citizens' groups should assume the responsibility for carrying on these programs. Harmful commercial amusements appealing to sexual drives of adolescents, unsupervised dance halls where teen-agers and adults mix and where liquor is sold, and certain movies, magazines, and books will push youths into troublesome adventures.

To counteract these dangers which lead youths to crime, a wholehearted teamwork of public and private agencies devoted to the task of crime prevention is necessary. These include schools, churches, parent-teacher associations, youth organizations, group work agencies (such as YMCA, YWCA, YMHA, Boy Scouts, Girl Scouts, and boys clubs), probation officers of the juvenile court, social workers, and policewomen and officers of juvenile bureaus of police departments. All these groups should assist parents and guardians in locating difficult children in danger of maladjustment, and in recognizing early symptoms of unhappiness, conflict, and asocial behavior.

Recent research studies show that a small percentage of multi-problem families are the source of more than 75 per cent of all juvenile delinquency. These families are characterized by desertion, alcoholism, divorce, mental illness, drug addiction, and crime. Their children tend to become asocial. Coordinated social services for these problem families, staffed by trained personnel, are able to help through counseling, casework and group work, and can prevent a good deal of deviant behavior. Child guidance and mental hygiene clinics need to have more therapeutic facilities.[18]

The development of youth activities, and social group work, as well as the strengthening of recreational facilities, promise desirable change. The cooperation of schools, churches and social agencies with the juvenile police is essential to help underprivileged and endangered children in slum areas.

An important part in delinquency control may be taken by newspapers, magazines, radio, television, and motion pictures in reporting on juvenile delinquency in terms of its causes and protection of youth, rather than stressing the sensational aspects, scandals, and a false heroism in delinquent behavior.

IX. ADULT DELINQUENCY AND SOCIAL WORK

The vast majority of adult offenders sentenced for felonies or minor crimes is kept in prisons or penitentiaries, segregated for years from normal life and left without responsibility for themselves and their families. Only a minority of younger prisoners is assigned to open institutions, such as prison farms and camps where life is less abnormal and the inmates are prepared for the return to law abiding

---

[18] Bradley Buell, *Community Planning for Human Services* (New York: Columbia University Press, 1952), pp. 334-341; New York City Youth Board, *Youth Board News,* Vol. 10, No. 1 (January 1958), pp. 1-4; and, William C. Kvaraceus and Walter B. Miller, *Delinquent Behavior* (Washington: National Education Association, 1959).

life, the goal of commitment. Only a small percentage of offenders committed to penal institutions are hardened criminals who have to be kept in prison for the protection of society. Long confinement within prison walls brings the prisoner into a state of mind which makes it rather difficult for him to accept a normal attitude toward life and toward society, although he is expected to react in this way upon his release from prison. In particular, young offenders, maladjusted or misled by gangs and older fellows, are often bedeviled by hard-boiled criminals in prison whenever they are not strictly separated from such elements, as they are in reformatories. Homosexuality is frequent in many penal institutions, a difficult problem for the administration, which is unable to provide outlets for normal drives of young, vigorous men. Much of the nervous tension, unrest, disorder, or violence is caused by sexual frustration and perversion.[19]

Penal institution are classified into prisons, penitentiaries, reformatories, and jails. They are divided into institutions of maximum, medium, and minimum security dependent upon the restraint they offer against a possible escape. Most city and county jails, prison farms, and forestry camps are of medium or minimum security type. In penal institutions religious services are offered by chaplains of the major faiths. These frequently also participate in the classification process of the inmates and assist in educational activities for the prisoners, library services, and counseling.

The honor system, used in some prisons, permits the offender to move up according to his attitude and cooperation, to live in sections which offer better opportunities to learn self-control, and to get acquainted with the outside community. The prisoner usually is assigned to work in a shop or on a farm similar to those he will be employed in after his discharge. Privileges accorded to him are based upon his adjustment to social demands, and, as a result, he accepts responsibilities for himself and for his neighbors. Open institutions are still rare, but they help to adjust the prisoner to normal life.

---

[19] For further study of adult crime and its treatment, see Harry E. Barnes and Negley K. Teeters, *New Horizons in Criminology* (Englewood Cliffs, N. J.: Prentice-Hall, Inc., 1949); Max Grunhut, *Penal Reform, A Comparative Study* (New York: Appleton-Century-Crofts, 1948); Kenyon J. Scudder, *Prisoners Are People* (New York: Doubleday, 1952); and, James V. Bennett, "Corrections," *Social Work Year Book* (1960), pp. 205-211.

The oldest, but most neglected, type of prison in our penal system is the county and city jail, of which there are about 3,900 in the United States. The jail serves as a place of detention for: (1) adult offenders after arrest, pending trial or release on bail; (2) witnesses who otherwise may not appear in court or who have asked for protection before the hearing; (3) convicted offenders before they are taken to a prison or penitentiary; and (4) offenders sentenced to jail as place of commitment. About three million citizens annually spend some time in jail. The basic problems of the jail are threefold: (1) It lacks the means of rehabilitation—it fails to understand and influence the convicted offender and, therefore, to prevent recidivism. The jail confinement does not deter many adult offenders from committing new violations of the law, nor does it change their attitudes or behavior; (2) It lacks adequate health facilities, medical and dental care, mental hygiene, and facilities for the treatment of alcoholism; (3) It costs society the wasteful expense, placed upon the public and private social agencies, of supporting the families of those confined to jail.[20]

The emotional situation of a convict is well described in the following excerpt from someone who experienced prison life:

From the very day he enters the county jail or the local prison, the prisoner is subjected to a comi-tragic, well-directed, and ruthless campaign to reduce him to the silent and lowest common level of prisondom. Once reduced, unquestioning obedience to orders and absolute subordination of individuality is the prime essential—that is, unless he has powerful friends, which the average prisoner has not. That such orders may be the spawn of archaic rules makes no difference whatsoever.

He is made to feel from the moment he enters the prison gates that he is an outcast, unclean—that he is but one of so many animals to be counted at certain times of the day and herded into place. He would not be human unless every atom of resentment, every antisocial instinct smouldered in sullen hatred.[21]

Under such circumstances, the usual results of a prison or jail experience on the prisoner are not rehabilitation, readjustment, and change of basic attitude toward society, but a retardation in maturity (similar to a feeling of being suspended in time) and frequently

---

[20] Myrl E. Alexander, "Let's Look at Our Jails," *Federal Probation* (September 1952), pp. 14-19; and *Jail Administration* (Springfield, Ill.: Thomas, 1957).

[21] "The Prisoner Speaks," *Annals,* Vol. 157 (September 1931), pp. 138-140.

actual regression. This is brought about because the prisoner experiences the confinement as a replica of his child dependency. For this reason, other means than prison and penitentiary confinement have to be sought to solve the social problem of crime. A stimulating account of the Chino Institution for Men, an open institution for adult offenders that prepares them for the return to the community and to decent civilian life, is given in Kenyon J. Scudder's, *Prisoners Are People,* which is recommended to the reader interested in understanding prison problems.[22]

The most advanced type of penal institutions is the reformatory, primarily intended for the reception of young adult male offenders and of offenders sentenced for the first time. It is frequently limited to persons up to twenty-five or thirty years of age. The Elmira (New York) reformatory served as the first example for this type of institution. At present, there are one or more reformatories in every state. Some of these institutions are built on the cottage plan, permitting individual treatment. Several reformatories, however, are still using the cell-block system and mass treatment; to help prevent the inmates from escaping some have watch towers that house sharpshooting guards. Progressive reformatories develop a conscientious program of clinical diagnosis, classification, and systematic adjustment similar to the process of treatment of juvenile delinquents.

Most penitentiaries, prisons, and reformatories are equipped with prison industries, including several types of workshops with modern machinery, as well as facilities for agricultural work. Usually the agricultural products and goods manufactured in prison industry are used exclusively in public institutions, such as hospitals, schools, and correctional facilities, in order to avoid competition with "free labor" and private industries on the open market ("state use system").

The modern concept of rehabilitation makes it necessary to give up the outdated approach of retaliation against the offender to take revenge for his attack against society. One of the essential elements in developing the reformatory into an institution of rehabilitation is to supplement the present technical, industrial facilities with pro-

---

[22] Robert M. Lindner, *Stone Walls and Men* (New York: Odyssey Press, 1946), pp. 418-422; and, K. Scudder, *op. cit.,* pp. 5-6, 273-282. See also Giles Mayfair and Dorrick Singleton, *The Offenders: The Case Against Legal Vengeance* (New York: Simon & Schuster, 1957); and, Gresham M. Sykes, *Society of Captives* (Princeton, N. J.: Princeton University Press, 1958).

grams for personal adjustment to emphasize therapy rather than punishment. Rehabilitation is, in fact, neither punishment nor retaliation, but social adjustment, education, and preparation of the offender for living a normal citizen's life. In order to achieve such re-education, social casework in correctional institutions is indispensable. We recognize that casework services are not available in many penal institutions, but at least the need for casework with prisoners is theoretically accepted. Offenders in prison or jail have, in general, a deep need for personal attention and help.

The nature of the penal institution certainly makes individual work with prisoners rather difficult, and it sets definite limits to the personal contact, which is the essential tool of social casework. In spite of these limitations, there are possibilities for individual work with the convict, provided that skilled, competent social workers are available. A number of state prisons and reformatories, and most Federal penal institutions, have social service departments with trained personnel, which offer the inmates not only medical care, psychological tests, general education and vocational training, but also social services. These facilities are important for achieving the goal of rehabilitation of the prisoner.

Intelligent wardens and superintendents of penal institutions accept the social worker as a vital part in the team of institutional personnel. There is no doubt that walls and bars of the prison are not conducive for letting the inmate cooperate in counseling and casework. But the social worker still can function successfully in such an authoritative setting if he is skilled enough to overcome the barriers which are erected by the prison environment. This applies to work with inmates who express the desire to consult the social worker, or who are referred to him by the medical officer, the psychologist, or by the classification clinic, when intensive casework seems necessary.[23]

In fact, the best time for the social worker to make contact with a prisoner is the period when he has just entered the prison or jail. The initial shock of the first day or night in the prison and of meeting with the other inmates makes the prisoner bewildered and scared and often hateful of everyone. The social worker will give him a chance to discuss the hard realities of prison life, his possibilities for his future, and his educational and vocational opportunities, limited as

---

[23] Elliot Studt, "Worker-Client Authority Relationship in Social Work," *Social Work,* Vol. 4, No. 1 (January 1959), pp. 18-28.

they might seem to the prisoner. The social worker has to determine how much help the inmate needs, and whether he is able to use social casework assistance at this time. Frequently the prisoner might hide his real feelings, and the social worker has to understand that he needs time before he is able to take advantage of casework service. The social worker certainly should not overwhelm him with suggestions and offers of assistance until the prisoner is really asking for his service. Sometimes he will need advice and help with specific problems, such as contact with his family and friends, arrangements of obligations he left behind, changes in the prison, assignment to a specific training unit, or transfer to other living quarters.

The main task of the social worker in prison is to help the convict in his own attitude towards his crime, sentence, and confinement. He will try to help him clarify his thinking about his own action, change his attitude toward society, and develop new plans for his future life. In this respect, the social worker might well be helpful in advice about the use of the prison library, vocational training and studies, as well as adaptation to the rules of the prison.

Finally, the social worker will have a substantial role in preparing the convict for his release and his return to the community. To this end, he helps him to take an honest attitude toward prison regulations, toward the request for work, and also attempts to explain to him that an important element for permitting his release is a new outlook toward society and its laws. Often, it is difficult for the social worker to convince the prisoner that he himself has the responsibility for his change and readjustment. It is easier for the convict to conform on the surface with official rules, but to remain unchanged in his mind. The social worker tries to bring the prisoner to the insight that, after release, his chance of success requires a definite change in his behavior, which, alone, results from a positive attitude towards society.

X. PAROLE

Parole may be defined as the release of a prisoner under supervision before the expiration of his sentence, with the provision that he may be returned to the prison if he violates the conditions of his parole. Whereas probation, as we saw, is a judicial decision of the court, parole is an administrative act usually made either by the parole board or the board of directors of the prison.

Parole was first developed in a convict colony in Australia in 1837, and was adapted in England and Ireland in 1840 by Sir Walter Crofton, the director of the Irish Convict Prisons. In the United States, the first parole system was introduced at Elmira Reformatory (New York) in 1877. Since that time, all states have developed programs of parole.

Parole requires that the prisoner be returned to the prison to finish his sentence if he commits a new crime or a serious technical violation of his parole. Examples are: failing to report to the parole officer, changing his job or home, leaving the community without permission of the parole authority, or indicating that he might commit another criminal act.

The decision on parole, which is of such vital importance for the prisoner, should be based upon an impartial, careful investigation of his personality and conduct. It should consider reliable information about the prisoner's background, his life experiences, family and neighborhood, his health, and the situation that will confront him after his release. In preparation of the release, the parole officer tries to ascertain whether the family of the prisoner and his neighbors will welcome him back and assist him in adjusting himself to normal life. He will enlist cooperation of social agencies, or other groups which may help the prisoner in this adjustment, especially in obtaining employment, so that he can support his family, maintain his self-respect and become, again, part of the community.

The supervision of the released prisoner by the parole officer is a responsible job. The case load of the parole officer should not be so large that it prohibits conscientious supervision. It requires trained and skilled personnel acquainted with human behavior, social casework, and conditions in correctional institutions, plus the ability to encourage the parolee to assume the responsibility for his life in the community. The parole officer also has to interpret the parolee's situation to the community, and he must be familiar with laws and regulations. At present, many parole officers do not meet these requirements, but it is hoped that courts and parole authorities will increasingly require adequate education and professional training for parole officers who carry such a heavy responsibility.[24]

---

[24] Kenyon J. Scudder, "Prisons Will Not Solve Our Crime Problem," *Federal Probation* (March 1954), pp. 32-39; and, L. E. Olin, *Selection for Parole: A Manual for Parole Prediction* (New York: Russell Sage Foundation, 1951).

It is essential that a workable parole system permit an indeterminate sentence so that the parole authority may set the date and the conditions of parole according to the progress made by each prisoner.

The advantages of parole are that the public receives protection through the supervision of the parolee, that it gives the prisoner an incentive for good behavior, and that it sends him into the community with the goal of being a law-abiding citizen, rather than with the intention of settling a score with society. Parole permits recommendation for release when favorable conditions are found and acts as a bridge between the abnormal environment of the segregated prison and the life under personal responsibility in the community. Parole makes our system of treatment of the offender less expensive than does long detainment in penal institutions and offers an opportunity to correct mistakes or injustices which have been made in judgment.[25]

The particular difficulty of parole lies in the fact that the parolee, after serving part of his sentence in a prison or penitentiary, returns to the community with a great handicap. Family, neighbors, employer, and co-workers learn that he has "served time." In addition to this shame, the parolee is pressed by the threat of being returned to the prison for violation of parole conditions. Sometimes parolees are returned to the prison for minor transgressions, such as forgetting to report to the parole officer, changing a job, drinking, or marrying without special permission. There is some question whether minor violations should not be overlooked by a capable parole officer and the return ordered only if a serious offense is committed. Often parolees are very lonely and looking for companionship. The parole officer assists them in finding connections, but in most instances he has to supervise so many people with different needs that it is hard for him to help the individual efficiently.

There are about 42,000 persons released each year on parole from penal institutions in the United States, and the number who have to be returned to the prison varies between 15 and 40 per cent of this group.[26]

---

[25] Sanford Bates, *Prisons and Beyond* (New York: Macmillan, 1936), pp. 250-251.

[26] Miriam Van Waters, "Adult Offenders," *Social Work Year Book* (1951), p. 41; Frank T. Flynn, "Courts and Social Work," *Social Work Year Book*

Prisoners under parole or after final discharge are assisted in many larger communities by private organizations which provide casework and usually material assistance. The oldest of these organizations is the Pennsylvania Prison Society. The social workers of these voluntary agencies help the released prisoner, particularly if the prisoner is a woman, by giving counsel, clothes, and financial assistance, and securing employment. Their work frequently includes the re-establishment of constructive relations with the family of the former convict. Private organizations have in this respect the advantage of being less distrusted by the offenders and his family, and being more flexible in their policies of assistance and help.

Prison societies, which sometimes assume a neutral name, such as "Service League," assist in gaining the cooperation of the community to give a hand to the returned prisoner and to offer him a chance for normal work and life. They provide information services and conduct research and studies and participate in suggestions for the improvement of legislation and penal institutions. Especially well known in this reform work is the Osborne Association, which for many years has organized important research and surveys of correctional institutions in the United States; it has stimulated penal legislation of the Federal government and the states. The American Prison Association, founded in 1870, also improves by forums, conferences, and professional proposals the standards of our penal institutions. In addition to social workers, probation and parole officers, also religious groups and civic organizations advocate further reform of the treatment of the adult offenders and the introduction of methods of effective rehabilitation in our correctional system.

Selected Bibliography

*Aichhorn, August, *Wayward Youth.* New York: Viking Press, Inc., 1952,

Alexander, Franz, and William Healy, *Roots of Crime.* New York: Knopf, 1935.

Banay, Ralph S., *Youth in Despair.* New York: Coward, 1948.

(1954), pp. 150-154; *National Prisoner Statistics* (July 1959), p. 2; and, David Dressler, *Practice and Theory of Probation and Parole* (New York: Columbia University Press, 1959).

*Barnes, Harry Elmer, and Negley K. Teeters, *New Horizons in Criminology*, 2nd ed. Englewood Cliffs, N.J.: Prentice-Hall, Inc., 1953.

*Bates, Sanford, *Prisons and Beyond*. New York: Macmillan, 1936.

Block, Herbert, and Arthur Nedderhoffer, *The Gang*. New York: Philosophical Library, 1958.

Blumer, Herbert, *Movies, Delinquency, and Crime*. New York: Macmillan, 1933.

Cavan, Ruth S., *Criminology*. New York: Crowell, 1955.

Chute, Charles L., and Marjorie Bell, *Crime, Courts, and Probation*. New York: Macmillan, 1956.

*Cohen, Albert K., *Delinquent Boys: The Culture of the Gang*. Glencoe, Illinois: Free Press, 1951.

Cohen, Frank J., *Children in Trouble*. New York: Norton, 1952.

*Deutsch, Albert, *Our Rejected Children*. Boston: Little, 1950.

*Ellingston, John R., *Protecting Our Children From Criminal Careers*. Englewood Cliffs, N.J.: Prentice-Hall, Inc., 1948.

Flynn, Frank T., "Courts and Social Work," *Social Work Year Book* (1954), pp. 149-154.

Furman, Sylvan S., *Reaching the Unreached*. New York: New York City Youth Board, 1952.

Glueck, Sheldon and Eleanor T. Glueck, *After-Conduct of Discharged Offenders*. New York: Macmillan, 1945.

————, *Delinquents in the Making: Paths to Prevention*. New York: Harper, 1952.

————, *Unraveling Juvenile Delinquency*. New York: Commonwealth Fund, 1950.

Goldberg, Harriet L., *Child Offenders: A Study in Diagnosis and Treatment*. New York: Grune, 1948.

Hakem, Michael, "A Critique of the Psychiatric-Approach to Crime and Correction," *Law and Contemporary Problems* (Autumn 1958), pp. 650-682.

Hassler, Alfred, *Diary of a Self-Made Convict*. Chicago: Regnery, 1954.

Healy, William, and Augusta F. Bronner, *New Light on Delinquency*. New Haven: Yale University Press, 1936.

*Hollingshead, August B., *Elmtown's Youth*. New York: Wiley, 1949.

*Lindner, Robert M., *Stone Walls and Men*. New York: Odyssey Press, 1946.

MacDonald, John M., *Psychiatry and the Criminal*. Springfield, Ill.: Thomas, 1958.

Neumeyer, Martin H., *Juvenile Delinquency in Modern Society*. New York: Van Nostrand, 1955.

*Pigeon, Helen D., *et al., Principles and Methods in Dealing with Offenders.* New York: National Probation Association, 1949.

*Polier, Justine W., *Everyone's Children: Nobody's Child.* New York: Scribner, 1941.

Reckless, Walter C., *The Crime Problem.* New York: Appleton-Century-Crofts, Inc., 1955.

*Redl, Fritz, *Understanding Children's Behavior.* New York: Columbia University Press, 1949.

*————, and David Wineman, *Children Who Hate.* Chicago: Free Press, 1951.

*Reinemann, John Otto, "Probation and the Juvenile Delinquent," *The Annals,* Vol. 261 (January 1949), pp. 109-119.

*Scudder, Kenyon T., *Prisoners Are People.* New York: Doubleday, 1952.

Sellin, Thorsten (editor), "Prisons in Transformation," *The Annals,* Vol. 293 (May 1954).

Shaw, Clifford R., and H. D. McKay, *Juvenile Delinquency and Urban Areas.* Chicago: University of Chicago Press, 1942.

Smith, A. Delafield, *The Right to Life: A Legal Approach to Society's Responsibility to the Individual.* Chapel Hill: University of North Carolina Press, 1955.

Studt, Elliot, "Worker-Client Authority Relationship in Social Work," *Social Work,* Vol. 4, No. 1 (January 1959), pp. 18-28.

Sutherland, E. H., and Donald Cressey, *Principles of Criminology.* Philadelphia: Lippincott, 1955.

Tannenbaum, Frank, *Crime and the Community.* New York: Ginn, 1938.

Tappan, Paul, *Contemporary Correction.* New York: McGraw, 1951.

*Teeters, Negley K., and John Otto Reinemann, *The Challenge of Delinquency.* Englewood Cliffs, N.J.: Prentice-Hall, Inc., 1950.

Van Waters, Miriam, *Youth in Conflict.* New York: Republic Printing Co., 1927.

Weeks, Herbert A., *Youthful Offenders at Highfields: An Evaluation of the Effects of the Short-Term Treatment of Delinquent Boys.* Ann Arbor: University of Michigan Press, 1958.

Whyte, William F., *Street Corner Society.* Chicago: University of Chicago Press, 1943.

Young, Pauline V., *Social Treatment in Probation and Delinquency,* 2nd ed. New York: McGraw, 1952.

14.

Recreation and
Leisure-Time Activities

I. HISTORICAL AND FUNCTIONAL DEVELOPMENT

Before the Industrial Revolution, the masses of the people in all countries toiled long hours in order to earn their livelihood. Only a small number of well-to-do persons of the ruling classes were able to enjoy leisure time. On Sundays and holidays, people gathered in the church for religious services and after service at the village square for talks, folk singing, dancing, and games, whenever tradition and mores allowed such enjoyment. Here in the United States, Calvinist and Puritan asceticism disapproved of "idle play" as sinful and as a waste of time for adults.

The impact of industrialization with the increasing use of water, steam, gas and electric power, and machinery, as well as the recent introduction of automation, have resulted in fundamental changes in the working methods and the ways of living. The mechanical production of most goods requires less manual effort and can be achieved in shorter working hours. It engages the worker, however, only in a limited part of the whole production process, lacks in variety of activities, particularly on the assembly line, and frequently makes the worker indifferent to the quality and value of the finished product. In the private household, as well as in various institutions, and

451

restaurants and hotels, considerable time is saved by the use of such mechanical appliances as gas, and electric stoves, refrigerators, washing machines, and vacuum cleaners. Health protection and sanitary standards have been raised by modern technical equipment in hospitals and clinics which also saves human energy and allows more efficient medical treatment and scientific research. The large-scale production of ready-made textiles and clothing, canned and frozen foods and bakery goods free the family of many time-consuming tasks of former generations. The widespread use of the family car makes the members of the family today more mobile than ever before.

In the beginning of the machine age, there was anxiety that man would be deprived of employment and lose his creative capacities if mechanical devices were used. But, today we understand the advantages of mass production in agriculture and industry, and of the precision machines which free men from drudgery in the production of goods and protect them from injury and often untimely death. The working week of five days, with shorter daily working hours, gives the working man and woman more leisure time for recreational activities and restful relaxation.

Recreation may be defined as an activity which gives joyful, satisfying experiences, and an opportunity for creative self-expression.[1] Relaxation, in the meaning of a "creative pause," is a period of peaceful silence, an anticipating readiness for renewed activity. For example, the breathing pause is not just a passive keeping still and stopping of breathing, but that part of the natural rhythm in which the opening up to a full easy inhalation is prepared. Relaxation restores the natural breathing rhythm, and the physical and mental balance and vigor. Applied relaxation brings release from nervous strain and fatigue caused by overtenseness and gives a feeling of ease and aliveness in work and play. Recreation combined with a healthful relaxation assures enjoyment of leisure time.

Watching children at play, the adult wonders about the amount

---

[1] Harold D. Meyer and Charles K. Brightbill, *Community Recreation* (Englewood Cliffs, N. J.: Prentice-Hall, Inc., 1956), pp. 21, 24-28; Robert Dubin, *Human Relations in Administration* (Englewood Cliffs, N. J.: Prentice-Hall, Inc., 1957), pp. 229-230; George D. Butler, "Recreation," *Social Work Yearbook* (1957), pp. 482-489; and, Paul F. Douglas, "Recreation in the Age of Automation," *The Annals,* Vol. 313 (September 1957).

of energy they spend without being exhausted. The older adult person, as a rule, does not have the agility and the quick physical and mental reaction of the young. Therefore, community recreation for children and young people must be of a different nature than that for older citizens. It is especially important for the younger generation to have outlets for their physical energy in sports. Playgrounds keep them off the streets and offer them not only something to do in their spare time but also something to enjoy. The adolescent needs other activities as well as the "work-out" to absorb his growing strength, to develop his skills and mental capacities. Competitive games, physical culture, and active sports develop not only physical fitness, but also a sense of fair play, of order, discipline, and responsibility. They strengthen the capacity of youth to adjust to changing life conditions, help him to overcome emotional disturbances and irrational behavior and to develop intelligent, logical judgment and social attitudes.

To become a well-rounded mature personality, youth also needs educational and cultural activities, such as are offered in many communities by organized youth groups. Discussion groups assist young persons in broadening their knowledge, to think logically, and to understand personal problems. The members of such youth groups profit not only from the knowledge that they acquire or the skill they learn, but from the confidence in their abilities. At the same time, they gain from participation in a group of their own age and they expand their interest beyond their own self to their fellow men.[2]

Recreational activities are as diverse as the personal interests and ambitions of the people who participate in them and are based upon their ethnic, religious, and cultural backgrounds. Social legislation which restricts child labor, collective bargaining agreements between industries and labor unions, statutes on maximum working hours, and legal retirement provisions secure for young and older persons an increasing amount of leisure time. Constructive use of the available free time becomes most essential.

Leisure time may be spent for individual study and education, for social activities, or for pleasurable entertainment, but sometimes

---

[2] August B. Hollingshead, "The Organization of Leisure-Time Services for Youth," Herman D. Stein and Richard A. Cloward (editors), *Social Perspectives on Behavior* (Glencoe, Ill.: Free Press, 1958), pp. 456-469; and, Arthur Williams, "Recreation," *Social Work Year Book* (1960), pp. 498-507.

all three goals may be combined. Among the educational pursuits, we find reading as a means of learning and stimulation of thought. Creative work in the arts, music, and literature plays an important part in educational leisure-time activities. Art work satisfies the individual's desire for self-expression, and, at the same time, contributes to the enjoyment of others. Hobbies give individual and social gratifications, for instance handicraft work, amateur photography, and gardening.

Dramatic performances, pageantry, choral concerts and symphonies are frequently sponsored by schools, churches, social clubs, and recreation departments. Sports, athletics, and competitive games are promoted by colleges, schools, youth organizations, and clubs.

Some individuals and groups may prefer outdoor recreation such as camping, swimming and hiking, fishing and hunting. Sailing and motor boating have become increasingly more popular in recent years. In 1958, for example, 4 per cent of all American citizens owned a sailing vessel or motorboat. Unfortunately, boating accidents also have dangerously multiplied, and sailing and motorboats should be driven only by persons who have learned to use them and who comply with water and boatcraft rules. Traveling, sight-seeing and nature studies often appeal to the young as well as to the adult.[3] A very popular social leisure-time activity of all ages has always been social and square dancing.

Social meetings of religious, cultural, political, and civic groups, further the interchange and clarification of ideas, sometimes also the promotion of educational, civic, or political causes. Watching ball games and the races, particularly our "national sport," baseball, are the most popular activities. Listening to the radio, records, and television also play an essential role in passive recreation today.

Women are especially active in cultural, educational, and welfare community programs, serve as volunteers often in leading positions, promote civic, religious, health, and welfare movements, and support Community Chest, United Fund, and other charity campaigns. Women's clubs, such as the League of Women Voters, advocate social reform and legislation and contribute to the improvement of schools, hospitals, clinics, and other public services. Other women's clubs have

---

[3] Martin H. Neumeyer and Esther S. Neumeyer, *Leisure and Recreation* (New York: Ronald, 1958), pp. 204-218.

bridge parties, hobby, beauty, and fashion shows, and welfare bazaars.[4]

II. ORGANIZATION OF RECREATION

Recreation, in its great variety, is made possible through systematic efforts of recreation and park commissions of the Federal, state, county, and city governments, and private social agencies, churches, labor unions, youth agencies, industries, and other civic organizations. However, commercial recreation and mass entertainment also are characteristic features of our industrial society. Their main media are radio, television, motion pictures, newspapers, journals, and periodicals. Parents and educators are much concerned with the destructive influence of certain comic books and horror stories and some radio and television programs which describe brutalities, crimes, and obscenities and seem to glorify lawlessness, shooting, killing, and gangsterism. Among commercial mass entertainments, ball games, horse races, wrestling matches, amusement parks, county fairs, and dance halls attract the largest crowds. In general, commercial recreation leads only to passive attendance, while social recreation tends to encourage active participation.

Radio and television are heard and watched by a large proportion of the population of the United States. Programs—with a few exceptions—are sponsored by commercial firms. Daily and weekly newspapers, journals, and magazines have a circulation of more than 140,000,000 in our country and influence the opinion and the taste of the population.[5]

In metropolitan areas, theaters and playhouses stage dramatic, dance, musical and opera performances, and the concert halls present orchestral and individual concerts, usually for a seasonal period. No public subsidies are given for these cultural activities, as in Europe. Circus, vaudevilles, and various shows and exhibitions, are part of county fairs and rural festivities. The motion picture theaters, however, have become the largest mass entertainment in our country. About 19,000 permanent cinemas operate in the United States, and

[4] John G. Galbraith, *The Affluent Society* (Boston: Houghton, 1958), pp. 334-336; and, Margaret Mead, "The Patterns of Leisure in Contemporary American Culture," *Annals* (September 1957), pp. 11-15.
[5] Neumeyer, *op. cit.*, pp. 325 and 326.

their weekly visitors are estimated at about 42,000,000 persons. Commercial dance halls with professional bands and orchestras invite to ballroom dancing and less frequently to square and folk dances.

Before the turn of this century, only a few recreational facilities were established in some large cities. During the twentieth century, many more facilities have been created and large masses of our population have gained the opportunity to enjoy their leisure time. When the organized labor movement was fighting for higher wages for the workers, it also fought to shorter daily working hours and free week-ends. The movement secured for workers and employees the long desired leisure time. Due to these social changes, recreation has been accepted as a legitimate responsibility of the community. Recreation programs have been expanded from services to children and adolescents, to programs for all age groups, including special facilities for handicapped people, such as the blind, crippled children, and senior citizens.

Recreation services are still offered by many private organizations, but these are, more and more, coming to be regarded as obligations of governmental authorities.[6] City planners in urban and rural development consider recreational facilities as being equally as vital as provisions for schools, hospitals, and adequate communication. Frequently, community recreation is administered by a special commission, or by boards of education, or park authorities. School properties, gymnasiums, playgrounds, and swimming pools are used for sports, gymnastics, games, contests, and festive performances. Some large industrial establishments provide leisure time opportunities for their workers and their families and a few even employ trained recreation leaders to organize sports and social affairs.

Municipal recreation centers operate under the direct guidance and control of the local population. Following democratic principles, they offer the best opportunity for the whole population to participate in healthy sports, games, and cultural leisure time activities. Thus, even those families who cannot afford the membership fees of private societies and sport clubs or the price for commercial entertainment and amusements, have access to recreation facilities. Public recreation also is, as a rule, supervised by trained leaders who are not

---

[6] George D. Butler, *Introduction to Community Recreation*, 3rd ed., Chapters 1, 3, and 6 (New York: McGraw, 1959).

concerned with fees or the profits of the establishment, but in the health and welfare of the people.

Numerous private recreation agencies pursue the same ideals in the interest of the population and maintain high standards of service to the community. Such organizations are, for example, the YWCA's, the YMCA's, settlement houses, the National American Red Cross, Girls Scouts, Camp Fire Girls, Boys Scouts, and, in rural areas, the 4-H Clubs and the Future Farmers of America. There are also many other religious and non-sectarian organizations, cultural and athletic societies, and women's clubs for youth and young adults which carry on recreational activities without profit motive. They are supported by membership fees, donations, and allocations from the local Community Chest or United Fund campaign. In rural regions, recreation facilities often are still limited, but the extension programs of the Federal Department of Agriculture, of state agencies, universities and colleges, and of the National Recreation Association are encouraging the expansion of recreation activities and the training of recreation leaders to work in agricultural areas.

Municipal, county, state, and Federal agencies are assuming an increasing responsibility for the establishment of camping grounds which offer inexpensive vacation opportunities. Camping has become widely accepted as a leisure time activity. It makes it possible for the urban population, especially children and youth, to return during vacations to nature and to enjoy primitive out-door living. Some social welfare and health agencies sponsor special camps for handicapped, retarded, and underprivileged children and convalescent camps for adults. Organized camps for healthy children, primarily for the age groups from nine to fourteen years, are an essential part of modern recreation; but many of them charge high fees and thus are not accessible to children of families with low income. There are about 12,000 resident vacation camps in the United States, receiving more than 4,000,000 children and adolescents a year. The majority open only for the summer months, but some operate on a year-round basis.[7]

---

[7] Hugh W. Ransom, "Camping," *Social Work Year Book* (1957), pp. 110-115; Kenneth B., and Susan H. Webb, *Summer Magic* (New York: Association Press, 1950); Ralph L. Kolodny and Virginia M. Burns, "Group Work

In the field of recreation, the relationship between governmental and private social agencies, which assume responsibility for leisure time activities, is not clearly defined. It is different in various states and communities. Though municipal authorities in urban centers assume, increasingly, the main responsibility for the establishment and maintenance of playgrounds and sport and athletic opportunities, there remain important tasks for private organizations in this field. The remarkable growth of public recreation under the leadership of municipal authorities, raises the question about whether or not private recreation agencies merely supplement governmental activities in this area. There is reason, however, to believe that recreation agencies of a private nature can still perform a constructive and necessary function. They could offer opportunities not available through public agencies, to develop high standards of performance, to serve as models for public recreation, and in training professional leaders in this field.[8] Some of the distinctive advantages of private recreation agencies, are their ability to make experiments in ways to pursue more constructive leisure time activities, and their greater freedom from official pressure which permits them to delve into "controversial issues."

In metropolitan regions, easily accessible day camps supplement the facilities of frequently overcrowded resident vacation camps. Day camps make it possible for younger children to participate who cannot easily adjust to life away from home, but who profit from play in the open air and relaxation in natural surroundings. Such day camps have the advantage of keeping the children in close contact with the family to which they return in the evening, and of being less expensive.

Camp counselors have a responsible social and educational job. They have to understand each child as an individual and have to be concerned with his personal needs, his health, and safety, as much as with his relationship to the other children in the group, and to

---

with Physically and Emotionally Handicapped Children in a Summer Camp," *Social Work With Groups* (New York: National Association of Social Workers, 1958); and, Elton B. McNeil (editor), "Therapeutic Camping for Disturbed Youth," *Journal of Social Issues,* Vol. XIII, No. 1 (1957), pp. 1-62.

[8] Ray Johns and David F. de Marche, *Community Organization and Agency Responsibility* (New York: Association Press, 1951), pp. 67-69; and, William Schwartz, "Camping," *Social Work Year Book* (1960), pp. 112-117.

the other members of the camp staff.[9] Camp leaders guide the children groups in physical as well as spiritual and educational activities and help them to make their stay an enjoyable, constructive experience and a period of social adjustment. The educational functions which vacation camps perform become more important with the steadily growing urbanization of our country.

III. SOCIAL IMPLICATIONS OF RECREATION

A more systematic and constructive spending of leisure time for the aged is now more necessary than in former generations. Every year, a larger number of men and women retire. More public and private resources for recreation of senior citizens are needed. Many retired people are quite able to volunteer their services to religious, cultural, educational, civic organizations, and to social agencies, and will find satisfaction to see that they can continue to be useful members of the community. Even if they have no economic worries, retired people who are in good physical and mental health want more, during old age, than just a place to live and rest in the sun. They want to make use of their previous experiences, of their knowledge and skills, for the benefit of the younger generation. Recreation for senior citizens, therefore, has to provide more than hobbies, radio, and TV to fill the hours of the aged; it has to take care of their physical well-being providing sufficient rest and relaxation, and has to offer them an opportunity to cultivate their creative abilities and to continue their cultural and civic interests. It is important that the retired person finds homogeneous companionship and new tasks so that he feels useful and respected in his community. The science of gerontology is making remarkable progress, but there is still need for further exploration and research to learn how to protect the health of the aged, and how to use more efficiently their skills, abilities, and social contributions.

Although a large proportion of our people takes advantage of recreation facilities, there are substantial differences in the way leisure time is spent in different regions of the United States and among the

---

[9] Characteristic illustrations are presented in Gisela Konopka, "The Method of Social Group Work," *Concepts and Methods of Social Work* (Englewood Cliffs, N. J.: Prentice-Hall, Inc., 1958), pp. 187-189, 190-191, and 195-196.

different social classes of the population. An interesting illustration of this fact is presented by Hollingshead and Redlich in their survey of New Haven, Connecticut.[10] They found that executives of banks and large industrial concerns, wealthy industrialists, and professional men, who represent the upper social class, and their families, mainly use restricted clubs. They play golf, and tennis, swim, dance, play cards, and attend social affairs and parties; their women are active on church and welfare agencies' boards, support youth and religious organizations, and help in charity drives. The upper-middle class consists of businessmen, employees in semi-executive positions, professional people without first-rank status and in salaried positions. The members of this class belong to neighborhood clubs, fraternities, and service societies, as well as to churches which enable them to engage in leisure-time activities similar to those used by the members of the upper class, but not within the same restricted clubs and circles. The third group, the "middle middle-class" includes the employees of commercial and industrial firms, shop owners, independent craftsmen, public servants, and professional people of modest income. The members of the middle middle-class and their families belong to churches, veterans societies, less exclusive service clubs, and other civic or occupational associations. They frequent general community recreation facilities more than do the two wealthier classes and are often to be seen on playgrounds, sport and athletic fields, swimming pools and community centers. The fourth group, the "lower-middle class," in the Hollingshead-Redlich study, includes nearly one-half of the entire local population. This group identifies itself either with the "middle-class" or with the "working class." It consists of semi-skilled employees, clerical and sales workers, and skilled manual workers. Among the women of this group, about 37 per cent classify themselves as active members of the labor force. This class, with their families, spends a good deal of its spare time on "do-it-yourself activities" in gardening, improvement of the house and the furniture, making dresses and curtains, and house equipment. The members of this class belong to labor unions and churches, but rarely to social or service clubs; they and their families use public recreation facilities, playgrounds, swimming halls, and community

---

[10] August B. Hollingshead and Fredrick C. Redlich, M.D., *Social Class and Mental Illness: A Community Study.* (New York: Wiley, 1958), pp. 66-135.

centers widely, and attend competitive games. The members of all levels of the "lower class," are mostly unskilled or only semi-skilled laborers. Many of them are aged people on relief, recipients of old-age insurance benefits, as well as sick and handicapped people. Among the younger members, some are unemployed. Those working, are employed in low-paid jobs, often in non-unionized shops and factories. The members of this class, and their families, do not belong to service organizations, veterans societies or social clubs. Their leisure time activities tend to be spent spontaneously, without previous planning. They scarcely use community recreation facilities, but pursue cheap commercial amusements, a beer hall or a neighborhood bar. Their children spill out into the streets to play in alleys and streets, in parking lots and public parks. Older children of this class and teen-agers go to public beaches, roller-skating rinks and amusement parks. Some join street gangs in the downtown area and are in danger of becoming involved in petty offenses which may lead to juvenile delinquency. Many families of the lower class resent their depressed economic status, their lack of funds and their poor housing conditions; they are hostile to the authorities and to the privileged classes of society, and they refuse to join the leisure time activities of the more privileged groups of society.

Hollingshead and Redlich emphasize that the findings of their research are not conclusive for other parts of the United States. In other cities, for instance New York, Chicago, and Philadelphia, settlement houses and neighborhood centers provide recreation facilities particularly for the youth of the "lower class" and attempt to serve this group and various minority groups, such as Negros, Mexicans, Puerto Ricans, and Orientals, who are not fully accepted into other recreation activities. This applies particularly to the Southern states where segregation in public schools is applied in recreation activities as well. The movement to achieve educational integration will certainly expand to include all fields of recreation in the future.

IV. LEADERSHIP IN RECREATION

In the field of recreation, volunteers play a very important role, more so than they do in most other areas of social welfare. Volunteers serve on boards of private recreation agencies, as well as on park and recreation commissions and boards of education. They influence the policies and programs of leisure time activities. Especially important, however, is the direct work volunteers perform on playgrounds, sport fields, swimming pools and in community and recreation centers. Among these volunteers, are members of youth groups, of religious and civic organizations, students, teachers, and members of parent-teacher associations and of service clubs. The need for volunteers is especially great because most recreation programs can employ only a limited number of paid leaders, and have to rely upon the assistance of volunteers therefore, due to the lack of adequate funds.

Professional leadership in the field of recreation is not based upon a unified theory. The YWCA's, the Girls Scouts, Jewish community centers, and some recreation departments of boards of education are interested in employing leaders who have had graduate social work education. Other agencies, such as the YMCA's and the Boys Scouts, have engaged personnel from George Williams College in Chicago, or special institutions, such as the Training Center in Scouting, or from the field of education. In certain recreation circles, there is the desire to ask for specialized training in recreation in colleges and universities, in connection with courses in physical education.[11] Trained social group workers are rarely found in rural programs, the 4-H Clubs or the "Future Farmers of America." Graduate students experienced in social work, with emphasis on group work and community organization, qualify well for leadership in the recreation field.

Personal requirements for positions in the field of recreation are a wholesome, dynamic, and outgoing personality. Good intelligence, mental alertness, and sound judgment also are required. Great devotion and a natural inclination to work with people, combined with a relaxed, cheerful disposition, and a well-controlled temperament are essential. The recreation leader's educational background should include physical education, sociology, social work, psychology, and knowledge of history and political science. Practical experience in recreation activities and in related fields are desirable. Also, a general skillfulness and flexibility is needed to handle unexpected situations.

A recreation leader, well prepared for service in this field, is of

---

[11] Neumeyer, *op. cit.*, pp. 430-440; Harold L. Wilensky and Charles N. Lebeaux, *Industrial Society and Social Welfare* (New York: Russell Sage Foundation, 1958), p. 297.

vital importance for the entire recreation program because his personality has far-reaching influence on the development of physical health and mental integrity of our youth and on the well-being of our grown-up population. It is not sufficient that we build more, and better-equipped recreation and community centers, sport and adult educational facilities, but that these institutions will be guided in a spirit of the democratic ideal of freedom, mutual understanding, and cooperation.

Selected Bibliography

Anderson, Jackson M., *Industrial Recreation: A Guide to its Organization and Administration.* New York: McGraw, 1955.

Baxter, Bernice, and Rosalind F. Cassidy, *Group Experience: The Democratic Way.* New York: Harper, 1943.

Blumenthal, Louis H., *Group Work in Camping.* New York: Association Press, 1937.

*Brighthill, Charles K., and Harold D. Meyer, *Recreation: Text and Readings.* Englewood Cliffs, N.J.: Prentice-Hall, Inc., 1953.

Butler, George D., *Introduction to Community Recreation.* New York: McGraw, 1949.

Corbin, H. Dan, *Recreation Leadership.* Englewood Cliffs, N.J.: Prentice-Hall, Inc., 1953.

Danford, Howard G., *Recreation in the Community.* New York: Harper, 1953.

Dewhurst, J. Frederick, *et al., America's Needs and Resources.* New York: Twentieth Century Fund, 1955.

*Dimmock, Hedley S., and Harleigh B. Trecker, *The Supervision of Group Work and Recreation.* New York: Association Press, 1949.

Hjelte, George, *The Administration of Public Recreation.* New York: Macmillan, 1940.

*Hunt, Valerie V., *Recreation and the Handicapped.* Englewood Cliffs, N.J.: Prentice-Hall, Inc., 1955.

Hutchinson, John L., *Principles of Recreation,* New York: Ronald, 1951.

Jenny, John H., *Introduction to Recreation Education.* Philadelphia: Saunders, 1955.

Jones, Anna M., *Leisure Time Education.* New York: Harpers, 1946.

Klein, Alan F., *Society-Democracy-and the Group.* New York: Woman's Press, 1953.

Lewin, Kurt, *Resolving Social Conflict.* New York: Harpers, 1948.

Lindeman, Edward C., *Leisure—A National Issue*. New York: Association Press, 1939.

Lippitt, Ronald, *Training in Community Relations*. New York: Harper, 1949.

Mannheim, Karl, *Man and Society in an Age of Reconstruction*. New York: Harcourt, 1944.

Merrill, Francis E., *Society and Culture: An Introduction to Sociology*. Englewood Cliffs, N.J.: Prentice-Hall, Inc., 1957.

*Meyer, Harold D., and Charles K. Brighthill, *Community Recreation: A Guide to its Organization*. Englewood Cliffs, N.J.: Prentice-Hall, Inc., 1956.

Mitchell, E. D., and B. S. Mason, *The Theory of Play*. New York: Ronald, 1948.

Nash, Jay B., *Philosophy of Recreation and Leisure*. St. Louis: Mosby, 1953.

Olds, Edward B., and Eric Josephson, *Young People and Citizenship*. New York: National Welfare Assembly, 1953.

Ostrow, Albert A., *How to Enjoy Leisure*. New York: Dutton, 1954.

Rainwater, Clarence E., *The Play Movement in the United States*. Chicago: University of Chicago Press, 1922.

Robbins, Florence G., *The Sociology of Play, Recreation, and Leisure*. Dubuque, Iowa: W. Brown, 1955.

Simkhovitch, Mary K., *Group Life*. New York: Association Press, 1940.

Slavson, Samuel R., *Recreation and the Total Personality*. New York: Association Press, 1946.

Stafford, George T., *Sports for the Handicapped*. Englewood Cliffs, N.J.: Prentice-Hall, Inc., 1947.

Tead, Ordway, *New Adventures in Democracy*. New York: McGraw, 1939.

Wrenn, C. Gilbert, and D. L. Harley, *Time on their Hands*. Washington: American Council on Education, 1941.

15.

Services for Special Needs

I. SERVICES TO VETERANS AND THE ARMED FORCES

Legislation for the welfare of veterans was enacted already in Colonial times. Numerous laws, which were changed after each major war, provided land grants, homestead privileges, medical care, and various types of pensions and monetary grants to veterans, their survivors, and dependents.[1] At present, veterans' services have two main goals: (1) to compensate the veteran and his family as much as possible for the sacrifice he has made for his country and to prevent his suffering economic loss from his military service; and (2) to demonstrate to the veteran and his family recognizance of gratitude of the nation for his risking his life or health in the service.[2]

The first group of measures includes compensation to disabled veterans and to survivors, medical care, hospitalization, vocational

---

[1] The history of veterans services in the United States has been discussed in Chapter 3.

[2] Eveline M. Burns, *The American Social Security System* (Boston: Houghton, 1949), p. 266; Gustavus A. Weber and Lawrence F. Schmeckebier, *The Veterans Administration* (Washington: Brookings Institution, 1934), pp. 4, 5, 320; Omar N. Bradley, "The Veterans' Administration," *National Conference of Social Work, Proceedings* (1946), pp. 353-359; and, Claribel H. Moncure, "Veterans' Benefits and Services," *Social Work Year Book* (1960), pp. 591-600.

rehabilitation, educational aid, and job reinstatement. The second category comprises mustering-out pay, preference in civil service positions, bonuses, priorities in housing, and loans for purchasing of homes, farms, and businesses. Emphasis has been placed by veterans' services on rehabilitation—helping the veteran to regain his position in the community.

The social and economic benefits granted to veterans and their families may be divided into five categories: (1) medical care, hospitalization, and social services; (2) compensation and pensions to disabled veterans and to survivors of deceased veterans, life insurance, and social insurance benefits protection; (3) education, training, and vocational rehabilitation; (4) job reinstatement, preferences in civil service positions, and employment services; and (5) economic privileges, including mustering-out pay, readjustment allowance, and loan guarantees for the purchase of a house, a farm, or a business.

By June 30, 1958, the veteran population in the United States was 22,727,000. About one out of every eight citizens was a veteran, and veterans with their families made up forty per cent of our total population.[3]

The major part of veterans' benefits is provided by the Federal government, because veterans, since the independence of our country, have been the largest group of "Federal wards." Our main discussion, therefore, will be concerned with the Federal program. But, most of the states also have established veterans' departments which supplement the Federal aid. Their activities are briefly indicated below.

A. Medical Care, Hospitalization, and Social Services for Veterans

In accordance with the current emphasis of veterans' services on rehabilitation, the Federal program provides free hospitalization and medical and dental care to veterans in need of treatment for service-connected illnesses and disabilities. The honorably discharged veteran may be admitted to a Veterans Administration hospital or to another authorized hospital. For nonservice connected illnesses, the veteran may be admitted to a hospital if he is unable to pay the cost

---

[3] The Administrator of Veterans Affairs, *Annual Report, 1958,* Chapter 17 (Washington: Government Printing Office, 1959), pp. 138-139.

of hospitalization and confirms this under oath, when beds are available. In emergencies, immediate hospitalization is granted. This includes prosthetic and other appliances, chaplaincy, library facilities, recreational activities, and rehabilitation, and social services. In 1958, the Veterans Administration operated 172 of its own hospitals, twenty of them for tuberculosis, 40 for neuropsychiatric, and 112 for general and surgical treatment.[4] Vocational training and special rehabilitation centers have been set up for blind, deaf, and hard-of-hearing veterans. Blind veterans also are entitled to seeing-eye dogs and electronic and mechanical equipment; legless veterans to payment up to $1,600 for the purchase of a special automobile.

The social worker has the function of helping the veteran in his rehabilitation by enabling him to use to his best advantage the various benefits to which he is especially entitled, and other community resources. Casework with the veteran who is ill or disabled deals with personal and family problems, employment, economic questions, particularly, with his attitude and feelings regarding his handicap, his relationship with others, and questions of his adjustment. The caseworker helps the patient to understand the nature of his illness and treatment, and to face obstacles within himself and in his environment which stand in the way of his rehabilitation. The patient is informed about facilities for occupational and physical therapy, vocational guidance and training, and opportunities to gain a general education. The social worker explains to the patient the doctor's advice and prescriptions regarding medication, proper diet, rest, and life habits and helps him to leave the hospital with confidence in his ability to re-establish himself.

In neuropsychiatric hospitals, the psychiatric social worker helps the veteran and his family to become familiar with the nature of his nervous disease, the expectation of the length of the treatment, and the time of discharge. Particularly important here is to make patient and family understand how essential the complete treatment is for the cure and the future life of the veteran.

To assist the men in the armed forces and their families in personal and social problems, the Army uses medical and psychiatric social

[4] E. Burns, *op. cit.*, pp. 267-268; and Virginia C. Karl, "Veterans' Benefits and Services," *Social Work Year Book* (1957), pp. 573-584.
Annual Report of Administration of Veterans Affairs, 1958 (Washington: Government Printing Office, 1950), pp. 5-7.

workers of its own staff, in cooperation with the Medical Service Corps; the Navy relies upon civilian social workers, and the Air Force on the Office of Community Services.[5] The American Red Cross offers family services to the dependents of the men in the armed forces.

Domiciliary care in special institutions is available for veterans who, because of their disability, are so severely incapacitated that they are unable to earn a living or are unwilling to live in the community.[6] Veterans in need of medical and dental treatment for service-connected ailments which do not require hospitalization are cared for at outpatient clinics. There, they receive medical, psychiatric, and dental treatment, and medical supplies and appliances. In order to make it unnecessary for veterans to travel distances, and to relieve the crowded hospitals and clinics, Hometown Medical Care Plans have been authorized in most states under which veterans may be treated by private physicians and psychiatrists. The Veterans Administration is authorized to reallocate hospital beds according to the shifting of the veteran population to other parts of the country.

Social services are available to veterans in domiciliary institutions and outpatient clinics, as well as in hospitals. Our American system of veterans' aid is characterized by the fact that large expenditures for veterans will be due when they become old and are in financial need, often forty years and longer after a war.[7]

B. Economic Compensation for Disabled Veterans and Their Families

Compensation for service-connected disabilities for veterans who have lost at least 10 per cent of their earning capacity is based upon degree of wartime disability and period of military service. The monthly compensation ranges from $18 to $190, but additional com-

---

[5] Elizabeth Wickenden, *The Military Program and Social Welfare* (New York: National Committee on Social Work in Defense Mobilization, 1955); and John H. Hurley, "National Defense and Social Welfare," *Social Work Year Book* (1957), pp. 380-381.

[6] In 1959, the Veterans Administration maintained seventeen Homes for domiciliary care for 17,500 veterans, and ninety-four mental hygiene clinics.

[7] Mildred Maroney, "Veterans Benefits," in Lewis Meriam and Karl Schlotterbeck (editors), *The Cost and Financing of Social Security* (Washington: Brookings Institution, 1950), pp. 96-97.

pensations for severe disabilities, such as blindness, loss of a hand, foot, or eye, permit a monthly compensation of $47 up to a maximum of $440. Veterans with disabilities rated at 50 per cent or more receive additional allowances for a wife, children, and dependent parents. After the veteran's death, his survivors are entitled to "dependency and indemnity compensation" ranging from a minimum of $122 a month for the widow in relation to the military pay of the veteran. One child receives $70 a month, two children $100, three children $130, each additional child $25, and dependent parents from $10 to 75 monthly.

For nonservice-connected disabilities a veteran with a permanent and total disability may receive a pension ranging from $66.15 to $135.45 a month, provided that he is in economic need, his annual income does not exceed $1,400 and he has no dependents, or $2,700 if he is married or has minor children. Pensions are also paid to the widow and minor children if need is proved. The difference between compensation and pension lies in the fact that the first is paid for all incapacities and is independent of income and financial status of the veteran, whereas pensions are paid only for total nonservice-connected disability and only to veterans or survivors whose income is lower than a statutory limit.[8] Since 1960, veterans have a choice for higher pensions if they have low incomes or dependents.

Veterans of World War I were protected through life insurance ranging from $1,000 to $10,000, and veterans of World War II were entitled to purchase the same amounts by National Service Life Insurance policies. There are more than 6,000,000 policies in force; both systems are administered by the Veterans Administration.

Survivors of veterans discharged before July 26, 1951, who passed away within three years after their discharge were entitled to their full social insurance benefits under the Old-Age and Survivors Insurance, whereby the veteran is deemed to have had monthly wages of $160 during his military service. Burial expenses for a deceased veteran are reimbursed to relatives or friends up to a maximum of $150.

The members of the Armed Forces receive dependents allowances similar to those provided for military personnel during World War II.

---

[8] George F. Rohrlich, "Veterans Pensions in Retrospect and in Prospect," *Social Service Review,* Vol. 31, No. 4 (December 1957), pp. 427-441.

TABLE IV

PATIENTS IN VETERANS HOSPITALS
June 30, 1958 *

Type of Medical Care	Patients in Veterans Hospitals			
	General and Surgical Hospitals	Tuberculosis	Neuro-psychiatric Hospitals	Total
All types	55,512	7,719	57,295	120,526
Tuberculosis ...	6,360	5,587	1,503	12,043
Psychiatric	6,360	25	52,883	59,268
Psychotic	4,067	5	49,958	54,036
Other psychiatric .	2,293	20	2,925	5,238
Neurological ...	4,199	62	658	4,940
General and surgical	39,959	2,095	2,221	44,275

* *Source:* Administrator of Veterans Affairs, *Annual Report 1958* (1959), p. 7.

C. Education and Vocational Rehabilitation

Under the *Servicemen's Readjustment Act of 1944* (so-called "G.I. Bill of Rights") and its amendments, a program of general *education and training* was made available to honorably discharged veterans with ninety days or more of service. The period of subsidized education varies from one to four years. Training may be performed in industry, business, and workshops providing apprentice or on-the-job training. War orphans 18 to 23 years of age receive educational assistance for three years.

Vocational rehabilitation is provided under the "Act Providing Vocational Rehabilitation of Disabled Veterans," of 1943 (Public Law 16) in order to restore the employability of disabled war veterans.[9] The training period for vocational rehabilitation is not limited, but after four years an approval of the Veterans Administration is required. The vocational training for veterans of World War II terminated in 1960, but, for Korean veterans it continues until 1968. Training allowance for disabled veterans is paid in addition to

---

[9] Roger Cumming, "Veterans Services," *Social Work Year Book* (1954), pp. 522-528; Virginia C. Karl, "Veterans Benefits and Services," *ibid.* (1957), pp. 573-584; and, Claribel H. Moncure, *op. cit.* (1960), 595-598.

disability compensation and retirement pay. The vocational rehabilitation plan is carefully supervised; courses have to be continued
so that the benefits will not be wasted and the training will suit the
individual needs of the veteran. In hospitals of the Veterans Administration and of the Navy, vocational guidance and counseling
are provided so that disabled veterans may prepare their rehabilitation training in advance.

D. Job Reinstatement and Preference in Civil Service

Before the end of World War II, the *Veterans Readjustment Act*
provided the right of the veteran to be re-employed in his former
job with special regulations of conflicting interests. In civil service
examinations and tests a special priority of 5 points for veterans
and of 10 points for disabled veterans made the eligibility for, and
the appointment of, veterans and their widows to civil service positions easier. These priorities apply to Federal civil service, but in
most states also to state and local government civil service jobs.

Special job counseling and placement services are available to the
veteran. Policies for effective placement of veterans are established
through the Veterans Placement Service Board, whose chairman is
the veterans' administrator. Veterans' employment representatives
serve in all state employment organizations and many local employment services. Particular attention is given to counseling and placement services for physically handicapped veterans who had been
prepared by vocational rehabilitation.

E. Economic Privileges

At the time of honorable discharge, the veteran receives mustering-
out pay and a special type of Federally financed unemployment
benefit, called "Readjustment Allowance." Since 1952, unemployment insurance benefits have been paid to veterans under two different programs: (1) The general state unemployment insurance
laws provide pay to veterans who have established benefit rights after
their return to civilian life or, in twenty states where unemployed
veterans receive insurance benefits, on the basis of "frozen wage
credits" earned before their military service. (2) *The Veterans
Readjustment Assistance Act of 1952,* provides weekly benefits to
unemployed veterans with active service after June 27, 1950, includ-

ing the Korean conflict, of $26 for twenty-six weeks. A veteran must first claim benefits for which he is eligible under a state unemployment compensation law or the Railroad Unemployment Insurance Act.

Self-employed veterans in trade, business, profession, or other vocations are entitled to readjustment allowance if they had net earnings of less than $100 in the previous month.

Veterans and widows of deceased veterans received help in building a home, establishing a business, or buying a farm by *guaranteeing* up to 60 per cent of the loan from private lending societies or individuals until 1960. For veterans of the Korean Conflict, these benefits are available until 1965. Veterans also receive priorities in housing located in public housing projects built with funds of the Lanham Act of 1950, and in securing homesteads on public land. Disabled veterans receive aid in obtaining suitable homes.

F. Organization of Veterans Administration

Federal Organization. Veterans' benefits are administered by the Veterans Administration. The policy-making body is the central office in Washington, D.C., which is responsible for the supervision of the entire program. The various fields of the administration, covering legal problems, claims, appeals, vocational rehabilitation, education, and life insurance, are assigned to staff units. Social services are a subdivision of the Department of Medicine and Surgery in the central, district, and regional offices. Social services are available to veterans receiving medical treatment and care.

Operating functions are decentralized and delegated to five district offices, to fifty-seven regional offices, and 532 field stations. They handle disability and death awards, training and education, and other benefits. Readjustment allowances are paid by the state unemployment compensation agencies, which are also reimbursed for their administrative costs incurred by this cooperation.

State Veterans' Programs. Although the Federal government assumes the basic responsibility for veterans' services, nearly all the states provide additional benefits to veterans. These services supplement the Federal benefits or continue them after their expiration. The benefits include information and counseling centers, preference in civil service or public employment, tax and license fees exemptions,

TABLE V

EXPENDITURES MADE BY THE VETERANS ADMINISTRATION
1939-1958

Fiscal Year	Total Expenditures
1939	$ 600,221,534.14
1940	$ 639,126,696.89
1941	$ 614,357,411.24
1942	$ 647,729,952.88
1943	$ 656,256,161.79
1944	$ 828,391,436.33
1945	$2,271,318,333.42
1946	$4,772,072,218.89
1947	$7,805,355,201.06
1948	$7,184,961,094.86
1949	$7,076,749,316.14
1950	$9,752,982,831.63
1951	$5,998,433,367.66
1952	$6,074,484,831.94
1953	$5,098,458,093.94
1954	$5,282,574,988.43
1955	$5,330,468,067.18
1956	$5,609,241,578.32
1957	$5,708,195,756.70
1958	$6,100,623,393.16

* *Source:* Administrator of Veterans Affairs, *Annual Report 1958* (Washington: Government Printing Office, 1959), Table 97, p. 280.

and domiciliary care in 33 state soldiers' homes. Other state benefits are financial aid to needy veterans, bonuses, pensions, and burial expenses to indigent veterans. Several states supply guarantees for loans to veterans for the purchase of a home, farm, or business, sometimes up to a higher maximum than the Federal program allows. In other state programs, land settlement, homesteads, or institutional care for children are available to veterans and their families.

The state veterans' departments or commissions administer or supervise these services for veterans, but, in a few instances, private veterans' organizations or the various state departments of public welfare are charged with providing benefits.

Community Services for Veterans. Among social agencies, some are particularly active in services for veterans. Through its local chapters, the American National Red Cross assists veterans in the presentation of claims for their legal benefits. The home service division of the chapters offer casework services, and, in special instances, financial aid to veterans and their families. Several veterans' organizations, such as the American Legion and the Veterans of Foreign Wars of the United States, also help veterans with filing their claims, in rehabilitation, in securing housing, loans for purchasing homes, farms and business, in obtaining employment or hospitalization, and in getting family and child welfare services.

Beyond the Federal and state programs, local community services assist the veteran and his family because the veteran should also receive the consideration and aid given to other citizens. Such services are offered by public and private agencies, such as the local health and welfare departments, the employment service, vocational rehabilitation centers, family and child welfare agencies, and mental hygiene and child guidance clinics.

II. PUBLIC HOUSING AND URBAN RENEWAL

A. Housing Needs and City Planning

Social welfare is deeply concerned with adequate housing; along with food and clothing, housing is one of the basic necessities of man, particularly for the maintenance of family life. The provision of adequate housing is a problem which must be considered by social, economic, and civic organizations. Two movements during the nineteenth century directed public attention to the problems of housing. The first movement was caused by the conditions of the slums and was aimed at housing reform. The second movement, "city planning," had as its objective the protection of good residential neighborhoods from the intrusion of factories and substandard construction.[10] It attempted to relate new dwelling to their sites, providing adequate space, privacy, sanitation, water, light, air, gardens, and an attractive exterior in order to develop healthy living quarters. It also considered the relationship of the neighborhood to the entire community—transportation, communications, hospitals, schools, and recreational facilities.[11] During past decades, both movements have

---

[10] Charles Abrams, *U.S. Housing—A New Program* (New York: Tamiment Institute, 1958); Robert M. Fisher, *Twenty Years of Public Housing* (New York: Harper, 1959); and, Francis X. Servaites, "Housing and Planning," *Social Work Year Book* (1960), pp. 302-310.

[11] Arthur Hillman, *Community Organization and Planning* (New York: Macmillan, 1950), pp. 111-129; Bryn J. Hovde, "Housing and City Planning," *Social Work Year Book* (1954), pp. 257-266; and, Lee F. Johnson, "Housing," *ibid.*, (1957), pp. 292-302.

found a joint objective in striving for the construction of healthy, comfortable houses in decent neighborhoods, in urban and rural areas, at a reasonable price, thus providing adequate housing for the entire population.

Housing needs are determined by two main factors. The rapid growth of cities in our industrial age has caused a deficit in the actual dwelling supply in relation to the increasing size of the population. This shortage was aggravated by the lack of civilian, residential construction during World War II. The other aspect of housing needs is a qualitative one. The National Housing Inventory, of 1957, revealed that, of 55,000,000 residential units, 76 per cent were in good condition, but 24 per cent were deficient or in need of major repairs.[12]

In cities, environmental deficiencies are created by the lack of organized, planned development, and the overuse of land, outmoded street patterns, "shack towns" in suburban areas, poor traffic conditions, and lack of adequate transportation, parks, playgrounds, and other recreational facilities.

B. Housing Legislation

Legislation in the field of housing began, on the local level, in New York City and a few other metropolitan cities in the 1860's. The legislation required fire protection, and correction of the worst slum conditions.[13] Land and building speculators, however, continued in big cities and industrial regions the business practice of constructing substandard tenements and of purchasing exemption from regulations by taking advantage of political corruption. Practical experience proved that private enterprise on a competitive market could not produce decent, sanitary, and sufficiently spacious, low-rent housing for low-income families without tax exemptions and substantial government subsidies. Housing legislation, therefore, approached the social need of adequate housing for families of low income through: (1) restrictive regulations, building codes, condemnation procedures for unsafe, unsanitary buildings, and zoning; (2) tax exemptions for

---

[12] U.S. Housing and Home Finance Agency, *Annual Report* (1957), p. 18.
[13] State legislation in the realm of public housing was first passed in New York. See Langdon W. Post, *The Challenge of Housing* (New York: Rinehart, 1938), pp. 81, 119-123.

adequate housing at low rents; (3) subsidies to private builders, corporations, and housing societies for the construction of good, low-rent dwellings to replace slums; (4) government intervention through financing of private construction by loans or guarantees; and (5) governmental housing construction of low-cost housing units.

In the Depression of the 1930's Federal housing legislation started with the *Home Loan Act of 1932.* Under the New Deal, the *National Housing Act of 1934* guaranteed mortgages, the Public Works Administration built low-cost housing projects, and the *U. S. Housing Act of 1937* provided Federal grants to local housing, which were expanded under later amendments. During World War II, additional war housing projects were financed under the *Lanham Act,* which created residential facilities for 8,000,000 persons. After the war, in 1947, the Housing and Home Finance Agency replaced the National Housing Agency. It consists of five divisions: (1) the *Federal Housing Administration* for sound home financing through loan insurance programs; (2) the *Public Housing Administration* for the administration of Federally aided low-rent public housing projects; (3) the *Federal National Mortgage Association* for home mortgages procured through secondary market facilities; (4) the *Community Facilities Administration* for loans to educational institutions and hospitals for housing of students, faculty, interns, and student nurses, and for public works of local or state governments; and (5) the *Urban Renewal Administration* for slum clearance, urban renewal planning and financing, and the rehabilitation of blighted areas.

C. Urban Renewal

City planning is devoted to the scientific development of cities along rational lines. It was devised to contribute to the health, amenity, convenience, and security of the citizens and to further commerce and employment.[14] The planning is carried on by local and regional planning commissions in cities and counties. These

---

[14] Catherine Bauer, "Housing in the United States," *International Labor Review* (July 1945), pp. 18-21; and Edward C. Branfield and Morton Grodzins, *Government and Housing in Metropolitan Areas* (New York: McGraw, 1958).

agencies are in charge of zoning, street and highway construction, and urban redevelopment, but, they often are hampered by inadequate budgets and stubborn resistance of special interests groups.

The population is slowly coming to recognize that a foresighted and constructive housing policy is one essential requirement in the cultural program of the nation. Housing reform was first the concern of a small group of social reformers and social workers, but, at present, legislative bodies, business, industry, labor, and veterans take part in the shaping of housing policy.

Family and children's agencies and leisure-time and recreation organizations cooperate with housing authorities and offer their services to families residing in housing projects. They develop recreation centers for children and young people, adult discussion groups, and art and drama clubs.

D. Housing for the Aged and Handicapped

Special housing needs exist for the older generation.[15] Old-age and survivors' insurance benefits, private annuities, public service retirement allowances, and industrial pensions establish a certain economic security for many of our senior citizens so that they do not have to look forward to a sad end in the poorhouse. However, the amount of monthly income derived from these programs is, in general, so modest that their free choice as to where they live still is rather restricted whenever their health conditions make it difficult to climb steep stairs, or to use old-fashioned heating, kitchen, and bathroom equipment. Their failing strength will prevent many old people from maintaining a clean household and getting adequate food, so that they will be endangered by malnutrition and illness. For the older generation, housing costs have been disproportionally high as was shown by research studies of the Social Security Administration. This research in eight large cities found that older people spent from 37 to 51 per cent of their total budget on rent, heating, and light. This high expense limits their purchase abilities for nutritious food, ade-

---

[15] Hertha Kraus, "Housing Our Older Citizens," *Annals* (January 1952), pp. 126-130; Gordon J. Aldridge and Fedele F. Fauri, *Social Welfare and the Aged* (Ann Arbor: University of Michigan, Institute for Social Gerontology, 1959); and, Wilma Donahue (editor), *Housing the Aging* (Ann Arbor: University of Michigan Press, 1954).

quate clothing, medical care, medicines, and cultural and recreational needs. It also makes it more difficult for the aged to maintain personal friendships and social contacts to relieve their loneliness.[16]

As we mentioned above, present community services are not sufficient. One essential improvement would be made if the present supply of low- and medium-cost housing facilities would be enlarged and improved in order to meet the particular needs of older persons. New housing projects should include single-story units, and well-lighted, airy apartments with modern home-management facilities. Homemaker and nursing services should be maintained in cooperation with community welfare agencies to make it easy for old people in such housing units to secure proper care, food, and medical attention. The experiments of cottage colonies or special apartment houses for the aged deserve careful attention and research follow-up.

Most older people prefer to live in their own homes, in familiar surroundings with their furniture and personal belongings. But many are in need of full-time domestic help, nursing care, and medical supervision over a long period of time. This may be provided by social agencies if the homes of the aged are not too widely scattered in the community, are readily accessible, and if housing arrangements permit the old people to care for themselves as much as possible and to assist their companions.

Senior citizens should not be forced to live in any specific type of residence. It may be expected, however, that many older people prefer quiet housing facilities of the low-rent type, to a mixed surrounding with noisy children and teen-agers whose habits are not conducive to the rhythm of life of the old. Such facilities also require good transportation so that relatives and friends may visit easily. The planning of good housing facilities for older couples or single persons could be included in public housing projects or in units financially supported by government. Senior housing apartments or cottages and companion apartments have been suggested as possible types which would be economical, would accommodate substantial

---

[16] "A Budget for an Elderly Couple," *Social Security Bulletin,* Vol. 11, No. 2 (February 1948), pp. 4-12; New York State Joint Legislative Committee on Problems of the Aging, *Age Is No Barrier* (1952), pp. 10-17, 117-119; and, Elizabeth Wickenden, *The Needs of Older People and Public Welfare Services To Meet Them* (Chicago: American Public Welfare Association, 1953).

numbers of older persons, and may be easily coordinated for house-keeping, cleaning, and laundry services provided by the management of such units.

Similar public housing needs exist for handicapped, blind, and crippled persons, who cannot obtain normal housing at prices they are able to pay. In some public housing projects, the rights of racial and religious minority groups have been protected by "no discrimination" clauses and a policy of management that gives particular consideration to their needs so that they are accepted as well as other families.

The setting up of a social service department in larger housing units under the public housing authorities has been successful in some instances. Social workers serve as a counselor, as the family case-worker, and as the group worker in this setting. In England and France, social workers are employed more frequently by housing authorities in large projects than here. It may be possible, however, to preserve good family relations and develop sound recreational and cultural life in housing projects by an intensive use of available social agencies in the community which may give special attention to the social needs of senior residents in new housing units.

The development of adequate housing for low- and medium-income groups of citizens requires construction by both private builders and under public auspices. Human needs for health, comfort, privacy, and safety must be satisfied; rents or purchase prices should be based upon the ability of the families to pay. Cooperation of surrounding communities is needed to afford education, worship, employment, safety from traffic and other hazards, health protection, recreation, welfare services, and shopping facilities. Families with several children, persons with special health problems, and migratory workers need special consideration and protection.

Rural housing reform is a particular problem because of the reluctance of farmers to make changes, and because of the high cost of rural construction. Under the *Housing Act of 1949,* the Department of Agriculture is entitled to give loans to farmers for housing improvement for which they are unable to obtain loans from banks or loan cooperatives (credit unions). The distribution is made through the Farmers Home Administration, and the loans may be used to build adequate housing for the farmers and their farm workers.

III. INDUSTRY AND SOCIAL WELFARE

In the field of modern industrial operations four aspects of social welfare seem to be of particular importance. First, there are the arrangements made (recently described as "industrial health and welfare plans") in plants, mines, and commerce in order to establish or to improve social security, health, and the general welfare of the employees and their families. Second, there is the function of public employment services in finding the best-suited worker for employers and the right jobs for workers seeking employment. Third, there is the use of social workers in industrial and commercial companies in order to assist the employees and their families in personal, health, and financial problems and difficulties. Finally, there is the relation of organized labor to social work and its participation in the responsibility for development and maintenance of community welfare services.[17]

A. Industrial Health and Welfare

The very nature of modern industry with its concentration of large populations in industrial centers around mills and mines has challenged both workers and employers in regard to measures of protecting life, health, and well-being of the workers. A number of older labor unions started as fraternal mutual aid societies; they made provisions to help their members during periods of sickness and unemployment by grants and loans, and to aid the survivors in case of death of the breadwinner. Some employers established medical clinics, pension plans, and life insurance protection for their employees. But, only a very small proportion of workers were covered by one or the other type of social protection before World War II. Organized labor, at first, had been opposed to company welfare plans because they endangered the organization of workers in labor unions and curtailed labor's mobility and bargaining strength. When union leaders, during the 1930's, succeeded in organizing mass-production industries, they were forced to promise their newly recruited mem-

---

17 Harold L. Wilensky and Charles N. Lebeaux, *Industrial Society and Social Welfare* (New York: Russell Sage Foundation, 1958); and, Jack W. Skeels, "Labor and Social Welfare," *Social Work Year Book* (1960), pp. 356-362.

bers that health, recreational, and retirement benefits, which earlier had been introduced by some companies, would be maintained.

During World War II, rapidly enlarged production created a search for manpower at a time when wage increases were restricted by the government's wage stabilization policy. Thus, many companies established pension and health service plans in order to attract workers. This factor seemed even more important because, under Old-Age and Survivors Insurance, the benefits were rather inadequate. They had been left at the 1935 level whereas the cost of living had greatly risen. "Fringe benefits" were a relatively simple solution to the problem of fixed wages because the cost of the plans in the face of excess profit taxes was nominal and could be written off as business expense. This also made the hiring of manpower easier.

The first plans were set up voluntarily by industry. After the Federal government completed a bargaining agreement with the United Mine Workers in 1946, which included a pension and welfare plan, such "fringe benefits" became a more common feature in collective bargaining because other unions felt they had to prove that they were able to obtain the same concessions from the employers as the mine workers. Before this change, some welfare plans had been financed by the workers themselves. The new pattern, which started with a collective agreement of the United Auto Workers at Toledo, Ohio, in 1935, meant that the welfare plans were financed entirely (though in some cases, in part) by the employers. Finally, in 1948, the National Labor Relations Board ruled that industrial pensions were "conditions of employment" and might be included in all collective bargaining contracts.[18]

Since this development, health and welfare plans have played an important role in our industry. There are three main types of plans: (1) pension or retirement plans providing annuities for workers retired after long service with the company, (2) voluntary health insurance plans, providing prepaid medical care and hospitalization for illness not covered by workmen's compensation protection, and (3) a combination of retirement annuities and health services.

Disability insurance benefits are provided in several plans which

---

[18] U.S. Department of Labor, "Health and Insurance Plans Under Collective Bargaining," *Bulletin No. 1221* (1956); and, Clark Kerr, *Social and Economic Implications of Private Pension Plans* (Berkeley: University of California Press, 1949), pp. 2-4.

supplement disability benefits under the Federal old-age, survivors, and disability insurance program. In some instances, also, supplementary unemployment benefits are paid, for example, to merchant seamen who are members of the National Maritime Union.

There is a great variety in structure, conditions, benefits, methods of administration, and financing among the more than 10,000 existing health and welfare plans. Numerous research studies have analyzed various features of these plans, and labor unions have accepted them as part of a broader concept of social security for their members.

Retirement or pension plans often are combined with a life insurance policy which is paid by the employer. During, and immediately after, World War II, 42 per cent of retirement plans were wholly financed by the employer; for the remaining 58 per cent, worker and employer shared the cost. An analysis of 346 retirement annuity plans by the Social Security Administration in October 1952, revealed that, only in 25.4 per cent of the plans, the employer alone paid the premiums, whereas in 74.6 per cent both workers and employers shared the expense for the annuity insurance. In nearly all plans, membership is dependent upon a longer period of work in the firm, most commonly five years, less frequently, one year. The majority of plans requires a minimum age of thirty years and no more than fifty-five to sixty, and usually sixty-five years. Frequently, employment may be continued with consent of the employer beyond the fixed retirement age; in this case, 18 per cent of the plans provided an increased annuity amount.

The annuity is determined in various rates by a percentage of annual earnings and the length of service with the company. Wages and salaries up to a certain limit are considered in computing the annuity. In those plans in which the workers contribute, their payment premiums often amount to 2 to 3 per cent of the first $3,000 annual wages and 2 to 5 per cent of the excess earnings. A large majority of private plans permits the employee, who leaves the company before retirement, to maintain his annuity rights (vesting) or to request a cash refund.

Frequently, annuity plans provide that in the event the death of the insured worker occurs before his retirement, his own contributions, sometimes with interest, will be paid back to his widow and orphans. The most common type of annuity plan is the "definite benefit" plan. Payments are deferred to retirement at a specified age, usually sixty-five years. Many plans allow for an earlier retirement, beginning at fifty-five years of age under a reduced annuity. Frequently, permanent disability is a condition of early retirement, and certain plans allow the payment of disability or invalidity benefits without age limit for employees unable to work. The trend in recent agreements has been to postpone annuity payments until actual retirement at which time an increased pension is paid.

The relation of private industrial retirement plans to the benefits of Old-Age and Survivors Insurance is an important question.[19] Some retirement annuity plans provide benefits computed by including old-age insurance benefits received under the Federal Old-Age and Survivors Insurance; others pay benefits in addition to whatever old-age insurance is drawn by the retired worker. Both supplement the public social insurance benefits, but the second type grants a larger additional monthly amount to the retired worker. In the financing of plans in which the employees share the expenses, an integration with Federal benefits is achieved by classifying a uniform benefit rate on the first $3,000 or $3,600 of annual earnings, with a higher rate on the excess amount. It is widely argued that private annuity plans should include Federal social security benefits so that they may be developed into a sound system.

There are, however, definite limitations to private retirement plans. They cover only a certain percentage of workers, leaving out, usually, the unorganized—those working in small firms, casual workers, and self-employed persons who may need a supplementation of Federal old-age insurance most. They limit the mobility of labor because, particularly under noncontributory plans, workers become eligible for benefits only if they remain for long years in the same industry or serve with the same employer. Thus, workers lose the initiative to change jobs for better conditions, higher pay, and promotions, which are considered vital elements in a well-functioning, fluid labor market. A private plan may put the older worker under strong pressure to keep his job and stay with his union because of fear of losing his pension.

---

[19] Arthur J. Altmeyer, "Social Security and Welfare Funds," in William Haber and Wilbur J. Cohen (editors), *Readings in Social Security* (Englewood Cliffs, N.J.: Prentice-Hall, Inc., 1948), pp. 132-136; Harold L. Wilensky and Charles N. Lebeaux, *op. cit.*, pp. 160-163; and, Harold W. Davey, *Contemporary Collective Bargaining*, 2nd ed. (Englewood Cliffs, N.J.: Prentice-Hall, Inc., 1959).

Another critical point is that private pensions are likely to vary from company to company, and among industries, due to the rhythm of regular employment, wages, age composition of workers, and financial reserves. Equalization of benefits is difficult under these circumstances.[20]

The sound organization of pension plans through collective bargaining is difficult because their technical and financial basis is complicated and requires special statistical experts. It also remains doubtful whether pension plans, especially of smaller firms, are able to guarantee the payment of annuities in case of insolvency, mass dismissal of workers, and other failures. Special provisions are needed to insure that private pension plans do not hinder the older worker in his search for a more satisfying job.

Private pension plans contribute to the social security of those employees who happen to be covered by these plans, but they are not the final solution of general security in old age. Organized labor and students of social security agree that a universal, complex, and adequate public system of old-age insurance is necessary for the protection of the total population. Without such a system, the demands of special groups and labor unions for particular benefits under specific conditions exercise pressure and threaten to result in unbalanced, unfair, overlapping, and competing arrangements which lack equity and are wasteful. The AFL-CIO considers private pension plans under collective bargaining only as a step to a governmental, comprehensive, and adequate public social security program.[21]

Health benefit plans are the second main type of private security programs developed in industry either by labor unions, collective bargaining, or companies under their own initiative. One of the first medical care plans was founded in New York by the International Ladies' Garment Workers' Union which, as early as 1912, established a union health center with free medical care for its members. Under collective bargaining, during and after World War

---

[20] Ewan Clague, *The Background of the Pension Problem* (U.S. Department of Labor, Bureau of Labor Statistics, 1949), pp. 5-6; and, Alfred M. Skolnik and Joseph Zisman, "Growth in Employee-Benefit Plans," *Social Security Bulletin,* Vol. 22, No. 3 (March 1959).

[21] C. Kerr, *op. cit.,* pp. 9-10; and, Kermit Eby, "Labor's Drive for Security," *Social Service Review,* Vol. 24, No. 1 (March 1950), pp. 17-18. The Forand Bill intends to provide health insurance for free hospital, surgical, and nursing home care to Social Security beneficiaries.

II, numerous medical care and hospital plans have been set up. They usually insure all employees of a company in a prepaid medical care and hospital plan, negotiated either with one or several hospitals, physician panels, or with a private insurance company, which assumes the payments for medical care, medicines, and hospitalization in case of illness and accidents not covered by workmen's compensation. Sometimes medical care plans are preceded by exploratory studies such as those the United Automobile Workers made in Cleveland in a Medical Research Institute in 1940. The benefits of industrial medical care plans are not uniform. In general, medical and surgical care, medicines, appliances, and hospitalization are provided free of charge or for a nominal fee. Less frequently, 50 to 60 per cent of the wage is paid during illness up to a maximum period, usually one year. Other health agreements limit the services of medical care to preventive measures, medical examination, and diagnosis; encourage the workers to join at their own expense a prepaid medical and surgical care program; or refer them for treatment to their own private physician. A number of prepaid medical care systems with clinic and hospital facilities is sponsored by unions or by cooperative societies.[22]

The cost of health, medical care, and hospital plans usually is shared between employers and workers, but some companies assume the entire payment of contributions, the chemical and metal industries for example. As a rule, medical treatment is limited to a maximum amount of expenses for surgery and delivery service, ranging from $25 to $100, and to a maximum hospitalization period ranging from twenty-one to seventy days.[23]

The largest voluntary health insurance system is the "Blue Cross Plan." It is, fundamentally, a hospital insurance, but, sometimes, it includes services of medical treatment. Commercial insurance com-

---

[22] Harold S. Vance, "Industry Looks at the Problem of Financing Health Services," President's Commission on the Health Needs of the Nation, *Building America's Health* (1952), Vol. 4, pp. 121-124; Franz Goldman and Evarts A. Graham, *The Quality of Medical Care Provided at the Labor Health Institute* (St. Louis: The Institute, 1954); and, Herman M. Somers and Anne R. Somers, "Private Health Insurance" *California Law Review*, Vol. 46, No. 3 and 4 (1958).

[23] Research Council for Economic Security, *Employee Benefit Plans* (Chicago: 1951); and, Agnes W. Brewster, "Voluntary Health Insurance and Medical Care Expenditures," *Social Security Bulletin*, Vol. 21, No. 12 (December 1958).

panies underwriting sickness insurance are the second group in order of magnitude, but their benefits are frequently limited to cash allowances for a certain number of days of illness or to a contribution to the hospital costs. Rarely is comprehensive medical care offered. The third group consists of surgical-medical plans, such as the Blue Shield, sponsored by state medical associations and used under contract by companies, labor unions, and consumer groups for securing medical treatment for their employees and members.

Independent medical care and hospitalization plans are organized either as industrial or nonindustrial plans. The first group comprises prepaid health care arrangements, financed either by the employer, or employer and workers, or employer and union, or by the union, or the workers alone. Nonindustrial health plans are organized by consumers, medical societies, and private medical group clinics or are community-wide institutions, such as the Health Insurance Plan of Greater New York.

Because our country has no compulsory health insurance program, voluntary prepaid medical care plans in industry have an important function to meet the medical needs of the population and to provide health education for the public, as well as information for research. They may be pioneers for a general health insurance or public health service system, which probably will be considered necessary in the future. The voluntary plans also may develop preventive dental care, dental clinics, home-nursing services, provisions for lengthy hospitalization for patients in need of such treatment, and particularly for expensive hospital accommodations which may not be included in a general health insurance program.

Retirement annuity, medical care, and hospitalization plans have been combined so that the employees receive substantial protection for their health and old age. An example of such a coordination is the program established for the soft coal industry, administered by a Welfare and Retirement Fund and a Medical and Hospital Fund [24] that have been set up under collective bargaining. In general, about one-half of the unions organized under the AFL-CIO have a health

---

[24] Margaret C. Klem and Margaret F. McKiever, "Program Developments and Benefit Trends in Voluntary Health Insurance," *Social Security Bulletin,* Vol. 11 (November 1948), pp. 4-5; and, Olin W. Anderson and J. J. Feldman, *Family Medical Care Costs and Voluntary Health Insurance* (New York: Health Information Foundation, 1956).

and welfare plan. Their benefits include, as a rule, provisions for life insurance, accidental dismemberment insurance, sick-leave benefits, wage-loss benefits for the period of incapacity due to illness or non-industrial accident, hospital expense benefits, medical care benefits, maternity benefits, and certain benefits for dependents.

To protect the interests of the workers insured in private employee health and welfare plans, the *Welfare and Pension Plans Disclosure Act of 1958* requires that the administrators publish a description of the organization and its operation and an annual financial report with the Secretary of Labor. The statute, however, has been criticized as not providing the promised protection to the labor force against fraud, embezzlement, and kickbacks. Further legislation may be necessary.

B. Public Employment Services

One of the social institutions which is of paramount importance for industry and labor is the public employment service. Local and a few state employment offices were established as early as the nineteenth century. The first state offices were opened in Ohio in 1890, in New York in 1896 and in Wisconsin in 1901. The particular employment problems of new immigrants which were emphasized by the Immigrants Protective Society under Grace Abbott in Chicago led to the setting up of an information service for immigrants in the U.S. Bureau of Immigration in 1907, which was changed into an employment office in 1914. The manpower problems of World War I resulted in the establishment of the U.S. Employment Service in the Federal Department of Labor.

It was only in the depths of the Depression, after the New Deal government had assumed responsibility, that the public employment services were reactivated. The *Wagner-Peyser Act of 1933,* developed, again, a national system of public employment services with financial support of Federal funds and with special emphasis on placement of war veterans and agricultural labor. Federal grants permitted the states to organize their employment bureaus and to introduce modern methods of placement with the use of aptitude and vocational tests for occupational classification, by employing qualified personnel. In 1939, the U.S. Employment Service was incorporated as "Bureau of Employment Security" in the Social Security Administration. After

Pearl Harbor, in December, 1941, the state employment offices were merged with the Federal service, because of the need of a uniform policy for war needs. After the war, in November 1946, the public employment services were returned to the states. They are operating now as state agencies, usually under the Department of Employment and in close cooperation with the state unemployment insurance administration.[25] The Bureau of Employment Security, including the U.S. Employment Service, was attached to the U.S. Department of Labor in 1950.

The function of the employment services is "to bring workers and employers together." They assist in the effective recruitment and placement of labor, helping workers to find suitable and, if possible, stable employment. As well, they help employers to find qualified employees. This function is carried out by registration and classification of workers desirous of finding jobs upon consideration of their vocational capacity. Employment services obtain from employers information on job openings and their requirements, and they refer job applicants, if necessary, to other employment offices where workers are needed. The employment service, thus, is the connecting link between the employer in need of labor and the worker in need of a job. Only seldom do employment services attempt to develop special training or retraining courses or to assume a role in the task of channeling the flow of labor to areas with better placement facilities.

C. Social Workers in Industry

During World War I, industrial social work in the United States developed under the name "industrial counseling" in a number of plants, particularly in war factories. Between the world wars, a few large companies—the Metropolitan Life Insurance Company, the Hawthorne Works of the Western Electric Company in Chicago, and the R. H. Macy department store in New York—employed industrial counselors. Their main function was to help the employees with personal and family problems, in questions of health, care of children, marital problems, and financial difficulties. Other companies

---

25 U.S. Bureau of Employment Security, *Counseling and Employment for Special Worker Groups* (Washington 1954); Arthur W. Motley, "Employment Services," *Social Work Year Book* (1957), pp. 232-239; and, William U. Norwood Jr., "Employment Services," *ibid.* (1960), pp. 240-245.

followed these examples. Whenever immediate help cannot be given by an interview or advice, the employee is informed about health clinics and hospitals, family service agencies, loan associations, and recreation and adult education facilities and is referred to those community resources which meet his need. Sometimes, the industrial counselor, in cooperation with the shop steward, will be able to adjust the difficulties the worker may have in relation to his supervisor, his fellow workers, or in regard to the type of his work assignment.[26] Although these activities require professional social work skill and thorough knowledge of social agencies, health facilities, and recreation in the community, only a few industrial counselors are trained social workers. The majority are factory operators who get along well with people or come from employment services, vocational guidance, and personnel agencies.[27]

With the development of defense production and the ensuing spread of war industries in World War II, many plants, yards, and docks engaged industrial counselors, particularly for women. Organized labor became concerned that industrial counselors in the plants might be biased in their approach to personal and work problems in favor of the employer who had hired them, and might lack understanding of, and sympathy for, labor unions. In some instances, the counselors or "welfare workers" even were accused of serving as labor spies for management so that the workers had no confidence in them. Therefore, both CIO and AFL developed, with the cooperation of local welfare councils, a new program of "union counselors" under their own sponsorship and control.[28] Social workers on the staff of the Welfare Council, or Council of Social Agencies, or on one of the affiliated organizations were asked to offer training to selected rank-and-file workers, who had the confidence of their fellow workers. The training courses do not attempt to make social workers out of

---

26 Mary Palevsky, *Counseling Services for Industrial Workers* (New York: Family Welfare Association of America, 1945), p. 4; and, B. A. Kogan, "Some Labor Union Enterprises in Public Health Economics," *American Journal of Public Health,* Vol. 38 (July 1948), pp. 945-946.

27 There is no specialization in industrial social work here such as has developed in France. See Harold L. Wilensky and Charles W. Lebeaux, *Industrial Society and Social Welfare* (New York: Russell Sage Foundation, 1958), p. 162.

28 Robert L. Kinney, "Union Counseling Bridges a Gap," *Survey Midnonthly,* (April 1945), pp. 106-108; M. Palevsky, *op. cit.,* pp. 5-8, 35-36.

rank-and-file union members. They aim, however, to give the volunteers an understanding of simple interviewing technique and of classification methods of social problems. The trainees are taught that grievances of a fellow worker about his work and his supervisor belong to the shop steward as representative of the union, and that questions of family disturbances and personal, social, psychological, and health problems should be referred to the proper social and health agencies in the community. The training courses, for this reason, include instruction about the public and private social agencies in the community, their function in the field of family and child welfare, health treatment, and relief, and about their policies and limitations.

The union counselors are able to answer simple legal and jurisdictional questions themselves. The active participation of union members in the counseling process is of significance. It represents a new, positive approach to their concern in social welfare. Serious social and personal problems, however, should be referred to the social agency best suited to help. The most advisable arrangement is that a union staff member or a social worker who enjoys the full confidence of labor serve on the staff of the Welfare Council or of the Community Chest so that any difficult questions may be referred to him. He contacts, then, the special social agency which is able to help the person or family in need of service. In some places, a central referral bureau for all inquiries from union counselors and their "clients" has been set up, but in other cities, the union counselor (union community service director) refers the inquiring workers directly to the competent social agencies. This integration of social services with labor union counseling has proved of value to union members to help them overcome family disturbances, to receive neglected medical and dental care, and to replace oppressing debts with reasonable loans. It also has helped to avoid unnecessary duplication of available community services by special institutions of labor unions.

Many problems (frequently concerning marital difficulties and health and child adjustment questions) brought to the attention of industrial counselors are the same as those encountered in family casework. The short period of training of union counselors, however, limits their information basically to a survey of community welfare and health organizations and to an understanding of the necessity of referring serious problems to a central, experienced representative, if possible a trained social worker. Only careful in-service training and refresher courses for the union counselors, and a conscientious consultant service by a trained social worker, guarantee reliable operation of this new system of making social agencies available to the bulk of the industrial working population.

The difficulty of preparing rank-and-file workers in plants sufficiently, within a short period, for counseling, has led to another approach in which professional social workers assume the task of industrial counseling. This has been experienced in the Workers Personal Service Bureau, organized through the Brooklyn Council for Social Planning in cooperation with eighty New York unions. In the factories, individual workers in need of advice, casework, or other services were approached by a group of union members and leaders who had been prepared by the social agency in a training course and in discussion groups. The emphasis in this approach was upon the fact that counseling of the workers and referral to community agencies should be the responsibility of professional social workers who were familiar with the methods of interviewing, casework, and the resources of the community.

In a number of industries, "in-plant counseling" either by industrial counselors employed by management or by union counselors who advise fellow workers with the consent of management during certain hours on working time, during lunch hours, or after work has been continued. However, industrial counseling does not play such an essential role in the stabilization of the labor force and in the improvement of workers' morale in peacetime as it did during the war.

A few labor unions have established professional social work under their own auspices. The National Maritime Union (AFL-CIO), in cooperation with the United Seamen's Service, has organized a Personal Service Department as a casework agency in New York. During World War II, branch units were operating in New Orleans and San Francisco. Casework is available to members of the American Merchant Marine who have family and other personal and health problems, and referrals are made to other social agencies when they may be of help to the seamen.

Trained, experienced social workers are also employed in some of the health and welfare plans administered under union auspices, for example, in the rehabilitation service of the United Mine Workers of America Welfare and Retirement Fund. They also are employed in

centers for aged and unemployed workers and their families founded
by the United Automobile Workers of America, and in the Community Service Activities of the AFL-CIO.

D. Organized Labor and Social Work

Labor unions in the United States have historically favored protective legislation with regard to child labor and women's work,
workmen's compensation, and old-age insurance. However, prior to
the Depression of the 1930's when the pressing need for unemployment insurance as well as for wage and hours legislation was clearly
demonstrated, their attitude was one of ambivalence toward this
type of social legislation.[29] Since the Depression a positive endorsement of social legislation, including collective bargaining, social security provisions, and extension of social insurance, has become the
unanimous attitude of organized labor in our country.

Originally, labor unions manifested substantial suspicion of, and
very little sympathy for, public and private social work. Even when
industrial workers, during World War I, substantially contributed
to Community Chest drives, they were indifferent about the aims
and methods of charitable agencies and the programs that the drives
supported. The social worker still was considered as a person doling
out largesse and being a representative of a wealthy, superior class,
instead of helping neighbors on a plane of equality. The rank-and-file
workers criticized their employers for paying low wages but boast-
ing of the generous contributions they donated to charities. They
found that private social agencies sometimes were used to discourage
persons in financial need from joining labor unions, and that relief
even was abused as a tool in order to break strikes. During World
War II, a change in this attitude took place. It began with the organization of war relief drives by both the AFL and the CIO in
order to help the suffering people of those countries which had been
attacked by the Axis powers. When these contributions reached an
annual amount of about $50,000,000, in 1942, the National War Fund
and the American Red Cross recognized the need of integrating this
important source of income into the general welfare campaign. It

---

[29] John A. Fitch, "Samuel Gompers and the Labor Movement," *The Survey*
(June 1950), pp. 291-292; and, Albert Deutsch, "Get Together, Labor and
Social Work," *Social Work Today* (April 1942), p. 13.

was evident that several competing drives would result in discontent and conflict among the population, and that only a unified, concerted appeal for war relief as well as domestic health and welfare services would be successful. Organized labor decided to join forces and to cooperate in the National War Fund, through special war relief committees of the AFL and the CIO. Representatives of labor groups were employed in Community Chests, and labor began to play a more significant role in social work.

This role was not limited to aiding the local, state, and national Community Chests and the Red Cross in the united fund raising appeals in factory, plants, docks, and union meetings. In view of the essential efforts of organized labor in raising the large amounts needed for domestic and foreign war relief activities, it was only natural that labor leaders were no longer satisfied with mere "window dressing" representation of labor on boards of social agencies, Community Chests, and Welfare Councils.[30] Their participation in fund raising campaigns, social welfare planning, and policy development of individual agencies led to understanding and a sincere interest among labor unions and their membership in social work. Labor representatives were able to interpret to union members the need for, and the value of, health and welfare services for their own families and for the whole working class, as well as for the sick, old, infirm, and needy children of the community.

In the postwar era, the interest of labor unions in the support of social services through participation in Community Chest campaigns has continued. Closely connected with this active help in raising the necessary funds for voluntary welfare and health agencies is the participation of labor representatives in community welfare councils, which are concerned with the planning of development, concentration, or expansion of social welfare, health and defense facilities. Labor feels that these services should not be handled by a few wealthy people alone, but by representatives of the common man as well. The third result of this sharing in participation of union representatives in policy-making boards and committees of social agen-

---

[30] Howard Keeler, "Unions in Social Work," *Social Work Year Book* (1951), pp. 518-519; Brent Taylor, "Labor Becomes a Big Giver," *Survey Graphic* (February 1943), pp. 47-48; and, Arthur Hillman, "Labor Joins the Chicago Council: Social Work and Labor Explore Their Common Ground," *Community,* Vol. 22, No. 3 (November 1946), pp. 48 ff.

cies (though it usually is only a modest participation in view of the economic and social importance of labor) is that union members and their families are more aware of, and more willing to use, the services of health and welfare agencies. Union members are independent people who are little accustomed to turning to public or private social agencies in time of difficulties. Union counselors have recently been able to dissipate the distrust of union members against social agencies and enable them to use services of the community. The experience of union representatives in social agencies has developed mutual respect between labor and social workers. The participation of organized labor in social work is increasingly accepted as a method for more effective interpretation of social work to the public, and as a fair and constructive relationship. Finally, the cooperation of unions in social work planning will bring into focus unmet needs of the community so that Community Chests and Welfare Councils will realize more easily where essential, actual health and welfare needs require new or expanded services.

Already, now, the "Community Services Committee" of the AFL-CIO is actively engaged in supporting the work of community welfare councils in planning and improving standards of social services, both on the Federal level, and in states and local communities. The fund raising for health and welfare is strengthened by the helpful recommendations of organized labor and active participation in campaigns and collections all over the country. The director of the Community Services Committee, Leo Perlis, is urging community chests and federated funds to allocate money for professional social work education.

Selected Bibliography

I. Services to Veterans and the Armed Forces

Aaronson, Franklin, and Hilda Rosenbloom, "State Aid to Veterans," *Social Security Bulletin,* Vol. 8, No. 2 (February 1945), pp. 12-20.

Bradley, Omar N., "The Veterans Administration," *National Conference of Social Work, Proceedings* (1946), pp. 353-359.

Burns, Eveline M., *The American Social Security System,* Chapter X, "Income Security Measures for Veterans," pp. 265-292. Boston: Houghton, 1949.

Cumming, Roger, 'Veterans' Benefits and Services," *Social Work Year Book* (1954), pp. 521-529.

Gray, Carl R. Jr., "The Veterans' Administration," *The American Annual,* 1st ed. (1952).

Hinshaw, David, *Take Up Thy Bed and Walk.* New York: Putnam, 1948.

Karl, Virginia C., "Veterans Benefits and Services," *Social Work Year Book* (1957), pp. 573-584.

Magnuson, Paul B., "Medical Care for Veterans," *Annals,* Vol. 263 (January 1951).

Maroney, Mildred, "Veterans' Benefits," in Lewis Meriam and Karl Schlotterbeck editors), *The Cost and Financing of Social Security.* Washington: Brookings Institution, 1950, pp. 96-119.

Rohrlich, George F., "Veterans Pensions in Retrospect and in Prospect," *Social Service Review,* Vol. 31, No. 4 (December 1957), pp. 427-441.

Ross, Elizabeth H., "Social Work's Responsibility for Veterans," *National Conference of Social Work, Proceedings* (1946), pp. 336-341.

Stipe, Jack H., "Social Services in the Veterans Administration," *Journal of Social Casework,* Vol. XXIX (February 1948), pp. 43-48.

United States Veterans Administration, *Reorganization of the Veterans Administration.* Washington: Government Printing Office, 1953.

Weber, Gustavus A., and Lawrence F. Schmeckebier, "The Veterans Administration: Its History, Activities, and Organization," *Service Monographs of the U.S. Government, No. 66.* Washington: Brookings Institution, 1934.

II. Public Housing and Urban Renewal

Abbott, Edith, *The Tenements of Chicago: 1908-1935.* Chicago: University of Chicago Press, 1936.

Abrams, Charles, *The Future of Housing.* New York: Harper, 1946.

Aronovici, Carol, and Elizabeth McCalmont, *Catching Up with Housing,* New Jersey: Beneficial Management Association, 1936.

Bauer, Catherine, "Housing in the United States, Problems and Policy," *International Labour Review,* Vol. LII, No. 1 (July 1945).

Breese, Gerald, and Dorothy E. Whiteman, *An Approach to Urban Planning.* Princeton: Princeton University Press, 1953.

Churchill, Henry S., *The City Is the People.* New York: Reynal, 1945.

Dahir, James, *Communities for Better Living; Citizen Achievement in Organization, Design and Development.* New York: Harper, 1950.

————, *The Neighborhood Unit Plan, Its Spread and Acceptance.* New York: Russell Sage Foundation, 1947.

Deutsch, Morton, and Mary E. Collings, *Interracial Housing.* Minneapolis: University of Minnesota Press, 1951.

*Fitch, James Marston, *American Building: The Forces That Shape It.* Boston: Houghton, 1948.

Foley, Donald L., *Neighbors or Urbanites?* Rochester, N.Y.: University of Rochester, 1952.

Goodman, Percival, and Paul Goodman, *Communitas: Means of Livelihood and Ways of Life.* Chicago: University of Chicago Press, 1947.

Hill, John G., "Fifty Years of Social Action on the Housing Front," *Social Service Review,* Vol. XXII, No. 2 (June 1948).

Johnson, Lee F., "Housing," *Social Work Year Book* (1957), pp. 292-302.

Kraus, Hertha, "Housing Our Older Citizens," *Annals,* Vol. 279 (January 1952), pp. 126-138.

Loring, William C., Frank L. Sweetser, and Charles P. Ernst, *Community Organization for Citizen Participation in Urban Renewal.* Cambridge, Mass.: Cambridge Press, 1957.

Mumford, Lewis, *City Development; Studies in Disintegration and Renewal.* New York: Harcourt, 1945.

————, *The Culture of Cities.* New York: Harcourt, 1938.

Post, Langdon W., *The Challenge of Housing.* New York: Rinehart, 1938.

Robbins, Ira S., "Housing Our Aging," New York State Legislative Committee on Problms of the Aging, *Age Is No Barrier* (1952), pp. 117-119.

Straus, Nathan, *The Seven Myths of Housing.* New York: Knopf, 1945.

————, *Two-Thirds of a Nation: A Housing Program.* New York: Knopf, 1952.

Wood, Edith Elmer, *Introduction to Housing: Facts and Principles.* Washington: U.S. Housing Authority, 1940.

*————, *Recent Trends in American Housing.* New York: Macmillan, 1940.

Woodbury, Coleman (editor), *Urban Redevelopment Study,* 2 Vols. Chicago: University of Chicago Press, 1953.

III. Industry and Social Welfare

*Altmeyer, Arthur J., "Social Security and Welfare Funds," in William Haber and Wilbur J. Cohen, *Readings in Social Security,* pp. 132-137. Englewood Cliffs, N.J.: Prentice-Hall, Inc., 1948.

Baker, Helen, *Employee Counseling—A Survey of a New Development in Personnel Relations.* Princeton: Princeton University, 1944.

Becker, Harry, *Labor's Stake in Employment and Retirement.* Detroit: United Auto Workers, 1949.

———— (editor), "Organized Labor and the Problem of Medical Care," *Annals* (January 1951).

Beyer, Clara M., "Labor Standards," *Social Work Year Book* (1954), pp. 308-320.

Coyle, Elisabeth F., "A Description of Industrial Counseling," *The Compass,* Vol. 25, No. 2 (January 1944), pp. 16-19.

Cruikshank, Nelson H., "Labor's Role in the Broad Field of Social Work and Community Responsibility." New York: Community Chests and Councils, 1950.

Davey, Harold W., *Contemporary Collective Bargaining.* 2nd ed. Englewood Cliffs, N.J.: Prentice-Hall, Inc., 1959.

Deutsch, Albert, "American Labor and Social Work," *Science and Society,* Fall (1944), pp. 289-304.

*Eby, Kermit, "Labor's Drive for Security," *Social Service Review,* Vol. XXIV, No. 1 (March 1950), pp. 13-18.

Evans, Elizabeth, "A Business Enterprise and Social Work," *The Compass,* Vol. 25, No. 2 (January 1944), pp. 11-15.

Fitch, John A., "Samuel Gompers and the Labor Movement," *The Survey,* Vol. 86, No. 6 (June 1950), pp. 289-292.

"Ford-UAW Pensions and Social Security Contract," *Monthly Labor Review,* Vol. 69 (December 1949), pp. 649-653.

Gage, Elena, "A Foundation for Industrial Counseling," *The Family* (July 1944), pp. 176-182.

*Goldner, William, *Pensions Under Collective Bargaining.* Berkeley: University of California, Institute of Industrial Relations, 1950.

Hillman, Arthur, "Labor Joins the Chicago Council: Social Work and Labor Explore Their Common Ground," *Community,* Vol. 22, No. 3 (November 1946), pp. 48 ff.

Katz, Alfred H., "Reaching Out to New Clients," *Survey Midmonthly,* Vol. 83, No. 3 (March 1947), pp. 74-76.

*Keeler, Howard, "Unions and Social Work," *Social Work Year Book* (1951), pp. 518-522.

Kerr, Clark, *Social and Economic Implications of Private Pension Plans.* Berkeley: University of California, Institute of Industrial Relations, 1949.

Kinney, Robert L., "Union Counseling Bridges a Gap," *Survey Midmonthly,* Vol. 81, No. 4 (April 1945), pp. 106-108.

Klem, Margaret C., and Walter J. Lear, M.D., "Industrial Health and Medical Programs," *Publication No. 15,* Washington: Federal Security Agency, Public Health Service, 1950.

Kornhauser, Arthur, Robert Dubin, and Arthur M. Ross, *Industrial Conflict.* New York: McGraw, 1954.

*Kramer, Kenneth L., "Labor's Goals for Social Security," *Social Work Journal,* Vol. 31, No. 1 (January 1950), pp. 16-19.

Kyle, Constance, "A Union Serves Its Members," *The Compass* (November 1944), pp. 7-8.

———, "Case Work in the National Maritime Union," *The Family* (October 1944), pp. 217-223.

Labor Participation in Organized Health and Welfare Activities Other Than Fund Raising. New York: Community Chests and Councils, 1943.

Lester, Richard A., *Labor and Industrial Relations.* New York: Macmillan, 1951.

Minkoff, Nathaniel M., "Trade Union Welfare Plans," *Monthly Labor Review,* Vol. 64, No. 2 (February 1947), pp. 201-214.

National Planning Association, *Pensions in the United States.* Washington: Government Printing Office, 1952.

New York State Department of Labor, *Union and Union-Management Health Insurance Plans in New York State.* Albany, N.Y.: January, 1949.

*Pavelsky, Mary, *Counseling Services for Industrial Workers.* New York: Family Welfare Association of America, 1945.

*Pohlmann, Kenneth E., "Rehabilitation of Disabled Miners," *American Journal of Public Health,* Vol. 42, No. 7 (July 1952), pp. 791-794.

Pollack, Jerome, "Kaiser-Fraser UAW-CIO Social Security Program," *Industrial and Labor Relations Review,* Vol. 6, No. 1 (October 1952), pp. 44-109.

Schmalz, Robert, and Henry Freeman, "Case Work Skills in a Worker's Service Bureau," *The Family* (March 1944), pp. 19-26.

Skeels, Jack W., "Labor and Social Welfare," *Social Work Year Book* (1960), pp. 356-362.

Spears, Ethel M., *Company Medical and Health Programs.* New York: National Industrial Conference Board, 1948.

United Mine Workers of America, Welfare and Retirement Fund, *Rehabilitation of the Disabled.* Washington: 1950.

*U.S. Department of Labor, Bureau of Labor Statistics "Collective Bargaining Provisions, Health, Insurance and Pensions," *Bulletin No. 908-17.* Washington: Government Printing Office, 1950.

———, *Health Insurance Plans Under Collective Bargaining, Bulletin No. 1221.* Washington: Government Printing Office, 1956.

Van Eenam, Weltha, and Martha E. Penman, *Analysis of 346 Group Annuities Underwritten in 1946-50*. Washington: Social Security Administration, 1952.

Van Kleeck, Mary, "Social Work on the Industrial Frontier," *The Compass* (November 1944), pp. 3-7.

Weinerman, E. Richard, *Labor Plans for Health: The San Francisco Survey*. San Francisco: Labor Council, 1952.

16.

International Social Welfare

INTERNATIONAL SOCIAL WORK is the youngest branch of social welfare activities. It is based upon the recognition that international cooperation in social welfare is needed in order to assure the well-being, social and economic security, and good health of human beings everywhere. This is indispensable before world peace and stability can be secured.

The United Nations is endeavoring to develop a peaceful world through intergovernmental action by relying on mutual cooperation, world trade, international courts, communication, and education. Social work contributes to these efforts its awareness of human needs, its respect for human dignity, and its skill in helping human beings, particularly in the relief of hunger and disease, in fighting catastrophes, and in rehabilitation services.

International social work in its narrower sense comprises welfare activities under the auspices of international agencies—governmental or voluntary—but social services in foreign countries may also be called international social work.

International social welfare organizations may be classified into four groups:

(1) Government agencies of international character (for example, the United Nations, World Health Organization, UNESCO, International Labor Organization, Colombo Plan, and Bureau for Technical Cooperation).

(2) Private international organizations (for example, the Interna-

500

tional Conference of Social Work, International Red Cross, International Child Welfare Union, World YWCA, International Social Service, International Rescue Committee, World Federation of Mental Health, and World Assembly of Youth).

(3) National government agencies extending their work to other countries (for example, the U.S. Children's Bureau, U.S. Public Health Service, and International Cooperation Administration).

(4) National private agencies extending their social service to other countries (for example, the Danish or Swedish Red Cross, Swiss Aid to Europe, the Dutch Interchurch Aid, American Friends Service Committee, American Joint Jewish Distribution Committee, Church World Service, Catholic Community Service Council, Unitarian Service Committee, and American ORT Federation).

I. HISTORY OF INTERNATIONAL SOCIAL WELFARE

The first international activities in social welfare developed about the mid-nineteenth century when representatives of private and public charities began to organize international conferences in order to share their experiences and thereby to learn of effective new methods in the field of social services. The content of the conventions was related to special problems which were reflected in their titles: International Congress of Charities, Corrections and Philanthropy; Penitentiary Congress; International Penal and Prison Congress; Universal Congress for the Improvement of the Fate of the Blind; International Congress of Public and Private Relief; and International Congress for the Protection of Discharged Prisoners.

After World War I, the International Conference of Social Work met for the first time in Paris, in 1928, and became the international forum of comprehensive character for the exchange of experiences and ideas in social welfare. The purposes of the International Conference are to bring social workers of all countries of the world together to improve, through the mutual exchange of knowledge, the social welfare systems and methods of social work. The first proposal of an International Conference was made by Dr. Clotilde Mulon of Paris, but the real organizer and founder of the International Conference was Professor René Sand of the University of Brussels (Belgium). Conferences were held, after the founding conference in

Paris, at Frankfurt-am-Main, in 1932, and in London, in 1936. After World War II, the fourth conference met in Atlantic City and New York in 1948, the fifth in Paris, in 1950, the sixth in Madras, India, in 1952, the seventh in Toronto, in 1954. The eighth was held in Munich in 1956, the ninth in Tokyo in 1958, and the tenth is to be held in Rome in 1961. Another international conference is scheduled in 1962 in Rio de Janeiro, Brazil.

The Conference maintains international headquarters in New York and regional offices in Paris and Bombay.

The original large-scale organization of many nations related to social welfare is the International Red Cross.[1] Its foundation was inspired by the vision of Henri Dunant, a young banker of Geneva. By accident, he came to the battlefield of Solferino in 1859 and was so shocked by the suffering of the wounded and dying soldiers on both sides that he wrote a book describing these horrors entitled "Un Souvenir de Solferino." He asked for humane treatment of the wounded. This book stirred public opinion in many countries and led to the Geneva Convention of 1864, at which the International Red Cross was founded. Its articles provide that under the guidance of an International Committee, composed of Swiss citizens, principles of humane treatment and medical care of wounded soldiers were to be established, and that hospitals, ambulances, doctors, and nurses caring for these patients should be respected as neutral institutions. The International Committee recognizes new national societies of the Red Cross, encourages all civilized nations to join the Geneva Convention, and attempts to secure the observance of this international law. The International Committee also organizes, if necessary, special agencies in periods of war for the relief of civilian populations, the communication with prisoners of war, including the sending of letters and parcels to these prisoners from their families. It arranges for visits and inspection of prisoner of war camps, and conducts special relief actions in case of major natural catastrophes.

After World War I, in 1919, the League of Red Cross Societies was formed as a federation of the national organizations, aside from the International Committee. The League consists of eighty-two national

---

[1] Martin Gumpert, *Dunant, The Story of the Red Cross* (New York: Oxford University Press, 1938); Ernest P. Bicknell, *With the Red Cross in Europe* (Washington: American National Red Cross, 1938); and, Dorothy Lally, "International Social Welfare, *Social Work Year Book* (1960), pp. 331-334.

Red Cross societies, promotes voluntary national Red Cross work, and encourages collaboration for the improvement of health, prevention of disease, and relief in case of epidemics, earthquakes, floods, and fires.

During World War I, Red Cross societies began to conduct large-scale relief actions. The American and British Red Cross organized hospitals, convalescent homes, dispensaries, and infirmaries in France, Belgium, Italy, and Greece. After the war, international relief actions were continued under the auspices of the International Red Cross, as well as by various national Red Cross societies and other relief organizations. A children's fund for the feeding of undernourished children and for the establishment of child welfare centers, summer camps, kindergartens, and various schools in many European countries characterizes a development of international welfare service.

Red Cross societies were joined in this effort during and after both world wars by other relief organizations, such as the American Friends Service Committee, the British Service Committee (Quakers), the American Jewish Joint Distribution Committee (A.D.C.), the International Save-the-Children Fund (now called the "International Child Welfare Union"), the American Relief Administration, the Near East Foundation, the European Children's Fund, and other philanthropic and humanitarian organizations.[2]

During the period between the two wars, the International Save-the-Children Fund was particularly active in developing child health and welfare services in Ethiopia, Central Africa, and the Balkan countries. The Near East Foundation assisted in the rehabilitation of Greece by setting up hospitals, orphanages, and schools. The Joint Distribution Committee continued its work for children, orphans, and medical care in eastern Europe. It was assisted by "O.S.E.," an international federation for the provision of medical care, hospitals, and dispensaries and for the training of Jewish doctors, nurses, and health personnel and by "O.R.T.," which is devoted to the vocational training of young Jewish persons to prepare them for immigration and resettlement.

---

[2] John Maloney, *Let There Be Mercy* (New York: Doubleday, 1944); Clarence Pickett, *For More Than Bread* (Boston: Little, 1953); Howard L. Brooks, *Prisoners of Hope* (New York: Fischer, 1942); and, Varian Fry, *Surrender on Demand* (New York: Random House, Inc., 1945).

During World War I, recreational services were developed by the American Young Women's Christian Association in various European countries. The international organization of the YWCA, called "World's YWCA," had already been founded earlier in England, in 1894, and helped during and after World War I in refugee and immigration aid. In 1921, it organized a nondenominational International Migration Service (now called "International Social Service") as an independent agency with headquarters in Geneva. The national YMCA's founded an International Committee in 1879 and carried on an extensive program of international service, mutual visits, and conferences; a YMCA committee for war prisoners' aid was active in both world wars.

A new stimulus to international cooperation came from the foundation of the League of Nations. The League had a standing committee on social welfare, and its secretariat established a section on "Social Questions and Opium Traffic." The Committee on Social Questions was particularly concerned with protection of women and children against prostitution ("Traffic in Women and Children"). This committee dealt also with methods of protecting children in the field of child labor, with measures to protect young people in periods of unemployment, and with the suppression of obscene publications. The committee published reports on child marriage, the status of illegitimate children, the setup of child welfare councils, guardianship for illegitimate children, and work in institutions and foster families for children. In the field of health protection the Health Organization of the League published information on epidemics in cooperation with the International Office of Public Health in Paris and set up special bureaus in Singapore and Rio de Janeiro for protective measures against communicable diseases and epidemics. With a permanent world-wide service for the dissemination of epidemiological information, the Health Organization assisted governments in the development of public health systems by interchange of experts and technical personnel and the assignment of specialists to other countries.[3]

---

[3] Harriet E. Davis (editor), *Pioneers in World Order* (New York: Columbia University Press, 1944); Martin Hill, *The Economic and Financial Organization of the League of Nations* (Washington: Carnegie Endowment, 1946); Arthur Sweetzer, "The Non-Political Achievements of the League," *Foreign Affairs* (October 1940); and, Carlile A. Macartney, *Refugees, the Work of the League* (London: League of Nations Union, 1936).

II. THE UNITED NATIONS RELIEF AND
REHABILITATION ADMINISTRATION
(UNRRA)

The United Nations Relief and Rehabilitation Administration (UNRRA) became the most dynamic force in the development of international social welfare. Founded on November 9, 1943, two years before the creation of the United Nations, in Washington, D.C., by forty-four nations, it was an international organization, that was called upon to solve relief problems of tremendous magnitude. The aggression of the Axis powers had, in three years, overrun thirty-five countries in Europe and Asia, destroying their economic and political systems. It left them in semi-starvation, ravaged by hunger, diseases, epidemics and despair, without sufficient food, clothes, and shelter, and lacking care for the sick and homeless. To assist the victims of the war and to restore, after their liberation, normal living conditions, morale, health, and hope was a task which could be undertaken only through the cooperation of all countries of the free world.

As early as in August 1940, Winston Churchill had announced that after the defeat of the Nazis, supplies of food, medicine, raw materials, and the means for reconstruction would be provided to the liberated countries by interallied collaboration. The Leith-Ross Committee (Allied Committee on Post-War Requirements) in London started work for relief and rehabilitation in Europe. The Middle-East Relief and Refugee Administration (MERRA) in Cairo, Egypt, established camps for refugees from the countries attacked by the Axis powers (Poland, Greece, Yugoslavia, Czechoslovakia). In the United States, President Franklin D. Roosevelt, in 1942, established the Office of Foreign Relief and Rehabilitation Operations under the able leadership of former Governor Herbert Lehman, of New York, which began relief work for civilians in North Africa in cooperation with the Allied armies.

The creation of UNRRA became a promise to the people in the invaded countries and to their underground fighters, giving them assurance that the nations of the free world would share their resources in food, clothing, medicine, and emergency supplies as soon as help possibly could be brought. The basic idea was that victory was not enough, that peace also had to be won.[4]

---

[4] United Nations Relief and Rehabilitation Administration, *The Story of*

When UNRRA was able to go into action, it curbed widespread starvation, prevented epidemics, and averted moral and economic collapse in all seventeen war-warped countries where its assistance was requested. It took over the refugee camps in the Middle East and began to bring food, clothing, medicine, and shelter for the hungry, sick, and homeless populations. This relief spelled the difference between life and death for millions of men, women, and children. It was the more urgent as the war was a global one spreading to Europe, Asia, the South Pacific, the Near East, and Africa. The entire population of the war-devastated countries was affected. Strategic bombing destroyed vast areas; the "scorched earth" policy of the Nazis increased the suffering of the civilian population already terrorized by concentration camps, and inhuman, criminal "biological extermination" which murdered millions of innocent human beings.

UNRRA's resources, though they amounted in total to more than three billion dollars, never were large enough to restore fully the shattered economy of the occupied countries. They could not rebuild the destroyed cities, public utilities, factories, mines, ports, railroads, and fishing fleets. But UNRRA put back into operation the segments of the national economy that were indispensable for the survival of the people, for carrying out of the relief program, and for the start of rehabilitation. In order to prevent starvation, UNRRA furnished food and medicine, doctors, nurses, and hospitals. In order to repair roads, bridges, and communications, it provided trucks, bulldozers, freight cars and repair supplies. Millions of refugees and slave laborers captured by the Axis powers were cared for in camps, children's homes, and reception centers.

The main mission of UNRRA was not only to provide relief but also to lay the groundwork for the economic and social recovery of the occupied countries, in order *to help people to help themselves*.[5] UNRRA's tasks were gigantic. It was the greatest of all re-

---

UNRRA (Washington: 1948), p. 3 ff; National Planning Association, *UNRRA: Gateway to Recovery* (Washington: 1944), pp. 12-17; and, Harold H. Hutcheson, "International Agencies for European Reconstruction," *Foreign Policy Reports,* Vol. XXIII, No. 9 (July 15, 1947), pp. 110-120.

[5] Herbert H. Lehman, "UNRRA on the March," *Survey Graphic,* Vol. 33, No. 11 (November 1944), pp. 436-440, 470-471; and, Martha Brandscombe, "The Children of the United Nations—UNRRA's Responsibility for Social Welfare," *Social Service Review,* Vol. XIX, No. 3 (September 1945), pp. 310-323.

lief and rehabilitation undertakings ever attempted in human history. It worked at a time when the world was in chaos and the supplies and materials that UNRRA urgently needed for its work were almost unobtainable because the fighting armies needed them also. UNRRA also had to struggle against the shortage of manpower, because, in all Allied countries, men were enlisted in the armed forces. It often faced jealousy and mistrust on behalf of the military authorities who thought that they could administer relief themselves. In order to carry on this difficult task more effectively, UNRRA created an international administration, which formed a loyal staff deeply devoted to the challenging cause of international aid.

At the end of the war, most nations were desperately in need of the means for survival and rehabilitation. UNRRA accepted the challenge to see to it that nations without foreign exchange would not be left without an adequate share in these scarce supplies so that they could prevent starvation and economic collapse.

At first, aid was limited to the invaded Allied countries without foreign exchange—Albania, Byelorussia, China, Czechoslovakia, Greece, Poland, the Ukraine, and Yugoslavia—then it was extended to Austria and Italy. Limited help also was given to Ethiopia, Finland, Hungary, Korea, and the Philippines. The occupied western European countries, France, the Netherlands, Belgium, Luxembourg, Denmark, and Norway, possessed foreign exchange and did not ask for UNRRA aid.

The administration of UNRRA was directed by a council composed of one representative of each of the nations which subscribed to the organization; the council decided the policy of the agency. A central committee composed of representatives of nine governments acted as executive board and made emergency decisions between council sessions. The executive responsibility and the appointment of the staff was vested in the Director-General—first, Herbert H. Lehman (now United States Senator), then, Fiorello H. LaGuardia (former Mayor of New York), and Major General Lowell W. Rooks. The staff included members from forty nations and totaled, at its peak, over 12,000 persons scattered around the globe. There were experts in administration, food and agriculture, transportation, construction, social welfare, public health, medicine, nursing, communications, finance, and accounting.

In contrast to other international agencies before UNRRA, such as the League of Nations or the International Labor Organization, which only recommended measures and legislation to their member governments, UNRRA was operating as an "action organization." It also became the testing ground for the collaboration of the Allies. The vast dispersion of its activities throughout the world made their administration and coordination difficult.

Starving, sick, and desperate people wanted quick action, but UNRRA could not draw upon tradition and former experience. UNRRA's international staff was willing to work under trying conditions and sacrifices. There was a wide delegation of authority from the executive branch to the missions and welfare teams.

UNRRA was financed by its member nations which had not been occupied by the enemy. They were asked to contribute 2 per cent of their national income for relief and rehabilitation, while all members agreed to share in the cost of administration. Other nations, private agencies, and individuals made voluntary contributions. The largest contributors were the United States with $2,700,000,000 (about 70 per cent), United Kingdom with $624,650,000, and Canada with $138,738,739. Most contributions were made in the form of commodity credits and supplies.[6]

In order to carry on its program, UNRRA bought $3,000,000,000 worth of food and supplies in many parts of the world, packed and shipped them in more than 6,000 cargo ships over every ocean. It moved into country after country as the Axis forces retreated. It seldom had enough of the many commodities the liberated countries were pleading for, and prompt delivery frequently was delayed by military obstacles, procurement decisions by national agencies, legislative actions in many countries, strikes, changing international policies, changes in government authority, and civil war.

The Council had established the principle that UNRRA supplies should be distributed without regard to politics, race, or religon. It was ordered that food and other supplies should be given without charge to anyone in distress who could not pay for them. But govern-

---

[6] George Woodbridge, *The History of UNRRA* (New York: Columbia University Press, 1950).

ments were permitted to sell goods to those who were able to pay for them in local currency so that the countries could rebuild their health, welfare, and community services. About one-half of UNRRA's total activities was devoted to the distribution of food. There was severe hunger in Europe and Asia, widespread malnutrition and hunger diseases. But actual starvation and threatening famines and epidemics were averted through UNRRA food (mostly bread grain, rice, fat, oils, dairy products, canned or powdered milk, sugar, meat, and vegetables). UNRRA also furnished agricultural tools, seeds, farm animals, and fertilizer to restore production.

UNRRA organized the largest international health program, so far known. It curbed epidemics across Europe and, with the exception of one cholera epidemic, in Asia. The medical staff counseled and assisted the governments of the liberated countries in the rehabilitation of their public health services, through the use of modern medical and sanitary methods, and installed UNRRA's own medical care only in the displaced persons' (DP) camps. UNRRA's health services prevented typhus, and other widespread contagious diseases, reduced malaria in Greece and Italy, and stopped cholera epidemics in China and Egypt in 1946 and 1947. Hospitals, nursing schools, and sanitary systems were established with modern medical supplies, and UNRRA taught doctors, nurses, and technicians how to use them.

The care of the refugees and displaced persons became a major task of UNRRA. By May 1944, UNRRA had taken care of 40,000 Yugoslav, Greek, and Polish refugees, partisans and their families, in tent camps in the Middle East and Northern Africa. In Germany, Austria, and Italy, UNRRA assisted the Allied military forces in the reception of about 8,000,000 refugees and slave laborers in assembly centers, and in their repatriation to their home countries. UNRRA also coordinated the work of voluntary social agencies of many countries, which provided refugee aid and immigration services. It set up a Central Tracing Bureau in order to find lost relatives, husbands, wives, children, and parents, and organized the repatriation of displaced persons and slave laborers who wanted to return to their native countries. Many needed hospitalization, medical and psychiatric treatment, and rehabilitation. Special children's centers were established for children who had lost their families. There were over 10,000 children in these centers in Germany (Aglasterhausen, Munich, Feldafing, and so on), and other thousands were brought back from German families where the Nazis had placed them.[7]

There were among the refugees and displaced persons more than 500,000, however, who for political or religious reasons, could not or did not want to return to their homeland. UNRRA did not force them to go back against their desire and, in June 1947, turned them over to the International Refugee Organization which had been set up for this purpose by the United Nations. In the DP camps, over forty private agencies worked with UNRRA in refugee aid. UNRRA was not responsible for the repatriation of prisoners of war or displaced persons who refused to be brought back to their native land. The International Red Cross Committee in Geneva and the Intergovernmental Committee on Refugees, created at the Evian Conference in 1938, in cooperation with the League of Nations High Commission for Refugees, had been organized before for these tasks.

In August 1946, the United States and the United Kingdom requested that UNRRA's activities be brought to a close; they did not want to continue relief and rehabilitation on an international basis. As a result, UNRRA's work was terminated at the end of 1947.

When UNRRA had to cease its work, other international agencies took over important phases with the assistance of substantial residual funds and some of UNRRA's trained personnel. These were the International Children's Emergency Fund (created upon the urgent request of the UNRRA Council by the United Nations), the International Refugee Organization, the World Health Organization, and the United Nations Food and Agricultural Organization.[8]

---

[7] Fred K. Hoehler, *Europe's Homeless Millions* (New York: Foreign Policy Association, 1945); Fred K. Hoehler, "Displaced Persons," in George B. de Huszar (editor), *Persistent International Issues* (New York: Harper, 1947), pp. 41-68; National Planning Association, *Europe's Uprooted People* (Washington: 1944); and, Jane Perry Clark Carey, *The Role of Uprooted People in European Recovery* (Washington: National Planning Association, 1948).

[8] W. Hardy Wickwar, "UNRRA in Retrospect," *The Social Service Review*, Vol. XXI, No. 3 (September 1947), pp. 363-374; Donald S. Howard, "After UNRRA—What?" *Survey Graphic*, Vol. 36 (April 1947), pp. 236-239, 264-269; and, Stephen S. Goodspeed, *The Nature and Function of International Organizations* (New York: Oxford University Press, 1959).

III. SOCIAL WELFARE UNDER THE UNITED NATIONS AND INTERGOVERNMENTAL AGENCIES

A. United Nations Activities

Under the provisions of the United Nations Charter, approved in 1945, the Economic and Social Council (ECOSOC) was authorized to develop a comprehensive system of international social welfare, dealing with humanitarian and social problems. It was to become "the international machinery for the promotion of the economic and social advancement of all peoples." Article 55 of the U.N. Charter does not limit responsibility to the improvement of social or health conditions, emergency situations, or international problems. This goal was to be accomplished, as well, by the promotion of higher standards of living, by attempting to secure full employment, by the development of conditions of economic and social progress, and by international cooperation among nations in solving problems of economic, social, health, and related character.

The Council promotes international cultural and educational cooperation, and it encourages universal respect for, and observance of, human rights and fundamental freedoms for all human beings without distinction as to race, sex, religion, or language. Within the framework of the Council, health and welfare questions are primarily the concern of the Social Commission. The Commissions on Human Rights, Economics and Employment, Status of Women, and Narcotic Drugs assume responsibility in related fields, of importance for the health and welfare of people and provided by community services.[9] The Council prepares draft conventions for international cooperation and makes recommendations to the General Assembly of the United Nations as well as to member governments with reference to social legislation, education, and health and cultural progress. The Council has the responsibility for coordinating the activities of the specialized agencies in the field of welfare, cultural relations, and health.

---

[9] The organizational structure of ECOSOC is shown in Chart 8. See also Martha Branscombe, "Responsibility for Co-ordination of Social Services at the International Level," *International Social Work,* Vol. 1, No. 1 (January 1958), pp. 40-44.

In the United Nations Secretariat, the Division of Social Welfare in the Department of Social Affairs is the staff unit which administers social service projects under the direction of ECOSOC and with the advice of its Social Commission. The work of the Division of Social Welfare, of the Technical Assistance Administration, and of UNICEF are the most important practical activities of the United Nations in international social welfare operations. They include research studies and reports on social problems, assistance in social welfare programs and social administration, consultant service to governments, information on social welfare practice, collection and provision of literature and films, scholarships for studies in foreign countries and fellowships for observation of social services in other countries, help in social welfare training, and increasing knowledge and skill in services for families, children, handicapped persons, correctional services, and housing. The work has shifted emphasis from emergency measures to international social welfare policy and long-term programs of social change, raising the levels of living and overcoming the traditional poverty, ill health and ignorance which still is the condition of one-half of the world's population. International seminars on social security, rural welfare, child welfare services, and teaching of social casework have been arranged under the auspices of the United Nations with the aid of the participating countries on various continents. At the request of governments, experts are sent to those countries which desire advice on such matters as child welfare, rehabilitation of handicapped persons, public assistance, casework or group work techniques, social insurance legislation and administration, prevention and treatment of delinquency, and community organization for health and social welfare.[10]

United Nations Children's Fund. Under its original title "United Nations International Children's Emergency Fund" this agency was established in 1946 at the urgent request of the UNRRA Council in order to carry on child feeding and child welfare services that could not be discontinued without grave damage to millions of chil-

---

[10] *Report on the World Social Situation* (Geneva: United Nations, 1957); Julia P. Henderson, "Urbanization and the World Community," *The Annals,* Vol. 314 (November 1957), pp. 147-155; Robert E. Asher, *et al., The United Nations and Promotion of General Welfare* (Washington: Brookings Institution, 1957); and, Hertha Kraus (editor), "International Social Welfare," Annals, May 1960, Vol. 329.

Chart 8. *United Nations: the Economic and Social Council and the Specialized Agencies.*

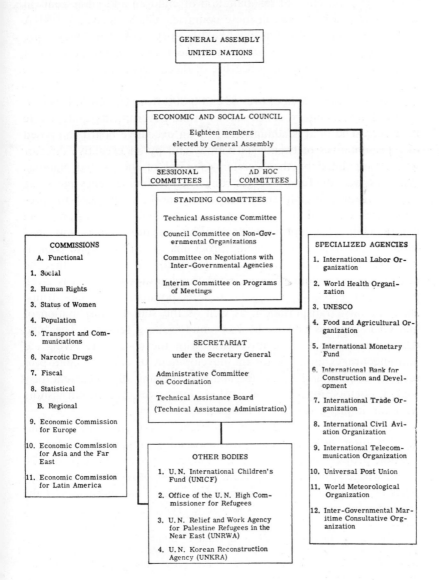

dren, pregnant women, and nursing mothers. The United Nations Assembly adopted provisions stipulating that UNICEF was to operate for the benefit and rehabilitation of children and adolescents in war-devastated countries, in those countries which received UNRRA assistance, and finally for child-health purposes where they were needed in general. The distribution of aid was to be on the basis of need, without discrimination because of race, creed, nationality status, or political belief.

UNICEF received, first, over $32,000,000 from UNRRA. It is now financed by voluntary contributions from governments and private resources. The fund is administered by an executive board composed of representatives of twenty-six nations and by an executive director who is appointed by the Secretary-General of the United Nations. After the war, the fund first was concerned with emergency measures of mass feeding of children and expecting mothers. In 1950, the program was changed to concentrate on children's aid of long-term nature, child health projects, particularly antituberculosis and antisyphilis vaccination, and training programs for child welfare personnel.[11] UNICEF applies the "matching principle": it requires that the government or voluntary agencies in the country where aid is given provide indigenous supplies, such as flour, potatoes, vegetables, fruits, sugar or fats, transportation, as well as the staff for distribution of UNICEF supplies and medical or child welfare services. The fund thus operates on a cooperative basis with the country receiving aid and encourages initiative for the development of effective child protection, child welfare services, and the training of competent personnel, doctors, nurses, social workers, midwives, and health visitors who can improve conditions immediately.

The fund assisted in the establishment of the International Children's Center, in Paris, which provides training, research, and demonstration projects in maternal and child services for doctors, nurses, social workers, and other professional personnel. UNICEF also supports a postgraduate training center for nurses and physicians at the All India Institute for Health and Public Hygiene in Calcutta. Its most

---

[11] Samuel K. Jacobs, "The United Nations International Children's Emergency Fund: An Instrument of International Social Policy," *Social Service Review,* Vol. XXIV, Nos. 2 and 3 (June 1950), pp. 143-172; (September 1950), pp. 347-373.

spectacular actions after the end of World War II, were mass feeding programs and the testing and antituberculosis vaccination of nearly 40,000,000 children in Europe, Asia, the Near East, Africa, Latin America and the Philippines which still are going on. UNICEF provides food, clothing, and drugs for children after various natural catastrophes.[12]

The following experience of a health worker on the island of Borneo illustrates international welfare services being administered under the auspices of UNICEF. In the tropical region near Simanggang, he discovered a seventeen-year-old boy, in a wooden cage suspended under the longhouse where the villagers live. The child was totally crippled with yaws, his body raw all over with sores. For seven hopeless years he had been caged in this way in order to protect the parents and other members of the family and the inhabitants of the village from contagion and from the intolerable smell of his rotting flesh. No medical treatment for this cruel disease was known in the isolated village. The cage was just big enough for the boy to sit in, but he could not get up or walk a bit. Food was passed through a small opening of the cage.[13]

The condition of this child is a brutal, cogent example of what a case of untreated yaws can do to a human being. The young Dayak was moved to the Kuching Hospital. There, elaborate plastic surgery has cured his continuous pain and helped him regain some use of his limbs. Today, one single shot of UNICEF penicillin, at a price of only fifteen cents, is all that is needed to cure a case of yaws, providing the disease is caught in time. In June 1953, vaccination campaigns, made under the auspices of UNICEF in Asia against this contagious disease, passed the 1,000,000 mark, and have been maintained since.

On October 6, 1953, the United Nations decided that UNICEF should continue on a permanent basis as an international child welfare organization directly within the framework of the UN.

---

[12] *UNICEF, Compendium,* Vol. 6 (1957); Maurice Pate, "UNICEF, A Year of Achievement in 80 Countries," *United Nations Review,* Vol. 1, No. 2 (August 1954), pp. 11-15; Spurgeon M. Keeny, *Half the World's Children* (New York: Association Press, 1957); and, Robert L. Heilbronner, *Mankind's Children: The Story of UNICEF* (New York: Public Affairs Pamphlet No. 279, 1959).

[13] "News of the World's Children," *United Nations Bulletin,* Vol. XIV, No. 12 (June 15, 1953), p. 439.

B. Intergovernmental Agencies

Under the auspices of the United Nations, the *International Refugee Organization,* in 1947, took over from UNRRA the care of about 700,000 displaced persons and refugees, located, for the most part, in assembly centers and camps in Central Europe to repatriate or resettle them. Both activities met with serious difficulties. The composition of the families of refugees, with small children or older dependents, and the age of others, prevented many from emigrating to countries which were willing to receive only single, young, healthy men or women suited for rural or industrial labor. Others were excluded from emigration by health conditions, particularly tuberculosis, crippling and contagious diseases, or vocational limitations. There were not sufficient funds to pay transportation even for those refugees who wanted to emigrate and had found a country willing to receive them. IRO adhered to the principle that no refugee should be compulsorily repatriated. The so-called "hard core" refugees, particularly old, handicapped, and sick persons, who, with few exceptions, were not admitted anywhere and could not migrate to other countries, finally had to be left where they were—mainly in Germany, Austria, and Italy.[14]

When IRO terminated its operations in 1952, the United Nations assumed the responsibility for the remaining 400,000 refugees and displaced persons who had neither been repatriated nor resettled, as well as for new religious and political refugees. In order to provide aid and international protection for these refugees, the Office of the United Nations High Commissioner for Refugees (UNHCR) was created in 1951. The High Commissioner has headquarters in Geneva and attempts to reach agreement between various nations to secure the rights and the legal status of refugees and emigrants. The Office attempts to facilitate the settlement of refugees in the country where they have sought asylum, to integrate them into this country's economy, and to make them self-supporting. When it proves impossible for the country of residence to absorb the refugees, migration is considered. The High Commissioner is not engaged in direct

---

[14] Edward B. Marks, Jr., "The Hard Core DP's," *The Survey,* Vol. 85, No. 9 (September 1949), pp. 481-486; and, Marie Dresden Lane, "Who Share Our Concern for These People: The Resettlement of Unwanted Refugees by the International Refugee Organization," *Social Service Review,* Vol. XXVI, No. 3 (September 1952), pp. 270-283.

migration and settlement services, but he negotiates with governments and voluntary agencies to enable the refugees to migrate to countries where they may find a new home.

Because the budget of the High Commissioner is not sufficient to supply financial aid even to the most needy groups of refugees, the United Nations General Assembly authorized the High Commissioner to issue a special appeal for a Refugee Emergency Fund. Refugees in need of help, in 1954, were still living in camps in Shanghai, Hong Kong, Palestine, Turkey, Greece, Italy, Trieste, Austria, and Germany. Their total number was estimated at 3,000,000; not included in this number were 7,000,000 refugees in India who fled from Pakistan after the partition of the country. A difficult problem are the new refugees in Western Germany who escaped from the territory behind the Iron Curtain and for whom international help seems to be required.[15]

The High Commissioner has set up branch offices in Washington, D.C., London, Paris, Brussels, Rome, Bad Godesberg (Germany), Vienna, Athens, Bogota (Colombia), and Hong Kong to work for the legal, economic, and social protection of refugees, provision of certificates, and for their admission to countries which are willing to receive them and their resettlement there.

Another serious problem of an international nature developed in 1948 when nearly 800,000 Arab refugees who had fled from Israel were in gravest need in the surrounding Arab countries and in Arab-controlled areas of Palestine. IRO was not able to assume responsibility for their care. The International Red Cross and the American Friends Service Committee organized emergency aid for food, clothes, houses, health services, and some vocational training. The United Nations finally were forced to set up a *Relief and Work Agency for Palestine Refugees in the Near East* (UNRWA), whose director is appointed by the Director-General of the United Nations, in consultation with the government members of an Advisory Commission composed of the representatives of France, Turkey, the United Kingdom, and the United States as permanent members, and of Jordan and Syria. In 1960, there were still over 900,000 refugees,

---

[15] Some of these refugees came as immigrants to the United States, under the provisions of the *Refugee Immigration Act of 1953*. See Walter A. Friedlander, "The New Refugees in Germany: A Challenge to Social Work," *Social Work Journal*, Vol. XXXIV, No. 4 (October 1953), pp. 157-160, 178.

one-third of them living in camps and tents, near Gaza in southern Palestine and in Jordan, Lebanon, and Syria.[16]

In December 1950, the General Assembly of the United Nations established the *United Nations Korean Reconstruction Agency* (UNKRA) in order to help relieve the sufferings of the Korean population and to repair the widespread devastation caused by the War. UNKRA rehabilitated agricultural production, food processing and preservation, industrial development, electric power, transportation, and communications. The organization helped in the rebuilding of schools, hospitals, children's institutions, fundamental education, health measures to prevent communicable diseases, housing projects, sanitation, and the establishment of social welfare services.

Among the specialized international agencies, the following operate programs which are related to social welfare and health:

(1) The *International Labor Organization* (ILO).

(2) The *World Health Organization* (WHO).

(3) The *Food and Agricultural Organization* (FAO).

(4) The *United Nations Educational, Scientific, and Cultural Organization* (UNESCO).

The organizations are independent in their administration and operation, and are directed by their own boards and councils. Their governing bodies, however, work in close cooperation with the United Nations.

1. International Labor Organization

This agency was organized in 1919, after World War I, and has assisted in the improvement of labor-management relations, the enactment of social legislation, and in the development of social security systems in many countries. The ILO recommended social insurance laws, the replacement of outdated poor relief by modern social assistance statutes, maternity and infant protection, child labor

---

[16] *United Nations Bulletin,* Vol. 14, No. 5 (March 1, 1953), p. 185; and Vol. 16, No. 9 (May 14, 1954), pp. 354-357. An analysis of this difficult problem is presented in Sibylla G. Thicknesse, *Arab Refugees: A Survey of Resettlement Possibilities* (London: Royal Institute of International Affairs, 1949); and, Joseph B. Schechtman, *The Arab Refugee Problem* (New York: Philosophical Library, 1952).

laws, and the protection of unmarrried women and illegitimate children.

Since social justice is a prerequisite for lasting peace, the ILO promotes improvement of labor conditions in all countries by encouraging economic progress and social legislation. It attempts to eliminate human suffering and deprivation, and recommends regulation of working hours, of labor supply, and prevention of unemployment and work injuries. It aims at obtaining an adequate living wage in all countries and social protection of workers and their families against sickness and disablement. The ILO advocates the protection of children, young persons, and women against damaging labor and of foreign workers against exploitation. It recognizes the principle of freedom of association and of labor union organization and supports vocational and technical guidance and education as well as rehabilitation.[17]

The administration of the ILO is vested in a body of delegates of sixty-six nations, representing not just governments, but also labor and management. The International Labor Conference serves as its parliament, to which, annually, each member country sends four delegates: one employer, one worker, and two government representatives. The "governing body" is the executive council of ILO; the International Labor Office, its secretariat, has its headquarters in Geneva. The ILO is financed by its government members and has been accepted as a "specialized agency" by the Economic and Social Council of the United Nations. Both the ILO and the United Nations share an interest in the strengthening of social security and the improvement of living standards and health conditions. ILO works in closest cooperation with ECOSOC for the protection of child and woman labor, and the development of social insurance, public assistance legislation, and family allowances.

2. World Health Organization

During the Conference in San Francisco in 1945, which created the Charter and founded the organization of the United Nations,

---

[17] James T. Shotwell (editor), *The Origins of the International Labor Organization* (New York: Columbia University Press, 1934); and, Bernard Beguin, "ILO and the Tripartite System," *International Conciliation No. 523* (May 1959).

Brazil proposed to include the protection of health into the goals of the United Nations. After preparation in Paris, an International Health Conference convened in New York in June 1946, through invitation by the United Nations. It approved the Constitution of the World Health Organization. It is the first world-wide health agency—a specialized agency of the United Nations—comprising ninety nations as members.[18] Its principal organs are the World Health Assembly, composed of representatives of all member countries and meeting each year, the Executive Board with eighteen members elected by the Assembly, and the Secretariat under the Director-General.

The WHO carries on the work of international health activities formerly organized by the International Office for Public Hygiene in Paris, the League of Nations, and UNRRA. Its objective is the attainment of the highest possible level of health for all the people on earth. The preamble of the WHO constitution defines health as "the state of complete physical, mental, and social well-being and not merely the absence of disease or infirmity." Six major programs of action include the promotion of maternal and infant hygiene, of nutritional diets, and of environmental hygiene, as well as campaigns against malaria, tuberculosis, yaws, typhus, trachoma, and venereal diseases. Many of these health programs are operated jointly with UNICEF when they are aimed at the protection of children, mothers, and youth, and with other organizations.

WHO is not content to help prevent diseases from crossing frontiers, but assists member governments in eradicating communicable diseases in source areas. It acts as a clearing-house for scientific information on health matters, keeps its members informed on latest developments, such as vaccines and nuclear radiation hazards, publishes an international pharmacopoeia on drugs and medicines and numerous technical publications. It operates a warning service on epidemic diseases anywhere in the world and recommends health regulations on international travel by land, sea, and air. WHO advises its members on the most effective ways of organizing health

---

[18] C. E. A. Winslow, "International Cooperation in the Service of Health," *Annals,* Vol. 273 (January 1951); Ritchie Calder, *Ten Steps Forward* (Geneva: WHO, 1958); Brock Chisholm, "Growing Up in a Changing World," *International Social Work,* Vol. 1, No. 3 (July 1958), pp. 25-29; and, Munray Morgan, *Doctors to the World* (New York: Viking Press, 1958).

services and sends on request international teams of physicians, nurses, teachers, and social workers to assist in health protection. It permits health workers to obtain advanced education abroad and assists governments in the improvement of training facilities for health personnel. WHO tries to break the vicious circle "disease breeds poverty, poverty breeds disease."

WHO has its headquarters at Geneva (Switzerland) and six regional offices, one for Africa (Brazzaville), for the Americas (Washington, D. C.), for the Eastern Mediterranean (Alexandria), for Europe (Copenhagen), for South East Asia (New Delhi), and for the Western Pacific (Manila). The delegates of the World Health Assembly are representatives of their government, and also experts in public health. All member nations contribute to WHO's annual budget according to a "scale of assessment." WHO is supported by the U. N. Technical Assistance Fund (annually for about $5,000,000), and takes an active part in the technical assistance program of the United Nations.[19] Its main emphasis is directed towards the development of efficient public health services (including demonstration projects), control of endemic diseases, fight against communicable disease, protection of the healthy growth of children, improvement of sanitation, and training of health personnel.

In 1948, a private international organization in the field of mental hygiene, the *World Federation for Mental Health,* was founded in London at the World Congress for Mental Health. The Federation supports the work of the United Nations, of the World Health Organization, and of the UNESCO, in cooperation with governments, professional associations, and private mental hygiene societies. Its goal is the promotion of mental health, in fostering the ability to live harmoniously in a world of tensions, and in providing information, popular education, and the training of professional personnel in the field of mental hygiene.

3. Food and Agricultural Organization

The United Nations Food and Agricultural Organization (FAO),

---

[19] Walter R. Sharp, *International Technical Assistance* (Chicago: Public Administration Service, 1952), pp. 73-77; H. L. Keenleyside, "Education or Catastrophe," *Adult Leadership,* Vol. 2, No. 7 (December 1953), pp. 4-7; and, Margaret Mead, *Cultural Patterns and Technical Change* (Geneva: UNESCO, 1957).

with headquarters in Rome, was established in 1945 with the purpose of abolishing famines and malnutrition through increased food production and a better distribution of agricultural products. As progress in sanitary facilities and medical care reduces mortality rates and, therefore, increases the population, it becomes necessary to augment the agricultural production by the use of scientific methods. In 1960, seventy-six nations were members of the organization. FAO furnishes technical information and instruction and conducts research and demonstration projects in crop and animal improvement and forest and fishery development. FAO assists countries on their request by improving methods of conservation, processing, and marketing of food.[20]

FAO thus works toward raising levels of nutrition and of standards of living by assistance in the improvement in the efficiency of agricultural production, husbandry, and fishing. It also helps provide better methods of distributing food and agricultural products and in the improvement of living and working conditions of the rural population. FAO contributes through its work toward an expanding and more abundant world economy.

The aim of the United Nations and its specialized agencies to secure to all mankind basic human rights, a decent standard of living, and health, social and economic security, can be achieved only if above all every man has sufficient food. For this reason the work of FAO is of such vital importance to human welfare.

4. UNESCO

As a specialized agency of the United Nations, UNESCO was established in 1945 in order to contribute to peace and security through international cooperation in the fields of education, science, and culture. Its organization structure is a general conference with representatives of all member nations, an executive board of eighteen members, and the secretariat under a director-general with headquarters in Paris. UNESCO strives to promote mutual understanding among peoples by the distribution of cultural, scientific, and educational information—through libraries, radio, movies, periodicals,

---

[20] United Nations Food and Agricultural Organization, *Essentials of Rural Welfare* (Washington, D.C.: 1949); and, W. Sharp, *op. cit.,* pp. 71-73.

and newspapers.[21] It encourages exchange of students, artists, scientists, international children and youth conferences, seminars, and research studies in philosophy, humanities, history, art, social, and natural sciences.

UNESCO is mainly concerned with the development of education, human values, and social behavior. UNESCO attempts to realize the idea of a world community by promoting special projects, such as international youth conferences, camps, schools, and children's villages. In a program of promotion of welfare in a rapidly changing world, its task is to emphasize the constructive, peaceful use of technical achievements. UNESCO's function is to apply the teachings of cultural anthropology, psychology, and sociology to the improvement of education, the abolition of illiteracy, the development of adult education and the encouragement of creative art and scientific research with full respect for indigenous cultural and religious values.[22]

UNESCO believes in equal opportunities for education for all human beings, in unrestricted pursuit of objective truth, and in free exchange of knowledge and ideas. It considers intellectual and moral solidarity as essential for world peace, and education for justice, liberty, and peace a duty of all nations. UNESCO attempts to develop mutual understanding and fundamental education, the spread of culture and of scientific knowledge. It has conducted research into the causes of political tensions, the concepts of liberty, democracy, and law, racial problems, and prejudice.

To preserve the independence, integrity, and fruitful diversity of the various cultures, UNESCO is prohibited from intervening in cultural questions which are the responsibility of its members. In the area of scientific cooperation, UNESCO has not been able to organize an international research institute of its own, but it supports international institutions, such as the Zoological Station at Naples and the High Altitude Research Stations in Switzerland.[23]

---

[21] Brenda M. H. Tripp, "UNESCO in Perspective," *International Conciliation, No. 497* (March 1954); and, Kenneth Soddy, *Mental Health and Infant Development* (New York: Basic Books, 1953).

[22] Frederick S. Dunn, *War and the Minds of Men* (New York: Harper, 1950), pp. 10-12; and, Harold E. Snyder, *When People Speak to People* (Washington: American Council on Education, 1953).

[23] Other specialized agencies which are less oriented toward health and welfare policies are the World Bank for International Reconstruction, the International Monetary Fund, the Universal Postal Union, the International

IV. THE TECHNICAL ASSISTANCE PROGRAM

Assistance in periods of mass distress—famine, flood, earthquakes, fire, and volcanic eruptions—has been the object of international relief for a long time. The rapid development of technology and natural science, however, has focused our attention upon the fact that more than half of the people of our world are living under conditions of hunger, poor health, and economic deprivation. For many decades, therefore, religious missionary groups, private philanthropy, and more recently, national and international public agencies have brought education, technical training and skills, and child and health services to countries in need of help.[24] During World War II, UNRRA provided organized methods of technical assistance to countries willing to accept such aid in the attempt to help themselves. As we discussed above, some of the main activities of the United Nations Secretariat in the field of social welfare and those of the specialized agencies in connection with the United Nations are devoted to the objective of assisting the peoples of the so-called "underdeveloped areas of the world" (which we might rather designate as "developing areas") to defeat the threat of hunger, disease, and want by production of more food, more clothing, better housing, and sanitation.

In his inaugural address, January 20, 1949, President Truman emphasized the need for raising living standards in underdeveloped countries by helping them to increase their production through technical improvement of their material resources, agriculture and industries, and the productive capacity of their people. The *Point Four Program* suggested that capital be invested for the economic develop-

Trade Organization, the International Telecommunications Union, the International Civil Aviation Organization, and the Inter-Governmental Maritime Consultative Organization. (See Chart 8): Structure of the UN Economic and Social Council.

[24] W. Sharp, *op. cit.,* pp. 1-23; William A. Brown, Jr. and Redoers Opie, *American Foreign Assistance* (Washington, D.C.: Brookings Institution, 1953); Robert T. Mack, Jr., *Raising the World's Standard of Living* (New York: Citadel, 1953); U.N. Department of Social Affairs, *Social Progress Through Community Development* (New York: United Nations, 1955); James W. Wiggins *et al., Foreign Aid Reexamined: A Critical Appraisal* (Washington: Public Affairs Press, 1958); and, Irwin T. Sanders *et al., Interprofessional Training Goals for Technical Assistance Personnel Abroad* (New York: Council on Social Work Education, 1959).

ment of underdeveloped countries through private, governmental, and international resources (for example, the International Monetary Fund), and the establishment or expansion of technical assistance so that the exchange and the application of scientific and professional knowledge, techniques, and skills would help the people to raise their living standards. The program was conceived as a cooperative enterprise of all countries through the United Nations and its specialized agencies.

President Truman's initiative was highly praised, but the realization of his idea was delayed by Congress. In 1950, the *Foreign Economic Assistance Act* approved the basic objective "to aid the efforts of the peoples of the underdeveloped areas to develop their resources and improve their working and living conditions by encouraging the exchange of technical knowledge and skills and the flow of investment capital." [25] Business pressure urged special treaties with foreign countries in order to secure capital protection for private investors.

The *Act for International Development* (1950) attempted to achieve a compromise between aid to underdeveloped areas for the development of their resources, by exchange of technical knowledge and skills, and by the investment of capital in these areas. The government was authorized to participate in international projects of technical assistance under the auspices of the United Nations and its specialized agencies or to conclude bilateral agreements with individual countries.

The administration of the Point Four Program was vested in the Technical Cooperation Administration (TCA) in the Department of State, and, in 1953, was transferred to the Foreign Operations Administration, in the Office of the Director of Mutual Security. It is now handled by the International Cooperation Administration, Department of State. Requests for technical assistance were made from countries in Europe, Asia, the Near East, Latin America, and Africa. After the approval of a project to which the foreign countries always contribute their own share in materials, supplies, personnel, and maintenance, other Federal agencies, such as the Department of Health, Education and Welfare or the Department of Agriculture,

---

[25] Frances K. Kernohan, "Organization for Foreign Social Policy," *Social Work Journal*, Vol. 34, No. 4 (October 1953), pp. 147-150, 173-176; and Dorothy Lally, *op. cit.*, pp. 328-331.

assume the execution of the project, usually in cooperation with a field mission of the International Cooperation Administration (ICA). Projects are divided into the categories of: (1) agriculture and natural resources development, (2) health, education, and welfare, and (3) industry and government services.[26]

Characteristic of many of the projects, especially from the point of view of social work, has been the cooperation among members of different nations and various professions in these "field teams." They are frequently composed of an agriculturist, an engineer, a doctor, a nurse, a plant pathologist, and a social worker, as well as indigenous experts in some of these professions.

The particular contribution of the social worker in the team is his professional experience and ability to recognize the most urgent social needs of the population and to assist people to find for themselves the best-suited solution for their problems. The social worker's qualification for this function is based upon his knowledge of human behavior and his understanding of the specific mentality of the people with whom he works. This concept helps him to accept the religious and cultural customs of people, which may be very different from his own. It enables him to help a foreign community to determine the extent and urgency of its problems and to activate all possible resources for their solution.

The development of such a program of technical assistance services, therefore, needs to be met in cooperation with the people of the community and in consideration of the importance of their religious and cultural values and their human dignity. The specific assignment of a social worker to the team is based upon his ability to awaken a sincere interest in the population for the betterment of their living conditions, to make them desirous for the changes which may be brought about in the program.[27] In cooperation with other

---

[26] A penetrating analysis of the structure, organization, and administration of the projects is to be found in W. Sharp, *op. cit.,* pp. 25-58; Technical Assistance Board, *The Expanded Programme of Technical Assistance for Economic Development of Under-Developed Countries* (New York: United Nations, 1953); and, Ernest B. Harper and Arthur Dunham, *Community Organization in Action* (New York: Association Press, 1959), pp. 501-536.

[27] Melvin A. Glasser, *The Role of Social Service in Raising the Standard of Living* (New York: American Association of Social Workers, 1953), pp. 28-34; Charles I. Schottland, "Social Work Issues in the Political Arena," *Social Wel-*

members of the team, the social worker has to use all his skill to explore and enlist the resources in the community which may help to solve urgent health and welfare needs. He has to evaluate their emotional, as well as their health and economic, implications so that the team may establish a working program for economic development, child health and welfare, delinquency prevention, rehabilitation of the handicapped, or whatever else is an urgent need of the community. Some technical assistance projects of this type already have demonstrated remarkable progress in the control of malaria, tuberculosis, yaws, and other diseases, in food production concerning the quality and quantity of nutrition, and improvements in educational methods, housing conditions, sanitation, water supply, and industrial development.

The same type of technical assistance projects has been carried on under the auspices of the United Nations and its specialized agencies with financial and technical aid from the United States. In 1949, ECOSOC submitted a program for international technical assistance to the General Assembly of the United Nations, which approved the proposal. Projects are carried on through the Food and Agricultural Organization, the World Health Organization, the United Nations Children's Fund, the International Labor Office, and UNESCO. Most of them are oriented toward the promotion of rural welfare; the organization of "social centers" or "community centers"; the improvement of production methods, and village and water development; the founding of cottage handicrafts and small-scale industries; and progress in education, vocational training, rehabilitation, public hygiene, and communications. In rural settings of developing nations, such as India, the Arab countries, and Egypt, the success of technical assistance depends essentially upon whether or not the people in the village can be encouraged to assume the responsibility for social change as their own project. In 1958, almost 7,800 experts were sent to 70 countries by the United Nations and the specialized agencies in technical assistance including ICA.

In view of the increasing importance of technical assistance for

fare Forum (1953), pp. 18-33; Hertha Kraus, "Identifying Professional Requirements for Social Service Abroad," Social Casework, Vol. 35, No. 4 (April 1954), pp. 147-152; and, M. S. Gore, "The Social Worker and the Community," International Social Work, Vol. 2, No. 4 (October 1959), pp. 25-28.

the developing countries, the United Nations established the "Expanded Technical Assistance Program." Its primary objective is to strengthen the national economy and the political independence of the country which applies for the assistance in development of agriculture and industries.

The country which requests aid under the Expanded Technical Assistance Program of the UN specifies the type of aid which it needs and prepares the work requested by its own means, as much as possible, in order to determine the needs, and to facilitate an agreement with the UN. The measures of the Expanded Technical Assistance Program must not be used as a means of interference in the internal affairs of the country which applies for assistance, and must be rendered without regard to religion, race, or religion in the country which desires aid. In most countries of the Far and Near East, and Africa, the education of social workers for work in rural villages has just begun. They are prepared for various skills —to aid in public assistance, child welfare, elementary and health education, home economics, sanitation, midwifery, and nursing service. They need personal qualities, such as resourcefulness, maturity, ingenuity, dedication to their people, and a deep sense of devotion to their work. In India, for example, in several demonstration projects, women workers live in villages in teams of three. One worker gives nursing and midwife service; the second teaches crafts, assists in general school education, and organizes adult classes; and the third works with children, especially with those of "toddler" age. Efficient supervision of such women workers requires trained, professional social workers to inspire and guide women and men workers in village improvement activities.[28]

The Social Commission of the Economic and Social Council of the United Nations characterized as essential elements in social welfare functions in the technical assistance programs the training of professional, technical, and auxiliary personnel for social service, community organization, the encouragement of self-help activities for the improvement of living standards, and the strengthening of public social welfare programs and statistical and research services.

---

[28] Dewey Anderson and Stephen Raushenbush, *A Policy and Program for Success* (Washington, D.C.: Public Affairs Institute, 1950), pp. 17-22; and, Eugene Staley, *The Future of Underdeveloped Countries* (New York: Harper, 1954).

It called for demonstration projects for proving the value of a simultaneous approach to social, economic, educational, and health problems. Experience in international social service confirms this emphasis on interprofessional teamwork as an important condition for successful work.

V. COMMUNITY DEVELOPMENT

After World War II, the newly independent nations faced the problem of how to accelerate the improvements in economic and social conditions of their communities. They lacked not only the material resources in agricultural or industrial production, but also the technical knowledge of how to organize their own productive capacities and how to use technical assistance offered them by their own provincial or national government and by international organizations and social agencies from abroad. The "Community Development Movement," as one of the most important attempts at technical assistance, achieved this goal.

"Community Development" has been defined as "the conscious process whereby small, geographically contiguous communities are assisted by the more developed, national and world community to achieve improved standards of social and economic life." [29] Although community development has been offered primarily to villages in rural areas, its techniques and experiences are applicable, also, to urban development, but different factors of community organization have to be considered. These ends are achieved primarily through the communities' own local efforts and through local community participation at all stages of goal-selection, mobilization of resources and execution of projects. It thus enables these communities to become increasingly self-reliant. At present, communities in different countries also have different levels of social and economic status

---

[29] "Mobilizing Resources for Social Needs" (Statement prior to the Ninth International Conference of Social Work, Tokyo, 1958), *International Social Work,* Vol. 2, No. 2 (April 1959), pp. 1-9. For other definitions see Arthur Dunham, *Community Welfare Organization: Principles and Practice* (New York: Crowell, 1958); Louis Miniclier, *et al., Community Development Review,* No. 10 (March 1958), pp. 1-77; Charles I. Schottland, "Community Development and Technical Assistance," *International Social Work,* Vol. 2, No. 1 (January 1959), pp. 46-52; and, Ernest B. Harper and Arthur Dunham, *op. cit.,* Part VI.

which are influenced by the mores, values, and basic philosophy of the country. If the more advanced countries want to help others to achieve better living conditions, the method must be agreed upon between the two partners. Agreement is necessary because community development may change the life of the local community fundamentally. The process of community development involves not only material, economic and technical progress, but also broader cultural and social change. It requires, therefore, that the team of experts who aid the community have full understanding of the values, the aims, and the real needs of the people, and are able to stimulate and encourage their initiative, enthusiasm and identification with the project of social and economic change. In some communities it will be more difficult than in others to bring the concept of self-help to life. It will be necessary to offer services and advice without creating dependency. Social workers will be useful on the team of experts due to their freedom from bias and prejudice, their training in accepting people where they are, and sharing with them the planning for constructive change, their awareness of the interrelation of social, economic, health, and emotional forces, and their knowledge of the use of community resources.

VI. INTERNATIONAL EXCHANGE OF SOCIAL WORKERS

The exchange of experts in various disciplines is an important part of technical assistance programs of the United Nations, the United States, and other international and national private organizations. In this connection, we merely want to mention the important contributions which physicians, public health officers, sanitary engineers, agricultural, transportation, industrial, and food experts, specialists in the treatment and prevention of diseases and epidemics, and laboratory technicians and nurses made toward the improvement of economic, social, and health conditions in developing areas. In the field of social welfare, the United Nations are primarily interested in the development of adequate services for family, youth, and child welfare, rehabilitation of handicapped persons, and housing and community planning. The specialized agencies of the United Nations have devoted their primary action to the improvement of physical and mental health, maternal and child care, education, rural welfare, employmènt security, and social insurance. In order to achieve progress in social welfare programs, many countries request that expert advisers be sent to assist them in the establishment and improvement of social services, in organization and administration, and assume teaching and demonstrations. These activities are designed as International Advisory Social Welfare Services.[30] They play an important role in the planning and development of welfare and health services, programs of public assistance and social insurance, rehabilitation and village centers, and social legislation. Consultants are selected on the basis of a request of the government, which wants to use their services and which has the right of approval. Experts are selected by the United Nations, the specialized agencies, governments, and voluntary social welfare organizations.

Another aspect of this exchange are Fellowship Programs under the auspices of the United Nations, national governments, and private agencies which enable social workers and students to observe or to study methods, organization, and operation of social welfare in another country. This International Exchange of Social Welfare Personnel provides opportunities for experienced, as well as young social workers and students to broaden their understanding, knowledge, and skills. Three methods of exchange are used: (1) fellowships for travel and observations of social agencies and institutions varying between three and nine months, (2) scholarships for formal academic education in schools of social work, as a rule for one or two years, and (3) a direct exchange of teachers, administrators, research or other specialists, experts in correctional work, directors of settlement houses, training schools, children's institutions, instructors and youth leaders.[31]

For American social workers and students of social work, some opportunities for teaching, study, and research are provided by

[30] Department of Social Affairs, *International Advisory Social Welfare Services* (Lake Success, N.Y.: United Nations, 1949); Social Security Administration, *Observation as a Way of Learning for International Social Welfare* (Washington: Government Printing Office, 1955); and, Barbara B. Palmer, "The Foreign Student: A Challenge to Social Work Education," *Social Service Review,* Vol. 31, No. 3 (September 1957), pp. 277-289.

[31] Department of Social Affairs, *International Exchange of Social Welfare Personnel* (Lake Success, N.Y.: United Nations, 1949), pp. 1-7; and, Marguerite V. Pohek, "What Can Casework Contribute to European Social Services?" *Social Work Journal,* Vol. 35, No. 1 (January 1954), pp. 15-18.

the Fulbright Educational Exchange Program. Such experiences strengthen mutual understanding between nations, professional knowledge, and cooperation in social welfare from which all countries benefit, the visitor as well as the host country. Careful preparation and professional and cultural orientation for international exchange deeply enhances its value.

An important interpretation of our concepts and programs of social welfare on the international level was achieved by social welfare attachés, who have been appointed by the Department of State since 1948. They informed government and private agencies about legislation and experiences in social welfare and helped public and private social agencies in their overseas relief and welfare programs. Social welfare attachés had been appointed on the staff of the Embassies in Paris, New Delhi, and Cairo, but are not maintained at present. This constructive, valuable service should be continued and extended to other embassies and legations.

VII. VOLUNTARY AGENCIES IN INTERNATIONAL SOCIAL WELFARE

Our discussion has already shown that the work of private social agencies of either international or national character, engaged in overseas work, is an important part of the present international social welfare activities. During the war and the period of emergency relief abroad, they were coordinated in the United States under the President's War Relief Control Board and its successor, the Advisory Committee on Voluntary Foreign Aid. Most of these agencies are also members of the American Council of Voluntary Agencies for Foreign Service, which includes religious and non-sectarian organizations and the relief services of the AFL-CIO. The relief work in Germany after the end of the war was carried on by the Army, the High Commissioner, and voluntary agencies that were admitted under a "Council of Relief Agencies Licensed for Operations in Germany" (CRALOG). Of particular importance proved to be the new "Neighborhood Centers" supported by the American Friends Service Committee, Church World Service, and the Unitarian Service Committee. The latter organization also conducted training institutes for social workers and teachers with the aid of the High Commissioner and of German social agencies.

Similar relief activities in Japan, Korea, and Okinawa are performed by organizations combined in LARA, "Licensed Agencies for Relief in Asia." These activities include the feeding of children and nursing mothers, clothing aid, and assistance in the reconstruction of welfare services, hospitals, orphanages, and schools. Very essential is the rehabilitation work in Korea, where the "United Nations Korean Reconstruction Agency" (UNKRA), financed from voluntary government contributions, is working together with various private organizations, including the American Korean Foundation, American Friends Service Committee, the Unitarian Service Committee, World Church Service, American Relief for Korea, "Houses for Korea," and the American Education Mission. In the United States, the National Social Welfare Assembly serves as coordinating body between public and private agencies devoted to international social services and develops cooperative programs in this area.

In 1929 an International Committee, now called the *International Association of Schools of Social Work,* was established. It arranges international and regional meetings in order to promote the standards of social work education throughout the world. Finally, an *International Federation of Social Workers,* which enlists as members national professional associations of social workers, was formed in connection with the International Conference of Social Work in Paris, in 1950. This international federation aims at the promotion of high standards of service and professional cooperation between social workers in all countries of the world.[32]

VIII. INTERNATIONAL ASPECTS IN SOCIAL WORK EDUCATION

Throughout the world, social work is performed within the framework of cultural, religious, economic, and social conditions which determine the different values and customs of the people who use social services. Most countries are convinced that the performance of social welfare functions requires special preparation and train-

---

[32] Charlotte E. Owen, "International Voluntary Social Work," *Social Work Year Book* (1949), pp. 252-260; Lyman C. White, *International Non-governmental Organizations* (1951); Joe R. Hoffer, "Conferences of Social Work," *Social Work Year Book* (1954), pp. 132-133; Ernest F. Witte, "Education for Social Work," (International Activities), *Social Work Year Book* (1960), pp. 235-236; and, Eileen L. Younghusband, "The U.N. Third International Survey of Training for Social Work, *International Social Work,* Vol. 2, No. 4 (October 1959), pp. 30-34.

ing.[33] But the basic responsibility for the care of people in need is not everywhere placed upon the community, or a government authority; in some countries it still rests with the family, the wider circle of relatives, with the church, or other religious or charitable agencies. Under these circumstances, it is difficult to establish a uniform definition of "Social Work" or "Social Worker" which would be recognized everywhere. But certain characteristics of social work are world-wide: (1) as a "helping process" for individuals, families, and groups, helping them to solve their economic, health, or personal problems; (2) as a "social function" for the benefit of the individual and the community, not the agency; (3) as an "enabling process," encouraging the use of community facilities and the development of sources for the betterment of the community.[34]

Social service being so closely interrelated with the economy and culture of the nation, the principles, methods, and concepts of social work in the United States discussed in this book cannot be applied rigidly in countries whose customs, values, and resources are different from our own. Social work has to be adapted to the cultural, economic, and climatic setting. Dean Donald S. Howard, speaking at the National Conference of Social Work, in 1952, explained these differences but emphasized that everywhere social work is the discipline, based upon a combination of a philosophy, knowledge, attitudes, and skills, that helps individuals, groups, communities, and societies attain the highest possible level of well-being, primarily by "helping them to help themselves." Social welfare, of course, also assists people who cannot help themselves—children, the aged, the crippled, the blind, and the sick.[35]

---

[33] Sir Ralph Cilento, "The World Moves Toward Professional Standards in Social Work," *Social Work Journal,* Vol. 29, No. 3 (July 1948), pp. 99-107; Walter A. Friedlander, "Some International Aspects of Social Work Education," *Social Service Review,* Vol. 23, No. 2 (June 1949), pp. 204-210; and, Katherine Kendall, "International Developments in Social Work Education," *Social Work Journal,* Vol. 32, No. 2 (April 1951), pp. 70-77.

[34] K. Kendall, *op. cit.,* pp. 73-74; Edward H. Spicer (editor), *Human Problems in Technological Change: A Casebook* (New York: Russell Sage Foundation, 1952); and, Cayetano Santiago, *Effect of Cultural Differences on the Value of American Social Work to Foreign Students* (New York: Council on Social Work Education, 1955).

[35] Donald S. Howard, "The Common Core of Social Work," *The Social Welfare Forum* (1951), pp. 14-36; and, Lester B. Granger, "Basic Human Needs," *Social Work Journal,* Vol. 34, No. 2 (April 1953), pp. 65-70, 87-88.

As we have seen, international social work agencies are aware of the necessity of training social workers, and they assist countries that either lack or have too few facilities for the training of social workers and auxiliary personnel. The social workers' and students' exchange program and the delegation of teachers and instructors to foreign countries are part of the process of education for social welfare. The United Nations has considered founding a research center or an international school of social work, but this project has not been carried out. Such a school would provide the opportunity to compare the philosophy and methods of social welfare of various nations.

The experiences of persons engaged in different aspects of foreign relief, rehabilitation, and international social welfare cooperation, as discussed in this chapter, have created a new spirit of mutual understanding, respect, and good will. The finding of a "common core of social work" has strengthened the conviction that all peoples of the world, whether rich or poor, have their right to self-respect, human dignity, self-determination, and freedom from want and fear. Social workers are conscious that in helping peoples abroad to overcome hunger, disease, and suffering, the well-being of all peoples can be directed toward the development and maintenance of world stability and peace. Social welfare has become an integral part of the world-wide efforts for the advancement of human progress.

Selected Bibliography

Abbott, Edith, "International Social Welfare," *The Compass,* Vol. 28, No. 4 (May 1947), pp. 3-36.

Alper, Benedict S., "Prevention and Control of Delinquency at the International Level," in *National Conference of Social Work, Proceedings* (1948), pp. 366-371.

*Asher, Robert S., *et al., The United Nations and Economic and Social Cooperation.* Washington, D.C.: Brookings Institution, 1957.

Barr, Stringfellow, *Citizens of the World.* New York: Doubleday, 1952.

Bicknell, Ernest P., *With the Red Cross in Europe.* Washington, D.C.: American National Red Cross, 1938.

*Bovet, Lucien, *Psychiatric Aspects of Juvenile Delinquency.* Geneva: World Health Organization, 1951.

Brooks, Howard L., *Prisoners of Hope.* New York: L. B. Fischer, 1942.

Brown, William A., and Redoers Opic, *American Foreign Assistance.* Washington: Brookings Institution, 1953.

Brugger, Florence, "What Are Profitable Imports for the United States," *National Conference of Social Work, Selected Papers in Group Work and Community Organization* (1952), pp. 80-90.

*Cilento, Sir Raphael, "The World Moves Toward Professional Standards in Social Work," *Social Work Journal,* Vol. 29, No. 3 (July 1948), pp. 99-107.

Corsi, Edward, "The Impact of International Tensions on People," *Social Welfare Forum* (1955), pp. 11-129.

*Daniels, Walter M. (editor), *Point Four Program.* New York: Wilson, 1951.

de Jongh, Jan F., "A European Experiment in Casework Teaching," *Social Casework,* Vol. 34, No. 1 (January 1953), pp. 9-17.

*de Schweinitz, Karl, *Social Security for Egypt.* Washington: Social Security Administration, 1952.

*Dunham, Arthur, *Community Welfare Organization.* New York: Crowell, 1958.

Farman, Carl H., and Veronica Marren Hale, *Social Security Legislation Throughout the World.* Washington: Social Security Administration, 1949.

*Fasteau, Irving J., "International Social Welfare," *Social Work Year Book* (1957), pp. 311-324.

Finer, Herman, *The United Nations Economic and Social Council.* New York: World Peace Foundation, 1946.

*Friedlander, Walter A., "International Aspects of Social Work Education," *Social Service Review,* Vol. XXXII, No. 2 (June 1949), pp. 204-210.

Fry, Varian, *Surrender on Demand.* New York: Random House, Inc., 1945.

Gerschenkron, Alexander, and Berthold F. Hoselitz, *The Progress of Underdeveloped Areas.* Chicago: University of Chicago Press, 1952.

*Glasser, Melvin A., "Social Service in Underdeveloped Areas: A Report on the International Conference," *Social Work Journal,* Vol. 34, No. 2 (April 1953), pp. 59-64.

Granger, Lester B., "Basic Human Needs," *Social Work Journal,* Vol. 34, No. 2 (April 1953), pp. 65-70, 87-88.

*Gumpert, Martin, *Dunant: The Story of the Red Cross.* New York: Oxford, 1938.

Hambidge, Gove, *The Story of FAO.* New York: Van Nostrand, 1955.

*Harper, Ernest B., and Arthur Dunham, *Community Organization in Action.* New York: Association Press, 1959.

Henderson, Julia P., "Urbanization and the World Community," *The Annals,* Vol. 314 (November 1957), pp. 147-155.

Hill, Martin, *The Economic and Financial Organization of the League of Nations.* Washington: Carnegie Endowment, 1946.

*Hoey, Jane M., "Professional Implications of International Social Work Developments," in Cora Kasius (editor), *New Directions in Social Work.* New York: Harper, 1954.

*Howard, Donald S., "The Common Core of Social Work," *Social Welfare Forum* (1951), pp. 19-36.

Hyman, Joseph P., *Twenty-Five Years of American Aid to Jews Overseas.* New York: American Jewish Joint Distribution Committee, 1939.

Jones, Rufus M., *A Service of Love in Wartime.* New York: Macmillan, 1920.

*Kasius, Cora, "Are Social Work Principles Emerging Internationally?" *Social Casework,* Vol. 34, No. 1 (January 1953), pp. 23-29.

*Kendall, Katherine A., "Social Work Education: A Responsibility of the Total Profession," *Social Casework,* Vol. 34, No. 1 (January 1953), pp. 17-23.

Kernohan, Frances K., "The Impact of the United Nations on Poverty, Ignorance, and Disease," *Social Service Review,* Vol. 29, No. 1 (March 1955), pp. 14-19.

*Kernohan, Frances K., Savilla M. Simons, and Charlotte E. Owen, "International Social Work," *Social Work Year Book* (1954), pp. 266-285.

Konopka, Gisela, "The Application of Social Work Principles to International Relations," *The Social Welfare Forum* (1953). New York: Columbia University Press, 1953, pp. 279-288.

Koselitz, Bert F., *The Progress of Underdeveloped Areas.* Chicago: University of Chicago Press, 1952.

Kraus, Hertha, *International Relief in Action: 1914-1943.* Scottdale, Pa.: Herald Press, 1944.

Lally, Dorothy, "Comments on the International Fellowship Program," *Social Welfare Forum* (1952), pp. 104-117.

*――――, "International Social Welfare," *Social Work Year Book* (1960), pp. 318-338.

Lane, Marie Dresden, "Public Assistance Concepts in an International Agency," *Social Security Bulletin,* Vol. 14, No. 5 (May 1951), pp. 3-9, 30.

Lie, Trygve, *Peace on Earth.* New York: Hermitage House, 1949.

Lubin, Isadore, "The Revolution in Human Affairs," *Social Welfare Forum* (1952), pp. 75-83.

McLaughlin, Kathleen, *New Life in Old Lands.* New York: Dodd, 1954.

Maloney, John, *Let There Be Mercy.* New York: Doubleday, 1951.

*Myrdal, Alva, *et al.*, *America's Role in International Social Welfare*. New York: Columbia University Press, 1955.

Nicholson, James T., "Effective Development in International Social Welfare Programs," *National Conference of Social Work, Selected Papers in Group Work and Community Organization* (1952), pp. 73-79.

*Pickett, Clarence, *For More Than Bread*. Boston: Little, 1953.

Pohek, Marguerite V., "Casework Seen Through European Eyes," *National Conference of Social Work, Selected Papers in Casework* (1952), pp. 94-109.

Potter, Pitman B., "The Social Services of the League of Nations," *Special Studies*, Vol. 6, No. 9. Geneva, Switzerland: Geneva Research Center, 1935.

Rees, Eltan, "Century of the Homeless Man," *International Conciliation*, No. 515 (November 1957).

*———, "The Refugees and the United Nations," *International Conciliation*, No. 492 (June 1953), New York.

———, *We Strangers and Afraid. The Refugee Story Today*. New York: Carnegie, 1959.

Rockefeller, Nelson A., "Building the Economic Basis for Better Living Throughout the World," *Social Welfare Forum* (1952), pp. 84-94.

Roosevelt, Eleanor, and Helen Ferris, *Partners—The United Nations and Youth*. New York: Doubleday, 1950.

Schechtman, Joseph B., *The Arab Refugee Problem*. New York: Philosophical Library, 1952.

*Sharp, Walter R., *International Technical Assistance*. Chicago: Public Administration Service, 1952.

*Simons, Savilla M., "International Social Work," *Social Work Year Book* (1951), pp. 245-259.

Snyder, Harold S., *When People Speak to People*. Washington: American Council on Education, 1953.

Staley, Eugene, *The Future of Underdeveloped Countries*. New York: Harper, 1954.

———, *World Economic Development*. Montreal: International Labor Office, 1944.

Spicer, Edward H., *Human Problems in Technological Change. A Casebook*. New York: Russell Sage Foundation, 1952.

Social Security Administration, *Social Workers Abroad Assess Their Training in the United States*. Washington, D.C.: Government Printing Office, 1955.

Stoessinger, John G., *The Refugee and the World Community*. Minneapolis: University of Minnesota Press, 1956.

United Nations, Department of Social Affairs, *International Advisory Social Services.* Lake Success, N.Y.: 1949.

————, *International Exchange of Social Welfare Personnel.* Lake Success, N.Y.: 1949.

*————, *Report on the World Social Situation.* New York: 1957.

*Warren, George L., "International Social Work," *Social Work Year Book* (1947), pp. 232-249.

White, Lyman C., *International Non-governmental Organizations.* New Brunswick, N.J.: Rutgers University Press, 1951.

Wickwar, W. Hardy, "Relief Supplies and Welfare Distribution: UNRRA in Retrospect," *Social Service Review,* Vol. XXI, No. 3 (September 1947), pp. 363-374.

Wilson, Francesca M., *In the Margins of Chaos.* New York: Macmillan, 1945.

Winslow, C. E. A., "International Cooperation in the Service of Health," *The Annals,* Vol. 273 (January 1951).

*Woodbridge, George, *The History of UNRRA,* 3 vols. New York: Columbia University Press, 1950.

Yates, Elizabeth, *Rainbow Round the World. A Story of UNICEF.* Indianapolis: Bobbs, 1954.

Yates, Lamartine, *So Bold an Aim.* Food and Agricultural Organization, 1956.

17.

Professional Aspects of Social Work

I. DEVELOPMENT OF THE PROFESSION

The forerunners of social work, individual citizens giving alms to people in need, and charities under auspices of the churches, were known in ancient times. But social work as a profession is young. It grew mainly from the Humanitarian Movement of the nineteenth century which attempted to improve the desperate conditions of the poor, to achieve social reform by legislation, and to awaken the social conscience of the public. The need for professional education in social work was emphasized in 1893 for the first time, by Anna L. Dawes at the International Congress of Charities, Correction, and Philanthropy, held in Chicago. In the Charity Organization Societies the necessity of preparation for charitable work was recognized, but it was not before 1898 that the first six-weeks' training course was set up by the New York Charity Organization Society. It later was extended to six months and developed into the New York School of Social Work, since 1940 affiliated with Columbia University.[1]

---

[1] Edith Abbott, *Social Welfare and Professional Education*, rev. ed. (Chicago: University of Chicago Press, 1942); Ernest V. Hollis and Alice L. Taylor, *Social Work Education in the United States* (New York: Columbia University Press, 1951), pp. 3-52; and, Nathan E. Cohen, *Social Work in the American Tradition* (New York: Dryden, 1958), pp. 8-15.

In Chicago, the Institute of Social Science opened in 1901 under the leadership of Graham Taylor, Sophonisba P. Breckinridge, and Edith Abbott, then became the School of Civics and Philanthropy, and later the School of Social Service Administration of the University of Chicago. Boston, Philadelphia, and St. Louis established similar schools of social work in 1904 and 1908. Since that time, the recognition of social work as a profession has made remarkable progress. Until academic education was begun, social workers were trained under an apprenticeship system without systematic, scientific knowledge. Their technical skill depended upon the executives of the charity agencies where they served as volunteers. During the first decade of this century the necessity of social reform as well as of competent individual service became evident in connection with social problems caused by mass emigration from European countries. The rapidly developing industrialization and urbanization of our country created social problems and human suffering that called for skillful personnel to administer social services. The great Depression of the 1930's brought unexpected economic distress to large masses of the population and showed that trained social workers were indispensable.

There were in most professions, for example in law, ministry, medicine, three stages in the development of professional education: (1) an apprenticeship under an experienced practitioner, (2) the establishment of private schools, and (3) the recognition of universities that a professional school should be part of their academic program.

The criteria for any profession have been stated as the following:

(1) Special competence, acquired through intellectual training, which develops skills and requires the use of independent, responsible judgment, not merely mechanical skills.

(2) Distinct techniques capable of communication through an orderly and specialized educational discipline, with application of knowledge and skills based upon academic learning.

(3) Practitioners who become conscious of common bonds and organize as a professional association for the promotion of high standards and of common interests.

(4) The professional association has concern for the development of standards of service for the profession as a whole as expressed by

a code of ethics, provision for specialized education, and the use of specialized knowledge and skill in order to apply them in the public interest.

(5) A professional person has a sense of personal responsibility and accountability to others in the same field for the kinds of standards he sets for himself.[2]

It was not until the end of World War I that social work began to be recognized as a profession. There is a marked difference in this respect from other professions, such as law, medicine, teaching, and the ministry. The recent changes in the attitude of the people toward public relief and charities, which we discussed earlier, led to new positive concepts with regard to the persons who performed new types of services. This historical fact explains the delay of the acceptance of social work as a profession in our country.

There is no longer any doubt that social work satisfies the criteria for a profession. The social worker has to study the scientific principles of human behavior and the structure and organization of social institutions. With these principles before him, he has to develop, under his own responsibility, knowledge and skill in working with people under specific social, economic, and emotional conditions. Social work has organized professional associations which maintain standards of performance and behavior embodied in a code of ethics. Social work recognizes its responsibility for competent service with integrity, for the welfare of human beings whom it serves.

The number of graduate schools of social work in the United States and Canada has increased, by 1960, to sixty-three (seven of them in Canada) and 109 undergraduate departments accredited by the Council on Social Work Education. About 11,400 graduate students were, in 1960, enrolled in schools of social work in the United States and Canada.

The youth of the social work profession explains the fact that at present more than half the persons employed in social work positions have not received professional education in social work. The

---

[2] Benjamin E. Youngdahl, "Social Work as a Profession," *Social Work Year Book* (1949), pp. 497-498; "Social Work at the Crossroads," *Social Work Journal*, Vol. XXXIV, No. 3 (July 1953), pp. 111-113; Nathan E. Cohen, "Social Work as a Profession," *Social Work Year Book* (1957), pp. 553-562; and, John C. Kidneigh, "Social Work as a Profession," *ibid.* (1960), pp. 563-573.

study, *Social Work Education in the United States,* by Ernest V. Hollis and Alice L. Taylor, raises the question whether it might be necessary to classify the functions in social agencies into those services which require graduate, professional training, and other activities which may be performed by persons who do not have graduate education, but are prepared for simpler, technical work.

In fact, the proportion of trained social workers is slowly increasing, and there is a growing awareness by social agency boards and public welfare commissions, as well as by the public, that professionally trained social workers are needed for the responsible, competent performance of social services. Thus, social work gradually is being accepted along with the older professions—the ministry, law, teaching, and medicine.

II. SOCIAL WORK EDUCATION

A. Undergraduate Education

Preparation for social work requires high school study with the qualifications to enter college. In college, undergraduate study includes a broad course in liberal arts with emphasis on social sciences, sociology, social welfare, history, philosophy, economics, psychology, political science, cultural anthropology, and physical and biological science.

Because the number of social welfare positions exceeds by far the present total number of professionally trained people in social work, a substantial group of social agencies employs persons upon graduation from college. These positions are mainly junior positions in public welfare departments, in recreation and leisure-time organizations, in probation services of juvenile courts, in institutions for children and adults, in personnel work in commerce and industry, in social security administration, unemployment insurance, workmen's compensation, and in public employment services.

The undergraduate program acquaints the student with the basic concepts and major findings of the social sciences, psychology, sociology, and economics. It also gives him an understanding of the importance of biology, genetics, history and principles of government, social philosophy, public health, and family problems. The undergraduate student gains a broad background of present society and of man as an individual and as a member of various groups. He then learns to arrive at some integrated perspective of the relations between human behavior and the demands of our society. He studies to be able to state his opinion clearly and interpret the facts and his ideas to other people.

On the basis of these studies, the student has the choice: (1) to apply for advanced, graduate, professional training in social work; (2) to use his preparation for accepting employment in a position which does not require graduate training; or (3) to consider this undergraduate program as preparation for informed, intelligent citizenship which brings him an understanding of social welfare concepts, the wide range of social problems, and the motivation to help solve them.[3] The last group may include businessmen, housewives, local officials, state legislators, teachers, labor leaders, and citizens in other occupations.

A typical, undergraduate social welfare major program includes the following courses:

(1) In lower division—general psychology, general economics, elementary statistics and research, introduction to sociology, history, biology, and anthropology.

(2) In upper division—concepts, history and system of social welfare, methods of social work, public assistance, child welfare, social security, social problems and social institutions, social legislation and reform, social philosophy, child and adolescent psychology, mental deficiency, abnormal psychology, social psychology. It also may comprise introduction to clinical psychology, municipal and state government, public administration, problems of poverty, labor economics, public finance and taxation, and crime prevention and correction. Other courses may deal with problems of juvenile delinquency, race relations and culture, migration, study of group behavior, community recreation, dynamics of culture, medical sociology, child hygiene, and housing and planning.

---

[3] Harold E. Wetzel, "Educational Priorities As Seen by the Undergraduate Department," Council on Social Work Education, *Education for Social Work, Proceedings* (1953), pp. 58-61; Katherine A. Kendall, *Undergraduate Preparation for the Social Services* (New York: Council on Social Work Education, 1954); and, Herbert Bisno, *The Place of the Undergraduate Curriculum in Social Work Education* (New York: Council on Social Work Education, 1959).

Some colleges offer in their programs facilities for their students to make observations in social agencies in order to know something of the practice of social welfare, under the name of "field experience." The value of these courses is disputed. The graduate schools of social work find that field work as clinical practice of social work processes is a vital part of graduate education, but is successful only through integration with academic courses in casework, group work, and community organization and by very responsible supervision. The attempt to provide practical experience of sufficient breadth and intensity in the undergraduate program poses the problem of securing conscientious and reliable field supervision, and of curtailing unduly the time required for a broad liberal education and a background in the social sciences and the humanities. Social agencies, on the other side, use in-service training, as well as seminars, institutes, and extension courses of universities, in order to supplement theoretical knowledge and skills of staff members who have no professional training.

B. Profesional Education for Social Work

Graduate training for social work requires, as a rule, the successful completion of two academic years of study in an accredited school of social work, leading to the granting of the master's degree. Prerequisite for acceptance to graduate school is the bachelor's degree, preferably in social welfare or in the social sciences, and personal qualification for the profession of social work. Most schools accept students older than thirty-five years only if they have demonstrated good capacity for social work. Graduate social work education is characterized by its close integration of academic courses in the school with practical field work in a selected social agency under careful supervision.

In the development of social work education, the schools considered for some time eight areas of particular importance, which are often called "The Basic Eight" but which no longer are accepted as a rigid program, and do not serve longer as the foundation of the curricula:

(1) Social casework (generic and specialized).
(2) Social group work.
(3) Community organization.

(4) Social research and statistics.
(5) Social welfare administration.
(6) Public welfare and child welfare.
(7) Medical information.
(8) Psychiatric information.

The aims of professional education in social work are to develop competence in three major areas: (1) conceptual and perceptual understanding; (2) skills in methods, procedures, and processes; and (3) personal professional qualities.[4]

The first category includes understanding of individual and group behavior, the significance of human behavior in relation to social environment, and the historical perspective of social welfare development and of religious, economic, political, and social movements. It requires a grounding in the social sciences, the structure and philosophy of government, the nature of social change, the causes and effect of cultural factors, and principles of social security. It also demands knowledge of the principles, objectives, and processes in social casework, group work, community organization, supervision, intergroup relations, public administration, social polices and planning, and social research. The curriculum includes the study of public relations, standards of social legislation; the administration of social welfare, community structure, and resources; the study of human growth; and the significance of physical, social, and emotional deviations from normal behavior.

The skills of professional social work require the ability to establish and maintain purposeful and constructive relationships with individuals, groups, and communities. The most important skill in the helping process is that of enabling an individual, a group, or a community to identify and clarify problems and needs, and to solve them by their own initiative in a socially desirable way. The social

---

[4] E. Hollis and A. Taylor, *op. cit.*, pp. 220-225; Charlotte Towle, *The Learner in Education for the Professions. As Seen in Education for Social Work*. (Chicago: University of Chicago Press, 1954), pp. 233-246; Ernest F. Witte, Katherine A. Kendall, and Ernest V. Hollis, "Education for Social Work," in Lloyd E. Blauch (editor), *Education for the Professions* (Washington: Office of Education, 1955); Ernest P. Witte, "Education for Social Work," *Social Work Year Book* (1960), pp. 223-240; and, Werner W. Boehm, *Objectives for the Social Work Curriculum of the Future* (New York: Council on Social Work Education, 1959).

worker learns to use his own resources in professional relationships based upon self-understanding, control of personal needs and feelings, and warmth of response. Other skills are those of social administration, planning, social action; use of scientific methods in research and practice; skill in teamwork with other professions; ability in communication, staff development, supervision, and volunteer and student training; and preparation for social work teaching, and social statesmanship.

The personal, professional qualities that graduate training aims to develop include genuine warmth, sensitivity to, and liking for people, and the capacity to identify with a variety of persons. A professional philosophy comprises a high degree of social conscience and conscientiousness, emotional, mental, and physical stability, maturity, self-security, imagination, resourcefulness, flexibility, as well as personal integrity, courage, and a sincere conviction about the values of social work. Professional concepts make the student capable of standing up for the rights of people even against hostile attitudes of the public. These qualities, furthermore, encompass conceptual thinking, open-mindedness, clarity of purpose, accuracy, courtesy in professional relationships, and a belief in the value of citizen participation and in the right of the individual, the group, and the community to make their own decisions within the framework of a democratic society.

It is easy to understand that these areas of professional competence can be fully developed only if academic classwork and clinical supervised field instruction are integrated. Field work requires, as a rule, two full days weekly for the first graduate year and three days weekly for the second year. Supervisors are either members of the university faculty or are staff members of the social agency where the student receives his field work training. In both instances an intensive cooperation between the teaching faculty and the field supervisor in observing the student's professional development and learning is maintained. Field work is designed to integrate the academic knowledge, practical understanding, and professional skill of the student by personal contact and direct work with clients.

A number of schools of social work have set up an advanced program beyond the level of the master's degree. This has been classified either as "the third year" with the aim of strengthening the professional skills of the student or as "the doctoral program," leading to a Doctor of Social Work or a Doctor of Philosophy degree. The latter program, as a rule, requires two more years of postgraduate studies, which offer a deepening and refinement of knowledge and skill, new knowledge directed toward definition and solution of professional problems (with the evaluation and testing of social work methods and hypothesis), and the broadening of professional perspective. The doctoral program integrates social work knowledge and methodology with those of other scientific disciplines; develops independent critical professional thought, and interprofessional relationships; and prepares primarily for teaching social work, for the administration of social welfare programs, and for social work research.[5]

For many years, the graduate schools of social work were organized as the American Association of Schools of Social Work (AASSW), whereas, other colleges, which offered undergradute programs, had formed the National Association of Schools of Social Administration (NASSA). Since 1952, the Council on Social Work Education has absorbed both associations. It represents, also, the agencies employing social workers, the professional membership association, and the public. The functions of the Council on Social Work Education are to establish standards and to accredit schools of social work, to aid in better selection and education of students and social workers, to improve social work education, to interpret social work to the public, and to help in continuing professional growth of employed social workers. The organizational structure is based in a council consisting of a House of Delegates, a Board of Directors, and four standing committees on (1) accreditation, (2) program, services, and publications, (3) schools and departments of social work, and (4) research.

III. REGISTRATION OR LICENSING OF SOCIAL WORKERS

Professionals in medicine, teaching, law, and nursing are recognized by an official license, certificate, or registration which is re-

---

[5] Charlotte Towle, Eveline Burns, and Eleanor Cockerill, *Social Work Education in the Post Master's Program* (*Guiding Principles*) (New York: Council on Social Work Education, 1953), pp. 9-11, 23-29; Charles Frankel, "Professional Education as University Education," *Social Service Review*, Vol. 32, No. 3 (September 1958), pp. 234-246; and, Ernest F. Witte, *op. cit.*, pp. 225-231.

quired before they can perform professional service. In France, Germany, Austria, and Sweden, social workers need a license in order to practice their profession.

In the United States, however, no license has yet been introduced, but suggestions have been made that licensing should be required or that the practice of social work should be restricted. In 1933, the California Conference of Social Welfare organized registration on a voluntary basis, requiring the passing of a carefully prepared examination. In 1945, a statutory system of official registration and certification for social workers replaced the voluntary program in California. Applicants who have completed successfully one year at an accredited graduate school of social work and who pass a written examination receive a certificate authorizing them to the title "Registered Social Worker" (R.S.W.). The Board maintains a register of social workers, conducts research, prescribes qualifications, gives examinations, and issues certificates. A certificate is suspended or revoked if a registered social worker is convicted of an offense involving moral turpitude, is a habitual drug addict, is declared insane or incompetent, advocates the overthrow of government by force, violence or other unlawful means, or has committed a dishonest or fraudulent act as a social worker resulting in substantial injury to others.

The value of the registration for the protection of the public and for the self-respect of professional workers depends partly upon the personnel practices of social agencies. In Los Angeles and in San Diego, the County Civil Service Commission uses registration as a basis for position classification, and the County Bureau of Public Assistance of Los Angeles, the largest single social work employer in California, requires registration. Another decisive factor for the value of registration is the continuing and increasing interest in the measure on the part of the public, the employing social agencies, and social workers themselves.[6]

There is no doubt that the present social services must be maintained and extended according to the changing needs of the people. The number of adequately trained social workers must be increased. The public will gradually come to recognize their own stake in

---

[6] Susan Pettes, *Licensing and Registration of Social Workers* (New York: American Association of Social Workers, 1953).

competent social work practice. After these requirements have been met, it seems desirable to introduce a licensing system, as in medicine, and to restrict social work practice to trained, competent, licensed practitioners.

IV. PROFESSIONAL ORGANIZATIONS IN SOCIAL WORK

Professional organizations of social workers have been in existence since 1918, when the American Association of Hospital Social Workers was founded, which became later the American Association of Medical Social Workers. It was followed by the National Association of School Social Workers in 1919. In 1921, the American Association of Social Workers, which succeeded the National Social Workers Exchange, became the largest organization in the field of social work. In 1926, the American Association of Psychiatric Social Workers was set up, and, in 1946, the American Association of Group Workers. Two study groups, the Association for the Study of Community Organization, beginning in 1946, and the Social Work Research Group, in 1949, pursued the special interests in these fields.

Since 1949, however, the professional representatives attempted to emphasize the common elements in social work and to achieve a coordination of all professional organizations of social work in the United States. This aim was accomplished by the merger of all seven organizations into the *National Association of Social Workers* on October 1, 1955. It now represents the united social work profession in our country. The purpose of the Association is the promotion of high quality and effectiveness in social work practice and the improvement of social conditions in our society. The organization and activities are designed to further a sound unification of objectives and action in social work, but with flexible diversification in line with the particular interests of the members of the Association, and with the changing needs of a growing profession. The Association publishes a quarterly professional journal, *Social Work,* and the *Social Work Year Book.* Among the objectives of the Association, are work for constructive social legislation, for adequate working conditions and salary, recruitment of able persons for the profession, and cooperation with other professional and civic organizations.[7]

---

[7] Nathan E. Cohen, "Social Work as a Profession," *Social Work Year Book* (1957), pp. 560-562; and John C. Kidneigh, *ibid.* (1960), pp. 568-571.

The Association accepts as members persons holding a degree from a graduate school of social work which is accredited by the Council on Social Work Education. Student members may join the Association in their second year of graduate studies. The Association has five sections: Medical Social Work, Psychiatric Social Work, School Social Work, Group Work, and Social Work Research. There are also committees on community organization and international social welfare. Other special interests can be served through the organization of committees or commissions. There are about 27,000 members organized in 150 chapters in all states and in Puerto Rico.

V. STANDARDS OF PROFESSIONAL PRACTICE

The principles of American social work arise from the beliefs in a democratic society. Foremost among them are the following:

(1) Firm faith in the dignity, worth and creative power of the individual.
(2) Complete belief in his right to hold and express his own opinions and to act upon them, so long as by so doing he does not infringe upon the rights of others.
(3) Unswerving conviction of the inherent, inalienable right of each human being to choose and achieve his own destiny in the framework of a progressive, yet stable, society.

Professional social work is built on an integrated body of knowledge distilled from physical, medical, psychological, and social science, and on technical methods derived from both this scientific knowledge and the tested experience of skilled practitioners.

Principles of ethical conduct of the social worker direct his relationship to the clients, to the social agency, to his colleagues, to the community, and to the profession of social work. These principles are embodied in a code of ethics, which together with standards for professional practice was adopted by the Delegate Assembly of the American Association of Social Workers in 1951.

Since social work is founded on belief in the value of the individual, it has a special responsibility to protect civil rights based upon democratic principles. Only by following this belief can social work discharge its professional obligations with intellectual integrity. The professional social worker has the moral responsibility to work toward the abridgement of discrimination for any reason. The civil rights of clients served by social workers and those of social workers themselves have to be protected in order to preserve human dignity and self-respect.

VI. SOCIAL WORKERS AND LABOR UNIONS

During the Depression years of the 1930's, social workers and clerical and technical employees of social agencies began to join labor unions which were interested in organizing staffs of social agencies into their membership. When many workers, without graduate social work education and degrees, were employed in public welfare agencies, but were not eligible to become members of the professional social work organizations, they began to identify themselves with the trade unions and felt that their work with the unemployed families was strengthened by their own participation in the labor movement. They felt the same insecurity in their own jobs which their clients experienced when they were fired as production decreased or business went down.

The political climate under the New Deal was favorable to trade unions. The *Norris-LaGuardia Act of 1932* and the *National Recovery Act of 1933* strengthened the bargaining rights of trade unions which were maintained by the *National Labor Relations Act of 1935* after the *National Recovery Act* was considered unconstitutional by the Supreme Court. Thus, the right of labor unions to organize workers was legally established and employers were prohibited to interfere through unfair labor practices.

The aim of the so-called "rank-and-file movement" was to improve working conditions and wages, to gain influence in the professional organizations, and to stimulate social action. Both AFL and CIO unions were included, but none of them consisted entirely of social workers and social agency personnel. In the AFL, two unions recruited social workers as members—the American Federation of Government Employees and the American Federation of State, County, and Municipal Employees. Some social workers in public welfare agencies were organized also in the United Public Workers of America, a CIO union.

Under the auspices of the CIO, workers in voluntary social agencies organized in the United Office and Professional Workers which established a National Social Service Division that coordinated the local chapters of the Social Service Employees Union. Together with United Public Workers of America, they formed a Joint Committee of Trade Unions in Social Work which arranged conferences and meetings at the time of National and State Conferences of Social Work. There were conflicts among the organized social workers over whether or not the typical trade union methods, such as striking, picketing, and demonstrations were appropriate means of fight for better wages and conditions, because their employers were either government agencies or private welfare boards, not industries, and because there was danger that their clients would suffer most from such measures.[8]

During the Second World War, the social workers in trade unions split on issues of participation in the war and on Nazi-Germany and the Soviet Union. After the War, in 1948, when the large labor unions united in the AFL-CIO, several groups of social workers left the United Public Workers of America and the United Office and Professional Workers of America which had many social workers as members, and joined the Industrial Union of Marine and Shipbuilding Workers. This split weakened the activity of social workers in labor unions and led to the demise of the two large social work unions.

At present, the largest number of social workers employed in public welfare agencies is organized in the American Federation of State, County, and Municipal Employees (about 12,000). Some social workers are in Federal agencies in the American Federation of Government Employees, both affiliated with the AFL-CIO. Social workers in private agencies are organized in the Community and Social Agency Employees (AFL-CIO), but their number is much smaller than that in public agencies, about 550 in 1959.

Unions of social workers have not limited their activities to collective bargaining, negotiations over salaries and working conditions, sick and vacation leave, and participation of union members in boards of agencies, but have concerned themselves as well with the policies

---

[8] Mary van Kleeck, *Creative America* (New York: Covici, 1936); Nathan E. Cohen, *Social Work in the American Tradition* (New York: Dryden, 1959), pp. 203-206, 279-280; and, John A. Fitch, "Professional Workers as Trade Unionists," *Social Work in the Current Scene* (New York: National Conference of Social Work, 1950).

of social agencies regarding other union-labor relations, and the client groups, and with the development of social legislation and services.[9]

These aspects of union activities have resulted in a number of conflicts between unions and the boards of directors of private and public welfare agencies. There have been questions raised over whether or not certain aspects of union membership, and particularly political postulates, are compatible with professional concepts and ideals. The professional organizations in social work, as well as in several other professions, do not oppose membership in labor unions with respect to improvement of salary and working conditions and collective bargaining. The 1946 Delegate Conference of the American Association of Social Workers recognized the right of social agency employees to bargain collectively and to be represented by a union of their choice. One particular difficulty in these negotiations is that a strike in a hospital or in a social agency involves serious dangers for patients and clients. Therefore, it should not be applied except as a means of last resort. These special emergency activities must be executed without causing irreparable damage to human beings.

Except among social workers in government agencies, collective bargaining, including social security provisions, is regarded as a proper form of union participation in presenting desirable working conditions to boards of social agencies. But not all boards have agreed to accept these suggestions, and the proportion of staff members organized in one or the other labor union at present varies greatly in the different states and regions. The activities of unions in social work have contributed to the recognition of the value of staff participation in policy formulation and in the development of new methods of practice in social agencies.

VII. VOLUNTEERS IN SOCIAL WORK

Volunteers have been the pioneers in all fields of social work, not only in group work, but also in casework, in health services, and in community organization (preceding professional, paid social workers). They started out by assisting people in financial stress who

---

[9] Wilbert E. Moore, "Unions in Social Work," *Social Work Year Book* (1949), pp. 519-520; Wayne McMillen, "Unions in Social Work," *The Compass* (July, 1947), pp. 6-8; and, Harold L. Wilensky, *Intellectuals in Labor Unions* (Glencoe, Ill.: The Free Press, 1956).

did not want to ask for poor relief; they founded relief societies, health organizations, schools for the blind and deaf, children's homes, day nurseries, recreation services, settlement houses, family welfare agencies, and the charity organization societies. They laid the foundations on which modern social work is built, and they recognized the need for the professional training of social workers in a complex society.[10]

The first paid employees in social agencies were volunteers who had formerly served without compensation. With the increase in the numbers of trained, paid staff workers, volunteers began to play a less important role in social agencies, particularly in casework and health agencies. During a later phase, professional social workers questioned the need for volunteers on their boards and committees and were afraid that they might interfere with their professional operations. More recently, however, this skeptical opinion has changed, and the genuine, intrinsic contribution of volunteers serving on the board of a social agency, to interpreting its work to the public, and in carrying out its program has been recognized again. A partnership between volunteers and professional workers is developing. This partnership has proved to be essential in the field of public relations (explaining the agency's work to the people), in the collection of money at fund-raising campaigns, in establishing policies on boards and committees, and in direct services to people with whom the agency deals.

The new relationship between volunteers and professional workers is based upon mutual respect and upon a sharing of responsibility between both. In order to do an efficient job, the volunteer needs to be sincerely interested in the work, must be willing to accept guidance, training, and supervision, and must feel responsible for carrying out the assignment given to him, so that he is no less dependable than a paid worker. However, the professional staff should express recognition of the value of the volunteer's work—respect for his desire to contribute his time and effort without demanding monetary compensation.

In large cities, volunteer bureaus under the auspices of the local community welfare council and special committees in smaller com-

---

[10] Robert F. Fenley, "Volunteers in Social Work Welfare," *Social Work Year Book* (1957), pp. 592-598; and, Eugene Shenefield, "Citizen and Volunteer Participation," *ibid.* (1960), pp. 157-162.

munities examine those agencies in which volunteers are needed. They encourage the application of volunteers at the bureau and promote their recruitment and training. They recommend the volunteers to those social agencies for which they are best suited.

Both women and men, and an increasing number of young people, individually and in groups, serve as volunteers in private and public social agencies. There are many types of service these people can perform, such as child care and hospital aids, group leaders, arts and craft instructors, clerical or typist help, automobile drivers, receptionists, entertainers, and librarians. They are especially important in civil defense planning for emergencies because services cannot be staffed with trained, professional workers alone.

The participation of volunteers in the field of recreation is particularly essential. Recreation agencies have to meet such a broad demand for leadership and guidance that they are never able to engage sufficient paid personnel. The executives in recreation also are willing to use services of volunteers on a broader scale than health and casework agencies are. Finally, recreational activities are such that the participation of volunteers in games, sports, gymnastics, arts and crafts, camping, and discussion groups is convenient. In leisure-time work, the large number of volunteers available, makes their effective selection, training, and supervision an increasingly important task for the trained professional worker.

VIII. SOCIAL WORK LITERATURE

The development of the social work profession is reflected in the substantial number of books and periodicals to which we have referred in the selected bibliographies. The current developments of social welfare are analyzed in the *Social Work Year Books,* the proceedings of the National Conference of Social Work, published under the title *The Social Welfare Forum* and *Selected Papers* in casework, in group work, and community organization. Other annual proceedings and year books are published by the Church Conference of Social Work, the National Conference of Catholic Charities, the National Conference of Jewish Communal Service, the National Probation and Parole Association, the U.S. Department of Health,

Education and Welfare, and many other Federal, state, and local organizations, and private health and welfare associations. An alphabetical list of periodicals which contain information on social welfare is conveniently found in the *Social Work Year Book* (1960) pp. 741-744.

IX. OUTLOOK

Social work, as a dynamic profession, is subject to changes that are influenced by the development of our society, our religious, cultural and sociological values, and by scientific progress. Certain trends which we illustrated in this book indicate important phases of the present situation, which may be briefly summarized here.

(1) Social work is still in need of a clarification of its purpose and philosophy. It has made progress in agreement among social workers in this respect and is developing a program of interpreting its aims so that the public might become aware of what social services mean for our society. The development of codes of ethics, personnel practice, and civil rights provides significant proof of the strength of professional ideas in social work.

(2) With the increasing recognition of social work and its contribution in solving social problems of our society, not only public and private social agencies, but also, industry, labor unions, commercial firms, hospitals, health agencies, churches, and the courts employ social workers and take advantage of their skill. In some instances, individual social workers operate in private practice as family or marriage counselors or in cooperation with psychiatrists or psychologists.

(3) Characteristic of present-day social work is its commitment to teamwork with other professions. Because social workers derive their knowledge from the sociologist's concept of the social process, the political scientist's knowledge of government and administration, the psychologist's comprehension of human behavior and mental functions, the anthropologist's understanding of cultural factors and personality differences, the geneticist's knowledge of hereditary influences, the economist's insight into the process of our economy, the psychiatrist's cognition of emotional illness and health, and the physiologist's observation of physical and nervous functions they

integrate their work with that of other professions. The interdisciplinary approach, the cooperation of several professions, in the prevention of pathological conditions in individuals and groups and in the treatment process promises further progress in the results of diagnosis and cure.

(4) Social workers are on the way to coordinating their own professional activities. They are attempting to clarify the common generic basis of the various types of social work, they have unified their professional organizations, and strengthened a comprehensive system of social work education and accreditation of its institutions.

(5) Social work is giving increasing attention to social work research. It no longer relies solely on research done by the social sciences, medicine, psychology, and anthropology but proceeds to assume responsibility in developing its own critical research, testing its methods and the results of its operations. The multi-discipline idea, accepted in social work, requires social workers to draw from the social and biological sciences basic data on human beings (their nature and behavior), on our society, and economic structure. However, social workers are contributing to this research their own concepts, observations, and experiences. This contribution includes an examination of the potentials and dynamic forces in the social group and in the community, the willingness to measure social needs and trends, and the effect of social work practice with an application of methods and knowledge of related scientific fields.

(6) Also, the international scene has been opened to social work, which, as a result, is developing world-wide concepts, has begun to recognize the impact of social problems in faraway countries, and is assuming responsibility for contributing its professional ideas, knowledge, and skills to the well-being of people everywhere. Social work is aware that in such an international climate, and under cultural, social, economic, and health conditions, often very different from our own, new concepts and new approaches are necessary. From the observation of foreign nations and from visitors to our country, social workers are learning other ways of meeting human problems and are re-evaluating our own methods and philosophy of social work. Social work has, through its international experiences, strengthened its conviction that the most effective and satisfactory way of helping people is to assist them to help themselves.

Selected Bibliography

*Abbott, Edith, *Social Welfare and Professional Education,* rev. ed. Chicago: University of Chicago Press, 1942.

*Anderson, Joseph P., *Opportunities in Social Work.* New York: Vocational Guidance Manuals, 1952.

*Bisno, Herbert, *The Philosophy of Social Work.* Washington: Public Affairs Press, 1952.

————, *The Place of the Undergraduate Curriculum in Social Work Education.* New York: Council on Social Work Education, 1959.

*Boehm, Werner W., *Objectives of the Social Work Curriculum of the Future.* New York: Council on Social Work Education, 1959.

————, *The Social Casework Method in Social Work Education.* New York: Council on Social Work Education, 1959.

Bower, Chester L., "Social Workers and the Community: A Challenge to Education," *Social Work Journal* (April 1953), pp. 71-73.

*Brown, Esther Lucile, *Social Work as A Profession,* 4th ed. New York: Russell Sage Foundation, 1942.

Bruno, Frank J., *Trends in Social Work as Reflected in Proceedings of the National Conference of Social Work, 1874-1946.* New York: Columbia University Press, 1948.

Butler, Ruth M., *An Orientation to Knowledge of Human Growth and Behavior in Social Work Education.* New York: Council on Social Work Education, 1959.

*de Schweinitz, Karl, *People and Process in Social Security.* Washington, D.C.: American Council on Education, 1948.

*Hamilton, Gordon, "Helping People—the Growth of a Profession," *Social Work as Human Relations.* New York: Columbia University Press, 1949, pp. 3-18.

Horwitz, John J., *Education for Social Workers in the Rehabilitation of the Handicapped.* New York: Council on Social Work Education, 1959.

*Hollis, Ernest V., and Alice L. Taylor, *Social Work Education in the United States.* New York: Columbia University Press, 1951.

Kahn, Alfred J. (editor), *Issues in American Social York.* New York: Columbia University Press, 1959.

*Kidneigh, John C., "Education for Social Work," *Social Work Year Book* (1951), pp. 158-170.

————, "Social Work as a Profession," *Social Work Year Book* (1960), pp. 563-573.

Lee, Porter R., *Social Work as Cause and Function.* New York: Columbia University Press, 1937.

Lurie, Harry L., *The Community Organization Method in Social Work Education*. New York: Council on Social Work Education, 1959.

Mencher, Samuel, *The Research Method in Social Work Education*. New York: Council on Social Work Education, 1959.

Murphy, Marjorie, *The Social Group Work Method in Social Work Education*. New York: Council on Social Work Education, 1959.

Pumphrey, Muriel W., *The Teaching of Values and Ethics in Social Work Education*. New York: Council on Social Work Education, 1959.

*Reynolds, Bertha C., *Learning and Teaching the Practice of Social Work*. New York: Farrar & Rinehart, 1942.

Studt, Elliot, *Education for Social Workers in the Correctional Field*. New York: Council on Social Work Education, 1959.

*Towle, Charlotte, *The Learner in Education for the Professions*. Chicago: University of Chicago Press, 1954.

Weissman, Irving, *Social Welfare Policy and Services in Social Work Education*. New York: Council on Social Work Education, 1959.

————, and Mary A. Baker, *Education for Social Workers in the Public Social Services*. New York: Council on Social Work Education, 1959.

Wilensky, Harold L., and Charles N. Lebeaux, *Industrial Society and Social Welfare*. New York: Russell Sage Foundation, 1958.

*Witmer, Helen Leland, *Social Work: An Analysis of a Social Institution*. New York: Farrar & Rinehart, 1942.

Youngdahl, Benjamin E., "Social Work as a Profession," *Social Work Year Book* (1949), pp. 497-506; and (1951), pp. 491-500.

Name Index

Name Index

574

Subject Index

Subject Index